S0-BJH-126

A Garland Series

The English Stage

Attack and Defense 1577 - 1730

A collection of 90 important works
reprinted in photo-facsimile in 50 volumes

edited by

Arthur Freeman

Boston University

A Serious Remonstrance
in Behalf of the Christian Religion

by

Arthur Bedford

with a preface
for the Garland Edition by

Arthur Freeman

Garland Publishing, Inc., New York & London

1974

Library of Congress Cataloging in Publication Data

Bedford, Arthur, 1668-1745.
A serious remonstrance in behalf of the Christian religion.

Reprint of the 1719 ed. printed by J. Darby, London.
1. Theater--Moral and religious aspects.
I. Title.
PN2047.B5 1974 792'.013 79-170478
ISBN 0-8240-0625-9

Printed in the United States of America

Preface

Arthur Bedford was born at Tiddenham or Tidenham, near Cheapstowe, Gloucestershire, some twenty-five miles from Bristol, in 1668, and went up to Brasenose College, Oxford, where he graduated B.A. in 1687/8 and proceeded M.A. in 1691. Ordained in 1688, he returned to his county and served as vicar of Temple-Church, Bristol, from 1692 to 1713. With the commotion initiated by Jeremy Collier's Short View *(1698) and its predictable replies, Bedford threw himself into the fray, at first with a relatively modest sermon preached 7 January 1705 at Temple-Church. Published as* Serious Reflections on the Scandalous Abuse and Effects of the Stage *by the congenial London printer William Bonny, now transplanted to Bristol and by 1703 "stark blind" (John Dunton), Bedford's sermon may have brought him to the attention of Wriothesley, Duke of Bedford, whose chaplain he became in the following year. It was occasioned, he says, by "the Acting of* Comedies *and* Tragedies *in* St. James's *Parish during the time of the Fair in the year 1704" and the actual building of "a* Play-house *in the City of* Bath, *and the great Apprehensions that such a Design was carried on this city [Bristol]."*

Inter alia, *the portent of a tempest which alarmed many in 1703 is evoked to warn citizens of Bristol of the course matters were taking. Bonny's advertisements comprise only attacks on the stage.*

But by 23 July 1705 a theatrical manager, Mr. Power, and his troupe had established a semi-permanent playhouse at Bristol, and had staged Love for Love *in defiance of Collier's extreme strictures and the antagonism alike of local authorities and clergy. One non-clerical opponent published a* Concio Laici or Layman's Sermon, *taking up cudgels where the Church had evidently left them (Bedford,* Evil and Danger, *pp. 12 ff.), but no copy of this attack has come to light. Conceivably it is the same "advertisement" cited as "lately shewn" in* Serious Reflections, *and printed to discourage further stage-playing. Subsequently there appeared* A Second Advertisement concerning the Profaneness of the Play-House, *of which only B^8 (16 pages, surely lacking the preliminaries) survives in the British Museum, and which is unreasonably attributed to Bedford by* BMC *and by Lowe. Its title implies a connection with the lost* Concio Laici, *and its tone is more obviously secular than Bedford's; nor is it mentioned in the advertisements to* Evil and Danger *(1706) which do include* Serious Reflections *and a prior essay on the misuse of sacred music in popular domain. We do reprint the text of* A Second Advertisement, *but offer no claim for Bedford's authorship.*

PREFACE

The first of Bedford's two major assaults on the stage, The Evil and Danger of Stage-Plays, *appeared in the following year, once more printed by Bonny at Bristol, but now on sale, by Henry Mortlake, at London. A kind of sequel of Collier's* Short View *("Immorality and Profaneness": "Evil and Danger"), it claims to include "almost Two Thousand* Instances, *taken from the* Plays *of the two last Years, against all the* Methods *lately used for their* Reformation." *Treating briefly of the events at Bristol, account is given of Mr. Power's first playing of* Love for Love *(23 July 1705), as well as of* The Provok'd Wife *(13 August following), for which the company were sternly admonished and fined, and a temporary end to professional theatre in that city effected.*

Reverend Bedford obtained the living of Newton St. Loe, Somersetshire, in 1713, and probably remained there as rector some eleven years, although he did not resign the place until 1737. In 1719 he offered to the world a treatise on the literal immorality of the drama which is exceeded for scholastic and precisionist zeal not even by its spiritual forefather Histriomastix. A Serious Remonstrance in behalf of the Christian Religion . . . against . . . English Play-Houses – *now printed, as Lowe-Arnott-Robinson omit to mention, at London, by John Darby, for booksellers in Bath, Bristol, and Oxford – cites "almost Seven Thousand Instances [of profaneness and im-*

morality] taken out of the Plays of the present Century, and especially of the five last Years," along with "above Fourteen Hundred Texts of Scripture, which are mentioned in this Treatise, either as ridicul'd and expos'd by the Stage, or as opposite to their present Practices," the latter catalogued in sixteen double-columned pages. Virtually unique of its kind, this exhaustive compendium speaks a long and desperately thorough immersion in the tainted literature (although as usual there is no indication of actual theatergoing), and may stand as a high-water mark of pietistic/diabolist anti-theatrical paranoia. In Evil and Danger *we learned that "God" is pronounced 23 times in* The Duchess of Malfi; *here we are confronted with the "wickedness" of even mock-sorcery, the "blasphemy" of Macbeth, and the unforgivable attribution to human agency of such heavenly action or forbearance as love, luck, and safety. The extent of Bedford's imagination in identifying transgression is astounding: "When correctly viewed," as Mr. Lehrer puts it, latterly,* "everything *is lewd."*

In 1724 Bedford came to live at Hoxam, and subsequently held the post of Lecturer of St. Botolph's, Aldersgate. In this capacity he preached a sermon on 29 November 1729, "occasioned by the erecting of a play-house in the neighborhood," printed (1730) by Charles Akers for J. Hooke, W. Meadows, and T. Cox. "The Erecting of a Play-

House *in the Neighbourhood obliges me to warn this Congregation of the great Evil and Danger in Frequenting them,*" *he explains, but full twenty-five years after his similar preachment at Bristol, Bedford was not above putting his rhetoric to second use. With a few minimal rephrasings and omissions of local or timebound allusions, and a few updatings (notably a longish attack, pp. 22-5, on* The Beggar's Opera*) the new sermon is the old sermon* verbatim. *In an appendix Bedford cites as "unanswered" his larger works of 1706 and 1719. A "second edition" (for John Wilford, the pamphlet specialist, 1735; not in Lowe-Arnott-Robinson, British Museum 1112.e.18[1]) is no more than the 1730 sheets with a cancel title.*

*The lucrative new playhouse in Goodman's Fields, opened by Thomas Odell 31 October 1729, was ordered closed on 28 April 1730 "because of the complaints of the Lord Mayor and Aldermen" (Nicholl, II, 284), but "under circumstances which are not clear, Odell commenced production again on 11 May and continued playing until the end of the regular season" (*London Stage, *III, xxii; cf.* MLN, *XXV [1930], 443-56). Garrick made his first London appearance here in 1741, and the playhouse was still in operation in 1742. It was demolished in 1746.*

Arthur Bedford is treated briefly by DNB, *slightly by* CBEL, *less by* NCBEL, *and summarily by Foster,* Alumni Oxoniensis, *and Nichols,* Illustrations. *Joseph Wood Krutch,* Comedy and Conscience after the Restoration *(rev. ed., New York, 1949) terms him "an industrious pedant," although Defoe "read him with approval." He was no narrow scholar: he wrote two books intelligently disputing Sir Isaac Newton's* Ancient Chronology, *made a mark as an orientalist, a critic of modern music, and an astronomer. Late in life he attended Frederick, Prince of Wales, as chaplain, and from 1724 onward was chaplain as well of Ashe's Hospital in Hoxam, where he took up his final residence and died (13 August 1745), aged 78, from the effects of making outdoor observations on the comet of that year.*

Serious Reflections *is reprinted from a copy at Yale (Beinecke Hag 12 2 v.2). It collates* A-1^4*(72 pp.), with vertical chainlines.* A Second Advertisement *is reprinted from British Museum 641.e.16 (3), collating* B^8*, with vertical chainlines. It is mostly uncut at the foot, but all leaves are guarded, slightly affecting a few inner margins. Although Lowe-Arnott-Robinson do not evidently regard this copy as imperfect, it seems almost certainly to lack preliminaries; but I know of no other copy.* The Evil and Danger of Stage-Plays *is reprinted from the Yale copy (Beinecke Haf 21 706b) collating* $A^7 B$-$P^8 Q^4$*. In this text* $B1^r$ *exists in two states, one (cancelled) bearing the inflammatory title "Hell upon Earth, or, the Language of the Play-House," which we print as an appendix* *from Lowe's copy, now at Harvard (Thr.417.06*). It should be noted that neither of the British Museum copies contains this leaf, as Lowe-Arnott-Robinson suggest.* A Serious Remonstrance *is reprinted from a copy at Yale (Beinecke Haf 21 7196) collating* $A^4\, a^4\, b^2\, B\text{-}Z^8\, Aa\text{-}Bb^8$ *(440 pp., vertical chainlines).* A Sermon, *1730, is reprinted from British Museum 225.h.11 (2.), collating* π^1 $A\text{-}E^4$ *(42 pp., vertical chainlines), compared with Harvard Thr. 417.30*.*

April, 1972 A.F.

A SERIOUS REMONSTRANCE In Behalf of the Christian Religion, AGAINST

The Horrid BLASPHEMIES and IMPIETIES which are still used in the *English* Play-Houses, to the great Dishonour of Almighty GOD, and in Contempt of the Statutes of this Realm.

Shewing their plain Tendency to overthrow all Piety, and advance the Interest and Honour of the Devil in the World; from almost Seven Thousand Instances, taken out of the Plays of the present Century, and especially of the five last Years, in defiance of all Methods hitherto used for their Reformation.

By *ARTHUR BEDFORD*, M. A.

Chaplain to the most Noble WRIOTHESLY Duke of *Bedford*, and Rector of *Newton St. Loe* in the County of *Somerset*.

Jer. 7. 8, 9, 10. *Behold, ye trust in lying Words, that cannot profit. Will ye steal, murder, and commit Adultery, and swear falsly, and burn Incense unto* Baal, *and walk after other Gods whom ye know not; and come and stand before me in this House, which is called by my Name, and say, We are delivered to do all these Abominations?* Cætera Deus avertat.

To treat Honour and Infamy alike, is an Injury to Virtue, and a sort of Levelling in Morality. I confess, I have no Ceremony for Debauchery; for to compliment Vice, is but one Remove from worshipping the Devil.——*Preface to* Collier's *Book of the Stage.*

LONDON:

Printed by JOHN DARBY, for HENRY HAMMOND, Bookseller in *Bath*; RICHARD GRAVETT, Bookseller on the *Tolzey* in *Bristol*; and ANTH. PIESLEY, Bookseller in *Oxford*. 1719.

A TABLE of the Chapters contained in this Treatise.

A Catalogue of above Fourteen Hundred Texts of Scripture, which are mentioned in this Treatise, either as ridicul'd and expos'd by the Stage, or as opposite to their present Practices.

Gen.

Levit.

Prov.

Texts

Texts out of the Apocrypha.

Texts out of the New Testament.

Acts

A

A Serious Remonstrance, &c.

CHAP. I.

The Preface.

WHEN the *primitive Fathers* dissuaded the *Christians* in their Times from going to the *Theatres*, they frequently urged this among other Arguments, That it was directly contrary to the (a) *Covenant*, which they had made to *God* in their *Baptism*, when they did solemnly promise and vow, that they would so far *renounce the Devil and all his Works, the Pomps and Vanities of this wicked World, and all the sinful Lusts of the Flesh*, as that they would *not follow nor be led by them.* Accordingly, they made it a matter of Conscience to avoid those *Shews*, which were intended for the Entertainment of the People. They (b) look'd upon the *publick Sports* and *Pastimes* of those Days, as the *Scenes*, not only of *Folly* and *Lewdness*, but also of *great Impiety* and *Idolatry*; as Places, where the *Devil* eminently ruled, and they reckoned all to be his *Votaries*, who went thither. *Ter-*

(a) Dr. *Bray* on the *Church-Catechism.*

(b) Dr. *Cave's Primitive Christianity*, Part 2. Chap. 2. p. 32.

tullian aſſures us,(*c*) that *upon any Man's Converſion to Chriſtianity, he immediately abſtained from the Stage,* and that *his abſtaining was a principal ſign of his Converſion.* And he ſaith at large, (*d*) That *all things conſider'd, it is no wonder, that ſuch People ſhould fall under the Poſſeſſion of the Devil. God knows* (ſaith he) *we have a ſad Example of this already: A certain Woman went to the Play-houſe, and brought the Devil home with her. And when the unclean Spirit was preſſed in the Exorciſm, and asked, How he durſt to ſet upon a Chriſtian? I have done nothing* (ſaith he) *but what I can juſtify, for I ſeiz'd her upon my own Ground.* And then he adds, *But how many Inſtances have we alſo of others, who have apoſtatiz'd from God, by this Correſpondence with the Devil?* (*e*) *What Communion hath Light with Darkneſs?* (*f*) *No Man can ſerve two Maſters, or have Life and Death in him at the ſame time.*

But to come to later Examples. Mr. *Collier* having (*g*) juſtly expos'd a *Comedy* call'd *The Provok'd Wife,* for burleſquing the Story of *The Serpent's beguiling Eve* in a ridiculous Manner, by a ridiculous Actor, and in a ridiculous Habit; the Author is pleas'd thus (*h*) to excuſe himſelf, That he *ſhall always make a great Diſtinction between his Reſpects to God and the Devil.* To which Mr. *Collier* replied, (*i*) *His Reſpect to God is ſomewhat familiar. But he mends the matter. He makes a very great Diſtinction between God and the Devil! Then it ſeems he hath ſome Regard for both of them; ſome Reſpect for the Devil. Truly, one would almoſt think ſo by his way of writing; and if we may argue from the Intereſt which he promotes, I am afraid, that the greateſt part of the Diſtinction will lie the wrong way.* And indeed he, who conſiders what our *Poets* have printed ſince, will find too great reaſon for ſuch an Apprehenſion.

(*c*) *Libro de Spectaculis, verſus finem,* pag. 700.

(*d*) *Ibid. cap.* 26.

(*e*) 2 *Cor.* 6. 14, 15, 16.

(*f*) *Matth.* 6. 24.

(*g*) *A ſhort View of the Stage,* pag. 77, 78.

(*h*) *A Short Vindication of the Relapſe, and the Provok'd Wife,* pag. 15.

(*i*) *A Defence of the Short View,* pag. 106.

The *modern Stage* hath done ſo much toward the *undermining Religion*, by their notorious Practices of *Swearing, Curſing, and Blaſphemy*; by their *miſapplying the Doctrines of Chriſtianity*; *expoſing Virtue, and encouraging Vice*; *vilifying the Magiſtracy and Clergy of this Land*; and by *teaching* the World *a ſort of profane and immodeſt Wit in Converſation*; and have ſo often declared themſelves *Enemies to all Reformation*, that the inſiſting on all theſe Particulars at large, would fill ſeveral Volumes in *Folio*. I ſhall not therefore tire either myſelf or the Reader, with what might be ſaid on each particular Head; but only obſerve the notorious *Profaneneſs* of the *Play-Houſes* in reference to two particular *Vices*, which all *Chriſtians* may be amaz'd at: namely, the *Reſpect and Eſteem which they pay to, and expreſs for the Devil*, and their *expoſing and vilifying the Great God, the Creator of Heaven and Earth*: And this will be ſhewn, as in other Inſtances, ſo particularly in the *Veracity* which they aſcribe, and the *Reverence* which they ſhew to the *Oracles of Satan*; and in their *contradicting, blaſpheming*, and *burleſquing* the *Sacred Scriptures*, the *Oracles of the Living God*.

The *paying any Reſpect to*, or *expreſſing any Eſteem for the Devil*, is a Crime too great for the Correction of a *Pen*, and too black to be deſcrib'd with *Ink*. It is that, which former *Chriſtian* Nations dared not to venture upon; and we may tremble to think how guilty we are. It is a Sin of the deepeſt Dye, and the Devils themſelves cannot invent a greater. The *Manichæans*, who thro Error attributed ſome part of the Creation to theſe *Infernal* Spirits, did never in any other Expreſſions preſume to ſuch an height of Impudence. To our ſhame be it ſpoken, it is committed by thoſe, who are liſted under *Chriſt's Banner*, and promiſed in their *Baptiſmal Vow* to continue his faithful Soldiers and Servants unto their Lives End; and at the ſame time did as ſolemnly renounce the *Devil* and all his Works: and how they can be accounted *Chriſtians*, who uſe ſuch Expreſſions, or are delighted to hear them, is beyond my Apprehenſion. That pretended *Chriſtians* ſhould ſink ſo low into the *Dregs of Paganiſm*, is ſtrange, when we conſider, how the *primitive Martyrs reſiſted unto Blood, ſtriving againſt this Sin*. But that we ſhould uſe any Expreſſions, which imply a divine Adoration of the *Devil*, is more abominable, when ſo many of our brave *Reformers* did burn at the *Stake*, rather than they would do the ſame toward the *Images* of *departed Saints*. The *Devil* is that accurſed *Spirit*, who firſt rebelled againſt GOD, and attempted to dethrone his *Maker*, who brought Mankind into a State of *Sin* and *Miſery*; who always oppoſed the Deſigns of GOD for our *Salvation*, and is continually contriving our *Ruin* and *Deſtruction*. Is this then the Being, who deſerves our *Prayers* and *Praiſes* with the moſt ſolemn *Acknowledgments?* What can be more *outrageous*, *daring*, *provoking*, and *blaſphemous?* The *Play-Houſes* have been accounted as *The Synagogues of Satan*; and if this can be proved upon them, it will be too evident, that they were not cenſured without a cauſe.

But OUR GOD is the Maker of the World, and all the Creatures which are therein; who gives us our Life, and every thing that we do enjoy; who hath preſerved us until now, and without whoſe Providence we connot live a Minute longer. It is He, who gave us the *Scriptures* as a Rule for all our Actions, and ſent his *Dearly-Beloved Son* from Heaven, to recover us out of that Condition into which we had plung'd ourſelves. And (*k*) *do* we *thus requite the LORD, O fooliſh People and unwiſe*, moſt horridly provoking and ungrateful? He knows all our Words and Actions. He hath promiſed infinite Rewards to ſuch as ſerve him, and hath threatned eternal Torments againſt thoſe who deſpiſe him. He can deliver this *Church* and *Nation* in our greateſt Dangers, or deſtroy us at once, when we think ourſelves moſt ſafe. And if we go on to ſlight, to expoſe, and to ridicule him for our Diverſion, or ſuffer ſuch things to paſs unpuniſhed; we ſlight his Mercies, we provoke his Juſtice, and dare him to pour out the fierceſt of his Vengeance upon us, until we are conſumed.

I ſuppoſe, that ſome of my Readers, who are not much converſant in the World, will hardly believe, that ſuch horrid Wickedneſs ſhould be ſuffered to be openly practiſed or repreſented by way of *Publick* Entertainment

(*k*) Deut. 32. 6.

and

and Diversion in a *Christian* Country, or that such Diversions should be countenanced or encouraged by any, who pretend to be concerned for the Honour of *God*, and the Peace of their own *Consciences*. But sad Experience shews the contrary in both respects; and the following Sheets will furnish us with too many flagrant Instances of the former melancholy Truth: *God* grant that they may help to put an effectual Stop to the latter.

Indeed, the plain Tendency of our *English Plays*, with very few Exceptions, seems to be, to destroy or confound the Notions of Good and Evil, to laugh us out of our *Virtue* and *Religion*, to turn the most serious and sacred things into a Jest, and in short to debauch and corrupt the Minds and Manners both of Men and Women, under pretence of diverting them. Now, tho this must needs be an acceptable Service to the *Devil*; yet we may conclude, that *God* will not always, nor probably much longer, suffer himself to be so affronted, nor the *Devil* and his Instruments thus to prevail.

Among other Causes of the monstrous *Impieties* of the *Stage*, I take their dealing so much with the *Devil* in their *Plays*, to have been partly occasioned by (*l*) a *Statute* design'd for their Reformation, which forbids the mentioning the sacred Name of GOD, or of *Christ Jesus*, or of the *Holy Ghost*, or of the *Trinity*, in any *Stage-Plays*, *Shew* or *Interlude* whatsoever. For tho the *Poets* and *Players* have been often guilty of the breach of this *Statute*, as will afterward appear; yet being restrained thereby for some time, from their shameful Practice of *profaning the Name of God*, they might possibly take occasion from thence to be the more free with the *Devil*'s Name, and (as if they had a mind even to outdo their former Impiety, and to shew themselves incorrigible) to put him in *God*'s place, especially in their *Oaths* and *Invocations*. Thus have they fallen from one Wickedness to another, and given the World a convincing Proof, that the Methods used for their Reformation, do cause them to invent new Sins, and make them more abominable.

(*l*) 3 Jac. 1. *Chap.* 21.

CHAP. II.

The Name of the Devil is frequently mentioned on the Stage; where Men are also turned into Devils, and crowned with Success.

THE first Crime which I shall observe that the *Poets* and *Actors* are guilty of, in order to carry on the Designs abovementioned, is, The using the Name of the *Devil* so very frequently, and upon all Occasions. They cannot but know, that this Method is very apt to make us lose our just Apprehensions of GOD; and therefore is it the more surprizing to find how the *Tragedies*, and especially the *Comedies*, are stuff'd with this Word: as if the Design was to wear off the Horror, and make the Object sit easy upon our Thoughts, as fit only for our Diversion. I might spend Sheets of Paper in such Quotations; but I shall only give a Specimen, in affirming, That besides all other Expressions of the same nature, this same Word is used nine and thirty times in (a) one *Comedy*, and three and twenty times in (b) one *Tragedy*: and I suppose, that it is needless to peruse any more

(a) The Man's bewitched, *p.* 1. *l.* 18. *p.* 3. *l.* 26. *p.* 6. *l.* 37. *p.* 11. *l.* 37. *p.* 12. *l.* 17. *p.* 21. *l.* 30. *p.* 23. *l.* 20. *p.* 31. *l. penult. p.* 34. *l.* 11. *p.* 37. *l.* 30, *and* 35. *p.* 38. *l.* 7, *and* 17. *p.* 39. *l.* 1, *and* 16. *p.* 40. *l.* 7, 13, 22, *and* 34. *p.* 43. *l.* 16. *p.* 47. *l.* 30. *p.* 48. *l.* 12. *p.* 49. *l.* 2. *p.* 50. *l.* 10. *p.* 51. *l.* 33. *p.* 52. *l.* 37. *p.* 53. *l.* 19, *and* 29. *p.* 54. *l.* 7, *and* 9. *p.* 58. *l.* 37. *p.* 59. *l.* 15, 33, *and* 37. *p.* 61. *l.* 21, 22, *and* 24. *p.* 65. *l. antepenult. and p.* 66. *l.* 35.

(b) The unfortunate Dutchess of *Malfi*, *p.* 2. *l.* 16, *and* 18. *p.* 5. *l.* 32. *p.* 7. *l.* 27. *p.* 8. *l.* 4, 10, *and* 33. *p.* 15. *l.* 26. *p.* 18. *l.* 17. *and penult. p.* 20. *l. antepenult. p.* 27. *l.* 12. *p.* 35. *l.* 27. *p.* 37. *l.* 18. *p.* 40. *l.* 8. *p.* 41. *l.* 30. *p.* 48. *l.* 10, *and* 30. *p.* 49. *l.* 14. *p.* 54. *l.* 30. *p.* 66. *l.* 26. *p.* 70. *l.* 11. *and p.* 73. *l.* 31.

more ſuch Quotations, ſince this whole Book may ſerve for farther Proof.

Beſides, the *Actors* frequently dreſs themſelves up in ſuch Habits, which may make them look like *Devils*, and be reputed as ſuch upon the *Stage*; and it is obſervable, that theſe *Devils* are always crown'd with Succeſs according to their Expectations, when they have been baffled in all their former Projects.

In (c) one *Play*, *Sprightly* endeavours to obtain *Leonora*; and for this purpoſe he employs his Man *Toby* in the Diſguiſe of a Girl. After this (d) he frames another Deſign for the ſame purpoſe, but they both miſcarry. At laſt (e) *Toby* puts on a black Mask, with Horns upon it, and whilſt the Houſe is in a Fright upon that Occaſion, *Sprightly* takes the Advantage, and carries off his Miſtreſs.

In (f) another *Play*, *Polite* endeavours to obtain *Iſabella*; and for this purpoſe he employs his Man *Roger* to carry a Letter in a *Bible* to his Miſtreſs. This being diſcovered, he runs away. The next Contrivance (g) is to carry a Letter in the Habit of a Beggar: For this he is ſeverely whipp'd. The (h) third Deſign is to ſcale the Houſe with a Ladder, a Rope, and a Dark Lanthorn, and for this he is toſs'd in a Blanket. The laſt Contrivance is (i) the ſame with the former. Accordingly, *Polite* is dreſs'd in a black diſmal Habit, with a large Pair of Horns upon his Head, a long Tail behind him, and a Flaſh of Fire before him, and then the Succeſs attends him according to his Expectation.

But the profane Expreſſions with which theſe Repreſentations are attended, make them the more intolerable. Thus (k) *Polite* ſpeaks to his Man; *We muſt prepare ourſelves for the fourth Attack. And ſince I am to repreſent the Devil, you muſt be my Imp, and contrive a Dreſs ſuitable.* To which *Roger* anſwers; *Never fear, Sir,*

(c) The Walking Statue, *at the beginning.*

(d) *Page* 52, &c.

(e) *Page* 60, &c.

(f) Love in a Wood, *Page* 9.

(g) *Page* 12.

(h) *Page* 19.

(i) *Page* 29. *line* 13. *and p.* 33. *l.* 22.

(k) *Page* 29. *line* 13.

I'll be Imp, Devil, or Beelzebub, or what you please, to ſerve ſo good a Maſter.

[God grant, that theſe Words may not be true hereafter, tho now they are ſpoken in Jeſt.]

On this Occaſion, the *Actors* never fail of commending the *Devil* himſelf. Thus *Toby* ſaith, (*l*) *I have better Luck now I am a Devil, than when I was a Woman: And ſome would from thence take occaſion to ſwear, that the Devil is the leaſt of the two Evils.* And in the other *Play,* (*m*) an antient rich *Knight*, and a *Merchant*, makes uſe of this Occaſion to call the *Devil* his *Old Friend.*

The ſecond Impiety is, The joining together the Name of GOD and the *Devil* at the ſame time. According to this Language, we may contradict the *Apoſtle*, and ſay, (*n*) That *Righteouſneſs hath Fellowſhip with Unrighteouſneſs*, and *Light hath Communion with Darkneſs*; nay, that in the *Play-Houſe Chriſt hath a Concord with Belial*, and GOD *hath* an *Agreement with the Devil.* Thus when the *Actors* ſpeak as if the *Devil* was preſent among them, they ſay, (*o*) *For Heaven's ſake*, and ſwear (*p*) *By the Life*, and (*q*) *By the Wounds of the Son of GOD.* And in the other, (*r*) the *Knight* ſaith, *The Devil! Hell! Fury! The Lord have Mercy upon me! The Devil! Oh!* But certainly this Prayer to GOD would better become them in private, and upon their *Knees*, than upon the *Stage*, on ſo profane an Occaſion.

The third Battery erected againſt *Heaven* at ſuch a time, is, The vilifying either of *Religion* in general, or of the *Chriſtian Religion* in particular. Thus *Roger* ſaith, (*s*) *What an odd kind of Jumble will appear in my Stratagems? I think I began with Religion, and am like to end*

(*l*) The Walking Statue, *p.* 63. *l.* 6.

(*m*) Love in a Wood, *p.* 33. *l.* 26.

(*n*) 2 *Cor.* 6. 14, 15, 16.

(*o*) The Walking Statute, *p.* 63. *l.* 20.

(*p*) Ibid. *p.* 62. *l.* 11. *and p.* 63. *l.* 1.

(*q*) Ibid. *p.* 62. *l.* 14.

(*r*) Love in a Wood, *p.* 29. *l.* 27.

(*s*) Ibid. *p.* 29. *l.* 27.

with

with the Devil. It will be a very pretty Tranſition in Hiſtory; eſpecially, ſince in the one he miſcarried, and in the other he ſucceeded. And (*t*) the *Knight* ſaith, *You Rogues! And are ye ſuch pitiful, cowardly, unchriſtian-ſoul'd Fellows, as to be afraid of the Devil!*

[From ſuch Abominations as theſe, Good LORD, in thy due time, deliver us.]

CHAP. III.

Witchcraft and Magick encouraged by the Stage.

ANother Method made uſe of at the *Play-Houſes*, is to entertain their Followers with *magical Repreſentations*, *conjuring*, or *conſulting* the *Devil*. This ſurely can be no great Diverſion, at leaſt no proper one for *Chriſtians*, and may be apt to fill the Heads of raw and ignorant Perſons with falſe and dangerous Notions, as if the *Devil's* Power and Knowledge was much greater than it is; inſomuch that they may come in time to think it their Intereſt to be upon good Terms with him; as we hear of many in our own Country, who have been ſo wicked, as to make Compacts with him, and as ſome of the *Indians* are ſaid to *worſhip* him for fear leſt he ſhould hurt them: and thus the *Worſhip* of GOD is of courſe laid aſide, and all hope of his Favour and Bleſſing is renounced and forfeited.

We are told, (*a*) That *the Soul, that turneth after ſuch as have familiar Spirits, and after Wizards, to go a whoring after them*, GOD *will even ſet* his *Face againſt that Soul, and will cut him off from among his People.* And when (*b*) *Saul* did ſeek to a Woman at *Endor*, who had *a familiar Spirit*, the Event is recorded: *So* Saul *died*

(*t*) The Walking Statue, *p.* 62. *l.* 28.

(*a*) *Levit.* 20. 6.

(*b*) 1 *Sam.* 28. 7, &c. compar'd with 1 *Chron.* 10. 13, 14.

for

for his Transgression, which he committed against the LORD, *and also for asking counsel of one that had a familiar Spirit, to enquire of it; therefore he slew him.* In (c) the *Apocrypha*, we are told, that GOD *hated* and *destroyed the* Canaanites *for doing most odious Works of Witchcraft*. And St. *Paul* (d) reckons *Witchcrafts* among *the Works of the Flesh*; and protests, *that they who do such things, cannot inherit the Kingdom of GOD*.

But that these Texts of *Scripture* signify nothing to restrain the *Stage* from setting out those *Hellish Studies* with the utmost Advantage, will appear from the various Methods in our modern *Plays*, which tend to promote them.

The First which I shall mention, is the using such Words, as signify *Compacts* or *Consulting* with him, in a sense which implies something most pleasant, delightful, and satisfactory. This is a bold way of ordering *Metaphors*; but nothing is more usual upon the *Stage*. The Design hereof can only be to dispel those black and dismal Apprehensions, which People justly entertain of the *Devil*, and his Actions; and by frequent Insinuations, to make them believe, that they have been mistaken in these Notions. The (e) Word in the *Hebrew Bible*, which we translate an *Inchanter*, is derived from another, which signifies a *Serpent*, and therefore plainly refers to the *Devil*, who is (f) often called by this Name. Thus (g) *when* Balaam *saw, that it pleased the LORD to bless* Israel, *he went not, as at other times, to seek for Inchantments*. For *Serpents*, in the *Hebrew*; that is, for *Devils*. Such Crimes as these were (h) capital among the *Jews*; and all (i) who did *such things*, were *an Abomination to the LORD*. And the Crime is not less among *Christians*. The *Stage-Poets* give the Words, which signify such *Vices*, a very different Turn. By

(c) *Wisd.* 12. 4.
(d) *Gal.* 5. 19, 20, 21.
(e) *Levit.* 19. 26. *Numb.* 23. 23. 2 *Kings* 17. 17. 2 *Kings* 21. 6. *and* 2 *Chron.* 33. 6.
(f) *Gen.* 3. 1, 2, 4, 13, *and* 14. *Rev.* 12. 9. *and Rev.* 20. 2.
(g) *Numb.* 24. 1.
(h) *Exod.* 22. 18.
(i) *Deut.* 18. 10, 11, 12.

(k) Be

(*k*) *Bewitching*, (*l*) *Magick*, and (*m*) *Inchanting*, they only signify something, which is most pleasant and desirable. A *Charm* is a Word which is taken in an ill sense in Prose, and signifies something done by the secret Operation of the *Devil*. Thus (as a *Stage-Poet* also expresseth it) (*n*) *Witches whisper their Charms*. At other times it signifies something which is most apt to engage Affections, particularly our Love and Admiration. The *Psalmist* saith, (*o*) *There be many that say, Who will shew us any good? LORD, lift thou up the light of thy countenance upon us. Thou hast put Gladness in my Heart, more than in the time, that their Corn, and Wine, and Oil increased.* On the *Stage* it is thus express'd, (*p*)

> *I never solid Joy cou'd find,*
> *Where I my charming* Sylvia *miss'd.*

Thus the Word is frequently used, when spoken of (*q*) a *Country Life*, (*r*) of *Drinking*, (*s*) of a *Dress*, (*t*) of *Gold*, (*u*) of an *Intrigue*, (*x*) of *Love*,

---

(*k*) The Humours of the Army, *p.* 59. *l.* 31. The Maid the Mistress, *p.* 40. *l.* 16. Almyna, *p.* 44. *l.* 3. The Female Advocates, *p.* 10. *l.* 25. The Modern Prophets, *p.* 21. *l.* 14. The Modish Husband, *p.* 19. *l.* 11. *and p.* 47. *l.* 8. The Squire of *Alsatia*, *p.* 15. *l.* 33. *and* Vice Reclaim'd, *p.* 14. *l.* 23.

(*l*) Almyna, *p.* 44. *l.* 3. The Faithful Bride of *Granada*, *p.* 59. *l.* 16. The Successful Pirate, *Prologue*, *l.* 5. The Wonder, *p.* 52. *l.* 29. *and* Woman is a Riddle, *p.* 56. *l.* 19.

(*m*) The Cruel Gift, *p.* 9. *l.* 32. The Maid the Mistress, *p.* 25. *l.* 10. The Rival Brothers, *p.* 78. *l.* 26. The Royal Convert, *p.* 65. *l. penult. and* Zelmane, *p.* 49. *l.* 16.

(*n*) The Unfortunate Dutchess of *Malfi*, *p.* 38. *l.* 30.

(*o*) *Psal.* 4. 6, 7.

(*p*) The Squire of *Alsatia*, *p.* 16. *l.* 25.

(*q*) The Humours of the Age, *p.* 25. *l.* 11. The Tender Husband, *p.* 22. *l.* 23. The Wonders of the Sun, *p.* 50. *l.* 23. *and Venus* and *Adonis*, *p.* 14. *l.* 6.

(*r*) The Wife of *Bath*, *p.* 62. *l.* 32. *and*, The Wonders in the Sun, *p.* 12. *l.* 33.

(*s*) Three Hours after Marriage, *p.* 55. *l.* 3.

(*t*) The Wife's Relief, *p.* 27. *l.* 5.

(*u*) Woman is a Riddle, *p.* 4. *l.* 35.

(*x*) The Wife of *Bath*, *p.* 62. *l.* 32. The Wonders of the Sun, *p.* 21. *l.* 19. *and p.* 22. *l.* 19. *and* Woman is a Riddle, *p.* 28. *l.* 7.

(*y*) of

(*y*) of *Men*, (*z*) of *Musick*, (*a*) of *Verses*, and (*b*) of *Women*.

And

(*y*) A Wife well manag'd, *p.* 12. *l.* 2. The Drummer, *p.* 32. *l.* 31. *and* The Metamorphosis, *p.* 47. *l.* 20, *and* 28. The Successful Pirate, *p.* 32. *l.* 20. The Tender Husband, *p.* 17. *l.* 2. *p.* 23. *l.* 5. *p.* 43. *l. ult. and p.* 49. *l.* 12. The Wife of *Bath*, *p.* 19. *l.* 21. *and p.* 53. *l.* 26. The Wife's Relief, *p.* 31. *l.* 35. The Wonder, *p.* 12. *l.* 16. Thomyris, *p.* 22. *l.* 36. *p.* 23. *l.* 9. *p.* 34. *l.* 2. *and p.* 41. *l.* 13. Three Hours after Marriage, *p.* 20. *l.* 7. Tunbridge-Walks, *p.* 22. *l. ult.* *Venus* and *Adonis*, *p.* 10. *l.* 23. *p.* 11. *l. penult. and p.* 17. *l.* 1. Wit at a Pinch, *p.* 27. *l.* 13. Wit without Money, *p.* 59. *l.* 24. Woman is a Riddle, *p.* 23. *l.* 11. *p.* 45. *l.* 13, *and* 22. *and p.* 50. *l.* 2, *and* Zelmane, *p.* 19. *l.* 2, *and* 16.

(*z*) The Wonders of the Sun, *p.* 56. *l.* 6. *and p.* 60. *l.* 9. *and* *Venus* and *Adonis*, *p.* 17. *l.* 21.

(*a*) The Victim, *Epilogue*, *l.* 1. *and*, The Wife of *Bath*, *p.* 28. *l.* 30. *and p.* 47. *l.* 32.

(*b*) Almyna, *p.* 44. *l.* 3. A Wife well manag'd, *p.* 7. *l.* 15. *and p.* 18. *l.* 4, *and* 9. Love's Contrivance, *p.* 20. *l.* 3. Love's Last Shift, *p.* 12. *l.* 12. *p.* 49. *l.* 16. *p.* 55. *l.* 23, *and* 37. *p.* 57. *l.* 12. *and p.* 65. *l.* 31. Myrtillus, *p.* 10. *l.* 1. The Faithful Bride of *Granada*, *p.* 37. *l.* 9. *and p.* 59. *l.* 16. The False Friend, *p.* 31. *l.* 9. The Gotham Election, *p.* 37. *l.* 27. *and p.* 70 *l.* 6. The Humours of the Age, *p.* 27. *l.* 20. The Humours of the Army, *p.* 7. *l. penult. p.* 65. *l.* 29. *and p.* 66. *l.* 16. The Maid's the Mistress, *p.* 50. *l.* 13. *and p.* 52. *l.* 24. The Mistake, *p.* 5. *l.* 4. *and p.* 44. *l.* 34. The Modern Prophets, *p.* 6. *l.* 33. *and p.* 62. *l.* 21. The Modish Husband, *p.* 60. *l.* 3. *and p.* 66. *l.* 10. The Perfidious Brother, *p.* 23. *l.* 20. *and p.* 38. *l. ult.* The Perplex'd Lovers, *p.* 10. *l.* 1. *p.* 17. *l.* 13. *p.* 23. l. 1. *and p.* 24. *l.* 23. The *Persian* Princess, *p.* 3. *l.* 12. *p.* 16. *l.* 13. *p.* 21. *l.* 6. *p.* 35. *l.* 4. *and p.* 59. *l.* 3. The Platonick Lady, *p.* 48. *l. ult.* The *Portsmouth* Heiress, *p.* 51. *l.* 10. The Pretender's Flight, *p.* 6. *l.* 3. *p.* 7. *l. antepenult. p.* 14. *l.* 18. *and p.* 38. *l.* 21. The Provok'd Wife, *p.* 15. *l.* 13. *and p.* 54. *l.* 3. The Relapse, *p.* 31. *l.* 28. *and p.* 46. *l.* 3. The Rival Brothers, *p.* 100. *l.* 21. The Royal Convert, *p.* 27. *l.* 30. *and p.* 29. *l. ult.* The Squire of *Alsatia*, *p.* 16. *l.* 26. *p.* 17. *l.* 37, *and* 42. *p.* 50. *l.* 32. *and p.* 52. *l.* 37. The Sultaness, *p.* 4. *l.* 22. *and p.* 49. *l.* 24. The Temple of Love, *p.* 18. *l.* 26. *and p.* 19. *l.* 25, *and penult.* The Tender Husband, *p.* 39. *l.* 3, *and* 14. *and p.* 44. *l.* 22. The Victim, *p.* 23. *l.* 32. *p.* 24. *l.* 17. *p.* 25. *l.* 17. *and p.* 27. *l. ult.* The Wife of *Bath*, *Epilogue*, *l.* 4. *p.* 1. *l.* 8. *p.* 4. l. 18. *p.* 18. *l.* 11. *p.* 19. *l.* 36. *p.* 33. *l.* 20. *p.* 42. *l. antepenult.*

And thus it is said that (c) *Vice itself hath power to charm.* In a late *Play*, a Woman comes in to Colonel *Manly*'s Room thro a false Door, his Man *Aspin* saith, (d) *he firmly believes that it is some Fairy or other*; that (e) it was a *Spirit*, and (f) *vanished according to custom*; nay, that it was (g) the *Devil himself*, or (h) a *Witch*. But lest these Expressions should seem formidable, the *Colonel* treats her in another Language, and saith, (i) *She is some Divinity come down from Heaven to bless him, and* he hath *offended her with* his *Rashness*; and he addresseth himself thus to her, (k) *What you are, neither Angel nor Goddess are Terms great enough to express.* Thus as the *Poets* borrow such *Metaphors*, when they speak of *Witches* and *Witchcraft*; so they all imply something which is very taking and delightful.

But we need not to insist upon Figures, when they speak their *Sense* in plainer Language. One tells us

---

penult. *p.* 45. *l.* 20. *p.* 46. *l.* 2. *p.* 51. *l.* 13. *p.* 53. *l.* 22. *and p.* 55. *l.* 4. The Wife's Relief, *p.* 18. *l.* 30. *p.* 20. *l.* 34. *p.* 21. *l.* 19. *p.* 27. *l.* 21. *p.* 30. *l.* 36. *and p.* 54. *l.* 9. The Wonder, *p.* 38. *l.* 19. *p.* 41. *l.* 15. *p.* 61. *l.* 20. *p.* 62. *l.* 13. *p.* 66. *l.* 24. *and p.* 68. *l.* 20. The Wonders of the Sun, *p.* 20. *l.* 21. *p.* 26. *l.* 11. *and p.* 52. *l.* 13. Thomyris, *p.* 6. *l.* 26. *p.* 10. *l.* 2. *p.* 16. *l.* 24. *p.* 18. *l.* 4. *p.* 20. *l.* 34. *p.* 24. *l.* 24. *p.* 26. *l.* 12. *p.* 36. *l.* 16. *and p.* 44. *l. penult.* Titus Manlius, *p.* 49. *l.* 9. *Tunbridge-*Walks, *p.* 23. *l.* 25. *p.* 27. *l.* 16. *and p.* 38. *l.* 3. *Venus* and *A-donis*, *p.* 12. l. 12. *and p.* 15. *l.* 6, *and* 16. Vice Reclaim'd, *p.* 9. *l. penult.* *p.* 12. *l.* 25. *p.* 13. *l.* 18. *p.* 41. *l.* 5. *and p.* 55. *l.* 10. U-lysses, *p.* 4. *l.* 14. *p.* 9. *l.* 25. *p.* 28. *l.* 12. *and p.* 45. *l.* 6. *and antepenult.* Wit at a Pinch, *p.* 3. *l.* 21, *and* 22. *p.* 12. *l.* 22. *p.* 13. *l.* 3. *p.* 18. *l.* 1. *and p.* 49. *l.* 27. Woman is a Riddle, *p.* 11. *l.* 4. *p.* 27. *l.* 3. *p.* 37. *l.* 21. *p.* 46. *l.* 14, 24, *and* 34. *p.* 47. *l. penult.* *p.* 48. *l.* 28. *p.* 49. *l.* 35. *p.* 92. *l. antepenult. and p.* 96. *l. ult.* and Zelmane, *Prologue*, *l.* 9. *p.* 9. *l.* 12. *p.* 11. *l.* 5. *p.* 17. *l.* 4. *p.* 23. *l.* 1. *p.* 24. *l.* 16. *p.* 41. *l.* 27. *p.* 42. *l.* 13. *p.* 53. *l. penult.* *and p.* 65. *l.* 8.

(c) Love's Last Shift, *p.* 57. *l.* 2.

(d) Woman is a Riddle, *p.* 1. *l.* 10.

(e) *Ibid.* *p.* 1. *l.* 17.

(f) *Ibid.* *p.* 1. *l. ult.*

(g) *Ibid.* *p.* 5. *l.* 1.

(h) *Ibid.* *p.* 37. *l.* 16.

(i) *Ibid.* *p.* 37. *l.* 13.

(k) *Ibid.* *p.* 37. *l.* 27.

of

(*t*) of the great *Power* of the *Devil*, (*u*) that he could *carry a Room thro the Air by Enchantment*. Another plainly intimates, (*x*) that what a *Wizard cannot hinder*, is impossible to be prevented. One (*y*) *young Lady of a good Fortune* talks of (*z*) *Raising the Devil*, to acccomplish her Ends. And another (*a*) wishes that she *had made a Contract to be a Witch*, that so she might *ease* herself by *Revenge*, and *perish with Joy*. One describes (*b*) the *Devil*, that he *wears Petticoats, and chuses the Shape of a Woman*, it being *a* Form *that best agrees with his infernal Qualities*. And certainly, to an *Actor*, as it is now manag'd, this is not a frightful Description. In another *Play* (*c*) a *Wizard* is describ'd, as one who, (*d*) like GOD, came *flying upon the Wings of the Wind, mighty in Spells, in Charms, and Magick Love*; and accordingly, when he did *aid* the *Actors*, then *Earth, Hell, and all aerial Demons join'd with* them to *blast* their Enemies.

From these Expressions, I shall proceed to their Actions, which are too sad a Demonstration of what I charge them with. Sometimes (*e*) *England* or (*f*) *Scotland* is the *Scene* for their *Enchantments*, and the Nation thereby represented as wholly addicted to such detestable Practices. Sometimes (*g*) the *Scene* is in distant Countries; and at another time (*h*) even in the *Sun* it self. And thus this *infernal Fiend* is not only said to (*i*) *rule in the Air*; but is so represented on the *Stage*, as if that Saying in our excellent *Te Deum* was spoken of him; as if the whole World was a *Temple* devoted to his Service, and both *Heaven and Earth was full of his Majesty, and of his Glory*.

(*t*) Woman is a Riddle, *p.* 84. *l.* 31.

(*u*) Ibid. *p.* 84. *l.* 24.

(*x*) The Pretender's Flight, *p.* 32. *l.* 14.

(*y*) Woman is a Riddle, *Drama*.

(*z*) Ibid. *p.* 93. *l.* 18.

(*a*) The Man of Mode, *p.* 204. *l.* 24.

(*b*) Woman is a Riddle, *p.* 5. *l.* 1.

(*c*) Lucius, *p.* 7. *l.* 14.

(*d*) Psal. 18. 10.

(*e*) The *British* Enchanters, *Dramatis personæ in fine.*

(*f*) Mackbeth.

(*g*) Hercules, Rinaldo, *and* Theseus.

(*h*) The Wonders in the Sun.

(*i*) The unfortunate Dutchess of *Malfi*, *p.* 15. *l.* 26.

In

In several of these *Plays* we have *Enchantments* (*k*) performed to the Life, attended with such Success, as may seem to the Audience to be more than the Effect of a natural Power. These *Enchantments* are perform'd with Rods or Wands, sometimes as (*l*) in reality, and at other times (*m*) only in a burlesquing manner, to make the *sacred Story* appear more ridiculous.

When *Moses* was appointed by GOD to deliver the *Children of Israel* out of *Egypt*, he had this Command, (*n*) *Thou shalt take this Rod in thine hand, wherewith thou shalt do signs.* And it is recorded (*o*) that he did so upon several Occasions. In the *Play-house*, these *Rods* are called (*p*) *Mystical* and (*q*) *inchanted Wands.* Sometimes the things done by them, are expresly said (*r*) to be some of the *Devil's Frolicks*; and at other times the Power of the *Almighty* GOD is ascribed to them.

In a very late *Play*, (*s*) a pretended *Conjurer* hath a long white *Rod* in his Hand, of which an *Actor* makes this Remark: *You may be sure there's a good deal of Virtue in that Rod; I fancy 'tis made of Witch-Elm.* After this the Conjurer asks, (*t*) *But where's my Rod?* Then (*u*) he *lays* his Rod *on* another's *Head*, whilst they who stand by are afraid of the Consequence. And (*x*) after that, he *walks about in a pensive Posture, waving his* Rod. And that we might not be ignorant of the Design both in this and other *Plays*, the Poet hath here given us a

---

(*k*) The *British* Enchanters, *p.* 1. *l.* 4. *p.* 4. *in fine, and p.* 16. Mackbeth, *p.* 41. *Act* 4. Theseus, *p.* 37. *l.* 1. *p.* 43. *in fine, and p.* 49. *Scene* 4.

(*l*) Rinaldo, *p.* 45. *l. antepen. p.* 47. *l.* 12. *and p.* 49. *l.* 32. The *British* Enchanters, *p.* 1. *in fine.* Theseus, *p.* 49. *l.* 1. *Sc.* 4.

(*m*) The Drummer, *p.* 22. *l.* 15, &c. *p.* 25. *l.* 10. *p.* 48. *l.* 16, *and* 18. *and p.* 51. *l.* 17. The Wife of *Bath*, *p.* 35. *l.* 10.

(*n*) *Exod.* 4. 17.

(*o*) *Exod.* 4. 2, 4, 20. & 7. 9, 10, 11, 12, 17, 19, 20. & 8. 5, 16, 17. & 9. 23. & 10. 13. & 14. 16. & 17. 5, 9. *Numb.* 20. 8, 9, 11.

(*p*) The Wife of *Bath*, *p.* 35. *l.* 10.

(*q*) The *British* Enchanters, *p.* 1. *l. penult.* Theseus. *p.* 49. *Sc.* 4. *l.* 1.

(*r*) The Wife of *Bath*, *p.* 26. *l.* 25.

(*s*) The Drummer, *p.* 22. *l.* 14.

(*t*) Ibid. *p.* 25. *l.* 10.

(*u*) Ibid. *p.* 48. l. 16.

(*x*) Ibid. *p.* 51. *l.* 17.

Key to underſtand his Meaning. For (y) when one ſaith, *I would not have you rally things that are ſerious*; he is anſwer'd, with an Oath, *Well enough! But where's the Jeſt or Rallying any thing elſe?* All the Wit conſiſts in the profane Alluſion; and without this, there could be no Diverſion for the Audience.

But for a farther Proof of this their Practice, I ſhall only add two Quotations out of another *Play*, which I hope will be ſufficient.

(z) *But one thing more, if 'tis within your Art,*
(*i. e.* of Conjuration)
(As what is not?) whoſe pow'rful Wand commands
The moſt obdurate, moſt lethargick Spirit;
From Air, Earth, Water, whereſoe'er reſiding,
Atone the Gods (i. e. the Devils) *for me and Hell's Great Queen.*

And in the next (a) Page the *High Prieſt* ſings;

By the Spirit in this Wand,
Which the Silver Moon commands,
By the pow'rful God of Night,
By the Love of Amphitrite.

[By the Myſtery of thy holy Incarnation; (*which was to deſtroy the Works of the Devil*:) By thy holy Nativity and Circumciſion; By thy Baptiſm, Faſting and Temptation; By thine Agony and bloody Sweat; By thy Croſs and Paſſion; By thy precious Death and Burial; By thy glorious Reſurrection and Aſcenſion, and by the Coming of the Ghoſt;

Good Lord, deliver us from ſuch Impieties as theſe.]

Here we have *Devils*, (b) ſome riſing from under the *Stage*; (c) others flying down from above; (d) others crossing

(y) Ibid. *p.* 11. l. 28.

(z) Alarbas, *p.* 24. *l.* 3.

(a) Ibid. *p.* 25. *l.* 25.

(b) Hercules, *p.* 40. *l.* 5. Rinaldo, *p.* 45. *l.* 18, *and* 21. *p.* 47. *l.* 7. *and p.* 49. *l.* 20, *and* 31. The *Britiſh* Enchanters, *p.* 16. *l.* 16. *and p.* 20. *l.* 10. Theſeus, *p.* 45. *Scene* 3. *l.* 1.

(c) The *Britiſh* Enchanters, *p.* 16. *l.* 17. *and p.* 33. *l.* 23.

(d) Ibid. *p.* 16. *l.* 18.

crossing to and fro, and (*e*) others flying away. Some (*f*) go off, and (*g*) others sink down and disappear. One of these Fiends (*h*) attacks a Woman, (*i*) takes a Sword from a Man, and flies away; and another (*k*) sits in a Boat. At one time (*l*) two *Spirits* enter, leading in a Prisoner; and at other times, there is (*m*) a dreadful, or an innumerable Host of *Spirits*. These are Eruptions of *Hell* with a Witness; and we may wonder, that the Smoke of them hath not darkned the Sun, and turn'd the Air into Plague and Poison.

Sometimes these *Spirits* act their Parts on the *Stage*, and sometimes (*n*) they continue in the Air. Some (*o*) draw up, and others (*p*) are drawn up in order of Battel. Some (*q*) fight in the Air, and some (*r*) on the *Stage*. Here we have (*s*) Guards of *Devils* (*t*) attending on their *Enchanters*; and (*u*) a Person thus attended is called a (*x*) *good Enchantress*.

At one time, these (*y*) *Furies* enter, carrying in the one hand a Knife, and in the other hand a Torch. At (*z*) another time they enter, (*a*) tormenting an *Actress*, and (*b*) afterwards carry her off. At one time (*c*) a Troop of *Devils* seize a Man, and carry him to an *Inchanted Palace*. At another time they (*d*) seize a Man, and carry him into *Hell*: And that neither Sex may escape, at another time (*e*) a Cavern opens, and several *Devils* appear, and carry a Woman under-ground, to the same

(*e*) Hercules, *p*. 30. *l*. 2.
(*f*) Theseus, *p*. 47. *in fine*.
(*g*) Rinaldo, *p*. 17. *l*. 5.
(*h*) Theseus, *p*. 37. *l*. *antepen*.
(*i*) Ibid. *p*. 39. *l*. 3.
(*k*) Rinaldo, *p*. 21. *Act* 2. *Scene* 1.
(*l*) Ibid. *p*. 31. *Scene* 6.
(*m*) Hercules, *p*. 30. *l*. 1. Rinaldo, *p*. 49. *Scene* 4. *l*. 7.
(*n*) The *British* Enchanters, *p*. 33. *l*. 21.
(*o*) Ibid. *p*. 33. *l*. 24.
(*p*) Ibid. *p*. 33. l. 22. & *penult*.
(*q*) Ibid. *p*. 34. *l*. 6.
(*r*) Ibid. *l*. 7.
(*s*) Ibid. *p*. 22. *l*. 14.
(*t*) Ibid. *p*. 24. *l*. 22.
(*u*) Ibid. *p*. 31. *l*. 14.
(*x*) Ibid. *Dramatis Personæ*.
(*y*) Theseus, *p*. 45. *Sc*. 3. l. 9.
(*z*) Ibid. *p*. 39. *l*. 17.
(*a*) Ibid. *l*. 21.
(*b*) Ibid. *in fine*.
(*c*) Hercules, *p*. 28. *l*. 16.
(*d*) The *British* Enchanters, *p*. 20. *l*. 10.
(*e*) Hercules, *p*. 40. *l*. 5.

place. At another time, they (*f*) ſtand in various Forms and Aſpects, guarding an *inchanted Palace*. And as in *Scripture*, (*g*) the *good Angels* are ſaid to be *miniſtring Spirits, ſent forth to miniſter unto them, who ſhall be Heirs of Salvation:* So upon the *Stage*, the *Devils* are repreſented as ready to attend upon the *Actors*, and make Diverſion for the *Audience*.

Here we have ſet before us an (*h*) *inchanted Iſland* and an (*i*) *inchanted Palace*, (*k*) plac'd upon a Rock, (*l*) guarded with *Devils*, and (*m*) delightful Gardens adjoining to ſuch a Palace. One of them (*n*) is plac'd upon the utmoſt Height of the moſt backward part of the *Stage*, with blazing Battlements. In the midſt of the Wall is ſeen a *Gate*, with ſeveral Arches, ſupported by Pillars of *Chryſtal*, *Azure*, *Emeralds*, and all ſorts of *precious Stones*. And thus the Habitation of *Devils* is repreſented as if it would vie with the (*o*) holy *Jeruſalem* in Heaven, when *fill'd with the Glory of GOD*.

Beſides, here is care taken, that the Audience may really look upon theſe things as the Effect of *Magick*. Accordingly (*p*) one of the *Palaces* ſuddenly diſappears, and nothing is left to be ſeen but a *dark Deſert*. The other (*q*) lofty *Palace*, with the whole Mountain, immediately vaniſhes away, and only leaves a vaſt Rock in the middle of the Sea; and (*r*) the whole Proſpect of the Garden vaniſheth in a moment, leaving in its place the View of a wild and open Country.

And now let us ſee what part theſe *Witches* act. One of them (*s*) frequently changes herſelf into the Shape of another Perſon, and then (*t*) again into her own. Another, (*u*) by her Enchantments, changes the *Scene*

(*f*) Rinaldo, *p.* 43. *Act* 3. *Scene* 1. *l.*6.

(*g*) Heb. 1. 14.

(*h*) Theſeus, *p.*47. *in fine*.

(*i*) Hercules, *p.*26. *l.* 23. Rinaldo, *p.*27. *l.*23. Theſeus, *p.*57. *Act* 5. *Sc.* 1.

(*k*) Hercules, *p.*36. *Sc.* 2.

(*l*) Rinaldo, *p.*43. *Act* 3. *Sc.* 1. *l.*6.

(*m*) Ibid. *p.*27. *Sc.*4.

(*n*) Ibid. *p.*43. *Act*.3. *Sc.*1.

(*o*) Revel. 21. 10, *to the end.*

(*p*) Hercules, *p.*30. *l.*1.

(*q*) Rinaldo, *p.*47. *l.*12.

(*r*) Ibid. *p.*49. *l.*32.

(*s*) Ibid. *p.*35. *l.*18. *p.*37. *l.* 8. *p.*39. *l.*13.

(*t*) Ibid. *p.*37. *l.*1, 24. *p.*41. *l.* 1.

(*u*) Theſeus, *p.*37. *l.*21.

into an horrid Deſert, full of frightful *Monſters*; and in revenge (*x*) ſets a whole Palace on fire with this Expreſſion (*y*):

Hell then is arm'd, full of Rage and Fury of my own Contrivance. Thus parting, I bid you the beſt Farewell.

Some *Witches* enter (*z*) flying, ſome (*a*) vaniſh, (*b*) eſpecially in the time of Danger; and ſome (*c*) fly away (*d*) with this Expreſſion:

Come, hover thro the filthy foggy Air;
To us fair Weather's foul, and foul is fair.

In the midſt of ſuch horrid Repreſentations as theſe, the Audience is told twice in the ſame Page (*e*) of the *Charms of Magick*, (*f*) the *Pleaſures of Witchcraft*, and *charming the Air* to *chear* the *Heart*, and make a Diverſion.

In one Play (for the quoting of one is enough) we have (*g*) *Muſick*, and (*h*) *Songs*, and (*i*) *Dances* for *Witches*; and (*k*) a whole Train of *Witchcraft* is imitated. In (*l*) their Diſcourſe they talk of commanding the Winds, and making foul Weather, to the diſtreſs of Mariners, and the Revenge of themſelves.

In one of theſe *Songs*, the *Witches* (*m*) give us an account of their merry way of living. In (*n*) another, they tell us, that *all things go fair for their Delight*. At another time, (*o*) *Hecate* being rais'd from *Hell* by the Witches, (*p*) deſcends, as it were, from *Heaven* in a

(*x*) Ibid. *p.*65. *l. ult.*
(*y*) Ibid. *p.*65. *Sc.*5. *l.*4.
(*z*) Mackbeth, *p.*3. *l.*21.
(*a*) Ibid. *p.*5. *l.*26. & *p.*44. *l.*6.
(*b*) Rinaldo, *p.*51. *l.*10.
(*c*) Theſeus, *p.*63. *l.*8. Mackbeth, *p.*1. *Act* 1. *l.*12.
(*d*) Mackbeth, *p.*1. *l.*10.
(*e*) The *Britiſh* Enchanters, *p.* 2. *l.*5, & *antepenult.*
(*f*) Mackbeth, *p.*44. *l.*6.
(*g*) Ibid. *p.*39. *l.*38. *p.*44. *l.*9.
(*h*) Ibid. *p.* 24. *l* 32. *p.* 25. *l.* 19. *p.* 39. *l.*38. & *p.*40. *l.*1,17, & 23.
(*i*) Ibid. *p.*25. *l.*19. *p.*26. *l.*6. & *p.*44. *l.*9.
(*k*) Ibid. *p.* 41, &c. *Act* 4. *Scene* 1.
(*l*) Ibid. *p.*3. *l.*23.
(*m*) Ibid. *p.*25. *l.*19.
(*n*) Ibid. *p.*40. *l.*18.
(*o*) Ibid. *p.*39. *l. antepenult.*
(*p*) Ibid. *p.*40. *l.*1.

Machine, with *singing* within. At another time, *Hecate* (q) endeavours to revive the Spirits of *Mackbeth* with *magical Performances*, after this Speech to the *Witches*:

Come, Sisters, let us chear his Heart,
And shew the Pleasures of our Art;
I'll charm the Air to give a Sound,
Whilst you perform your Antick Round.

Beside these short Flights, *Witchcraft* is commended at large in a (r) solemn *Song* for such a purpose. As,

Oh! what a dainty Pleasure's this,
To sail i'th' Air,
Whilst the Noon shines fair;
To sing, to toy, to dance and kiss!
Over Woods, high Rocks and Mountains,
Over Hills, and mighty Fountains;
Over Steeples, Tow'rs, and Turrets,
We fly by Night 'mongst Troops of Spirits.
No Rings of Bells to our Ears sounds,
No Howls of Wolves, nor Yelps of Hounds;
No nor the Noise of Waters Breach,
Nor Cannons Throats our Heights can reach.

[From all the Deceits of the World, the Flesh and the Devil, Good LORD, deliver us.]

To put this matter in a clearer Light, it will be requisite to compare some Places of *Scripture* with the Words and Actions in the *Play-house*.

The *Scriptures* speaking of the *Majesty* and *Glory of GOD*, tell us, (s) that *he made a Decree for the Rain, and a way for the Lightning and the Thunder*; that (t) it is *the LORD*, who *thunders in the Heavens*, and *the Highest*, *who gives his Voice*, and *shoots out* his *Lightnings*; that (u) *it is the glorious GOD*, *who maketh the Thunder*; and (x) he *maketh Lightnings with the Rain, and bringeth*

(q) Ibid. *p*.44. *l*.6.
(r) Ibid. *p*.40. *l*.23.
(s) *Job* 28. 26.
(t) *Psal*. 18. 13, 14.
(u) *Psal*. 29. 3.
(x) *Psal*. 135. 7.

eth

eth the Winds out of his Treasuries. In the *Play-house* we have (y) *Thunder and Lightning*, represented, sometimes as rais'd by (z) *Devils*, and sometimes by (a) *Witches*. We have also (b) an Addition of *Showers*, when the *Witches* speak thus to one another:

> *When shall we three meet again,*
> *In Lightning, Thunder, and in Rain?*

The *Scriptures*, speaking further of the *Majesty of* GOD, tell us, (c) *He made Darkness his secret place, his Pavilion round about him were dark Waters, and thick Clouds of the Skies*; even when *at the Brightness that was before him his thick Clouds pass'd; Hail-stones and Coals of Fire.* In (d) the *Play-house* the *Stage* is also darkned at a time, when *Thunder* and *Lightning* is represented as rais'd by the *Devil* (e); tho not only on such Occasions.

The *Scriptures* also speaking of the *Glory of* G O D, saith (f) he *maketh the Clouds his Chariots, and walketh upon the Wings of the Wind.* This Expression is imitated by an *Actress* on the *Stage*, when (g) she speaks of the *Devil*:

> *Hark! I am call'd; my little Spirit (see)*
> *Sits in a foggy Cloud, and stays for me.*

Accordingly, sometimes (h) a *Witch* appears in the *Clouds*. At other times (i) the *Devils* descend in *Clouds*. And to give (k) but one Instance at large, *A black Cloud descends, all filled with dreadful Monsters, spitting Fire and Smoke on every side. The Clouds covers two Actresses, and carries them up swiftly into the Air, leaving in their*

(y) Mackbeth, *p.*39. *l.*19. The *British* Enchanters, *p.*33. *l.*19.
(z) Alarbas, *p.*26. *l.* 13, 22. Rinaldo, *p.*45. *l.*23. The *British* Enchanters, *p.*16. *l.*19, *p.*33. *l. penult.* & *p.*34. *l.*8.
(a) Mackbeth, *p.*1. *Act* 1. *Sc.* 1. & *p.*3. *l.*21. The *British* Enchanters, *p.*1. *l.*5. & *antepenult.*
(b) Mackbeth, *p.*1. *l.*1.
(c) *Psal.* 18. 11, 12.
(d) Alarbas, *p.*26. *l.*13. The *British* Enchanters. *p.*16. *l.*19.
(e) Elfrid, *p.*35. *Act* 5.
(f) *Psal.* 104. 3.
(g) Mackbeth, *p.* 39. *l. penult.*
(h) Theseus, *p.*53. *Sc.*6.
(i) The *British* Enchanters, *p.* 33. *l.*20.
(k) Rinaldo, *p.* 15. *l. ult.*

places two frightful Furies, who having grinn'd at, and mock'd an Actor, sink down, and disappear.

The *Scriptures* say of GOD, (*l*) *There went up a Smoke out of his Nostrils, and Fire out of his Mouth devoured; Coals were kindled at it. He bowed the Heavens also, and came down; and Darkness was under his Feet. And he rode upon a Cherub, and did fly; yea, he did fly upon the Wings of the Wind.* In one (*m*) *Play* a *Witch* descends in a Chariot drawn by flying Dragons. In a second, (*n*) a Chariot descends, drawn by two Dragons, spitting Fire; from whence two *Devils* come out, who seize a Woman, and carry her off in the Chariot. In a third, (*o*) a Chariot descends swiftly, drawn by Dragons, into which an *Enchantress* enters. After this (*p*) the Chariot mounts into the Air, and vanishes with her, whilst in the midst of Thunder, she blasphemously attributes to her self the *Works* of GOD, and says: (*q*)

> *Up to th' etherial Heav'ns, where Gods reside,*
> *Lo! thus I fly to thunder on thy Side.*

Like to this is another *blasphemous Sentence* in a (*r*) later *Opera.*

> *When I return, you'll see*
> *Lightning and Thunder thrown by me:*
> *Tempests and Comets shall amaze;*
> *With dreadful Fires the World shall blaz*
> *Terror, Destruction ready stand,*
> *And Death in my revengeful Hand.*

And now, what *Christian* can be unconcern'd at such intolerable Affronts offer'd to his GOD? Or what can be a juster Reason for Indignation than such a daring Insolence? How can Resentment be better shewn? Or how can Aversion be more seasonably exerted, than when a *Creature* shall set himself up to be equal to the

(*l*) *Psal.* 18. 8, 9, 10.
(*m*) Theseus, *p.*65. *Sc.* 5.
(*n*) Hercules, *p.*36. *l.*21.
(*o*) The *British* Enchanters, *p.* 39. *l.*8.
(*p*) Ibid. *p.*39. *l.*12.
(*q*) Ibid. *p.*39. *l.*10.
(*r*) Hamlet, *p.*28. *l.*21.

Great

Great Creator? If it is a Wickedneſs, which GOD will not endure (*s*) to *think, that* GOD *is ſuch a one as our ſelves,* what Wickedneſs muſt it be to ſpeak as if we were like unto GOD? It was the (*t*) *Luciferian* Pride to think in this manner: *I will aſcend into Heaven. I will exalt my Throne above the Stars of GOD. I will aſcend above the Heights of the Clouds. I will be like the moſt High.* And if this Vice did caſt the fallen *Angels* out of *Heaven,* and turn'd them into *Devils,* it may alſo juſtly caſt us into that Place of Torments, which is reſerved for them. *O* therefore (*u*) *conſider this, ye that forget GOD, leſt he tear you in pieces, and there be none to deliver you.*

But tho the bare Repetition of theſe daring Impieties cannot but raiſe the Ferment of the Blood, if we have any Zeal left for GOD and Religion; yet that which follows, is much worſe. In another *Play* (*x*) a *Witch* deſcends from above in a Chariot drawn by two huge Dragons, out of whoſe Mouths iſſue Fire and Smoke, whilſt ſhe twice together addreſſes herſelf to the *Devil* in theſe Words:

Ye Furies moſt terrible,
Follow me,
Surround me,
With Faces moſt horrible.

The Chariot being deſcended, the *Dragons* ruſh forward, and draw her toward a ſuppoſed *King of Jeruſalem,* who advances to meet this Imp of the *Devil* with ſuch Expreſſions, as are only fit to be us'd to our *dear Redeemer* himſelf.

How timely, Charmer, art thou thus arriv'd
To cure the Wounds of my diſorder'd Soul!

[From all *theſe* Crafts and Aſſaults of the Devil;
From thy Wrath and everlaſting Damnation, *which theſe crying Sins do juſtly call for,*
Good Lord, deliver us.]

(*s*) *Pſal.* 50. 21.
(*t*) *Iſa.* 14. 12, 13, 14.
(*u*) *Pſal.* 50. 22.
(*x*) Rinaldo, *p.* 11. *Sc.* 5.

The *Scriptures* tell us, (r) that *the Devils believe and tremble.* In the *Play-House* he is called (s) a *merry Devil.* Accordingly when *Witches* are concerned, the *Devil* ſeldom fails to act his Part for their Diverſion, ſometimes (t) with the Sound of *Trumpets*, ſometimes (u) with *Martial Muſick* mix'd with Inſtruments of Horror, and ſometimes (x) playing on Inſtruments of War. Sometimes (y) they ſing alone, and ſometimes (z) *Muſick* is join'd with their Singing: ſometimes (a) there is a *Chorus*, and ſometimes (b) there is a *Dance* of ſuch *infernal Spirits.*

Our Bleſſed Saviour, who came to ſeek and to ſave the Souls, which were loſt, tells us very ſolemnly twice together, and confirms it by two Parables, that (c) *there is Joy in the preſence of the Angels of GOD, over one Sinner that repenteth.* When his Deſigns are fruſtrated, it is matter of Rejoicing on the *Stage.* Accordingly, here we have (d) *Hell* repreſented as a Jeſt, with *Tombs* and *Dungeons*, and alſo with Men and Women chain'd in Rows, and *Devils* for their Companions. Here we may obſerve them (e) flouriſhing their Inſtruments of Horror to make Diverſion, and (f) carrying a Man to the Place of *Torments*, with a *Flouriſh of Muſick ſounding Triumph*, in direct oppoſition to the *Joy of Angels* at a Sinner's Converſion.

[Lord, lay not ſuch Sins as theſe to our Charge, and puniſh us not, as we deſerve, for ſuch daring Provocations.]

When *David* was in the Cave, he ſaid, (g) *I cried unto thee, O LORD, and ſaid, Thou art my Refuge, and my Portion in the Land of the Living.* At another time,

(r) *James* 2. 19.
(s) Alarbas, *p.*38. *l.*14.
(t) The *Britiſh* Enchanters, *p.*33. *l.*19, *and* 35.
(u) Ibid. *p.*34. *l.*7.
(x) Ibid. *p.*33. *l.*21.
(y) Mackbeth, *p.*40. *l.*1.
(z) Ibid. *p.*42. *l.*8.
(a) The *Britiſh* Enchanters, *p.*23. *l. antepenult.*
(b) Ibid. *p.*24. *l.*8.
(c) *Luke* 15. 7, 10.
(d) The *Britiſh* Enchanters, *p.*22. *l.*11. Compare this Quotation with *Mede*, *p.*31. on *Prov.* 21. 16.
(e) Ibid. *p.*24. *l.*21.
(f) Ibid. *p.*20. *l.*10. & *p.*22. *l.*11.
(g) *Pſal.* 142. 5.

he said, (*h*) *In thee, O LORD, do I put my Trust, let me never be put to Confusion.* And when good King *Jehosaphat* was streighten'd by his Enemies, he said, (*i*) *O our GOD, wilt thou not judge them? For we have no Might against this great Company, that cometh against us; neither know we what to do; but our Eyes are upon thee.* Upon the *Stage* another King of *Jerusalem*, but not another *David*, nor another *Jehosaphat*, when besieged, saith to an *Enchantress*, (*k*) *In thee, and thee alone, my Soul confides.*

When (*l*) St. *John* in a Vision *saw War in Heaven*, the Devil *prevailed not, neither* after the first Battel *was his place found* there *any more.* This on the *Stage* is an undervaluing of his Power; and therefore he must not leave off in such manner, whilst the *Poets* are capable to assist him: but an *Actor* calls upon the *Posse* of *Devils* for another Battel, and sets GOD at defiance, whilst *Britain* is represented as the Place, where these things are acted.

(*m*) *Fly quick, ye Demons, from your black Abodes,*
And try another Combat with the Gods;
Blue Fires, and pestilential Fumes arise,
And flaming Fountains spout against the Skies.

And now, may we not use the Words of *Moses*, and say, (*n*) *Who is on the LORD's side? Let him come forth*, and endeavour to suppress such unparallel'd *Blasphemies.*

When GOD was willing to shew his *Justice* to the World in a remarkable manner, (*o*) he *rained* down *Fire and Brimstone* upon *Sodom* and upon *Gomorrah*; and at another time (*p*) *the Earth opened her Mouth, and swallowed up* Korah, Dathan, *and* Abiram. But to make a Mock of such dreadful Judgments, (*q*) *Raining of Fire* is represented on the *Stage*, and (*r*) *the Earth opens and*

(*h*) *Psal.* 25. 1.
(*i*) 2 *Chron.* 20. 12.
(*k*) Rinaldo, *p.*13. *l.*13.
(*l*) *Rev.* 12. 7, 8, 9.
(*m*) The *British* Enchanters, 33. *l.*29.
(*n*) *Exod.* 32. 26.
(*o*) *Gen.* 19. 24, 25.
(*p*) *Numb.* 16. 30, 31, 32.
(*q*) The *British* Enchanters, *p.*33. *l.*38.
(*r*) Rinaldo, *p.*45. *l.*22.

swallows

swallows up *Actors* (even pretended *Christians*) with *Thunder*, *Lightning*, *and amazing Noises*, whilst the *Devil* hath the Credit of the whole Performance.

These are Challenges to awaken the Vengeance of the *Almighty*, daring him to exert his *Omnipotence*, to do Right to his *Honour*, and to vindicate his *Divinity*, by severer Effects of his Wrath and Indignation. These are outrageous Provocations, enough to arm all Nature in Revenge, to exhaust the *Judgments* of *Heaven*, to burn our *Metropolis* once more for an Example, or to sink the whole *Island* into the Sea.

I cannot forbear giving another Instance of this nature. When GOD was pleased to vindicate his own Honour, and to shew that he would not be thus affronted, by sending (*s*) a most dreadful Storm, which fill'd us all with Horror and Amazement; wherein he manifested both his Anger and his Power; and made us sensible, to our Sorrow, that *this was his Hand*, and that *he did it*: yet so great was the *Obstinacy* of the *Stage* under such signal Judgments, that we are told, (*t*) *the Actors did in a few Days after entertain again their Audience with the ridiculous Plays of* The Tempest, *and* Mackbeth. And that (*u*) *at the mention of the* (*x*) *Chimneys being blown down, the Audience were pleased to clap at an unusual length of Pleasure and Approbation.* Thus they all agree to mock *the Great Governor* of the World, *who* alone *commands the Winds and the Seas, and they obey him.* As if they would outbrave the *Judgment*, throw *Providence* out of the Chair, place the *Devil* in his stead, and provoke GOD once more to plead his own Cause, in sending a greater Calamity upon us. And since we continue to repeat the same Provocations, what can we expect, but the severer Effects of divine Vengeance?

But to proceed: The Prophet *Micaiah* (*a*) describes the *Majesty* of GOD in this manner. *I saw the LORD sitting upon his Throne, and all the Host of Heaven standing by him, on his Right-Hand and on his Left. And the*

(*s*) November 26. 1703.

(*t*) A Representation of the Impiety and Immorality of the *English* Stage, *p*.5.

(*u*) *Collier*'s Dissuasive from the Playhouse, *p*.15.

(*x*) Mackbeth, *p*.20. *l*.2.

(*a*) 1 *Kings* 22. 19,20,21,22.

LORD

LORD said, Who shall persuade Ahab, *that he may go up and fall at* Ramoth-Gilead? *And there came forth a Spirit, and stood before the LORD, and said, I will persuade him. And the LORD said unto him, Wherewith? And he said, I will go forth, and I will be a lying Spirit in the Mouth of all his Prophets. And he said, Thou shalt persuade him, and prevail also. Go forth, and do so.* Now what Wretch, who is not smitten with the Pleasure of *Blasphemy*, would put the Words of God to the holy *Angels*, into the Mouth of the *Devil*, when he speaks to his *Witches?* But compare the Expressions:

> (*b*) *I shall e'er Night*
> *Raise from the Center such a Spright,*
> *As by the Strength of his Illusion,*
> *Shall draw* Mackbeth *to his Confusion.*

When our *blessed Saviour* rose from the Dead, and had thereby given a full Demonstration, that he had finish'd the Work of our Redemption, he met his Disciples, (*c*) *saying, All hail! and they came, and held him by the Feet, and worshipped him.* When the *Poets* represent a Juggle, and take that occasion to praise the *Devil* in a *set Hymn* for that purpose, and in such Acts of Adoration, as are due only to the *Divine Being*, they *crucify the Son of GOD afresh, and put him to open shame,* by using his Expression on such an occasion. Thus (*d*)

> *Hail, Pow'rs beneath, whose Influence imparts*
> *The Knowledge of infernal Arts;*
> *By whose unerring Gifts we move,*
> *To alter the Decrees above:*
> *Whether on Earth, or Seas, or Air,*
> *The mighty Miracle we dare.*
> *Whether on Beasts our Skill is shewn,*
> *Or human Forms; what's more than human own.*

(*b*) Mackbeth, p. 38. l. 34.
(*c*) *Matth.* 28. 9.
(*d*) The Metamorphosis, p. 14.

This

This is but the third part of the *Song*, which proceeds to enumerate the Works of the *Devil*, in imitation of (*e*) one of our most excellent *Psalms* of Praise; and concludes with *invoking the Help*, and *craving the Assistance* of these *Powers* beneath. But I need not to transcribe any more; since if GOD should enter into Judgment, all the Blood in the Nation is not able to atone for this.

I shall only add, what, I suppose, the *Poets* and *Actors* do not mind, namely, that the same (*f*) Word in the Original is used (*g*) by St. *John*, where he cautions us against some Men, that we should not bid them *God-speed*, or say *Hail* unto them. *For he that biddeth* them *God-speed*, or saith *Hail*, *is Partaker of their evil Deeds.* If then we are Partakers with the *Devil* in his Sins, we shall without Repentance, be Partakers with him in his Sufferings.

I suppose, it will be urg'd, in Vindication of the *Tragedy* of *Mackbeth*, That the consulting with *Witches* is discourag'd, because *Mackbeth* himself, the principal Person in the *Play*, came to an untimely End by consulting with them.

But to this it may be answered, *First*, That granting this to be true, yet here is no Discouragement of *Witchcraft* or *Magick*. The *Witches* act their Parts (*h*) at several times, and (*i*) make both their *Entrance* and their *Exit* by *Flying*. They (*k*) sing, they (*l*) dance, they (*m*) commend their way of Living, and seem to have nothing to disturb them; and their (*n*) Character is, *that they have more in them than mortal Knowledge.*

But *Secondly*, It is not true, that *Witchcraft* is here discouraged; for *Mackbeth* is not the only Instance in this Case. *Banquo* had his Fortune told him, that he should be (*o*) *less than* Mackbeth, *and greater*; and

(*e*) *Psal.* 104.
(*f*) Χαίρειν.
(*g*) 2 *John*, v. 10, 11.
(*h*) Mackbeth, *p.* 1. *l.* 1. *p.* 3. *l.* 22. *p.* 24. *l.* 32. *p.* 39. *l.* 19. & *p.* 41. *l.* 1.
(*i*) *Pag.* 3. *l.* 22. & *p.* 1. *l.* 14.
(*k*) *Pag.* 24. *l.* 32. *p.* 25. *l.* 18. *p.* 39. *l. antepenult.* *p.* 40. *l.* 1, 23. *p.* 42. *l.* 8.
(*l*) *Pag.* 26. *l.* 5.
(*m*) *Pag.* 40. *l.* 23.
(*n*) *Pag.* 10. *l.* 27.
(*o*) *Pag.* 5. *l.* 10.

that

that he should be (p) *not so happy, yet much happier.* The first part of these was true in himself, and the other Part in his Posterity. He was also told, (q) that *he should get Kings, but he should never be one.* Accordingly (r) he was kill'd, when his Son *Flean* escaped, and (s) *eight Kings* are supposed to be of his Race.

Mackduff also consults the *Witches*, and had these Answers (t):

1. *Saving thy Blood, will cause it to be shed:*
2. *He'll bleed by thee, by whom thou first hast bled.*
3. *Thy Wife shall, shunning Dangers, Dangers find,*
And fatal be, to whom she most is kind.

The first and third of these were fulfill'd, because upon the Death of *Banquo* (u) *Mackduff* flies for *England*; his Lady being afraid to travel, stays behind, keeps (x) herself and her Children in a strong Castle, where they were barbarously murder'd by *Mackbeth*'s Orders. The other (y) was fulfilled, when *Mackduff* kill'd *Mackbeth*, saying, *I have a Prophecy, which tells me, I shall have his Blood, who first shed mine.*

Neither doth the Story of *Mackbeth* any way discourage the consulting with *Witches*. They tell him, that he was (z) *Thane*, or Earl of *Glamis*: This (a) he knew. That he was (b) *Thane* of *Cawdor*: This (c) was true, but he did not then know it. And they tell him, That (d) he should be King, which (e) happen'd accordingly. When they were willing to deceive him to his own Destruction, they tell him three Prophecies to make him bold.

First, (f) *Beware* Mackduff,
Avoiding him, Mackbeth *is safe enough.*
This was true; for (g) *Mackduff* kill'd him.

(p) *Pag.* 5. *l.* 11.
(q) *Pag.* 5. *l.* 12.
(r) *Pag.* 33. *l.* 35.
(s) *Pag.* 43. *l.* 34.
(t) *Pag.* 26. *l.* 11.
(u) *Pag.* 37. *l.* 19.
(x) *Pag.* 51. *l.* 20.
(y) *Pag.* 59. *l.* 22.
(z) *Pag.* 4. *l.* 34.
(a) *Pag.* 5. *l.* 18.
(b) *Pag.* 4. *l.* 35.
(c) *Pag.* 6. *l.* 11.
(d) *Pag.* 4. *l.* 36.
(e) *Pag.* 23. *l.* 26. *p.* 26. *l.* 28.
(f) *Pag.* 43. *l.* 5.
(g) *Pag.* 59. *l.* 25.

The

The ſecond is: (*h*)
Be bold and bloody, and Man's Hatred ſcorn;
Thou ſhalt be harm'd by none of Woman born.
To which *Mackduff* anſwers, (*i*) that he
Was from his Mother's Womb untimely ript.

The laſt is: (*k*)
Mackbeth *ſhall like a lucky Monarch reign,*
Till Birnam *Wood remove to* Dunſinam.
And accordingly (*l*) the Soldiers carried Boughs before them, to conceal their Number.

And certainly, when the *Poets* make every tittle thus fulfill'd, they cannot do more to encourage ſuch *diabolical Conſultations.* But if *Mackbeth* was deſtroy'd for conſulting *Witches*, it will alſo be remembred, that he gain'd a Kingdom by the ſame Method; and this is a ſufficient Encouragement. If the Apprehenſions of temporal Death will not frighten Men from capital Crimes in leſſer Caſes, then certainly it will not in ſuch Caſes as this. Beſides, Men are willing to obtain their ambitious Ends, and either look not on ſuch diſtant Conſequences, or elſe they think to prevent them, by being forewarn'd. If *Mackbeth*'s Example ſignifies any thing, the Moral is this: A Man may gain a Kingdom by conſulting with *Witches*; but he is in danger of coming afterward to an untimely End. But leſt this ſhould be a Diſcouragement, the *Poet* takes care to revive the Spirits of thoſe who might be afraid; and boldly tells the Audience, (*m*) That

Thoſe, who expect, and do not fear their Doom,
May hear a Meſſage, tho from Hell it come.

Thus we ſee the Method of the *Stage-Poets*; they repreſent the worſt *Vices* in the beſt *Dreſs*, and make a faint Repreſentation to the contrary, as ſufficient to a-

(*h*) *Pag.* 43. *l.*9.
(*i*) *Pag.* 59. *l.*25.
(*k*) *Pag.* 43. *l.*17.
(*l*) *Pag.* 55. *l.*34. *p.*57. *l.*16, 28. *p.*59. *l.*35.
(*m*) *Pag.* 31. *l.*34.

tone

tone for all their Enormities. With this they endeavour to amuse the World, that they may not think them so bad as they really are: and thus they usually answer the Objections, which are brought against them; and when they drown the World with an overflowing Sea of Profaneness, they make for themselves the Cover of a Fig-Leaf.

It may also be objected in behalf of a late *Opera*, call'd *Rinaldo*, that (n) *Godfrey* and *Rinaldo* convert *Argantes* and *Armida*, and therefore may be allow'd, since it gives Christianity the preference.

In answer to which, it must be allow'd, That there are some, who (o) *call themselves* what they are not, when they are in reality *the Synagogue of Satan*. However (p) *Godfrey* calls himself and his Allies *Christians*, and (q) *Argantes* a *Saracen* gives him that Title: And *Almirena* (r) calls the *Saracens* the *proud Foe to their Religion*. But if we look into the Expressions of these *Christians*, we shall find nothing but *Paganism* or *Atheism*. *Rinaldo* calls *Cupid* (s) the *God of Love*, and (t) the *God of faithful Love*, and (u) prays to him accordingly, praising him also with this Expression, (x) *How mighty is thy Power, blind God of Love!* He prays to (y) *Jupiter* for his *Thunder*, to *revenge* himself, and calls him, (z) *the Thunderer charg'd with Lightning*. And (a) he speaks of *Pluto* and *Proserpina* as of real Beings. *Godfrey* prays (b) to *Fortune*, and *Almirena* calls upon (c) the *Gods* and (d) the *Powers* for Aid. She is also, like other Actors, upon the profane Strain, and calls (e) an *eternal View of Sorrow*, that which will end with Death at the farthest. *Rinaldo* treats his Mistress as a *Goddess* in profane Language, and undervalues *Heaven*,

(n) Rinaldo, *the Argument*.
(o) Revel. 2. 9.
(p) Rinaldo, *Act* 1. *Scene* 1. *l*. 5.
(q) *Pag*. 9. *l*.1. *p*.11. *l*.22. *p*.61. *l*.5.
(r) *Pag*. 5. *l*.21.
(s) *Pag*. 5. *l*. *ult*. & *p*. 15. *l*. 10.
(t) *Pag*. 19. *l*.14.
(u) Ibid.
(x) *Pag*. 5. *l*. *ult*.
(y) *Pag*. 19. *l*.16.
(z) *Pag*. 15. *l*.26.
(a) *Pag*. 17. *l*. 34.
(b) *Pag*. 25. *l*.26.
(c) *Pag*. 29. *l*.24.
(d) *Pag*. 15. *l*.24.
(e) *Pag*. 27. l.7.

when

when he compares it with her. His Expreſſions on this occaſion, will ſhew his *Religion.*

(f) Charm'd by the Magick of thoſe pow'rful Lips,
My hurrying Soul flies outward to thy Call:
I'm not profane; but if I kneel to thee,
My Idol's Brightneſs will my Guilt atone.
And again (*g*)
For thee alone, thou Goddeſs of my Wiſhes,
In humble Sacrifice my Offerings burn;
For thee my Incenſe ſmokes in Sighs of Love.
And (*h*)
Thy Preſence gives me Life, and Death thy Abſence.
And (*i*)
My Heav'n! my Soul's beſt half!

Neither is the *Female Chriſtian* much behind in Compliments of the ſame nature. (*k*)

How lovely terrible in thoſe dear Eyes
Shines the fierce Lightning of Love's brighteſt Heav'n!
And (*l*)
Thou art the Calm of Peace, when my poor Mind
Is toſs'd in Storms of War.

From the Expreſſions on other Occaſions, the Reader may obſerve the Methods uſed to convert theſe *Mahometans.* Now, here is not one word of *God* or of *Chriſt*, or one Argument in behalf of the *Chriſtian Religion.* No, the *Poet* finds another way for this Purpoſe; and *Godfrey* makes uſe of a *Conjurer*, inſtead of *Reaſon.* He tells *Rinaldo*, (*m*) that *There was a Man, who by his magick Skill could read the ſtarry Characters of Heaven*; and (*n*) *that this Man, by long familiar Converſe bound, was his faſt faithful Friend*, and therefore they would conſult him. Hereupon *Rinaldo* (*o*) confeſſes

(*f*) *Pag.* 13. *l.*27.
(*g*) *Pag.* 15. *l.* 1.
(*h*) *Pag.* 15. *l.*7.
(*i*) *Pag.* 35. *l.*13.
(*k*) *Pag.* 13. *l.penult.*
(*l*) *Pag.* 15. *l.*4.
(*m*) *Pag.* 19. *l.*3.
(*n*) *Pag.* 19. *l.*6.
(*o*) *Pag.* 19. *l.* 11.

his

his Hope, and calls him, (*p*) *The desired Magician, whose balmy Counsels were to cure his Sorrow.* Upon their Arrival at the Cave, *Godfrey* desires his Advice and Assistance in (*q*) Words of the highest Respect. The *Magician* gives him *Rods* (*r*) with this Expression:

Take these fatal Wands, and then return,
Secure of bearing Conquest where you go.

With these Wands (*s*) they vanquish the Spirits, (*t*) dissolve the enchanted Garden, the Mountain, and the Castle. They (*u*) vanquish *Argantes*, and then (*x*) *Armida* the Enchantress saith:

Their Valour cannot be more fam'd than ours,
Their Gods are sure more powerful.

Accordingly (*y*) she breaks her enchanted Wand, and both of 'em say to the *Christians*: (*z*)

Conquer'd by you, we would embrace your Faith.

So that here is a Conversion to *Polytheism* or *Christianity* (for the *Poet* makes no difference) and the whole *Play* affords us this only Lesson, That the merest *Pagans*, or the greatest *Conjurers*, are the best Christians.

But to conclude this Chapter with one of our *Opera's*. In that which is called *The Wonders of the Sun*, *Gonzales* and *Diego* are carried up by a *Machine* into the *Heavens*, where they meet with a *Devil*, who (*a*) is call'd, *The Demon of* Socrates; and, as we are told, did belong to the *World in the Sun*. Upon his (*b*) Entrance, he is not willing to deceive the *Audience*, or keep them in suspense; but he plainly tells them, that he was

---

(*p*) Pag. 21. l. 10.
(*q*) Pag. 43. l. 8.
(*r*) Pag. 45. l. 21.
(*s*) Pag. 45. l. 29.
(*t*) Pag. 47. l. 3.
(*u*) Pag. 59. l. 23.
(*x*) Pag. 61. l. 30.
(*y*) Pag. 63. l. 6.
(*z*) Pag. ibid. l. 9.
(*a*) The Wonders in the Sun, *Dramatis Persona.*
(*b*) Pag. 10. l. 32.

a *Devil*, by (*c*) affirming, That he taught the learned *Cardan* many things; *Trithmethius* too, *Cæsar*, *La Bresso*, and *the occult* Agrippa were all his Pupils, besides a new Cabal of wise young Men, call'd *the Rosicrucian Knights*, who were the very Keys of the close Locks of Nature. He taught *Gassendus* in *France*, and *Campanella*, who were under his Instruction. It is much that the *Poet* had not added, That he (*d*) *set* our blessed Saviour *on a Pinacle of the Temple*, *shewed him all the Kingdoms of the World, and the Glory of them*, and therefore might be the fittest Person to carry the *Actors* through these other Regions, and satisfy their Curiosity; tho perhaps this Story being recorded in a Book which the *Poet* seldom minds, did slip out of his Memory.

Having thus own'd himself to be a *Devil*, let us see how he is caress'd at his Entrance on the *Stage*.

(*e*) Gonzales *to* Diego, *Silence, you Rogue, and down upon your Knees; see who comes yonder.*

Diego answers, *I am shot, amaz'd, confounded; I never saw such a Creature in my Life.*

Then they both kneel; whereupon the *Devil*, imitating the (*f*) Speech of the *Angel* to St. *John*, very gravely answers, *You must not kneel to me, I am your Brother.* Upon this, *Gonzales* is equally guilty with the *Devil*, in burlesquing the *Scriptures*, and (*g*) applying the Speech of the Woman to *Elijah* on this blasphemous Occasion: *Oh! mock me not, bright Vision, I beseech thee.* And *Diego* replies in the Language of (*h*) St. *John* concerning our *Saviour*, (*i*) *O Lord! Sir! his Brother! what d'ye mean, Sir? He is not worthy, Sir! to wipe your Worship's Shoes, Sir! O Lord! you his Brother? sweet Sir!*

After this he is called (*k*) *Angel!* (*l*) *dear Angel!*

(*c*) Pag. 11. l. 18.

(*d*) *Matth.* 4. 5, 8.

(*e*) The Wonders in the Sun, p. 10. l. 34.

(*f*) *Revel.* 22. 8, 9.

(*g*) 2 *Kings* 4. 28.

(*h*) *Mat.* 3. 11. *Mark* 1. 7. *Luk.* 3. 16.

(*i*) The Wonders in the Sun, p. 11. l. 2.

(*k*) Ibid. p. 14. l. 5. p. 17. l. 21. p. 19. l. 14. p. 28. l. 28. p. 30. l. 11. p. 33. l. 20. p. 43. Act. 3. l. 1.

(*l*) Pag. 14. l. 5. p. 17. l. 21. p. 19. l. 14. p. 28. l. 28. p. 30. l. 11. p. 45. l. 4. p. 55. l. 19. p. 61. l. 25. p. 66. l. *antepenult.*

sweet

(m) ſweet Angel! (n) my kind Angel! (o) my better Angel! (p) my Angel! for that ſhall be the Name I'll call you. My Life depends wholly on you. (q) My charitable Angel! (r) My good Genius! (s) My ſweet Genius! (t) Good Sir! (u) My Life! (x) My Preſerver! (y) My Life's Preſerver! (z) My Life's chief Happineſs! (a) My Life's dear Guardian! (b) My heavenly Protector! (c) The Soul of Harmony! (d) My Comforter! (e) My only Comfort! and (f) my delicious Bleſſing! He tells the *Devil*, that (g) *the World admir'd* his *Fame*. Speaking of a ridiculous Song, he ſaith, (h) *'Tis all ſeraphical, and like your ſelf.* He prays (i) that *Heaven may requite* him *for* his *Kindneſs*, and confeſſeth his Obligation to the *Devil* in this Expreſſion: (k) *Oh! How ſhall I expreſs my Thanks, thou Quinteſſence of Goodneſs!* And, in concluſion, the *Devil* gives him this Admonition, (l) *When ſometimes you have an hour of Leiſure, think on me your Friend.* To which he makes this Anſwer, *That I'll not fail to do, my glorious Angel, and for ever bleſs the Occaſion.*

When (m) the *Phariſees* aſcribed our *Saviour's* Miracles to the Power of the *Devil*, and ſaid, That *he had an unclean Spirit*, they were tax'd by him as *blaſpheming againſt the Holy Ghoſt*, of which whoſoever was guilty, *ſhould not be forgiven, either in this World, or in the World to come.* Their *Sin* was unpardonable: I pray GOD, that thoſe *Sins* which I have mentioned, may not be ſo too. But I can ſcarcely think it poſſible for the Wit of Man, when aſſiſted by the *Devil* himſelf, to in-

(m) Pag. 14. l. 8. p. 27. l. 6. p. 29. l. 10. p. 33. l. 20.
(n) Pag. 15. l. 3. p. 18. *l. ult.*
(o) Pag. 11. l. 13.
(p) Pag. 13. l. 26.
(q) Pag. 27. Act 2. l. 1.
(r) Pag. 11. l. *ult.*
(s) Pag. 19. l. 24.
(t) Pag. 69. l. 23.
(u) Pag. 43. Act 3. l. 1.
(x) Pag. 35. l. 20.
(y) Pag. 18. l. *ult.*
(z) Pag. 55. l. 28.
(a) Pag. 56. l. *antepenult.*
(b) Pag. 27. l. 2.
(c) Pag. 35. l. 28.
(d) Pag. 43. Act 3. l. 1.
(e) Pag. 44. l. 14.
(f) Pag. ib. l. 25.
(g) Pag. 11. l. 22.
(h) Pag. 55. l. 18.
(i) Pag. 35. l. 28.
(k) Pag. 48. l. 19.
(l) Pag. 69. l. 19.
(m) *Mat.* 12. 31, 32. *Mark* 3. 28, 29, 30.

vent Words, which are more *profane*, *outrageous*, *daring*, *provoking*, and *blaſphemous*; and which in this Age of the World can be attended with greater Aggravations.

CHAP. IV.

The Devil honour'd by the profane Swearing of the Stage.

I Suppoſe that I have tired the *Reader*: however I have ſufficiently tired my ſelf, in giving an account of thoſe *diabolical Arts*, which are promoted on the *Stage*. I could gladly leave off, and go no further in ſuch an unpleaſant Study; but ſince it is the Cauſe of GOD and his *Glory*, I muſt proceed to diſcover other *Blaſphemies* and enormous *Vices* of the ſame nature.

The next Crime which I ſhall charge the *Stage* with, is, the Honour which they give to the *Devil* by *profane Swearing*. If I was to reckon up the whole *Catalogue* of *Oaths* that are uſed upon the *Stage*, it would be ſuch a black Liſt, which the World never ſaw the like before. And tho the Name of GOD is diſhonour'd by each of theſe, yet I ſhall chiefly take notice of thoſe in which the *Devil* is expreſly mentioned.

It is allow'd by all, that *common Swearing* is a very great *Sin*. It is directly againſt (*a*) the *third Commandment*, where we are told, that *the Lord will not hold him guiltleſs, that taketh his Name in vain*. In the old Law, he who (*b*) ſwore ignorantly or unawares, was guilty; and (*c*) he alſo, who heard it, and conceal'd the Crime. The Prophets look'd on this as one Cauſe of their Calamity: (*d*) *Becauſe of ſwearing the Land*

(*a*) *Exod.* 20. 7. *Deut.* 5. 11.
(*b*) *Levit.* 5. 4.
(*c*) *Levit.* 5. 1.
(*d*) *Jer.* 23. 10. *Hoſ.* 4. 2, 7.

did

did *mourn, and the pleasant places of the Wilderness were dried up*; and when (e) *Zechariah* saw *a flying Roll*, typifying *the Curse of GOD*, he was told, that it should destroy every one who was guilty of *Swearing*. When our *blessed Saviour* expounded the *Law*, he commanded us (f) *not to swear at all*; *but let our Communication be Yea, Yea, and Nay, Nay, since whatsoever is more than these*, ἐκ τοῦ πονηροῦ ἐστι, *cometh* from the Devil. And St. *James*, *above all things*, cautions us against it, (g) *lest* we *fall into Condemnation*. And to prevent any Freedom with such Expressions as have any Resemblance of *Oaths*, (h) our *Saviour* tells us, That *of every idle Word which Men shall speak, they shall give an account at the Day of Judgment: For by* our *Words* we shall be *justified, and by* our *Words* we shall *be condemned*.

As this Sin of *Swearing* is contrary to the third *Commandment*, so it is also contrary to the (i) first Petition of the LORD's *Prayer*, wherein we daily desire of GOD that his *Name* may *be hallowed*, sanctify'd, or reverently us'd amongst us. It is also contrary to the *Creed*, since they who are guilty, must either believe, that there is no GOD at all, or else that he is not *Almighty*, but unable to inflict the Penalty which he hath so solemnly denounc'd against this *Sin* in the third *Commandment*.

To this may be added, That this is a Sin, in which there can be no Delight nor Advantage; so that here the *Devil* doth not so much as tempt us by any Allurement; here he lays no Bait, but we give our Souls into his hands, without any thing in exchange for them.

But tho there is neither Profit nor Pleasure herein, yet our *Poets* are resolv'd to give it a Reputation; and I believe, they are the first that ever taught the *Actors* to vindicate such a Practice. However, they seem resolv'd to keep it in fashion, and plead for it to the utmost, notwithstanding what GOD himself hath said to the contrary. One *Actor* speaks of another, that

(e) *Zech.* 5. 3.
(f) *Mat.* 5. 34, 37.
(g) *Jam.* 5. 12.
(h) *Mat.* 12. 36, 37.
(i) *Mat.* 6. 9. *Luke* 11. 2.

(*k*) *no Man* was *better educated than he*, and gives this Reaſon for it; becauſe he would *ſwear with ſuch a Grace, as would make a Man's Heart leap to hear him.* Another ſaith, (*k*) that *Whoring and Swearing are* Accompliſhments *too genteel for a* Tradeſman. And a third, no leſs than a *Knight*, (*m*) calls it a *Gentleman-like Recreation.* He ſaith, that in the Country, *he was even grown a Sot for want of it*: For there, if *a Man did but* ſpeak *an Oath, the People did ſtart* with a due Senſe of the Guilt. And therefore he ſwears, That *a Man had better be a Vagabond* in the City of *London*, *than a Juſtice of Peace in the Country*; becauſe in the City they might be profane to the utmoſt, without Reſtraint or Cenſure.

The Word (*n*) *Heaven* or (*o*) *Heavens* is ſometimes us'd in *Scripture* for GOD himſelf, whoſe Throne and chief Reſidence is there. This the *Poets* know, and therefore (*p*) they uſe it in the ſame Senſe, and frequently

---

(*k*) The Drummer, p. 26. l. 9.

(*l*) The Man of Mode, p. 185. l. 1.

(*m*) She would if ſhe could, p. 91. l. 34.

(*n*) *Luke* 15. 21.

(*o*) *Dan.* 4. 26.

(*p*) Heaven *for* GOD, A Woman's Revenge, *Epilogue*, l. 12. p. 39. l. 11. p. 42. l. 25. p. 43. l. 21. p. 45. l. 21. p. 52. l. 15. p. 55. l. *penult*. p. 57. l. 16. p. 59. l. 26. *French* Cato, p. 10. l. 2, 10. p. 25. l. *penult*. p. 36. l. 25. p. 41. l. 9, 26. p. 46. l. *penult*. p. 47. l. 1. p. 56. l. 12. Ignoramus, p. 12. l. 32. p. 16. l. 10, 14. p. 50. l. 35. Lucius, p. 2. l. 29. p. 40. l. 26. p. 54. l. 5. She would if ſhe could, p. 91. l. 21. p. 107. l. 24. p. 110. l. 12. p. 116. l. 13. p. 118. l. 14. p. 132. l. 36. p. 134. l. 13. p. 140. l. 35. p. 153. l. 1. p. 154. l. 2. p. 156. l. 19, 23. p. 157. l. 34. p. 162. l. 7. The artful Husband, p. 9. l. 20. p. 26. l. 21. The Cobler of *Preſton*, p. 9. *l. ult.* p. 10. l. 9. p. 12. l. 30. p. 14. l. 25. p. 22. l. 19. p. 33. l. 14. The comical Revenge, p. 19. l. 21. *&* *penult.* p. 27. l. 5. p. 45. l. 3. p. 59. l. 1. p. 63. l. *penult.* p. 64. l. 33. p. 79. l. 25. The Contrivances, p. 8. l. 1. p. 17. l. 3. The cruel Gift, p. 10. l. 5. p. 17. l. 29. p. 20. l. 10, 15. p. 24. l. 22. p. 32. l. 3. p. 34. l. 6. p. 35. l. 21. p. 38. l. 20. p 39. l. 37. p. 41. l. 9. p. 47. l. 13. p. 49. l. 26. p. 51. l. 2. p. 52. l. 9. p. 53. l. 3. p. 63. l. 4. p. 64. l. 3. The Drummer, p. 43. l. 19. The Earl of *Mar* marr'd, p. 22. l. 20. p. 23. l. 15, 19, *&* *ult.* p. 31. l. 20. p. 32. l. 6. The fatal Marriage, p. 109. l. 10. p. 111. l. 32. p. 112. l. 9, 20, 21. p. 113. l. 13, 22. p. 118. l. 23. p. 119. l. 21. p. 124. l. 30. p. 151. l. 4. p. 154. l. 17.

p. 155.

quently (*q*) in the same *Play*, even (*r*) when they ridicule it at the same time.

(I have been the larger in the Quotations out of the *Plays* for the three Years last past, that the Reader may observe, how frequently they use any Word for GOD, in their paltry and trifling Matters, and sometimes in profane Expressions, and debauch'd Intrigues; that so their too much Familiarity with the *Supreme Being* may, if possible, breed a Contempt of him.)

---

p.155. l.9. p.157. l.27. p.158. l.27. p.170. l.20. p.172. l.17. p. *ult.* l. *ult.* The Man of Mode, p.204. l.13. p.205. l. *penult.* p. 218. l.17. p.237. l.23. p.262. l. 20. The Masquerade, p.25. l.12. The perfidious Brother, p.3. l.19, *& ult.* p.12. l 17. p.13. l.27. p. 14. l.24, 29. p.16. l.18. p.17. l. 17. p.42. l.25. p.47. l.3. The Pretender's Flight, p.20. l.13. p. 33. l.11. p.36. l.3. The Royal Convert, p.1. l.*ult.* p.30. l.15. p. 33. l.3. p.34. l.1. p.35. l.7. p.37. l.4. p.39. l.19. p.61. l.6. p.76. l.3. p.82. l.8. The Squire of *Alsatia*, p.8. l.10. p.14. l.10, 27. p.20. l.40. p.21. l.3, 5. p.32. l. 35. p.39. l.43. p.40. l.3. p.44. l.4. p.48. l.8, 21, 31. p.49. l.7. p.54. l.10. p.55. l.15. p.57. l.43. *spoken by a furious, malicious and revengeful Whore, who gives* God *Thanks, that she wants for nothing*, p.58. l.14. p.62. l.29. p.63. l.27. p.73. l.39. The Sultaness, p.3. l.14. p.9. l. 20, *& penult.* p.11. l.23. p.12. l.29. p. 17. l.7. p.21. l.34. p.22. l. 16. p.28. l.11. p.29. l.34. p.36. l.9. p.47. l.1. p.52. l.28. p.53. l.27. The Victim, p.5. l.4, 20. p.7. l. 27. p.13. l.9. p.18. l.26. p.25. l. 19. p.30. l.8, 26. p.32. l.24. p.36. l.32. p.42. l.6. p.43. l.3. *Titus Manlius*, p.7. l.5. Three Hours after Marriage, p.20. l.19. *on a most ridiculous Occasion*, p. 33. l.27. p.71. l.19. Wit at a Pinch, p.8. l.17. p.19. l.6. p.22. l.11. Woman is a Riddle, p 32. l.4. p.34. l.25. p.35. l.16. p.37. l.18. p.46. l.5. p.50. l.7. p.55. l. 14. p.93. l.22. *Above an hundred and ninety one times in all.*

Heavens for God. *French* Cato, p.2. l. *penult.* She would if she could, p.153. l.16. The comical Revenge, p.47. l.33. p.54. l. *penult.* p.55. l.8. p.79. l.31. The Contrivances, p.33. l.23. The Man of Mode, p.199. l.16. The Perfidious Brother, p.55. l. 12. The Squire of *Alsatia*, p. 43. l.12. Wit at a Pinch, p.23. l.4, *&c.*

(*q*) The Wonder, p.5. l.7. p.8. l.22. p.10. l.6. p.17. l.7, 16. p.18. l.15. p.24. l.24. p.41. l.14. p. 53. l. 10. p. 57. l. 22. p. 63. l. 4.

(*r*) The Amorous Widow, p. 23. l.9.

Now, becauſe the Word *Heaven* is put in *Scripture* inſtead of GOD, therefore the *Poets*, to burleſque and ridicule it the more, put alſo the Word *Hell* inſtead of the *Devil*. Thus their *Swearing* by *Heaven* is a *Swearing* by *GOD*, their *Swearing* by *Hell* is a *Swearing* by the *Devil*; and whenever they ſwear by *Heaven* and *Hell*, or join theſe two Words together, (which is too too common) they mean *GOD* and the *Devil*.

To prevent theſe enormous Practices, St. *James* cautions us, (*s*) that we ſhould *not ſwear by Heaven*. And our *bleſſed Saviour* (*e*) gives the Reaſon, together with the Prohibition, *For it is GOD's Throne*; and therefore (*u*) *Whoſoever ſweareth by Heaven, ſweareth by the Throne of GOD, and by him that ſitteth thereon*. But this will not reſtrain the *Actors*; for they frequently (*x*) *ſwear by Heaven*,

(*s*) *James* 5. 12.
(*t*) *Mat.* 5. 34.
(*u*) *Ibid.* 23. 22.
(*x*) A Woman's Revenge, p. 35. l. *antepenult*. p. 36. l. 10. Camilla, *p*.27. *l*.14. *French* Cato, *p*.15. *l*.5. *p*.19. *l*.3. *p*.23. *l*.10. Liberty aſſerted, *p*.66. *l*.30. Love at firſt Sight, *p*.15. *l*.41. *p*.55. *Act* 5. *l*.24. *p*.60. *l*. *antepenult*. *p*.63. *l*.28. Solon, *p*.54. *l*.15. *p*. 62. *l*.27. The artful Husband, *p*.23. *l*. 2, 8. *p*.67. *l*.17. The Cares of Love, *p*.17. *l*.20. *p*.19. *l*.14. *p*.20. *l*.13. *p*.23. *l*.31. *p*.26. *l*.34. The Conqueſt of *Spain*, *p*.3. *l*.5. *p*.14. *l*.11. *p*.15. *l*.27. *p*.22. *l*.33. *p*.26. *l*.32. *p*.44. *l*.15. *p*.51. *l*.31. *p*.55. *l*.4. *p*.58. *l*.5. The Earl of *Mar* marr'd, *p*.9. *l*. 26. *p*.17. *l*.7. *p*.20. *l*.26. *p*.29. *l*. 25. The faithful Bride of *Granada*, *p*.2. *l*.19. *p*.29. *l*.18. The faithful General, *p*. 28. *l*. 44. The Female Wits, *p*.2. *l*.15. *p*. 4. *l*.19. *p*.9. *l*.16. p.25. *l*.5. *p*. 32. *l*.3. *p*.45. *l*.3. *p*.52. *l*.17. *p*. 55. *l*. *ult*. *Engliſh* Cato, *p*.40. *l*. *penult*. *p*.46. *l*.20. Electra, *Act* 1. *Ver*. 489. *Act* 3. *Ver*. 185. *Act* 5. *Ver*. 67. Injur'd Virtue, *p*.12. *l*.4. *Sawny* the *Scot*, *p*.30. *l*.33. The Loyal Subject, *p*.66. *l*.29, 35. The Miſtake, *p*.41. *l*. 8. The Perfidious Brother, *p*.5. *l*.25. *p*.7. *l*.12. *p*.19. *l*.5. *p*.20. *l*.29, 30. *p*.24. *l*. 12. *p*.25. *l*.25. *p*.35. *l*.20. *p*.39. *l*.17. *p*.40. *l*.17. *p*.42. *l*.25. The Perplex'd Lovers, *p*.23. *l*. *antepenult*. The *Perſian* Princeſs, *Act* 1. *p*.1. *l*.1. The *Platonick* Lady, *p*.70. *l*.1. The *Portſmouth* Heireſs, *p*.28. *l*.20. *p*.49. *l*. *antepenult*. The Pretender's Flight, *p*.9. *l*.23. *p*. 12. *l*. *penult*. *p*.28. *l*.13. *p*.35. *l*. 25, & *antepenult*. *p*. 37. *l*. 19. The Rival Brothers, *p*. 84. *l*. 5. The roving Husband reclaim'd, *p*.61. *l*.10. *p*.62. *l*.18. *p*.63. *l*.15. The Royal Merchant, *p*.44. *l*.38. *p*. 48. *l*. 21. *p*. 59. *l*. 18. The

Squire

Heaven, (y) *by the Heavens*, or (z) *by their Life, and by all the Happineſs which they hope for.* And to do the ſame Honour to that (a) *Priſon*, where the *curſed Spirits* are *reſerved under everlaſting Chains of Darkneſs*, they alſo (b) *ſwear by Hell*, or (c) *by the moſt ſacred Stygian Lake.*

It is allowed by all, that the very Nature of an Oath is an Appeal to GOD, as an Evidence for the Truth of what is ſaid. But in the *Play-Houſe*, the very Form is adminiſtred in another manner, and the Devil is added to make the Solemnity the greater. (d) *Now ſwear, and call to witneſs Heav'n, Hell, and Earth.*

Beſides, it is allowed by all Divines, that we ought on any Occaſion to *ſwear* by none but GOD, becauſe an *Oath* is an Act of *Religious Worſhip*, in which we acknowledge many of his *Attributes*, ſuch as his *Juſtice*, his *Omnipotence*, his *Omniſcience*, and his *Truth*. And therefore in ſolemn Caſes, where an *Oath* is allowed, we are commanded (e) to *fear the LORD our GOD, to ſerve him, to cleave unto him, and to ſwear by his Name.* And (f) to *ſwear, The LORD liveth, in Truth, in Judgment, and in Righteouſneſs.* Nay, GOD challengeth this to himſelf, when he ſaith, (g) *I am the LORD, that is my Name, and my Glory will I not give to another, neither my Praiſe to graven Images.* And therefore the *ſwearing* by *Pagan Idols*, or by the *Devil*, is the ſetting them up inſtead of GOD, and aſcribing to them the *Attributes* of the *Divine Nature.*

Squire of *Alſatia*, *p.*10. *l.*37. *p.* 20. *l.* 33. *p.* 31. *l. antepenult.* *p.* 32. *l.* 38. *p.*37. *l.*2. & *p.* 67. *l.*17. The Sultaneſs, *p.*49. *l.*19. The Victim, *p.*48. *l.*7.

(y) The Man of Mode, *p.* 190. *l.* 4. *p.* 236. *l.* 5. *p.* 235. *l.* 2, 33, &c.

(z) Ibid. *p.*212. *l.*24.

(a) *Jude*, ver. 6.

(b) *Appius* and *Virginia*, *p.*44. *l.* 13. Arſinoe, *p.* 42. *l.* 14. *Phædra* and *Hippolytus*, *p.* 61. *l.* 13. The *Britiſh* Enchanters, *p.*35. *l.*32. The Gameſter, *p.*45. *l. ult.* The Lawyer's Fortune, *p.* 30. *l.* 1. The Perplex'd Lovers, *p.*20. *l.*24. Zelmane, *p.*34. *l.*14.

(c) Arminius, *p.*5. *l.*19.

(d) *Phædra* and *Hippolytus*, *p.*48. *l.*20.

(e) *Deut.* 6. 13. and *Chap.* 10. 20.

(f) *Jer.* 4. 2.

(g) *Iſa.* 42. 8.

However, notwithſtanding theſe Texts, or any thing which can be urged to the contrary, the *Actors* frequently ſwear by the *Pagan Idols:* Sometimes in general, (*h*) *By the Gods*, (*i*) *By the Immortal Gods*, or (*k*) *Before the Gods*; (*l*) *By all the Powers*, (*m*) *By all the Powers of Heaven*, or (*n*) *By all the Stars.* And ſometimes they *ſwear* more particularly, (*o*) *By Love* or *Cupid*, (*p*) *By* Hercules, (*q*) *By* Jupiter, (*r*) *By* Juno, (*s*) *By* Mars, (*t*) *By* Neptune, (*u*) *By* Oroſmades, (*x*) *By* Pallas, (*y*) *By the Sun*, (*z*) *By the all-ſeeing Sun*, (*a*) *By mighty* Thor, and (*b*) *By* Venus; and (*c*) ſometimes alſo *by* ſuch *Women* for whom they have a Reſpect and Eſteem.

Neither is this the Reſpect which they pay only to *Pagan Idols*; but they pay the ſame alſo to the *Devil*, as

---

(*h*) *Perolla* and *Izadora*, *p*.29. *l*.27. Solon, *p*. 56. *l*. 5. The *Britiſh* Enchanters, *p*.8. *l*.15,35. The Faithful General, *p*.28. *l*.46. *p*. 36. *l*. 42. *p*. 68. *l*.39. The Female Wits, *p*. 44. *l*. 9. The Gameſter, *p*.40. *l*.*ult*. The Pretender's Flight. *p*.29. *l*.6.

(*i*) The *Britiſh* Enchanters, *p*.15. *l*.22.

(*k*) Hydaſpes, *p*.34. *l*.25. *p*. 48. *l*.26.

(*l*) Zelmane, *p*.46. *l*.26.

(*m*) Squire of *Alſat*. *p*.31. *l*.34.

(*n*) Almahide, *Interlude* 2. *p*.2. *l*.24. Zelmane, *p*.39. *l*.22.

(*o*) Camilla, *p*. 7. *l*. *penult*. *p*.21. *l*.19. Liberty Aſſerted, *p*. 14. *l*.17. *Pyrrhus* and *Demetrius*, *p*.10. *l*.15. Solon, *p*.64. *l*.19. The Wonders in the Sun, *p*.52. *l*.8.

(*p*) The Fair Example, *p*. 9. *l*. 19. The Gameſter, *p*. 56. *l*. 11.

(*q*) Gibraltar, *p*.59. *l*.35. Solon, *p*.40. *l*.28. *p*.71. *l*.6. The Confederacy, *p*. 13. *l*. *penult*. The Female Wits, *p*.44. *l*.12. The Gameſter, *p*.31. *l*.11. The Maſquerade, *p*. 6. *l*. 21. The Wonders in the Sun, *p*.52. *l*.8. Ulyſſes, *p*. 4. *l*.29. *p*.30. *l*.3. *p*. 41. *l*.21. Woman is a Riddle, *p*.10. *l*.17,26. *p*.11. *l*.22.

(*r*) The Gameſter, *p*.52. *l*.12. Ulyſſes, *p*.11. *l*.17. *p*.12. *l*.25.

(*s*) The Amorous Miſer, *p*.45. *l*.3. Ulyſſes, *p*.40. *l*.18.

(*t*) The Baſſet-Table, *p*. 22. *l*. 11.

(*u*) Thomyris, *p*.44. *l*.13.

(*x*) Ulyſſes, *p*.41. *l*.21.

(*y*) Thomyris, *p*. 44. *l*. 13. Zelmane, *p*.4. *l*.18.

(*z*) Zelmane, *p*.27. *l*.27.

(*a*) The Royal Convert, *p*.23. *l*. 7.

(*b*) The Fair Example, *p*. 7. *l*. *antepenult*. The Loyal Subject, *p*.70. *l*.3. The Northern Laſs, *p*. 52. *l*.15. Ulyſſes, *p*.3. *l*. *penult*.

(*c*) Solon, *p*. 64. *l*.15. The Man of Mode, *p*.241. *l*.10.

if they would put GOD himſelf and his greateſt Enemy upon the ſame Level. Accordingly they ſwear (*d*) *By all the Powers of Earth, and thoſe of Hell*; (*e*) *By the Infernal King, the Fates and Furies*; (*f*) *By the Infernal Powers*; (*g*) *By the glorious Impudence of ſubſtantial Darkneſs*; (*h*) *By the Roſy Gills of the Devil*; (*i*) *By the Furies*; (*k*) *By the Eternal Furies*; (*l*) *By Hell*, and (*m*) *By the Devil.* In one (*n*) *Play* the *Scene* is *Hell*, and *Pluto* ſwears at large,

> *By the Horrors of the Deep,*
> *By* Chaos, *Darkneſs, Night, and Sleep,*
> *By all the Torments here below,*
> *By all the fiery Streams that flow.*

And in another *Play*, (*o*) a *Knight ſwears, By all thoſe Devils that have hitherto poſſeſs'd* the Female *Sex.*

Thus have we ſeen in what manner the *Actors* ſwear by the *Pagan Idols*, and by the *Devil*. It may not be improper to obſerve, how they manage their *Oaths*, when they *ſwear* by GOD himſelf. Of this they are frequently guilty. And whereas the others were generally in more weighty Matters, this is very often upon ridiculous Occaſions. Sometimes they repeat (*p*) an *Oath* as ſpoken by another; but moſt commonly (*q*) they are guilty of it themſelves. That they may extend the Divine

---

(*d*) *Appius* and *Virginia*, *p.* 9. *l.* 18.

(*e*) Ibid. *p.* 9. *l.* 19.

(*f*) *Phædra* and *Hippolytus*, *p.* 21. *l.* 21.

(*g*) The Lady's Laſt Stake, *p.* 74. *l.* 18.

(*h*) The Wonders in the Sun, *p.* 11. *l.* 33.

(*i*) Arſinoe, *p.* 42. *l.* 14. The Faithful Bride of *Granada*, *p.* 43. *l.* 3. The Gameſter, *p.* 45. *l.* 4.

(*k*) The Gameſter, *p.* 56. *l.* 1.

(*l*) Arſinoe, *p.* 42. *l.* 14. The Gameſter, *p.* 45. *l. ult.* The Lawyer's Fortune, *p.* 30. *l.* 1. The *Britiſh* Enchanters, *p.* 35. *l.* 32. Zelmane, *p.* 34. *l.* 14.

(*m*) An Act at *Oxford*, *p.* 26. *l.* 16. The Gameſter, *p.* 55. *l.* 9.

(*n*) Solon, *p.* 30. *l.* 10.

(*o*) The Comical Revenge, *p.* 62. *l.* 22.

(*p*) The Man of Mode, *p.* 20. *l.* 22.

(*q*) *See* the Evil and Danger of Stage-Plays, *p.* 34, &c. *where above fourſcore Inſtances of this nature are reckon'd up*; *to which may be added*, Hob, *p.* 17. *l.* 1. Love in a Sack, *p.* 11. *l.* 14. *p.* 17. *l.* 22. *p.* 27. *l.* 6. *p.* 30. *l.* 6. *p.* 44. *l.* 1. *p.* 48. *l. ult.* & *p.* 53. *l.* 10. *Sawny* the *Scot*, *p.* 47. *l.* 7, 22. The Amorous Widow, *p.* 35. *l.* 14. *p.* 36. *l.* 2. *p.* 50. *l.* 15, 23. *p.* 52. *l. penult.*

Divine Attributes farther than the *Godhead*, they (r) *swear by all that's Good:* and, to take away all Distinction between Good and Evil, they also *swear* (s) *By all that's Mischievous.* To make the Sacred Name of the LORD more contemptible, they *swear* (t) *By the Lord Harry.* And to ridicule an Oath, by the *Name* of GOD, they take care, that it is deliver'd, sometimes in a (u) *French*, and sometimes in a *Scotch* Tone, which they call in Derision (x) an *Heathen Dialect*. I need not multiply Quotations of this nature, when a (y) *French* Serving-Man in one *Comedy*, and (z) a *Scotchman* of the same Rank in another, shall each be guilty hereof above forty times, besides the profaning the (a) sacred Name of GOD upon other Occasions. And,

---

l. penult. p.53. *l.*30. p.71. *l.*28. p. 77. *l.* 3, 9. The Litigants, p.23. *l.*18. p. 24. *l.* 38. The Perplex'd Couple, p.8. *l.*1. The Wonder, p.7. *l.*2. p.13. *l.*27,30. p.15. *l.*20. p.77. *l.*25.

(r) Compare *Mark* 10. 18. *with* A Woman's Revenge, p.50. *l.* 7. The What-d'ye-call it, p. 10. *l.* 19. The Wife's Relief, p.47. *l.*28.

(s) Woman is a Riddle, p.52. *l.*7.

(t) The Masquerade, p.6. *l.*1. p.9. *l.*26. The Cobler of *Preston*, p. 19. *l. penult.* p.21. *l.*5. This is spoken by a Drunken Cobler, who had before used the Name of the LORD too freely, p.11. *l.*29. *and called for Strong Beer,* For God's sake, *as if he was a God* who delighted *in Drunkenness.* p. 19. *l. antepenult.*

(u) Sawny the *Scot*, p.21. *l.*24. p. 22. *l.* 22. The Humours of the Army, p.28. *l. ult.* p. 50. *l.* 14, 21. p.66. *l.*5. p. 68. *l.*33.

(x) The Wonder, p.43. *l.*29.

(y) The Comical Revenge, *Act* 1. *l.*6. p.10. *l.*3, 10, 32, & *antepenult.* p. 11. *l.*26. & *ult.* p.14. *l.*17,23,28. p.21. *l.*1,6,13. p.22. *l.*13. p.23. *l.*25, 28. p.39. *l.*27,31. p.40. *l.*25. p.59. *l. ult.* p.60. *l.*4,13,21,26, & *ult.* p.61. *l.*7. p.68. *l.*9,14. p.71. *l.*27,32. p.72. *l.*20,32. p.74. *l.*31. p.80. *l.*20. p.81. *l.*32. p.82. *l.*32. p. 83. *l.*3,5.

(z) *Sawny* the *Scot*, p.6. *l.*5, 16. p. 7. *l.*3, 9, 30. p.8. *l.*9, 12, 24. p.9. *l.*7. p.11. *l.*30. p.14. *l.*18. p.15. *l.*1,32. p.16. *l.*5,8. p.17. *l.*15,29. p.19. *l.*15. p.20. *l.*3. p.28. *l.*34. p.32. *l.*25,28, & *antepenult.* p.33. *l.*6. p.34. *l.* 16. p.35. *l.*13. p.36. *l.*12. p.38. *l.*2. p.40. *l.*18. p.49. *l.*23. p.50. *l.*29,30. p.53. *l.* 27,30. p.61. *l.* 26. p.62. *l.*11,17. p.63. *l.*19, 33, 34. p. 66. *l.* 11. p.72. *l.*3. p.74. *l.*6.

(a) Ibid. p.65. *l.*21. p. 67. *l.* 3.

to

to vilify it the more, the *Poets* put this Name into the Mouths of the most sawcy, silly, impertinent Fellows of the whole Company.

Sometimes the *Actors* swear (*b*) *By the Blood* of the Son of GOD, even (*c*) in a ridiculous *Scotch* Tone, or (*d*) their *Heathen Dialect*; and sometimes (*e*) by his Wounds, (*f*) even in the same manner. Sometimes they swear (*g*) by the *Body*, (*h*) by the *Death*,

---

(*b*) *See* The Evil and Danger of Stage-Plays, *p.* 37, *where* above fifty Instances of this nature are reckon'd up. To which may be added, Love in a Sack, *p.*26. *l.*15. *Sawny* the *Scot*, *p.*7. *l.*4. *p.*33. *l.* 24, 32. *p.*38. *l.*23. *p.*39. *l. antepenult.* *p.*48. *l.*23. *p.*49. *l.*16. *p.*54. *l.*26. *p.*58. *l.*7, 27. *p.*70. *l.*19. The Wonders in the Sun, *p.*10. *l.*4.

(*c*) *Sawny* the *Scot*, *p.*6. *l.*14. *p.*10. *l.*8. *p.*17. *l.*20. *p.*18. *l.*2.

(*d*) The Wonder, *p.*43. *l.*29.

(*e*) *See* The Evil and Danger of Stage-Plays, *p.*37. *where almost thirty Instances of this nature may be reckon'd up. To which may be added,* The Litigants, *p.*21. *l.* 28. The Wonders in the Sun, *p.*9. *l.*26. *p.*17. *l.*3. *p.*19. *l.*18. *p.*26. *l.*14.

(*f*) *Sawny* the *Scot*, *p.* 6. *l. antepenult.* *p.* 8. *l.* 31. *p.* 13. *l. penult.* *p.*15. *l.*33. *p.*27. *l.*32. *p.*33. *l.* 6, 18. *p.*34. *l.*11. *p.*35. *l.*1. *p.*36. *l.*17. *p.*40. *l.*3. *p.*56. *l.*7. *p.*64. *l.ult.* *p.*73. *l.*30.

(*g*) As you find it, *p.* 16. *l. antepenult.* Love at first Sight, *p.*25. *l.*30. *p.*26. *l.*16,40. The Wonders in the Sun, *p.*16. *l.*11.

(*h*) The Mistake, *p.*48. *l.*19. Hampstead Heath, *p.* 18. *l.* 26. The Basset-Table, *p.* 10. *l.* 12. Love at first Sight, *Epilogue*, *l.*5. *p.*39. *l.*7. *p.*43. *l.* 21, 32. *p.*47. *l.*1, & *antepenult.* *p.*50. *l.*15. *p.* 56. *l. penult.* *p.*63. *l.*21, 30, & *ult.* *p.*65. *l.*24. *p.*67. *l.*22. Solon, *p.*49. *l.*12. *p.*67. *l.*19. Gibraltar, *Sheet* E. *p.* 33. *l.* 10. *Sheet* F. *p.*45. *l.*26. *p.*52. *l.*14. *p.*54. *l.*35. *p.*55. *l.* 17, & *penult.* *p.* 60. *l.* 27. Love at first Sight, *p.*57. *l.*30. The Amorous Miser, *p.*11. *l.*3. *p.*13. *l.*19. *p.*14. *l.*23. The Amorous Widow, *p.*15. *l.ult.* *p.*27. *l.*18. *p.*46. *l.*5. The Basset Table, *p.* 39. *l.*31. The Biter, *p.*4. *l.*4. The Careless Husband, *p.*4. *l.*1. *p.*6. *l.*10. *p.*17. *l.*37. *p.*18. *l.*39. *p.*28. *l.*12,41. *p.*47. *l. ult.* *p.*55. *l.*7. *p.*62. *l.*30. *p.*64. *l.*3. The Cares of Love, *p.*43. *l.*25. *p.*48. *l.*27. The Confederacy, *p.* 14. *l.*9. *p.*33. *l.* 3. The Conquest of *Spain*, *p.*60. l.26. The Gamester, *p.*4. *l.*21. *p.*45. *l.*32. *p.*55. *l.*14. The Lady's Last Stake, *p.* 46. *l.*16. *p.*70. *l.*6. *p.*71. *l.*25. The Lawyer's Fortune, *p.*8. *l.*20. The *Persian* Princess, *p.* 6. *l.* 1. The *Portsmouth* Heiress, *p.* 31. *l.* 4. *p.*47. *l.* 10, 28. *p.*52. *l.*1. *p.*54. *l.*12. The Quacks, *p.*13. *l.*21. The Roving Husband Reclaim'd, *p.*39. *l.*22. The Temple of Love, *Epilogue*, *l.* 3.

by

(*i*) by the *Heart*, (*k*) by the *Flesh*, and (*l*) by the *Life* of our *Dear Redeemer*. And this they often join with *Words* of Contempt and Reproach, as if they look'd upon the *Incarnation* of our *Blessed Lord*, his Sufferings for the *Redemption* of fallen Man, and that stupendous Miracle of Mercy, to be the greatest Calamity which could befal the World. Thus they *swear* (*m*) by the *Blood* of *Christ, and Fire*; (*n*) by his *Death and Fire*; (*o*) by his *Blood, Death and Fire*; (*p*) by his *Blood and Thunder*; (*q*) by his *Death and Amazement*; (*r*) by his *Death and Confusion*; (*s*) by his *Death and Destruction*; and (*t*) by *Torture and Death*. And (that which is most blasphemously impious) because they are resolv'd (*u*) to make a *Concord between Christ and Belial*, they swear (*x*) by his *Death and Furies*; (*y*) by his *Death and Hell*; by

---

(*i*) Love at first Sight, *p*. 25. *l*.17. *p*.28. *l*.24, 30, 36. *p*.30. *l*.9. *p*.38. *l*.9. *p*.41. *l*. 3, 31. *p*. 42. *l*.4, 10, 16, *and penult*. *p*.47. *l*.5, 9, 32. *p*.48. *l*.7, 22. *p*.52. *l*.1, 14. *p*.53. *l*.24, 31. *p*.54. *l*.18, 21, *and penult*. *p*.60. *l*.17, 21, 26. *p*. 61. *l*.3. *p*.62. *l*.12. *p*.63. *l*. 3, 9, 12, 37. *p*.64. *l*.11, 18. *p*.65. *l*.9, 29. *p*. 67. *l*. 3, 7, 16, 25, 32. *Sawny* the *Scot*, *p*.54. *l*.33. The Amorous Miser, *p*. 25. *l*. 21. The Amorous Widow, *p*. 26. *l*. 3.

(*k*) Almahide, *Interlude* 2. *p*. 2. *l*.18. The Platonick Lady, *p*.30. *l*.27.

(*l*) Gibraltar, *Sheet* F. *p*. 43. *l*.1. *p*.44. *l*.18. *p*.56. *l*.17. The Amorous Miser, *p*.39. *l*.1. The Amorous Widow, *p*. 31. *l*. 21. The *Portsmouth* Heiress, *p*.36. *l*.13. *p*. 63. *l*. 7, 11, 13. The Wonders in the Sun, *p*.16. *l*.19. *and Epilogue*, *p*.2. *l*.6.

(*m*) The Wonders in the Sun, *p*.54. *l*.11.

(*n*) The Recruiting Officer, *p*. 32. *l*.24.

(*o*) The Gamester, *p*.52. *l*.14.

(*p*) The Confederacy, *p*. 13. *l*.8. *p*.67. *l*.22. *p*.50. *l*.30. *own'd to be an Oath*. Ibid. *l*.31. The Fair Example, *p*.34. *l*.18.

(*q*) The *Portsmouth* Heiress, *p*.38. *l*.1.

(*r*) Rosamond, *p*.2. *l*.14. The Fair Example, *p*.42. *l*.18. *p*.59. *l*.31. The Lady's Last Stake, *p*. 46. *l*. 10. The Mistake, *p*. 58. *l*. 1. The Wife of *Bath*, *p*. 61. *l*. 2.

(*s*) The Roving Husband Reclaim'd, *p*.41. *l*.7.

(*t*) The *Portsmouth* Heiress, *p*.45. *l*.26.

(*u*) 2 *Cor*. 6. 15, 16.

(*x*) An Act at *Oxford*, *p*. 36. *l*. *penult*. The Confederacy, *p*. 13. *l*.15. *p*.45. *l*.7. *p*.33. *l*.7. *own'd to be an Oath*, ibid. *l*.8.

(*y*) Gibraltar, p.54. l.27. The Beaux Stratagem, p. 65. l. 23. The Ladies Last Stake, p.36. l. 20.

(z) by his *Death and the Devil*; (a) by his *Death, Hell, and the Devil*; (b) by his *Death, Hell, and Furies*; and (c) by his *Wounds, Death, and the Devil*. In one *Play*, an *Actor swears* (d) by the *Life* of *Christ*, that he is *sure, the Devil is either in* himself, *or in his Spectacles*; and (e) wisheth *by Christ*, that *the Devil would come into his Presence*. One *swears* by the (f) *Wounds* of *Christ*, that the *Devil* is *among them*; and (g) another confirms it with an *Oath*, by the *Life* of *our Blessed Saviour*, that it is so *in good earnest*.

[Visit not, O LORD, for these things; and let not thy Soul be avenged on such a Blasphemous Nation as this.]

---

20. The Perplex'd Lovers, p. 35. l. 37. The Platonick Lady, p. 27. *l*. 6.

(z) Gibraltar, p. 38. l. *penult.* p. 49. *l*. 9. p. 58. l. 29. The Amorous Widow, p. 47. l. 19. The Confederacy, p. 29. l. *ult.* p. 50. l. 25. *own'd to be an Oath*, ibid. l. 26.

(a) The *Gotham* Election, p. 61. l. 26.

(b) Arsinoe, p. 35. l. *penult.* She wou'd if she cou'd, p. 139. l. 33. The *British* Enchanters, p. 29. *Act* 4. *l*. 4. The Faithful General, p. 53. l. 7. The Perplex'd Lovers, p. 22. l. 5. The Platonick Lady, p. 48. l. 14. The Wonder, p. 76. l. 29.

(c) The Man's Bewitch'd, p. 49. l. 1.

(d) The Walking Statue, p. 59. l. 18.

(e) Ibid. p. 62. l. *penult.*

(f) Ibid. p. 62. l. 14.

(g) Ibid. p. 62. l. 11.

CHAP.

CHAP. V.

The Devil honour'd by the profane Cursing of the Stage.

THE next Charge against the *Stage*, is their *profane Cursing*. And here the Reader must not expect that I should mention the whole Catalogue. The Monsters are too deformed to appear. I shall therefore only produce a few, in which the Honour of the *Devil* or his Interest is more immediately concern'd.

To do this effectually, the *Poets* first make bold with the Words *Salvation* and *Damnation*, and apply them to the ridiculous Concerns of the *Stage*. By the Word *Salvation* in the *Scriptures*, is usually meant, our being eternally Happy with GOD in the Kingdom of Heaven, there receiving the End of our Hopes, and the Reward of all our religious Duties. By the Word *Damnation* in the *Scriptures*, is usually meant, the being eternally Miserable with the *Devil* in Hell-Fire; being punished for all our *Sins*, and made the Objects of infinite Justice. But, to wear off all pious Sense of these things, the Expressions are used in the *Play-house* upon mean and trifling Occasions. To (*a*) *damn* a *Play*, or (*b*) to *curse* it,

(*a*) The Apparition, *Prologue*, l.22. The Artful Husband, *Prologue*, l. *antepenult*. Injur'd Virtue, *Epilogue*, p. 2. l. 5. The Beaux Stratagem, *Epilogue*, l. 4. The Busy-Body, *Prologue*, Verse 35. *and ult*. The Country Lasses, *Prologue*, l.21. The Force of Friendship, *Epilogue*, l. *penult*. The Perfidious Brother, *Epilogue*, l. 8, 30. The Perplex'd Couple, *Epilogue*, l.15. The Royal Convert, *Prologue*, p.2. l.8. Three Hours after Marriage, *Prologue*, l.10. Woman is a Riddle, *Prologue*, l.10.

(*b*) The Apparition, *Epilogue*, l. 35.

is

is to disapprove or to slight it. To *save a Poet*, is (*c*) to encourage him; and a *Play* that is disliked, is (*d*) said to be *damn'd*, or call'd in Derision (*e*) *damn'd grave* Stuff: and thus by a strange *Hyperbole*, they set up the Audience in the place of GOD, and represent the acting of every Play, as if it was the *Great Tribunal*. To *save* a Man, in the *Playhouse*-Language, is (*f*) to pay his Debts; as if there was no Hell but a *Goal*: And sometimes it signifies (*g*) to *commit Adultery* with him, as if there was no *Heaven*, but what consisted in Brutality and Uncleanness: and also (*h*) to *destroy* him, signifies no more but a refusal to gratify his Lust. One *Actress* saith, (*i*) As I *hope to be saved, nay, as I hope to be married*; as if Marriage on Earth was more desirable than the Joys of Heaven.

Thus by the Words (*k*) *cursed*, or (*l*) *damned*, they often mean only something which is very considerable, be it either good or bad.

Thus (*m*) an *Actor*'s Habit is call'd *a damn'd finical Dress*. Thus at another time, a Man's *Assurance* or *Impudence* is call'd by (*n*) this Epithet. And to confound all Distinctions of *Virtue* and *Vice*, they give the same Title to (*o*) good Counsel; and (*p*) *Temperance* is call'd *a being damn'd to abstain from Claret*. Thus they give the

---

(*c*) The Apparition, *Epilogue*, l. 42. The Force of Friendship, *Epilogue*, l. *penult.*

(*d*) The Man of Mode, p.240. l. *ult.* The Royal Convert, *Prologue*, p.2. *l*.8. Three Hours after Marriage, p. 23. l.8. p. 24. *l*. 21.

(*e*) The Royal Convert, *Prologue*, p.2. l.11.

(*f*) The Fatal Marriage, p. 121. *l*.38,39.

(*g*) Love in a Chest, p. 57. l. 27.

(*h*) Ibid.

(*i*) The Apparition, p. 19. l. 29.

(*k*) Man of Mode, p.236. l.6.

(*l*) A Woman's Revenge, p. 55. l. 33. She wou'd if she cou'd, p.92. l.33. The Artful Husband, p.44. l. *ult.* p.47. l. 10. p. 66. l. 20. The Cobler of *Preston*, p. 11. l.8. p. 17. l. *penult.* The Masquerade, p. 5. l.23. p.10. l.1. The Squire of *Alsatia*, p.10. l.29, 33. p.29. l. 19. p.32. l.34. p.34. l.33. The Man of Mode, p.264. l.28.

(*m*) Thomyris, p.32. l.26.

(*n*) Love in a Sack, p.12.l.18.

(*o*) The Squire of *Alsatia*, p. 34. l.33.

(*p*) The Apparition, p.2. l.15.

ſame Title to Perſons living, as (q) to a *young Man*, (r) to an *old Man*, (s) to a *Frenchman*, (t) to a *Muſician*, or (u) to a *Woman*; as if *Damnation* was ſomething which only happen'd in this Life. Thus a Servant is called (x) a *damnable Dæmon*. And to ridicule the Works of GOD, and his Providence, an *Actor* is ſaid to have (y) a *damnable Voice*. Nay, (as if there was no Diſtinction between a Man and a ſenſleſs Creature, and our Hope of Immortality was but a Romance) an *Actor* (z) wiſhes that the *Souls of the Dice* may be *ground* and *conſumed*; and (a) they wiſh *Damnation* to a *Pipe*, or ſuch things which have neither Life nor Senſe.

It is common among *Chriſtians* at parting to ſay, *God be-with you*. *Our Bleſſed Saviour* upon the Croſs, ſaid, (b) *Father, into thy Hands I commend my Spirit*. When St. *Stephen* was ſtoned, he ſaid, (c) *LORD Jeſus, receive my Spirit*. The Deſign of all our Prayers in our *Liturgy*, and in private, is, that we may obtain everlaſting Life, and GOD may take us to himſelf; and we are taught in the LORD's Prayer, (d) to ſay, *Thy Kingdom come*, and *deliver us from evil*; Ἀπὸ τȣ̃ πονηρȣ̃, from the *Evil One*, or from the *Devil*. The Petitions in the *Playhouſe* are the Reverſe to theſe, unleſs by the *Devil* they mean GOD himſelf. Sometimes they petition conditionally for themſelves, that (e) they may be *damn'd*, that (f) the *Devil* may *blow* their *Heads* off, (g) *burn* them,

(q) *Sawny* the *Scot*, p. 57. l. 11.

(r) Love in a Sack, p. 47. l. 16.

(s) *Sawny* the *Scot*, p. 23. l. 14. p. 57. *l*. 27.

(t) Ibid. p. 28. l. 16.

(u) The Amorous Widow, p. 6. *l*. 30.

(x) Love in a Sack, p. 29. l. *penult*.

(y) The Amorous Widow, p. 19. l. 11.

(z) The Comical Lovers, p. 47. *l*. 18.

(a) The Wonder, p. 73. l. *penult*.

(b) *Luke* 23. 46.

(c) *Acts* 7. 59.

(d) *Matth*. 6. 10, 13. *Luke* 11. 2, 4.

(e) The Roving Husband Reclaim'd, p. 11. l. 14. p. 38. l. 19. The Stage-Beaux toſs'd in a Blanket, p. 15. l. 1.

(f) The Baſſet-Table, p. 53. l. 6.

(g) The Roving Husband Reclaim'd, p. 15. l. 26. The Maid the Miſtreſs, p. 42. l. 5.

choak

(*h*) *choak* them, (*i*) *claw* them, (*k*) *drive* them *away*, (*l*) *botch* them, (*m*) *fill* their *Belly with Hog's Flesh*, (*n*) *foul* their *Lungs*, and (*o*) *take* them, and (*p*) their *Souls* (*q*) *for ever*; and that (*r*) *Hell* may receive them. And to make the *Sin* appear more national than (I hope) it is, when (*s*) one pray'd, that *the Devil* might *jump down* his *Throat*, he was answer'd with this *Encomium*, *There spoke the true Spirit of a* Briton.

Two of these Expressions I shall venture to transcribe at large.

(*t*) *Now the Devil be my Landlord, Hell my Winter-Quarters, and a Rope my Winding-Sheet.*

(*u*) *If my future self* (in the other World) *retains a Thought,*
And this excess of Fondness (from a General to his Prince) *is forgot*;
May Dæmons sink my Spirit as I rise,
And chase my Soul from promis'd Paradise.

(*h*) The Stage-Beaux toss'd in a Blanket, *Prologue*, l. *ult.*

(*i*) The Humours of the Army.

(*k*) An Act at *Oxford*, p. 58. l. 30. The Careless Husband, p. 16. l. *antepenult.*

(*l*) The Confederacy, p. 66. l. 32. Wit at a Pinch, p. 13. l. 20.

(*m*) The Earl of *Mar* marr'd, p. 6. l. 25.

(*n*) *Sawny* the *Scot*, p. 16. l. 9.

(*o*) Love at first Sight, p. 56. l. 12. She wou'd if she cou'd, p. 163. l. 5. Squire Trelooby, p. 5. l. 22. p. 9. l. 15. The Basset-Table, p. 12. l. 9. The Busy Body, p. 5. l. 5. The Comical Lovers, p. 51. l. 33. The Comical Revenge, p. 11. l. 29. The Earl of *Mar* marr'd, p. 3. l. 4. p. 27. l. 1. The Humours of Purgatory, p. 17. l. 15. p. 19. l. 9. The Pretender's Flight, p. 3. l. 11. p. 13. l. 5. The Stage-*Beaux* toss'd in a Blanket, p. 8. l. 32. The Wonder, p. 29. l. 29.

(*p*) *Sawny* the *Scot*, p. 6. l. 9. p. 50. l. 8. p. 62. l. 29. The Amorous Widow, p. 24. l. 12. p. 59. l. 15. The Litigants, p. 9. l. 10. The Wonder, p. 75. l. 29. p. 77. l. 10.

(*q*) The Double Gallant, p. 55. l. 9.

(*r*) The Loyal Subject, p. 57. l. 28.

(*s*) The Humours of the Army, p. 20. l. 7.

(*t*) The Wonder, p. 65. l. 28.

(*u*) Irene, p. 43. l. 33.

Sometimes they curse themselves absolutely, that they (x) may be *damn'd*, that (y) the *Devil* may *take* them, or (z) *Furies* may *seize* them. One (a) *invokes the Furies of Hell to her Breast, to heighten her Rage*; and (b) wisheth, that *all the* Furies may there make *their Abode*, and (c) *all the poisonous Serpents* may *send* her their *most envenom'd Snakes, and wound* her *Breast without Pity*. But most commonly these Expressions are levelled against others. Sometimes conditionally, that (d) the *Devil* may *take* them, or such-like Expressions; but most commonly their *Curses* are absolute, that others *may be* (e) *damned* (f) *for ever*, or (g) *for ever cursed*, that they may *go* (h) *to the Devil*, or (i) *to Hell*; or (k) be *sunk into Hell*, and *the Fiends* may *seize* them. That the *Devil* (l) may *be* their *Bedfellow*, (m) *break* their Necks, (n) *choak* them, (o) *creep into* their *Wombs*,

---

(x) Love at first Sight, p. 16. l. 21. The Biter, p. 13. l. 30. The Female Wits, p. 25. l. 4. The Lawyer's Fortune, p. 38. l. 13. The Stage-Beaux toss'd in a Blanket, p. 11. l. 9. p. 31. l. 25.

(y) A City Ramble; or, The Humours of the Compter, p. 26. l. 3. *Sawny* the *Scot*, p. 6. l. 9. p. 50. l. 8. p. 62. l. 29.

(z) *Pyrrhus* and *Demetrius*, p. 57. l. 3.

(a) *Titus Manlius*, p. 31. *in fine*.

(b) Ibid. p. 33. l. 4.

(c) Ibid. *in fine*.

(d) Ignoramus, p. 36. l. 25.

(e) A Woman's Revenge, p. 51. l. 32. The Artful Husband, p. 3. l. 14. The Man of Mode, p. 185. l. 30. p. 215. l. 25. p. 225. l. 16. p. 234. l. 26. The Masquerade, p. 4. l. *penult*. The Pretender's Fate, p. 10. l. 20. The Wonders in the Sun, p. 25. l. 11, *ult*.

(f) The Contrivances, p. 16. l. *penult*.

(g) The *British* Enchanters, p. 28. l. 7.

(h) Marplot, p. 12. l. 30. The Beaux Stratagem, p. 62. l. 31. The Country-House, p. 27. l. 17. The Wonder, p. 74. l. 8. Woman is a Riddle, p. 52. l. 28.

(i) The Contrivances, p. 17. l. 20.

(k) The Royal Convert, p. 43. l. 14.

(l) *Sawny* the *Scot*, p. 64. l. 16.

(m) Marplot, p. 16. l. 21.

(n) The Wonders in the Sun, p. 17. l. 19. p. 64. l. 21.

(o) *Sawny* the *Scot*, p. 8. l. 35.

(p) *go with* them, (q) *hang* them, (r) *have* them, (s) *foul* their *Fingers*, (t) *give* them *a Clap with a* French *Thunderbolt*, (u) *pare* their *Nails*, (x) *reward* them, (y) *run away with them*, (z) *ſeize* them, (a) *ſtretch* them, (‖) or *ſtuff their Bellies full of Hemp, and* his *Dam* may *ſpit it out again*. That the *Devil* may (b) *take* them (c) *all*, even (d) *with all the* Actor's *Heart*, who ſpoke it; or (e) *take the Gripe of their Fingers, and dreſs* their *Doublets*, (f) *take* their *Locks*, or (g) *waſh* their *Face with a foul Clout*. That the *Furies* may (h) *confound*, (i) *ſeize*, or (k) *tear* them: That (l) *the Gods* or *Furies may purſue* them, *haunt* them, *and ſeize* their *guilty Minds*. That

---

(p) Love in a Sack, p.48. l. *antepenult*. The Contrivances, p.19. l.5. The Country-Houſe, p. 21. l. 20. The Man's bewitch'd, p.40. l.33.

(q) The Beaux Stratagem, p. 53. l.9, 11.

(r) Ignoramus, p. 21. l. 3. The *Gotham* Election, p. 53. l. 23.

(s) *Sawny* the *Scot*, p.7. l.13.

(t) Ibid. p.64. l.22.

(u) Ignoramus, p.40. l.22.

(x) The Maſquerade, p. *ult*. l. 28.

(y) The Walking Statue, p.63. l. 21.

(z) The Pretender's Fate, p. 26. l.30.

(a) Ignoramus, p.15. l.31.

(‖) *Sawny* the *Scot*, p. 55. l. 18.

(b) A City Ramble, or, The Humours of the Compter, p. 25. l. 1. Ignoramus, p. 36. l. 25. Marplot, p.17. l. *antepenult*. p. 20. l.5. p. 34. l.7. p.35. l.13. p.40. l.32. p.41. l.5. p. 58. l. 23. The Beaux Stratagem, p. 34. l.29. p.48. l.1. p.53. l.15. The Buſy-Body, p.18. l.5. The Comical Revenge, p. 60. l. 3. The Country-Houſe, p. 10. l.6. The Man of Mode, p.266. l.5. The Maſquerade, p. 27. l. 10. The Modern Prophets, p.47. l. 10. p.51. l. 35. p.66. l. *penult*. The Perplex'd Couple, p.54. l. 31. The Perplex'd Lovers, p. 30. l.34. p.52. l.29. The Recruiting Officer, p.25. l.20. p. 31. l.16. The Wonder, p. 31. l. *penult*. The Wonders in the Sun, p. 60. l. 13. Wit at a Pinch, p.26. l.9. Woman is a Riddle, p.51. l.26.

(c) Ignoramus, p.67. l.6. p. 68. l.2. The Comical Revenge, p.60. l. *penult*.

(d) The Comical Revenge, p.21. l.6.

(e) *Sawny* the *Scot*, p. 17. l. 20.

(f) Ibid. p.42. l.3.

(g) Ibid. p.39. l.30.

(h) Love and Liberty, p.63. l. 14.

(i) *Appius* and *Virginia*, p. 3. l. *antepenult*.

(k) Elfred, p.38. l.32.

(l) The Victim, p.63. l.13.

(*m*) *Hell* may *confound* them, that *Perdition* may (*n*) *catch* them, or (*o*) *seize* them *all*, or (*p*) that they *may be taken to the Devil.*

When one *Actor* saith, (*q*) *God be with you*, another returns the Compliment in these Words, *Go to the Devil.* One wishes (*r*) that *the Devil had* his Fellow-*Actor*; another saith, (*s*) He *would see* him *at the Devil.* And to shew their Breeding, (*t*) when one saith, *The Devil take thee*; the other answers, *The Devil take you, if you come to that.* One saith, that (*u*) he *would willingly make a Present of* his *Share in* his *Wife to the Devil*: Another (*x*) desires the *Furies and Hell to reward an Actor.* One *Actor* stabbing another with this Expression, (*y*) *Down to the Devils, down*; *Hell is thy Home, and thus I send thee thither*: To which the other *dying*, replies, *Curses find thee, tho Death and Darkness hide thee from mine Eyes.* And another dying, saith, (*z*) *Furies confound you all.*

This is the constant *Playhouse Language*, in direct opposition to that Expression in our most excellent *Liturturgy*, "The Blessing of God Almighty, the Father, "the Son, and the Holy Ghost, be amongst you, and "remain with you always." Or rather to the Words of St. *Paul*, (*a*) *The Grace of our LORD Jesus Christ, and the Love of GOD, and the Communion of the Holy Ghost, be with you all*; *Amen.*

We have a single Instance of (*b*) a *Poet*, who makes an *Apology* for (*c*) his *Imprecations*, and hopes, that *they will not be thought too violent.* I am glad to see a Remorse

---

(*m*) A Wife well manag'd, p. 9. l. 28. The *Gotham* Election, p. 72. l. 19.

(*n*) The *Persian* Princess, p. 57. l. 16.

(*o*) The Perfidious Brother, p. 57. l. 12.

(*p*) The Fair Quaker of *Deal*, p. 56. l. 25.

(*q*) The Wonder, p. 74. l. 7.

(*r*) The Amorous Widow, p. 35. l. 17.

(*s*) Ibid. p. 50. l. 29.

(*t*) The Litigants, p. 31. l. 5.

(*u*) The Perplex'd Couple, p. 54. l. 25.

(*x*) The *Persian* Princess, p. 45. l. *ult.*

(*y*) Elfrid, p. 38. l. 28.

(*z*) Love and Liberty, p. 63. l. 14.

(*a*) 2 *Cor.* 13. 14.

(*b*) French Cato, *Preface*, p. 13. l. *antepenult.*

(*c*) Pag. 54. l. 27.

of

of Conſcience in one, and heartily wiſh it may be found in the reſt: and I muſt alſo own, that his *Imprecations* are only temporal, and not of ſo heinous a nature as thoſe which I have mentioned. However, to ſet this matter right, no *Curſes*, of what nature ſoever, ought to be admitted on the *Stage*. If (as the *Apoſtle* ſaith) (*d*) *we muſt not do Evil, that Good may come of it*; then we muſt not do Evil for our Diverſion: and where Words are forbid by GOD, as all *Swearing* and *Curſing* are, no Excuſe can be allowed. And if no *Stage-Diſcipline* can make it tolerable, how provoking muſt it be to GOD, when ſuch *Expreſſions* are ſo conſtantly uſed, put into the Mouths of their *top Characters*, as the Ornament of Speech, ſometimes with Applauſe, and always without Cenſure! Now profane *Curſing* is a *Sin* moſt poſitively forbidden by *GOD* in (*d*) the Holy *Scriptures*. Such *Language* ought not to proceed out of our Mouths, nor be harboured ſo much as in (*e*) in our *Hearts*. And nothing ſhould provoke us to it. We muſt not (*f*) *curſe* even thoſe who *curſe* us, who are our *Enemies*, who *hate* us, who *deſpitefully uſe* us, and *perſecute* us. We muſt not imitate ſuch, but GOD, who continually poureth out his *Bleſſings* upon all. We muſt not *render Evil for Evil, or Railing for Railing, but contrariwiſe Bleſſing; as knowing that we are called* of GOD *to inherit a Bleſſing*. And thus muſt we *overcome evil with good*. It was therefore fooliſh Advice which was given to *Job* in his Afflictions, that (*g*) he ſhould *curſe GOD and die*, and it was reſented accordingly. This *Sin* in ſome caſes among the *Jews*, was a (*h*) *capital Crime*, and the Son of *Shelomith* by the Command of GOD was ſtoned for the ſame. When (*i*) *Shimei curſed David*, tho whilſt he lived he forgave the *Sin*, as againſt himſelf; yet he would not paſs it by, as it related to GOD, or might have been of ill Conſequence to the Nation, but he gave Orders at his Deceaſe, that (*k*) the Man, who thus

---

(*d*) *Rom.* 12. 14. *James* 3. 9, 10.

(*e*) *Job* 31. 30. *Ecclеſ.* 10. 20.

(*f*) *Rom.* 12. 14. *Matth.* 5. 44, 45. *Luke* 6. 28. 1 *Pet.* 3. 9, 10. *Rom.* 12. 21.

(*g*) *Job* 2. 9, 10.

(*h*) *Exod.* 21. 17. *Levit.* 20. 9.

(*i*) 2 *Sam.* 16. 5, 6, 7, 10. *and Chap.* 19. 23.

(*k*) 1 *Kings* 2. 8, 9, 44, 45, 46.

cursed, should be put to *death*, who was executed accordingly. Nay, in such cases, which were not punished by Man, GOD himself was the Executioner of his Wrath upon them that were guilty; and therefore *David* saith, (*l*) that *for the Sin of their Mouth, and for the Words of their Lips, they shall be taken in their Pride; and for Cursing and Lying, which they speak.* And he tells us the sad Estate of such a *Sinner*, that (*m*) *As he loved Cursing, so it shall come unto him: As he delighted not in Blessing, so it shall be far from him. As he clothed himself with Cursing, like as with a Garment; so it shall come into his Bowels like Water, and like Oil into his Bones. It shall be unto him as the Garment, which covereth him; and for a Girdle, wherewith he is girded continually.* Where we may observe, that as the Words in the *Hebrew* are in the *future Tense*; so these and the following Verses contain rather a *Prophecy* than an *Imprecation*. When *Goliah* (*n*) *cursed David*, he and the whole Army were afterward destroyed; and Vengeance seems to be but the natural Effect of such Hellish Language. The *Curse* of GOD is a dreadful thing: As (*o*) *such*, who *are blessed of him shall inherit the Land*; so *they who are cursed, shall be rooted out.* Nay, they shall (*p*) *be cast into Hell, the Fire prepared for the Devil and his Angels.* He therefore (*q*) *whose Mouth was full of Cursing and Bitterness*, was always reckon'd as a wicked Man, and one who had *no fear of GOD before* his *Eyes*. To this I may add, that *Balaam*, (*r*) who was a notorious *Enchanter*, and who *loved the Wages* of other *unrighteous* Acts, dared not to be guilty of this *Sin*, tho he might receive his *House full of Silver and Gold* as a Reward; and therefore he refused it, without a special Leave from GOD himself, which was never granted. *How*, saith he, *shall I curse them, whom GOD hath not cursed? and how shall I defy them, whom the LORD hath not defied?* And therefore it is strange, how the *Poets* can make this a matter of Diversion, which (if they had any Sense of

(*l*) *Psal.* 59. 12.
(*m*) *Psal.* 109. 17, 18.
(*n*) 1 *Sam.* 17. 43, 49, 50, 51.
(*o*) *Psal.* 37. 22.
(*p*) *Matth.* 25. 41, 46.
(*q*) *Psal.* 10. 7. *Rom.* 3. 14, 18.
(*r*) *Numb.* 23. 8.

Religion) might rather be a cause for Terror and Astonishment.

A Reader, who hath any Notion of a GOD, can hardly imagine the *Stage* to be thus guilty; and therefore I shall conclude this Chapter, by quoting ten other Sentences more at large, out of ten several *Plays*, that so I may shew their Guilt, and excite (if possible) a just Indignation against them.

1. (s) *Furies* (that is, *Devils*) *arise and seize him with Distraction.*

2. (t) *O! would th' avenging Thunderbolt of* Jove
Fall down amain on this devoted Head,
And drive me headlong to th' infernal Powers; (that is, to the *Devil*).

3. (u) *Let him die, ye Powers, strike him dead,*
Dart all your Lightning at his cursed Head!
Tear him, ye Furies, tear him!
May the Furies alarm him!
May his Conscience disarm him!

4. (x) *Be trebly curs'd, and may th' infernal Powers*
Never release thee from the Wo thou'rt fond of.

5. (y) *I'll present this Paper*
In a just Rage to Rhadamanthus' *Throne,*
And raise against thee the united Pow'rs of Hell.
I'll display it as a Banner of my Vengeance
To the Furies. Drunk with Rage,
I'll stir up all the Monsters of Cocytus
To tear out thy Heart.

6. (z) *Guilt haunt him! Fiends pursue him! Lightning blast him!*
Some horrid, cursed kind of Death o'ertake him
Sudden, and in the Fulness of his Sins.

7. (a) *Heav'n dart its swiftest Vengeance on your Heads!*
And Hell's eternal Plagues be your Reward!
To you, ye Pow'rs of Heav'n and Hell, (that is, to GOD, and to the Devil) *I call.*

(s) Almyna, *p.*36. *l.*20.
(t) *Appius* and *Virginia*, *p.*58. *l.* 27.
(u) Camilla, *p.*25. *l.*1.
(x) Electra, *Act.*1. *Ver.* 295.
(y) Ernelynda, *p.*53. *l.*27.
(z) *Jane Shore*, *p.*47. *l.*7.
(a) Love and Liberty, *p.* 61. *l.* 7.

8.

8. (*b*) *The Devil take my Soul.*

9. (*c*) *Whip me, ye Fiends, plunge me in Seas of Sulphur;*
Let your eternal Fancies work new Torments,
And add them to the Pains of Hell.

10. When (*d*) the Disciples ask'd of our *Blessed Saviour*, if they *should command Fire from Heaven, and consume* his Enemies, *even as* Elias *did*; *He rebuked them, saying, Ye know not what manner of Spirit ye are of: For the Son of Man is not come to destroy Mens Lives, but to save them.* But this being forbidden, the *Stage* runs to the other Extreme, and (*e*) an *Actor* calls for *Fire from Hell to dress* his Guests.

Thus we may see how directly opposite the *Church* and the *Play-house* are to each other. In the one, we pray for *Mercies*; in the other, they call for *Judgments*. In the one, we put up our Petitions to GOD; in the other, they make their Addresses to the *Devil*. And therefore whilst these Diversions are encourag'd, the Interest of *Religion* must necessarily decline.

[Tho they curse, yet, Good LORD, bless thou; and turn from us all those dreadful Judgments, which they so loudly call for!]

(*b*) The Busy-Body, *p*.5. *l*.5.
(*c*) The Successful Pirate, *p*. 58. *l*.18.
(*d*) *Luke* 9. 54, 55, 56.
(*e*) The Country House, *p*.19. *l*.22.

CHAP.

CHAP. VI.

Representations of Divine Worship, as paid to the Devil upon the Stage.

THE next Charge against the *Stage*, is their Representations of *Divine Worship* and *Adoration* as paid to the *Devil*.

How near this *Sin* comes to the actual Worship of him, I leave the Reader to judge, who, I suppose, will conclude from Matters of Fact, that the *Stage*-Crimes of this Nature are of the deepest Dye, enough to turn all past Mercies into Judgments, enough to provoke GOD to vindicate his Divinity by the Effects of his Indignation, and enough to make us the Monuments of his Vengeance. The Impieties of this kind are beyond Expression. What was said of *Antichrist* in *Rome*, is now too sadly fulfilled of the *Devil* in our *Play-houses*, that here (*a*) he *opposeth and exalteth himself above all that is called GOD, or that is worshipped; so that he, as GOD, sitteth in Temples* dedicated to his Service, *shewing himself, that he is GOD.*

To represent this in a more lively manner, here is (*b*) the *Grove* of *Proserpina* for a *Scene*, with an *Altar at a distance*, and *Priests* attending on the Service of *Pluto and his Consort*, the *King* and *Queen* of *Hell*; or in plainer *English*, of *Beelzebub* and his *Assistant*. Then *two Priests enter with lighted Tapers in each Hand, after them the High-Priest* (like *Moses*) *with a Rod*, whilst all this Ceremony is only to give a more solemn Grace to *the Worship of the Devil.*

When GOD delivered the *Israelites* by *Moses*, he appointed several *Sacrifices* to be performed for his Honour. These *Rites* are imitated on the *Stage* with the utmost Solemnity on the aforemention'd Occasion.

(*a*) 2 *Thes.* 2. 4. (*b*) Alarbas, *p.* 24. *Scene.*

Thus,

Thus (*c*) the *High-Priest* saith,

Ho, Mirides, *the sacred Rites begin*
To our great Master Pluto (the Prince of the Devils) *and his Queen.*

Then follows solemn *Musick*, and afterwards,

Priest. *To the great Infernal Pair.*
Chorus. *To the great Infernal Pair.*
Priest. *Victims slay, and Incense spread.*
Chorus. *Victims slay, and Incense spread.*
Priest. *Feast the* (*d*) Dæmons *of the Air.*
Chorus. *Feast the* Dæmons *of the Air.*
Priest. *With the Savour of the Dead.*
Chorus. *With the Savour of the Dead.*
Priest. *Strike the barren Heifer deep.*
Chorus. *Strike her, strike her, strike her deep.*
Priest. *Strike her deep, and sure as Fate,*
Fast as everlasting Sleep,
Sure as injur'd Woman's Hate.
Grand Chorus. *Strike her, strike her, strike her deep,* &c.
High-Priest. *Hear,* Pluto'*s Royal Consort, hear.*
Chorus. *Hear,* Pluto'*s Royal Consort, hear.*

And to one, who interrupts him, the *High-Priest* answers,

Rash Man, no more, on Peril of thy Life.

But there are other *Sacrifices*, which are more peculiar to the *Stage*: As (*e*) *the Devil was a Murderer from the beginning*; so when a Murder is really design'd, an *Actor* saith (*f*),

To the Infernal King
We offer up this dreadful Sacrifice.

(*c*) Alarbas, *p.*24. *Scene.*

(*d*) *What* Dæmon *signifies in English may be known from the Dictionary, or from any School-Boy, who hath read this Verse in the* Syntaxis,

Dæmona non armis sed morte subegit Iesus.

Or it may be known from the Language of the Stage *in other Plays, as* Sawny *the* Scot, *p.*70. *l.* 2.

(*e*) *Joh.* 8. 44.

(*f*) *Appius* and *Virginia*, p. 10. l. 7.

Thus

Thus a tender and an affectionate Father murdering a virtuous Daughter, hath this Expression (g);

Thus with the sprinkling of this sacred Blood,
I consecrate thee to th' Infernal Pow'rs.

And to omit all other Instances, an *Actor* speaking of burning a Bundle of *Plays*, saith (h),

I'll make a Burnt-Sacrifice of them, by way of Oblation to the Devil, from whence they came.

From their Sacrifices let us proceed to their Expressions; and the first which I shall take notice of, is their *Ejaculations.* These in *Scripture*, and among *Christians*, are Speeches of a pious Soul to GOD on some particular Occasion. Thus the *Psalmist* (i) cries out with admiration, *LORD, what is Man, that thou art mindful of him! and the Son of Man, that thou visitest him!* In *Scripture* it is, *LORD, what is Man!* The *Actors* express it thus, *What the Devil* (k) *have we here!* (l) *is this!* or (m) *are you!* And when St. *Paul* was converted, he (n) *trembling and astonished said, LORD, what wilt thou have me to do?* This in the *Play-House* Language (o) is, *Why, what the Devil wouldst thou have me to do?* (p) *should I do?* or (q) *shall we do?* In *Scripture* it is, *What, LORD!* In the *Play-House* it is, *What, the Devil!* I need not multiply Quotations of this nature; however, I have directed to above (r) sixty Instances of this

(g) *Appius* and *Virginia*, *p.* 56. *l.* 23.

(h) The Perplex'd Couple, *p.* 9. *l. antepenult.*

(i) *Psal.* 144. 3.

(k) A Woman's Revenge, *p.* 46. *l.* 16.

(l) The Adventures of Half an Hour, *p.* 16. *l.* 18.

(m) Woman is a Riddle, *p.* 31. *l. penult.* & *p.* 85. *l. ult.*

(n) *Acts* 9. 6.

(o) Injured Love, *p.* 29. *l.* 24.

(p) The Squire of *Alsatia*, *p.* 20. *l.* 23.

(q) Wit at a pinch, *p.* 20. *l.* 14.

(r) A City-Ramble, or the Humours of the Compter, *p.* 11. *l.* 1. A Woman's Revenge, *p.* 25. *l. antepenult.* & *p.* 46. *l.* 16. Injured Love, *p.* 29. *l.* 13, 21. *p.* 33. *l.* 16. & *p.* 68. *l.* 18. Marplot, *p.* 21. *l.* 23. & *p.* 38. *l.* 14. *Sawny* the *Scot*, *p.* 41. *l.* 12.

this nature, which the Reader may turn to, if he thinks it worth his pains.

When our *Blessed Saviour* spoke of the distinguishing Providences which should happen at his coming, the *Disciples answered and* (s) *said, Where, LORD?* This in the *Play-House* Language (t) is, *Where the Devil?*

Thus in *Scripture* it (u) is, *How, LORD?* In the *Play-House* (x), *How, the Devil?* In *Scripture* it is,

---

12. & *p*.52. *l*.1. She wou'd if she cou'd, *p*.143. *l*.29. Love's last Shift, *p*. 43. *l*.12,14. & *p*. 52. *l*.12. The Adventures of Half an Hour, *p*.16. *l*.18. The Artful Husband, *p*.6. *l*.33. The Busy Body, *p*.67. *l. penult*. The Cobler of *Preston*, *p*. 10. *l*.27. & *p*.11. *l*. 22. The Comical Lovers, *p*.47. *l*.5. & *p*.48. *l*.26. The Comical Revenge, *p*.67. *l. penult*. The Country House, *p*.19. *l*.20. The Double Gallant, *p*.19. *l*.24. The Drummer, *p*.43. *l*.29. The Earl of *Mar* marr'd, *p*. 5. *l*. 21. The Fatal Marriage, *p*.101. *l*.9. The Female Advocates, *p*.52. *l*.13. *p*.62. *l*.6. & *p*. 65. *l*. 7. The Maid the Mistress, *p*. 52. *l*. 24. The Man of Mode, *p*.265. *l*.1. The Man's bewitch'd, *p*.47. *l*. 30. The Masquerade, *p*.27. *l*.1. The modern Prophets, *p*.42. *l*. 1. The Perplex'd Lovers, *p*.15. *l*.16. *p*.26. *l*.19,25. *p*.38. *l*.10. *p*. 50. *l*. 23. & *p*.51. *l*. 5, 16. The Platonick Lady, *p*.26. *l*. 1. & *p*.40. *l. penult*. The Pretender's Flight, *p*.10. *l*.16. The Rival Fools, *p*.7. *l*.34. *p*.8. *l*.9. *p*.38. *l. ult*. *p*.24. *l*.34. *p*.58. *l*.8. *p*.67. *l*.20. & *p*.68. *l*.18. The Squire of *Alsatia*, *p*.20. *l*. 23. *p*.21. *l*.29. *p*.24. *l*.25. *p*. 46. *l*.29. & *p*.65. *l*.20. The Wonder, *p*.30. *l*.22. *p*.45. *l*.13. *p*.50. *l*.12. *p*.64. *l*.29. *p*.72. *l*. 14. *p*.74. *l*.13. & *p*.76. *l*.1. Wit at a pinch, *p*.7. *l*.15. & *p*. 20. *l*.14. Wit without Money, *p*.69. *l*.6. Woman is a Riddle, *p*.9. *l*.27. *p*.31. *l. penult*. *p*.51. *l*.5. *p*.54. *l. penult*. *p*.85. *l. ult*. *p*.86. *l*.9. & *p*.87. *l*.8.

(s) *Luke* 17. 37.

(t) Love's last Shift, *p*. 25. *l*. 17. & *p*.51. *l*.7. Marplot, *p*. 26. *l*.8. & *p*.39. *l*.31. The Artful Husband, *p*.65. *l*.28. The Busy Body, *p*.19. *l*.6. The Comical Lovers, *p*.34. *l*.18. The Earl of *Mar* marr'd, *p*.27. *l*.26. The Female Advocates, *p*.60. *l*. 22. Wit without Money, *p*.66. *l*.12. Woman is a Riddle, *p*. 83. *l*.1. & *p*.86. *l*.2.

(u) *Psal*. 8. 1, 9.

(x) She wou'd if she cou'd, *p*. 136. *l*.3. The Artful Husband, *p*.37. *l*.17. Love's last Shift, *p*. 73. *l*.16. & *p*.77. *l*.2. The Busy Body, *p*.32. *l. penult*. The Country Lasses, *p*.20. *l*.20. The Humours of the Army, *p*.49. *l*.33. The Pretender's Flight, *p*. 30. *l*.1. The Squire of *Alsatia*, *p*.71. *l*.12. The Wonder, *p*.39. *l*.1. Three Hours after Marriage, *p*.59. *l*.2. Woman is a Riddle, *p*.87. *l*.11.

Why,

(y) *Why, LORD?* In the *Play-House* it is, (z) *Why, the Devil?* In the *Scripture* it is, (a) *Who, LORD?* And in the *Play-House*, (b) *Who, the Devil?*

Thus, for example, they expostulate concerning the Works of GOD, and express their Gratitude for being made Men, in this Language; (c) *Who the Devil taught you the Art of Reasoning?*

In the *Scriptures* it is common to say, *LORD!* when some weighty Matter is mentioned. This word is often used by the *Actors* (d) upon ridiculous Occasions; but most commonly, and especially in Cases of importance,

---

(y) *John* 13. 37.

(z) Injur'd Love, p.29. l.34. Love's last Shift, p.2. l.33. & p.5. l.4. Marplot, p.38. l.14. *Sawny* the *Scot*, p.41. l.12. The Busy Body, p.6. l.34. The Comical Lovers, p.48. l.12. The Humours of the Army, p.55. l. 29. The Man's bewitch'd, p.1. l.22. p.37. l.30. The Platonick Lady, p.40. l.11. The Wonder, p.76. l.1. Wit without Money, p. 69. l.6. Woman is a Riddle, p.87. l.11.

(a) *Psalm* 15. 1.

(b) A Wife well managed, p. 4. l.18. Marplot, p. 37. l. 14, 29. She wou'd if she cou'd, p.148. l.4. The Busy Body, p. 30. l.2. p.56. l.23. p.64. l.9. The Double Gallant, p.55. l.26. p. 57. l. 12. The Man's bewitch'd, p. 39. l.16. The Perplex'd Lovers, p.28. l.15. p.32. l. 28. The Platonick Lady, p. 66. l.23. The Pretender's Flight, p.20. l.22. The Squire of *Alsatia*, p.10. l. 41. p.35. l.40. The Successful Pirate, p.47. l.4.

(c) The Busy Body, p. 25. l. 30.

(d) A Woman's Revenge, p. 51. l.7,21. p.55. l.4. Injur'd Love, p.32. l.5. Love in a Sack, p.12. l.22. p. 30. l. 10. The Amorous Widow, p.12. l. 13. p.15. l.26. The Fatal Marriage, p.101. l.12. p.125. l.8. The Humours of the Army, p. 27. l. *antepenult*. The Humours of Purgatory, p.18. l.5. p. 45. l.14. The Lady's last Stake, p. 71. l.32. The Man's bewitch'd, p.54. l.24. The Masquerade, p. 7. l.28. The Man of Mode, p. 178. l. *ult*. p.179. l.34. p.218. l.26. p.219. l.18. p.223. l.11, 19. p.236. l.36,37. p.237. l.6, 11,28. p.241. l.28. p.245. l.17. p.247. l.7. p.248. l.18. The *Persian* Princess, *Epilogue* l. 5. The Platonick Lady, p.57. *Scene* l.2. The Rival Fools, p.35. l. 32. p.37. l.18. p.38. l.10. The Squire of *Alsatia*, p.2. l.12. p. 3. l.18. The Wonder, *Epilogue* l.13. Wit at a pinch, p.32. l. 10. p.46. l.1. p.50. l.13. Woman is a Riddle, p.25. l.19. p. 50. l.9. p.90. l.24. p.92. l.16. p.95. l.5.

they say, (*e*) *The Devil!* Sometimes they say, (*f*) *O LORD!* and sometimes, (*g*) *O the Devil!* Sometimes (*h*) *Ah LORD!* and sometimes (*i*) *Ah the Devil!*

As it is very common in *Scripture* for Persons in Misery to begin their Petitions with this Expression, *O LORD!* so from hence they learn upon the *Stage* to say (*k*) very frequently, and (*l*) especially when they are praying for Help, *O the Devil!* The Language in our *Liturgy*, is, *LORD have mercy upon us!* and certainly we never had more reason for it than now. But the Language of the *Play-House* (*m*) is, *The Devil take me*

(*e*) Ignoramus, *p.* 24. *l.* 26. Love in a Chest, *p.* 63. *l.* 27. Marplot, *p.*23. *l.*21. *p.*52. *l.*22. *p.*59. *l.*4. The Apparition, *p.* 27. *l.*22. *p.*56. *l.*13. The Beaux Stratagem, *p.*17. *l.*31. The Busy Body, *p.*13. *l.*9. *p.*28. *l.*22. *p.*48. *l.*25. The Double Gallant, *p.*34. *l.*27. *p.*79. *l.*10. The *Gotham* Election, *p.* 55. *l.* 13. *p.*72. *l.*9. The Lady's last Stake, *p.*32. *l.*13. *p.* 68. *l. ult.* The Maid the Mistress, *p.*3. *l.*6. *p.*49. *l.*24. The Man's bewitch'd, *p.* 34. *l.*11. *p.*38. *l.*7. *p.*39. *l.* 1. The Masquerade, *p.* 26. *l.* 21. The Perplex'd Couple, *p.*47. *l.* 28. *p.*52. *l.*33. Three Hours after Marriage, *p.*67. *l.*8. Wit at a pinch, *p.*5. *l.*19. Woman is a Riddle, *p.*90. *l.*26.

(*f*) Love in a Sack, *p.*20. *l.* 17. *p.*54. *l.*1,2. *p.*53. *l.*19, *ult.* *p.*57. *l.*10. *p.*58. *l.*10. The Amorous Widow, *p.*74. *l.*12. The Contrivances, *p.*18. *l.*21. *p.*19. *l.*7. The Double Gallant, *p.*56. *l.* 15. The Fatal Marriage, *p.* 127. *l.*33. The Humours of Purgatory, *p.*33. *l.*18. The Masquerade, *p.*8. *l.*28. The modern Prophets, *p.*71. *l.*45. The Rival Fools, *p.*37. *l.*35.

(*g*) Ignoramus, *p.* 65. *l.* 15. Love's last Shift, *p.* 22. *l.* 30. The Amorous Widow, *p.*21. *l.* 31. *p.*23. *l.*1. The Masquerade, *p.*19. *l.*8. The Perjuror, *p.* 30. *l.* 16.

(*h*) The Cobler of *Preston*, *p.*11. *l.*29. The Perplex'd Lovers, *p.*33. *l.*27.

(*i*) Marplot, *p.*15. *l.*16. The modern Prophets, *p.*51. *l.*27. *p.* 52. *l.*4. Woman is a Riddle, *p.*11. *l.*9.

(*k*) The Busy Body, *p.* 31. *l.*20. *p.*62. *l.*27. The Comical Lovers, *p.*56. *l.*3. The Country Wake, *p.* 30. *l. antepenult.* The Double Gallant, *p.*56. *l.*15. The Maid the Mistress, *p.* 41. *l.*24. The Man's bewitch'd, *p.* 37. *l.*35. *p.*48. *l.*12. *p.*53. *l.*29. *p.*61. *l.*21. The Perplex'd Couple, *p.*47. *l.*16. *p.*59. *l.*23. The Perplex'd Lovers, *p.*12. *l.*19. *p.* 47. *l.*4. The Platonick Lady, *p.*19. *l.*12. *p.*58. *l.*16. The Rival Fools, *p.*17. *Act* 2. *l.*9.

(*l*) Marplot, *p.*14. *l.*15. The Busy Body, *p.*17. *l.*30.

(*m*) The Double Gallant, *p.* 55. *l.* 9.

for ever. Thus when one says, (n) *Pray, Godfather, give me your Blessing*; the other answers, *My Blessing! The Devil choak you.*

Sometimes they say, (o) *LORD! LORD!* and sometimes, (p) *The Devil! The Devil!* Sometimes, (q) *O LORD! O LORD!* and sometimes, (r) *O the Devil! the Devil!* Sometimes, (s) *Ah Heaven!* (t) *O Heaven!* (u) *Heavens!* or (x) *Good Heavens!* and sometimes (y) *Hell!* (z) *O Hell!* or (a) *O Furies!* And sometimes they join them both together; (b) *O Heaven! O Hell!* Thus (c) an *Actor* leaves off praying to GOD, and addresses his Enemy;

> *Answer me, Heav'n! But hold! What will Heav'n answer me?*
> *Answer me, Hell! for Heav'n will damn Desire,*
> *And be a Hell within me.*

Besides, they have many new Expressions on this Occasion of *Ejaculations*, or sudden Passions; but it is observable, that they have all the same Meaning. Some-

---

(n) A Woman's Revenge, *p.* 29. *l.* 14.

(o) The Busy Body, *p.* 28. *l.* 26. The Man's bewitch'd, *p.* 8. *l. ult.* The Successful Pirate, *p.* 43. *l.* 4.

(p) The Platonick Lady, *p.* 48. *l.* 6.

(q) The Contrivances, *p.* 18. *l.* 21. *p.* 19. *l.* 7. The Man's bewitch'd, *p.* 35. *l.* 5. *p.* 51. *l.* 15. *p.* 52. *l.* 13.

(r) The Country Wake, *p.* 16. *l.* 14. The Wonder, *p.* 38. *l.* 31.

(s) The *Persian* Princess, *p.* 20. *l.* 25.

(t) Electra, *Act* 4. *verse* 8. *French* Cato, *p.* 43. *l.* 20. Lucius, *p.* 26. *l.* 22. *p.* 27. *l.* 33. *p.* 39. *l. ult.* *Sawny* the *Scot*, *p.* 55. *l.* 2. She wou'd if she cou'd, *p.* 91. *l.* 18. *p.* 94. *l.* 18. *p.* 118. *l.* 20. *p.* 132. *l.* 32. *p.* 149. *l.* 15. *p.* 156. *l.* 16. *p.* 157. *l.* 30. *p.* 163. *l.* 13. *p.* 165. *l.* 29. The cruel Gift, *p.* 49. *l.* 26.

(u) Lucius, *p.* 36. *l.* 10. *Sawny* the *Scot*, *p.* 55. *l.* 28. The Man's bewitch'd, *p.* 36. *l.* 23.

(x) The *Persian* Princess, *p.* 32. *Scene l.* 1.

(y) Elfrid, *p.* 23. *l.* 10. *p.* 43. *l.* 5. Jane Gray, *p.* 51. *l.* 3. The Apparition, *p.* 56. *l.* 13. The Double Gallant, *p.* 79. *l.* 4. The *Persian* Princess, *p.* 59. *l.* 23.

(z) Elfrid, *p.* 27. *l. penult.* *p.* 38. *l.* 5.

(a) Perplex'd Couple, *p.* 35. *l.* 13.

(b) Jane Gray, *p.* 49. *l.* 4.

(c) Elfrid, *p.* 21. *l.* 28.

times they are contained in a single Word; as, (d) *Amazement!* (e) *Confusion!* (f) *Damnation!* (g) *Death!* (h) *Devils!* (i) *Distraction!* (k) *Fire!* (l) *Fury!* (m) *Furies!* (n) *Ghosts!* (o) *Hell!* (p) *Perdition!* (q) *Plagues!*

(*d*) Perfidious Brother, *p.* 28. *l.* 17. *p.* 55. *l.* 8. Perplex'd Lovers, *p.* 9. *l.* 34. Sultaness, *p.* 30. *l.* 29.

(*e*) Injur'd Love, *p.* 54. *l.* 1. The Apparition, *p.* 48. *l.* 1. Artful Husband, *p.* 37. *l.* 17. Cruel Gift, *p.* 35. *l.* 14. Fatal Marriage, *p.* 165. *l. antepenult.* Perfidious Brother, *p.* 28. l. 1. *p.* 30. *l.* 32. *p.* 50. *l.* 29. *p.* 54. *l. ult.* Perplex'd Lovers, *p.* 5. *l. antepenult.* *p.* 20. *l.* 22. *p.* 25. *l.* 10. *p.* 31. *l.* 1. *p.* 50. *l.* 2. Platonick Lady, *p.* 25. *l. antepenult.* *p.* 55. *l.* 25. Rival Fools, *p.* 9. *l.* 21. *p.* 32. *l.* 28. *p.* 52. *l.* 5. Royal Convert, *p.* 5. *l.* 25. *p.* 59. *l.* 19. *p.* 50. *l.* 25. Successful Pirate, *p.* 35. *l.* 5. Walking Statue, *p.* 64. *l.* 15. Wife's Relief, *p.* 55. *l.* 2.

(*f*) *Appius* and *Virginia*, *p.* 33. *l.* 26. *p.* 59. *l.* 1. Elfrid, *p.* 41. *l.* 34. The Apparition, *p.* 21. *l.* 3. The Country Lasses, *p.* 63. *l. penult.* Perfidious Brother, *p.* 52. *l.* 5. Perplex'd Lovers, *p.* 21. *l.* 24. *p.* 31. *l.* 27. *Persian* Princess, *p.* 30. *l.* 27. Platonick Lady, *p.* 65. *l.* 6. Wife's Relief, *p.* 54. *l.* 38.

(*g*) Injur'd Love, *p.* 30. *l.* 15. *p.* 31. *l.* 31, *ult.* *p.* 32. *l.* 9. *p.* 44. *l.* 23. *p.* 60. *l.* 42. Love and Liberty, *p.* 15. *l.* 27. Artful Husband, *p.* 11. *l.* 10. *p.* 38. *l.* 15. *p.* 66. *l.* 12. Busy Body, *p.* 48. *l.* 18. Drummer, *p.* 53. *l.* 20. *p.* 54. *l.* 30. Fair Quaker of *Deal*, *p.* 58. *l. antepenult.* Lady's last Stake, *p.* 46. *l.* 16. *p.* 70. *l.* 6. *p.* 71. *l.* 25. The Man's bewitch'd, *p.* 44. *l.* 18. Perfidious Brother, *p.* 54. *l.* 26. *Persian* Princess, *p.* 6. *l.* 1. Platonick Lady, *p.* 64. *l.* 4, 15. Squire of *Alsatia*, *p.* 20. *l.* 32. *p.* 28. *l.* 11. *p.* 36. *l.* 1. Wife's Relief, *p.* 66. *l.* 36.

(*h*) Walking Statue, *p.* 58. *l.* 25. *p.* 64. *l.* 15.

(*i*) Love in a Wood, *p.* 34. *l. antepenult.* Lady's last Stake, *p.* 72. *l.* 30. Perplex'd Lovers, *p.* 10. *l.* 6. Platonick Lady, *p.* 27. *l.* 14. *p.* 56. *l.* 2. Successful Pirate, *p.* 24. *l.* 12.

(*k*) Rival Fools, *p.* 33. *l.* 3.

(*l*) Love in a Wood, *p.* 33. *l.* 27. *p.* 34. *l. antepenult.*

(*m*) *Appius* and *Virginia*, *p.* 16. *l.* 19. The Apparition, *p.* 47. *l.* 29. The Country Lasses, *p.* 63. *l. penult.* *Persian* Princess, *p.* 19. *l.* 13. Wife of *Bath*, *p.* 58. *l.* 37.

(*n*) Walking Statue, *p.* 58. *l.* 25.

(*o*) Elfrid, *p.* 23. *l.* 10. *p.* 43. *l.* 5. Jane Gray, *p.* 51. *l.* 3. Love in a Wood, *p.* 33. *l.* 17. *p.* 34. *l. antepenult.* The Apparition, *p.* 56. *l.* 13. Double Gallant, *p.* 79. *l.* 4. *Persian* Princess, *p.* 59. *l.* 23. Wife's Relief, *p.* 54. *l.* 12.

(*p*) Perfidious Brother, *p.* 20. *l.* 26.

(*q*) The Wife's Relief, *p.* 64. *l.* 14.

Racks!

(*r*) *Racks!* (*s*) *Spirits!* (*t*) *Torture!* (*u*) *Tortures!* (*x*) *Vexation!*

Sometimes the *Poets* join two words together on theſe occaſions. Thus becauſe *Hell* is deſcribed in *Scripture* to be (*y*) a *Lake, which burneth with Brimſtone and Fire*; thereſore they call upon (*z*) *Brimſtone and Fire!* (*a*) *Brimſtone and Smoke!* or (*b*) *Fire and Brimſtone!*

Thus they alſo cry out upon (*c*) *Blood and Deſtruction!* (*d*) *Blood and Fire!* (*e*) *Blood and Fury!* (*f*) *Blood and Furies!* (*g*) *Confuſion! Dire Confuſion!* (*h*) *Conjuration and Diſtraction!* (*i*) *Death and Confuſion!* (*k*) *Death and eternal Darkneſs!* (*l*) *Death and the Devil!* (*m*) *Death and Fire!* (*n*) *Death and Hell!* (*o*) *Death and Perdition!* (*p*) *Death and Tortures!* (*q*) *Fire and Furies!*

(*r*) Drummer, p. 53. l. 16. Wife's Relief, p. 66. l. 36.

(*s*) Walking Statue, p. 58. l. 25.

(*t*) Wife's Relief, p. 54. l. 12.

(*u*) Drummer, p. 53. l. 18. Wife's Relief, p. 64. l. 14. p. 66. l. 36.

(*x*) Wife's Relief, p. 64. l. 17.

(*y*) *Revel.* 19. 20. & 20. 10. & 21. 8.

(*z*) Country Laſſes, p. 32. l. 19. Modern Prophets, p. 9. l. 24.

(*a*) Fair Quaker of *Deal*, p. 56. l. 21.

(*b*) Apparition, p. 57. l. 28.

(*c*) Humours of Purgatory, p. 25. l. *penult.*

(*d*) Fair Quaker of *Deal*, p. 10. l. 22.

(*e*) The Contrivances, p. 18. l. 9.

(*f*) Comical Lovers, p. 46. l. 29. The Contrivances, p. 18. l. 9.

(*g*) The City Ramble; or, The Play-houſe Wedding, p. 55. l. 15.

(*h*) Walking Statue, p. 64. l. 15.

(*i*) Lady's laſt Stake, p. 46. l. 10. Wife of *Bath*, p. 61. l. 2.

(*k*) The Man of Mode, p. 254. l. 22.

(*l*) The Man's bewitch'd, p. 40. l. 7.

(*m*) The Beaux Stratagem, p. 10. l. 8. The Recruiting Officer, p. 32. l. 24.

(*n*) The Fair Quaker of *Deal*, p. 10. l. 11. The Ladies Laſt Stake, p. 36. l. 20. The Perplex'd Lovers, p. 35. l. 37. The Squire of *Alſatia*, p. 40. l. 42. p. 46. l. 3. p. 59. l. 7.

(*o*) The Perfidious Brother, p. 36. l. 10.

(*p*) Ibid. p. 41. l. 17.

(*q*) The Apparition, p. 23. l. 18. The Lady's Laſt Stake, p. 68. l. 11. The Recruiting Officer, p. 47. l. *penult.* p. 69. l. 6.

ries! (r) *Flames and Sulphur!* (s) *Flesh and Fire!* (t) *Furies and Death!* (u) *Furies and Distraction!* (x) *Furies and Fire!* (y) *Furies and Firebrands!* (z) *Furies and Hell!* (a) *Hell and Confusion!* (b) *Hell and Damnation!* (c) *Hell and Furies!* (d) *Hell and Tortures!* (e) *Horror and Confusion!* (f) *Lightning and Thunder!* (g) *Racks and Torments!* (h) *Thunder and Lightning!* or (i) *Tortures and Hell!*

Sometimes the *Poets* join three Words together on this Occasion. Thus they say; (k) *Blood, and Fire, and Fury!* (l) *Confusion, Death, and Horror!* (m) *Death, Hell, and the Devil!* (n) *Death, Hell, and Devils!* (o) *Death, Hell, and Furies!* (p) *Hell, scalding Lead, and Sulphurs!* or (q) *Tortures, Distraction, and Death!* I had not taken the pains to make this Collection from the *Plays* of the ten last Years, nor have tired the Reader with them, but only that he may observe, how the *Poets* rack their Wits on all occasions, to be most co-

---

(r) The Perfidious Brother, p. 22. l.11.

(s) The Masquerade, p.6. l.9.

(t) *Jane Gray*, p.31. l.16.

(u) A Wife well manag'd, p. 6. l.7.

(x) The Fair Quaker of *Deal*, p.52. l.14.

(y) The Country Lasses, p. 32. l.28.

(z) Love's Last Shift, p. 48. l. 4.

(a) Elfrid, p.41. l.2.

(b) Injur'd Love, p.28. l. 9. The Squire of *Alsatia*, p. 66. l. 37.

(c) Injur'd Love, p.55. l.10. The Busy-Body, p.48. l.21. Fair Quaker of *Deal*, p.43. l.29. The Humours of the Army, p. 69. l. 34. The Man of Mode, p. 201. l.19. The Man's bewitch'd, p.38. l.17. p.60. l.4. The Perplex'd Lovers, p.10. l.4. p. 44. l. *penult*.

(d) The Humours of the Army, p.23. l.26.

(e) Love and Liberty, p.9. l. *antepenult*.

(f) The Apparition, p. 54. l. 21.

(g) The Beaux Stratagem, p. 11. l.29.

(h) The Country Lasses, p. 32. l.36.

(i) *Jane Gray*, p. 20. l. 1. The *Persian* Princess, p.21. l.11.

(k) The Contrivances, p. 18. l. 9. p.26. l. *antepenult*.

(l) Perfidious Brother, p. 51. l. 14.

(m) *Gotham* Election, p. 61. l. 26.

(n) Fair Quaker of *Deal*, p. 43. l.5.

(o) The Wonder, p.76. l.29.

(p) *Jane Gray*, p.75. l.27.

(q) Sultaness, p.46. l.23.

piously and extravagantly Blasphemous. And he who will compare this with their horrid Oaths, will find reason to believe, that by the Word *Death*, they mean the *Death* of *Jesus Christ*, the only *Son* of *GOD*, even whilst they (r) thus *join* him *with Belial*; as if they resolved in this manner (s) to *crucify to themselves the Son of GOD afresh*, whilst they thus *expose him to open Shame*.

[LORD, lay not these, and such-like other Sins to our Charge.]

The next Impiety which I shall take notice of in the *Stage*, is their *Adjurations*.

When *Jesus Christ* gave his *Apostles* a Commission to preach the *Gospel*, he said unto them, (t) *These Signs shall follow them that believe: In my Name shall they cast out Devils; and they shall lay Hands on the Sick, and they shall recover.* Accordingly St. *Peter* cured the *lame Man* at the *Temple*, *saying*, (u) *In the Name of Jesus Christ of Nazareth, rise up and walk.* Thus St. *Paul* cast out a *Devil* from one possessed, saying, (x) *I command thee in the Name of Jesus Christ to come out of her.* And when (y) *certain of the vagabond Jews took upon them to call over them that had evil Spirits, the Name of the Lord Jesus*, they were made Examples for such a Presumption. Then *Devils* were expelled *In the Name of Christ*: But in these wretched Times, *Christianity* is almost expell'd *In the Name of the Devil*. This seems to be the reason of their common *Adjurations* on the *Stage*, not only (z) *In the Name of Goodness*; but also, to confound all Distinction between *Virtue* and *Vice*, (a) *In the Name of Fornication*, (b) *In the Name of Fury*, and

(r) 2 *Cor*. 6. 15.
(s) *Heb*. 6. 6.
(t) *Mark* 16. 17, 18.
(u) *Act*. 3. 6.
(x) *Act*. 16. 18.
(y) *Act*. 19. 13,16.
(z) Ignoramus, p. 39. l. 5. The Man's bewitch'd, p.60. l.31. Perplex'd Lovers, p. 6. l.23. p. 34. l.9. Wonder, p.72. l.27.
(a) Modern Prophets, p. 61. l. 36.
(b) Wife of *Bath*, p.10. l.3.

(*c*) *In the Name of Mischief.* Thus they *adjure*, (*d*) *In the Name of Beelzebub*, (*e*) *In the Devil's Name*, (*f*) *In the Great Devil's Name*, (*g*) *In the Name of Lucifer*, and (*h*) *In the Name of Satan*; and also (*i*) *In the Name of Horror*, (*k*) *In the Name of Madness*, (*l*) *In the Name of Nonsense*, (*m*) *In the Name of Thunder*, (*n*) *In the Name of Vanity*, and (*o*) *In the Name of Wonder.*

Another Act of Devotion paid to the *Devil* upon the *Stage*, is *praying* to him. This is an Act of *Adoration* due only to GOD, which (*p*) *the blessed Angels* refused; and the paying it to *Saints* departed, was one of the *Errors* which caused our Separation from the *Church of Rome*. And certainly the *praying* to an invisible Being, as present, is the owning of him to be in every place, and consequently ascribing to him an *Attribute* which is due to GOD alone.

The Quotations are almost innumerable; but I shall venture to transcribe some of them at large.

In (*q*) one *Play* the *Devils* are called

Black Fiends, that people this infernal Grove,
And by dire Contract with the Stygian Gods,
From stalking Ghosts extort th' uncertain Knowledge
Of hid Futurity.

(*c*) Wit without Money, p.69. *l.* 4.

(*d*) Masquerade, p. 27. l. 2. Three Hours after Marriage, p. 7. l.8.

(*e*) Love's Last Shift, p.73. l. 9. *Sawny* the *Scot*, p.36. l.18. p.49. l.15. City Ramble, or, Play-House Wedding, p.12. l.15. *Gotham* Election, p. 71. l. 2. Contrivances, p.19. l.15. Man of Mode, p.183. l.26.

(*f*) *Sawny* the *Scot*, p.7. l.1.

(*g*) Fair Quaker of *Deal*, p. 56. l.3.

(*h*) Perplex'd Couple, p. 34. l. 4.

(*i*) *Persian* Princess, p. 45. l. 22.

(*k*) A Woman's Revenge, p. 43. l. 7.

(*l*) Lady's last Stake, p. 9. l. 34.

(*m*) Ibid. p. 37. l.10. Wife of *Bath*, p.58. l. *antepenult.*

(*n*) Woman is a Riddle, p. 12. l. 14.

(*o*) Country House, p. 20. l. 26. Earl of *Mar* marr'd, p.17. l.21. Maid the Mistress, p. 8. l. 8. Pretender's Flight, p. 14. l. 13. Recruiting Officer, p. 8. l.8. Wife's Relief, p. 4. l.23. The Wonder, p. 34. l. *antepen.*

(*p*) *Revel.* 22. 8, 9.

(*q*) *Persian* Princess, *p.* 27. *Act* 3. *l.* 5.

And

And they are afterward pray'd to thus:

(r) *All kind Powers help me.*

In other *Plays* there are theſe Expreſſions:

(s) *Ye Furies, that have ſeiz'd my lab'ring Soul,*
Be ſtill but for a moment.

(t) *Ye Furies ſeize me*: that is, that ſo the Petitioner may be eaſed of his troubled Mind, as it is (u) there explain'd.

(x) *Riſe, Furies, riſe,*
Leave your grim King unguarded to attend me.

(y) *Furies,* Alecto, *aid my juſt Deſign.*

(z) *Ariſe, ye Furies, awake and rage.*

(a) *Furies, give over!*
Spare me! Spare my Lover!

[Spare us, good LORD, ſpare thy People, and let not theſe Iniquities be our Ruin.]

To theſe ſhort Quotations I ſhall only add (b) another more at large.

——— Come, all ye Spirits,
That wait on mortal Thoughts; unſex me here,
Empty my Nature of Humanity,
And fill it up with Cruelty: Make thick
My Blood, and ſtop all paſſage to Remorſe;
That no Relapſes into Mercy may
Shake my Deſign, nor make it fall before
'Tis ripen'd to effect: You murdering Spirits
(Where e'er in ſightleſs Subſtances you wait
On Nature's Miſchief) come and fill my Breaſts
With Gall inſtead of Milk. Make haſte, dark Night,
And hide me in a Smoak as black as Hell.

(r) *Perſian* Princeſs, *p.*28. *l.*12.
(s) *Appius* and *Virginia*, p.50. *l.* 6.
(t) *Pyrrhus* and *Demetrius*, *p.* 57. *l.*3.
(u) Ibid. p.57. *l.* 8.
(x) Rinaldo, *p.*49. *l.*29.
(y) *Britiſh* Enchanters, *p.* 30. *l.* 30.
(z) Thomyris, *p.*29. *l.* 14.
(a) Love's Triumph, *p.*24. *l. penult.*
(b) Mackbeth, *p.*11. *l.*26.

But the most amazing Instances are in cases of Revenge. Our *Blessed Saviour* commanded his Disciples (c) to *learn of* him, *for* he was *meek and lowly in Heart, and* so they should *find rest to* their *Souls.* Accordingly, when he hang'd on the Cross, he (d) prayed to his *Father,* that he would *forgive* his Persecutors; and after his example, St. *Stephen* (e) *prayed, saying, LORD, lay not this Sin to their Charge.* Thus in our daily *Prayer,* which *Christ* hath taught us, we say, *Forgive us our Trespasses, as we forgive them that trespass against us.* And St. *Paul* gives this Advice, (f) *Let all Bitterness, and Wrath, and Clamour, and Evil-speaking, be put away from you, with all Malice; and be ye kind one to another, tender-hearted, forgiving one another, even as GOD for Christ's sake hath forgiven you.* And (g) *Put on therefore (as the Elect of GOD, holy and beloved) Bowels of Mercies,* Kindness, *Humbleness of Mind, Meekness, Long-suffering, Forbearing one another, and forgiving one another; if any Man have a quarrel against* any, *even as GOD forgave you, so also do ye.* These being the direct Rules of *Christianity,* it is surprizing to find what a contrary Part the *Players act* in their *Devotions* to the *Devil.* Thus *Medea* (h) *calls for all sorts of Plagues to fall upon her Rival.* She (i) *invokes the Infernals to revenge her Injuries;* and (k) she speaks to the *Furies* in the words of (l) *our Saviour's* last *Prayer, Finish the Work; delay no longer.* And the Words on such Occasions are most blasphemous. Thus (m) in the same *Play:*

Ye Ghosts! come forth, and bring eternal Night,
And gaze upon the Sun, only to obscure it:
Ready Obedience pay to my Commands,
Let Fury and Disdain
Approach from their gloomy Abodes:
Come forth, ye Ghosts, and bring eternal Night.

(c) *Matth.* 11. 29.
(d) *Luke* 23. 34.
(e) *Act.* 7. 60.
(f) *Ephes.* 4. 31, 32.
(g) *Colos.* 3. 12, 13.
(h) Theseus, *p.* 39. *l.* 24.
(i) Ibid. *p.* 45. *Scene* 3. *l.* 9.
(k) Ibid. *p.* 47. *l.* 3.
(l) *John* 17. 4.
(m) Theseus, *p.* 39. *l.* 10.

And

And in other *Plays*;

(n) You I invoke, assisting Furies, next:
Let complicated Mischiefs tear them hence;
And may they perish by their dearest Friends.
O ye swift executing Furies, come,
Destroy, confound the Leaders, and their Troops,
In hideous Ruin overwhelm them all.
(o) Hear it, ye dreadful Judges of the Damn'd,
And in your adamantine Books record it;
That when from the Tarpeian *Rock he plunges*
To lowest Hell, he may have dismal Justice.
(p) Bid him (a Ghost) *arise, and bring Revenge to day,*
From its infernal Mansion.
(q) Ye Realms of Pluto, *and his gloomy Consort!*
Infernal Hermes! *you my potent Curses:*
And awful Furies, Daughters of the Gods!
O rise, assist, revenge a murder'd King.
(r) Foul Offspring of eternal Night,
Hell's darling Plague, Alecto, *rise,*
Rejoice, and see with me
The Fall of proud Arsinoe.
(s) Assist, ye Furies, from the Deep,
Revenge, Revenge prepare.

(t) Thus *Sempronius* dying, saith,

Gods! I'm distracted! This my Close of Life!
Oh for a Peal of Thunder, that would make
Earth, Sea and Air, and Heav'n and Cato *tremble!*

And to add more Instances of this nature:

(u) Ye horrid Fiends of Hell,
My bursting Bosom swell;
With Vengeance black and dire
This injur'd Heart inspire.

(n) Ajax, *Act* 4. *Ver.* 23.
(o) *Appius* and *Virginia*, p. 52. *l.* 21.
(p) Ibid. *p.* 56. *in fine.*
(q) Electra, *Act* 1. *Ver.* 117.
(r) Arsinoe, *p.* 18. *l.* 16.
(s) Ibid. *p.* 19. *l.* 11.
(t) Cato, *p.* 46. *l. ult.*
(u) Hydaspes, *p.* 68. *l.* 6.

Gods

(x) *Gods of Revenge arise.*
(y) *Rise, all ye Furies,*
Rise and direct me:
In you my Cure is;
Rise and protect me.
(z) *Rise, all ye Furies, that obey my Call,*
And shake your wiry Whips, to whet my Rage.
(a) *Instruct me, ye Furies; teach me, ye Fiends, what Punishment I shall devise.*
(b) *Furies and Hell reward the subtle Fiend.*
(c) *Assist, ye wrathful Powers, let posting Death*
Ride on the sickly Air, and make it breathe
Cramps, Pains, Sores, Poisons, ev'ry Name that bears
Antipathy to Life, or Health, or Ease.
(d) *First, sink him to Hell, seize him, ye Fiends!*

It is common for *Christians* to say of a Person dying, *LORD, receive his Soul.* Thus St. *Stephen*, when stoned, said, (e) *LORD Jesus, receive my Spirit*; and above all, our *blessed Saviour* when crucified, said, (f) *Father, into thy Hands I commend my Spirit.* In the Language of the *Play-house* it is thus express'd:

(g) *Immortal* Rhadamanthus,
The Tyrant comes; prepare him a Reception,
Which Hell ne'er saw before: Attend, ye Furies!
Attend, ye skreaming Ghosts of murder'd Romans!
Behold the Judge now sentenc'd in his turn,
And doom'd to Pains, at which the Damn'd will tremble,
And take their own for Joys.

And in another (h),
Furies tear thee, as thou hast torn my Quiet.
Down, Devil, down, and tell the Prince of Darkness,

(x) *Phædra* and *Hippolytus*, p. 29. *l*. 16.
(y) *Pyrrhus* and *Demetrius*, p. 42. *l*. 14.
(z) Rinaldo, *p*. 39. *l*. 3.
(a) Generous Husband, *p*. 55. *l*. 11.
(b) *Persian* Princess, *p*. 45. *l*. *ult*.
(c) Ibid. *p*. 46. *l*. 9.
(d) Royal Convert, *p*. 24. *l*. 19.
(e) *Act*. 7. 60.
(f) *Luke* 23. 46.
(g) *Appius* and *Virginia*, *p*. 63. *l*. 16.
(h) Elfrid, *p*. 38. *l*. 32.

Ordgar

Ordgar hath ſent a Fiend more black than him,
To fill the burning Throne of Hell's Dominions.

And in a third, (*i*)

——————— *Villain, get thee down*
To Hell, and tell them, that the Fray's begun;
And we will ſend ſuch Shoals of murder'd Slaves,
Shall glut their empty Regions.

Another Act of *Devotion* paid to the *Devil* on the *Stage*, is *Thankſgiving*. As GOD is the Author and Giver of all good Gifts; ſo he ought to have the *Praiſe* of all. In *Scripture*, we have innumerable Precepts and Examples for this purpoſe; and in our *Liturgy* we have ſeveral *Thankſgivings* placed together, to be offer'd up to GOD as occaſion ſhall require. But this Duty in the *Play-houſe* is paid to the *Devil*. Thus a pretended *Alderman* of *London*, being in expectation of ſucceeding in an *adulterous Deſign*, expreſſeth his Raptures in this manner, (*k*)

O all ye Demons, Spirits, Apparitions,
Heroes and Gods, and Demi-Gods and Men!
How ſhall my Heart
Expreſs the Joy that labours for a Vent?

The laſt Part of *Divine Adoration* paid to the *Devil* on the *Stage*, is, *The ſinging of Hymns* to him. The (*l*) *Primitive Chriſtians* did uſually meet together before Day, to ſing *Hymns* to *Chriſt*, as GOD. And St. *Paul* (*m*) adviſeth, that we ſhould *teach and admoniſh one another in Pſalms, and Hymns, and Spiritual Songs, ſinging and making Melody in our Hearts unto the LORD.* And certainly, none but ſuch Wretches as are given over to a *reprobate Senſe*, can endure to hear ſuch a *ſolemn Devotion* paid to the *Devil*, and join'd with ſuch *grave Muſick*, as would be much more proper for a *Divine Hymn* or Anthem. A long Quotation would amaze the

---

(*i*) *Perſian* Princeſs, *p.* 54. *l.* 27.

(*k*) Love in a Sack, *p.* 53. *l.* 2.

(*l*) *Pliny's* Epiſtles, *lib.* 10. *Epiſ.* 97.

(*m*) *Coloſ.* 3. 16.

Reader, and therefore I shall only give him (*n*) two Lines of what I have been forced to quote before; and perhaps it is to this which an Actor refers, when (*o*) he speaks of *an Hymn to the Devil*:

Hail, Powers beneath, whose Influence imparts
The Knowledge of infernal Arts!

[LORD, let not thy Vengeance be pour'd out upon us for these things!]

CHAP. VII.

The Divine Attributes, and the Works of Creation and Providence, ascribed to the Devil on the Stage.

THE *Attributes* of GOD are his essential Properties, according to the different manner of his working. They are expressed in *Scripture* by several Epithets, and such as may be best understood by our mean Capacities. Some of them are so peculiar to the *Divine Essence*, that the like are not to be found in the Creatures. Others are not so peculiar, but that there are some Shadows and faint Resemblances of them, either more perfect and immutable (I mean) comparatively, as in the good *Angels* and pious *Souls* departed; or more imperfect and mutable, as in *Men* on Earth. But all these were wholly and irrecoverably lost by the *Devil* and his accursed *Spirits*, when they fell from their original State of Innocency; insomuch that they retain the contrary Qualities in the highest degree.

As therefore (*a*) GOD *will not give* his *Glory to another*, *nor* his *Praise to graven Images*; so much less can

(*n*) The Metamorphosis, *p.* 14. *l.* 9.

(*o*) The Contrivances, *p.* 7. *l.* 4.

(*a*) *Isa.* 42. 8.

he

he endure that his *Attributes* ſhould be aſcribed to the *Devil.* But as he is a GOD *jealous* of his Honour, ſo we have cauſe to fear that he will *viſit* for ſuch *Iniquities* as theſe, upon Perſons or a Nation guilty, if not (b) *upon their Children*, and upon their Childrens Children *unto the third and fourth Generation.*

To make this Matter plainer, ſuppoſe *our Stage* ſhould ſet up ſome poor ſordid *Rebel*, dignify him with all the *King's Titles*, and call him *the King*, or *his moſt Excellent Majeſty*, or *King of* Great Britain, France, *and* Ireland, and *Defender of the Faith*, &c. can we imagine that any *Government* would endure ſuch Affronts, or paſs by ſuch daring Inſolence? And yet all this is but the putting up of one Creature in oppoſition to another. How then can we think, that GOD himſelf will wink at ſuch Crimes, when we exalt not only a *Creature*, but even his vileſt Enemy, in oppoſition to him, who is the *Creator* of us all?

However, none of theſe Conſiderations can reſtrain our *Poets* from ſuch a *blaſphemous Method*, or from treating the *Devil* with the ſame Appellations, which the *Scriptures* mention as proper only to the true GOD. And this will too ſadly appear, by comparing thoſe Expreſſions with what we find in our *modern Plays.*

The *Scriptures* ſay that GOD is (g) *everlaſting*, even (h) *from everlaſting to everlaſting*, (i) *the firſt and the laſt*, (k) *who inhabiteth Eternity*, (l) *eternal*, and (m) *immortal.* The *Players* call the *Devil* (n) *eternal*, and (o) *a more than mortal Power*; and from thence ſpeak of him like to this *Scripture*-Expreſſion, (p) *Thou ſhalt not tempt the LORD thy GOD.* Nay, tho St. *James* (q) tells us, That if we *reſiſt the Devil, he will flee from us*; yet upon the *Stage* we are told, (r) that it is a *Raſh-*

(b) *Exod.* 20. 5.
(g) *Gen.* 21. 33. *Rom.* 16. 26.
(h) *Pſal.* 90. 2.
(i) *Iſa.* 44. 6.
(k) *Iſa.* 57. 15.
(l) *Rom.* 1. 20.
(m) 1 *Tim.* 1. 17.
(n) The Gameſter, *p.* 56. *l.* 1.
(o) *Britiſh* Enchanters, *p.* 16. *l.* 2.
(p) *Mat.* 4. 7. *Luke* 4. 12. *Deut.* 6. 16.
(q) *Jam.* 4. 7.
(r) *Britiſh* Enchanters, *p.* 16. *l.* 2.

ness and *Frenzy* to resist him, from this very Consideration;

Forbear, rash Mortal, give thy Frenzy o'er,
For now thou tempt'st a more than mortal Pow'r.

The *Scriptures* say, that (s) *the LORD our GOD is a great GOD*, and therefore he is (t) *greatly to be praised*; that he is (u) *clothed with Honour and Majesty*; that he (x) hath *set* his *Glory above the Heavens*; that (y) *he is the King over all the Earth*; and (z) he *is above all, and through all, and in us all.* In the *Play-House* it is (a) *the Great Devil*, and (b) *the Awful Furies:* And thus he is represented as (c) something very extraordinary or considerable, insomuch that he who (d) gains him, gains every thing else into the bargain. And when the *Stage-Poets* would mention something very great and remarkable, the word (e) *Devilish* is the Epithet to express it by. When any Person is taken notice of in *Scripture*, as of very wonderful Abilities, the usual Expression is, (f) that *GOD is with him*, or (g) *in him.* A religious Person is said (h) to have (i) *Christ in him:* And the

(s) *Deut.* 10. 17. 2 *Chron.* 2. 5.
(t) 1 *Chron.* 16. 25. *Psal.* 48. 1. *Psal.* 96. 4. *Psal.*145. 3.
(u) *Psal.* 104. 1.
(x) *Psal.* 8. 1.
(y) *Psal.* 47. 7.
(z) *Ephes.* 4. 6.
(a) A Wife well managed, *p.* 13. *l.*16. Ignoramus, *p.* 67. *l.*6. *p.*68. *l.*2. *Sawny* the *Scot*, *p.*7. *l.*1. Earl of *Mar* marr'd, *p.*5. *l.*29. *p.*12. *l.*17. *p.*18. *l.*28. The Nonjuror, *p.*45. *l.*6.
(b) Electra, *Act* 1. *ver.*119.
(c) Comical Lovers, *p.* 61. *l.* 20. Country House, *p.*21. *l.*6. Double Gallant, *p.* 4. *l.* 1. *p.*8. *l.* 21. Fatal Marriage, *p.* 127. *l. penult.* The Man's bewitch'd, *p.*40. *l.*13. Cobler of *Preston*, *p.* 20. *l. penult.* The Contrivances, *p.* 7. *l.* 13. Country House, *p.*21. *l.*6. *p.* 22. *l.* 37. *p.* 23. *l.* 7. Perplex'd Couple, *p.*11. *l.*17. *p.* 24. *l.*15. *p.* 30. *l.*21. Wit at a pinch, *p.*7. *l.*20. *p.*34. *l.*27.
(d) Rival Fools, *p.*15. *l.*29.
(e) She wou'd if she cou'd, *p.*95. *l.*33. Adventures of half an Hour, *p.*18. *l.*15. Cobler of *Preston*, *p.*16. *l.*28. The Drummer, *p.*15. *l.*2. Squire of *Alsatia*, *p.*33. *l.*12. *p.*66. *l.*5.
(f) *John* 3. 2.
(g) 1 *Cor.* 14. 25.
(h) *Gal.* 4. 19. *Coloss.* 1. 27.
(i) *Acts* 2. 4.

Apostles on the Day of *Pentecost* are ſaid to be (*k*) *filled with the Holy Ghost*; which is alſo the Character of (*k*) other ſincere *Christians*. But (as if the *Poets*, by burleſquing thoſe ſacred Expreſſions, did their utmoſt to bring them into Contempt; and indeed each Perſon of the *Ever-bleſſed Trinity* mention'd in them) the *Play-Houſe* Language on ſuch an occaſion is, (*l*) *He is the Devil*, or (*m*) *The Devil is in him*. When any thing happens very remarkable, or any Perſon is overruled by ſome unexpected *Providence*, preſently (*n*) *The Devil is in it*, and the Glory is given to him alone. And when a Man meets with good Succeſs, either it is (*o*) *like the Devil*; or it is applauded after this manner, (*p*) *Sure he can conjure, and hath the Devil for his* Aſſiſtant.

Another Attribute given to GOD in *Scripture*, is his *Omnipreſence*. This is reckon'd by *Divines* to be *incommunicable* to any *Creature*. In this reſpect GOD and Chriſt is ſaid (*q*) to be *all in all*, and (*r*) to *fill all in all*. Thus (*s*) *the Heaven is* his *Throne, and the Earth is* his

---

(*k*) *Acts* 4. 8. & 9. 17. & 13. 9. *Epheſ.* 5. 18.

(*l*) The Gameſter, *p.*6. *l.*22. Modern Prophets, *p.* 12. *l.* 18. Recruiting Officer, *p.* 48. *l.* 10. *p.*49. *l.*37.

(*m*) Marplot, *p.*5. *l.*20. *Sawny* the *Scot*, *p.*19. *l.*1. Beaux Stratagem, *p.*63. *l.*25. The Biter, *p.*3. *l.*7. City Ramble, *p.* 12. *l.*28. Comical Lovers, *p.* 20. *l.*3,5. *p.*35. *l.*2. The Contrivances, *p.* 4. *l.* 17. Country Houſe, *p.*8. *l.*24. *p.*9. *l.*2. Fatal Marriage, *p.*100. *l.*16. Female Advocates, *p.* 16. *l.* 30. Humours of the Army, *p.* 61. *l.*12. The Litigants, *p.*26. *l.*6. The Man's bewitch'd, *p.*52. *l.*37. Modern Prophets, *p.* 33. *l.* 32. *p.*51. *l.* 23. Perplex'd Couple, *p.*10. *l.* 25. Perplex'd Lovers, *p.*36. *l.*15. *p.*38. *l.*1. Platonick Lady, *p.* 3. *l.*28. *p.* 63. *l.* 11. Recruiting Officer, *p.* 16. *l.* 21. Rival Fools, *p.* 7. *l.* 15. *p.* 28. *l.*12. *p.*35. *l.*32. *p.*41. *l. penult.*

(*n*) Ignoramus, *p.* 19. *l.* 4. She wou'd if ſhe cou'd, *p.* 134. *l.*2. Beaux Stratagem, *p.* 27. *l.* 14. *p.*54. *l.*7. The City Ramble; or, The Play-houſe Wedding, *p.* 56. *l. antepen.* Cruel Gift, *Prologue*, *l.* 16. Double Gallant, *p.*45. *l.*12. Fatal Marriage, *p.* 129. *l.* 33. Man of Mode, *p.*183. *l.*12. The Man's bewitch'd, *p.*61. *l.*24. Perplex'd Couple, *p.* 39. *l.* 1, 4. Pretender's Flight, *p.* 8. *l. antepenult.* Wit without Money, *p.*58. *l. ult.*

(*o*) Platonick Lady, *p.*21. *l.*4.

(*p*) Wit without Money, *p.*44. *l.* 23.

(*q*) 1 *Cor.* 15. 28. *Coloſſ.* 3. 11.

(*r*) *Epheſ.* 1. 23.

(*s*) *Iſa.* 66. 1. *Acts* 7. 49.

Foot-

Footstool; (t) he *fills Heaven and Earth*, and is both *near* and *afar off*. The *Psalmist* speaks of this with Admiration, (u) *Whither shall I go then from thy Spirit? or whither shall I flee from thy Presence? If I ascend up into Heaven, thou art there: if I make my Bed in Hell, behold! thou art there: If I take the Wings of the Morning, and dwell in the uttermost parts of the Sea; even there shall thy Hand lead me, and thy Right Hand shall hold me.* In the *Play-House* we are told of (x) *climbing the Devil knows where.* One *Actor* saith of another, (y) *This old Fellow is certainly the Devil; one can go no where, but one is sure to meet him.* And afterward, (z) *He haunted us like the Devil.* The common Expression is, (a) *The Devil and all*, or (b) *The Devil and all indeed:* who is accordingly represented, sometimes as (c) being *in all the Folks*, and (d) at other times as being more eminently in *some* particular Persons.

As therefore the *incommunicable Attributes* of the *Divine Essence* are thus profan'd; so it is no wonder, if the rest do meet with the same Treatment.

To begin therefore with the *Wisdom* and *Knowledge* of GOD: The *Psalmist* saith (e) that *his Understanding is infinite.* And the *Apostle* breaks out into this Exclamation, (f) *O the Depths of the Riches, both of the Wisdom and Knowledge of GOD! How unsearchable are his Judgments, and his Ways past finding out!* Accordingly,

---

(t) *Jer.* 23. 23, 24. 1 *Kings* 8. 27. *Isa.* 40. 12. *Acts* 17. 27.

(u) *Psal.* 139. 7, 8, 9, 10, 11, 12.

(x) The Wonders in the Sun, *p.* 44. *l. ult.*

(y) The Man's bewitch'd, *p.* 12. *l.* 20.

(z) Ibid. *p.* 23. *l.* 20.

(a) A City Ramble; or, The Humours of the Compter, *p.* 50. *l.* 10. The General cashier'd, *p.* 3. *l.* 20. Modern Prophets, *p.* 18. *l.* 34. *p.* 57. *l.* 31. Perplex'd Couple, *p.* 11. *l.* 14. Rival Fools, *p.* 15. *l.* 29. Wife's Relief, *p.* 13. *l.* 13.

(b) Modern Prophets, *p.* 18. *l.* 36.

(c) Perplex'd Lovers, *p.* 38. *l.* 1.

(d) Platonick Lady, *p.* 3. *l.* 28. The Litigants, *p.* 26. *l.* 6. Recruiting Officer, *p.* 16. *l.* 21. Rival Fools, *p.* 7. *l.* 15. *p.* 28. *l.* 12. *p.* 41. *l. penult.*

(e) *Psal.* 147. 5.

(f) *Rom.* 11. 33.

he alone is (g) said to be *wise in Heart*. He (h) *telleth the Number of the Stars, and calleth them all by their Names*. He (i) *seeth every thing which he made*, even (k) *every Imagination, and* (l) *the Thoughts, and* (m) *the Intents of the Heart*. He (n) *taketh the Wise in their own Craftiness*. He (o) *directs our Goings*, and (p) *no Man can teach* him. He alone (q) *declares* and *shews the things which are to come*, and (r) *reveals the deep and secret things*. He (s) *knows* what we *have need of*, and (t) *numbers the Hairs of* our *Heads*. He (u) *foreknew* who should be *his People*; but (x) no one can *know* his *Mind*. And this is the Account, which the *Scriptures* give us of GOD.

On the other hand, the *Play-House* not only tells us of (y) *a subtle Devil*, who is (z) *infallible*, and *right* in his Judgment and *Guesses*; one who (a) *knows what* is done, and (b) cannot easily be *made a Fool of*, or (c) *cheated*; insomuch that they (d) who *deal with the Devil* cannot be *outwitted*, but (e) they *know* all *Affairs* in general, and (f) every Particular, tho never so secretly managed. And when he is in a Man, he (g) causes him to know also, and (h) to guess aright concerning the things of this World. In the *Play-House* we are

(g) *Job* 9. 4. *Job* 12. 16. & *Rom.* 16. 27.
(h) *Psal.* 147. 4.
(i) *Gen.* 1, 31. *Prov.* 15. 3.
(k) *Gen.* 6. 5. *Job* 11. 11. & *Heb.* 4. 13.
(l) *Psal.* 94. 9, 10, 11. *Rev.* 2. 23.
(m) 2 *Chron.* 6. 30. *Prov.* 15. 11. *Jer.* 11. 20.
(n) *Job* 5. 12, 13. 1 *Cor.* 3. 19.
(o) *Prov.* 5. 21. & 20. 24.
(p) *Isa.* 40. 13.
(q) *Isa.* 41. 23. *Rev.* 4. 1.
(r) *Dan.* 2. 22.
(s) *Mat.* 6. 32.
(t) *Mat.* 10. 30.
(u) *Rom.* 8. 29. *Rom.* 11. 2. 2 *Tim.* 2. 19. 1 *Pet.* 1. 2.
(x) *Rom.* 11. 34. 1 *Cor.* 2. 11.
(y) Rival Fools, *p.* 29. *l. ult.*
(z) Marplot, p. 9. l. 15.
(a) Humours of Purgatory, p. 46. l. 7.
(b) A Woman's Revenge, p. 1. l. ult. p. 2. l. 1.
(c) Ibid. p. 37. l. 6.
(d) Humours of the Army, p. 23. l. 30.
(e) The Mistake, p. 26. *in fine.* p. 27. l. 1.
(f) Woman is a Riddle, p. 4. l. *antepenult.*
(g) The Drummer, p. 52. l. 31.
(h) Man of Mode, p. 181. l. 8.

also told, that (*i*) he *knows* whither we *go*, or (*k*) *climb*; and he is also represented as a most subtle Being (*l*) in discovering of *knotty Points*. He knows (*m*) what Adventures we undertake, and (*n*) *what to do with* those, who are in all other respects very cunning: and (*o*) what the *Devil himself cannot know*, is represented as impossible to be known by any.

Sometimes the *Actors* say, (*p*) *The LORD knows what*, sometimes (*q*) *Heaven knows what*; and at other times, (*r*) *The Devil knows what*: insomuch that one would almost think, that by these three several Expressions they meant the same Being. In one *Play* an *Actor* saith, (*s*) *When I marry, the Devil must be wiser than I take him to be.* But then for a Demonstration of the *Devil's Wisdom*, and a Conviction of one who would not believe it, he marries the Lady *Heartwell*, a rich Widow, before the end of the *Play*.

In another *Play* (for the quoting of two is enough) the (*t*) *Devil* is presently represented as *omniscient*. One who was so cunning as to know another's Business beforehand, or to know what was past, is called (*u*) *the Devil*, or is (*x*) said to be *like the Devil*. One who own'd (*y*) that he did *converse with the Devil*, tells to utter Strangers (*z*) their *Trades*, (*a*) their *Names*, (*b*) their *Courtship*, (*c*) a *Dog's Name*, and (*d*) what had happen'd; whilst they who wondered at such Knowledge, appeal to (*e*) the *Devil* for Information, how it

---

(*i*) The Apparition, p. 20. l. 28.
(*k*) Wonders in the Sun, p. 44. l. ult.
(*l*) Ibid. p. 59. l. 19.
(*m*) Marplot, p. 36. l. 22.
(*n*) Rival Fools, p. 35. l. 34.
(*o*) Love in a Sack, p. 35. l. 2.
(*p*) Cobler of *Preston*, p. 35. l. 2.
(*q*) Love's last Shift, p. 43. l. 22.
(*r*) Humours of Purgatory, p. 46. l. 7.
(*s*) Wit without Money, p. 16. l. 6.
(*t*) Recruiting Officer, p. 7. l. 16.
(*u*) Pag. 48. l. 10. p. 49. l. 37.
(*x*) P. 47. l. 16.
(*y*) P. 50. l. 13.
(*z*) P. 45. l. 31. p. 47. l. 24.
(*a*) P. 46. l. antepenult.
(*b*) P. 49. l. 34.
(*c*) P. 49. l. 27.
(*d*) P. 48. l. 8.
(*e*) P. 45. l. 32. p. 46. l. penult.

could

could be obtain'd. Things extremely difficult to be known, are deſcribed with this *Periphraſis*; (f) *Theſe Affairs are ſo irregular, that nothing leſs than the Devil can give any account of them.* And to mention but one Inſtance more, which is enough to turn the Blood into Water: When *our bleſſed Saviour* had talked with the Woman of *Samaria*, (g) *ſhe went her way into the City, and ſaith unto the Men, Come, ſee a Man, who told me all things that ever I did; is not this the Chriſt?* But this *Sacred Text* is thus burleſqued in the *Play-Houſe*: (h) *That Fellow is certainly the Devil, or one of his Boſom-Favourites; he hath told me the moſt ſurprizing things of my paſt Life.*

The next *Attribute* is *the Power of GOD.* This was clearly ſeen in (i) the Works of *Creation*, even by the *Heathens*; and is that which (k) we daily aſcribe unto him in *the LORD's Prayer.* The *Scriptures* ſay, (l) that *in his hand is Power and Might, and in his hand it is to make great, and to give Strength unto all*: That (m) *he doth whatſoever he pleaſeth*: He (n) *is able of Stones to raiſe up Children unto* Abraham; and (o) *with* him *all things are poſſible*: He is (p) *able to do abundantly more than we are able to ask or think*, and (q) *to ſubdue all things unto himſelf*, and (r) *acts according to the Counſel of his own Will.* And therefore St. *James* adviſeth us (s) to ſay, *If the LORD will, we ſhall live, and do this or that.*

On the other hand, the Expreſſions in the *Play-Houſe* are, (t) *As the Devil would have it, it happen'd ſo* or ſo: Or (u) it may be ſo, *if the Devil don't croſs it.*

(f) Recruiting Officer, *p.* 50. *l.* 37

(g) *John* 4. 28, 29.

(h) Recruiting Officer, *p.* 42. *l.* 31.

(i) *Rom.* 1. 20.

(k) *Mat.* 6. 13.

(l) 1 *Chron.* 29. 12.

(m) *Pſal.* 115 3. & 135. 6.

(n) *Mat.* 3. 9.

(o) *Mat.* 19. 26. *Mark* 14. 36.

(p) *Epheſ.* 3. 20.

(q) *Phil.* 3. 21.

(r) *Epheſ.* 1. 11.

(s) *James* 4. 15.

(t) *Gotham* Election, p. 28. l. 18. Modern Prophets, p. 49. l. 44.

(u) The Man's bewitch'd, p. 3. l. 26.

If any thing extraordinary happens, (x) *the Devil is in it*, and he is praised with this Encomium, (y) *To see what the Devil can do!* He is represented as (z) ordering our Affairs, and as (a) *sure to act* when and what he pleaseth. He (b) *fights* our Battels, and when (c) he assists, he raiseth the natural Courage beyond what is usual; and he is not to be (d) hindered, or (e) outdone by any human Endeavours. When he (f) *crosseth* any Affair, it is very difficult to succeed. What (g) he doth, cannot be hinder'd by any Creature. What he (h) can't do, is impossible to be done; and (i) what he can't prevent, is impossible to be prevented by any. And (k) they whom he compels, must act of necessity. He (l) forbids, and (m) prevents us, by his ruling Power in our Designs, which otherwise had been very likely to succeed; and (n) frustrates those things, which otherwise could not fail. He (o) enables us to bear a Fatigue, and (p) many things are perform'd by his Assistance, which had otherwise been impossible. And that the

---

(x) Marplot, p. 55. l. 15. Beaux Stratagem, p. 27. l. 14. p. 54. l. 7. The City Ramble, or, The Play-House Wedding, p. 56. l. *antepenult.* Double Gallant, p. 45. l. 12. The Man's bewitch'd, p. 61. l. 24. Perplex'd Couple, p. 39. l. 4. Wit without Money, p. 58. l. *ult.*

(y) Unfortunate Dutchess of *Malfi*, p. 18. l. *penult.*

(z) Three Hours after Marriage, p. 58. l. 3.

(a) Platonick Lady, p. 49. l. 14.

(b) Ignoramus, p. 56. l. *ult.*

(c) Rival Fools, p. 39. l. 32.

(d) Platonick Lady, p. 49. l. 14.

(e) Woman is a Riddle, p. 33. l. 6.

(f) The Contrivances, p. 4. l. 17. Rival Fools, p. 44. l. 31.

(g) The Man's bewitch'd, p. 54. l. 9. Perplex'd Couple, p. 53. l. 24.

(h) Ignoramus, p. 25. l. 14. The Country House, p. 1. l. *ult.* p. 8. l. 32. Double Gallant, p. 46. l. 4. Unfortunate Dutchess of *Malfi*, p. 40. l. 8. Wit without Money, p. 13. l. 29. p. 29. l. 22.

(i) Pretender's Flight, p. 32. l. 15.

(k) Recruiting Officer, p. 49. l. 37.

(l) Cruel Gift, p. 57. l. 8. Three Hours after Marriage, p. 58. l. 3.

(m) *Sawny* the *Scot*, p. 51. l. 25. The Apparition, p. 34. l. 12. Cruel Gift, p. 57. l. 8.

(n) Rival Fools, p. 48. l. 4.

(o) Perplex'd Couple, p. 10. l. 26.

(p) Rival Fools, p. 39. l. 33. p. 48. l. 4.

Glory

Glory of all human Actions may be aſcribed to him, (*q*) when a Perſon doth ſomething which is extraordinary, and ſucceeds, he is ſaid to be aſſiſted by the *Devil*. Nay, his Power is mentioned as the greateſt of all, (*r*) *Did you not ſucceed?* (ſaith an *Actor*:) The other anſwers, *No, the errant Devil prevented me: Nothing elſe could have done it*; that is, not GOD himſelf.

And from this Conſideration the *Players* endeavour to excuſe all Mankind, and bring them in guiltleſs in the Caſe of *Whoredom* and *Adultery*. For (as one of them ſaith) (*s*) *When two ſuch Fiends as the Devil and a Woman lay their heads together, what can a poor Sinner do?* Or to ſpeak in the Language of (*t*) another, *What could I do? The Devil was at one Ear, and the Woman at the other: Who could help falling?*

The next *Attribute* is the *Goodneſs* of GOD. The *Scripture* tells us, (*u*) that *there is none good ſave one, that is GOD*; that (*x*) *his merciful Kindneſs is ever more and more towards us*: and therefore we are exhorted to (*y*) *give thanks unto the LORD, for he is good, for his Mercy endureth for ever.*

In the *Play-Houſe* it is common to ſay of the *Devil*, that he is not ſo bad as (*z*) ſome *Men*, or (*a*) as ſome *Women*. Perhaps in one ſenſe this may be too true of the *Poets* and *Actors*; for (*b*) the *Devils* themſelves do *believe* that there is a GOD, and *tremble* to think upon him, whilſt theſe Men ſet up the *Devil* in *oppoſition* to GOD, and bid him Defiance, and ſtill go on without Fear, Wit, or Shame, as harden'd in their Impiety.

Ten of theſe Sentences I ſhall quote at large, becauſe the Reader may obſerve their good Breeding, fine Language, and Manners at the ſame time.

(*q*) Perplex'd Couple, p. 10. l. 25. The Wonder, p. 53. l. 19.

(*r*) The Apparition, p. 35. l. 11.

(*s*) Perplex'd Couple, p. 53. l. 24.

(*t*) Succeſsful Pirate, p. 43. l. 27.

(*u*) *Mat.* 19. 17.

(*x*) *Pſal.* 117. 2.

(*y*) *Pſal.* 136. 1. *Jer.* 33. 11.

(*z*) Humours of Purgatory, p. 12. l. 6.

(*a*) A Woman's Revenge, p. 17. l. 9.

(*b*) *James* 2. 19.

(c) *Devil! worse than Devil, thou very Priest.*
(d) ———————— *Tell the Prince of Darkness,*
Ordgar *hath sent a Fiend more black than him,*
To fill the burning Throne of Hell's Dominions.
(e) *There cannot in all ransack'd Hell be found*
A Devil equal to Mackbeth.
(f) *More envious than the Devil.*
(g) *Find me a Devil yet blacker than thy self.*
(h) *I must go home to my Wife, and I had rather go to the Devil by half.*
(i) *I declare it, that he that runs away from the Devil, should be brought to a Court-Martial, and condemn'd for a Coward.*
(k) *No, he did not say so bad as that neither: he only wish'd them all at the Devil.*
(l) *You shall be my Second, if you please; tho I had as lief be married to the Devil.*
(m) *Spleen, thou worst of Fiends below.*

I might add (n) more Quotations, but I suppose that these are too many already.

But a bare Negative is not a sufficient Encomium for the *Devil* in the *Play-house*, and therefore he is represented not only as positively *Good*, but as (o) the *Quintessence of Goodness*. For this reason an *Actor* is (p) at a loss how he *shall express* his *Thanks*, and prays for the *Devil*, that (q) *eternal Blessings* may *crown* him. Sometimes he is call'd (r) a *favourable Devil*; and sometimes (s) a *loving Devil*. Sometimes these *infernal* Spirits are

---

(c) A Wife well manag'd, *p.* 18. *l.*13.
(d) Elfrid, *p.*38. *l.*33.
(e) Mackbeth, *p.*47. *l.*1.
(f) Tartuffe, *p.*53. *l.*32.
(g) Rinaldo, *p.*31. *l.*31.
(h) The Beaux Stratagem, *p.* 55. *l. penult.*
(i) Humours of the Army, *p.* 12. *l.*14.
(k) Ibid. *p.*54. *l.*27.
(l) Ibid. *p.*59. *l.*22.
(m) Recruiting Officer, *p.* 4. *l.* 35.
(n) Sir Courtly Nice, *p.* 2. *l.* 43. The Cruel Gift, *p.*30. *l.*25. The Humours of Purgatory, *p.*7. *l. ult.*
(o) The Wonders in the Sun, *p.*48. *l.*19.
(p) Ibid.
(q) Ibid. *p.*43. *l.*9.
(r) The Man's bewitch'd, *p.* 43. *l.*17.
(s) The General cashier'd, *p.* 4. *l.* 10.

call'd

(*t*) call'd, the *all-kind Powers*: And, as it was the Character of our *blessed Saviour*, (*u*) that he *went about doing good*; *for GOD was with him*: so on the *Stage*, (*x*) a Man, who *little thought that it was in the Devil's power to do good*, is convinc'd of his Error by Experience, and retracts his Opinion.

The next *Attribute* is the *Truth* of GOD. The *Scriptures* say, (*y*) that *he is a GOD of Truth*. He is (*z*) *a faithful GOD, which keepeth his Covenant and Mercy to a thousand Generations*. His (*a*) *Judgments are true and righteous altogether*. And (*b*) he will *be true*, tho *every Man is a Lyar*. Neither is he only true in his own Nature; but his Word also is the same. (*c*) *Every* Part thereof *is pure*; and (*d*) more firm and certain than the Duration of *Heaven* and *Earth*: neither (*e*) shall *one jot or one tittle pass away, until all be fulfilled*.

When therefore the *Prophet Isaiah* would give a convincing Proof, that the Great JEHOVAH was the true GOD, he thus speaks of the *Idols*: (*f*) *Let them shew us what shall happen. Let them shew the former things, what they be, that we may consider them, and know the latter end of them, or declare us things for to come. Shew the things that are to come hereafter, that we may know that ye are Gods*. And again, (*g*) *Who, as I, shall call, and shall declare it, and set it in order for me, since I appointed the antient People, and the things that are coming, and shall come? Let them shew them*. This *Attribute* the *Devil* was always fond of, as that which might secure to him the *Worship* and *Adoration* of the *Pagan Multitude*. Thus he led them on in a blind Superstition and Ignorance, until his Frauds were brought to light, by the Publication of the *Gospel*. However, the *Devil* was

---

(*t*) *Compare* The *Persian* Princess, *p*.27. *Act* 3. *l*.5. *with p*.28. *l*.12.

(*u*) *Acts* 10. 38.

(*x*) The Apparition, *p*. 59. *l*. 2.

(*y*) *Deut*. 32. 4. *Jer*. 10. 10. *John* 3. 33.

(*z*) *Deut*. 7. 9. 2 *Chron*. 6. 14.

(*a*) *Psal*. 19. 9.

(*b*) *Rom*. 3. 4.

(*c*) *Prov*. 30. 5.

(*d*) *Matth*. 24. 35. *Mark* 13. 31. *Luke* 21. 33.

(*e*) *Matth*. 5. 18.

(*f*) *Isa*. 41. 22, 23.

(*g*) *Isa*. 44. 7.

a Fool in his *Oracles* to what he is in his *Plays*; and his *antient Priests* had not so much Cunning to help him out at a dead Lift, as our *modern Poets*. One speaking of (h) the real Truth of a Story, saith, *Why, there's the Devil of it!* as if the *Devil* was *Truth* itself. Besides, they utter (i) strange Prophecies, as from him, and take care (k) that they are all fulfilled. And thus, they not only make him *Omnipotent* and *Omniscient* (as before) but set up him, who (l) *was a Lyar from the beginning*, to stand in competition with (m) the *GOD of Truth*. Accordingly, he who doubted before, and said, (n) *What, can the Devil speak true?* is (o) kill'd; whilst the other, who believ'd it, was made a King, and (p) depended upon it in his greatest Dangers. And by the Encouragement of such an Example (q) another *Actor* consults the *Witches*, and depends upon their Answers, which were accordingly fulfilled, as a Proof of what was said before, (r) that *they* had *in them more than mortal Knowledge*.

The last *Attribute* which I shall mention, is the *Vengeance* of GOD. This in *Scripture* is (s) said to *belong* to him. Accordingly, we are told of his (t) *Anger*, *his hot Displeasure*, and (u) the *Fierceness of his Wrath*, which (x) *abideth* upon Unbelievers, and (y) *is revealed from Heaven against all Ungodliness*. But in the *Play-house* we hear of (z) *the swift executing Furies*.

(h) The Comical Lovers, *p.* 28. *l.* 33.

(i) Alarbas, *p.* 26. *l.* 14. Mackbeth, *p.* 4. *l.* 34, 35, 36. *p.* 5. *l.* 12, 13, 14. *p.* 26. *l.* 11, 12, 13. *p.* 43. *l.* 6. 10, 17, 34.

(k) Alarbas, *p.* 38. *l.* 9. Mackbeth, *p.* 3. *l.* 15. *p.* 6. *l.* 11. *p.* 23. *l.* 26. *p.* 33. *l.* 35. *p.* 44. *l.* 33. *p.* 45. *l.* 3. *p.* 51. *l.* 20. *p.* 59. *l.* 3, 7, 21, 22, 25, 35. *p.* 54. *l.* 13. *p.* 55. *l.* 22, 34, *&c.* *and p.* 57. *l.* 16, *&c.*

(l) *John* 8. 44.

(m) *Deut.* 32. 4.

(n) Mackbeth, *p.* 6. *l.* 13.

(o) Ibid. *p.* 33. *l.* 35.

(p) Ibid. *p.* 59. *l.* 21.

(q) Ibid. *p.* 26. *l.* 12. *p.* 59. *l.* 22.

(r) Ibid. *p.* 10. *l.* 27.

(s) *Deut.* 32. 35. *Psal.* 94. 1. *Rom.* 12. 19.

(t) *Psal.* 6. 1.

(u) *Hos.* 11. 9.

(x) *Joh.* 3. 36.

(y) *Rom.* 1. 18. *Matth.* 3. 7. *Rom.* 2. 5. *Ephes.* 5. 6.

(z) Ajax, *Act* 4. *Ver.* 31.

As they thus apply particular *Attributes*; so we may the less wonder to find, that they burlesque them all in general. Thus they are all applied jocosely to a Woman, when an *Actor* saith (*a*),

> *I mistrust your Mistress's Divinity; you'll find her Attributes but mortal.*

It is from the Consideration of the *Attributes* of GOD, that we learn to believe in him, to fear him, to love him, to obey him, and to imitate his Divine Perfections. But when these *Attributes* are given to another, the natural Consequence is, that all these religious Duties are to be paid to that other, and not to GOD.

And therefore, if (*b*) GOD will not suffer his *Glory* to be *given to another*, and (*c*) is a *jealous* GOD, how can we expect that he will endure the ascribing his *Attributes* to his greatest Enemy? but rather, that he should make us feel the severest Marks of his Displeasure for such a daring Impiety, unless we prevent it by a speedy Reformation?

(*a*) Comical Revenge, *p.* 15. *l.* 24.

(*b*) *Isa.* 42. 8.

(*c*) *Exod.* 20. 5.

CHAP.

CHAP. VIII.

The Scriptures perverted to the Honour of the Devil.

THE Author of *A Compleat Key to a late Farce,* intitul'd, *The What-d'ye-call it,* hath inform'd us of ſeveral Expreſſions therein, which are (*a*) ſo many *Banters* upon our antient and modern *Engliſh Poets,* and their Performances. But becauſe the freedom which they take, in *ridiculing the Scriptures,* hath been omitted, I ſhall mention ſome particular Inſtances, in which they are notoriouſly *perverted* to the *Honour of the Devil.*

This is ſo black a Charge, that the *Apoſtle* tells us, that they who are guilty of it, are (*b*) *ungodly and unſtable Men,* and that they do *wreſt* the Scriptures *unto their own Deſtruction.* And certainly, if any Crime can deſerve ſo heavy a Judgment, it muſt be this, which of all others is moſt abominable, even the introducing

(*a*) *As particularly upon* Shakeſpear, *p.*1. *l.*1. *p.*3. *l. ult. p.*4. *l.*12. *p.*9. *l.*3. *p.*11. *l.*1. *p.* 12. *l.*3. *p.*13. *l.*16. *p.*15. *l.*16. *p.*18. *l.*20. *p.*25. *l.*14. *p.*27. *l.*4. *Upon* Dryden, *p.*3. *l.*14. *p.*5. *l.*1. *and antepenult. p.*11. *l.*1. *p.*17. *l. penult. p.* 29. *l.*6. *p.*30. *l.* 3. *Upon* The Tragedy of *Jane Shore, p.*4. *l.*5. *p.*7. *l.*20. *p.*9. *l.*18. *p.* 14. *l.*11. *p.*15. *l.*1. *p.*19. *l.*4, 13. *p.* 21. *l.* 28. *p.*26. *l.*20. *Upon* The Diſtreſſed Mother, *p.*4. *l.*18. *p.*5. *l.*19. *p.*6. *l.* 1, 9. *p.*8. *l.* 19. *p.*17. *l. penult. p.*19. *l.*21. *p.*20. *l.*13. *Upon* Venice Preſerved, *p.* 6. *l.*9. *p.*17. *l.*15. *p.* 23. *l.*6. *p.* 24. *l.*10. *p.*30. *l.*24. *Upon* The Fair Penitent, *p.* 8. *l.*4. *Upon* The Earl of *Eſſex, p.*9. *l.*18. *p.* 14. *l.*1. *p.*21. *l.*28. *Upon ſome of* Otway's *Plays, p.*24. *l.*17. *p.* 28. *l.*18. *p.*29. *l.*1. *Upon* Cato, *p.*16. *l.*3. *Upon* Oroonoko, *p.* 18. *l.*20. *Upon* The Conqueſt of *Granada, p.*20. *l.*13. *Upon Mary* Queen of *Scots, p.*22. *l.*22. *p.*23. *l.* 22. *p.* 25. *l.* 19. *Upon Appius* and *Virginia, p.*23. *l.*6. *Upon* The Tender Husband, *p.* 27. *l.*4. *Upon a Play written by* Southern, *p.* 29. *l.* 6. *Upon* The Mourning Bride, *p.*31. *l.*3. *Upon* The Slip, *p.*32. *l.*12.

(*b*) 2 *Pet.* 3. 16.

those

those *Divine Oracles* to extol or excuse GOD's greatest Enemy, and exposing those *Texts* which represent him as he is.

Immediately after the History of the *Creation* of the *World* and *Man*, the *Scriptures* give us an Account of the Fall of our first Parents, and how they were seduced by the Subtilty of the Devil. The Design hereof was to bring us to a due Sense of our lost and undone Condition by Nature, that we might be humbled for the same, that we might strive to be recovered through Grace, and know from hence, who was our grand Enemy from the beginning. For these Reasons we are told, (c) that *the Serpent*, or the *Devil was more subtle than any Beast of the Field, which the LORD had made*; that by his Subtilty he (d) *deceived* our first Mother *Eve*, and (e) continues a cunning Adversary with various Wiles and *Devices*. And now, who that believes himself of Kin to *Adam* and *Eve*, would use their Memory coarsely, ridicule their Follies upon the Stage, and make a Jest of their Misfortunes? nay, mix the Story up with Smut and Banter, and apply the same to scandalous Purposes? Who that looks on the Account as deliver'd by the *Holy Ghost*, would treat it disrespectfully? Or who that looks on the *Devil* as laying thereby the Foundation of their own Destruction, would make it a Subject only for their *Sport* and *Pastime?* But this is the Treatment which it meets with upon the *English Stage*. Sometimes they droll upon (f) *Adam* alone in *Paradise*, sometimes upon (g) *Eve*, and sometimes upon (h) both together. In one *Play*, *Eve* is called (i) our *old Grandame*; in another she is called (k) *the Mother of Jilts, who cuckolded her Husband with the Serpent, and then pretended to Modesty*, concluding with a *Satire* upon (l) a Text of *Scripture*, whilst the Words

(c) *Gen.* 3. 1.

(d) 2 *Cor.* 11. 3. 1 *Tim.* 2. 14.

(e) 2 *Cor.* 2. 11.

(f) Country Lasses, *p.* 27. *l. antepenult.*

(g) The Apparition, *p.* 30. *l.* 24.

(h) Provok'd Wife, *p.* 70. *l.* 36.

(i) Adventures of half an Hour, *p.* 8. *l. penult.*

(k) Sir Courtly Nice, *p.* 14. *l.* 27.

(l) *Gen.* 3. 7.

before and after are skreened from common view, being too filthy to be tranſcribed. In another *Play*, an *Actreſs* (*m*) is called a *Cockatrice*, a *ſecond Eve*, more deceitful than the firſt. And it is ſaid of another, (*n*) *This Girl will debauch me, but ſhe is one of* Eve's *own Siſters, born of a Woman.* In another *Play*, an *Actreſs* is called (*o*) *a wicked Inſtrument, that ſtands like the Serpent at* Eve's *Elbow* to tempt her to ſin. Another calls an *Actor* (*p*) the *old Serpent, who made the firſt of the Female Sex to weep.* And to excuſe this old *Serpent*, (*q*) one *Actor* ſaith, *The Devil did leſs Miſchief in the Form of a Serpent to* Eve, *than in the Form of a* London *Gentleman to her Daughters.* And another tells us (*r*) of *ſuch a Myſtery of Iniquity* in the Play-houſe, *as the two grand Intriguers, the Woman and the Serpent, put together for Miſchief, never hatch'd before.* And that which is moſt blaſphemous, the whole Story of our firſt Parent's Fall is urged in the *Play-houſe* as an Encouragement to *Adultery*; for (ſaith an *Actor*) (*s*) *The Devil danced at the firſt Wedding, and ſo Cuckoldom has been in faſhion ever ſince.* Or elſe they tell us poſitively, that the *Devil* is not ſuch an Enemy now, as he was repreſented at firſt; for (ſaith an *Actor* to a Woman) (*t*) *Sure the Serpent parted with his Subtilty, and cloſed in the Fruit he gave thy Sex.*

We are told in *Scripture*, that (*u*) when GOD *drove out* our firſt Parents from *Paradiſe*, he *placed Cherubims and a Flaming Sword* at the Eaſt of the Garden of *Eden.* But to turn this whole Story into Burleſque, a *Colonel*, who went out with a lewd Deſign by Aſſignation, is brought into a dark Room, where he ſaith (*x*), *I dare not peep, for fear of being expelled my* Eden, *for*

(*m*) Adventures of half an Hour, *p.* 19. *l.* 14.

(*n*) The Lady's Laſt Stake, *p.* 4. *l.* 3.

(*o*) The Amorous Widow, *p.* 75. *l.* 9.

(*p*) The Apparition, *p.* 30. *l.* 24.

(*q*) The Country Laſſes, *p.* 10. *l.* 33.

(*r*) The Apparition, *p.* 39. *l.* 33.

(*s*) Marry or do worſe, *p.* 12. *l.* 18.

(*t*) *Portſmouth* Heireſs, *p.* 70. *l.* 1.

(*u*) *Gen.* 3. 24.

(*x*) Woman is a Riddle, *p.* 46. *l.* 12.

ſearching

ſearching after too much Knowledge; and afterwards (if I miſtake not the Metaphor) compares his Miſtreſs to the *Devil* in *Paradiſe*, as if that accurſed Spirit was the greateſt Good to be enjoyed there. Another will have alſo this *Paradiſe* to be the enjoyment of (y) his Miſtreſs's Company, and the *Cherubims* to be the *Devil*. For thus an *Actor* expreſſeth himſelf to an *Actreſs*, whom he calleth (z) *a Creature divinely Fair*, and (a) *the moſt deſerving Work of GOD's Creation.*

When a cloven-footed Guardian bars the Gate to this fair Paradiſe, think what Agonies my tortur'd Soul muſt bear.

When *Moſes* (b) was ſent to deliver the *Iſraelites*, he endeavoured to excuſe himſelf with this Expreſſion, *O my LORD, I am not eloquent, neither heretofore, nor ſince thou haſt ſpoken with thy Servant, for I am ſlow of Speech, and of a ſlow Tongue.* But he was anſwer'd, *Who hath made Man's Mouth? Or who maketh the dumb or deaf, or the ſeeing or the blind? Have not I the LORD?*

The *Players* expreſs it thus, (c) *No doubt the Devil's at your Tongue's end, to furniſh you with Speeches.*

GOD ſaith, (k) *Thou ſhalt fear the LORD thy GOD, and ſerve him, and ſhalt ſwear by his Name.*

The *Play-houſe* Form is thus:

(l) *By all the Pow'rs of Earth, and thoſe of Hell,*
By the infernal King, the Fates and Furies,
We ſwear.

Or thus:

(m) *By the moſt ſacred Stygian Lake I ſwear.*

(n) The Speech of *Elijah* to *Eliſhah*, was, *Go back again, for what have I done unto thee?* The Speech of one *Actor* to another, is, (o) *Thou Devil, what have I done unto thee?*

(y) The City Ramble, or, The Play-houſe Wedding, *p.* 60. *l.* 33.

(z) Ibid. *p.* 61. *l.* 3.

(a) Ibid. *p.* 61. *l.* 16.

(b) *Exod.* 4. 10, 11.

(c) The General caſhier'd, *p.* 23. *l.* 12.

(k) *Deut.* 6. 13.

(l) *Appius* and *Virginia*, *p.* 9. *l.* 18.

(m) Arminius, *p.* 5. *l.* 19.

(n) 1 *Kings* 19. 20.

(o) The Country Laſſes, *p.* 66. *l.* 37.

In

In *Scripture* (p) *the Heaven* is ſaid to be the *Throne* of GOD, and (q) he is ſaid to be *in Heaven.* And that we, (r) *when we are abſent from the Body, are preſent with the LORD,* where (s) the Soul of the *righteous Man enters into Peace,* when his Body *periſheth.* In the *Play-houſe,* (t) a Man ſpeaking of his own Death, ſaith, He ſhall go *up to the Devil.* At another time a *Song* is commended with this Expreſſion, *I would not give a Fig for a Song that is not full of Sin and Impudence.* The Concluſion whereof runs thus (u):

No ſawcy Remorſe
Intrudes in my Courſe,
Nor impertinent Notions of Evil:
So there's Claret in ſtore,
In peace I've my Whore,
And in peace I jog on to the Devil.
All ſing, *So there's Claret,* &c.

After the *Chorus* ended, the firſt concludes again,
And in peace I jog on to the Devil.

When (x) our *bleſſed Saviour* was tempted, the Devil *ſhewed him all the Kingdoms of the World, and the Glory of them. And ſaith unto him, All theſe things will I give thee, if thou wilt fall down and worſhip me.* But he was repelled with this Anſwer, *Get thee hence, Satan, for it is written, Thou ſhalt worſhip the LORD thy GOD, and him only ſhalt thou ſerve.* In the *Play-houſe,* an *Actor* bringing Gold to his Wife, ſaith, (y) *Fall down and worſhip me.* Another (z) being in Want, who was rewarded with the utmoſt Succeſs at the end of the *Play,* frames a Colloquy between himſelf and the *Devil,* but concludes in a different Strain.

Actor. *The Devil puſhes me forwards. Be quiet. I tell you, Satan, I will go no further.*

(p) *Iſa.* 66. 1.
(q) *Pſal.* 115. 3. *Matt.* 6. 9. *Luke* 11. 2.
(r) 2 *Cor.* 5. 8.
(s) *Iſa.* 57. 2.
(t) The Fair Quaker of *Deal,* p. 58. l. *penult.*
(u) Provok'd Wife, p. 36.
(x) *Matth.* 4. 8,9,10.
(y) Ignoramus, p. 21. l. 12.
(z) Female Advocates, p. 14. l. *ult.* p. 15. l. 1, &c.

The Devil anſwers: *You want Money, and* Transfer *will lend you Money, which will make you wicked, and him an Uſurer. I think that's killing two Birds with one Stone.*

The Actor replies: *Old Gentleman, we are both your humble Servants, and I will for once take your Advice. You have been drawing me in to be drunk, and do what you will with me now.*

Our *bleſſed Saviour* (*a*) denies that *Satan* is *divided againſt* his own Intereſt. An *Actor* ſwears *by GOD*, uſes our *Saviour*'s Words, and gives him the Lye at the ſame time. (*b*) *I think the Devil plays Booty againſt himſelf, and tells you of my Sins.*

Our *bleſſed Saviour*, (*c*) ſpeaking of the Love which we owe to GOD, ſaith, It muſt be *with all the Heart.* In one *Play* (*d*) an *Actor* ſaith of two Perſons, *They are gone with all my Heart, even to the Devil.* And when it was anſwer'd, *How! to the Devil!* The Reply was made, *Ay, to the Devil. Who cares?* In a ſecond *Play*, an *Actor* ſaith (*e*) of a Woman, *I could wiſh that the Devil would take her, with all my heart.* And in a third, we have another Dialogue to the ſame purpoſe (*f*):

Be gone. Anſwer, *Where, Sir? To Dinner?* Reply, *Yes, to the Devil.* Anſwer, *To the Devil? Yes, Sir, with all my Heart.*

When many *Devils* had (*g*) poſſeſs'd a Man, his name was called *Legion, for they were many.* The *Actors* (*h*) dwell upon the Word, and apply it too truly to themſelves. (*i*) *There are at leaſt twenty Devils in her.* (*k*) *I think each of you has twenty Devils in you.*

(*a*) *Matth.* 12. 25, 26.
(*b*) The Comical Lovers, p. 25. l. 3.
(*c*) *Matth.* 22. 37.
(*d*) The City Ramble, or, The Play-houſe Wedding, p. 55. l. 17.
(*e*) Comical Revenge, p. 21. l. 6.
(*f*) Perplex'd Couple, p. 22. l. 28.
(*g*) *Mark* 5. 9, 15. and *Luke* 8. 30.
(*h*) Man of Mode, p. 266. l. 5.
(*i*) The Female Advocates, p. 53. l. 22.
(*k*) Ibid. p. 53. l. 26.

Why,

(*l*) *Why, what a many Devils there are! Certainly she has a Legion in her.* And another adds, (*m*) *Now the Devil's a creeping into her mouth, Sir; you may see a little of his Tail hang out: It looks for all the world as if it were a Sting, Sir.*

In the LORD's Prayer we call upon GOD, saying, (*n*) *Forgive us our Trespasses, as we forgive them that trespass against us.* The Reason is, because (*o*) it is *Blasphemy* to insinuate, that any *can forgive Sins, but GOD alone.* The *Players* value not the *Blasphemy*, but pervert the Petition thus, (*p*) *The Devil forget and forgive you all.*

When St. *Paul* desired the *Romans* to devote themselves to a religious Life, he said, (*s*) *I beseech you, Brethren, by the Mercies of GOD.* The Expression in the *Play-House* is, (*t*) I pray you, *By the more dreadful Torments of the Damn'd.*

St. *Paul* saith, that (*u*) *every Creature of GOD is good, and nothing to be refused, if it be received with Thanksgiving: For it is sanctified by the Word of GOD, and by Prayer.* The *Play-House* expounds it thus: (*x*) *Every Creature of GOD is good; every thing is good in its kind: Cards are harmless Bits of Paper, Dice insipid Bones, and Women were made for Men.* At another time (*y*) *saying Grace* before Meat is ridiculously apply'd to Marriage: And in a third *Play* (*z*) a *Serving-Man* makes an impertinent *Grace*, and proceeds with the mention of *the Devil's Name*, as if the Food was *sanctified* thereby.

St. *James* saith, (*a*) *Let* a Man *pray in Faith, nothing wavering; for he that wavereth, is like unto a Wave of*

(*l*) The Man's bewitch'd, *p.* 52. *l.* 37. *Sawny* the *Scot*, *p.* 32. *l.* 33, *penult.*

(*m*) *Sawny* the *Scot*, *p.* 42. *l.* 15.

(*n*) *Mat.* 6. 12. *Luke* 11. 4.

(*o*) *Mark* 2. 7. *Luke* 5. 21.

(*p*) *Sawny* the *Scot*, *p.* 58. *l.* 28.

(*s*) *Rom.* 12. 1.

(*t*) *Appius* and *Virginia*, *p.* 40. *l.* 4.

(*u*) 1 *Tim.* 4. 4.

(*x*) The Basset-Table, *p.* 48. *l.* 17.

(*y*) Amorous Widow, *p.* 26. *l.* 21.

(*z*) *Sawny* the *Scot*, *p.* 36. *l.* 13.

(*a*) *James* 1. 6.

the

the Sea, that is driven to and fro, and toſſed: But let not that Man think, that he ſhall receive any thing of the LORD. An *Actor* ſaith, and perhaps too truly, (*b*) *I would pray, but the Devil takes away my Heart, from having any Confidence in Prayer.*

The ſame *Apoſtle* (*c*) utterly denies that GOD is the Author of Sin: *Let no Man ſay, when he is tempted, I am tempted of GOD; for GOD cannot be tempted with Evil, neither tempteth he any Man. But every Man is tempted, when he is drawn away of his own Luſts and enticed.* But as the *Scriptures* vindicate GOD, ſo the *Play-Houſe* vindicates the *Devil*, and lays the blame upon ourſelves almoſt in the ſame Language. (*d*) *My Plot*, ſaith an Actor, *was hopeful, and nothing but the Devil could fruſtrate it.* But for this he is reprimanded, and taught better Manners in the following words: *When Fools miſcarry of their Folly, they always lay the blame upon the Devil.*

The ſame *Apoſtle* alſo tells us, (*e*) that *the Devils believe and tremble.* An *Actor* takes an occaſion to burleſque this *Scripture*, in ſpeaking to another as if he was the *Devil*; (*f*) *Old* Beelzebub *remember that, and tremble:* whilſt the Devil himſelf is repreſented as (*g*) *ſinging*, and very merry.

St. *Peter* alſo tells us of the *Devil*, (*h*) that he *goeth about as a roaring Lion, ſeeking whom he may devour*; and therefore we ought to *reſiſt* him, being *ſtedfaſt in the Faith.* This in the *Play-Houſe* is applied to a ſingle Actor, and ſometimes to (*k*) more, with very little Alteration, and ſerves for a profane Jeſt; tho I doubt there is too much Truth in it. But when they ſpeak of the *Devil* himſelf, they repreſent him in another manner. As for example, (*l*) *Look ye, fair Lady, the Devil is a very modeſt Perſon; he ſeeks nobody, unleſs they ſeek*

(*b*) Unfortunate Dutcheſs of *Malfi*, *p.* 70. *l.* 11.
(*c*) *James* 1. 13, 14.
(*d*) The Apparition, *p.* 34. *l.* 12.
(*e*) *James* 2. 19.
(*f*) Buſy Body, *p.* 24. *l.* 7.
(*g*) Squire of *Alſatia*, *p.* 28. *l.* 6.
(*h*) 1 *Pet.* 5. 8.
(*i*) The Biter, *p.* 52. *l.* 10.
(*k*) The General caſhier'd, *p.* 23. *l.* 26.
(*l*) Recruiting Officer, *p.* 50. *l.* 32.

him first: Besides, he is chain'd up like a Mastiff, and can't stir, unless he be let loose.

St. *Jude* saith, (m) that as for the *Angels which kept not their first Estate, but left their own Habitation, GOD reserved them under Chains of Darkness to the Judgment of the great Day:* He turned them into *Devils*. In one *Comedy* (n) a fine Lady declares her *Chastity*, that she did *not deal altogether so much in the Flesh.* To which the profane Spark, endeavouring to debauch her, makes this Answer; *Nay, now thou talk'st like a fallen Angel, repining at the Loss of Paradise.* A pretty Compliment to his *Mistress*, to compare her to the *Devil!* A fine, but usual Description of *Paradise*, to compare it to a *whoring Intrigue!* And an excellent Occasion to burlesque the *Scriptures* at the same time!

In another *Comedy* (o) an *Actor* being reckon'd (p) *a celebrated Christian*, speaks of those *Chains of Darkness* as if they were nothing but a *Poetical Romance*, and sets himself up in GOD's stead, to execute his Vengeance on these accursed Spirits:

I'll force ten thousand Hells to save my Bride.
I'll shake the Realms where Pluto *reigns,*
And make his Devils feel the Pains
Alcides *taught 'em once before.*

[From Hardness of Heart, and Contempt of thy Word and Commandment, Good LORD deliver us.]

(m) *Verse* 6.
(n) *Portsmouth* Heiress, *p.* 11. *l.* 6.
(o) Rinaldo, *p.* 25. *l.* 29.
(p) Dramatis Personæ.

CHAP

CHAP. IX.

Religion, Virtue, and the Worſhip of GOD, vilified on the Stage.

THE Deſign of GOD in revealing his Will to fallen Man, was to recover him out of that Eſtate into which he was plunged, bring him to the true Knowledge of his Maker, and promote the ſincere Practice of *Religion* and *Virtue*, together with his true Worſhip both in publick and private.

The Deſign of the *Play-Houſe* is to promote a looſe and inconſiderate ſort of Life, to make *Religion* uncreditable and paſs for ill Education, to diſcountenance all Virtue, and either aboliſh all Notions of GOD and his *Worſhip*, or bring in ſuch as are moſt vile and heretical.

For a Proof of this, I ſhall firſt ſhew how they treat the falſe *Religions*, and then their Behaviour to the true one.

As to falſe *Religions*, I ſhall only mention *Judaiſm*, *Popery*, and *Mahometaniſm*; which laſt two are the two *Antichriſts*, the one in the *Weſtern*, and the other in the *Eaſtern* Parts of the World. And add to theſe, *Paganiſm* itſelf. And if it can be proved, that they ſpeak reſpectfully of *Jews*, *Turks*, *Infidels*, and *Hereticks*, whilſt *Chriſtianity* is burleſqued by them at the ſame time; all ſober Perſons muſt conclude, that they are gone into the moſt daring and provoking Methods which can be imagined.

As for *Judaiſm*, one Quotation may be enough; (*a*) where a Wife reproving her Husband for *Curſing*, ſaith, *A very Chriſtian-like Saying truly!* To which he anſwers, *Don't tell me of Chriſtian:* And then ſwears by the *Blood* of GOD, that he'll *turn Jew*. Perhaps it

(*a*) The Country Houſe, p. 17. l. 25.

may be ſaid, that the *Actor* was in a Paſſion; however the *Poet* was calm, and ought to prevent his *Actors* from being profane. And whilſt *Judaiſm* is the Sport of the *Stage*, the *Satire* is directly levelled at *Chriſtianity*.

As for *Popery*, an *Actor* ſaith to his *Miſtreſs*, (*b*) *I'll turn Catholick, any thing, ſo you'll be my Saint.* Here he confeſſes too truly, that his *Religion* is yet to be choſen, whilſt ſhe ſets herſelf in GOD's ſtead, and burleſques a moſt ſacred Duty, in ſaying, *But can I grant your Prayer, if I don't underſtand your Petition?*

In another *Play* a (*c*) *Popiſh Prieſt* intrigues with an *Actreſs*, who at laſt makes this Confeſſion, (*d*) making both *Abſolution* and *Martyrdom* at the ſame time the Jeſt of the *Stage*: *Well, Doctor, your Religion is ſo pure,* (that is, Popery) *methinks I am ſo eaſy after an Abſolution, and can ſin afreſh with ſo much Security, that I'm reſolved to die a Martyr to it.* How far this Argument may prevail with others, I ſhall not determine; but I think it the moſt forcible, which can be offer'd to Men of a *Play-Houſe* Temper, and is to ſuch all *Bellarmine* in *Epitome*.

The next *Religion* is *Mahometaniſm*. This ſeems to be a great Favourite of the *Poets*. Therefore the *Turks* are called (*e*) the *True Believers*, and (*f*) the *Faithful*. Their *Prieſts* are called (*g*) *holy Prieſts*, and (*h*) *the pious grave Expounders of our Laws*. The *Alcoran* is called (*i*) *our* or (*k*) *the holy Alcoran*, which *ſpeaks plain*, and (*l*) *the Alcoran's juſt Laws*. The Form of an *Oath* is thus, (*m*) *Give him the Alcoran, and on that let him ſwear to ſpeak the Truth.* The Expoſtulation thereon is thus, (*n*) *Do you not ſwear and promiſe by your Prophet? By all contain'd within this holy Alcoran?* And the Infe-

(*b*) Country Laſſes, *p.* 7. *l.* 28.

(*c*) Beaux Stratagem, *p.* 30. *l.* 10, 21. *p.* 52. *l.* 22.

(*d*) Ibid. *p.* 46. *l.* 20.

(*e*) Almyna, *p.* 8. *l.* 4.

(*f*) Ibid. *p.* 40. *l.* 3, 23.

(*g*) Ibid. *p.* 1. *l.* 1.

(*h*) The Sultaneſs, *p.* 13. *l.* 13.

(*i*) Almyna, *p.* 2. *l.* 7. *p.* 45. *l.* 16.

(*k*) Ibid. *p.* 6. *l.* 28. Faithful Bride of *Granada*, *p.* 30. *l.* 15.

(*l*) Faithful Bride of *Granada*, *p.* 54. *l.* 16.

(*m*) Ibid. *p.* 51. *l.* 4.

(*n*) Almyna, *p.* 6. *l.* 27.

rence is, (o) *Upon the Alcoran the Slave accused him, therefore* it must be true. And *Mahomet* is called (p) *the Prophet*, (q) *our Prophet*, (r) *our great Prophet*, (s) *our holy Prophet*, (t) *our holy Mahomet*, and (u) *our mighty Prophet*, who (x) *shews his Justice.* He is represented as (y) *knowing*, as (z) *teaching us to believe. Our Prophet's Notion* (a) is true. It is as this (b) *our Prophet says* (c) *in his Alcoran*, and (d) *his Law.* He (e) makes Marriages. He is described as (f) *coming to Judgment*, and (g) *Paradise* is his. Concerning *Inspiration* and *Conversion*, he is thus extol'd:

> (h) *An enlightned Ray from* Mahomet
> *Has turn'd my horrid Purposes, and brought*
> *Repentance, which possesses now my Soul.*

And again;

> (i) *Sure our great Prophet has enlarg'd my Soul,*
> *I speak from him inspir'd, it must be so:*
> *I feel the sacred Glowings in my Bosom.*

(o) Faithful Bride of *Granada*, p. 57. l. 18.
(p) The Sultaness, p.30. l.21.
(q) Almyna, p. 3. l. 3. p.5. l.11,17,23. p.6. l.19. p.7. l.5. p.9. l.19, *antepenult.* p.21. l. 3. p.25. l. *ult.* p.39. l.17. p. 44. l.11. Irene, p.35. l.26. p.50. l.30. Faithful Bride of *Granada*, p.1. l. *antepenult.* p.5. l.7. p.27. l.16. p.34. l. *ult.* p. 52. l.12. p.53. l.23.
(r) Abra-Mule, p. 24. l. 15. Almyna, p. 2. l. 4. p. 20. l. 5. p. 28. l. 9. Faithful Bride of *Granada*, p. 20. l. *antepenult.* p.40. l.9. p.41. l.9. p.48. l.11.
(s) Almyna, p.63. l.16. The Sultaness, p.30. l.5.
(t) The Sultaness, p.24. l.31.
(u) Faithful Bride of *Granada*, p.13. l.10. p.8. l.2.
(x) Ibid. p.48. l.11.
(y) Ibid. p.20. l. *antepenult.* p. 52. l. 12.
(z) Ibid. p.41. l.9.
(a) Almyna, p.9. l. *antepen.*
(b) Ibid. p.9. l.19.
(c) Ibid. p.44. l.11.
(d) Irene, p.35. l. 26.
(e) Faithful Bride of *Granada*, p.13. l.10.
(f) Almyna, p.39. l.17.
(g) Ibid. p.25. l. *ult.*
(h) Faithful Bride of *Granada*, p.26. l.15.
(i) Almyna, p.28. l.9.

They pray to him thus: (*k*) *O Prophet*, (*l*) *Teach me to bear*, or (*m*) *Hear me, Prophet*; or (*n*) *great Prophet*. One dying ſays (*o*),

O holy Prophet! take me to thy Care.

Or thus, (*p*) in another Caſe;

How willingly would I haſte to my Exit,
And bleſs our Prophet for eternal Reſt!

Or thus (*q*);

O Prophet! let the Widow's Prayer aſcend,
Accept of our imperfect pious Rites.

They (*r*) *ſwear by* his Name, (*s*) in a *ſolemn* manner; and look upon it afterward as ſacred. Thus an *Actor* ſaith of himſelf, (*t*) *Have I not ſworn by* Mahomet? And (*u*) of another,

By Mahomet *thou ſwor'ſt, and he has heard:*
In Heav'n thy broken Vow recorded ſtands.

They bleſs in his Name thus (*x*),

Long may our Prophet ſpare your noble Life.

They curſe in his Name, and put his *Vengeance* before that of GOD himſelf thus; (*y*) *May our Prophet's Curſe, and that of the Moſt High*, fall on him.

And of the *Seraglio* it is ſaid (*z*),

'Tis fenc'd by Mahomet's *ſevereſt Laws.*

(*k*) Faithful Bride of *Granada*, p. 6. l. 23.
(*l*) Ibid. p. 57. l. 2.
(*m*) Ibid. p. 43. l. 2.
(*n*) Ibid. p. 40. l. 9. p. 15. l. 12.
(*o*) Almyna, p. 63. l. 16.
(*p*) Faithful Bride of *Granada*, p. 5. l. 7.
(*q*) Ibid. p. 24. l. 16.
(*r*) Ibid. p. 27. l. 16.
(*s*) Almyna, p. 20. l. 5.
(*t*) Ibid. p. 43. l. 15.
(*u*) Ibid. p. 32. l. 19.
(*x*) Ibid. p. 5. l. 23.
(*y*) Ibid. p. 7. l. 5.
(*z*) The Sultaneſs, p. 1. l. 9.

And the Inference immediately ſollows, that therefore

'Tis Sacrilege, 'tis Height of Profanation,
For vulgar Feet to tread in it.

Now if we would know the reaſon of ſo much Honour and Eſteem paid to ſuch an Impoſtor, we may have it from the Mouth of an *Actor*, who ſaith (a) that he *honours* Mahomet *for the handſome proviſion which he has made for Lovers in the other World, ſuch as freſh Miſtreſſes every Day in the Week*; and therefore he ſwears that *Mahomet ſhall always have* his *good Word.*

The laſt Religion is *Paganiſm.* This is the *Poets* Darling. The primitive *Fathers* did often urge againſt the *Heathens*, that the *Gods* whom they ador'd, were but ſo many Devils; and therefore when our bleſſed Saviour came into the World, their *Oracles* ceaſed, and thus was he *manifeſted* to (b) *deſtroy the Works of the Devil.* Now the *Poets* rack their Invention, that the Honour loſt among the *Pagans* may be recovered in the *Playhouſe.* Accordingly, here we have (c) *Temples* in their Honour, (d) *Oracles* given, which are fulfilled, tho ſtrange and myſterious, and Acts of divine Worſhip paid to them. In one (e) *Play*, *Bacchus* is own'd as a *God*; in (f) another, as the *Jolly God of Pleaſures*; and accordingly he is adored and invok'd with crowning the Goblet, and *Pagan* Superſtitions. In one (g) *Play*, after a Clap of *Thunder*, the *Scene* opens above, and diſcovers *Pallas* in the Clouds; the *Actors* all kneel, and one after another put up their ſeveral Petitions; nay, they are exhorted ſo to do in this Expreſſion:

She ſhakes her dreadful Ægis *from the Clouds,*
Bend, bend to Earth, and own the preſent Deity.

(a) The Comical Lovers, *p.* 46. l.1.

(b) 1 *John* 3. 8.

(c) Alarbas, *p.*24. *l.*1. Love the Leveller, *p.*35. The Temple of Love, *Act* 1. *Scene* 1.

(d) Alarbas, *p.*26. *l.*18. The Fickle Shepherdeſs, *p.*8. *l.*1. *p.*7. *l.* 12. Royal Convert, *p.* 54. Temple of Love, *p.*30,34.

(e) The Amorous Miſer, *p.*40. l. 1.

(f) Ulyſſes, *p.*6. *l.*21.

(g) Ibid. *p.*35. l.5.

In another (*h*) *Play* is repreſented a *Temple* dedicated to *Diana*, with an *Altar*, and *the holy Fire burning*, a *Chorus* on each ſide, and the *Prieſts behind* them, whilſt in the Song there are theſe Words:

We bend, Diana, *to thy Shrine,*
Spotleſs Goddeſs, Power Divine,
All Nature ſhall with us thy Praiſes join.
Hence, ye profane, far hence be gone,
Our ſacred Rites are now begun.

In another (*i*) *Play* is repreſented a magnificent *Temple*, in the midſt an Image of *Jupiter* in *Gold*, arm'd with *Thunderbolts*, ſtanding upon a large *Pedeſtal*, with an *Altar* flaming with *Sacrifices*, and ſeveral Perſons kneeling before it, whilſt the *Prieſts* wait round it, crown'd with *Gold*, and *Choriſters* on each ſide in *White* and in *Rows*, and an *Hymn* is ſung to *ſoft Muſick*, beginning with theſe Words:

O King of Gods! Immortal Jove! *To thee*
Our grateful Incenſe, and our Hymns we raiſe.

In the primitive Times, there were many thouſand *Chriſtians* put to death; which Puniſhment they willingly choſe, rather than they would offer *Incenſe* to the *Pagan Idols:* But their Examples are out of mind, and we commit the Sin without any ſcruple. Now he who conſiders (*k*) the great Care of GOD to forbid the *Jews* every thing which had a tendency to *Idolatry* or *Pagan Superſtition*, may wonder to ſee their *Temples*, their *Prieſts*, their *Altars*, and their *Devotions* thus repreſented on the *Chriſtian Stage*. And tho, bleſſed be GOD, there is not the ſame danger of *Paganiſm*; yet *Atheiſm* is too often the unhappy Conſequence. For when *Men* ſee theſe *Idols* worſhipped with the ſame or greater Devotion than what is given to the true GOD, they are apt to think, that all *Religions* are alike; and

(*h*) The Victim, *p.* 60. *per totum.*

(*i*) The Faithful General, *p.* 25. *Act* 3.

(*k*) Spencer *de Ritualibus Judæorum, per totum.*

that

that it is not the Excellency of any, but only the Education or Fashion of the Country, which makes the difference.

The *Scriptures* enjoin us, for this reason, (*l*) to *make no mention of the Names* of other *Gods*, neither to *let them be heard out of our Mouths.* They forbid us (*m*) to *swear by them*, to *serve them*, and to *bow* our *selves down unto them*, because such things will be (*n*) *a Snare unto us.* Besides, GOD tells us, (*o*) that he is *the LORD, that is* his *Name, and* he *will not give* his *Glory to another, nor* his *Praise to graven Images.* Nay, *Origen* assures us, (*p*) That the *Christians* in his Days *contended even to Death, rather than they would call* Jupiter *a God; and behaved themselves with that Reverence and Piety toward* GOD, *that they would not attribute to him any of those Names which the Poets gave to any of their imagined Deities.* But our present *Actors* regard no *Christian* Examples, and endeavour to out-vie even *Paganism* itself in this Particular. Here the *Pagan Gods* and *Goddesses* are represented as (*q*) *mighty*, (*r*) *almighty*, (*s*) *auspicious*, and (*t*) *awful*; as (*u*) *blessed*, and (*x*) *bounteous*; as (*y*) *celestial*, (*z*) *dreadful*, (*a*) *equal*, and (*b*) *eternal*; as (*c*) *Guardians of the Just*, and (*d*) such as

---

(*l*) *Exod.* 23. 13. *Deut.* 12. 3. *Judg.* 2. 2. *Psal.* 16. 4. *Isa.* 44. 9, *to* 21. *Hos.* 2. 17. *Zech.* 13. 2.

(*m*) *Jos.* 23. 7.

(*n*) *Exod.* 23. 33. *chap.* 34. 12. *Deut.* 7. 16.

(*o*) *Isa.* 42. 8.

(*p*) *Contra* Celsum, *lib.* 1.

(*q*) Lucius, *p.* 17. *l.* 21. The Force of Friendship, *p.* 20. *l.* 18. The Victim, *p.* 53. *l.* 4.

(*r*) The Faithful General, *p.* 59. *l.* 42.

(*s*) Ibid. *p.* 69. *l.* 35.

(*t*) Injur'd Virtue, *p.* 9. *l.* 25. *Phædra* and *Hippolytus*, *p.* 11. *l.* 11. Ulysses, *p.* 12. *l.* 6. *p.* 20. *l.* 23.

(*u*) Conquest of *Spain*, *p.* 14. *l.* 26.

(*x*) *Appius* and *Virginia*, *p.* 5. *l.* 12. Etearchus, *p.* 54. *l.* 17. *Perolla* and *Izadora*, *p.* 47. *l.* 6. *Phædra* and *Hippolytus*, *p.* 38. *l.* 23. The Distressed Mother, *p.* 67. *l.* 18. The Victim, *p.* 17. *l.* 28. Thomyris, *p.* 52. *l.* 31.

(*y*) Ulysses, *p.* 63. *l.* 10.

(*z*) The Royal Convert, *p.* 51. *l.* 7.

(*a*) The Force of Friendship, *p.* 27. *l.* 23.

(*b*) *Appius* and *Virginia*, *p.* 17. *l.* 30.

(*c*) Ulysses, *p.* 63. *l.* 10.

(*d*) Hydaspes, *p.* 22. *l.* 4.

always guard them; as (*e*) *good*, (*f*) *gracious*, and (*g*) *great*; as (*h*) the *greater and leſſer Powers*, who (*i*) *favour Right*, and (*k*) not only *reign beneath*, (*l*) *governing this great World, and ruling the Heart of Man*; but alſo (*m*) *ruling in Heaven and in Earth*. According to the *Play-houſe* Language, theſe *Pagan Idols* are the (*n*) *immortal Gods*, who *gave us* our *Being*; they are (*o*) *indulgent*, (*p*) *juſt*, nay (*b*) *all-juſt*, and (*r*) ſuch, whoſe *Juſtice our weak Thoughts muſt not pretend to weigh*. They are (*s*) *knowing*, (*t*) *mighty*, (*u*) *merciful*, and (*x*) *kind*. They (*y*) *ordain* whatſoever ſhall come to paſs, and which (*z*) their *Preſcience foreſaw*. They are (*a*) *powerful* to aſſiſt us, and (*b*) *pity* us in our Afflictions. They

---

(*e*) Etearchus, *p*.66. *l*.26. The Diſtreſſed Mother, *p*. 31. *l*. 16. The Falſe Friend, *p*. 24. *l*. 25. The Succeſsful Pirate, *p*.50. *l*.17.

(*f*) *Appius* and *Virginia*, *p*. 20. *l*.7. Ulyſſes, *p*.36. *l*.36. *p*. 47. *l*.22. *p*. *ult*. *l*. *penult*.

(*g*) Manlius Capitolinus, *p*.58. *l*. 4. Oedipus, *p*.48. *l*.2. *p*.71. *l*. 10.

(*h*) Ulyſſes, *p*.28. *l*.24.

(*i*) Ibid. *p*.30. *l*.31.

(*k*) Royal Convert, *p*.51. *l*.7.

(*l*) *Appius* and *Virginia*, *p*.17. *l*. 30.

(*m*) Ulyſſes, *p*.28. *l*.24.

(*n*) *Appius* and *Virginia*, p. 25. l. 8, *penult*. p.27. l.21. p. p.55. l.34. Arminius, p.5. l.31. Arſinoe, p.39. l.22. p.47. *l*.16. French Cato, p.13. l.8. p.21. *l*. 7. p.29. *l*.5. Craſus, p.7. *l*. *ult*. Fortune in her Wits, p.22. l.26. Oedipus, p. 37. l.13. *Phædra* and *Hippolytus*, p.12. l.15. p.49. l. 16. The Faithful General, p. 34. l.19. p.52. l.27. p.64. l.36. p.68. l.4. The Victim, p.4. l. 10. p. 29. l. 2. Ulyſſes, p. 28. l. 17.

(*o*) *Perolla* and *Izadora*, p. 26. l.29.

(*p*) French Cato, p.43. l.14. Injur'd Virtue, p.32. l.20. p.54. l. *penult*. Manlius Capitolinus, p.1. l. *ult*. p.37. l.9. Oedipus, p.68. l.1. The *Britiſh* Enchanters, p. 30. l. 33. The Falſe Friend, p.37. l.23. The Victim, p.41. l.23. p.56. l.26.

(*q*) *Perolla* and *Izadora*, p. 59. l.1.

(*r*) French Cato, p.10. l.11.

(*s*) *Perolla* and *Izadora*, p. 18. l.9.

(*t*) Lucius, p.17. l.21. The Force of Friendſhip, p.20. l.18. The Succeſsful Pirate, p.36. l.21. The Victim, p.53. l.4.

(*u*) The Victim, p.59. l.10.

(*x*) Manlius Capitolinus, p. 14. l.10. The *Perſian* Princeſs, p.33. l.14.

(*y*) Ajax, p.21. l.27.

(*z*) Ulyſſes, p.34. l.30.

(*a*) Titus Manlius, p.27. l.3. p.51. l.8.

(*b*) *Phædra* and *Hippolytus*, p.33. l.16. p.63. l. 34. The Faithful General, p.28. l.3.

bear

(*c*) *hear our Prayers*, and *give Victory*. They are (*d*) *righteous*, (*e*) *sacred*, and (*f*) *unerring*. Their (*g*) *Power* is *boundless*, and *Wisdom infinite*. They (*h*) *afford us providential Means in pity of our Infirmities*, and (*i*) are *Witnesses of* our *Devotions*.

Here *Cupid* is represented as (*k*) *a God*, as (*l*) *the God of Love*, as (*m*) *mighty*, (*n*) *almighty*, and (*o*) *powerful*, altho (*p*) *an Infant*. He is called (*q*) *gentle*, (*r*) *great*, and (*s*) *liberal*. He is said to be (*t*) a *God* who commands, and (*u*) *governs all*, and one (*x*) who *brings us Joys which never shall decay*. He is called (*y*) the *God of resistless Furies, who oft in Female Hearts with Triumph sees the unlook'd-for Changes of his wanton Power*; (*z*) *The Creator of Heaven and Earth, Delight of Gods above, to whom all Nature owes her Birth*, and (*a*) one *whom no Power can withstand*, but he *rules from the Skies to the Center*. And an *Actor* declares, that (*b*) he is *actuated*

(*c*) Solon, p.71. l.33. Zelmane, p.13. l.5.

(*d*) *English* Cato, p.58. l. 10. *French* Cato, p.15. l. *ult.* Oedipus, p. 28. l. 9. *Phædra* and *Hippolytus*, p. 38. l. *penult.* p. 48. l.16. p.64. l.28. The Force of Friendship, p.23. l.12. The Victim, p.32. l.33. Ulysses, p.1. l.19. p.11. l.1. p.57. l.30.

(*e*) Titus Manlius, p.27. l.3.

(*f*) *Phædra* and *Hippolytus*, p.38. *l.*18, *penult.*

(*g*) Solon, p.51. l.26.

(*h*) *Perolla* and *Izadora*, p. 28. l.6.

(*i*) Ibid. p.29. l.27.

(*k*) Arsinoe, p. 16. l. 12, 20. Love and Liberty, p.17. l.12. The Pretender's Flight, p. 5. l. 26.

(*l*) *French* Cato, p.31. l.7. Hydaspes, p.16. l.28. p.26. l.19. p.48. l.15, 17. p.58. l.14. The Faithful Bride of *Granada*, p.11. l. 11.

(*m*) Solon, p.19. l.12. p.29. l.29. Manlius Capitolinus, p.19. l. 8.

(*n*) Liberty asserted, p.52. l.1. Perplex'd Couple, p. 36. l. 26. The Roving Husband reclaim'd, p. 29. l. 10. The Royal Convert, p.29. l.29.

(*o*) Liberty asserted, p.46. l. 23. Love's Last Shift, p. 83. l. 4.

(*p*) Love's Last Shift, p. 83. l. 4. Cares of Love, p.19. l.20.

(*q*) Hydaspes, p.78. l.8.

(*r*) Liberty asserted, p.46. l.27.

(*s*) Injur'd Love, *a Comedy*, p.16. l.7.

(*t*) The Perplex'd Couple, p. 38. l. *ult.*

(*u*) Titus Manlius, p.55. l.31.

(*x*) Lucius, p.13. l.5.

(*y*) *Perolla* and *Izadora*, p. 27. l.31.

(*z*) *British* Enchanters, p.16. l. 31.

(*a*) Ibid. p.19. l. *antepenult.*

(*b*) Woman is a Riddle, p. 36. l.6.

by that Deity Cupid. Accordingly we are told of the (*c*) *mighty*, and (*d*) *the almighty Power of Love*, which is said to be (*e*) *the greatest Power that Nature knows*. And to give him one of the Titles of our *blessed LORD and Saviour*, he is (*f*) pray'd to, to be the *Mediator*.

In *Scripture* it is said of GOD, (*g*) *He disappointeth the Devices of the Crafty; so that their Hands cannot perform their Enterprize. He taketh the Wise in their own Craftiness; and the Counsel of the Froward is carried headlong.* In the *Play-house* this is (*h*) attributed to *Cupid* alone, as the *Effect* of his *Power*. For *who* (saith an *Actor*) *has conquered the Learned and the Brave, and frustrated their Resolutions, but he?*

In *Scripture* we are told of (*i*) the peaceable Reign of *Christ* under the Gospel, That *the Wolf shall dwell with the Lamb, and feed together; and the Calf, and the young Lion, and the Fatling, shall lie down together, and a little Child shall lead them. For the Earth shall be full of the knowledge of the LORD, as the Waters cover the Sea.* In the *Play-house*, all this is attributed to the *mighty Power of Love*, or *Cupid*. For (*k*) (saith an *Actor*) *He can unite the Wolf and the Lamb, force the Lion to forget his Majesty, and in amorous Dalliance sport with the bounding Kid.*

In *Scripture* (*l*) it is said, that *GOD hath chosen the base things of the World to confound the wise; and GOD hath chosen the weak things of the World to confound the things which are mighty: that no Flesh should glory in his Presence.* In the *Play-house* we are (*m*) told of the *wanton Boy* (Cupid), that he

> ——— ——— *Delights to bend the Mighty,*
> *And scoffs at the vain Wisdom of the Wise.*

(*c*) The Female Advocates, p. 44. l. *antepenult.* Love and Liberty, p. 20. l. 9.

(*d*) *Pyrrhus* and *Demetrius*, p. 38. l. 28.

(*e*) Love Triumphant, p. 21. l. 2.

(*f*) *Portsmouth* Heiress, p. *ult.* l. *antepenult.*

(*g*) *Job* 5. 12, 13.

(*h*) The Cares of Love, p. 19. l. 18.

(*i*) *Isa.* 11. 6, 7, 8, 9. *Isa.* 65. 25.

(*k*) The Fickle Shepherdess, p. 15. l. 13.

(*l*) 1 *Cor.* 1. 27, 28.

(*m*) The Royal Convert, p. 29. l. 29.

Here

Here the *Fates* are represented as (*n*) *appointing our Deaths*, as (*o*) *decreeing* a Man *for high Command*, as (*p*) *eternal*, (*q*) *impartial*, and (*r*) *propitious*; as such whose (*s*) *Laws are unalterable*, and every thing happens according as *Fate* has (*t*) *doom'd it*, or (*u*) *determin'd it for us*.

Here *Jupiter* is represented as (*x*) a *God*, as (*y*) *mighty*, and (*z*) *almighty*; as (*a*) an *Avenger*, and (*b*) of *awful Majesty*; as (*c*) the *Creator of the World*, with (*d*) his *forming Hand*, and (*e*) the *Commander* of the same. Here he is represented as (*f*) *dreadful* in Majesty, (*g*) *eternal* in his Being, and also in (*h*) his *Will*, as (*i*) *in Grandure above*, the (*k*) *Great*, and (*l*) *the great Olympian God*, *whose* (*m*) *Power doth extend beyond the Heaven's remotest Circuit*; as (*n*) *immortal*, (*o*) *impartial*,

---

(*n*) Arsinoe, p.38. l. *antepen.*
(*o*) *French* Cato, p.3. l.12.
(*p*) Force of Friendship, p.40. l. 6.
(*q*) Conquest of *Spain*, p.27. l. 14.
(*r*) Irene, p.32. l.31.
(*s*) *French* Cato, p.26. l. 1.
(*t*) The Force of Friendship, p.40. l.6.
(*u*) Ibid. p.43. l.10.
(*x*) Abra-Mule, p. 35. l. 16. The Artful Husband, p.26. l.17.
(*y*) Alarbas, p.15. l.15. *Appius* and *Virginia*, p. 52. l.11. Love and Liberty, p.57. l.32. *Pyrrhus* and *Demetrius*, p.31. l. 8. Solon, p.12. l. 16.
(*z*) Ajax, p.18. l. *penult.* Solon, p.12. l. 16. The Faithful General, p.26. l.13.
(*a*) Ulysses, p.30. l.3.
(*b*) *Phædra* and *Hippolytus*, p. 7. l.15.
(*c*) The Faithful General, p. 26. l.12.
(*d*) *Appius* and *Virginia*, p. 12. l.30.
(*e*) *Persian* Princess, p. 48. l. 5.
(*f*) Solon, p.40. l.28.
(*g*) Oedipus, p.44. l.5. The Faithful General, p.26. l.12.
(*h*) *Appius* and *Virginia*, p. 46. l.14.
(*i*) Arsinoe, p. 40. l. 2. p. 48. l.1.
(*k*) Ajax, p.42. l.22. Antiochus, p. 32. l. *ult.* p. 34. l. 4. *Appius* and *Virginia*, p.10. l. *ult.* p.17. l.30. p.51. l.25. p.56. l. 16. Ulysses, p.28. l.22.
(*l*) Electra, p.10. l.10.
(*m*) Antiochus, p.34. l.4.
(*n*) Oedipus, p.25. l.13. *Perolla* and *Izadora*, p.46. l.29. The Faithful General, p.25. *Act* 3. l.1. p.65. l.40. The Victim, p.2. l.24. p.50. l.19.
(*o*) *Persian* Princess, p. 48. l. 5.

imperial,

(p) *imperial*, and (q) *just*. Here he is called, (r) the *Father of Gods*, and (s) *Men*, and therefore (t) *King of* both, (u) who *knows the Crimes and Injuries of others*, and accordingly first (x) *scourges the flagitious World, and then forgives*. Here he is called (y) the *Supreme*, the (z) *Thunderer*, who (a) *prepares his Thunder*, even (b) his *sacred Thunder*, and (c) is *Vindictive*, (d) *who in his Hand doth roll the three-fork'd Bolt,*

Preparing to discharge his sacred Thunder.

To set this matter in a clearer Light, it will be requisite to produce some of the *Playhouse Language*, and compare it with *Scripture* Expressions; and accordingly I shall only take three Passages out of one *Tragedy*.

The *Scripture* speaks (e) thus of *Christ*.

I was set up from everlasting, from the beginning, or ever the Earth was. When there were no Depths, I was brought forth, when there was no Fountains abounding with Water. When he gave to the Sea his Decree, that the Waters should not pass his Commandment, when he appointed the Foundations of the Earth: Then I was by him, as one brought up with him; I was daily his delight, rejoicing always before him.

The *Play-house* (f) expresseth it thus:

So Jove *look'd down upon the War of Atoms,*
And rude tumultuous Chaos, *when as yet*

(p) *Phædra* and *Hippolytus*, p. 32. l. 30. p. 33. l. 9. The *British* Enchanters, p. 30. l. 33. The Faithful General, p. 25. *Act* 3. l. 1. Ulysses, p. 59. l. 9.

(q) Ulysses, p. 3. l. 9.

(r) The Victim, p. 45. l. 26. Ulysses, p. 28. l. 22.

(s) *As before.*

(t) *British* Enchanters, p. 30. l. 33. The Faithful General, p. 25. *Act* 3. l. 1. p. 65. l. 40.

(u) The Faithful General, p. 65. l. 40.

(x) Fortune in her Wits, p. 19. l. 15.

(y) *Appius* and *Virginia*, p. 5. l. 4. p. 9. l. 13. The Faithful General, p. 26. l. 12.

(z) *Phædra* and *Hippolytus*, p. 12. l. 26. The Faithful General, p. 26. l. 13. Ulysses, p. 34. l. 35.

(a) Ulysses, p. 34. l. 35. p. 35. l. 7, 25.

(b) Injur'd Virtue, p. 13. l. 22.

(c) Ulysses, p. 34. l. 35.

(d) *Appius* and *Virginia*, p. 9. l. 13.

(e) *Prov.* 9. 23, *to* 32.

(f) Ulysses, p. 42. l. 1.

Fair

Fair Nature, Form and Order had no Being,
But Discord and Confusion ruin'd all.
Calm and serene upon his Throne he sat,
Fix'd there by the eternal Law of Fate,
Safe in himself, because he knew his Power;
And knowing what he was, he knew himself secure.

The *Scriptures* speak (g) thus of *GOD*'s over-ruling *Providence.*

Herod *and* Pontius Pilate, *with the* Gentiles *and People of* Israel, *were gathered together: For to do whatsoever the Hand and the Counsel* of GOD *had determined before to be done.*

The *Play-house* (h) expresseth it thus:

——————*'Tis certainly decreed,*
Fix'd as the Laws, by which Imperial Jove,
According to his Prescience and his Power,
Ordains the Sons of Men to Good or Evil.

The *Scripture* speaks (i) thus of GOD's Protection in Dangers.

If I ascend up into Heaven, thou art there: If I make my Bed in Hell, behold thou art there. If I take the Wings of the Morning, and dwell in the uttermost Parts of the Sea; even there shall thy Hand lead me, and thy Right Hand shall hold me.

The *Stage* (k) expresseth it thus:

In stormy Seas, in those dread Regions, where
Swarthy Cimmerians *have their dark Abode,*
Divided on this World, and Borderers on Hell;
Even there the Providence of Jove *was with me,*
Defended, chear'd, and bore me thro the Danger.

I have been so long in describing the Respect paid in the *Play-house* to this chief *Idol* among the *Pagans*, that I shall be the shorter in my Observations on the rest.

(g) *Acts* 4. 27, 28.
(h) Ulysses, p. 59. l. 9.
(i) *Psal.* 139. 8, 9, 10.
(k) Ulysses, p. 61. l. 1.

However,

However, here we have *Mars* repreſented as (*l*) the *God of War* and (*m*) *Battels*, and a (*n*) *Guardian God, to* whom we *chiefly owe* our *Preſervation*.

Here we have *Nemeſis* repreſented as (*o*) *juſt*, and (*p*) one who *knows the Crimes and Injuries* of others.

Here we have *Pluto* repreſented as (*q*) a great Being, (*r*) *reverſing the Sentences paſs'd upon Men*.

And here we have *Thor* repreſented as a (*s*) *mighty* God, *who wields the Thunder*.

There are three *Acts* of Worſhip due to GOD alone, which in the *Play-Houſe* are frequently paid to *Pagan Idols*.

Firſt, *Prayer* to them. Sometimes they pray to (*t*) the Gods in general, and ſometimes in particular to (*u*) *Bacchus*, to (*x*) *Cupid*, to (*y*) *Diana*, to (*z*) *Hymen*, to (*a*) *Jove*, and to (*b*) the *Moon*. And as (*c*) the *Jews* were blamed in *Scripture* for *burning Incenſe* to her by the name of *the Queen of Heaven*; ſo in the *Play-Houſe* ſhe is called (*d*) *Queen of Darkneſs*, and *Queen of Night*. They alſo pray to (*e*) *Neptune*, to (*f*) *Pallas*,

(*l*) *French* Cato, p. 28. l. 11.
(*m*) Ibid. p. 31. l. 7.
(*n*) Fortune in her Wits, p. 17. l. 6.
(*o*) Ulyſſes, p. 3. l. 9.
(*p*) Ibid.
(*q*) Solon, p. 29. l. 28. p. 30. l. penult.
(*r*) Ibid. p. 30. l. penult.
(*s*) The Royal Convert, p. 23. l. 7.
(*t*) Arſinoe, *p.* 2. *l.* 1, *penult. p.* 3. *l.* 15, 18. *p.* 9. *l.* 8. *p.* 12. *l.* 3, 15. *p.* 13. *l.* 10. *p.* 18. *l.* 17. *p.* 19. *l.* 16. *p.* 25. *l.* 1. *p.* 33. *l.* 4, 22. *p.* 40. *l.* 8. *p.* 43. *l.* 17. *p.* 47. *l.* 16. Fortune in her Wits, *p.* 22. *l.* 26. *Perolla* and *Izadora*, *p.* 26. *l.* 29. *p.* 34. *l.* 12. *p.* 43. *l. ult. p.* 47. *l.* 6. *p.* 63. *l.* 11. Solon, *p.* 11. *Scene* 2. *l.* 2. *p.* 56. *l. ult. p.* 65. *l.* 8. *Britiſh* Enchanters, *p.* 8. *l.* 19. *p.* 30. *l.* 33. Zelmane, *p.* 13. *l.* 5.
(*u*) Ulyſſes, *p.* 6. *l.* 19.
(*x*) Arſinoe, *p.* 4. *l.* 4. *p.* 42. *l.* 2. A Woman's Revenge, *p.* 20. *l.* 1. Myrtillo, *p.* 9. *l.* 4. *p.* 16. *l.* 7. *Perolla* and *Izadora*, *p.* 27. *l.* 31. Northern Laſs, *p.* 72. *l.* 9. *Portſmouth* Heireſs, *p.* 21. *l.* 12. *p.* 25. *l.* 7. *p.* 28. *l. antepenult. p. ult. l.* 24.
(*y*) Fortune in her Wits, *p.* 26. *l.* 25.
(*z*) The Roving Husband reclaim'd, *p.* 27. *l.* 15.
(*a*) *Perolla* and *Izadora*, *p.* 46. *l.* 30. Solon, *p.* 70. *l.* 14. Faithful General, *p.* 26. *l.* 12. The Victim, *p.* 45. *l.* 24. Ulyſſes, *p.* 28. *l.* 22.
(*b*) Arſinoe, *p.* 1. *l.* 1.
(*c*) *Jer.* 44. 25, 26, 27.
(*d*) Arſinoe, *p.* 1. *l.* 1.
(*e*) Ulyſſes, *p.* 28. *l.* 22.
(*f*) Ibid. *p.* 35. *l.* 7.

to

to (g) *Pluto*, to (h) the *Stars*, and to (i) *Venus*. Thus a Petitioner begins;

> (k) *Supreme! First Cause! Eternal Source of Being!*
> *Almighty* Jove! *Original of Power, and Lord of Nature!*
> *Thus tamely could'st thou see thy Shrines profan'd?*

Secondly, *Praising* of them, especially with *Hymns*, giving them *Thanks*, and *ascribing* to them the *Blessings* which Men enjoy. These *Acts* are perform'd sometimes in general to (l) *the Gods*; sometimes with (m) Scripture-Expressions; and sometimes in particular to (n) *Aurora*, to (o) *Cupid*, to (p) *Diana*, to (q) the *Fates*, to (r) *Fortune*, to (s) *Jove*, to (t) *Mars*, and to (u) the *Stars*. Two Examples may suffice, the one (x) to *Jupiter* thus:

> *O King of Gods! Immortal* Jove! *to thee*
> *Our grateful Incense, and our Hymns we raise;*
> *May the tun'd Spheres with us agree,*
> *May Heaven and Earth join Harmony,*
> *To sing aloud their mighty Ruler's Praise.*

(g) Ibid. p. 28. l. 22.
(h) Arsinoe, p. 25. l. 5.
(i) Fortune in her Wits, p. 25. l. 2. Lucius, p. 4. l. 18. The Female Wits, p. 52. l. ult. *Portsmouth* Heiress, p. 40. l. 3. Ulysses, p. 15. l. 14.
(k) Faithful General, p. 26. l. 12.
(l) Ulysses, p. 63. l. 10.
(m) *Mat.* 26. 49. & 27. 29. & 28. 9. *Mark* 15. 18. *Luke* 1. 28. *John* 19. 3.
(n) *Venus* and *Adonis*, p. 9. l. 1.
(o) A Woman's Revenge, p. 20. l. 1. Myrtillo, p. 9. l. 4. p. 16. l. 7. *British* Enchanters, p. 19. l. 7. Titus Manlius, p. 55. l. 31.
(p) The Victim, p. 60. *Scene and Chorus.*
(q) Irene, p. 32. l. 31.
(r) *British* Enchanters, p. 28. l. *penult.* p. 29. l. 9.
(s) Solon, p. 2. l. 6. p. 12. l. 16. Faithful General, p. 25. *Act* 3. l. 1. The Victim, p. 45. l. 24.
(t) Fortune in her Wits, p. 17. l. 6. *Venus* and *Adonis* p. 22. l. 24.
(u) Rival Brothers, p. 18. l. 22
(x) Faithful General, p. 25. l. *penult.*

And the other to (y) *Fortune*, thus:

> *To* Fortune *give immortal Praise*
> Fortune *deposes, and can raise:*
> *All is as* Fortune *shall bestow*,
> *'Tis* Fortune *governs all below.*

Thirdly, *Swearing* by them. Sometimes they *swear* by (z) the *Gods* in general, and sometimes in particular, by (a) *Cupid*, by (b) *Hercules*, by (c) *Jove* and (d) *Juno*, by (e) *Mars*, by (f) *Neptune*, by (g) *Pallas*, and by (h) *Venus*. Sometimes by (i) *all the Powers*, sometimes by (k) the *Stars*, which they call at the same time (l) their *Guardian Stars*. And sometimes by the antient *Idols* of these Kingdoms, as by (m) *Thor*, and by (n) *Woden*.

Besides, The Respect always paid to the *Priests* of these *Pagan Idols*, is also as remarkable. They are (o) *clothed* in *white*, adorned with *Crowns* of Gold, with many Attendants, standing at their Altars, in most magnificent Temples, and performing their Devotions in the

(y) *British* Enchanters, *p.* 28. *l. penult. p.* 29. *l.* 9.

(z) *Perolla* and *Izadora*, *p.* 29. *l.* 25. Solon, *p.* 56. *l.* 5. The *British* Enchanters, *p.* 8. *l.* 35. The Faithful General, *p.*28. *l.*46. *p.*36. *l.*42. *p.* 68. *l.* 39. Female Wits, *p.* 44. *l.* 9. The Gamester, *p.* 40. *l. ult.* Pretender's Flight, *p.* 29. *l.* 6.

(a) Liberty asserted, *p.* 14. *l.* 17. Lucius, *p.*12. *l. penult.* Solon, *p.*64. *l.*19.

(b) Fair Example, *p.* 9. *l.* 19. The Gamester, *p.* 56. *l.* 11.

(c) Gibraltar, *p.*59. *l.*35. Solon, *p.* 40. l. 28. *p.* 71. *l.* 6. The Confederacy, *p.*30. *l. penult.* Female Wits, *p.* 44. *l.*12. The Gamester, *p.*31. *l.*11. The Masquerade, *p.*6. *l.*21. The Victim, *p.*50. *l.*19. Ulysses, *p.* 4. *l.*29. *p.*30. *l.*3. *p.*41. *l.*21. Woman is a Riddle, *p.* 10. *l.* 17, 26. *p.* 11. *l.* 22.

(d) The Gamester, *p.* 52. *l.*12. Ulysses, *p.*11. *l.*17. *p.*12. *l.*25.

(e) Amorous Miser, *p.*45. *l.*3. Ulysses, *p.* 40. *l.* 18.

(f) Basset-Table, *p.*22. *l.*11.

(g) Ulysses, *p.* 41. *l.* 21.

(h) Fair Example, p.7. l. *antepen.* Loyal Subject, p. 70. l. 3. Northern Lass, p.52. l.15. Ulysses, p. 3. l. *penult.*

(i) Zelmane, p. 46. l.26.

(k) Ibid. p. 39. l. 22.

(l) Ibid. p. 4. l. 18.

(m) Royal Convert, p.23. l.7. p. 30. l. 30

(n) Ibid. p.18. l. 8.

(o) Faithful General, p. 25. *Act* 3. Royal Convert, p. 77. l.18. The Victim, p. 60. l.1.

the most ſolemn manner imaginable. When (*p*) their *Gods* are angry, the *Prieſts* tell the People what muſt be done to appeaſe them; and when this is done, they are appeaſed accordingly. And even a *Princeſs* accoſts them in this Language (*q*),

> *Appear, ye Prieſts, ye dreadful holy Men,*
> *Ye Miniſters of the Gods.*

Now the Reaſon of all this is too plain, namely, becauſe the *Poets Chriſtianity* is *Pagan Idolatry.* And this will too ſadly appear, by viewing ſome of the Characters, who paſs for the beſt of *Chriſtians* upon the *Stage.* In the *Tragedy* of *The Lady* Jane Gray, there are three *Proteſtant* Characters; the *Duke of Suffolk*, the *Lord Guilford*, and the *Lady Jane* herſelf. The firſt of theſe imitates *Paganiſm*, in calling (*r*) upon *the Gods.* The ſecond ſwears (*s*) by *Tortures and Hell*, and (*t*) *by the heavenly Pity in* a Woman's *Soul.* He invokes (*u*) the *Powers*, (*x*) the *bleſt Powers*, and (*y*) the *Immortals*: and to confound the Diſtinctions between *Proteſtantiſm* and *Popery*, he prays in this manner (*z*);

> *O all ye Saints, that wear immortal Crowns!*
> *Spirits of Martyrs, that bright Angels are!*

And to ſhew that Heaven is not always minded, he (*a*) calls a temporal Crown a *ſacred and immortal Sound.* And the third, who is the *Poet's* chief Favourite, and who bears the principal Character, ſpeaks of *Eternity*, as if it laſted (*b*) no longer than this preſent Life.

(*p*) The Victim, p. 30. l. 1. p. 61. l. 11.
(*q*) Royal Convert, p. 77. l. 13.
(*r*) Jane Gray, p. 10. l. 9.
(*s*) P. 20. l. 1.
(*t*) P. 33. l. *antepenult.*
(*u*) P. 25. l. 1.
(*x*) P. 41. l. 4.
(*y*) P. 41. l. 21.
(*z*) P. 72. l. 14.
(*a*) P. 27. l. 31.
(*b*) P. 29. l. *ult.* p. 32. l. 29.

In a later *Tragedy*, (*c*) *Lucius* the King, and (*d*) *Roſalinda* the Queen, are frequently ſaid to be *Chriſtians*, and they both together declare (*e*) that they will rather die than renounce their *Religion*. But to ſhew what the Religion of *Lucius* is, he calls the Enjoyment of his Queen (*f*) *the Summit of his Hopes, and Height of Bliſs*. He ſaith, that (*g*) *in* her his *Joys are ever blooming, ever young*. He calls her (*h*) an *everlaſting Charmer*, he (*i*) invokes the *immortal Powers*, he (*k*) *ſwears by Glory and by Love*; and (*l*) addreſſes himſelf to the Pagan *Gods* and *Goddeſſes* in theſe words:

> *Haſte all ye Loves and Graces to my Aid;*
> *Dwell on my Voice, and languiſh in my Eyes.*
> *Bright* Cytherea, *from thy Heav'n look down,*
> *Grant,* Venus, *grant, that her Heart may move;*
> *For me thy Slave make her my Votary.*
> *Propitious now thou ſhalt my Goddeſs be,*
> *And I'll devote my happy Hours to thee.*

On the other hand, *Roſalinda* the Queen ſpeaks of *Eternity* (*m*) as if it was only in this World, and declares that (*n*) ſhe had *but one dear Concern, one Wiſh in Life*, and that was *to make the Royal* Lucius *ever* hers. She ſpeaks of the *Fates* (*o*) in the *Pagan* Language, and (*p*) prays to them, and alſo (*q*) to *all that's bleſſed*. She (*r*) calls upon *Cupid*, as (*s*) a *God*, and calls him (*t*) *Great Love*, confeſſing that his Authority is abſolute.

(*c*) *Lucius* the firſt Chriſtian King of *Britain*, p. 10. l. 30. p. 45. l. 11, 14, 23. p. 46. l. *antepenult*. p. 47. l. 33. p. 49. l. 7. p. *ult*. *in fine*.

(*d*) Lucius, p. 2. l. 10, 21. p. 45. l. 11, 14. p. 46. l. *antepen*. & *ult*. p. 47. l. 33. p. 49. l. 7. p. *ult*. *in fine*.

(*e*) P. 45. l. *antepenult*.

(*f*) P. 21. l. *penult*.

(*g*) P. 22. l. 6.

(*h*) P. 22. l. 8.

(*i*) P. 23. l. 28.

(*k*) P. 12. l. *penult*.

(*l*) P. 4. l. 16.

(*m*) P. 38. l. *ult*. p. 52. l. 2.

(*n*) P. 13. l. *ult*.

(*o*) P. 41. l. 21.

(*p*) P. 13. l. *penult*.

(*q*) P. 28. l. 30.

(*r*) P. 22. l. 4.

(*s*) Ibid.

(*t*) P. 22. l. 11.

She

She (*u*) ſwears *by the Powers that govern all.* She (*x*) prays to *the Powers*, and calls them (*y*) *mighty Powers*, (*z*) *eternal Powers*, (*a*) *heavenly Powers*, and (*b*) *the Powers who inſpire her Breaſt:* and if all other Quotations were omitted, her Religion is declared in one Expreſſion, (*c*) *I bow to the informing Powers.*

But when *Chriſtianity* is ſhewn upon the *Stage* in oppoſition to *Paganiſm*, it meets with a different Treatment. An *Actor*, who was alſo the *Author*, calls *Chriſtianity* (*d*) *this poiſonous Weed*, (*e*) *this pernicious Chriſtian Sect*, (*f*) the *Chriſtian Magick*, (*g*) *that accurſed Worſhip*; and calls a Chriſtian Woman, (*h*) *Baſe Chriſtian.* Another calls her (*i*) *this Chriſtian Witch*; and her Religion (*k*) *this Chriſtian Madneſs*, (*l*) *this baſe Chriſtian miſchief-making Sect*, and (*m*) *this accurſed Sect*; and a third in the ſame *Play* calls it (*n*) this mad *Chriſtian Frenzy.*

In (‖) another the being a *Chriſtian* is deſcribed by being *abandon'd*, and *loſt to Honour*, and *falling from every great and godlike Thought*, and *wrought upon* by *ſome whining coward Prieſt.* And (†) another tells us, That the *Crocodiles* in *Ægypt* might be *Chriſtians.*

But beſides theſe Strokes againſt *Chriſtianity* in particular, the *Poets* take a due care upon all occaſions to laſh *Religion* in general. One *Actreſs* very *gravely and courteſying* asks this Queſtion, (*o*) *Pray, Sir, what Religion are you of?* To which he anſwers, *What Religion am I of!——Marry, Sweetheart, that's an odd Queſtion!——Why, I am of——What Religion am I of!——Why, I am a Stockjobber.* Another makes this An-

(*u*) Lucius, p. 28. l. 6.
(*x*) P. 14. l. 3. p. 27. l. 32. p. 28. l. 16. p. 35. l. 28.
(*y*) P. 11. l. 34. p. 37. l. 33. p. 48. l. 22.
(*z*) P. 14. l. 4.
(*a*) P. 29. l. 26.
(*b*) P. 48. l. 22.
(*c*) P. 11. l. 4.
(*d*) Injur'd Virtue, p. 2. l. 21.
(*e*) P. 2. l. *penult.*
(*f*) P. 27. l. 20.
(*g*) P. 49. l. 15.
(*h*) P. 27. l. 14.
(*i*) P. 30. l. 28.
(*k*) P. 3. l. 10.
(*l*) P. 44. l. 25.
(*m*) P. 63. l. 9.
(*n*) P. 73. l. 22.
(‖) Royal Convert, p. 51. l. 21.
(†) Three Hours after Marriage, p. 68. l. 13.
(*o*) Woman is a Riddle, p. 19. l. 8.

ſwer; *Religion! O dear, I never meddle with theſe matters: I am an honeſt poor Fellow, and go to Church among my Neighbours.* Thus *Religion* is made the Jeſt of the *Stage*, whilſt the *Actors* declare that they have none at all. Another ſaith, that in the caſe of Ambition, (q) *no fooliſh Bonds ſhould cramp his Soul with Scruples and religious Toys.* Another tells us, (r) That the *Religion* in our *Country is Folly*, whilſt the *Scene* is laid in *England*; and another is concern'd, (s) that *a genteel Woman ſhould be a Saint, when Religion is out of faſhion.* For this reaſon one who makes a pretence to *Religion* is call'd (t) *a Prieſt-rid Boy, nurs'd up with Bugbears and religious Tales*; or (u) *a religious Dotard, who mortifies and feeds on barren Virtue.* A *Father* ſaith of his Daughter, (x) to a Suitor, That as for *Religion, ſhe ſhould be of any Religion to pleaſe him.* And when another (y) ſaid, *He did not care whether* a Woman *had any Religion at all*; he gives this Reaſon for ſuch a profane Expreſſion: *O by all means, 'tis beſt that a Wife ſhould have no Religion; when they get that in their heads, they never mind any thing elſe.*

Beſides, That the *Players* may ſtrike effectually at the root of all *Religion*, they repreſent all Pretenders to it as the moſt *wicked* Perſons upon Earth, and ſcruple nothing which may ſerve to blacken their Character. They tell us, that ſuch are notoriouſly guilty of (z) *lying*, (a) *abuſing their Apprentices*, (b) made up of *Religion* and *Pride*; (c) will not touch a *Card* for fear of the *Devil*, and yet are always *ſwearing, curſing, and hectoring* in the Family. One *Actor* ſaith of another,

---

(p) Marry or do worſe, p. 36. l. 32.

(q) Pretender's Flight, p. 26. l. 1.

(r) Love for Love, p. 4. l. 7.

(s) Provok'd Wife, p. 15. l. 7.

(t) Pretender's Flight, p. 27. l. 15.

(u) Perfidious Brother, p. 23. l. 5.

(x) Perplex'd Couple, p. 8. l. 19.

(y) The Apparition, p. 17. l. 25.

(z) An Act at *Oxford*, p. 9. l. 33.

(a) Ibid. p. 12. l. *penult.*

(b) Ibid. p. 42. l. 12. *Hampſtead*-Heath, p. 47. l. 5.

(c) An Act at *Oxford, and Hampſtead*-Heath, ibid.

he is (*d*) *a ſtrange Mixture, a perpetual Sermon-Hunter, repeats and ſings Pſalms continually, and prays ſo loud and vehemently, that he is a Diſturbance to his Neighbours, he is ſo heaven-ward pious, and ſeems ſo very a Saint.* But then he is immediately *curs'd* for *a damn'd godly Knave*, as they call him; and that we may beware of ſuch as pretend to *Religion*, he is immediately repreſented as the greateſt Villain in Nature. Another *Actor* ſaith, (*e*) *The Noiſe of ſuch a Houſe is a perfect Nuſance, for the whole Family are either ſwearing or ſinging of Pſalms.* Certainly they who pray and ſing *Hymns* to the *Devil*, are offended becauſe others pray to GOD, and ſing Pſalms to his Glory; and therefore they expoſe the one, that they may the better eſtabliſh the other. In one *Comedy* an *Actor* tells another, that ſuch a Perſon (*f*) *prays* much; to which this Anſwer is immediately return'd, *That's a bad ſign; a religious Cloke is the beſt Cover for Infirmities.* I pray GOD in his due time to deliver us from ſuch Repreſentations; but now (*g*) *Religion* is frequently inſinuated to be only a Cloke for Wickedneſs, that ſo the Profeſſion may be a Scandal. (*h*) GOD is deſcribed as the *Author* of *Sin*, particularly of *Adultery*, and (*i*) the *Devil* as one who aſſiſts us in our juſt Deſigns. (*k*) The *Zeal* to ſave Souls is curs'd. (*l*) Preaching the Word of GOD is expoſed. (*m*) All that is ſpoken by a Man full of Intrigues, ſeems like a Sermon. And (*n*) the very reading of a Sermon in private, is compared to reading

---

(*d*) Squire of *Alſatia*, p. 9. l. 38.

(*e*) An Act at *Oxford*, p. 42. l. 12. *Hampſtead*-Heath, p. 47. l. 5.

(*f*) Love at firſt ſight, p. 19. l. 35.

(*g*) Gibraltar, p. 8. l. 19. *Portſmouth* Heireſs, p. 6. l. 4. Love at firſt ſight, p. 48. l. 24. Roving Husband reclaim'd, p. 13. l. 10. Stage-Beaux toſs'd in a Blanket, p. *ult. in fine.*

(*h*) The Roving Husband reclaim'd, p. 59. l. 7.

(*i*) *Britiſh* Enchanters, p. 30. l. 30.

(*k*) Stage-Beaux toſs'd in a Blanket, *Prologue* p. 2. l. 15.

(*l*) Solon, p. 26. l. 31. The Baſſet-Table, p. 3. l. 8. p. 48. l. 10. The Rival Brothers, *Epilogue in fine.*

(*m*) Tender Husband, p. 25. l. 29.

(*n*) The Confederacy, p. 11. l. 27.

of a Bill for Money, when there is nothing to pay it.

Neither is it only a Senſe of revealed *Religion*, but even of natural, which the *Poets* endeavour to deſtroy: Some of the *Heathens* oppoſed *Plays*, as things of pernicious Conſequence; and therefore the *Players* think their Cauſe will not do well, until they can ſink *Chriſtianity* to a degree below *Paganiſm*; and then Men will be *lovers of Pleaſure more than lovers of GOD*. They ſtrive to ſtifle *Conſcience*, deſtroy all Notions of GOD and *Judgment*, *Heaven* and *Hell*, *Good* and *Evil*, and baniſh whatſoever hath a tendency to grave and ſerious Thoughts. Many (*o*) Inſtances of this nature may be produced, fitter for the Hands of a *common Hangman*, than for *publick View*; and therefore I muſt beg the Reader's pardon for producing two, that he may the better gueſs at the reſt. The firſt is the Diſcourſe of a Father to his Son, (*p*) who ſcrupled to break his *Oath*:

What, is the Sot grown Religious? Sirrah, I ſhall be aſhamed of you, and diſown you, if I find any more of theſe conſcientious Qualms.

The other is (*q*) a Man ſpeaking of himſelf:

What an unpoliſh'd thing was I before? On a Sunday *in the Afternoon not a Card, not a Dice, no Diverſion; and for the Evening, that forſooth muſt be ſpent in roaſting Apples, a long Chapter*, &c.

The Inference from hence naturally follows, That ſince *Religion* is a ſcandalous Thing, a dull heavy Employment, and in ſhort a Cheat; therefore we muſt down with it, let the *Profeſſors* be of what *Perſuaſion* ſoever. In (*r*) *one Comedy* a *Prologue* is exactly calculated for this purpoſe, to ſcourge in their turns all Pretenders to *Religion*, *Zeal* and *Honeſty*; but particularly all *Preachers*, let them belong either to the *Church* or

(*o*) An Act at *Oxford*, *p.* 17. *l.* 26. Gibraltar, *Sheet* E. *p.* 38. *l.* 1. Hampſtead-Heath, *p.* 20. *l.* 1. Love at firſt Sight, *p.* 24. *l.* 23. *p.* 49. *in fine.* Squire Treelooby, *Prologue*, *l.* 3. The Baſſet-Table, *p.* 9. *l.* 15. *p.* 46. *l.* 7. The Lawyer's Fortune, *p.* 45. *Signature* G 3. *l.* 8.

(*p*) Fortune in her Wits, *p.* 34. *l.* 27.

(*q*) The Fair Example, *p.* 10. *l.* 5.

(*r*) The Stage-Beaux toſs'd in a Blanket.

the

the *Dissenters*; and for this purpose the *Speaker* is dress'd in a ridiculous Habit, one half like a Minister of the *Church* of *England*, and the other half like a *Dissenting Teacher*; and sometimes points to one side, sometimes to the other; representing both as the greatest Villains in Nature. Indeed the *Title-Page* tells us, that the *Prologue* is against *Occasional Conformity*, otherwise no one who reads the *Prologue* could believe it, unless in this sense; they would have Men totally abstain from both, and therefore reflect on such as on any occasion resort to either.

But the *Church of England* seems to be the chief Mark at which they aim; and therefore all who frequent her Worship, especially on Week-Days (*Plays* being then acted) are (*s*) censured and ridicul'd. Neither can the Persons (*t*) concerned therein, or even the (*u*) Place adjoining, be free from Reflections. In one *Play* (*x*) a *Knight* speaking of a religious Education, describes it in this manner: *You must know, I was afraid of being damn'd in those days; for I kept sneaking cowardly Company, Fellows that went to Church, said Grace to their Meat, and had not the least Tincture of Quality about them.* Such blasphemous Expressions as these are enough to cause GOD to take the Gospel from us. In one *Comedy*, (*y*) a *Lady* saith, *She is going to Church*; from whence this Observation is (*z*) afterward made, *I know Women of your Principles have more Pride than those who have no Principles at all.* In (*a*) another there is this Expression: *The Church! I scorn your words, Sir; I deal in no such Cattle. I want no Luck in Horse-Flesh.* To which this answer is return'd, *I like your Cause the better for not having to do with the Church.*

Our blessed Saviour, when he shewed his utmost Concern for the Honour of GOD, could not find out a fitter Object, than the Place appointed for his Worship,

(*s*) An Act at *Oxford*, *p.* 11. *l. ult. p.* 17. *l.* 27. Hampstead-Heath, *p.* 15. *l.* 13.

(*t*) The Fatal Marriage, *p.* 103. *l.* 32.

(*u*) Three Hours after Marriage, *p.* 68. *l.* 10.

(*x*) The Provok'd Wife, *p.* 18. *l.* 14.

(*y*) The Careless Husband, *p.* 5. *l.* 9.

(*z*) Ibid. *p.* 6. *l.* 12.

(*a*) The Roving Husband reclaim'd, *p.* 23. *l.* 16.

and

and accordingly expoſtulates thus with the *Jews*, (*b*) *Is it not written, My Houſe ſhall be called of all Nations the Houſe of Prayer?* The *Poet* not only burleſques this *Scripture* and the Houſe of *GOD*, but alſo takes the Opportunity to ſet up the *Play-houſe* in oppoſition to it; and banters *Sin*, *Repentance* and *Mortification*, at the ſame time, (*c*) thus:

We'll turn the Pit into a Houſe of Pray'r;
And then, where oft you've ſinn'd, you may repent in,
And all come thrice a Week to keep your Lent in.

As the *Church of GOD* is the Place for *Religious Worſhip*; ſo upon the *Stage* it is too often repreſented as a Place for Amorous Intrigues, and a Receptacle for Villains. One *Actor* (*d*) asks this Queſtion, *Could you think our Buſineſs* at the Pariſh-Church *was to hear your Teacher ſpin out an Hour over a Velvet Cuſhion?* One expreſſeth (||) thus his Zeal for the fourth Commandment; *Two and fifty Days are loſt every Year, for want of Balls and Opera's on a* Sunday. Another (*e*) ſwears, ſaying, *Sunday is a vile Day, I muſt confeſs.* And (*f*) *a Man muſt have very little to do at Church, that can give an account of the Sermon.* And (*g*) *To mind* either the *Prayers* or the *Sermon*, is *to mind what one ſhould not do.* But (*h*) if he did not mind the Ladies, he *deſerved to be excommunicated.* In another *Play*, (*i*) *Aimwell* tells his Man, that he *muſt pimp for* his *Maſter*; who anſwers, that he *may do execution in a Country Church*: and that both Time and Place may be equally ridicul'd, (*k*) the Day is ſaid to be *Sunday.* Thus the Publick Solemnities of Religion are made a Jeſt, as if it was a ridiculous piece of Ignorance to pretend to the Worſhip of GOD. The *Playhouſe* is repreſented as a *Church*, and the Church

---

(*b*) *Matth.* 21. 13. *Mark* 11. 17. *Iſa.* 56. 7.

(*c*) Love the Leveller, *Epilogue in fine.*

(*d*) Squire of *Alſatia*, *p.* 50. *l.* 24.

(||) The fine Lady's Ayres, *p.* 20. *l.* 26.

(*e*) The Relapſe, *p.* 18. *l.* 32.

(*f*) Ibid. *l.* 42.

(*g*) *Pag.* 19. *l.* 27.

(*h*) *Pag.* 18. *l. penult.*

(*i*) The Beaux Stratagem, *p.* 15. *l.* 26.

(*k*) Ibid. *p.* 13. *l.* 13.

rather

rather as a *Stew*, whilst *Women* and *Men* are the only Deities to be there adored by each other. After a great deal of profane Discourse upon this Subject, the Man asks his Master, (*l*) *When were you at Church before, pray?* The Master answers, *Um! — I was there at the Coronation!* The Man asks, *And how can you expect a Blessing by going to Church now?* The Master answers, *Blessing! Nay,* Frank, *I ask but for a Wife.* And the Reply is, *Truly, the Man is not unreasonable in his Demands.* After this, their Landlord tells another Guest, that he (*m*) *fancied* he had *two Highway-Men* (meaning these two) *in the House* just now. Another answers, invoking the *Devil* according to the *Play-house* Language, *How d'ye smoke them?* The Landlord replies, *Why, the one is gone to Church.* And he is immediately answer'd, *That's suspicious, I must confess.* And yet this Man carries on his Intrigues at *Church*, he is the principal Person of Figure on which the Plot, Name and Humour of the *Play* depends, and marries the principal *Actress* of the *Play* according to his desire, (*n*) with *Ten thousand Pounds* Fortune; and (*o*) the Estate and Title of a *Lord* unexpectedly falls to him, as a greater Reward for the Mischief which he did to *GOD* and *Religion.* And his Man, who assisted him (*p*) as a *dear Brother in Iniquity*, doth also (*q*) meet with a Wife and *Two thousand Pounds*, as a Gratification for his carrying on the same Design.

To draw this matter nearer to the Life, a *Clergyman* is represented in the same *Play*, and treated with the utmost Scorn and Contempt, to make his *Person*, his *Character*, and his *Religion* despised. Upon his (*r*) first Entrance at the Inn, he is the Buffoon of the Company. After this, two Serving-men treat his Character in the vilest manner. (*s*) *Why*, (saith one) *the Mother of all this Mischief is a Priest.* The other answers, *A Priest!* The first replies, *Aye, a damn'd Son of a Whore of* Baby-

(*l*) Beaux Stratagem, *p.*16.*l.*16.
(*m*) Ibid. *p.*17. *l.*30.
(*n*) *Pag.*25. *l.*3. *p.*50. *l.* 17. *l.* 23. *p.*25. *l.*14. *p.*69. *l.*24. *p.*68. *l.*23,30.
(*o*) *Pag.* 67. *in fine.*
(*p*) *Pag.* 4. *l.*24.
(*q*) *Pag.*3. *l. antepenult. p.*20.
(*r*) *Pag.*28. *l.*30.
(*s*) *Pag.*31. *l.*9.

lon; adding, that (*t*) *he tells Lyes as if he had been a Traveller from his Cradle*, and (*u*) that he had perverted a Maid-Servant: *For* (ſaith he) *I am afraid, he has made her a Whore and a Papiſt.* Upon his next entrance, he addreſſes the ſame Servant thus, (*x*) *Save you, Maſter* Scrub. To which he anſwers, *Sir, I won't be ſaved your way. I hate a Prieſt. I abhor the* French, *and I defy the Devil. Sir, I am a bold* Briton, *and will ſpill the laſt Drop of my Blood to keep out Popery and Slavery.* And he afterwards goes on in (*y*) Language of the ſame nature. At his next appearance, the *Prieſt* turns *Pimp*, and (*z*) endeavours to debauch the Maid of the Houſe for this purpoſe. And (*a*) when ſhe anſwers, *Is that nothing? It would be both a Sin and a Shame:* He replies, *Here is twenty Lewidores for your Shame, and I will give you an Abſolution for your Sin.* After this (*b*) ſhe is adviſed by him to bring the *Parties* together, and *leave the Sins* with themſelves. To which ſhe anſwers, *Well, Doctor, your Religion is ſo pure! Methinks I am ſo eaſy after an Abſolution, and can ſin afreſh with ſo much ſecurity, that I am reſolv'd to die a Martyr to it.* Then he (*c*) agrees to let in another Man inſtead of the firſt, and (*d*) effects it. After this he addreſſes himſelf to a Highwayman, and a Houſebreaker, and (*e*) ſaith, *I will ſecure your Body and your Soul too. I will make you a good Catholick, and give you an Abſolution.* Which Offer is thus replied to, (*f*) *Then you and your Abſolution may go to the Devil.* And *Scrub* takes this occaſion to ſay, (*g*) That he *left the Prieſt* and the Highwayman *diſputing about Religion.* At another time he is (*h*) *arreſted as a Traytor againſt the Government*, and on this occaſion curſes an *Actor*, that (*i*) *the Devil* might *hang* him, and (*k*) *take* him. And now, who would not take all this to be a Reflection upon a *Popiſh Prieſt?* But *Exitus acta probat.*

(*s*) Beaux Stratagem, *p.*31. *l.*9.
(*t*) *Pag.*31. *Lin.*17.
(*u*) *Lin.* 20.
(*x*) *Pag.* 44. *l. antepenult.*
(*y*) *Pag.* 45. *l.* 17.
(*z*) *Lin.*27.
(*a*) *Lin.* 35.
(*b*) *Pag.*46. *l.*16.
(*c*) *Pag.* 53. *l.*34.
(*d*) *Pag.*58. *l.*23.
(*e*) *Pag.*62. *l.*26.
(*f*) *Pag.* 62. *l.*31.
(*g*) *Pag.*63. *l.*34.
(*h*) *Pag.*52. *l.*20.
(*i*) *Pag.*53. *l.*9.
(*k*) *Pag.*53. *l.*15.

It

It must not pass off so. For, that the *Church of England* may bear her share of the Scandal, he afterwards enters upon the *Stage* (*l*) with a *Common-Prayer-Book*, (*m*) with the Consent of both Parties, to marry (*n*) a supposed *Lord* (*o*) of her Communion, to (*p*) a rich Fortune, the principal *Actress* of the Play, who was (*q*) acquainted with our *Liturgy*, (*r*) a Frequenter of our *Service*, and (*s*) who was seldom absent on a *Sunday* either Morning or Afternoon: and this is his last *Exit*.

But this is not the only Instance in which the *Clergy* of the *Church of England* meet with such a Treatment on the *Stage*. Of this they have been (*t*) formerly guilty, and still continue to go on in the same method. As the Ministers of the *Gospel* are the Ambassadors of GOD and *Christ*, so they meet with the same usage. Indeed, since GOD is *blasphemed* every day almost upon the *Stage*, as *Christ* is *undervalued*, and *Religion* is *undermined*, so as far as it relates only to their own Persons, they who are concerned in that sacred Function may the better bear it. (*u*) *It is enough for the Disciple, that he be as his Master, and the Servant as his Lord*; and therefore since they vilify the *Master of the House*, *how much more* will they do the same by *those of his Houshold*? If the Account which the *Stage* gives of the *Clergy* be true, they are the greatest Monsters in nature, the Bane of Mankind, the Contrivers of all sorts of Mischief, and there is no Wickedness but they have the greatest hand in it. We are told (*x*) by a *Stage* Poet, that *Priests of all Religions are the same*; and therefore what they speak of one, is easily applied to all the rest. Nay, it is usually spoken in such general terms as may be applied with-

(*l*) Beaux Stratagem, *p.*65. *l.*32.

(*m*) *Pag.* 65. *l.*31, 26. *p.*66. *l.*8. *p.*67. *l.*25, 29.

(*n*) *Pag.*29. *l.*26.

(*o*) *Pag.* 15. *l.*30, &c.

(*p*) *Pag.*25. *l.*30. *p.*50. *l.*17. *p.*68. *l.*23, 30.

(*q*) *Pag.*11. *Act* 2. *l.*4.

(*r*) *Pag.*11. *Act* 2. *l.*1. *p.*22. *Act* 3. *l.*16.

(*s*) *Pag.*36. *l.*2.

(*t*) *Collier's* Short View of the Stage, *p.*97. *chap.* 3. *per totum.*

(*u*) *Matth.* 10. 24, 25. *Luke* 6. 40.

(*x*) *Dryden*, in his *Absalom* and *Achitophel.*

out any *Alteration.* They know that the Transition from one Religion to the other is natural, the Application is easy, and the Audience is but too well prepared. Thus formerly, (y) the Author of *Don Sebastian* aimed at the *Bishops* thro the sides of the *Mufti*, and only borrowed the Name of the *Turk*, that he might with Impunity make the *Christian* more ridiculous. *Dominick* in *The Spanish Friar*, is rail'd at, push'd off the *Stage* by the Rabble, and makes a dishonourable *Exit*; but this Correction is not given him as a *Papist*, but as a *Priest*.

In a late *Farce*, Father *Bernardo*, a Romish *Priest*, and a Confessor, is notoriously guilty of adulterous Designs, which are exposed upon the *Stage*; but then a due care is taken, that the latitude of Expression shall bring in all others guilty, as (z)

Well, for a thorough-pac'd Whoremaster, commend me to a Priest. And (a)

Devil, worse, if worse can be than Devil, thou very Priest.

In another *Play*, (b) Fabian *enters in a Friar's Habit*, with this Atheistical Cant and Reflection: *I am never the nearer being a Saint, for putting on the Habit of Piety. The Profession and the Practice of it are two things in the Schools, and wise Men distinguish them into several Interests.* Upon this he discovers three villanous Designs, which he had in his head. And in the Conclusion another *Actor* makes the Inference (c),

I love a Plot where the Clergy's concerned. They will be always sure of the Benefit without the Danger, &c.

From *Romish* let us proceed to *Pagan* Representations. In one *Comedy*, (d) the *Author* discovers some *horrid Impieties*, which he fathers upon the *Priests* of *Isis*, and would gladly excuse his Mismanagement with a *non putaram* in the *Preface.* However, his Expressions are in general terms, and the *High-Priest* himself is so kind as

---

(y) *Collier's* Short View of the Stage, *p.* 103.

(z) A Wife well manag'd, *p.* 17. *l.* 22.

(a) Ibid. *p.* 18. *l.* 13.

(b) The Fatal Marriage, *p.* 116. *l.* 25.

(c) Ibid. *p.* 117. *l.* 37.

(d) Love the Leveller, *p.* 20. *l.* 14. *p.* 25. *l.* 3, 30. *p.* 27. *l.* 22. *p.* 29. *l.* 11. *p.* 30. *l.* 21. *p.* 31. *l.* 2. *p.* 37. *l.* 28. *p.* 38. *l.* 24. *p.* 49. *l.* 3. *p.* 50. *l.* 21. *p.* 52. *l.* 3. *p.* 57. *l.* 9.

to

to discover the Author's Design, by talking of (*e*) *Cannon Bullets* and *Gunpowder*, the use whereof is well known in *England*, but was never heard of in *Egypt*, whilst the *Priests* of *Isis* were there. Nay, had the *High-Priest* kept the *Poet*'s Counsel; yet the Walls betray him, and one of the *Scenes* being (*f*) a *Chocolate-House*, brings the *Plot* nearer home, and shews at least that there was a double Entendre.

Another *Poet* lays the Scene at *Byzantium* in *Greece*; but when the *Actors* speak of the *Priests*, their Words are unconfined to any Nation. I shall therefore transcribe some Expressions at large, that the Reader may make his own Reflections.

(*g*) *Thy dreaming Priesthood.*
(*h*) ———————— *None dare dispute*
The sacred Slander, when the Priestly Power
Has preach'd and pray'd it into Orthodox:
Nay, should the Emperor himself oppose it,
They'll represent him as the Peoples Foe,
Make him Conspirator against himself,
And prove it is Religion to dethrone him.
'Tis an old pious Fraud, but still it takes;
Such Doctrine suits a Rabble. Answer, *And a Priest.*
Both are alike for Faction, fiery, rash,
Still prone to change, and ever in the wrong.
No Arts the Prince and People can divide,
Till you engage the Priesthood on your side.
And again, (*i*) ——— *'Twas but an Oath,*
And Interest may unbind that feeble Tye:
That Case the pious Priesthood have resolv'd.
And (*k*) *Still our Teachers would our Reason blind,*
And prove Almighty Justice rules Mankind:
But should we plead from this unequal Doom,
They would refer us to a World to come.
Unerring Guides they all pretend to be,
Yet know as little of the Way as we.

(*e*) Love the Leveller, *p.* 38. *l.* 24.
(*f*) Ibid. *p.*56.
(*g*) The Faithful General, *p.* 26. *l.* 14.
(*h*) Ibid. *p.*43. *l.*22.
(*i*) Ibid. *p.* 49. *l.*40.
(*k*) Ibid. *p.*56. *l.*22.

This

This is a two-edged Sword, and ſtrikes not only at the *Clergy*, but alſo at the *Providence*, *Power*, and *Juſtice* of that GOD, whoſe Servants they are. And if he was not infinite in *Mercy*, he would make the Utterers of ſuch Expreſſions *Examples* to others, and Objects of his *Juſtice*.

In a late *Play*, Dr. *Wolf*, a *Nonjuror*, is brought upon the *Stage*, and juſtly expoſed for his Enormities. In the *Prologue* (*l*) we are told, that there is no Reflection upon Parties, and therefore every one might be eaſy. But the *Clergy* muſt feel the *Poet*'s Laſh in the *Epilogue*; who (*m*) asks this Queſtion,

When Prieſts turn Traytors, where's the mighty matter?

And it is obſervable, that the words *Prieſts* and *Traytors* are printed in large Capitals, to make them more remarkable, and the Affinity more evident. Thus no Teacher of *Religion* can eſcape the Poets Laſh, let him be either *Schiſmatick* or *Heretick*, *Proteſtant* or *Papiſt*, *Turk* or *Pagan*. Here we are taught, that they are all alike, all *Rogues* and *Villains*; and therefore what is ſaid of one, the Reader may interpret of any as he pleaſeth. *Teachers* of all Perſuaſions are expoſed, and *Atheiſts* (*n*) are recorded, as the *brave Examples* for us to *follow*.

But there is another Mark, at which *they ſhoot out their Arrows, even bitter Words*; namely, the *Clergy* of the *Church* of *England*. Theſe general Innuendoes are not thought ſufficient to do them a Miſchief; but as they make the moſt conſiderable Figure in the Nation, ſo they are the moſt cenſur'd and reflected on. They are introduced on the *Stage* to join the *Lovers* in Marriage, and this is well known to be an Office peculiar to them. Accordingly, they are (*o*) mentioned with ridiculous Names, and either (*p*) compared to, or (*q*) joined with

(*l*) The Nonjuror, *Prologue*, *l.* 1.

(*m*) Ibid. *Epilogue*, *l.* 11.

(*n*) Love at firſt Sight, *p.* 9. *l.* 3.

(*o*) An Act at *Oxford*, *p.* 36. *l.* 22. A Woman's Revenge, *p.* 40. *l.* 23. She wou'd if ſhe cou'd, *p.* 166. *l.* 8. The Amorous Miſer, *p.* 56. *in fine*. The Lawyer's Fortune, *p.* 67. *l.* 5.

(*p*) Love's Contrivance, *p.* 34. *l.* 23. The *Portſmouth* Heireſs, *p.* 72. *l.* 22.

(*q*) The Pretender's Fate, *p.* 2. *l. ult.*

Hangmen

Hangmen and *Executioners*. The Poets (r) greedily catch at all Opportunities which preſent to expoſe their Order, and neither (s) the *Biſhops*, nor (t) the inferior *Clergy* can eſcape their continual Banters. The *Epithets* beſtowed on them are always full of Contempt and Reproach, as (u) *ſome ſtrong-back'd Paſtor*, (x) *a jolly red-nos'd Parſon*, (y) *a dreaming*, or (z) *a whining coward Prieſt*. If Hypocriſy is expoſed, (a) a great part thereof falls to their ſhare. When (b) an *Actor* ſaith of his Son, *I can't tell what to breed him to, that don't require much Strength of Body, nor Application of Mind*, then the *making of him a Parſon* is the next thing talk'd of. The Affronts put upon them, (c) mentioned in the Margin, are too many to be tranſcribed, and ſuch as need the Patience of the *Church of England* to bear with them. I ſhall only mention (d) one, by which we may obſerve the *Stage* Favourites, whilſt the *Clergy* are thus abuſed.

Go on, in time you may arrive to ſay Grace at the Table of ſome overgrown Atheiſt, skrew your Face into a formal Mould, and ſtudy caſuiſtical Divinity, to juſtify the Sins of your Patron by the Canon-Law, and be the Jeſt of the Family. You may ſometimes have their publick Encouragement, but never once their private Approbation. The very Chamber-Maids will laugh at you in their turn. Women love a Fellow of Spirit, and Life, and Vigour. A dozen

(r) The Earl of *Mar* marr'd, *p.* 15. *l.* 22. *p.* 17. *l.* 9.

(s) The Comical Revenge, *p.* 51. *l.* 21.

(t) Ibid. *p.* 49. *l.* 20. The Drummer, *p.* 3. *l.* 5. Woman is a Riddle, *p.* 32. *l.* 9. *p.* 37. *l.* 5. *p.* 54. *l.* 13.

(u) A Woman's Revenge, *Epilogue*, *l.* 23.

(x) Love's Laſt Shift, *p.* 5. *l.* 17.

(y) The Cruel Gift, *p.* 59. *l.* 24.

(z) Royal Convert, *p.* 51. *l.* 23.

(a) Love's Laſt Shift, *p.* 5. *l.* 17.

(b) The *Gotham* Election, *p.* 40. *l. penult.*

(c) An Act at *Oxford*, *p.* 36. *l.* 2. *p.* 40. *l.* 9. *p.* 25. *l.* 29. Hampſtead-Heath, *p.* 45. *l.* 9. Squire Trelooby, *Prologue*, *l.* 17. *Epilogue*, *l.* 19. The Amorous Miſer, *p.* 54. *l.* 6. *p.* 56. *l. antepenult.* *p.* 58. *l.* 30. The Gameſter, *p.* 61. *l.* 11. *Portſmouth* Heireſs, *p.* 7. *l.* 3. *p.* 41. *l.* 21. The Miſtake, *p.* 50. *l.* 10. The Stage-Coach, *p.* 3. *l.* 6. The Royal Merchant, *p.* 24. l. 15.

(d) The Maſquerade, *firſt printed Anno* 1717. p. 16. l. 31.

Intrigues, two or three Bastards put out in the City, and the nice management of a Box and Dice, will prevail more in your behalf than your nonsensical musty Formalities.

The *Clergy* receiving their Education in the *Universities*, the Poets endeavour accordingly to vilify those Seminaries of Learning. *The Stage-Beaux toss'd in a Blanket* (e) shews a poor Revenge upon a *College Servitor*; but *An Act at Oxford* seems wholly design'd to expose every Member from the highest to the lowest. Above (f) twenty Instances may be produced from this very Comedy. 'Tis true, the *Players* cared not to act it under this Name, and affront so great a Body in *wholesale*: the *Poet* therefore minces the matter in another *Play* called *Hampstead-Heath*, where a great part of these Insolences went off by *retale* with little Amendments. Here we are told, that (g) a *Servitor's Business is to pimp for Gentlemen-Commoners.* That they are (h) *wretched Scoundrels*, and *sorry Dogs*. That (i) *the Tutors are crabbed Fellows*, and only teach a *parcel of crabbed Authors.* Nay, that (k) the *Doctors* themselves have *no Divinity*. In another (l) *Play* the *Members* of the *University* are described as hunting after Women, even to a *Proverb*; and it is said of a Father, (m) that *he put* his Son *early to the University, where he staid three Years to small purpose.* In another, (n) a Father saith of his Son, *They had almost spoil'd him at the College, they cramm'd him so with your Logicks, and your Ethnicks, the Boy had been ruin'd.* In another (o) an *Actress* gives her *Opinion of the University Students*, that they are commonly *slovenly Fellows*, without any *Ingenuity*, their *Provision* is very *wretched*, and their *Conversation* is no better;

(e) *Pag.* 9. *l. penult.*

(f) *Pag.* 2. *l.* 18, 25, *penul.* p. 3. l. 6. p. 4. l. 4, 13, 27. p. 6. l. 10, 29. p. 7. l. 25, 30. p. 8. l. 12. p. 10. l. 4. p. 20. l. 20. p. 23. l. 19. p. 27. l. 30. p. 33. l. 31. p. 35. l. 32. p. 40. l. *ult.* p. 45. l. 29. p. 46. l. 6. p. 51. l. 6. p. 55. l. 11.

(g) *Pag.* 12. *l.* 14.

(h) *Pag.* 31. *l.* 12.

(i) *Pag.* 1. *l.* 12.

(k) *Pag.* 51. *l.* 4.

(l) Woman is a Riddle, p. 6. l. 22.

(m) Ibid. p. 7. l. 31.

(n) The Wife's Relief, p. 6. l. 22.

(o) Female Wits, p. 7. l. 3.

better; but yet they *are all proud, becauſe they have been at Oxford.* And accordingly *Oxford* is immediately cenſured as a *Place* fit only to *improve Beggars, and ſpoil Gentlemen, to make them vain, and think* that *no body hath Wit but themſelves.* Another (p) ſaith of them, *They are* Putts, *mere* Putts. *They are all Scholar Boys, and nothing elſe, as long as they live there: And yet they are as confident as if they knew every thing; when they underſtand no more beyond* Magdalen-Bridge, *than mere* Indians. And another ſpeaks (q) thus to an *Actor:*

Thou art a ſcholaſtick Pedant, and nothing will down with thee but Collegiate Formality: You muſt have every thing ſquar'd by Rules from your Claſſicks. The old Fool your Father muſt needs give you Learning, to make you a Blockhead. Your Precepts of Morality, and your Natural Philoſophy, will never recommend you to the Sparks of this Age. A Scholar is not admitted into Converſation, unleſs ſometimes at a Tavern, where they make him the Fool of the Company, and are merry at his expence. I wiſh your Logical, Ethick, and Metaphyſical Works had all been burnt with their Authors, like a Company of old muſty Cynical Coxcombs, as they are. And to ſhew that they have no more Reſpect for the greateſt Member than for the meaneſt, (r) one of the *Actors* is pleaſed to tell the Audience, That he *maintains at preſent a matter of fifty ſleeping Doctors in both Univerſities, that do nothing but dream.*

Had not the *Univerſities* been the Nurſeries both for *Religion* and *Learning*, and of the utmoſt conſequence to train up Perſons for the Service of GOD in the Work of the Miniſtry; perhaps they had not been ſo reflected on. But this makes the *Poets* perſiſt in affronting ſuch Venerable Bodies, without any fear of their juſt Reſentment.

I have tired the Reader with an Account, how the *Poets* expoſe the Time, and Place, and Perſons ſet apart for the publick Exerciſe of *Religion*, and alſo the training up of others for this purpoſe. As for *Religion* itſelf,

---

(p) Squire of *Alſatia*, p. 2. l. 16.
(q) The Maſquerade, p. 16. l. 25.
(r) The Fair Example, p. 27. l. 34.

(s) an Actor declares, that it is the *common Topick for the Raillery of our Wits*, and that *Atheism* is their *distinguishing Mark*; and their *Plays* do shew it to be so indeed. Another saith, (t) that if a Man *hath but the Faith of a Lover* toward his Mistress, it is *no matter for his Religion* toward his GOD; or (u) it is *Religion* enough for a Man to tell his Name. Another confesses (x) that *Money is the only Deity, except* a Woman, which he *adores*. And another saith, that (y) the *Horses shall* learn *Religion* at his House; which perhaps they may soon do, and have as much as their Teacher.

I shall trouble the Reader but with one Instance more. In one *Play* Captain *Rainer* is the principal Man of Figure throughout the whole; the *Drama* saith, he is *free and well bred*, and in the end he marries *Le Bell*, the principal Woman and great Fortune, from whence the *Play* took its Name: and therefore what he saith, (z) is the more material, which I shall set down at large.

In the old Remains of Truth, Improbity and Hypocrisy are painted the darling Principles of the Fortunate. A dissembled Virtue, like a dissembled Passion, hath commonly the best effect. Gravity and an affected Zeal goes farther in the eye of the World, than Sincerity and Plain-dealing; and were I to wrong a Man in his Estate, or a Woman in her Fortune, it should be still under the hypocritical Cant of Devotion. To this it is answer'd, *A pretty Religion you profess, truly!* And he immediately replies; *Religion! Ay, there's another Topick now! Religion and Reformation! Prithee, what hath Religion to do with a Man of Figure? Conscience resides among poor Rogues; Men of Quality are above it.*

As for their *Piety* towards GOD, I shall only mention some Expressions in one *Play*, where (a) an *Actor*

(s) Woman is a Riddle, *p.* 5. *l.* 14.

(t) Marplot, *p.* 8. *l.* 1.

(u) Female Advocates, *p.* 17. *l.* 6.

(x) Woman is a Riddle, *p.* 17. *l.* 5.

(y) The Country-House, *p.* 9. *l.* 31.

(z) *Portsmouth* Heiress, *p.* 5. *l. penult.*

(a) The Wife's Relief, *p.* 35. *l.* 13.

saith

ſaith of *Gold*, that it is a *King-creating, Beauty-buying, Virtue-giving Deity*; and makes (*b*) this Inference at the end of an *Act*:

> *Wonder not then, fond Man doth Wealth adore;*
> *What other Deity ſhould he implore?*

In another place (*c*) a Perſon is recommended as *one of the beſt Women in the Town*: but the Anſwerer takes care to expoſe her for the ſame reaſon; *Pious enough! But what have we to do with Saints, on this ſide of the Grave?*

In (*d*) *Scripture* the *Preaching* of the Word of GOD is eſtabliſhed as the ordinary Means of Salvation; and for this purpoſe (*e*) the *Apoſtles* received their Commiſſion from *Chriſt* himſelf. Upon the *Stage* (*f*) it is frequently banter'd; and when a Man talks ſerious, he (*g*) is called a *Pulpit-Devil*, according to their *fine Language*.

To proceed: Our *Bleſſed Saviour* ſaith, (*h*) *If any Man will come after me, let him deny himſelf, and take up his Croſs, and follow me.* But to expreſs it in the Language of the *Stage*, (*i*) *That will be a deviliſh Self-denial.*

Our *Bleſſed Saviour* frequently commends *Faſting* and *Abſtinence*, and (*k*) particularly tells us, that unclean *Spirits* are *caſt out* by it. Upon the *Stage* (*l*) the ſtarving of a Horſe is expreſs'd by his *learning Religion*; and theſe Precepts of *Chriſt* are repreſented as worſe than the *Inquiſition*. For to ſpeak in their Language, (*m*) *The Inquiſition only oppreſſes the Conſcience, but this is againſt the Devil and all.* And thus if even *Chriſt* himſelf

---

(*b*) Wife's Relief, *p.* 27. *l.* 8.
(*c*) Ibid. *p.* 10. *l.* 21.
(*d*) *Rom.* 10. 14——17.
(*e*) *Mat.* 28. 18, 19, 20. *Mark* 16. 15, 16. *Luke* 24. 47, 48.
(*f*) Love's laſt Shift, *p.* 1. *l.* 1. *p.* 8. *l. antepenult.* *p.* 23. *l.* 16. Man of Mode, *p.* 187. *l.* 3.
(*g*) Jane Gray, *p.* 51. *l.* 1.
(*h*) *Mat.* 16. 24. *Mark* 8. 24. *Luke* 9. 23.
(*i*) Humours of the Army, *p.* 57. *l.* 22.
(*k*) *Mat.* 17. 14——22.
(*l*) The Country-Houſe, *p.* 9. *l.* 31.
(*m*) Perplex'd Couple, *p.* 11. *l.* 14.

ſpeaks againſt the Intereſt of the *Devil*, the *Stage* will not endure it. And *Temperance* is alſo thus expoſed by a pretended Prieſt, (*n*) *He that drinks but to ſatisfy Nature, is damn'd.*

In *Scripture*, *Prayer* is repreſented as a chief Act of Religious Worſhip, and due to GOD alone. On the *Stage* it is often paid to other Objects, as to *Pagan Idols*, nay to *Men* and *Women*, and alſo to the *Devil* himſelf, with the moſt humble Poſture of Devotion. The Quotations are almoſt endleſs, and therefore I ſhall omit them. This Word is (*o*) often uſed on the *Stage* upon very unfit Occaſions, and (*p*) ſometimes ridicul'd. Sometimes by (*q*) *Prayer* they mean *Curſing*: ſometimes (*r*) by *giving ear* to a Man's *Prayer*, is meant committing Adultery. An *Actor* alſo (*s*) ſpeaks thus to his Father:

> *The Shrine of all my Off'rings, Pray'rs and Thanks,*
> *And God of my Obedience here on Earth;*
> *O let me bend beneath your Feet for ever,*
> *And kiſs the ſacred Ground your Steps have bleſs'd.*

And (*t*) another ſpeaks thus to his Wife:

> *At this fair Shrine my ev'ry Hour of Life*
> *To come ſhall offer Pray'rs and Penitence,*
> *To render Satisfaction for my Crime.*

In *Scripture* (*u*) we are thus exhorted: *Offer unto GOD Thankſgiving, and pay thy Vows unto the Moſt High; and call upon me in the Day of Trouble.* In the *Play-Houſe* an *Actreſs* ſaith, (*x*) *Offer thy Vows to me.*

In *Scripture* (*y*) we are commanded to *pray without*

(*n*) Unfortunate Dutcheſs of *Malfi*, *p.* 49. *l.* 8.

(*o*) Abra-Mule, *Epilogue l.* 3. Jane Shore, *p.* 17. *l.* 14. Love the Leveller, *Epilogue l. antepen.*

(*p*) The Wonder, *p.* 14. *l.* 23.

(*q*) She wou'd if ſhe cou'd, *p.* 100. *l.* 14.

(*r*) Roving Husband reclaim'd, *p.* 47. *l.* 14.

(*s*) Jane Gray, *p.* 17. *l.* 3.

(*t*) Love and Liberty, *p.* 50. *l.* 25.

(*u*) *Pſal.* 50. 14, 15.

(*x*) The Baſſet-Table, *p.* 57. *l.* 34.

(*y*) 1 *Theſſ.* 5. 17.

ceaſing.

ceasing. On the *Stage* (z) an *Actor* speaking of another's Consent, saith, *I'll ask it without ceasing*.

Our *Blessed Saviour* (a) commands us to *watch and pray, that* we may *not enter into Temptation*, and *may escape* when he enters into *Judgment*. Of this an *Actor* saith, (b) *I have lain in my Bed, watching and praying three whole Nights together, and cursing and swearing six more, and all to no purpose*.

And as GOD is the Object of our *Prayers*, so is he often said to be the Object of our *Devotion*. In *Scripture* (c) a *devout Man, and one that feared GOD continually*, is joined together, as being the same thing. On the *Stage* (d) we hear of paying even hourly *Devotion* to a (e) Woman. And sometimes (f) by *paying Devotion* is meant the committing of Adultery.

The whole Design of the *Scriptures* is (g) to bring Men to *Repentance*, and turn them from their Sins unto GOD. But this is (h) the perpetual Droll of the *Stage*, where it (x) always relates to Man, and (y) the Concern is for such things as are no Crimes at all. Thus one cries out, (z) *Forgive, forgive an humble Penitent*; and yet the Person address'd to, is only a Woman. Here

---

(z) The Country Lasses, *p*. 45. *l*. 3.

(a) *Mat*. 24. 42. & 25. 13. & 26. 41. *Mark* 13. 33, 34, 35, 37. & 14. 38. *Luke* 21. 36.

(b) Wit at a pinch, *p*. 31. *l*. 22.

(c) *Acts* 10. 2.

(d) Comical Lovers, *p*. 29. *l*. 27.

(e) Sir *Courtly Nice*, *p*. 13. *l*. 5. The Drummer, *p*. 40. *l*. 28.

(f) She wou'd if she cou'd, *p*. 97. *l*. 33. *p*. 107. *l*. 11. *p*. 138. *l*. 16.

(g) *Ezek*. 14. 6. & 18. 30. *Mat*. 3. 2, 8, 11. & 4. 17. & 9. 13. *Mark* 1. 4, 5, 15. & 2. 17. & 6. 12. *Luke* 3. 3, 8. & 13. 3, 5. & 15. 7. & 24. 47. *Acts* 2. 38. & 3. 19. & 5. 31. & 8. 22. & 11. 18. & 13. 24. & 17. 30. & 19. 4. & 20. 21. & 26. 20. *Rom*. 2. 4. 2 *Cor*. 7. 9, 10. 2 *Tim*. 2. 25. *Heb*. 6. 1, 6. & 12. 17. 2 *Pet*. 3. 9. *Revel*. 2. 5, 16, 21, 22. & 3. 1, 19.

(h) Rinaldo, *p*. 53. *l*. 15. Faithful General, *p*. 68. *l*. 49.

(x) Injur'd Love, *a Comedy*, *p*. 59. *l*. 30. Irene, *p*. 58. *l*. 29. *British* Enchanters, *p*. 29. *l*. 23. The different Widows, *p*. 23. *l*. 38. Roving Husband reclaim'd, *p*. 43. *l*. 4.

(y) The Artful Husband, *p*. 67. *l*. 34.

(z) Alarbas, *p*. 40. *l*. 12.

(*i*) by a *bitter Repentance* is meant being managed by a Wife. Sometimes (*k*) it ſignifies being willing to be married, or (*l*) ſorry for being married, eſpecially (*m*) becauſe thereby an opportunity of *Whoring* is loſt. And accordingly we are told, (‖) that he who marries in order to live honeſt, makes a bad bargain; ſince he *purchaſeth a ſhort Pleaſure with a long Repentance, and Loſs of Liberty.* Sometimes they decry this Duty in general, and (*) ſometimes apply it to Stage-Intrigues. Thus (*n*) one ſaith, *How deliciouſly a Man lives here, without fear of the Stool of Repentance!* But moſt commonly they encourage one another in Sin, becauſe they conclude they may repent at any time. I ſhall give ſeveral Inſtances at large, to ſhew that it is their frequent Practice.

(*o*) *I thank Heaven, that I have ſo much Grace left, that I can repent, when I have no more Opportunities of being wicked.*

(*p*) *Well, we muſt all ſin, and all repent, and there's an end on't.*

(*q*) *I am the worſt Man in the world at repenting, till the Sin be throughly done.*

(*r*) *I don't know whether I ſhould repent of my Sins, before I am condemn'd to be hang'd, or after.*

(*s*) *A Villain*, but a repenting Villain; *Stuff, which Saints in all Ages have been made of.*

(*t*) A Woman is commended, becauſe *ſhe hath Senſe enough to know, that ſhe may be a Saint, when ſhe cannot be a Sinner.*

(*i*) She wou'd if ſhe cou'd, p. 101. l. 27.

(*k*) Perplex'd Couple, p. 56. l. 12.

(*l*) Marplot, *Epilogue* l. 26. Modiſh Husband, *Epilogue* l. *antepenult.*

(*m*) Gibraltar, p. 38. l. 7.

(‖) Ibid. p. 38. *Sheet* E. l. 7.

(*) Roving Husband reclaim'd, p. 43. l. 4.

(*n*) The Wonder, p. 28. l. 1.

(*o*) Love's laſt Shift, p. 77. l. 11.

(*p*) Comical Lovers, p. 26. l. 7.

(*q*) Ibid. p. 51. l. antepenult.

(*r*) Humours of the Army, p. 60. l. 28.

(*s*) Provok'd Wife, p. 70. l. 12.

(*t*) The Wife's Relief, p. 53. l. 23.

I'd

(*) *I'd give half my Estate, to have that Fellow's Throat cut; I'd fling that Sin into the Scale, and repent in gross.*

[Let thy Goodness, and Forbearance, and Long-suffering, O LORD, lead them to Repentance, before it is too late.]

The *Scriptures* (u) require of us *Sincerity* in all our Duties. This is condemn'd (x) upon the *Stage* as (y) unsuccessful, and called (z) *the passionate Nonsense of Sincerity.* I shall add also some Quotations on this Subject.

(a) *To repent of Follies past, and be sincerely honest, is the only way to procure Contempt.*

(b) *Sincere! O hideous! What a thing have you named? No, no, Sir! Well-bred People are never sincere. 'Tis modish to flatter, lye and deceive. I hate your out-of-fashion'd good Qualities. Sincerity is altogether of vulgar Extraction.*

(c) *Give me as much Pleasure, I say, as my Constitution requires; as much Wit and Sincerity, as will qualify me for Company; and just as much Morality, as will secure me from the Talons of the Law; and let Fortune take her Chance.*

But beside the Ordinances of GOD, there are three things which are of the utmost use to us in a *Religious Life*; namely, *Reason*, *Conscience*, and *Consideration.*

As for our *Reason*, in this we differ from the Beasts of the Earth, and (d) in this we are made after the *Image* of GOD. This (e) upon the *Stage* is not only call'd *a Bubble*, but is reckon'd worse than Brutality.

(*) Ibid. p. 57. l. 16.

(u) *Jos.* 24. 14. 1 *Cor.* 5. 8. 2 *Cor.* 1. 12. & 2. 17. & 8. 8. *Ephes.* 6. 24. *Philip.* 1. 10. *Tit.* 2. 7. 1 *Pet.* 2. 1, 2.

(x) *Portsmouth* Heiress, *p.* 5. *l. penult. &c.*

(y) The Masquerade, *p.* 1. *l.* 11.

(z) Ibid. *p.* 9. *l.* 2, 5.

(a) Love at first sight, *p.* 64. *l.* 25.

(b) Perplex'd Couple, *p.* 7. *l.* 7.

(c) *Portsmouth* Heiress, *p.* 5. *l.* 13.

(d) *Gen.* 1. 26, 27.

(e) Perplex'd Couple, *p.* 36. *l.* 25.

(*f*) *Do you prefer your Nature to your Reason?* Answ. *Yes.* Reply. *Why?* Answ. *Because my Nature makes me merry, my Reason makes me mad.*

As for a *good Conscience*, it is what the *Scriptures* constantly recommend (*g*) to us, as the chief Cause of our Comfort and Hope. The Definitions of *Conscience* on the *Stage* are very different. One saith (*h*) that *Conscience is a domestick Thief.* And (*i*) another calls it, *The Childrens Bauble.* And the Inferences are as remarkable.

(*k*) *Prithee, Woman, what have we to do with Conscience? It is time enough to talk of that, when we have got an Estate.*

(*l*) *Conscience is the Childrens Bauble. Will Conscience keep a Coach and Six? Will Conscience buy a Title? Will Conscience maintain a grand Equipage? Will Conscience make a Courtier? O fie! fie! fie! Conscience is good for nothing at all: it is like a Ruff, out of the fashion.*

(*m*) *Conscience! Dost talk of Conscience, Friend? Where hast thou learnt that damn'd Fanatick Cant; fram'd to keep Fools and Blockheads still in awe, and make the Slaves of Chance the Slaves of Will?*

(*n*) *Qualms and Strugglings, which Fools call Conscience.*

> (*o*) *I question not but your Religious Dotards,*
> *Who mortify, and feed on barren Virtue,*
> *Were they to know these Deeds, would call me Villain.*
> *But let them rail, and pride themselves in Conscience;*
> *Whilst I each Bliss within my Grasp surprize,*
> *I'll leave to them Reversions in the Skies.*

(*f*) Provok'd Wife, *p.* 11. *l.* 26.

(*g*) *Acts* 23. 1. & 24. 16. *Rom.* 13. 5. 2 *Cor.* 1. 12. 1 *Tim.* 1. 5, 19. 2 *Tim.* 1. 3. *Heb.* 10. 22. & 13. 18. 1 *Pet.* 2. 19. & 3. 16.

(*h*) Love for Love, *p.* 43. *l.* 32.

(*i*) The Artful Husband, *p.* 29. *l.* *antepenult.*

(*k*) A Woman's Revenge, *p.* 25. *l.* 3.

(*l*) The Artful Husband, *p.* 29. *l.* 33.

(*m*) Earl of *Mar* marr'd, *p.* 3. *l.* 26.

(*n*) Faithful Bride of *Granada*, *p.* 20. *l.* 2.

(*o*) Perfidious Brother, *p.* 23. *l.* 5.

Reli-

(p) *Religion! Ay, there's another Topick now! Religion and Reformation! Two things that make a mighty Bustle in the World, without any considerable Progress; preach'd up every where, and follow'd no where.* (We may thank the Stage for that!) *Prithee, what has Religion to do with a Man of Figure? Conscience resides among poor Rogues; Men of Dignity are above it.*

(q) *Conscience, they say, has a Sting; but has not Love a greater? O Yes! Villains can suffer Shame, and live after it; but Lovers cannot brook Despair.* (†) *By your favour, Conscience, 'tis very necessary for my Quiet.*

(r) *The squeamish Fears of idle Conscience.*

(s) *No, my Conscience shan't starve me neither.*

(t) *And now, Conscience, I defy thee.*

(u) *I have been in a lamentable Fright, Sir, ever since your Conscience had the Impudence to intrude into your Company.* Answ. *Be at peace; it will come there no more: I have kick'd it down stairs.*

It is observable, that these Expressions come from the *Poets* chief Favourite, who was rewarded with the utmost Success at last, by marrying according to his Desire, and obtaining thereby two thousand Pounds *per annum*. And the Morality of the *Play*, which may be learnt, is this:

That younger Brothers should be careful to run out their Fortunes as fast, and as ill as they can; then petition their elder Brothers for a Maintenance: and if this be refused, they may make no conscience of cheating such Brothers to the utmost, and this is the way to raise their Fortunes again. For, as he blasphemously applies it, (x) *Providence takes care of Men of Merit.*

The third Help to a Religious Life is (||) *Consideration*

(p) *Portsmouth* Heiress, *p.* 6. *l.* 9.

(q) Ibid. *p.* 26. *l.* 3.

(†) The Maid the Mistress, *p.* 17. *l.* 25.

(r) Pretender's Flight, *p.* 25. *l. antepenult.*

(s) The Relapse, *p.* 12. *l.* 33.

(t) Ibid. *p.* 28. *l.* 34.

(u) Ibid. *p.* 28. *l.* 40.

(x) The Relapse, *p.* 12. *l.* 14.

(||) *Gen.* 24. 63. *Josh.* 1. 8. *Psal.* 1. 2. & 5. 1. & 19. 14. & 49. 3. & 63. 6. & 77. 12. & 104. 34. & 119. 15, 23, 48, 78, 97, 99, 148. & 143. 5. 1 *Tim.* 4. 15.

or *Meditation.* This is often (y) pressed upon us in the Holy Scriptures, for this (z) very End and Purpose. It is confirm'd by (a) Examples, (b) the Character of a blessed Man, and (c) *David* tells us the Effect of this Duty upon his own Life. But the Language of the Stage is very particular on this occasion. A rambling Expression is (d) a *Contemplation.* By (e) *Meditation* is either meant a Contrivance for *Whoredom* and *Adultery*, or the actual Commission of it; or at least the plotting how to carry on a leud Design, or a base Intrigue: and the same may also be said of (*) *Contemplation*. But when these words are taken in a good Sense, the *Actors* express themselves thus:

> (f) *The noble Savage takes Revenge at will*
> *Nor from past Actions ever feels Remorse:*
> *'Tis only Man that's plagu'd with Thought.*
> (g) *Every serious Thought is so much Time wasted.*
> (h) *Hang Thinking.*
> (i) *Banish Consideration: 'Tis as inconsistent with the Gentlemen of this Age, as Devotion.*

But neither *Reason*, nor *Conscience*, nor *Consideration*, is sufficient without the *Grace* of GOD to make them effectual. This was (k) promised by the *Prophets* as the

---

(y) *Deut.* 4. 39. & 8. 5. & 32. 5, 29. *Job* 37. 14. *Psal.* 50. 22. & 119. 15, 23, 48, 78, 95, 97, 99, 148. *Eccles.* 5. 1. *Isa.* 1. 3. & 5. 12. & 41. 20, 22. & 43. 18. *Hag.* 1. 5. 1 *Tim.* 4. 15. 2 *Tim.* 3. 7. *Heb.* 3. 1. & 7. 4. & 10. 24. & 12. 3.

(z) 2 *Sam.* 12. 24. *Ezek.* 12. 3. & 18. 14, 28.

(a) *Gen.* 24. 64.

(b) *Psal.* 1. 2.

(c) *Psal.* 119. 59.

(d) The Metamorphosis, *p.* 17. *l.* 2.

(e) Amorous Widow, *p.* 20. *l.* 6. *p.* 27. *l.* 35. False Friend, *p.* 24. *l.* 1. Generous Husband, *p.* 23. *l.* 14. Lying Lover, *p.* 45. *l.* 8.

(*) Fair Quaker of *Deal*, *p.* 13. *l.* 24. The Metamorphosis, *p.* 17. *l.* 2.

(f) Faithful Bride of *Granada*, *p.* 20. *l.* 4.

(g) Humours of the Age, *p.* 26. *l.* 2.

(h) The Lying Lover, *p.* 39. *l. antepenult.*

(i) Vice reclaim'd, *p.* 27. *l.* 35.

(k) *Zech.* 12. 10. 1 *Pet.* 1. 10.

Privilege of the Gospel; and is (*l*) the Gift of GOD, which (*m*) came by *Jesus Christ*. This is (*n*) sufficient for us, (*o*) to turn us from Sin unto GOD. This is (*p*) the Ground of all our Hope. By this (*q*) we are justified, and (*r*) shall be saved. And to this Grace of GOD (*s*) all that we do or have is ascribed. By Grace in *Scripture* is meant the Favour of GOD; in the Play-House it signifies (*t*) the Favour of a Prince; and (*u*) applied to the Transactions there, when an *Actor* saith of himself, *I have abundance of Grace in me, that I find.*

But the worst is yet behind. In *Scripture* (æ) *the Grace of GOD, which bringeth Salvation, teacheth us to deny Ungodliness and worldly Lusts, and to live soberly.* In the *Play-House* it hath a contrary Turn. Here it is an accomplish'd Character, (*) for a Man (as they say) to *swear with such a Grace, as would make another's Heart leap to hear him.* And (†) when another refuseth to be a *Whore* for Money, it is imputed to want of *Grace.* Thus an *Actress* saith, (*x*) *I am call'd by the Name of her, who was an Example of Chastity.* But the Answer is, *I hope you have more Grace, than to let it go farther than your Name.* And (*y*) another saith, *The Day of Grace is expired:* the meaning whereof is, a Woman can have patience no longer with one, who will not make her a Whore.

In another *Comedy* (‖) the utmost Perfection of *Grace* is lodg'd in an *affected amorous old Widow.* In (*z*) another, *Phædra* reads her Husband a Lesson of Obedience to her, gives him several Directions for this

(*l*) *Psal* 84. 11.
(*m*) *John* 1. 17.
(*n*) 2 *Cor.* 12. 19.
(*o*) *Acts* 26. 18.
(*p*) 2 *Thess.* 2. 16.
(*q*) *Rom.* 2. 24. *Tit.* 3. 7.
(*r*) *Rom.* 5. 21. *Ephes.* 2. 5, 8. *Tit.* 2. 11.
(*s*) 1 *Cor.* 15. 10.
(*t*) Irene, *p.* 58. *l.* 29.
(*u*) The Comical Lovers, *p.* 58. *l.* 17.
(æ) *Tit.* 2. 11, 12.
(*) The Drummer, *p.* 26. *l.* 11.
(†) A Woman's Revenge, *p.* 31. *l.* 23, *ult.*
(*x*) The Cares of Love, *p.* 10. *l. antepenult.*
(*y*) Injur'd Love, *a Comedy*, *p.* 16. *l.* 24.
(‖) The Biter, *p.* 5. *l.* 23.
(*z*) Solon, *p.* 26. *l.* 31.

purpose,

purpose, and then concludes thus; *Be sure remember what hath been said, and may* Juno *give you Grace to apply it aright.* Here *Preaching* is ridicul'd, the *Honour* due to GOD is given to a *Pagan Goddess*, and the Notion of *Grace* expos'd; so that there is a triple Discharge against *Religion* in a single Sentence.

It is impossible in modern Words to express a just Resentment of such dreadful Profaneness, and therefore I shall only add the Words of (z) the Apostle: *There are certain Men crept in unawares, who were before of old ordained to this Condemnation, ungodly Men, turning the Grace of our GOD into Lasciviousness, and denying the only LORD GOD, and our Lord Jesus Christ. But these speak evil of those things which they know not; but what they know naturally as brute Beasts, in those things they corrupt themselves.*

[From the Punishment, which such daring Impieties do deserve, Good LORD deliver us.]

(z) Jude, *ver.* 4, 10.

CHAP.

CHAP. X.

The Liturgy, and the Articles of the Christian Faith, burlesqued by the Stage.

AS the *Bible*, and the Grand Truths of *Religion*, cannot escape the Severity of our *Stage-Poets* Reflections; so it is the less wonder that they make bold with our *Liturgy*, and ridicule many Expressions in the Form appointed for our publick Devotions. But if the Fear of GOD cannot restrain the one, it cannot be expected that any Regard to Man, or the *Penalty* of (*a*) the *Statute* against *depraving* the *Common-Prayer*, can restrain the other.

To begin with *Baptism*. This is (*b*) a *Sacrament* instituted by *Christ* himself, whereby we are admitted into the visible *Church*, *in the Name of the Father, and of the Son, and of the Holy Ghost*; whereby our Sins are remitted, and we are made Members of *Christ*, the Children of GOD, and Inheritors of the Kingdom of *Heaven*. And if we were not worse than *Heathens*, we should always value that Ordinance which made us *Christians*. But yet an *Actor* speaks of it in a most vile manner; (*c*) *They led me to a neighbouring Horse-Pond, and there baptiz'd me.*

In *Baptism* our *Church* requires *Godfathers* and *Godmothers*, as Sureties for the Religious Education of the baptiz'd Child. These are supposed by some Divines to be (*d*) the *faithful Witnesses* mentioned in the Prophet *Isaiah*; but it is certain, that they were in the *Primitive Church*. This upon the *Stage* is apply'd to a

(*a*) 1 Eliz. chap. 2.

(*b*) *Mat.* 28. 19. *Mark* 16. 16. *Acts* 2. 38. & 22. 16. *Rom.* 6. 3, 4. *Gal.* 3. 27. *Col.* 2. 12. 1 *Pet.* 3. 21.

(*c*) The Perplex'd Couple, *p.* 41. *l.* 26.

(*d*) *Isa.* 8. 2.

lend

leud Purpoſe; and on ſuch an Occaſion, one *Actor* tells another (*e*),

I have been a kind of Godfather to you yonder: I have promis'd and vow'd ſomething in your Name, which I think you are bound to perform.

The firſt thing which the *Godfathers* promiſe in behalf of the Child, is, That he ſhall renounce the *Devil* and all his Works. This is ſo directly contrary to the *Play-Houſe* Deſign and Intereſt, that they take care, if poſſible, to render it ineffectual. Thus (*f*) an *Actreſs* ſpeaks of a Woman to another; *She is in a brave way of defying you, and all your Works:* and yet they were contracted at leaſt in Marriage at the end of the *Play*. Another ſaith, (*g*) *Swearing and Lying are a ſort of Godfathers in Love.* The Application of the Metaphor is, What they do is profane, and we muſt not give any credit to it.

In another *Play* (*h*) two *Engliſh Colonels* declare, that they *renounce all Women, except* one, *as heartily as ever they renounc'd the Devil.* But leſt they ſhould be ſuppoſed to have really renounced the *Devil*, they explain their Meaning in other places of the ſame *Play*; That (*i*) *none but Madmen are in love with one particular Object*, and that (*k*) *Marriage and Conſtancy* is a *purchaſing of long Repentance with the Expence of Liberty.* This is the ſame in effect as if they had ſaid, 'Tis true, in their *Baptiſmal Vow* they renounced the *Devil*, but it was never done heartily: At beſt it was a mad Trick, it might have coſt them their Liberty, and they are ſorry for it ever ſince. And (*l*) another ſaith, *I have no buſineſs to keep me from the Temptation of the World, the Fleſh, and ſo forth: Therefore prithee, dear Infernal, take me into thy Service, and my Soul is thine, without any more ado.*

(*e*) The Old Batchelor, *p.* 49.
(*f*) Man of Mode, *p.* 212. *l.* 33.
(*g*) *Portſmouth* Heireſs, *p.* 49. *l.* 13.
(*h*) Gibraltar, *Sheet* E. *p.* 36 *l.* 34.
(*i*) Ibid. *p.* 3. *l.* 3.
(*k*) Ibid. *Sheet* E. *p.* 38. *l.* 7.
(*l*) *Portſmouth* Heireſs, *p.* 10. *l.* 24.

The

The next thing which our *Godfathers* promise, is, That we shall believe all the *Articles* of the *Christian Faith*. The words of the Answer are, *All this I stedfastly believe.* Upon the *Stage*, (m) an *Actor* saith, *All this I firmly believe, and am resolved to die in this Faith.* And if we would know what great Truth this is which is thus assented to, it is, that the *Actresses* are all *Hypocrites.*

It was the Wisdom of our Reformers, to compose a *Catechism* to be learn'd by Children, in which the Nature of their *Baptismal Vow* should be taught them betimes, and they should learn their Obligation to a Religious Life from thence. Upon the *Stage*, (n) the word *Catechism* is applied to *Love-Intrigues.* And because our *Catechism* begins with this Question, *What is your Name?* therefore (o) when an *Actor* saith of another, *He has Religion enough to say his Catechism*, he means no more than telling his Name; as if that was sufficient, and Men should trouble their Heads no farther.

In our *Confession* and *Litany*, we acknowledge, that we are *miserable Sinners:* which Words are (p) also made the Jest of the *Playhouse.*

Immediately after our Confession follows a most excellent *Absolution*, which, when rightly used, is a Privilege (q) given by *Christ* himself for the Good of the *Church.* But this is ridicul'd upon the *Stage*, to make the Ministry itself more contemptible.

Thus it is (r) said of an *Actor*, that his *Heaven*, *at least his Priest, is his Claret Glass; for to that he confesses all his Sins, and from it receives Absolution and Comfort.*

In another *Play*, a pretended *Priest* offers an *Absolution* both to a Waiting-Maid, and a Highway-Man, and a vile use is made of it on both Occasions. The one hardens herself in Sin thereby, and the other rejects it with Scorn and Contempt.

(m) Woman is a Riddle, *p.* 30. *l.* 22.

(n) Love for Love, *p.* 27. *l.* 37. The Fair Example, *p.* 61. *l.* 26. The Wonder, *p.* 50. *l.* 2.

(o) The Female Advocates, *p.* 17. *l.* 6.

(p) The Generous Husband, *p.* 51. *l.* 6.

(q) *Matth.* 16. 19. *John* 20. 23.

(r) Sir Courtly Nice, *p.* 12. *l.* 37.

The *Priest* (s) sollicits the Waiting-Maid to bring a *Count* into her Mistress's Closet, and leave them together. She scruples it, because *it would be a Sin.* He answers, (t) *I will give you an Absolution for the Sin:* and she consenting, saith, (u) *Well, Doctor, your Religion is so pure! Methinks I'm so easy after an Absolution, and can sin afresh with so much Security, that I am resolved to die a Martyr to it.* And on this occasion both the *Priesthood* and the *Liturgy* is become the Droll of a Serving-Man: (x) *There has been the Doctor with a Temptation in one Hand, and an Absolution in the other, and Gipsey has sold herself to the Devil.*

As to the *Highway-Man*, he tells the Priest, *You come before your time; I am not condemn'd yet.* But yet the other presently answers, without any farther Questions, (y) *I'll give you an Absolution.* To which the other some time after replies, *Then you and your Absolution may go to the Devil.*

The next Instance is our *Litany*, which they thus expose.

(z) *From all such Petticoat Devils, deliver us, I pray.*
(a) *By the Spirit in this Wand,*
Which the Silver Moon commands.
By the powerful God of Night,
By the Love of Amphitrite.
(b) *By all the Powers of Earth, and those of Hell;*
By the infernal King, the Fates and Furies.
(c) *By those sad Sighs, by those poor streaming Eyes,*
By that dear Love, which makes us now unhappy,
By the near Danger of that precious Life.
(d) *By all the Pain that wings my tortur'd Soul,*
By all the dear deceitful Hopes you gave me.
(e) *By all my Zeal, by all my anxious Cares,*

(s) The Beaux Stratagem, *p.* 45. l. 34.
(t) *Lin. antepenult.*
(u) Ibid. *p.*46. *l.*19.
(x) Ibid. *p.*48. *l.*27.
(y) Ibid. *p.*62. *l.*28.
(z) *Sawny* the *Scot*, *p.* 3. *l.* 28.
(a) Alarbas, *p.*25. *l.*26.
(b) *Appius* and *Virginia*, *p.*9. *l.* 18.
(c) *Phædra* and *Hippolytus*, *p.* 18. *l.*8.
(d) Ibid. *p.*32. *l.*6.
(e) Ibid. *p.*53. *l.*19.

By those unhappy Crimes I wrought to serve you,
By those old wither'd Limbs and hoary Hairs,
By all my Tears.

I shall now proceed to the *Creed*, which we commonly call the *Apostles Creed*, or the *Articles* of the *Christian Faith*, which begins with these words, *I believe in GOD.* On the *Stage*, GOD is excluded as the Object of our *Faith*, and an *Actress* saith of her Lover, (*f*) *I only will believe in my* Antonio.

Another saith, (*g*) *I am a downright believing Puppy.* Another tells us, that (*h*) *Faith is the main Point of Religion*; but then by *Religion* he means only an Intrigue, as if all *Religion* consisted in that. Another (*i*) saith of a Man, *He is grown such an Atheist of late, he'll believe nothing.* But this is spoken only of a Trifle, and yet express'd as if every such thing is a GOD. Another saith, (*k*) *You believe me on my Journey to Hell*; and is thus answer'd, *You have a strong Faith, and that may contribute much toward your Salvation:* as if the *Faith* whereby we are saved was so insignificant. And (*l*) another saith, upon a very poor occasion, *All this I firmly believe, and am resolved to die in that Faith.* One saith of a Woman, (*m*) *Her Beauty will make thy Joys immortal.* The answer is, *I can't believe either in the Immortality of her Beauty, or your Passion.* But the Reply is, *Look on her then, and be converted.* Thus the Joys of *Heaven* are debased, the *Creed* profaned, a Woman is made a Goddess, and the Scripture-Expressions are applied to her at the same time. And another saith, (*n*) *Here's trying a Man's Faith indeed! What, Do you think I had the Faith of a Stock or of a Stone?* As if Stupidity

(*f*) The Conquest of *Spain*, *p.*52. *l.*31.
(*g*) The Lady's Last Stake, *p.* *p.*28. *l.*11.
(*h*) Marplot, *p.*56. *l.*26.
(*i*) The Provok'd Wife, *p.*65. *l. penult.*
(*k*) The Man of Mode, *p.*186. *l.* 9.
(*l*) Woman is a Riddle, *p.*30. *l.* 29.
(*m*) The Country Lasses, *p.* 41. *l.*4.
(*n*) The Comical Lovers, *p.* 40. *l.*1.

was ſo great an Excellency. Here (*p*) *Faith*, (*q*) *Unbelief*, and (*r*) *Believing* ſoars no higher than the *Stage*; and (*s*) *Infidelity* is of the ſame nature. An (*t*) *Infidel* or an (*u*) *Unbeliever* is alſo one, who values not the *Amours* or *Intrigues* which are carried on in that place. And thus they deal in general terms by the *Chriſtian Faith*.

In the ſecond Part of the *Creed* we have an Account of the *Death* of *Chriſt*: He was *crucified*. To turn this into Ridicule, an *Actor* ſaith upon the *Stage*, (*a*) *Then I'll be crucified*. The End for which he ſhed his Blood, was for the Salvation of Mankind; and therefore he can never be ſufficiently loved, admired and adored by us. The *Actors* (*b*) ſpeak thus of a Woman:

To Amarillis *your Devotion pay. The Balſam that heal'd your Woes flow'd from her rich Veins. Each Drop is a Ranſom for a Prince.*

And now, how muſt it grieve us to obſerve, that in a *Chriſtian* Nation, the *Son of GOD* is *crucified afreſh, and put to open Shame?* Our total Deſtruction cannot make amends for theſe things, if GOD ſhould enter into Judgment. The *Poets* know how to uſe other words, if they thought fit; but they rack their Invention to be as profane and blaſphemous as poſſible, eſpecially if they can but find a way to eſcape with Impunity.

(*p*) The Artful Husband, *p*.10. *l*.30. *p*.28. *l*.20. The Careleſs Husband, *p*.58. *l*.35. The Cid, *p*.3. *l*.10. Marplot, *p*.56. *l*.26. The Comical Lovers, *p*.39. *l*. *antepenult*. *p*.40. *l*.1. The Provok'd Wife, *p*.67. *l*. 1. The Sultaneſs, *p*.28. *l*.35.

(*q*) The Cruel Gift, *p*. 62. *l*. 26.

(*r*) The Artful Husband, *p*.10. *l*. 32,33. The Wife's Relief, *p*. 14. *l*.30.

(*s*) The Perplex'd Couple, *p*. 57. *l*.28. *Portſmouth* Heireſs, *p*.52. *l*.3. The Wife's Relief, *p*.14. *l*.30. The Wonder, *p*.33. *l*. 5.

(*t*) The Artful Husband, *p*.28. *l*.18. The different Widows, *p*. 45. *l*. 3. The Double Gallant, *p*.29. *l*.1. Vice Reclaim'd, *p*.21. *l*. *ult*. *p*.55. *l*.32.

(*u*) Injur'd Love, *a Tragedy*, *p*.17. *l*.17.

(*a*) The Provok'd Wife, p. 56. l.23.

(*b*) The Fickle Shepherdeſs, p.44. l.26.

In

In the last Part of our *Creed* are contained the two grand Motives to a religious Life, namely, the *Resurrection* of the Body, and the *Life Everlasting*. As for the *Resurrection*, it may be proved from (c) several plain Texts of *Scripture*. However, our *Poets* would fain insinuate the contrary. The being in a Dungeon is called, (d) being *buried in everlasting Darkness*. *Death* is called (e) *a sinking never to rise again*; (f) *lying for ever in the Grave*, and not *waking again to feel such racking Tortures*; (g) a *shrinking into the Arms of Death, and sleeping for ever*; (h) a *sleeping to Eternity*; (i) *sleeping so sound, that they never wake*; (k) *sleeping for ever in the Grave*, and (l) being *sunk for ever in endless Night*. One saith, (m) *Death seals up the Eyes for ever*. And another saith of an *Actress*, supposed to be dead, (n) *We'll bury her deep enough, and she shall rise at the Devil's Arse of the Peak*.

As for the *Life Everlasting*, nothing can be more plain. It is the Encouragement proposed for all our Duties, the End of all our Hopes; and (o) *Christianity* itself, without it, would be the most wretched State. And it is so plainly (p) reveal'd, that it never admitted of any dispute. However, the *Poets* would fain teach us

(c) *Job* 19. 25, 26. *John* 5. 28, 29. *and John* 11. 25. *Acts* 17. 18, 31. *Acts* 23. 6. *Acts* 24. 15, 21. *Rom.* 8. 11. 1 *Cor.* 15. *per totum.* 1 *Thes.* 4. 16, 17.

(d) The Faithful Bride of *Granada*, p. 43. l. 24.

(e) Abra-Mule, p. 59. l. 12.

(f) Faithful Bride of *Granada*, p. 29. l. 12.

(g) Perfidious Brother, p. 29. l. 31.

(h) Perplex'd Lovers, p. 29. l. 28.

(i) Recruiting Officer, p. 59. l. 28.

(k) The Royal Convert, p. 68. l. 24.

(l) Zelmane, p. 36. l. 3.

(m) *Persian* Princess, p. 16. l. 20.

(n) *Sawny* the *Scot*, p. 67. l. 29.

(o) 1 *Cor.* 15. 19.

(p) *Matth.* 19. 16, 29. *Mat.* 25. 46. *Mark* 10. 17, 30. *Luke* 10. 25. *Luke* 18. 18, 30. *Joh.* 3. 15, 16, 36. *Joh.* 4. 14. *Joh.* 5. 24, 39. *Joh.* 6. 27, 40, 47, 51, 54, 58, 68. *John* 10. 28. *John* 12. 25, 50. *John* 17. 2, 3. *Acts* 13. 46, 48. *Rom.* 2. 7. *Rom.* 5. 21. *Rom.* 6. 22, 23. *Gal.* 6. 8. 1 *Thes.* 4. 17. 1 *Tim.* 1. 16. 1 *Tim.* 6. 12, 19. *Tit.* 1. 2. *Tit.* 3. 7. 1 *John* 2. 17, 25. 1 *John* 5. 11, 13. *Jude*, *ver.* 21.

the contrary. Sometimes they ridicule it; and by (q) being *immortal*, they only mean being hang'd. Thus they say, (r) *He that is committed to* Newgate, *is in a fair way to Immortality.* Sometimes they doubt of it: Thus (s) one asks,

> *Who can resolve me, what's beyond this Span?*
> *Perhaps I may return to my first Nothing.*

And sometimes they roundly deny it. Thus (t) we are told, that *Nature produces nothing that is immortal, but a Chancery-Suit.*

But the daily Method is to insinuate the contrary, by speaking of the things in this World, as if they were eternal, immortal, and everlasting. Thus they strain their Hyperboles into Profaneness, and so to draw insensibly the Minds of the Auditors from the other World, because the excellent things which are spoken of that, is applied to this. This is a sly and a subtle Poison; end is the more dangerous, because it is the less observed. For this reason I shall be the larger in the References in the Margin.

Sometimes when they only mean at most for so long a space of time as the World lasts, they call it (u) *Eter-*

(q) The Lying Lover, p. 49. l. 19.

(r) The fine Lady's Airs, p. 16. l. 25.

(s) The Conquest of *Spain.* p. 66. l. 22.

(t) The Successful Pirate, p. 13. l. 15.

(u) *Cinna*'s Conspiracy, p. 19. l. *penult.* *Jane Gray*, p. 65. l. 14. Irene, p. 6. l. 23. p. 14. l. 14. Love the Leveller, p. 34. l. 20. Manlius Capitolinus, p. 57. l. 15. Marry or do worse, p. 2. l. 21. Oedipus, p. 10. l. 18. *Rosamond*, p. 3. l. 3. Solon, p. 11. l. *antepenult.* p. 12. l. 8. The Amorous Miser, p. 7. l. 7. *British* Enchanters, p. 38. l. 20. The Cares of Love, p. 5. l. 6. The Comical Revenge, p. 58. l. 12. The Conquest of *Spain*, p. 36. l. 33. p. 65. l. 35. The Faithful General, p. 29. l. *penult.* p. 58. l. 11. The Maid the Mistress, p. 4. l. 32. The Mistake, p. 22. l. 19. p. 47. l. *penult* and *ult.* The Royal Merchant, *Epilogue*, l. 26. Successful Pirate, p. 35. l. 19. Ulysses, p. 28. l. 3.

nal,

nal, (*x*) *Eternally*, (*y*) *Everlasting*, (*z*) *For Ever*, or, (*a*) *Immortal*.

Sometimes when they mean only, for so long a space of Time as a Person speaking or spoken to lives, they call it (*b*) *Endless*, (*c*) *Eternal*, ——— *Eter-*

(*x*) The Tender Husband, p. 30. l. 8.

(*y*) Liberty Asserted, p. 24. l. 5. Love and Liberty, p. 53. l. 24. Manlius Capitolinus, p. 48. l. 13. *Phædra* and *Hippolytus*, p. 23. l. 23. The City Ramble, p. 64. l. 19. Conquest of *Spain*, p. 28. l. 28. The Faithful Bride of *Granada*, p. 41. l. 19.

(*z*) Love the Leveller, p. 34. l. 20. The Conquest of *Spain*, *Epilogue*, l. 9. The Cruel Gift, p. 20. *l.* 18.

(*a*) *French* Cato, *Prologue*, l. 10. Hamlet, p. 88. l. *antepenult*. Hydaspes, p. 44. l. 16. Injur'd Love, *a Comedy*, p. 59. l. 41. Irene, p. 8. l. 28. Love and Liberty, p. 57. l. *penult*. *Phædra* and *Hippolytus*, p. 34. l. 26. Solon, p. 56. l. 33. The Careless Husband, p. 63. l. 6. The Conquest of *Spain*, p. 2. l. 30. The Cruel Gift, p. 10. l. *ult*. The Distressed Mother, p. 20. l. 8. The Generous Husband, p. 31. l. 8. The Man of Mode, p. 190. l. 33. p. 243. l. 1. The Succesful Pirate, *Prologue*, l. 17. The Sultaness, p. 25. l. 11.

(*b*) *Phædra* and *Hippolytus*, p. 36. l. 6. Conquest of *Spain*, p. 14. l. 35. The Cruel Gift, p. 1. l. *antepenult*. *Portsmouth* Heiress, p. 46. *l. ult*.

(*c*) Cato, p. 37. l. 25. *French* Cato, p. 8. l. 15. p. 15. l. 6. p. 31. l. 6. p. 44. l. 5. p. 47. l. 6. Fortune in her Wits, p. 19. l. *ult*. Hamlet, p. 12. l. *penult*. Injur'd Love, *a Comedy*, p. 57. l. 37. Irene, p. 26. l. 26. p. 38. l. 11. Liberty asserted, p. 4. l. 32. Love and Liberty, p. 13. l. 32. p. 48. l. 34. Love at first sight, p. 58. l. 17. p. 63. l. 29. Marry or do worse, p. 6. l. 21. p. 64. l. 14. *Phædra* and *Hippolytus*, p. 16. l. 4. p. 36. l. 6. *Pyrrhus* and *Demetrius*, p. 50. l. 12. Rinaldo, p. 27. l. 7. Sir Courtly Nice, p. 2. l. 6. p. 40. l. 22. *twice*. Solon, p. 64. l. 20. The Amorous Widow, p. 10. l. 17. Love's last Shift, p. 40. l. 28. p. 41. l. 37. p. 54. l. 10. The Apparition, p. 55. l. 32. The Artful Husband, p. 10. l. 17. *British* Enchanters, p. 16. l. 10. p. 35. l. 34. The careless Husband, p. 45. l. *penult*. p. 51. l. 23. Cobler of *Preston*, p. 5. l. 18. p. 21. l. 10. The comical Lovers, p. 10. l. 26. p. 27. l. 7. The comical Revenge, p. 58. l. 12. The Confederacy, p. 24. l. 5. Conquest of *Spain*, p. 7. l. 28. p. 31. l. 9. The Contrivances, p. 5. l. 19. The different Widows, p. 52. l. *antepenult*, p. 57. l. 26. The distressed Mother, p. 10. l. 9. The double Gallant, p. 17. l. 2. Fair Quaker of *Deal*, p. 1. l. 21. The faithful Bride of *Granada*, p. 13. l. 16. p. 40. l. 27. The faithful General, p. 27. l. *penult*. p. 34. l. 51.

(*d*) *Eternally*, (*e*) *Ever*, (*f*) *Everlasting*, (*g*) *Everlastingly*, (*h*) *Everliving*, (*i*) *For Ever*, ——— ——— *For*

l. 51. p. 45. l. 37. p.62. l. *ult.* p. 63. l. 13. p. 70. l. 16. The False Friend, p.22. l.21. p.58. l. *ult.* The Fatal Marriage, p. 124. l.21. Fickle Shepherdess, p.18. l.5. p.37. l.13. Force of Friendship, p. 6. l. 22. p.27. l. *antepenult.* The General cashier'd, p. 32. l. 8. Generous Husband, p. 14. l.6. Humours of the Age, p. 45. l. 24. The Maid the Mistress, p.2. l.27. p. 40. l.17. Man of Mode, p.191. l.28. Perplex'd Couple, p. 58. l.23. Perplex'd Lovers, p. 42. l.26. *Portsmouth* Heiress, p.28. l. 10. The Pretender's Flight, p.27. l.20. Provok'd Wife, *Epilogue*, l.25. The Relapse, p.3. l.2. p.18. l.8. Royal Convert, p. 74. l. 26. The School-Boy, p.17. l. *ult.* p.31. l. 5. The Sultaness, p.20. l.35. p.28. l.35. The Victim, p. 19. l. 16. p.30. l.21. The Wife's Relief, p. 68. l.12. Ulysses, p. 19. l. 28. p. 59. l.6.

(*d*) Marplot, *Prologue*, l. 10. Love at first Sight, p. 49. l. 28. p. 51. l. 8. p.62. l.33. Squire Trelooby, p. 54. l. 23. Artful Husband, p. 5. l. 21. Careless Husband, p.38. l.31. The comical Lovers, p.9. l.9. Country Lasses, p. 2. l. 25. p. 24. l. 18. Fair Quaker of *Deal*, p.1. l.21. Faithful Bride of *Granada*, p.13. l.16. p.40. l. 27. The Gamester, p.45. l.16. p.67. l.1. Generous Husband, p.6. l.30. p.27. l.15. The Maid the Mistress, p. 5. l.32. Man of Mode, p.200. *l.*16. The Mistake, p.42. *l.* 25. Perfidious Brother, p. 49. l. 5. Perplex'd Couple, p. 57. l. 27. The Roving Husband reclaim'd, p.33. l.13. Successful Pirate, p. 16. l.8. The Wife's Relief, p. 11. l.17. Wit at a Pinch, p.14. l. 11. Woman is a Riddle, p.28. l.2. p.53. l.12.

(*e*) Lucius, *p.* 22. *l.* 6. City Ramble, *p.* 68. *l.* 5. Conquest of *Spain*, *p.* 16. *l.*11. Faithful General, *p.* 28. *l.*9. *p.* 69. *l.*31. Fatal Marriage, *p.*152. *l.*37. Female Advocates, *p.* 11. *l.* 25. Female Wits, *p.*36. *l.*16. The General cashier'd, *p.*39. *l.*2. Man of Mode, *p.*252. *l.*25. Masquerade, *p.*24. *l.*39. The Victim, *p.*23. *l.*24. The Wonder, *p.*59. *l.*2. Thomyris, *p.*41. *l.*12. Ulysses, *p.*60. *l.* 23. Faithful Geral, *p.* 72. *l.*17.

(*f*) Jane Shore, *p.*60. *l.*19. Irene, *p.*39. *l.*36. Love's Last Shift, *p.* 49. *l.* 1. Love the Leveller, *p.* 39. *l.* 16. *p.* 65. *l.*23. Manlius Capitolinus, *p.* 55. *l.* 6. Rosamond, *p.* 23. *l.* 15. The Apparition, *p.*34. *l. penult.* Artful Husband, *p.*1. *l.*19. Basset-Table, *p.* 36. *l.* 19. *p.*58. *l.*31. Busy-Body, *p.*63. *l.*24. *p.*65. *l.* 18. Careless Husband, *p.*55. *l.* 22. The Contrivances, *p.* *ult.* *l.*13. Cruel Gift, *p.* 17. *l.* *ult.* Different Widows, *p.* 44. *l.* 7. Faithful Bride of *Granada*, *p.*12. *l.*18. *p.*43. *l.*24. Faithful General, *p.*5. *l.*5. Fatal Marriage, *p.* 141. *l.*28. Force of Friendship, *p.*38. *l.*11. The Gamester, *p.*60. *l.*4.

l. 4. The Man's bewitch'd, *p.* 28. *l.* 25, 29. Successful Pirate, *p.* 16. *l.* 7. The Wonder, *p.* 22. *l.* 11. Zelmane, *p.* 28. *l.* 23. *p.* 49. *l.* 25. *p.* 61. *l.* 12.

(*g*) The artful Husband, *p.* 42. *l.* 1. Country Lasses, *p.* 40. *l. penult.* The General cashier'd, *p.* 42. *l.* 14. Northern Lass, *p.* 70. *l.* 45. Provok'd Wife, *p.* 29. *l.* 9.

(*h*) The Force of Friendship, *p.* 4. *l.* 26.

(*i*) Abra-Mule, *p.* 7. *l.* 1. Jane Gray, *p.* 54. *l.* 12. Love's Last Shift, *p.* 46. *l.* 37. *p.* 53. *l.* 22. *p.* 70. *l.* 9, 31. Manlius Capitolinus, *p.* 14. *l.* 10. *Perolla* and *Izadora*, *p.* 56. *l. ult.* *British* Enchanters, *p.* 42. *l.* 26. Careless Husband, *p.* 33. *l.* 33. The Cid, *p.* 60. *l.* 14. Comical Lovers, *p.* 59. *l.* 4. *p.* 71. *l.* 35. Comical Revenge, *p.* 15. *l.* 22. *p.* 20. *l.* 28. The Confederacy, *p.* 48. *l.* 10. Conquest of *Spain*, *p.* 4. *l.* 22. The Contrivances, *p.* 16. *l. antepenult.* *p.* 27. *l.* 12. Country-House, *p.* 6. *l.* 33. *p.* 27. *l.* 18. Country Lasses, *p.* 17. *l.* 8. *p.* 48. *l.* 14. Cruel Gift, *p.* 61. *l.* 31. *p.* 65. *l.* 16. Distressed Mother, *p.* 13. *l.* 25. *p.* 14. *l.* 3. *p.* 35. *l.* 11. *p.* 63. *l.* 15. Double Gallant, *p.* 36. *l. ult.* *p.* 37. *l.* 16. *p.* 54. *l.* 34. *p.* 63. *l.* 36. Fair Quaker of *Deal*, *p.* 53. *l.* 7. Faithful Bride of *Granada*, *p.* 35. *l.* 14. *p.* 46. *l. penult.* Faithful General, *p.* 8. *l.* 51. *p.* 25. *l.* 11. *p.* 26. *l.* 44. *p.* 35. *l.* 31. *p.* 58. *l.* 1. *p.* 62. *l. penult.* *p.* 65. *l.* 36. *p.* 67. *l.* 50. *p.* 68. *l.* 6. The False Friend, *p.* 26. *l. penult.* Fatal Marriage, *p.* 124. *l. ult.* *p.* 163. *l.* 4. Female Advocates, *p.* 23. *l.* 9. *p.* 28. *l.* 23. *p.* 37. *l.* 22. The Female Wits, *p.* 45. *l.* 22. Fickle Shepherdess, *p.* 39. *l.* 10. Force of Friendship, *p.* 21. *l.* 13. *p.* 24. *l.* 25, 26. *p.* 30. *l.* 13. The Gamester, *p.* 24. *l.* 19, 27. *p.* 66. *l.* 23. The General cashier'd, *p.* 45. *l.* 28. *Gotham* Election, *p.* 37. *l.* 27. Humours of the Age, *p.* 57. *l. penult.* Humours of the Army, *p.* 22. *l. antepenult.* *p.* 33. *l.* 16. The Lady's Last Stake, *p.* 44. *l.* 37. *p.* 63. *l.* 9. The Lawyer's Fortune, *p.* 21. *l.* 16. The Maid the Mistress, *p.* 2. *l.* 32. *p.* 9. *l.* 32. *p.* 11. *l. ult.* The Man's bewitch'd, *p.* 35. *l.* 4. *p.* 36. *l.* 13. *twice.* *p.* 52. *l.* 24. *twice.* *p.* 52. *l.* 28. *p.* 53. *l.* 34. *p.* 62. *l.* 30. Man of Mode, *p.* 248. *l.* 4. Metamorphosis, *p.* 2. l. 25. *p.* 24. *l.* 29. *p.* 54. *l.* 1. The Mistake, *p.* 2. *l.* 24. *p.* 32. *l.* 4. *p.* 36. *l.* 16. *p.* 40. *l.* 30. Modern Prophets, *p.* 66. *l.* 7. Northern Lass, *p.* 22. *l.* 37. *p.* 29. *l.* 38. *p.* 57. *l.* 19. *p.* 65. *l.* 5. *p.* 71. *l.* 4. Perfidious Brother, *p.* 22. *l.* 2. *p.* 23. *l.* 18. *p.* 24. *l. penult.* *p.* 27. *l.* 20. *p.* 30. *l.* 18. *p.* 39. *l.* 8. & *antepenult.* *p.* 46. *l.* 13, 20. *p.* 47. *l.* 1. *p.* 48. *l.* 21. Perplex'd Couple, *p.* 51. *l.* 17. Perplex'd Lovers, *p.* 32. *l.* 33. *p.* 48. *l.* 11. *Persian* Princess, *p.* 52. *l.* 17. Platonick Lady, *p.* 57. *l.* 12. *p.* 65. *l.* 2. The Quacks, *p.* 29. *l.* 18. Recruiting Officer, *p.* 22. *l.* 7. The Relapse, *p.* 3. *l.* 2. Rival Fools, *p.* 30. *l.* 23. *p.* 39. *l.* 1. *p.* 44. *l.* 11. *p.* 57. *l.* 20, 25, 31. *p.* 66. *l. ult.* Royal Convert, *p.* 31. *l.* 18. *p.* 67. *l.* 14, 26. The Roving Husband reclaim'd, *p.* 45. *l.* 26. The School-Boy, *p.* 30. *l.* 29. Squire of *Alsatia*, *p.* 26. *l.* 4. *p.* 61. *l.* 18. *p.* 63. l. 37. *p.* 67. *l.* 30, 37. *p.* 72. *l. penult.* Successful Pirate, *p.* 16. *l.* 20. *p.* 21. *l.* 24. *p.* 25. *l.* 8. *p.* 32. *l.* 22.

(*k*) *For Ever and Ever*, (*l*) *Immortal*, (*m*) *Never ending*, (*n*) *To all Eternity*, (*o*) *To Eternity*, (*p*) *To the last Existence of my Soul's eternal Entity*, or (*q*) *It is founded on the Basis of Eternity.* Sometimes they droll (*r*) ironically upon the word *Eternal*. Here we are told of *Joys immortal* in a (*s*) *Kiss*, or even in (*t*) a *Duel*. *To* (*u*) *immortalize*, relates only to this World; and even (*x*) *to save from everlasting Torments*, looks no farther. A Man is (*y*) blasphemously called an *everlasting Goodness*. Nay, to bring the Notion as low as possible, we are told more than once, and even upon a leud Occasion, that (*z*) *each Moment is Eternity*.

It was a gross Error of *Mahomet*, to make the Joys of the other World consist in Sensual Pleasures: And for this, every Christian speaks of him with Abhorrence. But our *Stage-Poets* run lower than this, and represent the Sensual Pleasures of this Life as equal to Heaven itself, and even without any Regard to the Crimes forbidden in the 7th Commandment. For this

---

p.36. *l. penult.* p.48. *l.*7. *twice.* The Sultaness, p.10. *l. ult.* p.23. *l.*17. p.43. *l.*19. Tender Husband, p.37. *l.*16. The Victim, p.27. *l.*7. The Wife's Relief, p.6. *l.*7. The Wonder, p. 24. *l.*8. p.42. *l.*22. p.54. *l.*13. p.71. *l.* 28. Theseus, p. 11. *l.* 19. Thomyris, p.46. *l.* 19. *Venus* and *Adonis*, p.22. *l.* 16. Ulysses, *Prologue*, *l. penult.* p.4. *l.*16. p.48. *l.*26. p.51. *l.*22. p.57. *l.*1. p. 59. *l.* 15, 16, 19. Zelmane, p.17. *l.*14. p.19. *l.*24. p.40. *l.*17. p.41. l.31. p.48. *l.*10. p.50. *l.* 28. p.55. *l.*1. p.67. *l.*5.

(*k*) *British* Enchanters, p. 27. *l.* 3.

(*l*) Ajax, p.42. *l.*2. Hamlet, p. 30. *l.* 14. Beaux Stratagem, p.60. *l. penult.* *British* Enchanters, p.22. *l.*9. Country Lasses, p. 17. *l.* 1. p. 41. *l.*5. Double Gallant, p. 68. *l.*22. Successful Pirate, p. 31. *l.* 24, 27, 33. p.45. *l.* 7.

(*m*) Perfidious Brother, p. 10. *l.*32. Successful Pirate, p.33. *l.*9.

(*n*) The Man's bewitch'd, p. 49. *l.*33.

(*o*) The Relapse, p.8. *l.*41.

(*p*) Careless Husband, p. 35. *l.* 36.

(*q*) Wife of *Bath*, p.32. *l.*25.

(*r*) The General cashier'd, p. 36. *l.*19.

(*s*) Force of Friendship, p.29. *l.* 13.

(*t*) Ibid. p.39. *l.*28.

(*u*) Busy-Body, p.60. l.29.

(*x*) The Confederacy, p. 63. *l.* 21.

(*y*) Fatal Marriage, p. 153. *l.* 2.

(*z*) Old Batchelor, p.28. Successful Pirate, p.34. *l.*13.

reason, they stile it in the general (*a*) *immortal* and (*b*) *endless Joys*, or (*c*) *an immortal Flame*. Thus two Lovers going to Execution express themselves (*d*):

'Tis hard, 'tis wondrous hard, that we must die,
In sight of all the Happiness we wish,
The endless Joys which mutual Love would give.

Thus also (*e*) an Husband speaks to his Wife:

Thy wondrous Beauties kindle in my Soul
An everlasting Sense of fresh Delight:
My Heart surpriz'd each day with new Attractions,
Still sees itself beyond its utmost Wishes.

And (*f*) another Dialogue is as remarkable, where a Husband taking his Wife in his Arms, saith thus:

The utmost Blessing that my Thought can reach,
Is folded in my Arms, and rooted in my Heart.
Answer. *There let it grow for ever.*
Reply. *Well said*, Amanda, *let it be for ever.*
Would Heaven grant that——
Answer. *'Twere all the Heav'n I'd ask.*

And thus (*g*) a *Lover*, in hopes of enjoying his Mistress, saith, *That he is a happy Man for ever.*

According to this Language, *Whoredom* is called (*h*) *immortal Pleasures*; and (*i*) the *Actors* are said to *feed upon it for ever*, and (*k*) to be *undone for ever* without it. And one speaking to a *Jilt* concerning a whoring Intrigue, saith, (*l*) *Thou wilt oblige me for ever.*

(*a*) *Phædra* and *Hippolytus*, *p.* 22. *l.* 18.
(*b*) Ibid. *p.* 23. *l.* 4.
(*c*) Manlius Capitolinus, *p.* 11. *l.* 28. *British* Enchanters, *p.* 14. *l.* 4. *p.* 31. *l.* 10.
(*d*) Faithful Bride of *Granada*, *p.* 41. *l.* 4.
(*e*) Manlius Capitolinus, *p.* 13. *l.* 6.
(*f*) The Relapse, *p.* 2. *l.* 23.
(*g*) Comical Lovers, *p.* 15. *l.* 22.
(*h*) Rival Brothers, *p.* 72. *l.* 1.
(*i*) The Mistake, *p.* 44. *l.* 23.
(*k*) Love and Liberty, *p.* 33. *l. ult.*
(*l*) Amorous Widow, *p.* 43. *l.* 20.

This (ſaith an Actor) *is* (*m*) *a beauteous, an immortal Feaſt,*
Jove *might transform himſelf once more to taſte;*
Neglected leave his Heaven again, to prove
The more extatick Joy of mortal Love.

And that we may ſee what Senſe our *Poets* have of the Marriage-Vow, they thus deſcribe *Adultery* (*n*):

——*Joys, Raptures, Extaſies,*
Which tho they but a Moment laſt,
Give us of Immortality a Taſte.

Others ſay of it, (*o*) That *it is an eternal Round of Joy.* It is (*p*) *immortal Pleaſures.* It is (*q*) *everlaſting Joys.* One ſaith, (*r*) *I'll love thee everlaſtingly*; and another ſaith, (*s*) *I wiſh it were in my power eternally to oblige you:* and both mean no more than being guilty of this abominable Vice.

Theſe are ſtrange Deſcriptions of the Joys of another World, and the everlaſting State of Happineſs with GOD in the Kingdom of Heaven. A *Turk* would bluſh to hear them; and every one, who pretends to Chriſtianity, ſhould abhor them. Theſe Notions would have ſuited with the former State of *Sodom* and *Gomorrah*; and (*t*) *except the LORD of Hoſts had left unto us a very ſmall Remnant, we might have been like* them.

The Belief of theſe two *Articles* of our *Faith*, namely, the *Reſurrection of the Body*, and the *Life everlaſting*, had the greateſt Influence upon the *Primitive Chriſtians* in time of Perſecution. This made them die with *Chriſt* rather than deny him, and continue faithful to Death, that ſo they might inherit the Crown of Life. Thus the noble Army of Martyrs praiſed GOD

(*m*) Love and Liberty, *p.* 32. *l. ult. p.* 33. *l.* 1.
(*n*) Wife's Relief, *p.*21. *l.*21.
(*o*) Fair Example, *p.*59. *l.* 16.
(*p*) Ibid. *p.* 59. l. 31.
(*q*) Amorous Widow, *p.* 61. *l.* 18.
(*r*) Wife's Relief, *p.* 27. *l.*27.
(*s*) She wou'd if ſhe cou'd, *p.* 109. *l.* 21.
(*t*) *Iſa.* 1. 9.

on

on Earth, and now they praiſe him in Heaven. They then (*u*) knew the Promiſes, and now they know the Performance. This made their Memory ſo precious in all Ages, and their Examples recorded for our Imitation. But whilſt the *Church* ſpeaks moſt honourably of *Martyrdom*, the *Stage* uſes the (*x*) Word for a different purpoſe, and in a temporal ſenſe. It was always a Maxim grounded upon (*y*) *Scripture*, That not the Puniſhment, but the Cauſe makes a *Martyr*; and this Cauſe muſt be a Zeal for the Glory of GOD, and a Love of Religion. On the (*z*) *Stage* we are told of *dying a Martyr for a Secret*; and (*a*) *Virginity* itſelf is call'd *a Load of Martyrdom*. Inſtead of dying unto GOD, here Men are ſaid to *fall* as *Martyrs* (*b*) to a *Man*, (*c*) to *Pride*, (*d*) to *Falſhood*, or (*e*) to *Good Manners*, (*f*) to the *Idol Honour*, or (*g*) to a Woman's *Folly*; as if theſe were the Objects of their Devotion. But moſt commonly they are ſaid to be *Martyrs* to (*h*) *Love*, or to (*i*) a *Woman*. Thus the moſt ſolemn Expreſſions of Religion are proſtituted to *Courtſhip* and *Romance*. Thus a Miſtreſs is made a *GOD* Almighty, and worſhip'd even to *Martyrdom* itſelf, as if there was no farther Proſpect. Neither is it a ſingle Inſtance at a time; but (*k*) even *Crouds of martyr'd Slaves* are ſaid to be ready to *die* for one Woman. Inſtances worſe than all

---

(*u*) *Mat.* 5. 10, 11, 12. & 10. 22. & 10. 33. 2 *Tim.* 2. 11, 12. 1 *Pet.* 4. 12, 13, 14. & 4. 19. *Rev.* 2. 10.

(*x*) Love and Liberty, *p.* 6. *l.* 6. *p.* 20. *l.* 2. The Force of Friendſhip, *p.* 39. *l.* 7. Succeſsful Pirate, *p.* 61. *l.* 10.

(*y*) 1 *Pet.* 4. 15, 16.

(*z*) Injur'd Love, *a Comedy*, *p.* 56. *l.* 1.

(*a*) The City-Ramble, *p.* 40. *l.* 21.

(*b*) Marplot, *p.* 6. *l.* 21. Force of Friendſhip, *p.* 36. *l.* 30.

(*c*) *Pyrrhus* and *Demetrius*, *p.* 31. *l.* 30. The Country Laſſes, *p.* 69. *l.* 8.

(*d*) The Country Laſſes, *p.* 58. *l.* 4.

(*e*) Sir *Courtly Nice*, *p.* 43. *l.* 5.

(*f*) The Faithful General, *p.* 49. *l.* 38.

(*g*) The Wife's Relief, *p.* 15. *l.* 26.

(*h*) Cruel Gift, *p.* 56. *l.* 3. *p.* 60. *l.* 18. Force of Friendſhip, *p.* 32. *l.* 2. Wife's Relief, *p.* 43. *l.* 26.

(*i*) Arſinoe, *p.* 13. *l.* 17. Succeſsful Pirate, *p.* 24. *l.* 13. *p.* 26. *l.* 7.

(*k*) The Gameſter, *p.* 19. *l.* 11.

this

this might be given; but one ſhall ſuffice, (*l*) where a marry'd Woman is ſollicited for a Debauch, and told by her Gallant, that he will *die a Martyr, rather than diſclaim* his Paſſion. And thus we have *Adultery* dignified with the Title of *Martyrdom*; as if it was as honourable to periſh in the Defence of Whoring, as for the Faith of *Chriſtianity*. The *Primitive Chriſtians*, when they ſpoke of thoſe noble Champions, often call'd them the *bleſſed Martyrs*. Upon the *Stage*, (*m*) to be a *Martyr* ſignifies only to be unhappy. In *Eccleſiaſtical Hiſtory* we have recorded the moſt terrible Torments which the *Martyrs* did cheerfully undergo: All this on the *Stage* is compared to the hearing of (*n*) a bad Play.

In (*o*) one *Play* an *Actor* asks this Queſtion, *Who would die a Martyr to Senſe, in a Country where the Religion is Folly?* And (*p*) at the end of the ſame *Play*, the fine *Angelica* ſaith thus of her Lover: *Men are generally Hypocrites and Infidels. They pretend to worſhip, but they have neither Zeal nor Faith. How few, like* Valentine, *would perſevere even unto Martyrdom, and ſacrifice their Intereſt to their Conſtancy!* Here we have the *Religion* of the Country expos'd as a *Folly*, and *Worſhip, Zeal, Faith*, and *Sacrificing*, refer'd only to the Perſon ſpeaking, or at fartheſt to the Sex. And they are tax'd as *Hypocrites* and *Infidels*, who have different Notions. Thus we have not only *Martyrdom* ridiculed, but alſo the Language of the *Scriptures* profaned at the ſame time; and a *Woman* expoſeth herſelf in the Temple of *Satan* to be worſhip'd as a GOD.

To name but one Inſtance more. In (*q*) another *Play* an *Actor* ſaith, *For your Comfort, Marriage, they ſay, is holy.* Bnt to this it is anſwer'd, *Ay, and ſo is Martyrdom, as they ſay; but both of them are good for juſt nothing, but to make an end of a Man's Life.*

And now, if theſe things are right, what muſt we think of the *Great Articles* of our *Faith*, the *Reſur-*

(*l*) Love for Love, *p*.42. *l*.3.

(*m*) Comical Lovers, *p*. 28. *l*. 14.

(*n*) The Maid the Miſtreſs, *l*. 8. *Prologue the ſecond*, *l*. 34.

(*o*) Love for Love, *p*. 4. *l*. 7.

(*p*) Ibid. *p*.78. *l*. 26.

(*q*) Love Triumphant, *p*. 72.

rection

rection of the Body, and the *Life Everlasting?* But if it is otherwise, how can any People in a Christian Nation endure to hear their *Religion* thus daily exposed, not only without Resentment, but with Satisfaction?

CHAP. XI.

Virtue exposed by the Stage.

IN the last Chapter I gave an Account how the *Poets* degenerate from *Christianity*, by their exposing of *Religion*. I shall now discover how they sink even below *Paganism*, which will too evidently appear from their exposing of *Virtue*.

Tho the *Heathens* were led only by the Light of Nature, yet both the *Greeks* and *Latins* wrote very excellently upon *moral* Subjects. When GOD at first revealed his Will, he gave to the *Israelites* the *ten Commandments*, which is called *the moral Law*; and afterward other Exhortations, which were agreeable thereto. When our *Saviour* was upon the Earth, he charged us, saying, (a) *Think not that I am come to destroy the Law and the Prophets; I am not come to destroy, but to fulfil.* The *Apostles* treat on such *Topicks* as excellently as the *Prophets*; and therefore the Precepts of *Morality* are what *Heathens*, *Jews*, *Turks*, and *Christians* of all Persuasions are fully agreed in. But the Language of the *Play-Houses* being peculiar from all the World besides, may be seen in these following Particulars.

First, They represent *Virtue* as nothing but an Appearance only. He is *virtuous* in the *Play-House Language*, who hath a good Reputation; and he is *vicious*, who is so unfortunate as to expose himself to Censure. He who is as *vicious* as the worst, let him but keep it private, is in their opinion as *virtuous* as the best. In (b)

(a) *Mat.* 5. 17.

(b) An Act at *Oxford*, p. 25. l. 3. l. 24. *Hampstead*-Heath, p. 29.

one *Play*, an *Actor* speaking of *Adultery*, saith, *We will be both virtuous, that is, we will be secret, and the World shall never know the contrary.* In another (*c*) there is much to the same purpose spoken upon the same Subject: *Will these conscientious Qualms be never reconciled to Love?* that is, to Adultery. Answer. *And if it should be known.* Reply. *'Twould prove a Sin: But if it should not, then you are innocent and virtuous.* Answer. *Then Virtue is nothing but a Name.* Reply. *What else? She is innocent, who is reputed to be such; and leud, whom every body believes to be so.* In a third there is also (*d*) this Expression: *What is a Crime to the Wicked, may not be so to the Godly. If you guard well the Appearance, half the Duty of Religion is preserv'd, and you avoid the Scandal. Now the Crime, as to Men, is none, if not known; and in many reputed Crimes the Scandal is all the Offence: as particularly in a private Amour, where there is no Injury.* If such *Communications* do not *corrupt Good-Manners*, and such *Arguments* do not directly tend to confound all Notions of *Virtue* and *Vice*, I know not what can. In one *Play* (*e*) a Woman saith to another, *I have conquer'd my Virtue.* And she is answer'd, *I would not dissuade you; be as wicked as you will, but be a little discreet too.* In another, (*f*) one of the same Sex saith, *I'll promise to keep a good Reputation, and that's the most fashionable Virtue.* Besides, we are told, that (*g*) the *Pleasure of Virtue is not so much in the thing, as in the Reputation of having it:* and (*h*) that *there is nothing in that Religion, which debars a Man of his Pleasure.* 'Tis well known, that the *Heathens* taught different *Morals*, and declared that Man's chief Happiness in this Life consisted in the Practice of *Virtue*. The Prophet *Isaiah* (*i*) pronounceth an heavy *Woe against them, that* do but *call Evil Good, and Good Evil; that put Dark-*

(*c*) Love at first sight, *p.* 39. *l.* 16.

(*d*) The Stage-Beaux toss'd in a Blanket, *p.* 57. *l.* 24.

(*e*) The Modish Husband, *p.* 31. *l.* 10.

(*f*) *Tunbridge*-Walks, *p.* 11. *l.* 21.

(*g*) Careless Husband, *p.* 34. *l. antepenult.*

(*h*) *Portsmouth*-Heiress, *p.* 6. *l.* 21.

(*i*) *Isa.* 5. 20.

4 *ness*

ness for Light, and Light for Darkness; that put Bitter for Sweet, and Sweet for Bitter. The *Actors* render themselves liable to this Woe: They ascribe the Name of *Virtue* to *Vice.* Winking at the Adultery of an Husband, is stiled (*k*) *the most convenient piece of Virtue that ever a Wife was mistress of.* In (*l*) another *Play* a notorious *Whore* is publickly convicted before a Mock-Justice of the Peace, who makes this Apology for the Fact; *She hath committed a little Country Folly, as she privately confesseth. What's that! It may stand in rank with what they call Virtue here.*

Besides, they condemn *Virtue*, as something laid aside for many Years. And the very Women, without any regard to Character, talk at this rate on the *Stage.* (*m*) One saith, *We should regard the Character of Virtue, the Men like us the better for't.* But she is answer'd, *Not at all: 'Tis so out of fashion, it passes rather for a Disguise than a Dress.* And tho at some times they say, that *Virtue* is nothing but a *Reputation*; yet lest that should look like too great an Encomium, they tell us that (*n*) *Reputation's a Jest.* And then add, *What have Men of Estates to do with Reputation? Let those value the World's Censure, who want its Assistance. A Gentleman ought to be free, careless, and good Company.* And (*) another saith, *Indeed that Jewel Reputation is but a fanciful Business. One shall not see a homely Creature in Town but wears it in her Mouth as monstrously as the* Indians *do Bobs in their Lips; and it becomes them both alike.*

Besides, they are sometimes guilty of cursing even (*o*) *Virtue* and (*p*) *Morality*, and load both with Epithets full of Disgrace. Thus they say (*q*) *dull Morality*, (*r*) *dull* or (*s*) *sullen Moralist*, or (*u*) *musty* and (*x*) *unpolish'd Morals.*

(*k*) Careless Husband, *p.* 6. *l.* 33.
(*l*) Northern Lass, *p.* 46. *l. antepenult.*
(*m*) Modish Husband, *p.* 31. *l.* 23.
(*n*) Humours of the Age, *p.* 3. *l.* 31.
(*) Careless Husband, *p.* 15. l. 1.
(*o*) Cato, *p.* 51. *l.* 15. Provok'd Wife, *p.* 26. *l.* 34.
(*p*) Provok'd Wife, *p.* 37. *l.* 9.
(*q*) Solon, *p.* 57. *l.* 26.
(*r*) Cruel Gift, *p.* 2. *l.* 20.
(*s*) Faithful General, *p.* 62. *l.* 23.
(*u*) *Portsmouth* Heiress, *p.* 31. *l.* 5.
(*x*) Solon, *p. ult. l. antepen.*

Morals. A good Man is call'd (y) a *poor silly virtuous Wretch.* According to their Language, it is (z) *dear damn'd Virtue*; (a) *the lazy Virtue of some dreaming Hermit*; (b) *meager*, (c) *merciless*, or (d) *most inhuman Virtue*; (e) *Rigid* or (f) *Romantick Virtue*; (g) *Savage*, (h) *Severe and Scrupulous*, (i) *Spiteful* and (k) *Stubborn Virtue*, or (l) *Thoughtless Virtue, which a Man must be taught to repent of.*

But bare Epithets are not sufficient to carry on the Design, and therefore the *Poets* and *Actors* speak their minds more plainly upon all occasions, and exclaim against *Virtue* itself. I hope, that there will be no danger in exposing the Poison, and therefore I shall add several Quotations, that the Reader may see how it is their constant Practice.

(m) *How miserable were it to be virtuous, if such a Wretch as this could prosper?*

(n) *Virtue! Can you feed upon it?*

(o) *Some virtuous Devil.*

(p) *We virtuous Devils.*

(q) *I own myself a Libertine, a mortal Foe to that dull thing call'd Virtue, that mere Disease of sickly Nature. Pleasure's the End of Life; and while I am Mistress of myself and Fortune, I will enjoy it to the height.*

(r) *Virtue! with a Pox to't.*

(y) *Phædra* and *Hippolytus*, p. 2. l. 34.

(z) Marry or do worse, p. 51. l. 16.

(a) Cruel Gift, p. 1. l. 2.

(b) Manlius Capitolinus, p. 47. l. 13.

(c) Jane Gray, p. 34. l. 16.

(d) Ibid. p. 33. l. 10.

(e) *Phædra* and *Hippolytus*, p. 18. l. 6.

(f) Cruel Gift, p. 1. l. 1.

(g) *French* Cato, p. 51. l. 2.

(h) Rival Brothers, p. 100. l. 7.

(i) The Lady's last Stake, p. 73. *l. ult.*

(k) *Perolla* and *Izadora*, p. 40. l. 14.

(l) Conquest of *Spain*, p. 56. l. 1.

(m) A Woman's Revenge, p. 39. l. 9.

(n) Fortune in her Wits, p. 50. l. 3.

(o) Love at first sight, p. 8. l. 17.

(p) Love's last Shift, p. 28. l. 23.

(q) Ibid. p. 57. l. 14.

(r) Love the Leveller, p. 22. l. 6.

(s) *To lose Money, and long of this Virtue,* (with an Oath) *I wonder how this Virtue crept into my House: I am sure, I never gave it any encouragement.*

(t) Take, take, ye Gods, your meager Virtue back,
Your slender Diet. 'Tis too thin to live on.

(u) *What good hath your Virtue done you?*

(x) *Virtues in a Wife are good for nothing, but to make her proud, and put the World in mind of her Husband's Faults.*

(y) *He is of a ready Wit, pleasant Conversation, throughly skill'd in Men: In a word, he knows so much of Virtue, as makes him well accomplish'd for all manner of Vice.*

(z) *I protest, I had rather still be vicious than owe my Virtue to Necessity.*

(a) *I think, as the World goes, they may be proud of marrying their Daughter into a virtuous Family.* To this it is answer'd with an Oath, *Virtue is not the Case.* And when it was replied, *Where she may have a good Example before her Eyes,* this Expression was farther exposed by drolling upon the Name of GOD.

(b) *Teach him to repent his thoughtless Virtue.*

(c) *O Virtue! Virtue! what an Enemy art thou to a Woman's good Inclinations?*

(d) *How happy are we,*
Who from Virtue are free,
That curbing Disease of the Mind;
Can indulge ev'ry Taste,
Love where we like best,
Not by dull Reputation confin'd!

(s) Love the Leveller, p. 22. l. 12.
(t) Manlius Capitolinus, p. 47. l. 13.
(u) The careless Husband, p. 6. l. 4.
(x) Ibid. p. 19. l. 9.
(y) The comical Revenge, p. 15. l. 2.
(z) Ibid. p. 16. l. 34.
(a) The Confederacy, p. 32. l. 35.
(b) The Conquest of *Spain*, p. 56. l. 2.
(c) Fatal Marriage, *p.* 145. *l.* 18.
(d) The fine Lady's Airs, *p.* 47. *l.* 13.

(*e*) *I can hardly have ſo ill an opinion of her Underſtanding, as to think, that ſhe'll build any thing upon Virtue in this Age.*

(*f*) *Virtue is an Impoſſibility, the moſt Rigid halt in the Performance. 'Tis Air, Whimſey, a Jeſt.*

(*g*) *He is fallen in Love with her purely for her Virtue.* Anſwer, *That's a ſign of a diſtemper'd Appetite indeed. 'Tis like a Woman with Child, that longs for a thing out of ſeaſon.*

(*h*) *Give me a Man, that has agreeable Faults, rather than offenſive Virtues.*

(*i*) *He is a ſad Dog; he is a ſneaking young Puppy, that dares not get drunk, thinks Fornication a Sin, and never ſleeps till he has ſaid his Prayers.*

(*k*) *None of your muſty Morals.*

(*l*) *She is mad with Whimſeys of Virtue.*

(*m*) *Thou art even fond of Virtue for the ſake of the Solitude.* Anſwer, *And thou art fond of Vice for the ſake of the Scandal.* Reply, *Ay, ay, you may give it what Names you pleaſe: but the dear Felicity of Life is conceal'd under thoſe hideous Titles, like a good Face under a bad Vizor. And as there is no Preferment to be had without Intereſt; ſo there is no Pleaſure to be had without Scandal.*

(*n*) *Wit is the moſt impertinent thing that belongs to a Woman, except Virtue.*

(*o*) *What Notions of Virtue do we Women take up, upon the Credit of old fooliſh Philoſophers? Virtue is its own Reward. Virtue's this, Virtue's that —— Virtue's an Aſs, and a Gallant's worth forty on't.*

(*p*) *Virtue! Virtue is no more like the thing that's call'd ſo, than 'tis like Vice itſelf. Virtue conſiſts in Goodneſs, Honour, Gratitude, Sincerity, and Pity; and not in peeviſh, ſnarling, ſtrait-lac'd Chaſtity. True Virtue,*

(*e*) Humours of the Age, *p.*8. *l.* 32.

(*f*) Ibid. *p.*42. l. 5.

(*g*) Ibid. *p.*55. *l. penult.*

(*h*) Lying Lover, *p.*6. *l.* 21.

(*i*) The Maſquerade, *p.*9. *l.*32.

(*k*) The Metamorphoſis, *p.* 3. *l.* 12.

(*l*) Modiſh Husband, *p.* 12. *l.* 12.

(*m*) *Portſmouth* Heireſs, *p.* 7. *l.*6.

(*n*) Modiſh Husband, *p.* 28. *l.* 5.

(*o*) Provok'd Wife, *p.*3. l. 15.

(*p*) Ibid. *p.*32. *l.*35.

when-

whenever it moves, still carries an intrinsick worth about it, and is in every Place, and in each Sex of equal value. So is not Continence, you see.

Among all the *Plays* which have been printed, there is one, which is said in the *Title-Page* to be *writ by a Club of Ladies in vindication of virtuous Plays*; and therefore the Character which they give of *Virtue*, must be the more remarkable, which is to be seen in their own Words.

> (q) *Nothing's so hard, but may in time be won:*
> *Virtue's a Race that's difficult to run.*

This is spoken for an encouragement in an adulterous Design; and a little before, (r) *There is such a Pother with her Virtue! I fancy, she'll be cheap.*

(s) *Virtue! was it that you would say?* Answer, *No, Madam; sure you don't think me such a Brute.*

(t) *The Virtue which you boast of so much, I own is a very fine thing, if one could have it insur'd: but it often happens, that Women grow weary of it, when no body cares to take it from them.*

To these I shall add some Expressions which are spoken by a (u) *Gentleman* of *good Breeding*, and who makes an honourable *Exit* by marrying the great Fortune in the *Play*. I must confess, his Sentences are remarkable. (x) *Give me as much Pleasure, I say, as my Constitution requires; as much Wit and Sincerity, as will qualify me for Company; and just as much Morality, as will secure me from the Talons of the Law; and let Fortune take her choice.* And (y) a little after, *Urge your Virtue to a Courtier, and he'll receive you as a young Lord doth a begging Relation. Urge your Virtue to a Lawyer, and you may plead your Cause yourself. Urge your Virtue to a Woman, and she'll inquire into your Estate. In short, Virtue is like a Man's Coat of Arms, of no value to any but himself; and he that depends to rise by that one Quality alone,*

(q) The Roving Husband reclaim'd, *p.* 13. *l.* 18.
(r) Ibid. l. 10.
(s) Ibid. *p.* 32. *l.* 22.
(t) Ibid. *p.* 52. *l.* 13.
(u) *Portsmouth* Heiress, Rainer *in the Drama.*
(x) Ibid. *p.* 5. *l.* 13.
(y) Ibid. *l.* 23.

may even be reduced to starve with his Mistress. To this it is answer'd, *Excellent Satire this! Prithee, where hast thou learnt it?* And he immediately replies, *From the old Remains of Truth, where Improbity and Hypocrisy are painted the darling Principles of the Fortunate.*

Thus the *old Remains of Truth* are strangely misrepresented by the *Stage*, to condemn all *Morality*, and encourage *Hypocrisy*. Accordingly in (z) another *Comedy*, an *antient Philosopher* speaks in very different Language from his real Character, and concludes the *Play* with this Instruction to the Audience from his own Example:

Unpolish'd Morals I'll no longer prize.

And an antient King speaks (*a*) the same Language to his first Minister of State:

Hence with thy hungry, dull, untimely Morals;
The fond, deluding Sophistry of Schools.

There are two things which are generally the main Motives to the Practice of *Virtue*. *First*, That it is *good* and commendable in itself: and, *Secondly*, That it makes a Man be had in *Honour* and *Reputation* in the World. Now the Notion of *Goodness*, as well as *Grace*, upon the *Stage*, may be had at once from (*b*) an Uncle's Advice to his Nephew.

Be a good Boy; Game, whore, rake, get Bastards and Claps, and be very extravagant for one Year at least. I vow to GOD, I could weep to see how ungracious the young Rogue is!

And as for *Honour* and *Reputation*, they can afford it no better Epithets, than that it is (*c*) *cruel*, and (*d*) *sullen*; and at other times they speak more largely, in such Language as this.

(z) Solon, *p. ult. l. antepenult.*
(*a*) Royal Convert, *p.* 23. *l.* 22.
(*b*) The Masquerade, *p.* 5. *l.* 22.
(*c*) Perfidious Brother, *p.* 10. *l. penult.*
(*d*) *Phædra* and *Hippolytus*, p. 17. l. 34.

These

(e) *Those stubborn Principles of Faith and Honour, and I know not what, that have corrupted his Temper.*

(f) *Honour, what is it? but an empty Sound,*
That leads you by false Hopes to waking Dreams;
A Phantom, that eludes your greedy Arms,
And feeds your Pride alone, to starve your Pleasure;
An Idol, a vain Rattle, a blab Echo.

(g) *Honour! Why, what's that? There is no such thing now in Nature.*

(h) *Honour, I say, is good for nothing, but to spoil Conversation.* And it is therefore cursed in the same place.

(i) *Honour is a Foe, that labours in the Mind, and keeps the Soul in a perplex'd Disguise.*

(k) *Let those, who bind themselves to Honour's Rules,*
Die, as they live, unthinking honest Fools;
Who covet vain Reports of Honesty,
Unenvy'd let them take the Fame for me,
Success in Fraud pays well for Infamy.

(l) *I was afraid you had got that whimsical Notion of Honour in your Head, that makes Fools keep their Words to their own undoing.*

(m) *Honour is a meer Bubble, made use of by all the World, like a Masking Habit, to deceive one another.*

(n) *What are Reason and Honour? Bubbles.*

(o) *That Fantom of Honour, which Men in ev'ry Age have so contemn'd, they have thrown it amongst the Women to scrabble for.*

(||) *Honour is a publick Enemy.*

(e) Cato, p. 7. l. 10.

(f) Love and Liberty, p. 18. l. 29.

(g) Love the Leveller, p. 22. l. *penult.*

(h) Marplot, p. 7. l. 5.

(i) Marry or do worse, p. 64. l. 12.

(k) The Apparition, p. 13. l. 20.

(l) Ibid. p. 16. l. 9.

(m) The Maid's the Mistress, p. 50. l. 16.

(n) Perplex'd Couple, p. 36. l. 25.

(o) Provok'd Wife, p. 32. l. *antepenult.*

(||) Love for Love, p. 43. l. 32.

(*p*) *What is Honour? A noisy Nothing. A stalking Shade. When 'tis lost, no one finds it, and Heaven be praised, there is none look after it now; and when they have it, 'tis used like their Clothes, fond of it at first, till they find something they like better, and then it is gone with a Fadding.*

(*q*) *Honour is like a huge Giant of Ice, that melts before our warm Desires: 'Tis a Fantom to frighten Girls. It appear'd once to me in the form of a Wife, and I have hated it ever since.*

Indeed, we are told, (*) that it is *impossible to find Honour in a Poet*; but then it is pity that they should be suffered to corrupt others, and make them as bad as themselves.

The short of this matter is, the *Stage* resolves all *Religion* and *Morality* into two things, namely, *Pleasure* and *Profit*. As to *Pleasure*, the Quotations would be endless; and as to *Profit*, their Notion is, (*r*) *We must be getting every way, tho it be by evil Means.* Accordingly, they lay down this as a Maxim, (*s*) *The wise Man never thinks of right or wrong, so he gets the Money.* I shall only add two Quotations in this case, which are the Advice of a Father to his Son, and in one *Play* is this (*t*):

But what hast thou to do with ill-tim'd Honesty?
Observe me well, and treasure in thy Soul
The experienc'd Wisdom of thy Father;
Let Interest be thy bright unerring Guide,
The secret darling Purpose of thy Heart.
Believe me, Boy, she reigns Supreme below;
Honour and endless Pleasure wait around her;
When she commands, smile on the Man thou hatest,
Caress him to inevitable Ruin.
From foolish Pity guard thy well-taught Mind.
Think not of Friendship more than of a Word,
Which once gone forth is lost in idle Air.

(*p*) The Roving Husband reclaim'd, p.32. l.22.

(*q*) The Wife's Relief, p. 2. l. 38.

(*) A Woman's Revenge, p. 3. l.8.

(*r*) *Wisdom* 15. 12.

(*s*) The artful Husband, p.29. l. 33.

(*t*) The Cruel Gift, p.4. l.4.

In

In another *Play*, a Father gives his Son his own Example, which he calls (u) an *Original Receipt to make a Fortune by*. Which was *pimping* for others, *cheating* in all sorts of Games, and *defrauding* of Orphans, by being their Executors: and after a Page of such *Morality* as this, the Conclusion follows, *Do that, and thou wilt win my Heart for ever.*

But besides the general Discouragement which the *Stage* gives to *Virtue*, it may not be improper to mention some particular Instances, and shew how they represent those which relate to ourselves and our Neighbours.

As to the *Virtues* which relate to ourselves, the first which I shall name, is *Chastity*. This is a Duty (x) recommended in *Scripture*, both in (y) Body, Mind, Affections, (z) Words, and (a) Behaviour; and (b) that we should preserve it in our selves and others, insomuch that (c) such a *chaste Conversation* among *Christians* may by GOD's Blessing be a Method to convert the *Heathens*. This on the *Stage* hath a very different Turn. Sometimes it is represented as (d) an *Impossibility*, sometimes as (e) a bare *Fancy*, and sometimes as (f) *want of Grace*. The late (g) Expression concerning *Honour*, that it is a *noisy Nothing*, and a *stalking Shade*, which *no body minds*, was particularly meant of this *Virtue*; nay, they represent it as the *Sin of Ingratitude*. *Rather than be tax'd with such a Crime* (saith an Actor) *she'll be yours for nothing, at least for no Money*. Another tells us (h) that *of all Fatigues, there's none like following a virtuous Mistress*. Sometimes they call it (i) *a foolish kind of Virtue, which the Principles of the Ladies would fain get*

(u) Rival Fools, p. 2. l. 1, &c.
(x) *Tit.* 2. 5.
(y) 1 *Thess.* 4. 4, 5. *Job* 31. 1. 1 *Cor.* 7. 34.
(z) *Col.* 4. 6.
(a) 1 *Pet.* 3. 2.
(b) 1 *Cor.* 7. 2, 35, 36.
(c) 1 *Pet.* 3. 1.
(d) As you find it, *p.* 33. *l.* 30.
(e) The careless Husband, *p.* 34. *l. antepenult.*
(f) The Cares of Love, *p.* 10. *l.* 34.
(g) The Roving Husband reclaim'd, *p.* 32. *l.* 22.
(h) The Contrivances, *p.* 1. *l.* 4.
(i) The fine Lady's Airs, *p.* 13. *l.* 16.

rid of. One saith, (*k*) by way of ridicule, *Here's a Rout with a virtuous Jade, commend me to a pretty Whore.* And another, (*l*) *A Woman that is more chaste than I would have you, what is she good for? A sullen thing, that makes it her Business and Pride to war with the Flesh. She has cold Blood in her Veins perhaps, and if it be natural, 'tis a lazy Disease, and not a Virtue.* If a chaste Conversation might convert the *Heathens*; then the scandalous Language of the *Stage* is enough to confirm them in their Errors, and prejudice them the more.

And as *Chastity* is commended in *Scripture* when in single Persons; so *Constancy* in a married State meets with the same Character: (*m*) *The Bed undefiled is honourable among all Men*; and perhaps was never ill treated, except by the *English Stage.* The *Poets* call it (*n*) *Dull Constancy,* (*o*) *the Scandal of Constancy,* or (*p*) *the passionate Nonsense of Constancy,* or (*q*) *a being restrained by idle Rules, which sullen Honour dictates.* Their Descriptions also are remarkable. One saith, (*r*) *Constancy is an Argument of a narrow Soul. To be confin'd to one Embrace, is like trotting down every Saturday to the same Country House. Repetition renders the World dull and insipid; and when People are tired with one another, they ought to change by consent. Variety would make Life easy, and Love a greater Pleasure.* And another adds, (*s*) *Constancy is but a dull sleepy Quality at best. They will hardly admit it among the manly Virtues.* The Character which they give of it, is, that it is impracticable. Thus saith one, (*t*) *Constancy at my Years! 'Tis not a Virtue in season. You might as well expect the Fruit of Autumn ripens in the Spring.* Or else, that it is disreputable; so that (*u*) *None that have the least value for their Reputation,*

(*k*) Humours of the Age, p. 56. *l.* 12.

(*l*) The Roving Husband reclaim'd, p. 62. l. 9.

(*m*) *Wisdom* 3. 13. *Wisd.* 4. 1, 2. *Heb.* 13. 4.

(*n*) Injur'd Love, *a Comedy,* p. 2. *l.* 8.

(*o*) The careless Husband, p. 43. l. 26.

(*p*) The Masquerade, p. 1. l. 8.

(*q*) Royal Convert, p. 73. l. *antepenult.*

(*r*) Humours of the Age, p. 28. l. 24.

(*s*) Recruiting Officer, p. 10. l. 11.

(*t*) The Man of Mode, p. 202. l. 10.

(*u*) The modish Husband, p. 15. l. 19.

will pretend to so dull a Virtue as Constancy. And in the Conclusion of (*x*) one *Play*, being the *Moral* of the whole, we are advised to let loose the Reins, and suffer Men to live like Beasts. For,

Constraint alone creates a roving Mind;
They prove most constant, that are least confin'd.

To guard us from such *Vices* as these, GOD was pleased to implant another *Virtue*, even *Modesty*, in Man, especially in the Female Sex, which serves for Ornament and Defence, and is a Guard against all Temptations. St. *Paul* (*y*) recommends *modest Apparel, with Shamefacedness and Sobriety*, as their peculiar *Ornament*, and *that which becometh Women professing Godliness.* This upon the *Stage* is called (*z*) a *sickly, sneaking Virtue*, and (*a*) a *mopish thing, which by overclouding a Woman's Charms, makes them useless to herself, and unprofitable to those who live with her.* And we are told, (*b*) *for certain*, that *there is not upon Earth so impertinent a thing as a Woman's Modesty.* One describes it thus, (*c*) *Modesty is a starving Virtue, an old thredbare Fashion of the last Age, and would sit as odly on a Lover now, as a picked Beard and Mustacho's.* Another saith, (*d*) *Modesty commended! Why so? when it is out of the Fashion. Why, we have scarce so much as the Name of it left. Indeed, there's here and there a Country Girl pretends to something like it; but then she is a Fool to be sure, and is laugh'd at by every body.* Another saith, (‖) *I warrant you for Blushing; we have left that foolish Modesty off long since; 'tis of no use to Men of our Vocation.* And it is observable, that he and his Companions are crown'd with success at last. Another saith, (†) *Modesty! Here's a Fellow now! Prithee, what doth Modesty signify? Did it ever get a*

(*x*) An Act at *Oxford*, p. *ult.* l. *penult.*

(*y*) 1 *Tim.* 2. 9, 10.

(*z*) Solon, *Epilogue*, *l.* 36.

(*a*) Injur'd Love, *a Comedy*, p. 11. l. 25.

(*b*) Provok'd Wife, p. 39. l. *antepenult.*

(*c*) Double Gallant, p. 33. l. 11.

(*d*) The Masquerade, p. 9. l. 38.

(‖) The Slip, p. 6. l. 28.

(†) *Tunbridge-Walks*, p. 8. l. 12.

Courtier

Courtier's Place? But to pretend to Modesty at this Age! why, the Women have laid it aside now, (we may thank the *Players* for that) *and are resolv'd to be out of countenance with nothing.* And therefore he (*) *thanks Heaven,* that *Modesty is an Infamy, which* his *Family can't be branded with.* And the Obscenity in every *Play,* and almost in every *Character,* shews, that this is their real opinion; and this is the cause that there is so little Modesty in the World.

Another *Virtue* which is misapplied, is *Fasting.* This is recommended to us (e) by the *Prophets* and (f) *Apostles,* and also by (g) *Christ* himself. It is also recommended to us by the (h) Example of *Christ,* and (i) his Apostles, and other holy Men and Women both (k) under the Old and (l) New Testament. And the reasons for which we are exhorted to it, are these; because it is a Means to (m) turn away the Anger of GOD, to (n) cast out the Devil, and (o) free us from his Temptations. However, it doth not escape wholly without Censure upon the *Stage,* where (p) a Man almost drunk, when he can have no more Wine brought him, is represented as *fasting for the Sins of the day.*

Another *Virtue* is *Gravity.* This in *Scripture* is commended in (q) Clergy and Laity, in (r) Old and Young, in (s) Parents and Children, and in Men and (t) Women. But this is condemn'd in the *Play-house,* as (u) not

(*) *Tunbridge-Walks,* p. 8. l. 18.

(e) *Isa.* 58. 6. *Joel* 1. 14.

(f) 1 *Cor.* 7. 5.

(g) *Matt.* 6. 16, 17, 18. *Matt.* 9. 14, 15. *Mark* 2. 18, 19. *Luke* 5. 33, 34, 35.

(h) *Matth.* 4. 2. *Luke* 4. 2.

(i) *Act.* 14. 23. 2 *Cor.* 6. 5. 2 *Cor.* 11. 27.

(k) *Judg.* 20. 26. 1 *Sam.* 7. 6. 1 *Sam.* 31. 13. 2 *Sam.* 1. 12. 2 *Sam.* 12. 16, 22. 1 *Chron.* 10. 12. 2 *Chron.* 20. 3. *Ezra* 8. 21, 23. *Neh.* 1. 4. *Neh.* 9. 1. *Esth.* 4. 3. *Psal.* 35. 13. *Psal.* 69. 10. *Psal.* 109. 24. *Jer.* 36. 9. *Dan.* 9. 3. *Jonah* 3. 5, 7. *Zech.* 8. 19.

(l) *Luke* 2. 37. *Act.* 10. 30. *Acts* 13. 3. *Acts* 27. 9.

(m) *Joel* 2. 12, 13, 14.

(n) *Matth.* 7. 21. *Mark* 9. 29.

(o) 1 *Cor.* 7. 5.

(p) Love at first sight, p. 43. l. 5.

(q) 1 *Tim.* 3. 4, 8. *Tit.* 2. 7.

(r) *Tit.* 2. 2.

(s) 1 *Tim.* 3. 4.

(t) 1 *Tim.* 3. 11.

(u) The Royal Convert, *Prologue,* l. 32.

fit

fit to be seen, read or heard; and therefore it is no wonder that we have so little of it there.

Another *Virtue* is *Humility*. This is a Duty (x) frequently required in *Scripture*, and recommended to us by the Example of (y) the *Apostles*, but above all by the Example of (z) GOD, and (a) *Christ*. The (b) design of GOD's Corrections, is to work this Grace in our Hearts. It is the way (c) to obtain Mercy and a Blessing; and the want of it hath brought down (d) Judgments, sometimes on particular Persons, and sometimes on whole Nations. The Commendation which it meets with upon the *Stage*, is this; (e) *What in the name of common Sense have you to do with Humility? Will you never have enough of it?* If *Humility* is a Fault, the *Poets* and *Actors* are seldom guilty of it, and therefore I confess may more boldly expose it.

Another *Virtue* is *Patience*. This (f) *Bastard Patience*, as the *Poets* call it. To the Practice hereof we are (g) frequently exhorted in the *Holy Scriptures*. Here we are told (h) the happy effects of it both in this World, and also (i) in the World to come. And we

---

(x) *Micah* 6. 8. *Coloss*. 3. 12. 1 *Pet*. 5. 5.

(y) *Acts* 20. 9.

(z) *Psal*. 113. 6.

(a) *Matth*. 11. 29. *John* 13. 14, 15, 16.

(b) *Deut*. 8. 2, 3, 16.

(c) *Levit*. 26. 41, 42. 1 *Kings* 21. 29. 2 *Kings* 22. 19, 20. 2 *Chron*. 7. 14. 2 *Chron*. 12. 6, 7, 12. 2 *Chron*. 32. 26. 2 *Chron*. 33. 12, 13. 2 *Chron*. 34. 27, 28. *Job* 22. 29. *Ps*. 9. 12. *Ps*. 10. 17. *Psal*. 34. 2. *Psal*. 69. 32. *Prov*. 15. 33. *Prov*. 16. 9. *Prov*. 18. 12. *Prov*. 22. 4. *Prov*. 29. 23. *Isa*. 57. 12. *Matth*. 5. 3. *Matth*. 18. 4. *Matth*. 23. 12. *Luke* 6. 20. *Luke* 14. 11. *Luke* 18. 14. *James* 4. 6, 10. 1 *Pet*. 5. 5, 6.

(d) *Exod*. 10. 3. 2 *Chron*. 33. 23, 24. 2 *Chron*. 36. 12. *Jer*. 44. 10, 11. *Dan*. 5. 22.

(e) The Careless Husband, *p*. 28. *l*. 11.

(f) The Cruel Gift, *p*. 3. *l*. 37.

(g) *Psal*. 37. 7. *Luke* 8. 15. *Rom*. 12. 12. *Col*. 1. 11. 1 *Thess*. 5. 14. 1 *Tim*. 3. 3. 1 *Tim*. 6. 11. 2 *Tim*. 2. 24. *Tit*. 2. 2. *Heb*. 12. 1. *James* 1. 3, 4. *James* 5. 7, 8, 10, 11. 1 *Pet*. 2. 20. 2 *Pet*. 1. 6. *Rev*. 2. 2, 3, 19. *Rev*. 3. 10.

(h) *Eccles*. 7. 8. *Psal*. 40. 1. *Luke* 21. 19. *Rom*. 5. 3, 4. *Rom*. 8. 25. *Rom*. 15. 4. 1 *Thess*. 1. 3, 4. 2 *Thess*. 1. 4, 5. *Heb*. 6. 15. *Rev*. 13. 10. *Rev*. 14. 12.

(i) *Rom*. 2. 7. *Heb*. 6. 12. *Heb*. 10. 36.

have not only (*k*) the Apostles, but also GOD himself for our Example, who is therefore called, (*l*) *the GOD of Patience.* An *Actor* (*m*) describes it thus, *Tell me not of Patience. 'Tis the Beggar's Comfort, and what they apply to ease their Misfortunes.* And another adds, (*n*) *Nam'st thou Patience, my Soul disdains the Thought.*

Another *Virtue* is a serious *Preparation for Death*, and for another World. To this we are (*o*) exhorted in *Scripture* as our only Wisdom, and the one thing necessary, which ought to be the proper Business of our whole Lives; so that if we do it aright, we are happy, or otherwise we are wretched for ever. And now, let us see how the *Stage* expresseth it self on this occasion.

(*p*) *My Lady dying! I am not yet prepared to bear her Company. I'll e'en shift for one. I would not willingly leave this wicked World, before I have tasted a little more on't.*

(*q*) *Don't kill me now. I am not ready. I am not prepared. I might be undone by it.* Words too true to be made the Jest of the *Play-house.*

(*r*) *Indeed, Sir,* (saith one) *I am not sufficiently prepared for the next World.* To this it is answer'd, *That's nothing, Madam, you and I shall go Hand in Hand, as we usually say. I'll teach you how to live there.*

I shall now conclude this Chapter with their Notions of such *Virtues* as relate to our Neighbours. And of these I shall only mention three, namely, *Truth* and *Honesty* to all, and *Obedience* to Parents. As to the first of these, we are exhorted in *Scripture* (*s*) to *speak every Man Truth with his Neighbour:* and in this we resemble *GOD the Father*, who is called (*t*) *the GOD of Truth*; and *GOD the Holy Ghost*, who is called (*u*) *the Spirit of*

(*k*) 2 *Cor.* 6.4. 2 *Cor.* 12.12. 2 *Tim.* 3.10.

(*l*) *Rom.* 15.5.

(*m*) The Artful Husband, *p.* 13. *l.* 1.

(*n*) The Faithful General, *p.* 1. *l.* 2.

(*o*) *Deut.* 32.29. *Matth.* 24. 42,43,44. *Mark* 13. 35,36,37. *Luke* 12.35,36,37,38,39,40.

(*p*) Female Wits, *p.* 61. *l.* 12.

(*q*) The Mistake, *p.* 28. *l.* 25.

(*r*) Love at first sight, *p.* 49. *l.* 11.

(*s*) *Ephes.* 4. 15, 25.

(*t*) *Deut.* 32. 4.

(*u*) *John* 14.17. *Joh.* 15.26. *Joh.* 16.13. 1 *John* 4. 6.

Truth.

Truth. Of this, one Quotation shall suffice; (*x*) *Fie, Fie,* (saith an *Actor*) *the keeping of one's Word is a thing below the Honour of a Gentleman.*

As for *Honesty* in *Scripture*, it is a just, upright, and *sincere* dealing between Man and Man. Our *Blessed Saviour* commends it, as (*y*) the substance of all *the Law and the Prophets.* The Apostles frequently (*z*) press it in their Epistles. It was a Duty which they (*a*) practised, and (*b*) a Qualification for the Office of a Deacon, and also (*c*) a Means to profit by the Word of GOD. What the *Stage* means by the *Honesty* which is there commended, may be known by this Example. In a (*d*) late *Comedy*, (*e*) more lately reprinted, *Freeman* and *Courtall* have the Character of *two honest Gentlemen of the Town.* They are mentioned as such in the *Drama*, and crown'd with Success according to their Desires at the end of the *Play.* Now they begin the *Play* by entering together (*f*) upon the *Stage*, and immediately fall into discourse together (*g*) concerning their whoring Intrigues with their old Acquaintance: they (*h*) complain, that there is little hopes of new, and (*i*) call it a wicked Town for that reason. They (*k*) follow two Women, whom they never saw before; they (*l*) talk wantonly, and intrigue with them, and are ready upon receiving a strange Letter, to intrigue with others. And they have also (*m*) very leud and dishonest Designs with a married Woman; to prevent the discovery whereof, (*n*) one goes into a Closet, and (*o*) the other goes under a Table.

(*x*) She wou'd if she cou'd, *p.* 113. *l.* 7.

(*y*) *Mat.* 7. 12.

(*z*) *Rom.* 12. 17. *Rom.* 13. 13. 2 *Cor.* 8. 21. 2 *Cor.* 13. 7. *Phil.* 4. 8. 1 *Thess.* 4. 12. 1 *Tim.* 2. 2. 1 *Pet.* 2. 12.

(*a*) *Heb.* 13. 18.

(*b*) *Acts* 6. 3.

(*c*) *Luke* 8. 15.

(*d*) She wou'd if she cou'd, *printed Anno* 1710.

(*e*) *Reprinted Anno* 1715.

(*f*) P. 1. *alias* 89. *l.* 1.

(*g*) P. 1. *alias* 89. *l.* 14.

(*h*) P. 1. *alias* 89. *l.* 15.

(*i*) P. 1. *alias* 89. *l.* 16.

(*k*) P. 103. l. 6.

(*l*) P. 104. l. 9.

(*m*) P. 153. l. 29. p. 155. l. 13.

(*n*) P. 155. l. 10.

(*o*) P. 156. l. 31.

As

As to their ſeparate *Characters*, *Freeman* is (*p*) notoriouſly guilty of *Swearing*; he (*q*) banters upon *hardneſs of Heart*. He tells the Audience (*r*) how odious *a thing it is to be thought to love a Wife in good Company*; and ſaith, (*s*) that he would *break the whole Ten Commandments, rather than diſappoint* a Woman *of breaking one*.

On the other hand, *Courtall* not only (*t*) *ſwears* moſt notoriouſly, but he alſo (*u*) invokes the *Devil*. He banters on the word (*x*) *Infidel*, and (*y*) upon the *Lord*'s Prayer, nay (*z*) upon GOD, upon GOD's *Mercy*, and upon himſelf as a poor Sinner, in one Breath. When he was apprehenſive of being diſcovered, he ſaith, (*a*) *Now out comes all my Roguery*, meaning his ſwearing and forſwearing. He ridicules an honeſt conjugal Affection (*b*) with words ſo obſcene, that they muſt be omitted, and (*c*) calls *Conſtancy a forgetting all Shame*. He (*d*) commends the *Hopes* of *Variety*, and tells the Audience, that a *ſingle Intrigue in Love is as dull as a ſingle Plot in a Play*; and (*e*) farther adds, that *the keeping a Man's Word* is a *diſhonourable* thing. A (*f*) Waiting-Woman gives him notice of her Miſtreſs's baſe Intentions, which he receives very kindly. He (*g*) tells of his leud Courſes, and (*h*) calls a being common to all, *a Chriſtian Liberty*: and that the Audience may have the Notion of *Honeſty* from a Perſon of his Character, he adds, (*i*) that *wheedling* with a Man, whilſt a leud Deſign is carried on with his Wife, is both *neceſſary and honeſt*. And leſt Proſe alone might not

(*p*) P.129. l.4. p.144. l.28. p.145. l.5,21. p.146.l.8. p.151. l.6. p.168. l.15.
(*q*) P.96. l.20.
(*r*) P.134. l.29.
(*s*) P.144. l.19.
(*t*) P.114. l.4,15. p.117.l.16. p.121. l. 18, 26. p.135. l.4. p. 144. l.26. p.146. l.31. p. 148. l. 29. p. 164. l. 38. p. 167. l. 1.
(*u*) P.148. l.4.
(*x*) P.95. l.30.
(*y*) P.102. l.7.
(*z*) P.116. l.13.
(*a*) P.121. l.18.
(*b*) P.132. l.1.
(*c*) P.105. l.26.
(*d*) P.117. l.28.
(*e*) P.113. l.7.
(*f*) P.90. l.31.
(*g*) P.92. l.13.
(*h*) P.93. l.19.
(*i*) P.95. l.12.

not be sufficient to give a due notion of Honesty, a (*k*) *Song* explains it in these words:

> *A Catch and a Glass,*
> *A Fiddle and a Lass,*
> *What more would an honest Man have?*

Thus we see, according to the *Play-House Language*, an *honest Gentleman* is a *swearing, drunken, smutty, whoring, atheistical* Rattle. And when it is applauded on the *Stage*, it is taken in this sense. Such Persons make honourable Exits, and are rewarded with the most agreeable Women, and the richest Fortunes. But when *Honesty* is taken in the *Scripture* and the common Sense, it meets with a different Treatment. In such Cases they load it with *Epithets* full of Contempt and Reproach. Thus they call it (*l*) *blunt*, (*m*) *dull*, (*n*) *ill-tim'd*, or (*o*) *stubborn*, or (*p*) *the squeamish Fits of Honesty*. An honest Man is call'd (*q*) an *unwary honest Fool*. Thus an *Actor* saith, (*r*) *They'd make us honest, that is, they'd make us Fools*. I am the longer on this Subject, because there is less Danger in the Poison; and the Reader may thereby guess, how much more might have been said upon the rest. However, I shall only add some Quotations concerning *Honesty* and *Villany*.

As for *Honesty*, they speak of it thus:

(*s*) *Be honest! ha, ha, ha! I thank you, Sir, I love no such starving Virtue.*

> (*t*) *Let those, who bind themselves to Honour's Rules,*
> *Die, as they live, unthinking honest Fools:*
> *Who covet vain Reports of Honesty,*

(*k*) She wou'd if she cou'd, *printed* 1715. *p*. 165. *l*. 16.

(*l*) Solon, *p*. 49. *l*. 4.

(*m*) Irene, *p*. 29. *l*. 26.

(*n*) Cruel Gift, *p*. 1. *l*. 4.

(*o*) Faithful General, *p*. 42. *l*. 39.

(*p*) Marry or do worse, *p*. 21. *l*. 19.

(*q*) Faithful Bride of Granada, *p*. 18. *l*. 28.

(*r*) Stage-Beaux toss'd in a Blanket, *Prologue*, *p*. 2. *l*. 15.

(*s*) A Woman's Revenge, p. 7. l. 18.

(*t*) The Apparition. p. 13. l. 20.

Unenvy'd let them take the Fame for me:
Success in Fraud pays well for Infamy.

(u) *I wonder how Men can be such Fools to be honest; when Roguery thrives so well: Look where you will, 'tis that sways the World;*

And prosp'rous Villany abounds with Store,
Whilst honest Men are shunn'd, despis'd, and poor.

These two are not only in Verse, but at the End of *Acts*, when the Person speaks alone, and then goes out, that the Audience may have time to make a due Improvement.

(x) *This Virtue* (Freedom) *is enough to make me bear with all the Inconveniences of honest Company.*

(y) *Reform, and live honest.* Answer. *That's the way to be starv'd.*

(z) A Father's Advice to his Son:

But what hast thou to do with ill-tim'd Honesty?
Observe me well, and treasure in thy Soul
The experienc'd Wisdom of thy Father:
Let Interest be thy bright unerring Guide,
The secret darling Purpose of thy Heart.
Believe me, Boy, she reigns supreme below;
Honours and endless Pleasures wait around her:
When she commands, smile on the Man thou hatest,
Caress him to inevitable Ruin.
From foolish Pity guard thy well-taught Mind:
Think not of Friendship, more than of a Word
Which, once gone forth, is lost in idle Air.

(a) Thus they rail more particularly at honest Love: *What, turn'd Chymist in Love! Extracting Patience from the mere Necessity of a Woman's Inconstancy!* (with an Oath) *that a Man of Sense should be thus Ass-rid, and never feel himself gall'd! Wilt thou never be wise?*

(u) Ibid. p. 37. l. 11.
(x) The Comical Revenge, p. 15. l. *penult.*
(y) The Confederacy, p. 4. l. 9.
l. 35.
(z) The Cruel Gift, p. 1. l. 4.
(a) *Portsmouth* Heiress, p. 47.

And

And as they expose *Honesty*, so they commend *Villany* such Language as this:

(*b*) *Ay, but he's a Villain too!——No matter, the likelier to thrive.*

(*c*) Spoken also by one alone at the End of an Act:

I question not but your religious Dotards,
Who mortify, and feed on barren Virtue,
Were they to know these Deeds, would call me Villain:
But let them rail, and pride themselves in Conscience;
Whilst I each Bliss within my Grasp surprize,
I'll leave to them Reversions in the Skies.

(*d*) Spoken by one in Sackcloth of himself: *A Villain, but a repenting Villain! Stuff, which Saints in all Ages have been made of.*

The last *Virtue* which I shall mention, is *Obedience to Parents.* This is (*e*) frequently commended in *Scripture*, and frequently expos'd on the *Stage*, and especially in the Case of Love. This is a fine Lesson for young Ladies that hear it, and see it acted to the Life. (*f*) *He ask'd* (saith one) *in a surly manner——and I answer'd him as surlily. What tho he be my Father, I am not bound Prentice to him: So I told him in plain terms, if I were minded to marry, I'd marry to please myself, not him.* Answer. *And were you this undutiful and graceless Wretch to your Father?* Reply. *Then why was he graceless first?* There is more to this purpose, but too filthy to be seen. (*g*) Another saith, *If he was my Father, I should take a great pleasure to plague him.* And a third saith, (*h*) *My Heart begins to fail me*; and asks this Question, *Shall I resist my Father?* To this it is answer'd, *When he resists Nature. Are you to be a Goslin all your Life? Are you not of Age to be* married? *And doth he think you are made of Marble?* If the Disposal of Children in Mar-

(*b*) The Apparition, p. 16. l. 37.

(*c*) Perfidious Brother, p. 25. l. 5.

(*d*) Provok'd Wife, p. 70. l. 12.

(*e*) *Exod.* 20. 12. *Deut.* 5. 16. *Prov.* 23. 22. & 30. 17. *Mat.* 15. 4, 6. *Mark* 7. 10, 13. *Ephes.* 6. 1, 2. *Colos.* 3. 20.

(*f*) Love for Love, p. 55. l. 4.

(*g*) The Quacks, p. 5. l. 1.

(*h*) Ibid. p. 6. l. 19.

 riage

riage is the great Concern of Parents, and that upon which their own Comfort, the Comfort of their Children, and the Honour of their Family depends; and if they would have them dutiful in this Caſe, they ought to keep them from the *Play-Houſes*.

By this we may obſerve, how excellently the *Stage* promotes *Virtue*, and endeavours to reclaim the Age. Let every Man live as he pleaſeth: Let them *ſwear*, *curſe*, and *blaſpheme*: Let them be guilty of *Whoredom* and *Adultery*, be *drunk*, *impudent* and *ſhameleſs*, and never mind either *Death* or *Judgment*; then the *Actors* will thrive, their *Houſes* will be full, and then (which GOD forbid) they will effect their intended *Reformation*.

CHAP. XII.

Atheiſm and Profaneneſs promoted by the Stage.

AS the *Stage* vilifies *Religion* and the *Worſhip* of GOD, ſo it endeavours to promote *Atheiſm* and *Infidelity*. The Scriptures tell us, (*a*) That *the inviſible things of GOD, even his eternal Power and Godhead, are clearly ſeen, being underſtood by the things which are made: ſo that* the very Heathens, who had only the Light of Nature, and *denied it, were without Excuſe*. It is therefore a more (*b*) *abominable Wickedneſs* and *Folly*, to think *in our Hearts, That there is no GOD*: And what then muſt it be to expreſs it, and plead for it publickly in Words? If Men can be brought to be of this opinion, it immediately follows, that the *Holy Scriptures* are a Cheat, *Religion* is an Impoſition, and Men may live as they pleaſe, without any regard to a future State. However, the *Actors* ſpeak ſo freely upon moſt Occaſions, as if they thought there was no GOD at all. We are

(*a*) *Rom.* 1. 20.

(*b*) *Pſal.* 14. 1. *Pſal.* 53. 1.

told,

told, (*c*) that *in these days Religion is the common Topick for the Raillery of our modern Wits, and* that *Atheism is their distinguishing Mark.* And therefore as the *Poets* set up so much for Wits, we may be sure that they will take care that nothing shall be out of Character, which can evade the Penalty of the Law. Accordingly, in one *Play* (*d*) there is a remarkable *Dialogue* to this purpose; containing the Advice of a wealthy grave Knight to his Nephew, at his first setting out in the World.

'Nephew. *I am intirely free from the Prejudice of Education and Priestcraft.*

To this the Uncle objects, *Then the grave Dons will say, you are both a Dunce and an Atheist, Sirrah.* However, he himself makes the Answer: *But I think a little Spice of Infidelity sits smartly upon a young Fellow.*

Nephew answers; *Sir, I will wear my Faith, my Reason, and my Clothes, in the newest Cut.*

The Uncle replies, *Do so, you young Heretical Rogue! You do! The Boy has Fire: Ay, this is Life, Spirit, Soul.*

In another *Play* an *Actor* (*e*) tells us his own Religion; *I seldom trouble the Gods, except it be to swear by them.* A third saith, (*f*) *The Wits were Atheists in old Times, and* they were *brave Examples* for the Moderns to imitate, which *we follow'd till of late.* A fourth swears, that (*g*) if he *descends into the dark Corners of the Devil,* he will not trouble his head about it. And another adds, (*h*) *Pray let me request you to forget to say your Prayers, whilst these* (Women) *are Courtiers: Or if you will needs think of Heaven, let it be no higher than their Eyes.*

[Turn us, O LORD, in Mercy; that we may not experimentally know thee to be GOD by thy Justice, and our own Confusion.]

(*c*) Woman is a Riddle, p. 5. l. 14.

(*d*) The Wife's Relief, p. 22. Scene 3. l. 6.

(*e*) Love the Leveller, p. 5. l. 6.

(*f*) Love at first sight, p. 9. l. 3.

(*g*) The Amorous Miser, p. 9. l. 22.

(*h*) The Loyal Subject, p. 44. l. 18.

In the Times of gross Ignorance, it was the grand Design of the *Devil* to delude the Pagan World into Superstition: But since the clear Light of the Gospel hath appeared, and the Errors of Superstition have been so fully detected, his great Intention is to promote *Atheism*. Then he would fain make the World believe, that there were many GODS; and now he would fain introduce this Opinion, that there is no GOD at all. This seems to be the present Design, and the *Players* seem to concur with him in the promoting of it. But this being so notoriously gross, that it will hardly go down with any, there is another Aim, namely, to introduce *Profaneness*; and in this he is too successful. Here the *Players* act their Parts to the utmost in his Service. Every Quotation in this Book might serve for an Example; and therefore in enlarging on this Subject, I might transcribe the whole again. It is a melancholy thing to consider, how guilty the *Poets* are of a Crime so (i) often complain'd of; they put no difference between the things that are *holy*, and the things that are *profane*. The Word in *Scripture* generally signifies an Offence committed either against (k) the Divine Majesty, or something which immediately relates to him, as (l) his *Holiness*, or (m) his *Holy Name*. It signifies an Offence against (n) his *Covenant*, (o) the *Hallow'd*, or (p) the *Holy Things*, his (q) *Ordinances*, his (r) *Sabbaths*, his (s) *Sanctuary*, or his (t) *Temple*. Upon the *Stage*, the Word is used in trifling matters: A private House is a *Temple*, the robbing thereof is (u) *Sacrilege*, and a Person is call'd *profane* for this reason. It is said of a Woman, that *her* (x) *sacred Limbs had been pro-*

(i) *Ezek.* 22. 26. & 42. 20. & 44. 23.

(k) *Ezek.* 22. 26.

(l) *Mal.* 2. 11.

(m) *Levit.* 18. 21. & 19. 12. & 20. 3. & 21. 6. & 22. 2, 32. *Ezek.* 36. 20, 21, 22, 23. *Amos* 2. 7. *Mal.* 1. 11, 12.

(n) *Mal.* 2. 10.

(o) *Levit.* 19. 8.

(p) *Levit.* 22. 15. *Ezek.* 22. 16.

(q) *Levit.* 22. 9.

(r) *Nehem.* 13. 17, 18. *Ezek.* 22. 8. & 23. 38. *Mat.* 12. 5.

(s) *Levit.* 21. 12, 23. *Ezek.* 23. 39. & 24. 21. & 25. 3.

(t) *Acts* 24. 6.

(u) Beaux Stratagem, p. 61. l. 37.

(x) Manlius Capitolinus, p. 9. l. 28.

fan'd

fan'd with Irons: and what could have been ſaid more, if they had believ'd her to be a Goddeſs? Nay, a Woman ſaith of herſelf, (y) *Every idle Tongue profanes me now*; that is, ſpeaks of her. Thus to *profane the Paſſion of Love*, is either (z) to deſcribe it imperfectly, or to (a) miſrepreſent it. Thus even (b) a *Perriwig* is ſaid to be *profan'd* by *the Touch of a Hat*. And as every Trifle is thus idoliz'd, ſo on other occaſions they make light of the *Sin* itſelf, as it refers to GOD. The Senſe of the Divine Majeſty is loſt; and an *Actor* ſaith that of himſelf, which is too true of all the reſt: (c) *Now I have put on the Outſide of Profaneneſs, I would willingly wear it to ſome purpoſe.* Certainly the Advice of the *Apoſtle* can never be better apply'd, than in this Caſe: (d) If we would *exerciſe* our *ſelves unto Godlineſs*, and delight therein, we muſt *refuſe* ſuch *profane Fables*. We muſt *avoid* all ſuch *profane and vain Babblings, for they will increaſe unto more Ungodlineſs; and their Word will eat as doth a Canker*, ſtill growing worſe and worſe, until the Vitals of *Religion* are deſtroy'd. And indeed it is too notorious, that formerly they dared not to be guilty of *Blaſphemy*; but ſince they have ventured upon ſuch a Liberty, they go on in defiance both of GOD and Man, inſomuch that no Method hitherto attempted hath been able to reſtrain them.

(y) Faithful Bride of *Granada*, p. 46. l. 18.

(z) Royal Convert, p. 19. l. 7.

(a) The Victim, p. 28. l. 13.

(b) The Man of Mode, *Epilogue*, l. 26.

(c) The different Widows, p. 8. l. 22.

(d) 1 *Tim.* 4. 7. 1 *Tim.* 6. 20. 2 *Tim.* 2. 16.

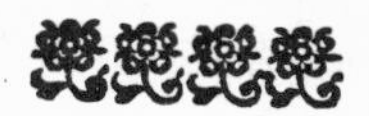

CHAP. XIII.

Vice encouraged by the Stage.

AS the *Stage* exposeth *Virtue*, so it also encourageth *Vice*; and is in this respect as equally guilty as in the other. For the Proof of this, I shall first produce some general Quotations, and leave them to the Consideration of the Reader.

(*a*) *We ought to sin seasonably, to drink in* Spain, *and whore in* London, *where the Wenches are good and cheap, and the Tax free.*

(*c*) *For a Look and a Chink of this,* (Money) *who now-a-days would not be a Sinner?*

(*d*) *I hate to sin like a Porter, that's damnable; but to sin in State, and like a Gentleman, I hope, is venial.*

(*e*) *Vice, when dress'd by him,* (an Actor) *hath Charms about her.*

(*f*) *Thou art fond of Vice, for the sake of the Scandal.* Answ. *Ay, Ay, you may give it what names you please; but the dear Felicity of Life is concealed under these hideous Titles,* (by calling it Vice, &c.) *like a good Face under a frightful Vizor. And as there is no Preferment to be had without Interest, so there is no Pleasure to be had without Scandal.*

But to be more particular: To this end they apply the *Act of Parliament* passed in a late Reign for *Toleration* of the *Protestant Dissenters*. If a Man can commit a *Sin* without a Scruple, they say, he hath his Liberty by *Law*, and may go on. Thus *Liberty of Conscience* is

(*a*) Gibraltar, *p.* 6. *l.* 14.
(*c*) Ibid. *p.* 22. *l.* 25.
(*d*) Love at first sight, *p.* 14. *l.* 16.
(*e*) Ibid. *p.* 50. *l.* 23.
(*f*) *Portsmouth* Heiress, *p.* 7. *l.* 8. *Spoken by the well-bred Gentleman.*

render'd

render'd as a *Liberty* to act without any *Conscience* at all. Here is a bold Reflection on the *Legislative Power*, and if such a *Liberty* is not restrain'd, it may prove of pernicious consequence. This *Act of Parliament* is particularly applied to encourage *Adultery*; (g) *Women cannot please long* (saith an Actor) *if they affect an Arbitrary Sway*, (to keep their Husbands to themselves) and the Reason which he gives, is, because there is *Liberty of Conscience*. Another also (h) speaks more fully to the same purpose: *Every Man after his own Fancy, I say. You are for a Whore, I am for a Bottle. As long as there is Liberty of Conscience abroad, why should not every Man be damn'd in his own way?* These are their Reports upon the *Statutes* of this *Realm*. Blessed be GOD, we have good *Laws* made for the suppressing of *Immorality* and *Profaneness*: These *Laws* have also been put in execution, and some of the *Actors* have felt the smart of them. At this they are angry, and cannot forbear to shew their Resentments against the *Law-makers*, and render them ridiculous: (i) *I* (saith one) *will petition the House of Commons to prove me a Cuckold, and be divorc'd by Act of Parliament*. I wish they would *petition* for their further Regulation, or others would *petition* for their total Suppression; and hope, that either the one or the other may in time be granted. The *Parliament* made an *Act* against *profane Swearing and Cursing*: To this (k) one of the *Actors* refers: *We pay for Swearing, and we pay for Drinking*. And another infers from thence, That *thus is Vice, by the Dexterity of our Councils, made the Supporter of Religion and the Laws*. All their Efforts cannot abolish such *Acts of Parliament*, and therefore they thus endeavour to ridicule them.

But for a further Encouragement of *Vice*, they represent *Persons* extremely *vicious* with Names of Respect and Esteem, and give them Characters in the *Drama*, as if they were the most accomplish'd Persons.

(g) Love's Contrivance, *p.* 17. *l. antepenult.*

(h) Gibraltar, *Sheet* E. *p.* 39. *l.* 25.

(i) *Hampstead*-Heath, *p.* 48. *l.* 21.

(k) Gibraltar, *p.* 6. *l.* 18.

In

In one *Play* (*l*) a Gentleman of *Shropſhire* is honour'd by the Name of *Worthy*, who owns that he did endeavour to debauch his own Miſtreſs: and in another *Play*, one of the ſame Name determines the Point thus (*m*) in defence of *Pimping*; *Right! but where there is a Neceſſity, a Chriſtian is bound to help his Neighbour.* Thus *Chriſtianity* is proſtituted to the *Stews*, and our conſcientious Obligations terminate in Leudneſs; and all this is promoted by Men of *Figure*.

In another *Play* the firſt *Actor* mention'd in the *Drama* is call'd by the Name of *Conſtant*; and who would not now expect a virtuous Behaviour? But yet at his firſt Entrance upon the *Stage*, he (*n*) banters all *Reformation*; he (*o*) ſwears at length, he confeſſeth himſelf lewd, (*p*) that he hath *more Fleſh and Blood than Grace and Self-denial*, and (*q*) he loved a marry'd Woman, the Lady *Brute*, *more than ever a Martyr did his Soul*. His *Conſtancy* is only a continual (*r*) ſolliciting of this Lady to commit Adultery with him. He (*s*) urgeth his own *Conſtancy* and *Truth* as Arguments that he ſhould ſucceed in ſuch a baſe Deſign, and prefers Debauchery before Marriage. (*t*) *There is* (ſaith he) *a poor ſordid Slavery in Marriage, that turns the flowing Tide of Honour, and ſinks it to the loweſt Ebb of Infamy. 'Tis a corrupted Soil: Ill-nature, Avarice, Sloth, Cowardice and Dirt are all its Product.* But he alſo ſaith at the ſame time, (*u*) that *Conſtancy* (by which he means Whoring) *is a brave, free, haughty, generous Agent, which cannot buckle to the Chains of Wedlock.* Thus *Vice* is diſtinguiſh'd by Names of Reſpect, whilſt a (*x*) *Juſtice* of the Peace, who ſhould ſuppreſs it, is call'd by a Name of Reproach, and deſcribed as one *who lives by Extortion and Connivance*; as if the Government did place

(*l*) Recruiting Officer, *p.* 6. *l.* 9.

(*m*) The Relapſe, *p.* 33. *l.* 24.

(*n*) Provok'd Wife, *p.* 14. *l.* 36.

(*o*) Ibid. *p.* 15. *l.* 7.

(*p*) Pag. 15. l. 6.

(*q*) P. 15. l. 14.

(*r*) P. 32. l. 16. *ad finem.* P. 33, 34. *per totum.* p. 52. l. 36. *ad finem.* p. 53, 54.

(*s*) P. 53. l. 29.

(*t*) P. 34. l. 1.

(*u*) P. 33. l. *ult.*

(*x*) The Humour of the Age, *Drama.*

ſuch

ſuch in theſe Offices, whoſe Circumſtances without them were the moſt mean and deplorable.

The Characters of *Freeman* and *Courtall*, two *honeſt Gentlemen of the Town* in one *Play*, have been already deſcribed, and need no Repetition.

In another *Play* (for I ſhall quote but one more) (y) *Belfond junior* is deſcribed to be *ſomewhat given to Women, and now and then to Good-Fellowſhip*; *but an ingenious well-accompliſh'd Gentleman, a Man of Honour, and of an excellent Diſpoſition and Temper.* How theſe *Characters* can conſiſt together, is ſtrange. However (z) he had a Child by one Whore, whom he turn'd off, and left to ſtarve, and then he debauch'd another, and was diſcover'd in the Fact. The next is his Uncle, (a) *a Man poſſeſs'd* (as the Poet tells us) *with all Gentleman-like Qualities.* He is angry with a Father for reproving his Son, and for this reaſon calls him (b) *Shame of the Family,* with more Language of the ſame nature. On this occaſion he alſo ſaith, that (c) *Rigour makes nothing but Hypocrites*; and (d) *too much Straitneſs in the Minds of Youth, like too much lacing of the Body, will make them grow crooked.* He (e) vindicates his Nephew, ſaying, *He is, as all young Fellows, I believe, are, given to Women*; *but 'tis in private. No common Whoremaſter*; *and in ſhort, keeps as good Company as any in* England. And again, (f) *He doth no ungentleman-like things. What if he doth wench a little, and is now and then extravagant in Wine? Where's the great Crime?* And (g) he afterward confeſſeth, that he himſelf had been guilty of the ſame.

To theſe we may alſo add *Truman* in the ſame *Play*, who is (h) ſaid to be a *Friend* to *Belfond junior, and a Man of Honour and Fortune*; and yet (i) he plainly

(y) The Squire of *Alſatia, Drama.*
(z) Ibid. *Termagant* in the *Drama.* P. 14. Act 2. Scene 1. p. 20. l. 14. p. 40. l. 8.
(a) *Drama.*
(b) P. 22. l. antepenult.
(c) P. 12. l. 42.
(d) P. 13. l. 3.
(e) P. 11. l. 27.
(f) P. 12. l. 8.
(g) P. 12. l. 21.
(h) Ibid. *Drama.*
(i) Ibid. p. 45. l. 3.

con-

confesseth, that he had *enjoy'd a Lady in most lewd Dalliance.*

To instance but in one Woman: The fine *Angelica*, a Lady of thirty thousand Pounds Fortune, talks (*k*) saucily to her Uncle, and (*l*) smuttily to her Suitor; she (*m*) burlesques the Scriptures, and (*n*) most profanely and immodestly makes herself, as well as her Sex, the Objects of *Zeal*, *Faith*, and *Perseverance even to Martyrdom*; adding, that the *Men* who act otherwise, *are* either *Hypocrites or Infidels*.

And yet this is not all: The *Poets* not only represent their principal *Actors* as most scandalously vicious; but also take care to reward them with good Wives and Fortunes at the End of the *Play*. Or if they meet not with such Success, which is but seldom; yet they are never punished as they deserve. This was fully charg'd upon them by Mr. *Collier*, in a whole Chapter on this Subject; but nothing which can be said, will cause them to amend: there must be some other Method to reclaim them.

As for later Examples; there are no greater Persons in one *Comedy* than *Wilmot* and *Vincent*. These (*o*) endeavour to debauch *Leonora* and *Jacquelinda*, two *Spanish* Ladies. For this purpose they form several Intrigues, (*p*) first with *Guzman*, and then (*q*) with *Blincarda* their Governess. They (*r*) frequently own themselves to be notorious *Whoremongers*; and yet (*s*) they are afterward rewarded by marrying these two Ladies, with two thousand Pounds each for their Portions.

In an old *Play*, but still frequently acted, *Valentine* loves *Angelica*, and is so well rewarded by her, that the *Comedy* takes its Name from them both. He is the

---

(*k*) Love for Love, p. 16. l. 27. p. 17. l. 4.
(*l*) P. 68. l. 13.
(*m*) Ibid.
(*n*) P. 78. l. 28.
(*o*) Gibraltar, p. 35. l. 4.
(*p*) P. 12. l. 34.
(*q*) P. 22. Act 3. l. 1.
(*r*) P. 3. l. 7, & penult. p. 4. l. 28. p. 5. l. 8, 12. p. 6. l. 35. p. 8. l. 3. p. 9. l. 5. p. 18. l. antepenult. p. 36. l. 12, 28. p. 38. l. 1, 5. p. 39. l. 24. p. 56. l. 3. p. 58. l. 4.
(*s*) P. 68. l. 10.

Hero of the whole Performance, and (*t*) recommended as a Perſon of many *Virtues*. 'Tis true, he was hearty in his Affection to *Angelica*. He was (*u*) indeed Fifteen Hundred Pounds in Debt to one Man, with (*x*) half a dozen Duns, who came in a Morning, (*y*) and ſeveral others, to the value of Four Thouſand Pounds. This made him (*z*) under Confinement; and therefore in his caſe, to be in love with a Lady of Thirty Thouſand Pounds, muſt need be a great Commendation. But abating this one Character, he is altogether compounded of Vice. He is a (*a*) *Prodigal*, and unnatural, and ſpent all his Subſtance in riotous Living. He was (*b*) ſcandalouſly guilty of whoring, and (*c*) ſeems to glory in it. He is (*d*) undutiful. He (*e*) curſes, and (*f*) ſwears. He (*g*) talks profanely, and applies to himſelf the words of our *Saviour*, (*h*) *I am the Truth*; as if in the midſt of his pretended Madneſs, he was really ſmitten with the Pleaſure of Blaſphemy: And yet this Libertine is crown'd for the Man of Merit, he hath his Wiſhes thrown into his Lap, and makes the happy *Exit* by obtaining his Miſtreſs, who (*i*) receives him with profane Raptures on that occaſion.

In a later *Play* (*k*) *Dick* is a *Gameſter*, (*l*) he diſowns his Mother, (*m*) and ſteals from her. (*n*) His Mother gives him the vileſt of Characters, and (*o*) his Diſcourſe with his Man, ſhews him to be a Villain, and publickly known to be ſuch. He (*p*) *ſwears* moſt horridly, and

(*t*) Love for Love, p. 77. l. 20.

(*u*) P. 5. l. *penult.*

(*x*) P. 4. l. 28.

(*y*) P. 7. l. *ult.* p. 20. l. *penul.* p. 21. l. 5.

(*z*) P. 8. l. 3.

(*a*) P. 1. l. 7, &c. p. 4. l. 28. p. 5. l. *penult.* p. 8. l. 17.

(*b*) P. 5. l. 19.

(*c*) P. 6. l. 34, 39.

(*d*) P. 53. l. 6. p. 76. l. 5.

(*e*) P. 12. l. 36.

(*f*) P. 33. l. 8.

(*g*) P. 22. l. 11, 17. p. 30. l. 36.

(*h*) *John* 14. 6. P. 51. l. 2. p. 52. l. 31. p. 57. l. 22.

(*i*) P. 78. l. 28.

(*k*) The Confederacy, *Drama.*

(*l*) P. 12. l. 21. p. 13. l. 28. p. 14. l. 22. p. 32. l. 27. p. 33. l. 16. p. 44. l. 23.

(*m*) P. 31. l. *antepenult.*

(*n*) P. 2. l. 37, *penult.* p. 12. l. 14. p. 13. l. 21. p. 35. l. 9, 14. p. 71. l. 6, 16, 20.

(*o*) P. 3. l. 38.

(*p*) P. 13. l. 8, 15, 19. p. 14. l. 9. p. 32. *l. penult.* p. 33. l. 3, 7. p. 45. l. 7.

is

is guilty of many other *Vices*. However, he also (q) marries *Corinna*, a Maiden of a great Fortune, and unexpectedly receives (r) Ten Thousand Pounds from his Mother, Mrs. *Amlet*. The whole *Plot* turns upon him; since *The Confederacy*, from whence the *Play* took its Name, is only a Combination between him and *Brass* his Man, for all sorts of Mischief.

In another *Play* there are three remarkable Instances of this nature.

First, Capt. *Rainer* is publickly debauched from the beginning to the end. At (s) his first entrance upon the *Stage*, he rails against *Religion* and *Reformation*, and carries his Cause with a very trivial opposition. He (t) pleads for *whoring*, and (u) endeavours to debauch every Woman almost which he meets: Acquaintance or Strangers, or in Masks, are all alike to him, so (x) extravagant is he in his Amours. This is (y) the *free* and *well-bred* Gentleman, the principal Person in the *Comedy*, who (z) in the end marries the Lady from whence the *Play* took its Name, with Ten Thousand Pounds Fortune.

Secondly, *Venture* (a) forges *Lyes* and *Intrigues* to steal a Fortune. He (b) courts *Lucia*, supposing her to be the *Portsmouth Heiress*, and afterwards marries her. However, (c) she proves a great Fortune; and thus all his Tricks and Cheats are crown'd with success.

Lastly, *Feignwel* (d) forges Lyes of *Freemont*, (e) debauches *Maria*, then he (f) slights her and courts another. But (g) in the end he marries *Maria*, who had a Thousand Pounds. So that these are their *Exits* after all their Rogueries.

(q) P.72. l.12.
(r) P.72. l.5.
(s) *Portsmouth* Heiress, p. 5. l. 19.
(t) P.4. l.27. p.9. l.29.
(u) P.10. l.23. p.17. l.6. p. 31. l.23. p.32. l.10, 19.
(x) *Drama*.
(y) *Drama*.
(z) P.67. l.5.

(a) P.12. l. 26. p.14. l.8.
(b) P.52. l.19.
(c) P.69. l.7.
(d) P.27. l.15. p.40. l.15. p. 44. l.28.
(e) Maria *in the Drama*, p. 26. l.6.
(f) Feignwel *in the Drama*,
(g) P.71. l.28.

In another *Play*, (*h*) *Volatile* loſes all his Subſtance at gaming. However, (*i*) he games again, and wins; and at laſt, for a farther Encouragement, (*k*) he gains *Arabella*, the Object of his Wiſhes.

In another *Play*, (*l*) *Reynard*, for the obtaining of his Miſtreſs, gets falſe and forged Deeds of Eſtates; but (*m*) the Cheat proves ſo well, that he married *Belinda* with her Father's conſent, who was the principal *Actreſs* in the *Play*, and (*n*) Heireſs to a conſiderable Eſtate, both real and perſonal.

It would be endleſs to mention all the Inſtances of this kind, ſince there are few *Plays* without ſome. I ſhall therefore proceed to thoſe particular Commendations which they give of ſeveral *Vices*, that ſo it may be evident, how they carry on the ſame Deſign in words at length, as well as in ſuch Repreſentations.

As for *Sin* in general, they ſpeak of it upon ridiculous occaſions, and in a ridiculous manner. One ſaith, (*o*) It is *too great a Sin to compare* one Woman with another. They make our very Duties to be *Sins*: *'Twere a Sin in me* (ſaith one) *to learn dull Patience.* They look upon the preventing of Sin in others, to be a *Sin* in itſelf. Thus (*p*) an *Actor* ſaith, that *a good motherly Woman of his Acquaintance, talking of the Sins of the Times, told him with Tears in her Eyes*, that Whoredom and Adultery was in part prevented, *to the utter Decay and Diſcouragement of Trade and Induſtry.* And another ſaith immediately before, (*q*) That *London* was *grown a wicked Town*, becauſe they had not ſuch Notices, where they might be debauched, as formerly.

St. *John* tells us, (*r*) that *Sin is the Tranſgreſſion of the Law* of GOD; but in the *Play-houſe* we learn, that it is a *Sin* and a *Wickedneſs* when his *Law* is not tranſgreſs'd.

(*h*) The Wife's Relief, p. 2. l. 4.
(*i*) P. 34. l. 32.
(*k*) P. 63. l. 33. p. 64. l. 32.
(*l*) *Tunbridge-Walks*, p. 45. l. 30.
(*m*) P. 54. l. 29. p. 56. l. 27.
(*n*) P. 58. l. 20.
(*o*) Comical Revenge, p. 22. l. 7.
(*p*) She wou'd if ſhe cou'd, p. 90. l. 2.
(*q*) Ibid. p. 1. *alias* 89. l. 17.
(*r*) 1 *John* 3. 4.

The

The first *Vice* which I shall mention, which they do constantly and notoriously recommend, is *Whoredom* and *Adultery*. The *Poets* put no difference between these, but plead for them both alike. The Description which they give of a *Whore*, is (*s*) that she is one *of the Ladies kept by publick-spirited Men for the good of the whole Town*. Where-ever the word *Love* is in the *Title-Page*, there the Intrigues of this nature are represented in the Book, and drawn up even into a *Science*. One of the *Comedians* made this Observation, (*t*) that *Whores were dog-cheap at* London, *and a Man might but step into the* Play-house *Passage, and pick up half a Dozen for half a Crown*. In short, these Intrigues are the *Plots* upon which the *Plays* turn, both *Comedy* and *Tragedy*, and wherein their Wit is shewn; so that we may as certainly expect to find such Instances, as to find both Men and Women in the *Drama*. For this reason, they frequently plead for *Adultery*, sometimes in (*u*) *Men*, and (*x*) sometimes in *Women*, and (*y*) sometimes in both; and seem wonderfully pleased with (*z*) one of the married Couple, who will wink at such Crimes in the other. At other times, they (*a*) speak against *Chastity*, as (*b*) a *foolish thing*, as *out of fashion*, and as *the worst thing in the world to keep*. And they represent (*c*) *Constancy* to each other, as a *scandalous* Vice in the eye of

(*s*) The Man of Mode, p. 242. l. 12.

(*t*) Gibraltar, p. 6. l. 9.

(*u*) Love at first sight, p. 1. l. *ult.* p. 12. l. 24. The Biter, p. 44. l. *antepenult.* Busy-Body, p. 5. l. 1. Modish Husband, p. 27. l. 32. *Portsmouth* Heiress, p. 42. l. 9. The Roving Husband reclaim'd, p. 23. l. 16. p. 47. l. 6. Tender Husband, p. 48. l. 19. p. 49. l. 4.

(*x*) Hampstead-Heath, p. 28. l. 25. *Perolla* and *Izadora*, *Epilogue*, l. 13. *with Smut following it.* Solon, p. 25. l. 18. p. 48. l. 21. The Cares of Love, p. 3. l. 24. Provok'd Wife, p. 40. l. 35. Tender Husband, p. 49. l. 22. Three Hours after Marriage, p. 14. l. 6.

(*y*) Love at first sight, p. 43. l. 13, 26. Love the Leveller, p. 8. l. 12. The Biter, p. 44. l. 21. Conquest of *Spain*, p. 4. l. 33. *Portsmouth* Heiress, p. 50. l. 17. The Roving Husband reclaim'd, p. 31. l. 17.

(*z*) Careless Husband, p. 6. l. 33.

(*a*) The Contivances, p. 1. l. 8.

(*b*) The Wife's Relief, p. 20. l. *antepenult.* The Masquerade, p. 1. l. 11.

(*c*) The Careless Husband, p. 43. l. 26.

the

the World. At other times, they (*d*) ſtrongly plead for *Whoredom*, and (*e*) extol the Office of a *Pimp*, or a *Procurer*, as a Buſineſs of Weight, Merit, and Authority; a civil Employment, fit to make a Man a Privy-Counſellor, and as no common Bleſſing to Mankind. Here the *Auditors* are taught, in words at length, and not in Figures only, how to debauch the Women with whom they converſe; and their Expreſſions are gilded over with all the *Art* and falſe *Rhetorick* imaginable. Here they are taught how to ſollicit the Lady herſelf, and ſometimes how to intrigue with the Waiting-Gentlewoman, both by fair Words and Bribes, to betray the young Miſtreſs, or enſnare her Affections. Here they are taught how to employ even their Waiting-Men to intrigue with the Servants of the Family for the ſame purpoſe, and to be let in at the Doors, or, rather than fail, to ſcale the Windows. The Method of Diſguiſes and conveying Letters, is drawn up into a Science; and there are ſuch Inſtances of every Particular in our mo-

(*d*) Gibraltar, p. 3. l. 3, 34. *Sheet* E. p. 35. l. 4. *at large. Sheet* F. p. 38. l. 1. *Sheet* H. p. 49. l. 27. Love at firſt ſight, p. 3. l. 4, *&c. to the end.* p. 4. l. 9. Love the Leveller, *Epilogue*, l. 1. The Baſſet Table, p. 55. l. 1, *&c.* The careleſs Husband, p. 43. l. 34. The comical Revenge, p. 32. l. 39. p. 34. l. 2. The Fair Example, p. 40. l. 26. Generous Husband, p. 22. l. 33. Humours of the Age, p. 29. l. 12. Man of Mode, p. 185. l. 1. p. 228. l. 15, 27. p. 238. l. 36. Modiſh Husband, p. 12. l. 20. *Portſmouth* Heireſs, p. 5. l. 1. p. 50. l. 17. Provok'd Wife, p. 40. l. 35. The Relapſe, p. 58. l. 2. The Rival Brothers, p. 12. l. 1, &c. *with many ſtrange Flights to this purpoſe.* The Roving Husband reclaim'd, p. 28. l. *ult.* Squire of *Alſatia*, p. 11. l. 24. p. 12. l. 8. *Compare alſo* p. 27. l. 4. *with the Explanation* p. 56. l. 15. p. 70. l. 4. The Wife's Relief, p. 45. l. 28. *Venus* and *Adonis*, p. 11. l. 16.

(*e*) An Act at *Oxford*, p. 11. l. 12. *Repeated in* Hampſtead-Heath, p. 13. l. 26. Gibraltar, p. 7. l. *penult.* p. 10. l. 23. p. 13. l. 30. p. 40. *Sheet* F. l. 13. p. 55. *Sheet* H. l. 23. Marry or do worſe, p. 9. l. 5, 11. She wou'd if ſhe cou'd, p. 90. l. 7. Artful Husband, p. 68. l. 20. Beaux Stratagem, p. 15. l. 25. Cares of Love, p. 26. l. 2. Sir Courtly Nice, p. 12. l. 2. p. 47. l. 7. The Contrivances, p. 1. l. 1. The fine Lady's Airs, p. 7. l. 26. The Generous Husband, p. 34. l. 30. The Maid's the Miſtreſs, p. 22. l. 1. p. 30. l. 33. p. 31. l. 5. The Modiſh Husband, p. 9. l. 9. Perplex'd Couple, p. 41. l. 2.

dern *Plays*, that I think it not ſafe to direct to them even in the Margin.

Here Men are taught (*f*) how to be impudent, and take no Denial. Here are (*g*) Contrivances for whoring repreſented, with (*h*) *Evaſions* to avoid Suſpicion, and a dreadful Tincture of *Smut*, ſometimes in (*i*) common Diſcourſe, and ſometimes in (*k*) *Verſe*; where the force of the *Muſick* doubles the Miſchief, and from whence the Singing-Maſters furniſh themſelves with *Songs* to teach the *Ladies* for their *better Breeding*, and ſometimes for their *utter Ruin*. When they uſe (*l*) Expreſſions with a *double Entendre*, they have ſometimes (*m*) ſuch Actions as ſhew their Meaning. Nay, (*n*) ſuch things as are forbidden to be ſpoken, are afterwards printed at large. All theſe *Myſteries of Iniquity* put ſuch Notions into the Minds of the Hearers, and leave ſuch Impreſſions, which otherwiſe they had not known; and which ſome, who ignorantly have gone to the *Play*-

---

(*f*) The Careleſs Husband, p.20. l.26,34. p.22. l.8.

(*g*) Gibraltar, *Sheet* E. p. 40. l.18. *with many others.*

(*h*) Love at firſt ſight, p. 43. *Scene* 2. *with many others.*

(*i*) Gibraltar, p. 24. l. 4, 11. p.40. *Sheet* E. l.1. p.56. *Sheet* G. l. 4. p. 57. l. 16. Hampſtead-Heath, p.53. l.14. *Perolla* and *Izadora*, *Epilogue*, l. 15, &c. Solon, p.25. l.28. The Amorous Miſer, p.3. l. 25, &c. p. 5. l.23. The Baſſet-Table, p. 47. l. 5. p. 55. l. 14. p. *ult.* l. 25. The Biter, p.12. l.2. p.59. l.25. *Britiſh* Enchanters, p. 31. l. 28. The Confederacy, p. 38. l. 28. The fair Example, p. 59. l. 10. The Female Wits, p. 62. l. 17. The Lawyer's Fortune, p. 41. l. 19. The Loyal Subject, p.47. l.12. The Metamorphoſis, p.22. l.18. Northern Laſs, *Prologue*, l.19. *Epilogue*, l.23. p.3. l.19. p.7. l.8. p.30. l.29. p.39. l.35. p.40. l.12. p.47. l.11. p.54. l.31. p.56. l.2. p.65. l.17. *Portſmouth* Heireſs, p. 10. l. 1, &c. p.32. l. 28. Rival Brothers, p.78. l.5. p.79. l.26. Ulyſſes, p.46. l.3.

(*k*) Arſinoe, p.26. l.11, p.45. *in fine.* The Biter, p.17. p.45. The Loyal Subject, p.46. *Song* 2, and *Song* 4. Northern Laſs, p. 44. l. *penult.* p.55. l.14. The Quacks, p.28. The Royal Merchant, p.28. l.30. p. 30. l.29.

(*l*) The careleſs Husband, p. 8. l.21. Northern Laſs, p. 66. l. 2. The Quacks, p. 26. l. 25. p.29. l.2. The Stage-Coach, p. 2. l. *penult.* What-d'ye-call-it, p. 36. l. 10.

(*m*) The careleſs Husband, p. 8. l.21. *A Compleat Key to the* What-d'ye-call-it, p.30. l.16.

(*n*) The Quacks, *Epilogue the firſt.*

houſe,

house, have afterwards ingenuoufly confefs'd. Here are all forts of *Love-Stories* related to pleafe the *Fancy*, and all forts of Devices fhewn which *Satan* can invent to infnare and ruin the well-meaning, but too unwary Girl. And when *Whoremongers* have learned their Parts on the *Stage*, they will quickly act them in another place. In (*o*) one *Comedy*, *Fetcher*, a *Pimp*, tells his Mafter, that he *found* his *Wenches for* him, and afterwards acquaints the Audience, how he came by this curfed Skill: (*p*) *I am read, I am Book-learned. The reafon that Pimps fo often mifcarry, is, becaufe they don't read Hiftory, they don't grow acquainted with Stratagems. I for my part read Hiftory, and thou fhalt fee I'll do thy Bufinefs rarely.* Now as (*q*) *Plays* by the *Poets* are *accounted the genuine Hiftory of the Age*; fo I fuppofe they are fpoken of by this intriguing Pimp: but I am fure that they are exactly adapted for fuch a curfed purpofe.

I fuppofe that all Perfons who have any *Modefty* left, cannot but have a juft Abhorrence againft fuch Expreffions, which plead for thefe notorious *Vices*, and for this reafon I fhall mention the more.

(*r*) *Wife and Miftrefs, are like Love and Mufick at the fame time; they give a Relifh to each other.*

(*s*) Spoken by a Lord: *To be true to one's Wife, is fo unbred in a Man of Quality.*

(*t*) Spoken by a Wife: *This little time fhall finifh him a compleat Husband. Intrigue affift me! and I'll act a Revenge that might have been worthy of the moft celebrated Wife in* Boccace.

As for *Whoredom*, it is called (*u*) *immortal Joys*, and (*x*) *the diftinguifhing Mark of a fine Gentleman*; fo that one would think the *Poets* to be in good earneft in pleading for Debauchery, when they put fuch Expreffions as thefe into the *Actors* Mouths.

(*o*) Gibraltar, p. 5. l. 8.

(*p*) Ibid. p. 40. *Sheet* E. l. 16.

(*q*) An Act at *Oxford*, *Preface*, p. 5. l. *ult.*

(*r*) *Portfmouth* Heirefs, p. 42. l. 9.

(*s*) The Modifh Husband, p. 27. l. 32.

(*t*) Three Hours after Marriage, p. 14. l. 6.

(*u*) *Venus* and *Adonis*, p. 11. l. 16.

(*x*) The Wife's Relief, p. 45. l. 28.

(y) *He that leaves his Wench for fear of Mishaps,*
May he beg all his days, be cracking of Lice,
And die in conclusion of Clap
(z) *Make much of every wanton Girl,*
Which needs but little courting;
Her value is above the Pearl,
That delights in being most abominably wicked.

(a) One swears to a Woman, that he *thinks* he *shall do* her the heartier Service when guilty of Whoredom.

(b) *A generous Mind abhors the least Restraint.*
Variety and Liberty (in Whoredom) *we want.*

(c) *'Tis Men of Sense that run rambling, and only dull Fools that marry.*

(d) *Whoring is a Vice too genteel for a Tradesman.*

(e) *Let them think what they will, Leudness is the business now.*

(f) *The Pleasures of Love, and the Joys of good Wine,*
To perfect our Happiness wisely we join.

(g) *I see, Education corrupts us; and the nearer we go to Nature,* (that is, the more common we are, like brute Beasts) *we are the more honest.*

(h) A Father's Advice to his Son: *If thou canst not make her a Wife, be sure you make something of her.*

(i) *Sure you would not have me commit Fornication.* Answer; *Why, if you did, Child, 'twould be but a good friendly part, if it were only to keep me in countenance, whilst I commit Adultery.*

(k) *Virtue* (spoken of whoring) *is its own Reward. There is a Pleasure in doing Good, which sufficiently pays itself.*

(y) The comical Revenge, p. 32. l. 39.
(z) Ibid. p. 34. l. 2.
(a) Ibid. *p.* 70. *l.* 4.
(b) Generous Husband, *p.* 25. *l.* 7.
(c) Humours of the Age, *p.* 29. *l.* 12.
(d) Man of Mode, *p.* 185. *l.* 1.
(e) Ibid. *p.* 228. *l.* 14.
(f) Ibid. *p.* 238. *l.* 36.
(g) The Modish Husband, *p.* 12. *l.* 20.
(h) Ibid. *p.* 22. *l.* 33.
(i) The Provok'd Wife, *p.* 40. *l.* 35.
(k) The Relapse, *p.* 58. *l.* 2.

He

(*l*) *He has as fair a Reputation as any Gentleman about* London. *'Tis true, he's a Good-Fellow, but no Sot: He loves Mirth and Society without Drunkenness: He is, as I believe all young Fellows are, given to Women; but 'tis in private, and he is particular, no common Whoremaster, and in short, keeps as good Company as any Man in* England.

(*m*) *Infamy! Nay, there you wrong him. He does no ungentleman-like things. Prithee, consider Youth a little. What if he does wench a little? Where's the great Crime? All young Fellows will do it.*

Among all the *Comedies* which have been printed, there is one (*n*) which is said in the *Title-Page* to be *written by a Club of Ladies in vindication of virtuous Plays.* I shall therefore transcribe what these *modest Ladies* speak of *Adultery*, with a *virtuous Design*, as they tell us, to *reclaim* a *Roving Husband*, that the Reader may the better judge of other *Performances* upon the *Stage*.

(*o*) Spoken by Women, the first married, the other single. *'Tis mightily out of the mode to love one's Husband, and 'tis Alamode to love some body else.* Answer, *It's a strange Fashion, methinks.* Reply, *Only the prettiest in the World; nothing pleases me like it.* Upon this (*p*) a Text of *Scripture* is immediately quoted, for proof of this Doctrine.

(*q*) Spoken by a Lord: *We Men of Quality are much in the right to secure Money enough for our Mistress, when we are weary of our Wives: For thou know'st, 'tis a nauseous thing to have it said, that a Man of Quality should love his Wife above half a Year.*

(*r*) *Virtue will allow of more than Love or Discretion.*

(*s*) Spoken by a Colonel endeavouring to debauch a married Woman: *I desire nothing from you, but what is for your Good.* ——— *'Tis Love, almighty Love has never given me Rest, since I saw you.* Here an Attribute of GOD is ascribed to a *Pagan* Idol.

(*l*) Squire of *Alsatia*, *p.* 11. *l.* 27.

(*m*) Ibid. *p.*12. *l.*8.

(*n*) The Roving Husband reclaim'd, *in the Title-Page.*

(*o*) P.17. l.25.

(*p*) *Prov.* 9. 17.

(*q*) P.25. l.18.

(*r*) P.28. l.*ult.*

(*s*) P.29. l.8.

(*t*) Spoken by a marry'd Woman concerning Adultery: *If marry'd Folks must have no Pleasure but from one another, they had as good be condemn'd to the Gallies, and the Town would be but a despicable Place.*

(*u*) Spoken by a *Widow* and the *Colonel*: Widow. *She* (whom the Colonel would debauch) *fancies, 'tis ordained for Wives to suffer without Thought of Return.* Colonel. *She is much to be pity'd; for she, I believe, knows not what it is to be really happy,* (that is, to commit Adultery.) Answ. Widow. *Therefore she is not to be pity'd, for she knows not what she wants, or else I warrant she would not be so backward.* The Widow proceeds with a Tincture of *Smut*, which I must omit.

(*x*) Spoken by a Man: *My Heart I can give but to one, and that must be a Woman, that neither seeks mine, nor any one's else: My Body I can dispose of in several places.*

(*y*) Spoken to a marry'd Woman by a Lady: *Neither can I imagine what makes you take such pains to be true to a Man, who is false to you; for to my knowledge your Husband has a Mistress now ready to lie in.* Here a Person of Quality is represented as a *Pimp*.

(*z*) Spoken by the same Lady: *I am for the modern way. Love a little, not long, but often; and never make myself uneasy for any Man. The Virtue you so much boast of, I own, is a very fine thing, if one could have it insur'd; but it often happens, Women grow weary of it, when no body cares to take it from them: And lest this should be your Chance, you had as good give it* (commit Adultery) *while you may be thank'd for it, as keep it, and cry it about the streets, when no body will buy it.*

(*a*) Spoken by the Devil, when rais'd by a Fortune-teller:

Just such a one is allotted for thee,
Which if you refuse, you ne'er happy will be:
Ne'er think 'tis a Sin, (Adultery) *of a truth I do know*
'Tis the Will of the Fates, and they will have it so.

(*t*) The Roving Husband reclaim'd, *p.* 31. *l.* 17.
(*u*) P. 33. l. 16.
(*x*) P. 47. l. 6.
(*y*) P. 51. l. antepenult.
(*z*) P. 52. l. 11.
(*a*) P. 59. l. 5.

Here

Here *Adultery* is repreſented as the only Way to Happineſs, as irreſiſtible, and what the Fates or GOD decrees, and is conſequently the Author of it. 'Tis true, that this is ſpoken by a *Devil incarnate*; and this (I ſuppoſe) the virtuous Authors think to be a ſufficient Apology.

(*b*) Spoken by the Colonel: *If you love me, how can you ſee me dying for that, which you can with ſo much Eaſe and Pleaſure grant? A Woman that is more chaſte than I would have you be, what is ſhe good for? A ſullen thing, that makes it her Buſineſs and Pride to war with the Fleſh*, (according to our Baptiſmal Vow:) *ſhe has cold Blood in her Veins, perhaps; and if it be natural, 'tis a lazy Diſeaſe, and not a Virtue.*

Beſides, in this *Virtuous Play* there is contain'd great ſtore of *Smut*, (*c*) both in *Verſe* and *Proſe*, ſpoken without diſtinction (*d*) by a Widow, (*e*) by a Colonel, and (*f*) by a Perſon of Quality. I hope the Authors intended not to affront their Modeſty; but 'tis pity that the Ladies, when they write, muſt follow the Faſhion.

If then a *Comedy* written by Ladies is ſo offenſive, tho they are naturally more modeſt than the other Sex, what muſt we think of thoſe which are written by Men? If a *Comedy* written *in vindication of Virtuous Plays* is ſo ſcandalous, what muſt we think of thoſe who have no ſuch Deſign in view? And if it is thus with a *Play* printed after thoſe which are moſt profane have been expoſed, what muſt we think of the *Plays* when the Poets went on without controul?

Of all the *Sins* againſt the ſeventh Commandment, there is none more deteſtable than that of Inceſt. The *Scripture* calls it (*g*) a *Fornication, which is not ſo much as named among the Gentiles.* Upon the *Stage* it is ſpoken of in a very different Stile (*h*):

Think'ſt thou to awe me with that Fantom Inceſt?
Such empty Names may fright thy coward Soul;
But know, that mine diſdains them.

(*b*) The Roving Husband reclaim'd, *p.* 62. *l.* 8.
(*c*) P. 40. l. 5.
(*d*) P. 3. l. 19.
(*e*) P. 35. l. 6.
(*f*) P. 53. l. 11.
(*g*) 1 *Cor.* 5. 1.
(*h*) Royal Convert, *p.* 62. *l.* 22.

The laſt *Vice* which I propoſed to mention of this nature, is *Pimping*. An *Actor* upon the *Stage* ſwears, (*i*) *by the Honour* thereof, as if it was no leſs than GOD; and another ſaith of ſuch a Perſon, (*k*) that *Lovers, forgetting the blind God, ſhall fall down and worſhip him.*

Other Expreſſions of the Sin itſelf are moſt abominable: as (*l*) *This Pimping is certainly the moſt pleaſing, and the moſt obliging Vocation in the World. 'Tis a good Bargain, they ſay, when all ſides are pleaſed, and here the Obligation's link'd together. And let the World ſay what they will, I ſay, your true Pimp is a Man of Parts.* With an Oath, *I'll make it appear, that Gallants themſelves are* inferiour to a *Pimp.*

(*m*) *I had an Ambition to be of ſome honourable Profeſſion, ſuch as People of Quality undertake: as for inſtance, Pimping. A Pimp is as much above a Doctor, as a Cook is above a Scullion.*

(*n*) *Pimps manage the great Buſineſs of the Nation.*

(*o*) *A Trade and Induſtry, the Decay whereof* is mention'd *with Tears in* the Speaker's eyes.

(*p*) *She's an indefatigable Sollicitrix in her way of Buſineſs, an excellent Perſon.*

(*q*) *Every Man in his own Sphere.* Anſw. *Right! And therefore you muſt pimp for your Maſter.*

(*r*) *Is there any thing of more Authority than a Pimp? What brings Men to more Preferment?*

(*s*) *Pimping is the moſt honourable and profitable of all Profeſſions.*

(*t*) *I only wiſh it was my Fate to ſerve ſome Stateſman in Buſineſs: For Pimping often toſſes a Man into a Place*

(*i*) The Maid the Miſtreſs, *p.* 22. *l.* 1.

(*k*) Gibraltar, *p.* 13. *l.* 30.

(*l*) Marry or do worſe, *p.* 9. *l.* 5.

(*m*) Sir *Courtly Nice*, *p.* 12. *l.* 2.

(*n*) Ibid. *p.* 47. *l.* 7.

(*o*) She wou'd if ſhe cou'd, *p.* 90. *l.* 7.

(*p*) The Artful Husband, *p.* 68. *l.* 20.

(*q*) The Beaux Stratagem, *p.* 15. *l.* 25.

(*r*) The Cares of Love, *p.* 26. *l.* 2.

(*s*) The Contrivances, *p.* 1. *l.* 1.

(*t*) The Fine Lady's Airs, *p.* 13. *l.* 16.

of

of Three Hundred a Year, when Money ſhall be refuſed, Merit expulſ'd, and Relations thought impudent for pretending to it.

(u) *Pimp! Madam, don't ſpeak diſreſpectfully of my Calling. Pray, what is a Pimp?*

(x) *O Pimping, Pimping! What a Calling's thine? that like the Bee from Poiſon can'ſt ſuck Honey, and from the gripingeſt Fiſt extract their Wealth.*

(y) *Thus every way the Pimp is ſure to thrive;*
And whilſt his Money laſts, in Credit live.

(z) *Here's he, that diſpoſes of all things here. What a ſucceſsful Quality is Pimping?*

(a) *Pimp like a Man of Honour. 'Tis the ſhorteſt way to Preferment.*

And now can any Man think, that the *Poets* or *Actors* ever read or mind ſuch Places of *Scripture*, which ſpeak againſt (b) *Adultery*, (c) *Fornication*, and (d) *Whoredom*; and exhort us to avoid all ſuch Diſcourſes as have a tendency thereto? The *Scriptures* tell us, (f) that theſe *Sins* expoſe us to the Judgments of GOD, and tend to the Ruin both of Soul and Body; and if ſuch Men thought hereon, they would not thus venture to debauch our Youth, and turn our Cities into ſo many

---

(u) The Generous Husband, p. 34. l. 30.

(x) The Maid the Miſtreſs, p. 30. l. 33.

(y) Ibid. p. 31. l. 5.

(z) The Modiſh Husband, p. 9. l. 9.

(a) The Perplex'd Couple, p. 41. l. 2.

(b) *Exod.* 20. 14. *Lev.* 20. 10. *Deut.* 5. 18. *Pſal.* 50. 18, 21. *Jer.* 7. 9, 10. & 13. 27. & 23. 10, 11. *Prov.* 6. 26, 32. *Ezek.* 23. 45. *Hoſ.* 2. 2, 3. & 4. 13, 14. *Mal.* 3. 5. *Mat.* 5. 27, 28, 29, 30. & 15. 18, 19. *Mark* 7. 20, 21. *Luke* 18. 19, 20. 1 *Cor.* 6. 9, 10. *Gal.* 5. 19, 21. *Heb.* 13. 4. *James* 4. 3, 4. 2 *Pet.* 2. 13, 14.

(c) *Ezek.* 16. 15, 28, 29, 58, 59. *Acts* 15. 20, 29. *Rom.* 1. 21, 24, 29. 1 *Cor.* 59, 10, 11. 1 *Cor.* 6. 13, 18. 2 *Cor.* 12. 21. *Coloſſ.* 3. 5, 6. 1 *Theſſ.* 4. 3. *Heb.* 12. 15, 16. *Jude* ver. 7. *Rev.* 2. 20, 21, 22.

(d) *Lev.* 19. 29. *Numb.* 25. 1, 3. *Deut.* 22. 20, 21. & 23. 17. *Prov.* 23. 27, 28. *Jer.* 13. 27. *Hoſ.* 4. 10, 11. *Nah.* 3. 3, 4. 1 *Tim.* 1. 9, 10. *Rev.* 21. 8. & 22. 15.

(f) 1 *Cor.* 15. 33. *Epheſ.* 5. 3, 4, 11, 12. & 4. 29, 30. 1 *Theſſ.* [illegible] 2.

Places

Places like *Sodom* and *Gomorrah*, lest when others may be destroy'd with Fire and Brimstone, they also should perish in the flames. But he who compares their Practice with the Scriptures, hath cause to think, that these *Vices* are so frequently promoted, because they are so frequently forbidden; and the *Actors* are so plainly guilty of corrupt Communication, because GOD hath so plainly caution'd us to avoid it.

[From Fornication and all other deadly Sin, and from those who thus endeavour to promote it, Good LORD deliver us.]

In the *Scriptures* we are caution'd to avoid (g) *Rioting and Drunkenness*, being *Vices* unbecoming of the Gospel, and exclusive of *Heaven*. Upon the *Stage* (h) several *Songs* are sung in praise of *Drunkenness*, and it is frequently commended at large in Prose. Here it is call'd (i) *a Gentleman-like Recreation*, (k) *the distinguishing Mark of a fine Gentleman*, and (l) *the only true Pleasure of Life*. To initiate young People into this *Vice*, they plead thus: (m) *He is a Good-Fellow, but no Sot; he loves Mirth and Society without Drunkenness: he is, as I believe, all young Fellows are, and in short keeps as good Company as any Man in* England. Or thus: (n) *He does no ungentleman-like things. Prithee consider Youth a little. What if he is now and then somewhat extravagant in Wine, where's the great Crime? All young Fellows in this drinking Country will sometimes be forced upon it.* Or thus: (o) *The Intention of the Donor is, that I should*

(g) *Deut.* 29. 19, &c. *Prov.* 23. 20, 21. & 28. 7. *Luke* 21. 34. *Rom.* 13. 12, 13, 14. 2 *Cor.* 5. 9, 11. 2 *Cor.* 6. 10. *Gal.* 5. 19, 21.

(h) She wou'd if she cou'd, *p.* 151. *l.* 24. *p.* 165. *l.* 17. Amorous Miser, *p.* 39. Artful Husband, *p.* 48. *l.* 1. Comical Revenge, *p.* 30. *l.* 13. *p.* 31. *l.* 18. *p.* 32. *l.* 13, 39. *p.* 43. *l.* 20. Man of Mode, *p.* 238. *l.* 36. Provok'd Wife, *p.* 36.

(i) She wou'd if she cou'd, *p.* 91. *l.* 37.

(k) The Wife's Relief, *p.* 45. *l.* 28.

(l) Cobler of *Preston*, *p.* 23. *l.* 6.

(m) Squire of *Alsatia*, *p.* 11. *l.* 24.

(n) Ibid. *p.* 12. *l.* 8.

(o) Injur'd Love, *a Comedy*, *p.* 62. *l.* 37.

spend

spend my Money in drinking his Health: I cannot do otherwise in Conscience. These Sentences seem design'd to settle the *Consciences* of young Beginners: and then there are other Lessons, such as these; (p) *A Tavern is a safe Retreat from Business and Care: There the Mind's secure, and shifts itself into a better Habit.* Or, (q) *A smiling Glass removes the Thoughts of coming Cares. Old Time steals softly by, and Night steals through his crazy Hands, e'er Noon seems fully past.* Sometimes they ridicule the *Sin* thus: (r) *Drunkenness is not so damnable a Sin to me, as it is to many. Sorrow and Repentance are sure to be my first Work the next Morning.* And what is this *Sorrow* and *Repentance*, but a ridiculous Management by a Wife? But to compleat all, they bid defiance to all sober Admonitions, and say, (s) *Let those sensless Fools preach up Sobriety, who know not the Pleasure of a Debauch.* I shall only add, That when (t) the *Rich Man* in the *Gospel* said to his Soul, *Take thine ease, eat, drink, and be merry*; then GOD call'd him *Fool*, and told him, that that *very Night* his *Soul should be required of* him. But upon the *Stage* (u) a *mock Justice* of the *Peace*, instead of giving good Examples, punishing Evil-doers, and rewarding such as do well, turns to these Excesses, bids GOD defiance, argues with himself in a Language directly agreeing with this *Fool*, and ushers it in with the *blasphemous Pretence* of his Eyes being open'd, and an extraordinary Revelation.

In the *Scripture* (x) a Sense of *Shame* and *Guilt* is reckon'd as a great Promoter of Virtue, and an Inciter of us to Religious Duties. And where (y) this is wanting, a Man will stick at nothing, and is in the high road to Ruin and Destruction. The *Poets* give it a different Turn, and say, (z) *Impudence never fails of Success*

(p) Love at first sight, *p.* 3. *l.* 13.

(q) Ibid. *p.* 3. *l.* 4.

(r) The Comical Revenge, *p.* 11. *l.* 5.

(s) The Humours of the Age, *p.* 4. *l.* 8.

(t) *Luke* 12. 16, 17, 18, 19, 20, 21, 22.

(u) The Northern Lass, *p.* 38. *l.* 20. *p.* 39. *l.* 24.

(x) 2 *Chron.* 30. 15.

(y) *Jer.* 5. 3, 4. & 6. 15. & 8. 12.

(z) The Perplex'd Couple, *p.* 5. *l.* 19.

with

with the Women. It passes for Wit, Humour, nay and Courage too, in young Fellows, and why not in old? Of this I shall only give one Instance (which I hope is sufficient) where (*a*) an *Actor* speaks thus: *All this shall not make me out of love with my Virtue. Impudence has ever been a successful Quality, and 'twould be hard indeed, if I should be the first that did not thrive by it.* And to shew that it was a *successful Quality*, the *Poet* takes care to reward him with a Lady and a Fortune at the end of the Play, and crown him with Success to his own satisfaction.

In the *Scriptures* we are caution'd to avoid (*b*) *Lying*, it being (*c*) not of GOD, but (*d*) of the Devil, and (*e*) the Character of a wicked Man. Besides, (*f*) several Punishments, both in this World and in the other, are threatned against such as are guilty hereof. In the *Play-House* the Sense hereof is (*g*) express'd after this manner:

> *In Confidence and Lyes some Hope is left;*
> *'Twere hard to be found out in the first Theft.*

In our *Litany* we pray to *GOD* to deliver us *from Battel and Murder, and from sudden Death.* In the *Scriptures* (*h*) *Murder* and *Revenge*, and even every thing which hath a tendency to such Crimes, is positively forbidden. Upon the *Stage*, especially in *Tragedies*, the *Hearers* are taught to delight in Blood; and *Fight-*

(*a*) The Double Gallant, *p.* 33. *l.* 25.

(*b*) *Lev.* 19. 11. *Job* 34. 6. *Prov.* 14. 5, 25. & 19. 22. & 30. 8. *Isa.* 63. 8. *Jer.* 9. 3, 5. & 23. 14. *Acts* 5. 3, 4. *Ephes.* 4. 25. *Colos.* 3. 9. *James* 3. 14.

(*c*) *Numb.* 23. 19. 1 *Sam.* 15. 29. *Tit.* 1. 2. *Heb.* 6. 18.

(*d*) *John* 8. 44.

(*e*) *Psal.* 40. 4. *Psal.* 58. 3. *Mic.* 6. 11, 12.

(*f*) *Psal.* 63. 11. & 101. 7. *Prov.* 6. 16, 17, 19. & 19. 5, 9. & 29. 12. *Isa.* 28. 15, 18. & 44. 25. & 59. 2, 3, 4. *Jer.* 30. 36. *Hosea* 4. 2. *Amos* 2. 4. *Nahum* 3. 1. *Rom.* 1. 25. 1 *Tim.* 1. 10. *Revel.* 21. 8, 27. & 22. 15.

(*g*) The Man of Mode, *p.* 246. *l.* 6.

(*h*) *Exod.* 20. 13. *Deut.* 5. 17. *Gen.* 9. 6. *Numb.* 35. 30, 31. *Mat.* 5. 21—26. *Rom.* 12. 18, 19, 20, 21. *Gal.* 5. 19, 21. 1 *Tim.* 1. 9. *Revel.* 21. 8. & 22. 15.

ing is recommended as (*i*) *the distinguishing Mark of a fine Gentleman.* There is scarce a *Comedy* without Instances of *Whoring*: and scarce a *Tragedy* without Instances of *Murder* and *Revenge*, nay, Plots and Contrivances to bring about such Designs. If the Reader views but one (*k*) *Act* mention'd in the Margin, he may have a small Taste of all the rest, and perhaps may think it needless to search for more. Besides, we have several Instances of Self-Murder, and I do not remember one, which is afterward exposed as a Crime. Such Sights, *Bloodshed* and *Cruelty*, being shewn on the *Stage*, do by degrees occasion the *Spectators* to be fierce and outrageous; and Men do there learn to be inhuman. It is very observable in this Case, that the greatest Persecutions which were ever raised against the *Christians* were begun and carry'd on in *Heathen Rome*, where they had their *Theatres*, and their *Tragedies* were most frequently acted. This made them more savage and barbarous, insomuch that the Martyrdom of the Saints soon became their Diversion, and Christians were in reality brought forth to be devour'd by *wild Beasts*; and thus to make pastime for those, who had pleased themselves with such Resemblances. And since the Reformation, it is as remarkable, that the most dreadful Persecutions against the *Protestants*, and all the cursed Designs to destroy our Religion, have either been begun, or at least been approved and promoted by that City. This is that *great Whore*, who hath diverted herself by the *Theatres* and *Jubilees*: And as she was addicted to such Sports and Pastimes; so it may the less be wonder'd at, that in all Ages she hath made herself (*l*) so *drunk with the Blood of the Saints.*

In the *Scriptures* we are (*m*) forbidden to *swear falsely*, and also (*n*) commanded to *perform unto the LORD our Oaths*, because (*o*) there are heavy Judgments to be

(*i*) The Wife's Relief, p. 45. l. 28.

(*k*) *Perolla* and *Izadora*, *Act* 2. *beginning in* p. 13.

(*l*) *Revel.* 17. 6.

(*m*) *Levit.* 6. 3. & 19. 12. *Jer.* 7. 9, 10. *Hos.* 10. 4. *Mat.* 5. 33.

(*n*) *Deut.* 23. 21, 22, 23. *Psal.* 66. 13, 14. & 116. 14, 18. *Eccles.* 5. 4, 5.

(*o*) *Exod.* 20. 7. *Deut.* 5. 11. *Zech.* 5. 4. 1 *Tim.* 1. 10.

inflicted

inflicted upon ſuch as are guilty; and that we may have the greater Veneration for an *Oath*, we are particularly commanded in our private Converſation (p) *not to ſwear at all.* The *Players* to their daily *Oaths* add a Commendation of the *Sin*, and ſay, (q) that *Swearing is a Vice too genteel for a Tradeſman*; and that (r) the *keeping of an Oath* is a *fooliſh Scruple* for a Man to be troubled with.

The *Scriptures* ſpeak often againſt thoſe who (s) are *given to Pleaſure*, that (t) it *choaks the good Word of GOD*, that (u) when *Men ſerve divers Luſts and Pleaſures*, they are guilty of all Iniquity; that (x) many are *lovers of Pleaſures more than lovers of GOD*; and that (y) it is much better to *chuſe Affliction* in this World, *than to enjoy the Pleaſures of Sin for a ſeaſon.* The whole Deſign of the *Play-houſe* is to act contrary hereto. I might mention hundreds of Inſtances; but I ſhall only quote (z) one, where the *Scriptures* are burleſqu'd, other *Vices* taught, and the Fall of our firſt Parents made the Jeſt of the Performance at the ſame time.

Dominion over an Husband! Who taught you that Doctrine? Anſwer, *Doctrine do you call it? 'Tis a Right that all Women ought to aſſume: 'Tis a Legacy left us by our firſt Mother* Eve. Reply, *But I hope you'll make a ſoberer uſe of it than ſhe did.* Anſwer, *What uſe, but to make it ſubſervient to my Pleaſures?*

In the *Scriptures*, *Pride* is repreſented as (a) a grievous Crime, which (b) caſt the *Angels* out of Paradiſe, and turned them into *Devils*, which (c) GOD hates, and (d) reſiſts, which (e) goeth before Deſtruction, which (f) cauſeth Contention, and (g) Shame, and (h) is hateful both to GOD and Man. In the *Play-houſe*

(p) *Matth.* 5. 34. *Jam.* 5. 12.
(q) Man of Mode, *p.* 185. *l.* 1.
(r) She wou'd if ſhe cou'd, *p.* 106. *l.* 16.
(s) *Iſa.* 47. 8.
(t) *Luke* 8. 14.
(u) *Tit.* 3. 3.
(x) 2 *Tim.* 3. 4.
(y) *Heb.* 11. 25.
(z) The perplex'd Couple, *p.* 20. *l.* 34.
(a) *Prov.* 18. 12.
(b) *Iſa.* 14. 12, 13, 14, 15.
(c) *Prov.* 6. 16, 17.
(d) 1 *Pet.* 5. 5.
(e) *Prov.* 16. 18.
(f) *Prov.* 13. 10.
(g) *Prov.* 11. 2.
(h) *Prov.* 8. 13. *Pſ.* 101. 5.

it

it is represented as (*i*) the only guard to *Virtue*. An *Actress* saith of an *Actor*, whom she marries at last, (*k*) *He is a pretty Fellow, I like his Pride*: and it is reckon'd as a great Fault in another, (*l*) that *he wants Ambition; and which is worse, he talks of Virtue, Conscience, and Religion*.

In the *Scriptures* we are commanded (*m*) to be tender of our Neighbour's Reputation as well as of our own; and in this, as well as in other Particulars, to do to others as we would have them do to us. Our *Plays* abuse all Orders and Degrees of Men among us, without any manner of distinction; and advise their Hearers to follow their Example. I shall here insert at large (*n*) one of their Precepts to this purpose.

When Mens Backs are turn'd, if you have any Scandal to load them with, then be sure to remember them; nay, forget your own Name sooner than theirs: For, let me tell you, Scandal is the very Pam in Conversation, and you should always lead it about for the good of the Board. Spare no body. Every one is pleased to see his Neighbour liew'd. If you have but Stock enough to pay your Club in that, you may keep Company with the highest Flyer of them all. Nay, (*o*) one of the *Poets* being apprehensive, that this Liberty of the *Stage* began to decline, and that they must not use their abusive Talents in publick, as they had done formerly, he therefore (*p*) adviseth others to *rail at*, and expose their Neighbours in private, from the highest to the lowest; and tells us, that this is the true way to work a *Reformation*. Their way to reclaim one *Vice*, is by the commission of another; and *doing Evil that Good may come*, is esteemed among them as a *Virtue*.

(*i*) The Tender Husband, *p.* 1. *l.* 8.

(*k*) The Beaux Stratagem, *p.* 9. *l.* 28.

(*l*) Abra-Mule, *p.* 16. *l.* 4.

(*m*) *Exod.* 20. 16. *Deut.* 5. 20. *Ps.* 15. 1, 2, 3. *Ps.* 50. 16, 20, 21. *Matth.* 7. 1, 2, 3, 4, 5, 12.

(*n*) The fair Example, *p.* 10. *l.* 31.

(*o*) The Biter, *Epilogue*, *p.* 1. *l.* 23.

(*p*) Ibid. *Epilogue*, *p.* 2. *l. penult.*

The

The last *Vice* which I shall mention, is *Theft*. This is particularly (*q*) forbidden in the *Holy Scriptures*. It is (*r*) a shameful *Vice*, which (*s*) destroys the Soul, and (*t*) renders a Man unfit for the Kingdom of Heaven: and therefore (*u*) the Prophet pray'd, that no Temptation might make him guilty of it. In the *Play-house*, *Theft* is encouraged both by Recommendation and Example. In (*x*) one *Comedy* there is a bold Stroke: *How strangely the World is alter'd? Of old, Good-Morrow, Thief, was as kindly received, as now, Your Honour. The* Spartans *and the* Arabians *held it lawful; so grew* Arabia *happy,* Sparta *valiant.* In another (*y*) *Comedy*, *Dick the Gamester* readily finds the way to his Mother's Box: and if Children and Apprentices can do the same, the *Play-houses* may be full of Auditors, whilst others do pay for them.

Thus we see, that as the Expressions are various, by which *Vice* is commended; so the chief *Plot*, Design and Humour of most *Poets*, runs this way. Their finest *Gentlemen* and *Ladies* are leud, profane, and debauch'd; and these are caress'd, applauded, and rewarded with the chief Success. And as the Friends of the *Plays* do count them (*z*) *the genuine History of the Age*; so if their Notion is true, this Nation is the most *atheistical*, *profane*, and *debauched*, that ever was known since the World began. A Person of a sincere Character is hardly to be met with, and all manner of Wickedness is crown'd with Success. Here is nothing which GOD can be pleased with, but every thing conspires to provoke his Wrath, and force him to enter into Judgment. Indeed, a full Account of all the *Plays* would swell into a *Folio*, and therefore I shall only epitomize one of them, by which the Reader may judge of the rest.

(*q*) *Exod.* 20.15. *Lev.*19.11. *Deut.*5.19. *Psal.*50.18. *Jer.* 7. 9,10. *Matt.*19.18. *Mark* 10.19. *Luke* 18.20. *Rom.* 2. 21. *Rom.* 13.9. *Ephes.*4.28. 1 *Pet.*4.15.

(*r*) *Jer.* 2. 26.

(*s*) *Prov.* 9. 17, 18. *Prov.* 29. 24.

(*t*) 1 *Cor.* 6. 10.

(*u*) *Prov.* 30. 9.

(*x*) The Metamorposis, *p.* 15. *l.* 13.

(*y*) The Confederacy, *p.* 31. *Act* 3. *l.* 1, &c.

(*z*) An Act at *Oxford*, a *Comedy*, *in the Epistle Dedicatory*, *p.* 5. *l. ult.*

In

In a late *Play*, called *The Wonder, or, A Woman keeps a Secret*, might above all others have been expected a *Scheme* of *good Morality*, modeſt *Characters*, and a fair *Repreſentation* of the *Britiſh Kingdoms*, eſpecially if we peruſe the *Dedication*, and conſider, that the Author was a Woman: And therefore if this is faulty, what muſt the reſt be?

In this *Play*, our Nation is repreſented as moſt debauch'd, eſpecially the *Women*. Thus (*a*) *Frederick*, a *Merchant* in *Portugal*, ſaith, *I own, wenching is ſomething more difficult here than in* England, *where Womens Liberties are ſubſervient to their Inclinations, and Huſbands ſeem of no effect, but to take care of the Children which their Wives provide.* And a *Lady* adds, (*b*) *What pleaſant Lives Women lead in* England, *where Duty wears no Fetters but Inclination?*

Beſides, the only Perſons of theſe three Kingdoms repreſented in the *Play*, are *Colonel Briton* and his Man *Gibby*. The *Colonel* firſt appears in a (*c*) Riding-Habit. He lodges with *Frederick*, a Merchant, and (*d*) immediately begins to talk of *whoring*, and intrigues for that end. He declares himſelf acquainted with ſuch ſort of Practices, and profeſſeth a violent Inclination that way. He ridicules (*e*) both *Religion* and *Marriage* at once, and calls it *the ſacrificing of his Body for the good of his Soul.* He brings *Iſabella* into *Violante*'s Houſe, being (*f*) *an intire ſtranger to her Name and Circumſtances.* He comes the ſame Evening after her, and (*g*) declares his Affection to her. He receives a Letter from her, but (*h*) thinking that it came from another, is reſolved to take up with her alſo, and (*i*) puts his Man to obſerve her Houſe at parting. After this, (*k*) he would fain entice her into his Lodgings, and debauch her; and (*l*) confeſſes, that he had *not been* in Portugal *four and twenty Hours, and had three Intrigues* (as he ſuppoſed) *upon his Hands*

(*a*) The Wonder, *p*.6. *l*.17.
(*b*) P.8. l.18.
(*c*) P.5. l.9.
(*d*) P.6. l.8.
(*e*) P.7. l.3.
(*f*) P.17. l.27.
(*g*) P.24. l.30.
(*h*) P.27. l.25.
(*i*) P.28. l.24.
(*k*) P.41. l.6.
(*l*) P.48. l.27.

already, on which occasion he repeats his vicious Inclinations. And if we can judge either from the Name of this Person, his Character, or the Expressions in this *Play*, the People in these Kingdoms are generally like him.

The *good Morality* is the other thing to be consider'd, which must be taken from the *Actors* and their *Success*, or from their *Expressions*. The *principal Actor*, from whom *Morality* must be learn'd, is also this *Colonel Briton*. His Character is, (*m*) that he is *a Gentleman of excellent Principles, and strict Honour*; and what can be proposed for Imitation with greater Advantage? I shall add, that he is the *Poet*'s Favourite, crown'd with Success on a sudden beyond his Expectation, and marries a principal Lady of the *Play*, even *Isabella*, a Person of (*n*) *extraordinary Beauty*, with (*o*) *Ten Thousand Pounds* for her Fortune, and without any Settlement, tho (*p*) he was not acquainted with her above two Days. However, this Darling is (*q*) *leud*, and (*r*) *intriguing* to the uttermost. He (*s*) *swears*, he (*t*) *curses*, he (*u*) *takes the Name of GOD in vain*; he (*x*) *invokes the* Devil, and (*y*) is guilty of *Smut* and Immodesty in his Addresses to his Mistress. And these are the only *Virtues* which can be learnt from his Example.

The next to him is *Felix*, who (*z*) is of a noble Family; and he (*a*) like the *Colonel*, marries (*b*) *Violante*, with (*c*) *Twenty Thousand Pounds* for a Fortune, whilst both these Weddings are without consent of Parents. As to his Morals, he is (*d*) supposed to be guilty of Murder in a Duel, and (*e*) he still retains the same passionate Temper. He (*f*) looks upon *the chief Blessings of this*

(*m*) The Wonder, *p*. 61. l. 4.
(*n*) P. 8. l. 29. p. 17. l. 29. p. 66. l. 17.
(*o*) P. 50. l. 31.
(*p*) P. 48. l. 27.
(*q*) P. 6. l. 8, &c. p. 27. l. 25.
(*r*) P. 27. *l*. 25. p. 28. *per totum*. p. 41. l. 6. p. 48. l. 27.
(*s*) P. 51. l. 13. p. 61. l. 19. p. 63. l. 15. p. 64. l. 5.
(*t*) P. 63. l. 2. p. 64. l. 29.
(*u*) P. 49. l. 28.
(*x*) P. 50. l. 12. p. 64. l. 29.
(*y*) P. 41. l. 6, &c. p. 49. l. 11, 26.
(*z*) *Dramatis Personæ*.
(*a*) P. 74. l. 7.
(*b*) P. 78. l. 13.
(*c*) P. 78. l. 19.
(*d*) P. 2. l. 1, 27.
(*e*) P. 65. l. 9.
(*f*) P. 5. l. 1.

Life

Life to be a Friend and a Mistress. Besides, he (g) *swears*, he (h) *curses*, he (i) invokes the *Devil*, and (k) is jealous in the highest degree. And when (l) his Wife's Fortune is denied, because it was a stolen Bargain, the Law is immediately urged as a Remedy. Thus from the Example of both Ladies we learn Disobedience to Parents in the case of Marriage; and (m) the Moral is unfolded, because *every Man's Happiness consists in chusing for himself*. The (n) *Colonel*, the (o) *Ladies*, and (p) their Servants, talk immodestly, and Smut, without Distinction, and without Reproof. Both (q) the *Ladies* contrive to carry on their Intrigues without the discovery of their Parents; and *Violante*, who acted so honourably in keeping the Secret, did (r) never fail to invent a Lye as nicely as (s) the Waiting-Maids, when it would serve for her purpose. From her (t) Conversation with *Felix*, we may observe, that the utmost causes of Suspicion in a Woman are groundless. And lest the inferior Trade of *Pimping* might be discouraged, *Gibby*, who (u) was employed by the *Colonel* in all these Intrigues, is (x) rewarded with success suitable to his Condition, and (y) continues in the Service. Thus our Nation is represented to be as the *Stage* would have it; and the *Morality* taught in the *Play-houses* is in some respects the same with that which was practised in *Sodom* and *Gomorrah*, before they were destroyed with *Fire and Brimstone*.

(g) The Wonder, p.25. l.16. p.39. l.12. p.60. l.22. p.62. l. 1, 17, *penult*. p.70. l.2. p.72. l.5. p.73. l.*penult*.

(h) P.62. l.7,24,33.

(i) P. 39. l.1. p.60. l.21. p. 72. l.14. p.73. l.23.

(k) P.22. l. 27, &c. p.61,62, 63, 64, &c.

(l) P.78. l.18.

(m) P.79. l.2.

(n) P.6. l.8, &c. p.27. l. 25. p.41. l.6, &c. p.49. l.11,26.

(o) P.8. l.17. p. 19. l. *penult*. p.41. l.18, &c. p.49. l.5,9.

(p) P.8. l.28, *ult*. p.30. l.29. p.31. l.1,3. p.55. l.24.

(q) *Compare* p.3. l.4. *and* p. 4. l.12. *with* p.9. l.10. p.10. l. 28. *and* p.19. l.1.

(r) P.55. l.7. p.72. l. 8, &c. *and* l.31.

(s) P.54. l.1,7,19.

(t) P. 25, 26, &c. p. 63, 64, &c.

(u) P.28. l.19. p.43. l. 4. p. 45. l.2.

(x) P.79. l.10.

(y) P.79. l.13.

If we look into the Expressions, *Revenge* is (z) taught thus: *I have nothing left except Revenge upon my Rival.* —— *Oh that some Miracle would reveal him to me, that I through his Heart might punish my Infidelity!*

Pimping is (a) recommended in these words: *It is a thriving Trade. I remember a Country-Man of my own, who by going on such Errands came to great Preferment.*

Whoring, Intriguing, and *Assignations,* are (b) thus described in Verse at the end of the *Scene,* to make it more *emphatical* and *sententious:*

> *Thus we improve the Pleasures of the Day,*
> *Whilst thoughtless Mortals sleep their Time away.*

Hasty Marriage without Consideration is (c) thus extolled at the end of the 4th *Act,* as the Sum of all:

> *She who for Years protracts her Lover's Pain,*
> *And makes him wish, and wait, and sigh in vain:*
> *To be his Wife, when late she gives consent,*
> *Finds half his Passion was in Courtship spent.*
> *Whilst they who boldly all Delays remove,*
> *Find every Hour a new Supply of Love.*

And now let the Reader judge, if there is so much *Vice* and *Profaneness* in a *Play,* the Dedication whereof will suppose the *Poet* and *Actors* to be most cautious; what may be expected in others, where the only Design is to please a meaner *Audience?*

Secondly, If there is so much *Vice* and *Profaneness* in one *Play,* what may be supposed to be in all those which are continually acted in *London,* and afterward printed and dispersed throughout the whole Nation?

It is therefore very evident, that the *Scriptures* and the *Stage* are directly contrary to each other. The *Scriptures* recommend *Virtue,* and the *Stage* recommends *Vice:* And as (d) we cannot *serve GOD and Mammon,*

(z) The Wonder, P. 33. l. 1.
(a) P. 45. l. 4.
(b) P. 28. l. *penult.*
(c) P. 59. l. 14.
(d) *Matth.* 6. 24.

because

becauſe they are *contrary Maſters*; ſo for the ſame reaſon it is admirable, how any Perſon, who believes the *Scriptures*, and pretends to *Chriſtianity*, can take any Pleaſure in a *Play-houſe* Diverſion.

CHAP. XIV.

The Stage a declared Enemy to all Reformation.

THE next Charge which I ſhall draw up againſt the *Stage*, is their poſitive declaring againſt all *Reformation*, either in themſelves or others, and the Means whereby it may be effected. This ſhews their Obſtinacy in the higheſt degree; and that tho ſometimes there may be a pretence, yet there is always but little proſpect of their Amendment. Here *Law* and *Divinity*, *Judge* and *Juries*, *Charges* and *Sermons*, *Lords* and *Commons*, *Magiſtrates* and *Clergy*, are all valued alike. Let them endeavour to reform the World if they dare; they ſhall ſoon hear of it from the *Stage*, and be affronted, cenſured, deſpiſed, and expoſed; and what is but whiſper'd in other places, is there ſhewn barefaced.

Firſt, The preſent Age is frequently derided by the *Actors*, becauſe (bleſſed be GOD) there have been great Endeavours uſed for a *Reformation* of Manners. Too much of this Language may be ſeen in (*a*) *Prologues* and *Epilogues* made for this purpoſe, where the *Actors* addreſs themſelves to the *Pit*, and ſpeak for the Information of the *Audience*. I ſhall only give the Reader a taſte thereof from (*b*) one of their *Epilogues*.

With Zeal and Sin at once we're ſtrangely warm'd,
And grow more wicked as we grow reform'd.
Oh! 'tis a bleſſed Age, and bleſſed Nation,
When Vice walks Cheek by Jole with Reformation!

(*a*) Rival Brothers, *Prologue.* The Female Wits, *Prologue.*

(*b*) Stage-Beaux toſs'd in a Blanket, *Epilogue*, *p.* 3. *l.* 7.

Sometimes it is called in Derision (*c*) a *Reforming Age*, and (*d*) a *Saint-like Age*. Our *modern Societies* for putting the *Laws* in execution, are described as such who (*e*) *are not sincerely reformed*; but endeavour to *mend others more than themselves*. *A modern Reformer* is (*f*) one, who *can see other Mens Faults better than his own*, and called (*g*) a *Stock-jobber*, a *State-Botcher*, *the Terror of strolling Strumpets*, *City Reformer*, *chief Beggar-hunter*. He who is *zealous* to suppress *Profaneness*, is stiled (*h*) *a Bustler for Reformation*, and 'tis well if (*i*) he can escape without Censure. The Name of an *Informer* in the (*k*) *Play-house Language* is as odious as those of *Traytor*, *Cheat*, *Knave*, *Coward*, *Rascal*, *Thief*, and *Varlet*. Here we are told, that (*l*) *in the crying out against Immoralities*, *the Accusers have nothing to brag of*, *but both Prisoners and Evidence are equally guilty*. One tells us, (*m*) that if we *reform*, *and live honest*, *it is the way to be starv'd*. Another *principal Actor* in a *Play* hath a bold Stroke at large. (*n*) *Religion! Ay, there's another Topick now. Religion and Reformation! Two things that make a mighty stir in the World, without any considerable progress, preach'd up every where, and follow'd no where. 'Tis as easy to reform the Follies and Vices of the Age by Scandal*, (that is, by preaching against *Vice*, and informing against Offenders) *as it is to persuade a young Fellow of my Inches, that there's any thing in that Religion that reins him from his Pleasure*. This is in short, *Religion* is a Cheat, and *Reformation* is impossible. And lastly, another hearing *Vice* only reproved, breaks out into (*o*) this *Sarcastical*

(*c*) Rival Brothers, *Prologue*, *l.* 2. The Lawyer's Fortune, *p.* 9. *l.* 16.

(*d*) An Act at *Oxford*, *p.* 8. *l.* 22. Hampstead-Heath, *p.* 10. *l.* 20.

(*e*) As you find it, *p.* 67. *l.* 22.

(*f*) *Portsmouth* Heiress, *p.* 48. *l.* 1.

(*g*) An Act at *Oxford*, *p.* 3. *l.* *penult.* Hampstead-Heath, *p.* 3. *l.* 25.

(*h*) The Lawyer's Fortune, *p.* 19. *l.* 10.

(*i*) The Quacks, *p.* 15. *alias* 11. *l.* 1.

(*k*) Love's Contrivance, *p.* 12. *l.* 18.

(*l*) As you find it, *p.* 32. *l.* 24.

(*m*) The Confederacy, *p.* 4. *l.* 35.

(*n*) *Portsmouth* Heiress, *p.* 6. *l.* 9.

(*o*) Love at first sight, *p.* 14. *l.* 21.

Ex-

Expreſſion: *Oh! I am ſick, perfectly ſick, out of order! Did you obſerve that Religious Air with which ſhe ſpoke?* And then proceeds with an Oath; *'Tis ſo unlike a Gentlewoman, that a Country Lady, who had been three ſhort Minutes only at Court, would be heartily aſhamed to talk ſo, when ſhe went down again to her Husband.*

It may be obſerved, that upon a particular Occaſion (*p*) thirty two *Engliſh* Temporal *Lords*, nine *Biſhops*, and ſeven *Judges*, did by a *Certificate* under their Hands teſtify their Approbation of the *Deſign of the Societies for Reformation of Manners*; which they look'd upon to be *ſo great and noble, ſo much for the Honour of GOD, the Advancement of Piety and Virtue, and the Publick Good both of Church and State, that* they thought *it could not fail of being approved of by all Good Men.* Thus alſo five Temporal *Lords*, thirteen *Biſhops*, and nine *Judges* of the Kingdom of *Ireland*, did in the ſame manner teſtify their Concurrence therewith. But if all the World approves thereof, yet ſince it tends to the Deſtruction of *Vice*, the *Players* will oppoſe it.

The only Method which the *Plays* promote for a *Reformation* of Manners, is to let every Man alone, to do what he pleaſes, and to go on without conſtraint. Of this I ſhall give ſome Inſtances, where the whole Tendency of the *Plays* runs this way; and the finiſhing Stroke being in *Verſe*, preſſes the *Moral* more home upon the Minds of the *Audience*.

The *Scriptures* ſpeak (*q*) very poſitively concerning a due Education of *Children* and *Youth*, and (*r*) that *Severity* is ſometimes neceſſary. It is true, that theſe Admonitions are conſiſtent with Prudence; ſo that every Man is at liberty to act as ſhall moſt conduce to the main End. But the *Players* will not allow of *Severity* upon any occaſion, as may be ſeen by this Example.

In a late *Comedy* there are (*s*) two *Brothers*; the eldeſt is ſaid to be *leud, abominably vicious, ſtubborn and obſtinate, being bred up with great Rigour and Severity.* The

(*p*) An Account of the Societies for Reformation of Manners, *in the beginning.*

(*q*) *Prov.* 22.6. *Epheſ.* 6.4.

(*r*) *Prov.* 13.24. & 19.18. & 22.15. & 23.13, 14. & 29.15, 17.

(*s*) Squire of *Alſatia*, *Drama.*

other is an *ingenious well-accomplish'd Gentleman, a Man of Honour, and of an excellent Disposition and Temper; being bred up from his Childhood with all the Tenderness, and Familiarity, and Bounty that can be.* Now this well-accomplish'd Gentleman had a Child by one Whore, whom he turn'd off, and then lay with another, and was detected in the Fact: and (*t*) was often extravagant in Wine. His Conversation on the *Stage* (*u*) gives us his Character at large, so that it could be no Secret; and (*x*) one Whore pulling out the other by the hair before Father and Uncle, discovers all to his Relations. Now the *Virtue* was, that (*y*) the one was rakish in good Company; and the *Vice* consisted not in the Fact, but in the Acquaintance. To set this matter right, the *Uncle* blames (*z*) the *Father* for his *Severity*, saying, *Rigour makes nothing but Hypocrites:* and adds, (*a*) *I had as lieve govern a Dog as a Man, if it be by Fear. This* (saith he) *I take to be the difference between a good Father to Children, and a harsh Master over Slaves.* The *Uncle* owns (*b*) that his Nephew was guilty of *Whoredom* and *Drunkenness*, and (*c*) vindicates him in both, as (*d*) only *Gentleman-like Actions.* Indeed, for fashion-sake, the *Uncle* did once (*e*) give the *Nephew* good Advice. This was chiefly brought in to save the *Poet's* Credit, and this alone is reckon'd sufficient for both *Poet* and *Actor.* After this, the younger Brother (*f*) brings Women in *Masks* to his *Uncle's* House: the Father (*g*) suspects them to be *Whores*; but the *Uncle* (*h*) trusts to the Nephew's Honour, and gives them the Liberty of his House, without any Examination. Upon this, the *Poet* supposeth the younger Brother reform'd, who is happily marry'd to a good Fortune with a large Settlement.

As for the wicked elder Son, the *Uncle* adviseth his Father, (*i*) *You see Severity will do nothing. In short,*

(*t*) Squire of *Alsatia*, p. 12. l. 10.
(*u*) P. 14. l. 15—23.
(*x*) P. 22. l. 13.
(*y*) P. 11. l. 29.
(*z*) P. 12. l. 42.
(*a*) P. 13. l. 7.
(*b*) P. 11. l. 27.
(*c*) P. 12. l. 9.
(*d*) P. 12. l. 9.
(*e*) P. 30. l. 23.
(*f*) P. 65. l. 3.
(*g*) P. 65. l. 8.
(*h*) P. 65. l. 14.
(*i*) P. 64. l. 32.

give

give him his Liberty and a good Allowance. There now remains no other way to reclaim him. And (k) *use him kindly, and forgive him.* Accordingly (l) the *Father* forgives him at first sight; but the former Severity had spoil'd him, and it was too late. For tho he had but just escaped from Ruin, yet he resolves to go on, and saith, (m) *I intend to have my Swing at Whoring and Drinking, as* others *had.* Upon this the *Father* owns his Mistake as to *Severity*, both in the Case of the (n) *younger* and (o) the *elder Brother*: and the *Uncle* (p) concludes the whole in this manner; *You that would breed your Children well, by Kindness and Liberality endear them to you: And teach them by Example*; that is, let them whore, and be drunk without Correction, and vindicate them when guilty. For

Severity spoils ten for one it mends:
If you'd not have your Sons desire your Ends,
By Gentleness and Bounty make those Sons your Friends.

When Parents have educated their Children, (q) the next Care is to dispose of them sutably in Marriage; and upon this the Happiness of the Family doth greatly consist. The *Play-House* Direction is not to cross them; and their Reason is, because it is to no purpose. Thus (r) in a late *Play*, Sir *Jealous Traffick* keeps up his Daughter from the sight of all Men, designing to settle her with a *Spaniard*. However, ways are found out to marry her in disguise to another, whom she loved. Upon this, the Father is reconciled, and concludes the whole with this Saying (s):

By my Example let all Parents move,
And never strive to cross their Childrens Love;
But still submit that Care to Providence above.

(k) Squire of *Alsatia*, p. 70. l. 5.
(l) P. 72. l. 24.
(m) P. 74. l. 5.
(n) P. 65. l. 37.
(o) P. 75. l. 7.
(p) P. 75. l. 13.
(q) *Ecclus.* 7. 25.
(r) The Busy-Body.
(s) P. 72. l. 16.

When

When People are marry'd, the *Stage*-Method is to let the Women run into all Extravagancies without controul, as the best way to reclaim them.

In (*t*) one *Comedy*, *Clerimont*'s Wife loses five hundred Pounds in one Night, and (*u*) had leud Inclinations, which (*x*) the Husband discovers. However (*y*) he forgives all, and returns into a good Humour; saying, That

They only, who gain Minds, true Laurels wear;
'Tis less to conquer, than convince the Fair.

There are some other Instances in the *Play* concerning Education; but (*z*) the *Moral* at the end clears all:

You've seen th' Extremes of a domestick Life,
A Son too much confin'd, too free a Wife;
By generous Bonds you either should restrain,
And only on their Inclinations gain.
Wives to obey must love, Children revere,
While only Slaves are govern'd by their Fear.

In a later (*a*) *Play*, *Carizales* an old *West-Indian*, very rich, and settled here, marries *Lucia*, *Fortfil*'s youngest Daughter of fifteen Years of Age, and accordingly locks her up. Upon this there happens the utmost Cause for Jealousy; and he, when alone, argues thus upon it: (*b*) *To what purpose has been all this Circumspection? Wherefore these Locks, Walls and Bars?* After this (*c*) he saith, *Vengeance I claim, and Vengeance I will execute myself; but it shall not be a common and ordinary Punishment: As I have been singular in my Actions, my Revenge shall be the same. It must fall then upon myself——myself. I am most guilty of this Offence.* Accordingly in the End of the second Act, (*d*) we are told the Reason of all this:

(*t*) The Tender Husband, p. 3. l. 5.
(*u*) P. 49. l. 11, &c.
(*x*) P. 51. l. 1.
(*y*) P. 53. l. 27.
(*z*) P. 62. l. 10.
(*a*) The Generous Husband, *Drama*, p. 2. l. 7. p. 3. l. 1.
(*b*) P. 56. l. 21.
(*c*) P. 58. l. 28. *See also* p. 60. l. 5. p. 62. l. *antepenult.*
(*d*) P. 25. l. 7.

A

A generous Mind abhors the least Restraint.

And in (e) the End of the whole *Play*, there is more to the same purpose:

In vain we Nature strive by Art to force,
She must return with the more rapid Course;
And if your Wife doth not herself restrain,
Believe me, all your Guards and Locks are vain:
Let all her Ways be unconfin'd,
And clap your Padlock on her Mind.

That is, let Persons be exposed to all manner of Temptations, and then deliver them, if you can, from the Evil.

Here we see the *Stage*-Method for Families. Because some ridiculous Managements, which they represent, may miscarry, therefore there must be no Government at all; no Curb, no Restraint, and no Severity: and every one must do what they please. It is no wonder, that the Youth, who hear *Plays*, prove so refractory; since they are taught to despise all Family-Rule and Authority. And indeed it is a wonder, if it should be otherwise.

The next Particular is the putting the publick *Laws* in execution against *Vice* and *Profaneness*. This was always look'd upon as an excellent Method for *Reformation*; and is (f) what GOD himself approves of, as the Design and End of Government.

To give but one Instance: Among the various Methods which our *Lawgivers* have establish'd for the preventing of *Vice*, the imprisoning of Malefactors, the trying them afterward for their Crimes, and bringing them to publick Punishment, was always thought very proper to prevent further Mischief, to reclaim the Offenders, and to give Examples, that others may beware. But all these Methods upon the *Stage* are turn'd to Ridi-

(e) The Generous Husband, p. 63. l. 8.

(f) *Rom.* 13. 3, 4, 5. 1 *Tim.* 1. 8, 9, 10.

cule,

cule, that ſo the Good intended, may, if poſſible, be prevented.

Accordingly, in a late Comedy, (g) a Man is condemn'd for Murder, whilſt the other was alive and unhurt. Another (h) for Robbery, when he himſelf was robb'd : and the Proceedings are (i) thus deſcrib'd, to make all ſuch ridiculous; *The Juſtice was drunk that committed him, the Judges ſevere and in haſte, the Jury an hungry, and ſo the Knave was caſt.* Some (k) make the *Penitential Pſalm*, which is ſung at the *Gallows*, to be only a matter of *Merriment*, and a Banter. Among the Priſoners order'd for Execution, one (l) banters upon a *Prayer-Book*; another (m) makes a ridiculous *Confeſſion* of his *Sins*, to expoſe all Seriouſneſs at ſuch a time; and a third, being (n) an old *Bawd*, ſaith, *My Comfort is, I ſhall die a good Proteſtant, and make a very decent End*; with many (o) ſuch jeſting Expreſſions. To bring *Religion* into Contempt on this occaſion, a *Perſon* is introduced (p) to viſit the Malefactors, who (q) picks two Priſoners Pockets at the ſame time. He alſo drolls upon (r) *Repentance*, (s) is very free with ridiculing Expreſſions on the occaſion, and particularly burleſques the *Sacred Scriptures.*

And now it may not be amiſs to let the World ſee what pains is alſo taken at ſuch a time to expoſe *Death* itſelf, and a Preparation for it. One Priſoner (u) ſaith, *Methinks we ſhould have little ſtomach to beg, and are to be hang'd within theſe three Hours.* To this it is anſwer'd, *Why, you whining Cur, then we have the more need to beg, that we may drink at parting.* Another ſaith, (x) *We'll have it all in Drink, and then be hang'd till we are ſober.* And a third ſaith to a Priſoner, (y) *I little*

(g) A Woman's Revenge, or a Match in *Newgate*, p. 50. l. 30.
(h) P. 51. l. 10.
(i) P. 51. l. 18.
(k) P. 52. l. 27. p. 53. l. 28.
(l) P. 54. l. 34.
(m) P. 58. l. 14.
(n) P. 55. l. 2.
(o) P. 55. *per totum.*
(p) P. 56. l. 9.
(q) P. 57. l. 6. p. 59. l. 8.
(r) P. 58. l. 28.
(s) P. 56. l. 11.
(t) P. 58. l. 11.
(u) P. 52. l. 1.
(x) P. 52. l. 27.
(y) P. 57. l. 17.

thought

thought you should have had need to have minded Heaven so soon. However, whilst they expose the Laws of Man, they shew what little Regard they have to the Laws of GOD, and that future Rewards and Punishments are no more valu'd than the present.

And as this is their way of treating on the Execution of the Laws; so it is easy to guess, what Respect they pay to such as put them in execution, especially against *Immorality* and *Profaneness.* Perhaps their *Hearers,* being so well acquainted with their *Oaths* and *Curses,* have paid in another place for what they have learnt at the *Play-Houses,* and therefore the *Magistrates* must be ridiculed. The Affronts are very frequent, which they put upon the *Judges, Aldermen, Justices of the Peace, Juries, Informers,* and all such as endeavour to *reform* the *Corruptions* either of the *Nation* or the *Play-House.* Others are afraid of *Justice*; these bid it defiance. Others pay a Respect to *Magistrates*; these despise them. And certainly this is a great Obligation for the future, as well as a Reformation from what is past.

To begin with the *Judges:* These act by *his Majesty's Commission,* and therefore the Affronts pass'd upon them have a double Stroke. Thus they insult the *Royal Authority,* as well as such who are employ'd thereby. When a *Judge* is represented, (z) the very Name must be ridiculous. They give him this Character, that he is (a) *antient* and *hard-hearted,* (b) *sparing of his Words and Sentences, nodding on the Bench, with a tedious dull Plea before him.* Nay, the (c) going into *Westminster-Hall,* or into any other throughout their *Circuits,* is represented so very ridiculous, that it is too scandalous to relate it. And as one reflects on all *Superiours,* (d) that because *we are apt to imitate* them, therefore *the very Footmen grow profane:* So another reflects on all the *Judges,* (e) that *those Gentlemen of the long Robe have*

(z) An Act at *Oxford,* p. 16. l. 18.

(a) The Confederacy, p. 2. l. 22.

(b) Love at first sight, p. 53. l. 16.

(c) An Act at *Oxford,* p. 16. l. 18.

(d) Woman is a Riddle, p. 5. l. 12.

(e) The Man of Mode, p. 182. l. 2, &c.

not

not been wanting by their good Examples to countenance the crying Sin of the Nation.

In a late *Play*, beside the (g) *Swearing* and (h) *Cursing*, there is a *Judge*, (i) who appears like a Cat upon the *Gutter* of the House; and (k) when he is taken thence, (l) he looks out from the *Vent-hole of the Cellar*, and (m) when he was almost got out, tumbles in again. Then (n) whilst he is hearing of a Cause, falls asleep upon the Bench: And his own Son saith of him, (o) *My Father is such an unaccountable Man, that the only way to recover him to his Senses, is to amuse him with a Cause in the Air.*

Mr. *Collier* (p) in his Reply to Mr. *Dennis* concerning the *Abuse of the Clergy* by the *Stage*, hath these words: *When the Badge of a Man's Office, which should give him Credit, is shewn ridiculous, I fancy, he hath reason to complain. If the Poet is of another mind, let him practise the same Liberty upon a Judge or a Lord Mayor, and see how the Jest will take.* He then thought, that they would not dare to do it; but now we see, that they dare to do any thing.

Neither do the *Aldermen* escape any better than the *Judges*. Their Election is thus described; (q) *Being cramb'd up into Offices among the Worshipful:* and a *Mayor* is call'd (r) one, who *upon the City's Charge* is *made drunk at least for a whole Year.* These have also (s) ridiculous *Names*, and sometimes (t) as ridiculous *Epithets*. They are rank'd with (u) *Taylors*, nay with (x) *Pimps*

(g) The Litigants, *Act* 1. *Sc.* 1. l. 1. p. 21. l. 28. p. 23. l. 18. p. 24. l. 38.

(h) P. 9. l. 10. p. 31. l. 5, 6. p. 33. l. *antepenult.*

(i) P. 24. *l.* 12.

(k) P. 25. l. 14.

(l) P. 26. l. 2.

(m) P. 26. l. 33.

(n) P. 34. l. 12.

(o) P. 29. l. 15.

(p) P. 23.

(q) The Faithful General, p. 41. l. 45.

(r) The Tender Husband, p. 21. l. 25.

(s) An Act at *Oxford*, p. 30. l. 1. Love the Leveller, p. 6. l. 15. The Lawyer's Fortune, p. 11. l. 28.

(t) The Lawyer's Fortune, p. 12. l. 3.

(u) An Act at *Oxford*, p. 17. l. 4. *Hampstead*-Heath, p. 19. l. 12.

(x) Love the Leveller, p. 6. l. 15.

and

and Pickpockets; and deſcribed as ſuch, who (*n*) will *give Money* for *Titles of Honour*, who take *Bribes*, and excuſe all *Offenders*, who can but pay. Such who (*o*) *wiſh one another at the Devil*, are in the *Poets Language* fit for *Aldermen*. In one Play (*p*) the Poet joins together without diſtinction *Cheats and Cuckolds*, *Aldermen and Cullies*; and when he deſcribes them, he tells us, that they all are

> *Creatures a Muſe ſhould ſcorn, ſuch abject Traſh*
> *Deſerves not Satire's, but the Hangman's Laſh:*
> *Wretches ſo far ſhut out from Senſe of Shame,*
> Newgate *or* Bedlam *only can reclaim.*

The next are the *Juſtices of the Peace* in the Country. Theſe are alſo mention'd by (*q*) ridiculous Names, repreſented as (*r*) expoſing themſelves, and affronted by others with all imaginable Rudeneſs in ſome whole Pages together, and call'd (*s*) *the Reforming Juſtices, who make* at leaſt *two hundred Pounds a Year of Whores and Pickpockets*, and (*t*) live by *Extortion* and *Connivance*. They are expoſed, as (*u*) guilty of *Whoredom*, as (*x*) talking *Smut*, and in love with young Girls; as (*y*) receiving of *Bribes*, and for the ſake hereof excuſing groſs Offenders, but ſeverely puniſhing ſuch as have nothing to pay. Thus they make the *Magiſtrates* the Jeſt of the *Play-Houſes*, and (*z*) ſend them away with a diſhonourable *Exit*. And they alſo repreſent their Vices, not as particular to a few, but common to all, and indeed *the conſtant Humour* of the Age.

(*n*) Squire *Trelooby*, *Prologue*, p. 2. l. 3.

(*o*) The Fair Example, p. 1. l. 10.

(*p*) The Careleſs Husband, *Prologue* 1. l. 7.

(*q*) An Act at *Oxford*, *Drama*, *Name* 4. *Hampſtead*-Heath, *Drama*, *Name* 4. The Humour of the Age, *Drama*, *Name* 4. The Northern Laſs, *Drama*, *Name* 3, 4.

(*r*) The Humour of the Age, p. 5, &c. p. 14, &c. p. 38, &c. An Act at *Oxford*, p. 37. *Hampſtead*-Heath, p. 41.

(*s*) An Act at *Oxford*, p. 56. l. 19. *Hampſtead*-Heath, p. 57. l. 28.

(*t*) The Humour of the Age, *Dramatis Perſonæ*.

(*u*) Ibid. p. 6. l. 22.

(*x*) Ibid. p. 15, 43.

(*y*) Ibid. p. 38. l. 7.

(*z*) Ibid. p. 7.

In one *Play* (*a*) *Roger*, puff'd up with a Conceit of his being transform'd into a Gentleman, cannot forbear making his Reflections on this occasion. *When* (saith he) *I am in a Commission of the Peace and Quorum, I will get me a Clerk, a good sensible Fellow, much wiser than my Worship; he shall do all the Business, and I'll have all the Credit, and the best half of the Fees.*

In (*b*) another *Play* a *Constable* speaking of a *drunken Sot*, saith, He *is guilty of no Crime but what Justice may wink at; for our whole County consists of walking Vessels of* October. *Now to accuse one Vessel to another, for no other Crime but being full, would be downright false Heraldry.*

In a third, Sir *Paul* is introduced as a *Justice of the Peace*, who was at first very *zealous* to *reform* the *Vices* of the Age; but soon turns to be a great *Debauchee*, after serious Debates and Resolutions. He then tells the Audience, that (*c*) he *will take a new Course of Life directly*, and blasphemously pretends to *Illuminations*, as if the *Scripture*-Notion of Repentance was a turning from Virtue to Vice. Accordingly he resolves upon *Rioting*, *Drunkenness*, and *Whoring*. His arguing with himself is remarkable, (*d*) to turn Prodigal in point of Conscience, and (*e*) caress the Debauchees, as Men of the greatest Virtue. After this, *Vexhem* the Constable brings (*f*) a *Whore* before Sir *Paul*, who imprisons the Constable, and saith, (*g*) *Now, Lady, whereas you were brought before me as a Delinquent, I retain you as my Mistress.* Accordingly (*h*) he provides for her. He is (*i*) very angry, because she was stolen away for a Fortune; then (*k*) he is jested at for being a *Commissioner* of the Peace. He is (*l*) taken in a *Spaniard*'s Habit, searching after his Whore: He is (*m*) carry'd to his own House

(*a*) The Metamorphosis, *p.* 27. *l.* 3.
(*b*) The Cobler of *Preston*, *p.* 26. *l.* 18.
(*c*) The Northern Lass, *p.* 37. *l.* 16.
(*d*) P. 38. l. 20.
(*e*) P. 39. l. 24.
(*f*) P. 46.
(*g*) P. 46. l. 31.
(*h*) P. 56. *in fine.*
(*i*) P. 63.
(*k*) P. 63. l. 23.
(*l*) P. 69.
(*m*) P. 69. l. 33.

for

for *Justice*, where he is ridiculously treated; then (*n*) he abuseth another Magistrate by the name of *Upstartical Justice*; and at last (*o*) he bribes the Constable to silence his Information.

In another *Play*, there is an antient *Knight* who had the Character of (*p*) *a grave, sober, discreet Magistrate; an unwearied Opposer of Leudness and Debauchery, and a zealous Promoter of a Reformation of Manners*; and yet he is made the sole Diversion of the Audience. To represent him as bad as possible, he frequently (*q*) *swears*, (*r*) *curses*, and (*s*) *takes the Name of GOD in vain*, even (*t*) imploring his Assistance in an *adulterous* Design. He saith, (*u*) that the Woman whom he intended to debauch, was the Object of his *Adoration*. He (*x*) invokes the *Demons, Spirits*, and *Apparitions*, upon this occasion. He (*y*) dresses himself like a *Chimney-Sweeper*, to accomplish his Designs; and then (*z*) he goes into a Sack to hide himself, where (*a*) he is discovered, and makes a dishonourable *Exit*.

To give an Instance more at large: In a later *Play*, printed *Anno* 1717. the *Scene* opens, and (*b*) the *Constable* saith, *If I carry my Point* (Money) *what signifies a little Perjury? There's many an honest Man keeps a Wife and Family by it*. Then he lays open such Villanies in a *Justice* of the Peace, which the World never heard of, except on the *Stage*, that the *Audience* may be prejudiced beforehand, and the Office render'd contemptible. *Ay*, (saith he) (*c*) *you don't know what a good Trade a Justice of the Peace is*. Then (*d*) he saith, *I will in a short Digression lay open to you the whole Mystery of Iniquity*, which

---

(*n*) The Northern Lass, *p*.71. *l*. 12.

(*o*) P.71. *l*.40.

(*p*) Love in a Sack, *p*. 33. *l*. 12.

(*q*) P. 11. *l*. 14. *p*. 17. *l*.22. *p*.26. *l*.15. *p*.27. l.6. *p*.36. *l*.9. *p*.44. *l*.1. *p*.48. *l*. *ult*.

(*r*) P.11. *l*.12. *p*.16. *l*.7. *p*. 48. *l*.4, *antepenult*.

(*s*) P.12. *l*.22. *p*.16. *l*.15. *p*. 27. *l*.22. *p*.29. *l*.18. *p*. 30. *l*.6. *p*.34. *l*.6. *p*.53. *l*.10. *p*.54. *l*.1, 2. *p*.57. *l*.10. *p*.58. *l*.10.

(*t*) P.54. *l*.14.

(*u*) P.14. *l*.14. *p*.23. *l*.4.

(*x*) P.53. *l*.2.

(*y*) P. 41, &c.

(*z*) P.56. *l*.15.

(*a*) P.57. *l*. *penult*. &c.

(*b*) The Perjuror, *p*.2. *l*.11.

(*c*) P.2. *l*.18.

(*d*) P.3. *l*.1.

is thus in his own words: (s) *You must know, here is an old Fellow qualified with Ill-nature and Avarice, by the help of a little Money and some Interest, gets into the Commission: He entertains a Clerk, some broken Attorney (for they make the best Clerks) he consequently has more Sense than the Justice, at least more Law; and for their Honesty, they are generally upon a Par. The Fees are divided into four parts, the Justice has two, the Clerk one, and the favourite Constable another. Besides which, the Justice out of his own Dividend allows twenty Shillings a Week to a Couple of* Finders, (*which are vulgarly called* Informers) *and a handsome Treat now and then to the Watchmen, for knocking Gentlemen down in the Streets, and swearing Riots against 'em the next morning.* Thus *every Man is willing to make the best of his Place. We inferior Magistrates can plead both great and antient Examples. Every Man must have his share of Profit. The Commonwealth is a great Machine, composed of many great and small Wheels, and every one must be pleas'd. Why, Sir, here is this old Justice, if he had fifty in Family, it would not cost him Twopence all the Year for Bread and Meat. Sunday-Morning is his Market-Day, when he never fails to take from Butchers, Bakers and Poulterers, (who venture to sell to poor Workmen, that can't buy on a Saturday-Night) Beef, Bread and Fowl enough to maintain his House the ensuing Week.*

It is easy to observe the reason of all this Scandal thrown upon the *Magistrates* of the Land, namely, because they receive *Information* against *Offenders*, and put the *Laws* in *Execution*, which are made to prevent the *profaning* of the *LORD's-Day*. These are Crimes never to be forgiven; but the guilty must expect from the *Stage* the utmost Severity which either *Satire* or the *Father of Lyes* can invent.

When the *Justice* appears in Person, he tells the Audience, (t) that *the Constable ow'd to him all that* he *was worth*, and that (u) he himself had taken *Meat from the Butcher, Cabbages from the Herb-Woman, and Bread from the Baker*, for his own use; and to prevent their

(s) The Perjuror, *p.3. l.7.* (u) *P.9. l.13.*
(t) *P.8. l. penult.*

com-

complaining, the *Constable shall swear a Riot against them.* Then he saith, (*x*) *I'll teach 'em to sell things on a Sunday, a pack of profane Wretches; and yet I hope they won't have the Grace to leave it off.* After this, the *Clerk* tells the *Justice,* (*y*) *There is one Goodman* Conscience *desires to speak with* him. The *Justice* answers, He is *not at Leisure,* that he had *heard of such a one;* but *he* could *not live in the City,* and the *Justice knew no such Person at the other end of the Town.* That (*z*) he *had such an Acquaintance formerly; but it was a great while ago:* But he *had no acquaintance with him since* he *was sworn into the Commission,* neither did he *desire it.* Adding, (*a*) *He is a troublesome Fellow, this same* Conscience, *and I must put him off.* And therefore he orders the *Clerk,* (*b*) *If ever* Conscience *comes again, tell him, I am not at home.*

After this, (*c*) the *Constable* brings *Actors* before the *Justice.* They (*d*) whisper. The (*e*) *Constable* answers, *Yes, yes, and please you. I'll swear as much as your Worship thinks fit against them. You know, Sir, I was never backward of serving your Worship upon any occasion. But what would you be pleased to have me swear?* The *Justice* (*f*) bids him *swear what comes uppermost. I only desire to bind them over. I shall be satisfied with my Fees, and five Pieces after to stifle the Indictment.* Upon this, to make all Attempts for a *Reformation of Manners* ridiculous, the *Justice* (*g*) declares, *I am for a thorough Reformation; and with the Zeal of an upright Magistrate will pursue it. I have ferretted every Hole, Crack, and Cranny in the Parish, that Vice could but put its Head into. There is not a Bawdy-house in the Parish that I am not acquainted with. I visit them twice or thrice a Week at least. Let me alone for Lewdness. If there be a Whore more than ordinary in the Parish, I presently scent her out, I warrant you. Let me alone with the leud Women. I love to have the management of them myself.* Upon this,

---

(*x*) The Perjuror, *p.* 10. *l.* 2.
(*y*) *P.* 10. *l.* 8.
(*z*) *P.* 11. *l.* 4.
(*a*) *P.* 11. *l.* 9.
(*b*) *P.* 11. *l. penult.*
(*c*) *P.* 12. *l.* 12.
(*d*) *P.* 13. *l.* 3.
(*e*) *P.* 13. *l.* 16.
(*f*) *P.* 14. *l.* 2.
(*g*) *P.* 14. *l.* 17.

(*h*) the *Execution* of the *Law* against *profane Swearing* is made the *Jest* of the *Stage*. Then two Women being brought before the *Justice*, he (*i*) expresses his leud Inclination to them both, and (*k*) owns it again. The *Actress* (*l*) rebukes him for it, and (*m*) he is made the Scoff both of *Constable* and others. The *Justice* adds, (*n*) *'Tis not the Sin, but the knowledge of it, that distinguishes the Thief.* And (*o*) *the World is all a Cheat, and Virtue but a Disguise, which, 'tis true, should never be thrown off, but where a Man knows his Company. Do but devoutly cast your Eyes upwards, and it is no matter where your Hands are.* And when he is threatned to be discover'd, he twice, (*p*) on two occasions, saith, He can *forswear it*. The (*q*) Conclusion of the *Play* is a direct Invective against *prosecuting* all *Offenders*; because the *Magistrates* are equally guilty; (Malice and Scandal can forge any thing in the *Play-house*, if it serves the Interest of *Vice* and *Profaneness*) and the last Speech to the *Justice* hath these Words: (*r*) *For the future, I would have you less zealous against publick Follies, and begin a Reformation in your own Family. Forbear to persecute your Neighbours, and correct your self.*

To mend the matter, the *Author* thinks himself under a necessity to declare in a *Preface*, that he *meant not this of any particular Person*. And, indeed, this may be true, if he design'd it to expose all the *Magistrates* in the Kingdom. And in the (*s*) *Prologue* he adds:

> *Our Author lashes not a* Whig *or* Tory,
> *But common Vices in fictitious Story.*

Now, it is not common for a *Justice* of the Peace to be so vile a Wretch, as he is here represented. Perhaps, there is not such an Instance in the Kingdom; or if there was, he could not hold his Commission long under so just and good a Government. But it is common

(*h*) The Perjuror, *p.19. l.12.*
(*i*) *P.22. l.9. p.23. l.10.*
(*k*) *P.27. l.22.*
(*l*) *P.27. l.18.*
(*m*) *P.28. l.5,6,8,16.*
(*n*) *P.28. l.20.*
(*o*) *P.29. l.19.*
(*p*) *P.30. l.2. p.31. l.9.*
(*q*) *P.32. l.14.*
(*r*) *P.32. l.9.*
(*s*) *Prologue, l.16.*

for the *Justices* of the Peace, (being encouraged by *His Majesty's* Royal *Proclamation*, read frequently in open Court) to execute the *Laws* against *Immorality* and *Profaneness*; and this is therefore what the *Poet* lashes, whilst he raiseth so much Scandal for no other purpose.

These Examples are so full, that we cannot wonder if the *Stage Poets* abuse all other inferior Officers. The principal among those who stick in their stomachs, are the *Informers*. The *Magistrates* act only by Evidence; and therefore if these can but be discouraged, the *Laws* and all other *Officers* will signify nothing. Accordingly, in two different *Plays* (for the Humour must not be lost) one *Driver* is represented as a *Reformer of Manners*, and informs the Audience, that he is (*t*) *a Scourge to publick Leudness, but privately in love with Whoring, and a Member of the Calves-Head-Club*. That he is (*u*) extremely *malicious*, and (*x*) *makes Two Hundred Pounds a Year of Whores and Pickpockets*. After this, he is represented as guilty of (*y*) *Cursing*, and (*z*) is buffeted and abused. Others speak of him, as (*a*) a *City Reformer, and chief Beggar-hunter*; as (*b*) *Carrion, fit only for Crows to feed upon*; and that (*c*) such a Man is *impudent* even to a Proverb. In other *Plays* an *Informer* is called a (*d*) *canting* Fellow, with *no more Religion than an* English *Whore*, and (*e*) one who is *in want*; and accordingly *swears* for no other reason but to get a Maintenance.

The Design of forming *Societies for Reformation of Manners* was most great and noble, and their Success has been very evident in most places, especially in and about

---

(*t*) An Act at *Oxford*, *p*. 5. *l*. 1. Hampstead-Heath, *p*. 5. *l*. 9.

(*u*) An Act at *Oxford*, *p*. 29. *l*. 33. Hampstead-Heath, *p*. 29. *l*. 33.

(*x*) An Act at *Oxford*, *p*. 46. *l*. 19. Hampstead-Heath, *p*. 47. *l*. *penult*.

(*y*) An Act at *Oxford*, *p*. 23. *l*. 9. *p*. 24. *l*. 11, 17, 25. Hampstead-Heath, *p*. 25. *l*. 26.

(*z*) Ibid.

(*a*) An Act at *Oxford*, *p*. 3. *l*. *penult*. Hampstead-Heath, *p*. 3. *l*. 24.

(*b*) An Act at *Oxford*, *p*. 37. *l*. 28. Hampstead-Heath, *p*. 42. *l*. 20.

(*c*) An Act at *Oxford*, *p*. 50. *l*. 1.

(*d*) The Lawyer's Fortune, *p*. 9. *l*. 12.

(*e*) Faithful Bride of *Granada*, *Epilogue*, *l*. 10.

London, to the admiration of all good Men. However, these very Methods are subject to the *Play-house* Scorns. (*f*) *What signifies* (saith an *Actor*) *your reforming Society? The noble Exploit of demolishing a poor Sunday Apple-Stall!* Here's *Impiety* against *GOD*, as well as *Disrespect* to *Man*. A Care for the Observance of the *Fourth Commandment* signifies nothing with them; and indeed they aim to destroy not only that, but all the rest.

As to their treatment of *Juries*, *Bailiffs*, and other *Officers*, I shall give but one Quotation of each, because I have trespassed so long already upon this Subject.

The Juries.

(*g*) *I* (saith an *Actor*) *am one of the Grand-Jury, and consequently very malicious, and can hang thee right or wrong.*

The Bailiffs.

(*h*) *A* Middlesex *Bum-Bailiff is an Impudence ten degrees beyond the Devil.*

Other Officers.

(*i*) *Are you fit to appear in Offices in this Saint-like Age? A notorious leud Liver, and a Scandal to Reformation!* To this it is answer'd, *Why, who is fitter to be employ'd, than he that supports the Trade of the Nation?* Here *Vice* is caressed as our *Support*, and necessary for *Trade*; and could the *Actors* have their will, the most *profligate Wretches* should have all the Places of Trust, and *Profaneness* alone should be a Qualification for Preferment.

If then such must feel the *Poet*'s Lash, who endeavour to reform *Vice* in other places, tho they let the *Stage* alone, what usage must they expect, who attempt to reclaim the *Play-houses*? They shall have Dirt enough cast at them, that some at least may stick; and whoever

---

(*f*) Hampstead-Heath, *p.* 5. *l.* 11. An Act at *Oxford*, *p.* 5. *l.* 5.

(*g*) An Act at *Oxford*, *p.* 29. *l.* 31. Hampstead-Heath, *p.* 33. *l.* 19.

(*h*) An Act at *Oxford*, *p.* 9. *l. ult.*

(*i*) An Act at *Oxford*, *p.* 8. *l.* 22. Hampstead-Heath, *p.* 10. *l.* 20.

escapes,

escapes, they have their share. One (k) *Comedy* is from the beginning to the end on this Subject, and the *Epilogue* is very scandalous. Here an Enemy to the *Stage-Immoralities* is censured, despised, brought in guilty of Whoredom, and makes a dishonourable *Exit.* I thought, that *Tossing in a Blanket* was an Office too mean for a *Poet:* however upon occasion he can stoop so low; and accordingly he treats the Censurer of his *Vices* more like a *Dog* than a *Christian*, that so the *Title-Page* and the *Play* may be both of a piece. It is well that the *Law* secures *His Majesty's Subjects*, and restrains the Malice of the *Poets*; but by this we may observe what they would be at, if they had a *Power* proportionable to their own *Inclination.*

Sometimes they reflect on the *Reformers* of the *Stage* in their *Epistles Dedicatory*, and *Prefaces*, as (l) Enemies to the *Church* and *present Government*, and as (m) *snarling Zealots*; and tell us, that (n) now *the Liberty of the Stage declines*, and that *Plays, as tho they were not dull enough before, must now, to oblige the affected Zeal and Humour of some kind of People, be robb'd of all the Life and Pertness* (that is, the Blasphemy and Profaneness) *which is in them.*

They tell us also in their *Acts*, that such who oppose them, (o) do *rail*, they are (p) *Whigs*, they are (q) an *hypocritical* Party, nay (r) *inveterate Hypocrites*, who are Enemies to the *Stage*, and say, that (s) *if the Stage did not make it its business to expose Knaves and Hypocrites, they would say nothing against it.* (t) *Do you think* (saith one concerning an Enemy to the *Stage* Vices) *that any Man alive could say so many severe things against both Sexes, without having a sufficient Experience of those Evils and Frailties in himself?* They represent such, as guilty of (u) *Whoring*, and tell them, (x) that *if they*

(k) The Stage-Beaux toss'd in a Blanket.

(l) An Act at *Oxford*, *Epistle Dedicatory*, p. 4, &c.

(m) Zelmane, *Epistle Dedicatory.* p. 1. l. 7, &c.

(n) *Portsmouth* Heiress, *Preface*, l. 3, &c.

(o) The Gamester, *p.6. l.16.*

(p) Ibid.

(q) The Stage-Beaux toss'd in a Blanket, *Title-Page*, p. 43. l. 18. p.58. l.29. p.59. *l.*2.

(r) Ibid. p.49. l.17.

(s) Ibid. p.50. l.9.

(t) Ibid. p.57. l.14.

(u) Ibid. p.56. l. 29. *to the end of the Play.*

(x) Ibid. p.49. l.18.

are ſuch Zealots for Morality, they ſhould firſt reform themſelves. In their Cenſures they have no regard to Truth or Equity. If they can render ſuch Perſons deſpicable, it is no matter how they effect it: Nay, it is obſervable, that theſe Reflections may with equal force be applied againſt the preaching of the Word, and all Inſtructions in *Religion:* And indeed, if the *Stage-Poets* had their wills, it is to be doubted, that all would fare alike. In their *Prologues* and *Epilogues,* they are ſometimes (y) wholly upon this Subject, when they ſpeak more particularly to the Audience. There is one Quotation that I ſhall venture to tranſcribe, for the ſake of the *excellent Engliſh* and *ſmooth Running* of the Verſe, which is almoſt as remarkable as (z) the *Poet*'s Scurrility.

Sure we've ſcap'd the Informer's Inquiſition;
The Diſeaſe is bad, and he a damn'd Phyſician:
Him no Motive does to Reformation lead
But Want; he ſwears, becauſe it gets him Bread.
He culls the Ill, and earns from thence his Food;
He, with mending, he's ruin'd if the World is good.
No, great Examples ſhall reform the Stage:
Muſt we learn Manners from the vileſt of the Age?

Had this come from a *School-Boy,* it would have deſerved *Correction;* but as it comes from a *Stage-Poet,* it is very fine, and deſerves a *Plaudite.* It is abuſive, and therefore excellent. I have heard of ſome *Children,* who learn to curſe, before they can ſpeak plain; and the *Poet* writes ſcurrilouſly, when he cannot write Senſe. Had he been a Child, he might have learn'd better Manners; but as he is old, I doubt, it will be the more difficult to reclaim him.

Thus we ſee, that they ſpare neither *Writers* nor *Reformers,* (a) ſuch *thoughtleſs Criticks of the Age,* as they

---

(y) The Faithful General, *Prologue.* The Female Wits, *Prologue.* The Rival Brothers, *Prologue.* The Stage-Beaux toſs'd in a Blanket, *Epilogue.*

(z) The Faithful Bride of *Granada, Epilogue, l.* 8.

(a) The Faithful General, *Epilogue, l.* 1.

term

term them. Sometimes they have (*b*) a fling at them, and away again to another Subject; and ſometimes they ridicule both them and the preaching of the Word of GOD together, as if both were alike Enemies to the *Stage*: and from hence we may explain what they offer on ſuch occaſions with a *double Entendre*. Some Inſtances of this nature may bear a publick View, and therefore let the *Reader* judge of theſe two.

(*c*) *To th' Stage the Army of Reformers come,*
Sworn Foes to Wit, as Carthage *was to* Rome:
Their Ears ſo ſanctified no Scenes can pleaſe,
But heavy Hymns, and penſive Homilies.

And (*d*),

With force and fitting freedom Vice arraign;
Tho Pulpits flatter, let the Stage ſpeak plain.

It will not be amiſs to give the *Reader* a taſte of their *fine Language* in Proſe as well as Verſe. And becauſe I will not tire him with many Quotations, I ſhall only take a few out of (*e*) one particular Comedy, The *Author* begins very roundly in (*f*) the *Epiſtle Dedicatory*, and tells us, that *the Stage hath no Enemies, but ſuch as are Hypocrites, and real Enemies to Virtue.* And he gives this reaſon, *Becauſe the Stage is a profeſſed Enemy to them and their darling Vices.* This is a bold Aſſertion; and the Falſhood is as evident as the Enmity. However, there is much more to the ſame purpoſe in the *Play* itſelf.

In (*g*) one place, an Oppoſer of the *Stage-Vices* is call'd, *A Man of looſe Principles, who can be guilty of arrogating to himſelf a Righteouſneſs above all Men, as well as a Judgment and Senſe ſuperior to all the Men of Wit in Town.*

(*b*) Squire Trelooby, *Prologue*, l.22. The Biter, *Epilogue*, l.24. *and in the end*. The careleſs Husband, p.53. l.10. The Gameſter, p.6. l.16. The Stage-Coach, *Epilogue*, l.7. Zelmane, *Preface*, p.1. l.8.

(*c*) Squire Trelooby, *Prologue*, l. 3.

(*d*) Ibid. l.17.

(*e*) The Stage-Beaux toſs'd in a Blanket.

(*f*) P.2. l.18.

(*g*) P.29. l.8.

In

In (*h*) another place, an Enemy of the *Stage-Vices* is represented as endeavouring to debauch a Woman of the same Temper. He speaks thus: *Put off the Veil. I know you are an Hypocrite.* She answers, *Nay, now you begin to be abusive. An Hypocrite!* And he replies, *Nay, I am sure of it; for almost all our Party are so.*

I shall only add some Expressions which I find in the same Play, and only in the two following Pages.

(*i*) *They ought to abhor the Play-house, since they so often see their ugly Faces there.*

(*k*) *The Stage-Glass is not made to flatter Fools and Knaves, and therefore they and their Friends are for breaking the honest Mirror.*

(*l*) *Fools and Knaves have a real Quarrel with the Stage; not that it shews their Pictures deformed to themselves, but to every body else.*

And (*m*) *The greatest Pique Men have to the Stage, is, because their Follies and Vices are too conspicuous, and too well beloved.*

And now, since there is such a publick daring Method to prevent all *Reformation*, what can we infer from hence, but that without infinite Mercy, this Nation is ripe for Ruin and *Destruction*?

[Which GOD prevent.]

(*h*) The Stage-Beaux toss'd in a Blanket, p. 58. l. 29.

(*i*) P. 2. l. 37.

(*k*) P. 2. l. 39.

(*l*) P. 2. l. *penult.*

(*m*) P. 3. l. 4.

CHAP.

CHAP. XV.

Heaven, the Abode of GOD, exposed on the Stage.

AS the *Poets* on all occasions endeavour to undervalue *Religion* and *Reformation*, and as they extol *Profaneness*; so they also lessen the Joys of *Heaven*, which is the Reward for the one, and the Torments of *Hell*, which is justly due to the other.

When GOD was pleas'd in his Holy Word to persuade Men to turn from their Sins unto him, and to lead *godly, righteous, and sober Lives*, he also revealed the great Rewards which he should give to those who obey him, and urged it as an Argument to persuade us, or indeed to constrain us. It is called (*a*) *an Inheritance incorruptible, undefiled, and that fadeth not away, reserved in Heaven for* the Servants of GOD; (*b*) *a Crown of Glory, that fadeth not away*; (*c*) *a Crown of Righteousness*; (*d*) *a Crown of Life*; (*e*) *a being ever with the LORD*, and (*f*) *seeing him as he is*; (*g*) our *Hire*, and (*h*) our *Reward*. And from hence we are exhorted (*i*) to turn from Sin, (*k*) to the Practice of all manner of

(*a*) 1 *Pet.* 1. 4.
(*b*) 1 *Pet.* 5. 4.
(*c*) 2 *Tim.* 4. 8.
(*d*) *James* 1. 12. *Rev.* 2. 10.
(*e*) 1 *Thess.* 4. 17.
(*f*) 1 *John* 3. 2.
(*g*) *Mat.* 20. 8.
(*h*) *Psal.* 58. 11. *Prov.* 11. 18. *Isa.* 40. 10. & 62. 11. *Mat.* 5. 12. & 6. 1. & 10. 41, 42. *Luke* 6. 23, 35. 1 *Cor.* 3. 8, 14. *Col.* 2. 18. & 3. 24. *Heb.* 10. 35. & 11. 26. 2 *Joh.* 8. *Rev.* 22. 12.
(*i*) *Ezek.* 18. 21, 22, 27, 28. 1 *John* 3. 2, 3, 4.
(*k*) *Psal.* 15. per tot. *Psal.* 24. 4, 5. & 37. 39. *Rom.* 2. 7, 8, 10, 11. & 8. 1. 1 *Cor.* 15. 58. 2 *Cor.* 7. 1. *Tit.* 2. 11, 12, 13. *Heb.* 12. 14. 2 *Pet.* 1. 4, 5, 6, 7, 8, 9, 10, 11. 2 *Pet.* 3. 14.

Duties,

Duties, (*l*) to Perſeverance in them, and (*m*) to *endure Temptations*. The *Players* endeavour by various Methods to fruſtrate theſe Encouragements and Admonitions of GOD himſelf, and to prejudice their *Auditors* againſt them all.

For firſt in their *Plays* they frequently diſpute and doubt whether there be any other World or not, and ſometimes argue againſt it. This is doing their utmoſt to prove GOD to be a Lyar. A few Quotations may be ſufficient for the Proof of this. One *Actor* ſaith poſitively, (*n*) *He that truſts to Futurity, is an Aſs for his pains.* Another (*o*) arguing about the State of the Soul, ſaith, *Where ſhall I find it? The Learned can't agree where to place it; therefore I'll have no trouble about that.* Another asks this Queſtion (*p*):

> *Who can reſolve me, what's beyond this Span?*
> *Perhaps I may return to my firſt Nothing.*

And another (*q*) argues thus with himſelf:

> *Bend, ſupple Conſcience, when Life's to be gain'd;*
> *That may be certain, what's hereafter, feign'd:*
> *We know not what's on th' other ſide o'th' Skreen,*
> *Beyond yon dreadful Curtain to be ſeen.*

But the *Poets* ſeem in doubt, that this is too groſs to be impoſed on the World. A future State is too plainly revealed, to be contradicted; and therefore they generally take other Meaſures.

Firſt, They repreſent the Joys thereof as inconſiderable, and not worth the minding, or the parting with temporal Pleaſures for their ſakes. Accordingly in one *Play* (*r*) a *Supper* upon *Free-Coſt* is three times com-

(*l*) *Mat.* 10. 22. *Luke* 22. 28, 29, 30. *Rev.* 2. 10.
(*m*) *James* 1. 12.
(*n*) The Litigants, *p.* 1. *l.* 1.
(*o*) The Man's bewitch'd, *p.* 29. *l.* 28.
(*p*) The Conqueſt of *Spain*, *p.* 66. *l.* 22.
(*q*) Jane Grey, *p.* 64. *l.* 15.
(*r*) The Humours of Purgatory, *p.* 42. *l.* 3, 23. *p.* 43. *l.* 15.

pared

pared to the Kingdom of *Heaven*; which is thus deſcribed in another (s):

I tell you how the Men above
Enjoy their Pleaſures, and their Love:
Ever Ranging,
Ever Changing,
Bumpers Drinking,
Never Thinking;
Thus they riot, thus they rove.

Had this come from a Follower of *Mahomet*, it might have been excuſable; but it ſounds too groſs from Profeſſors of *Chriſtianity*. And indeed the *Poets* write more agreeably to the *Alcoran*, than to the *Holy Scriptures*. Thus for example, the *Pſalmiſt* ſpeaks of GOD; (t) *Whom have I in Heaven but thee? and there is none upon Earth that I deſire beſides thee.* An *Actor* ſpeaks thus of a Wife; (u) She is *all my Soul could wiſh for, but the Addition of a Father's Bleſſing.* Another ſpeaks thus to his Miſtreſs; (x) *I think, I have obtained the Summit of my Happineſs in the Fruition of thy Charms.* A third calls a Woman, (y) *Thou Sum-Total of my Happineſs.* And another ſaith (z);

————*Do I accept her?*
With greater Rapture, than the Wretch that's freed
From Death's convulſive Pangs, embraceth Heav'n.

I ſuppoſe that there can be no danger in producing ſuch Strains as theſe, and therefore I ſhall add ſome more.

(a) *An immortal Spring of Joy.*
(b) *I prize no Joy above her.*

(s) The Comick Maſque, *p.* 10. *l.* 32.
(t) *Pſal.* 73. 25.
(u) Love's laſt Shift, *p.* 77. *l.* 31.
(x) The Maſquerade, *p.* 28. *l.* 34.
(y) The Drummer, *p.* 32. *l.* 32.
(z) Liberty aſſerted, *p.* 25. *l.* 29.
(a) *Pyrrhus* and *Demetrius*, *p.* 12. *l. ult.*
(b) Thomyris, *p.* 44. *l. ult.*

Soul

(*c*) *Soul of Pleasure, Heav'n and you must grant the Blessing.*

(*d*) *You are my Soul's Ambition: I have no Wish above ye.*

(*e*) *Blest will be my Condition, if you can love me.*

(*f*) *It is Life to be with her, and worse than Death to be without her.*

(*g*) *Not Saints to Heav'n with more Submission bow.*
I have no Will, but what your Eyes ordain;
Destin'd to love, as they are doom'd to reign:

That is, condemn'd to live with GOD in Heaven.

(*h*) *So much, so tenderly your Slave adores,*
He hath no Thought of Happiness but yours.

Neither are the Men only guilty of this Extravagancy; but the *Women* also treat the *Men* with the same Language. One saith to her Husband, (*i*) *I find all Joys in thee.* Another (*k*) saith to her Suitor, *All my Joy's in thee alone.* And a third, as modest as a Virgin Muse in these days, expresseth herself (*l*) thus at the Thoughts of being marry'd: *Oh! I am raised from the Anguish of a black Despair to a Heaven of Hope and Happiness.*

In one *Play* a Shepherd (*m*) prays his Mistress to *bless a Lover*, and at another time the *Shepherdess* is as forward to say, (*n*) that *where this Love is away, there is no Delight*, and consequently no Blessing. If all this is not monstrously impudent, and the highest Affront to the Modesty of the Female Sex, it will be hard to assign what is.

But to proceed: In another *Play*, suffering for a Mistress is call'd (*o*) a *sweet Martyrdom.* When a Lover courts his *Mistress*, and is refused, this is stiled (*p*) the *falling*

(*c*) Thomyris, *p.*53. *l.*13.
(*d*) Camilla, *p.* 35. *l.* 4.
(*e*) Ibid. *p.*35. *l.*19.
(*f*) Clotilda, *p.*4. *l.*18.
(*g*) *British* Enchanters, *p.*7. *l.*8.
(*h*) Ibid. *p.*7. *l.*29.
(*i*) *Phædra* and *Hippolytus*, *p.* 32. *l.* 18.
(*k*) Myrtillus, *p.*21. *l.*7.
(*l*) The Perplex'd Couple, *p.* 63. *l.*15.
(*m*) Love's Triumph, *p.* 8. *l.* 35.
(*n*) *British* Enchanters, *p.* 17. *l.* 20.
(*o*) Arsinoe, *p.*14. *l. ult.*
(*p*) *Pyrrhus* and *Demetrius*, *p.*31. *l.*18.

a Martyr to her Pride: as if they, who ſuffered for the Cauſe of *Chriſtianity*, were diſappointed in their Endeavours and Expectations. And the *Moral*, *Deſign*, and *Concluſion* of one whole *Play*, is to equal the Joys of *Love* with the Joys of *Heaven*, and to illuſtrate the Similitude, becauſe we (*q*) obtain them both by Sufferings.

Our preſent Joy is ſweeter by paſt Pain:
To Love and Heav'n by ſuff'ring we obtain.

When Lovers are crown'd with Succeſs, they declare their Satisfaction in the moſt extravagant Expreſſions: That (*r*) they do *not envy Jove* in his ſupreme *Grandeur*, but count themſelves as happy as a GOD; they (*s*) declare themſelves bleſſed, with a *Hail happy Hour!* and call it (*t*) a compleat Joy, and a bleſſed Day, when the Lovers meet their *Miſtreſſes*. Their Satisfaction, when they obtain their Wiſhes, are call'd (*u*) Joys that never pall, and (*x*) never waſte, (*y*) endleſs Pleaſures and golden Treaſures, (*z*) a Pleaſure beyond expreſſion, in which all is Joy, and all is Bleſſing. It is poſſible to produce (*a*) ſome *Strains* upon this occaſion, which have a Tincture of *Smut*; tho I cannot forbear to tranſcribe others, which have a mixture both of *Impudence* and *Blaſphemy*.

(*b*) *Bleſs'd above meaſure, our Joys are compleat.*
(*c*) *My Sighs with Pain reſpiring,*
Are only breath'd for thee:
'Tis what my Soul's deſiring,
Thy Love's a Feaſt for me;
The ſweeteſt Bliſs, the deareſt Treaſure.

(*q*) *Compare* The *Britiſh* Enchanters, *p. ult. l. penult. with Rom.* 8. 18. 2 *Cor.* 4. 16, 17. *Heb.* 2. 10.

(*r*) Arſinoe, *p.* 48. *l.* 1.

(*s*) Camilla, *p.* 37. *l.* 2.

(*t*) Love's Triumph, *p.* 8. *l.* 35. *Britiſh* Enchanters, *p.* 38. *l.* 15.

(*u*) Clotilda, *p.* 2. *l.* 22, 23.

(*x*) Ibid. *p.* 23. *l.* 16.

(*y*) *Pyrrhus* and *Demetrius*, *p.* 36. *l.* 15.

(*z*) *Britiſh* Enchanters, *p.* 19. *l.* 3.

(*a*) Hydaſpes, *p.* 30. *l.* 31.

(*b*) Almahide, *Interlude* 2. *in the End.*

(*c*) Ibid. *p.* 56. *l.* 12.

The

(d) *The Stars have given me Rest,*
And Love yields all I want:
This sighing Soul, this tortur'd Breast,
Hath all that Heav'n can grant.

Our *blessed Saviour* asks this Question, (e) *What shall it profit a Man, if he shall gain the whole World, and lose his own Soul?* We know what Answer a *Christian* would make. An *Actor* on the *Stage* hath this Expression (f);

Let Dotards rail, and pride themselves in Conscience:
Whilst I each Bliss within my Grasp surprize,
I'll leave to them Reversions in the Skies.

But, *Secondly*, the *Poets* represent the *Joys* on *Earth* as preferable to the *Joys* in *Heaven*. This may be proved from what hath been already mentioned, and therefore I shall give but one more Instance in each Sex. A *Virgin Actress* hath this Expression; (g) *In what or where the Joys of Heaven consist, lies deeper than a Woman's Line can fathom; but this we know, a Wife must in her Husband seek for hers.* And an *Actor* gives (h) this Reason for the Preference:

They taste of Death, who do at Heav'n arrive;
But we this Paradise approach alive.

These Flights are much too high, and therefore I shall descend to others, where the *Poets* set both upon a *Par*. And here I might produce a great Variety of Instances, where sometimes (i) a *Woman* beloved, and sometimes (k) a *Man*, sometimes (l) *Love* in general,

---

(d) Hydaspes, *p.*72. *l.*23.
(e) *Mat.* 16. 26. *Mark* 8. 36.
(f) The Perfidious Brother, *p.*23. *l.*9.
(g) The False Friend, *p.* 28. *l. penult.*
(h) The Man of Mode, *p.* 200. *l.*27.
(i) The Victim, *p.*35. *l. ult.* *p.*36. *l.* 1, 2. Titus Manlius, *p.* 55. *l.*29.
(k) Myrtillo, *p.*21. *l.*7. The Man of Mode, *p.*186. *l.*25. *p.* 259. *l.* 7. The Royal Convert, *p.*23. *l.*4. Titus Manlius, *p.* 55. *l.* 29.
(l) The Mistake, *p.*36. *l.*30.

and ſometimes (*m*) *Love* in particular is equal'd to the Delights of Saints and Angels in the other World.

In one *Play* a Man is call'd by a Woman, (*n*) *My everlaſting Love*, and a Woman is call'd by a Man, (*o*) *My Life, my Soul*, and (*p*) *My all that's charming*; and is addreſs'd to with theſe Expreſſions, (*q*) *My Heart, my Soul, and Body into the bargain, is at your Service*; and (*r*) *my Heart is all thy own.* In another a Woman is call'd (*s*) *The Sum-Total of my Happineſs.* And in a third, a *Chriſtian King* compliments his *Queen* with this Expreſſion, (*t*) *The Summit of my Hopes, my Height of Bliſs*; as if *Marriage* was the greateſt Expectation of a *Chriſtian.*

When Lovers obtain their Miſtreſſes, they expreſs themſelves with ſuch Raptures as theſe.

(*u*) *I am bleſs'd.*
(*x*) *I can want nothing here; poſſeſſing thee,*
All my Deſires are carry'd to their Aim
Of Happineſs: there's no room for a Wiſh,
But to continue ſtill this Bleſſing to me.

(*y*) *Thus kneeling, let me receive the mighty Bleſſing. For now I have obtain'd the End of all my Wiſhes. I know no Happineſs beyond this.*

(*z*) *'Tis ſhe, for whom I have ſigh'd and ſearch'd ſo long. Now I am bleſs'd indeed.*

If I quoted to the utmoſt, I might fill a Volume in reciting ſuch Expreſſions. But as none can doubt the Truth of this Charge, who ever ſaw or heard a *Play*; ſo I ſhall mention but two other Inſtances.

(*a*) *Take me to your Arms; for here's the greateſt*

(*m*) The Cruel Gift, *p.* 35. *l.* 15. Wit at a pinch, *p.* 18. *l.* 5.
(*n*) The Wonder, *p.*22. *l.*11.
(*o*) Ibid. *p.*22. *l.*12.
(*p*) Ibid. *p.*12. *l.*16.
(*q*) Ibid. *p.*41. *l.*23.
(*r*) Ibid. *p.*71. *l.*5.
(*s*) The Drummer, *p.*32. *l.*32.
(*t*) Lucius, *p.*21. *l. antepen.*
(*u*) The *Portſmouth* Heireſs, *p.*53. *l.*4.
(*x*) The Fatal Marriage, *p.* 154. *l.*34.
(*y*) The Perplex'd Couple, *p.* 67. *l.*12.
(*z*) The Platonick Lady, *p.*70. *l.* 1.
(*a*) The Maid the Miſtreſs, *p.* 49. *in fine.*

R *Bliſs*

Bliss that Life or Nature (that is, GOD himself) *can bestow.*

(*b*) *Every Good that Nature* (that is, GOD himself)
can bestow,
And ev'ry Charm is center'd sure in thee.

Besides, the *Poets* in this case make no distinction between Good and Evil; between a chaste Love, and a brutish Lust. *Whoredom* is call'd (*c*) *Immortal Pleasures,* (*d*) *Joys Immortal,* (*e*) which *raise the Soul to* Heaven above, and (*f*) a *Revelling in Pleasures Imperial.* Thus an *Adulteress* is (*g*) *ador'd* by a Man, and an *Adulterer* is call'd (*h*) her *Soul's Delight*, by the very Woman whom he debauches.

In (*i*) one *Play*, an *Actor* being willing to commit *Incest*, expresses his Lust by calling it *the enjoying* his *Heaven one Moment*; and further paraphraseth on this Expression:

That Moment were Eternity in little;
A mighty Sum, but taken on Content,
To save the tedious telling o'er and o'er.

Now a *tedious Eternity*, or *Computation* of Time in *Heaven*, is such a profane Description, the like whereof is scarcely heard of, except in the *Play-House*. And it is much to be doubted, that they who can delight to hear it so represented, will never be admitted into it.

Besides, (*k*) the Temptations to *Whoredom* are said to be irresistible; so that GOD himself cannot blame those who are guilty. And in the same *Play*, when (*l*) *Gonzales* was

---

(*b*) The Perplex'd Lovers, *p.* 18. *l.* 25.

(*c*) The Rival Brothers, *p.* 73. *l.* 3.

(*d*) *Venus* and *Adonis*, *p.* 11. *l.* 16.

(*e*) Ibid. *p.* 15. *l. antepenult.*

(*f*) Woman is a Riddle, *p.* 10. *l.* 26, 28, &c. *compared with p.* 11. *l.* 19. *p.* 49. *l.* 22. *antepenult.*

(*g*) Love in a Sack, *p.* 14. *l.* 14. *p.* 23. *l.* 4.

(*h*) Rosamond, *p.* 15. *l.* 7.

(*i*) Love Triumphant, *p.* 34. *l.* 4.

(*k*) The Wonders in the Sun, *p.* 39. *l.* 10.

(*l*) Ibid. *p.* 15. *l.* 27.

carry'd

carry'd into the *Planetary Region*, and told of *Pimping* there, he admired at it, ſaying, *I thought this had been a little too near Heaven to uſe that Folly, as being ſo notorious in our World:* But he was ſoon ſilenc'd with this Anſwer; *Worlds, for that matter, Friend, are much alike. Beſides, what you call Folly, is a Virtue here.*

Here it is too evident, what Notions our *Poets* have of another World, and how the general Strains of Courtſhip or Leudneſs in almoſt every *Play*, are in ſuch words, than which nothing can be more profane and extravagant. Every *Hyperbole* is skrew'd up to *Blaſphemy*. It is *Heaven* itſelf, or more than *Heaven*, to enjoy an *Actor* or an *Actreſs*; and *Hell*, or worſe than *Hell*, to be deprived. *Eternity* is comprehended in a Moment. And the Expreſſions which ſhould be abhor'd with the utmoſt Indignation, are received with an unuſual Satisfaction. The *Hero*'s Miſtreſs, or his Whore, is no leſs than his *Deity*, whilſt ſhe is pleaſed to be worſhipped as ſuch, and contented to take to herſelf the Honour due to GOD alone. She diſpoſes of his Reaſon, preſcribes his Motions, and commands his Intereſt. On the other hand, the *Women* lay aſide all Senſe of Decency and Modeſty; and addreſs themſelves to Men in the ſame Language. Thus, to uſe an *Actreſs's* words, (*b*) *Lovers adore their Objects.* What Sovereign Reſpect, what Religious Addreſs, and what idolizing Raptures are we peſter'd with? *Shrines*, and *Offerings*, and *Adorations*, are nothing upon ſuch ſolemn Occaſions. Thus Love and Devotion, thus Ceremony and Worſhip are confounded, and the *Sparks* are taught to court their Miſtreſſes, as others ſay their Prayers.

In *Scripture*, the Salvation of our Souls is repreſented as (*c*) the *End of* our *Faith*, our *Hope*, and our *Endeavours*. Upon the *Stage* a *Serving-Man* thus ſpeaks to a *Prieſt*, who afterward appears to marry his Miſtreſs to a Lord: (*d*) *Sir, I won't be ſaved your way; I hate a Prieſt, and I defy the Devil.*

Our *bleſſed Saviour* (*e*) tells us a Parable of *Lazarus*,

(*b*) The Wonder, *p*.38. *l*.25.
(*c*) 1 *Pet*. 1. 9.
(*d*) The Beaux Stratagem, *p*. 44. *l*. *penult*.
(*e*) *Luke* 16. 21, 23.

that he *desired to be fed with the Crumbs which fell from the rich Man's Table*, and was afterward *carry'd by the Angels into* Abraham's *Bosom*. To ridicule the first Expression, (f) *What* (saith an Actor) *would those poor Ladies, that are confin'd at Court, give for the Crumbs of Lovers, that sigh and fall from your Table?* And to undervalue the other, (g) *Shall she* (a Maiden) *lie in the Arms of such an enervate Cripple? She had better lie in* Abraham's *Bosom*: As if it was a Place of exquisite Misery.

Our *blessed Saviour* also in his most excellent *Prayer* for the whole Church, immediately before his Crucifixion, hath these words (h):

This is Life eternal, that they may know thee, the only true GOD, and Jesus Christ, whom thou hast sent.

Upon the *Stage*, an *Actor* finding that his Mistress loves him, saith (i);

> *This, this is Life indeed! Life worth preserving!*
> *Such Life as* Juba *never felt till now.*

And a little after (k);

> *My Joy! my Best-belov'd! my only Wish!*

And now, if GOD should (l) *swear in his Wrath, that they* shall never *enter into* that *Rest* which they despise, nor enjoy more than what they wish for; how wretched and miserable must such Men be to all Eternity?

(f) The Roving Husband reclaim'd, *p.*32. *l.*16.

(g) The Amorous Miser, *p.*12. *l.* 24.

(h) *John* 17. 3.

(i) Cato, *p.* 49. *l.*17.

(k) Ibid. *p.* 49. *l.*25.

(l) *Psal.* 95. 11.

CHAP.

CHAP. XVI.

Hell, the Priſon of the Devils, magnified on the Stage.

AS the *Poets* endeavour to expoſe and vilify *Heaven*, the Abode of GOD; ſo they take as much pains to magnify *Hell*, the Priſon of the *Devils*. If *Satan* is the God whom they ſerve, and the King whoſe Intereſt they endeavour to promote, it cannot be expected but they will endeavour to ſet off the Place of his Confinement to the utmoſt advantage, repreſent it as a *Palace*, and turn the *everlaſting Chains of Darkneſs* into *Ornaments of Gold*. And therefore, becauſe this Method doth more directly tend to the Honour of the *Devil*, I ſhall be the larger in detecting the Impiety of it.

(*a*) It may not be improper in a word or two to conſider what a frightful Idea the *Holy Scriptures* give us of *Hell*. It is deſcribed by all the Circumſtances of Terror, by every thing dreadful to Senſe, and amazing to Thought. The Place, the Company, and the Duration, are all Conſiderations of Aſtoniſhment. It is compared in *Scripture* to (*b*) *Tophet*, and (*c*) the Valley of the Son of *Hinnom*, where the Children were moſt barbarouſly burnt in the Fire to the Idol *Moloch*.

The Place in Scripture is call'd (*d*) *the loweſt Hell*, (*e*) *outer Darkneſs, where there is weeping and gnaſhing*

(*a*) *Collier*'s Short View of the Stage, *p.* 191.

(*b*) *Iſa.* 30. 33.

(*c*) *Mat.* 5. 22, 29, 30. & 10. 28. & 18. 9. & 22. 15, 33. *Mark* 9. 43, 45, 47. *Luke* 12. 5. *James* 5. 6. *where the word* Gehenna, *or Hell, is derived from two* Hebrew *words, which ſignify*, The Valley of *Hinnom*. *See Levit.* 18. 21. & 20. 2. *Joſh.* 15. 8. 2 *Kings* 23. 10. *Jer.* 7. 31, 32. & 19. 5.

(*d*) *Deut.* 32. 22. *Prov.* 7. 27. *Iſa.* 14. 9. *Mat.* 11. 23. *Luke* 10. 15.

(*e*) *Mat.* 8. 12. & 13. 30, 42.

of Teeth, (*f*) *the Lake of Fire, and the ſecond Death*; (*g*) a place of *Torments*; (*h*) a *fearful Judgment, and fiery Indignation, which ſhall devour the Adverſaries*; (*i*) *Snares, Fire and Brimſtone, and a horrible Tempeſt,* which *ſhall be* the *Portion* of the Wicked; and (*k*) *a Lake of Fire burning with Brimſtone.*

The Company for which it is prepared, are (*l*) the *Devil and his Angels*, and all others who ſhall be *accurſed* of GOD; and the duration of this *Fire* and *Puniſhment* is (*m*) *everlaſting, where* (*n*) *the Worm* of Conſcience *never dies, and the Fire* of GOD's Judgments cannot be quenched. And therefore it is called (*o*) *unquenchable Fire*, (*p*) *everlaſting Deſtruction from the Preſence of the LORD, and from the Glory of his Power*; and (*q*) a *Priſon*, from whence there is no *coming out, until the utmoſt Farthing* is *paid*, which can never be done. And why hath GOD given us this ſolemn Warning? Is it not to awaken our Fears, and guard our Happineſs? Is it not to reſtrain the Diſorders of our Appetite, and to keep us within the Bounds of Reaſon and Duty?

And as for the *apoſtate Angels*, the *Scriptures* inform us of their loſt Condition; of their Malice and Power; of their active Induſtry and Experience; and all theſe Qualities correſponding to their depraved State, the Antiquity of their Being, and Fall, and the Miſery of their Puniſhment. The *Devil* is deſcribed as (*r*) a *Sinner*, (*s*) a *Lyar*, and *a Murderer from the beginning*; as (*t*) a *ſubtle* Adverſary, and (*u*) with perpetual *Enmity*. He is called (*x*) *a ſtrong Man armed*, (*y*) an *Enemy*, (*z*) a *great red Dragon*, (*a*) a *roaring Lion, who walketh about*

(*f*) *Revel.* 20. 14.
(*g*) *Luke* 16. 23.
(*h*) *Heb.* 10. 27, 31.
(*i*) *Pſal.* 11. 6.
(*k*) *Revel.* 19. 20. *Revel.* 20. 10, 15.
(*l*) *Matth.* 25. 41.
(*m*) *Matth.* 25. 41, 46.
(*n*) *Iſa.* 66. 24. *Mark* 9. 44, 45, 46, 47, 48.
(*o*) *Matth.* 3. 12.
(*p*) 2 *Theſſ.* 1. 7, 8, 9.
(*q*) *Matth.* 5. 25, 26.
(*r*) 1 *Joh.* 3. 8.
(*s*) *Joh.* 8. 44.
(*t*) *Gen.* 3. 1.
(*u*) *Gen.* 3. 17.
(*x*) *Matth.* 12. 29. *Luke* 11. 21.
(*y*) *Matth.* 13. 39.
(*z*) *Rev.* 12. 3.
(*a*) 1 *Pet.* 5. 8.

ſeeking

ſeeking whom he may devour, (b) the *Prince*, and (c) the *God of this World*, (d) the *Prince of the Power of the Air*, and *the Spirit which worketh in the Children of Diſobedience*; (e) *Principalities and Powers, the Rulers of the Darkneſs of this World, and ſpiritual Wickedneſs in high places.* We are told of (f) his *Devices*, (g) his *Snares*, and *taking* Men *captive at his will*; and that (h) for this purpoſe he *transforms* himſelf *into an Angel of Light*. We are therefore exhorted to (i) *be ſober and vigilant*, to (k) *reſiſt* him, to (l) *give no place* to him, and (m) to *put on the whole Armour of GOD* for this purpoſe. And for our encouragement, we are told, that (n) *Chriſt Jeſus* will aſſiſt and *ſuccour* us, who (o) came into the World to conquer and *deſtroy* the *Devil* and all his *Works*. Beſides, we are told of the Puniſhment which ſhall be inflicted on the *Devil* and all his Angels. That (p) they ſhall be *judged* by the Saints, and (q) they are already *delivered into Chains of Darkneſs, to be reſerved unto the Judgment of that great Day*. And why are they painted at in all the formidable Appearances imaginable, and their Miſery thus deſcribed? Is it not to alarm our Caution, and put us upon the utmoſt Defence, that we are not ſeduced by them to fall into the ſame Condemnation?

Let us now ſee how our modern *Poets* repreſent theſe unhappy *Spirits*, and their Places of Abode. Why, very entertainingly! They who have a true taſte for Atheiſm, can never be better regaled. Here they rally upon *Hell* and *Damnation* with a great deal of Air and Pleaſantry, and only deſign by it to make Diverſion for the Audience: and here it is ſet before their Eyes in different Repreſentations, but all for Sport and Paſtime.

(b) *Joh.* 12. 31. *Joh.* 16. 11.
(c) 2 *Cor.* 4. 4.
(d) *Epheſ.* 2. 2.
(e) *Epheſ.* 6. 12.
(f) 2 *Cor.* 2. 11.
(g) 2 *Tim.* 2. 26.
(h) 2 *Cor.* 11. 14.
(i) 1 *Pet.* 5. 8, 9.
(k) *Jam.* 4. 7.
(l) *Epheſ.* 4. 27.
(m) *Epheſ.* 6. 10, 11, 12, 13, 14, 15, 16, 17.
(n) 2 *Cor.* 12. 7, 8, 9. *Heb.* 2. 18.
(o) *Heb.* 2. 14. 1 *Joh.* 3. 8.
(p) 1 *Cor.* 6. 3.
(q) 2 *Pet.* 2. 4. *Jude, ver.* 6.

In one *Play*, (*r*) as a Woman is going along the *Stage*, a Cavern opens, and ſeveral *Devils* appearing, carry her under-ground. After this, we have (*s*) for the *Scene* a *Deſart, and Hell appears open at a diſtance.* Then (*t*) an *Actor* enters into *Hell*, encounters the *Devils*, puts them to flight; and, to ſhew that the Puniſhments are not eternal, he (*u*) leads out the Woman, who was carried thither in the aforeſaid manner.

But becauſe the Story of *Hercules*'s leading *Omphale* out of *Hell*, thus repreſented on the *Stage*, owes its Original to the *Heathen Poets*, therefore our *modern Writers* labour to repreſent the *Scripture*-Account thereof as no more than a *poetical Romance*. If *Hercules* cannot be advanced upon an equal foot with our *Redeemer*, who *deſcended into Hell* to free us from the Torments thereof; then the *Scriptures* ſhall be thruſt down to the ſame level with the Writings of *Heſiod* or *Ovid*. For thus ſaith an *Actor*:

(*x*) *I'll force ten thouſand Hells to ſave my Bride;*
I'll ſhake the Realms where Pluto *reigns,*
And make his Devils feel the Pains
Alcides *taught 'em once before.*

And to clear up the matter, this *Actor* is a *Chriſtian Hero* upon the *Stage*.

Another ſaith in another *Play*, (*y*) *The Plagues that Heathen Poets feign in their fabulous Hell, are all really doubled upon me.* And a third ſaith (*z*),

Wiſh the whole Frame of Nature were diſſolv'd,
That all things to a Chaos were reſolv'd:
There is ſome Charity in this Deſire,
Since with our Loſs, our Sorrows would expire.

According to this Notion, there is an end of Puniſhment, when the World is diſſolv'd; and the Account

(*r*) Hercules, p. 40. l. 5.
(*s*) Hercules, p. 44.
(*t*) Hercules, *ibid.*
(*u*) Hercules, p. 46.
(*x*) Rinaldo, p. 25. l. 29.
(*y*) The Apparition, p. 60. l. 26.
(*z*) The comical Revenge, p. 44. l. 38.

of

of *Christ's* coming to take Vengeance upon ſuch as know him not, depends upon a like foundation with what the *Poets* affirm of *Æacus*, *Minos*, and *Rhadamanthus*, in the other World. According to this, the future Reſemblance of *Tophet* in *Scripture* muſt be no better grounded than the *Story* of *Styx* in *Homer*; the *Lake of Brimſtone*, and that of *Phlegethon*, is alike dreadful; and we have as much reaſon to believe the Torments of *Tantalus* and *Prometheus*, as thoſe of the *Devil* and the Damn'd. Theſe are lamentable Conſequences! And yet I cannot ſee how the *Poets* can avoid them, whilſt they make a Jeſt of both, and treat them alike. In one *Play*, *Hell* is (*a*) call'd *A mere Glaſs-Houſe, where the Devils are continually blowing up Mens Souls on hollow Irons, and the Fire never goes out.* And muſt (*b*) our *Saviour's* Deſcription of *Hell*, (*where the Worm dieth not, and the Fire is not quenched*) be thus derided, and put into the Mouth of a Madman? Is not the drolling upon the Vengeance of a juſt GOD, and the Miſeries of the Damn'd, a ſad Inſtance of Irreligion, and a ſadder Proſpect? Beſides, is not the Effect of ſuch an Entertainment very admirable? To ſee *Hell* thus play'd with, is a mighty Refreſhment to a leud *Conſcience*, and a biaſs'd Underſtanding. It heartens the young Libertine. It confirms the Well-wiſhers to *Atheiſm*, and makes *Vice* bold and enterprizing. Such Diverſions ſerve to diſpel the Gloom, and varniſh over the Horrors of the Shades below, and are a ſort of Inſurance againſt Damnation.

But the *Poets* fearing that they cannot make their Audience wholly disbelieve it, take other methods to trifle with, and extenuate the Miſeries of it. For this reaſon the word *damn'd* is frequently applied to things which are inſignificant, and always to things which relate only to this Life.

Sometimes they give this *Epithet* to one another, as to (*c*) a

(*a*) The unfortunate Dutcheſs of *Malfi*, p. 48. l. 31.

(*b*) *Mark* 9. 43, 44, 45, 46, 47, 48.

(*c*) A Woman's Revenge, p. 47. l. 14. Ignoramus, p. 52. l. 3. Injur'd Virtue, p. 47. l. 26. The artful Husband, p. 47. l. 10. Cobler of *Preſton*, p. 38. l. 21. Humours of Purgatory, p. 41. l. 9.

Man

a *Man*, (d) a *young Man*, to (e) an *old Man*, to (f) a *French Man*, to (g) a *Musician*, and to (h) any *Woman* without distinction. Thus a *Woman* is call'd (i) the *damn'd cunning Devil*, or (k) the *damn'd She-Devil*, and a Servant is call'd (l) a *damnable Demon*; tho it is observable that they never treat the Devil himself in such a manner. Sometimes they give this Epithet to (m) their own *Plays*, and (n) *Poetry*. Sometimes to *Virtue* itself, and those things which should make them better, as to (o) *good Counsel*, to (p) *Gravity*, and to (q) *Temperance*. This is the Character (r) which they give of the Life of a Fish in Water, because the Liquor in which he lives is but small. And in short, they give this Epithet (s) to many other Particulars, too

---

Man of Mode, p.225. l.20. The Masquerade, p.24. l.8. Perfidious Brother, p.28. l.22. Squire of *Alsatia*, p.10. l. 29, 33. p.29. l.19. p.32. l.34. p.49. l.11. p. 66. l.9. p.70. l.24. p.74. l.36. Three Hours after Marriage, p.23. l. 8.

(d) *Sawny* the *Scot*, p. 57. l. 11.

(e) Love in a Sack, p. 47. l. 16.

(f) *Sawny* the *Scot*, p.23. l. 14. p.57. l.27.

(g) Ibid. p.26. l.16.

(h) A Woman's Revenge, p. 35. l.31. Ignoramus, p.44. l. 36. The Amorous Widow, p.6. l.30. Artful Husband, p.38. l.2. Comical Revenge, p. 21. l. 5. The cruel Gift, p. 128. l.2. p. 133. l.15. The Masquerade, p. 10. l.1. Perplex'd Lovers, p.13. l.12. Squire of *Alsatia*, p. 13. l.22. p.22. l.13.

(i) The Perplex'd Lovers, p. 13. l.12.

(k) Squire of *Alsatia*, p. 22. l. 13.

(l) Love in a Sack, p.29. l. *penult.*

(m) Love the Leveller, *Epilogue*, l.15. Man of Mode, p. 240. l. *ult.* The Masquerade, p. 4. l. 14.

(n) Three Hours after Marriage, p.24. l.21.

(o) Squire of *Alsatia*, p. 34. l. 33.

(p) Royal Convert, *Prologue*, p. 1. *in fine.*

(q) The Apparition, p.2. l.5.

(r) Squire of *Alsatia*, p. 61. l. 1.

(s) *As to an Assurance or Impudence*, Love in a Sack, p. 12. l.18. *To Beer*, The Cobler of *Preston*, p. 11. l. 8. *To Cheats or Tricks*, The Humours of Purgatory, p. 39. l. 14. *To Cant*, The Earl of *Mar* marr'd, p. 3. l. 27. *To the Day*, The Man of Mode, p. 264. l.28. *To Curiosity*, Woman is a Riddle, p. 4. l.32. *To Dancing*, The Man of Mode, p.236. l.25. *To double Meaning*, The Cruel Gift, *Epilogue*, p.2. l.14. *To a Dress*, Thomyris,

too tedious to be named. Sometimes (*t*) this Expression, and (*u*) another of the same derivation, signifies only *very much*. According to the Language of the *Play-house*, (*x*) to *damn*, or (*y*) to *curse*, signifies no more than for a Man to disapprove thereof; and (*z*) to *save a Poet*, is only to encourage his Performance. Sometimes (*a*) *Damnation* is wish'd to those things which have neither Life nor Sense. And one *Actor* saith to another, (*b*) *I'll see you damn'd*, as if it would prove a satisfaction. Besides, (*c*) *damning* or *saving* is applied to a *Play*, and the Actions of our *dear Redeemer* attri-

---

Thomyris, p. 32. l. 26. The Squire of *Alsatia*, p. 26. l. 11. *To Drudgery*, The Squire of *Alsatia*, p. 44. l. 38. *To Flambeaux*, Woman is a Riddle, p. 52. l. 26. *To Fortune*, The Man's bewitch'd, p. 54. l. 28. *To a Grate*, The Wonder, p. 6. l. 11. *To Hyde-Park*, A Woman's Revenge, *Epilogue*, l. 14. *To Jealousy*, She wou'd if she cou'd, p. 93. l. 3. p. 130. l. 4. *To an Intrigue*, Woman is a Riddle, p. 85. l. 19. *To a Lampoon*, The Man of Mode, p. 185. l. 11. *To a Look*, Love's last Shift, p. 9. l. *penult*. *To a Madman*, The Busy-Body, p. 15. l. 21. *To a Mistake*, The Cobler of *Preston*, p. 17. l. *penult*. *To a Picture*, The Artful Husband, p. 68. l. *antepenult*. *To a Shell*, The Rival Fools, p. 56. l. 13. *To Sticks*, Lucius, *Epilogue*, p. 1. l. *ult*. *To a Story*, The Man of Mode, p. 203. l. 26. *To a Dish of Tea*, The Masquerade, p. 6. l. 33. p. 8. l. 1. *To the Time of Night*, The Man of Mode, p. 236. l. 6. *To Trouble*, She wou'd if she cou'd, p. 92. l. 33. *To a Voice*, The Amorous Widow, p. 19. l. 11.

(*t*) A Woman's Revenge, p. 55. l. 33. Artful Husband, p. 44. l. *ult*. p. 66. l. 20. The Masquerade, p. 5. *l*. 23.

(*u*) Woman is a Riddle, p. 25. l. 13.

(*x*) Injur'd Virtue, *Epilogue*, p. 2. l. 5. Lucius, *Epilogue*, p. 2. l. 11. The Apparition, *Prologue*, l. 22. The artful Husband, *Prologue*, l. *antepenult*. The Beaux Stratagem, *Epilogue*, l. 4. The Busy-Body, *Prologue*, *verse* 35. *ult*. The Country Lasses, *Prologue*, *l*. 21. Force of Friendship, *Epilogue*, l. *penult*. Perfidious Brother, *Epilogue*, l. 8, 30. Perplex'd Couple, *Epilogue*, l. 15. Royal Convert, *Prologue*, l. 29. Three Hours after Marriage, *Prologue*, l. 10. p. 23. l. 20. Woman is a Riddle, *Prologue*, l. 10. p. 23. l. *antepenult*.

(*y*) The Apparition, *Epilogue*, l. 35.

(*z*) The Apparition, *Epilogue*, l. 42. The Force of Friendship, *Epilogue*, l. *penult*.

(*a*) The Wonder, p. 73. l. *penult*.

(*b*) Humours of Purgatory, p. 18. l. 20.

(*c*) The Wonder, *Prologue*, l. 6.

buted

buted to the *Audience*, who ſit on the Benches, like *Chriſt* himſelf on the *Clouds*, when he *ſhall come to judge the Quick and the Dead.* What ſuch a familiarity with the Word upon the *Stage* ſhould mean, is unaccountable, unleſs it is to bring it into contempt; and that the Audience ſhould the leſs regard or fear it at another time, eſpecially when the Thoughts of a future Miſery might put a reſtraint on them, whilſt they are running into it.

Another way of extenuating the Torments of Hell, is by ſuppoſing that they may be eaſed, or wholly removed by ſome particular Enjoyments there. Thus an *Actor*, courting of his Miſtreſs, hath (*d*) this Expreſſion:

I would deſcend to Hell, could Hell retain you;
But Hell would be no Hell when you were there.

Another method of Extenuation, is by Compariſons. In theſe the *Poets* conſtantly make the Torments here on Earth, to be worſe than the Torments of *Hell.* Inſtances of this nature may be found in very many of our *Plays*, and therefore I ſhall venture to tranſcribe the more.

(*e*) *Why ſhould we fear worſe Pains to feel?*
The married Wretch has ſure no other Hell.
(*f*) *Stones, Furies, Wheels are ſlight to what I ſuffer,*
And Hell itſelf's Relief.
(*g*) *Would I were a League under-ground, or in any other Hell but this.* Spoken by one who was teaz'd with the Courtſhip of an old Widow.
(*h*) *I muſt go home to her,* (meaning his Wife) *and I had rather go to the Devil by half.*
(*i*) *To want Money is the Devil.*
(*k*) *The Devil has done his worſt, and I am a Cuckold.*

(*d*) Elfrid, p. 12. l. 31.
(*e*) Jane Gray, p. 76. l. 21.
(*f*) *Phædra* and *Hippolytus*, p. 55. l. 30.
(*g*) The Amorous Widow, p. 47. l. 33.
(*h*) Beaux Stratagem, p. 55. l. *penult.*
(*i*) The Contrivances, p. 20. l. 4.
(*k*) Double Gallant, p. 43. l. 5.

What

(*l*) *What I have borne for thee* (a Lover) *Hell cannot match.*

(*m*) *'Tis worse than Hell to think she is disloyal.*

(*n*) *The Devil certainly takes care to give me all the Plagues he can.* That is, the sight of fine Women without any farther enjoyment.

(*o*) *Whate'er the Damn'd or the Despairing feel,*
The sharpest Punishments of angry Jove
Are all contain'd at once in jealous Love.

(*p*) *Now that I feel a Hell within my Breast,*
Let all the Furies here make their abode.

(*q*) *Not one drop of good Drink! There's the Devil.*

In these Flights the *Poets* sometimes represent the *Devils* and damned Spirits, as senseless of their own Miseries; but pitying and much concerned for those in this World: and thus (*r*) their *Trembling* and Terror is not upon their own account, but for others. Thus an *Actor* saith (*s*),

Come, ever-glorious, ever-honoured Race, (of Souls departed)
And thou, old awful Appius *at their Head,*
Ascend from Hell, with all Hell's Rage about you:
Come and survey this miserable Breast;
And here's a Sight will turn your Rage to Grief,
And send you back to Hell with such a Tale,
As shall have power to move the Damn'd to Pity.

Another saith, (*t*)
Attend, attend, ye Ghosts of murder'd Romans;
Behold your Judge now sentenc'd in his turn,
And doom'd to Pains, at which the Damn'd will tremble,
And take their own for Joys.

(*l*) The Man's bewitch'd, p. 52. l. 28.

(*m*) Perfidious Brother, p. 41. l. 12.

(*n*) The Pretender's Flight, p. 22. l. 7.

(*o*) The Victim, p. 52. l. 29.

(*p*) Titus Manlius, p. 33. l. 3.

(*q*) Wit without Money, p. 25. l. 21.

(*r*) *James* 2. 19.

(*s*) *Appius* and *Virginia*, p. 32. *l. antepenult.*

(*t*) Ibid. p. 63. l. 16.

And another, (u)

Ye mighty Gods, where will you find new Scourges,
When you inflict such Punishments, that Hell
Feels some Remorse, and Fiends themselves drop Tears?

According to this Notion, the *Damn'd* are not so miserable in themselves, but they are astonish'd at the Torments of others, and have an allay of Comfort in thinking that some Persons are more wretched than they. However, that there are degrees of *Torments* in *Hell*, is most certain; but that some are in a state of Joy, when compared with others, is a Note beyond *Ela*, and savours too much of the *Play-house* Extravagancy.

However, to strain it higher yet, the *Actors* are neither afraid nor ashamed to set themselves up above GOD, and threaten to inflict greater Torments than those which are the Effects of infinite Justice. For thus one saith, (x)

Nay, all the Horrors Devils can invent,
Shall prove to her less fatal than my Rage.

And again, (y)

——————— *So will I torture thee,*
The Damn'd themselves shall start to hear thy Groans.

And another raiseth himself to the same pitch, (z)

From my Invention Torments shall have Birth,
That shall so terrible to Nature seem,
Ev'n Hell's dire Furies will my Zeal esteem,
And copy from my Wit.

However, the rendring of *Hell* a less Evil, is not sufficient. The *Poets* take all imaginable care to represent it as a positive Good. For this reason it is called (a) *the amorous Hell*. And because the blessed State of Saints departed

(u) The successful Pirate, p. 36. l.21.
(x) Injur'd Virtue, p.33. l.26.
(y) Ibid. p.51. l.26.
(z) Ibid. p.44. l.26.
(a) Antiochus, p.46. l.18.

departed is (*b*) often called *the Kingdom of Heaven*, where God reigns over them in a more eminent manner, and fills them with Joy and Happineſs; therefore *Hell* is alſo in oppoſition called (*c*) *a triumphant Kingdom*, and (*d*) the *burning Throne of Hell's Dominions*. And there is not only (*e*) a *King*, but alſo a *Queen* of theſe infernal Regions, who are owned as ſuch, and to whom the *Actors* pray, and offer up *Sacrifices* accordingly.

For ſuch Reaſons as theſe an *Actor* declares in behalf of himſelf and his Company, that (*f*) if they were *led to the Gates of Hell*, there was none of them who *would ſtay behind*. And their Language on this occaſion is very remarkable.

(*g*) *Would you have any Service where I'm going?*
Anſ. *Where's that?*
Reply. *I'll tell you in your Ear. To Hell, my Lord. Reſolve to go and bear me Company.*

(*h*) A Coachman ſaith in another *Play*, *If a Gentleman and a Lady have a mind to ride in a Coach together to the Devil, ſo they pay us honeſtly for carrying them, our Conſcience is diſcharg'd.*

And in another, (*i*)

Why, if the Devil has carried her away, Sir, where can we run? Anſwer, *To Hell, you Dog.*

And again, (*k*)

Carry my Wife to London! Anſwer, *Carry her to the Devil.*

Another (*l*) ſpeaks of *Hell* as if it was a place of Pleaſure and Delight, and reſembled the *Play-houſe*, where a Man muſt pay Money to be admitted. *When I* (ſaith an *Actor*) *go to Hell, I mean to carry a Bribe: For good Gifts evermore make way for the worſt Perſons.*

(*b*) *Matth.* 5.20. *Matt.* 7.21. *Matt.* 8.11. *Matt.* 18.3.
(*c*) Rinaldo, p.27. l.10.
(*d*) Elfrid, p.38. l.35.
(*e*) Alarbas, p. 24, 25, 26, 27. Solon, p.30. l. *penult.* Ulyſſes, p.28. l.22.
(*f*) The General caſhier'd, p.21. l.13.
(*g*) Jane Gray, p.68. l.9.
(*h*) Injur'd Love, p.62. l.29.
(*i*) The Man's bewitch'd, p. 54. l.9.
(*k*) Ibid. p.66. l.9.
(*l*) The unfortunate Dutcheſs of *Malfi*, p.59. l.22.

But to conclude this Chapter with comparing a few Texts of *Scripture* on this occasion. (*m*) Our *Blessed Saviour*, and (*n*) his *Apostle* tell us, that the Torments of *Hell* are eternal, and (*o*) therefore it will *profit a Man* nothing, *if he shall gain the whole World, and lose his own Soul*; neither can any *exchange* be *given for* the *Soul*. The *Stage* makes a Jest of all this; and therefore (*p*) here we have Persons *rescued from the dark Jaws of Hell*; and (*q*) upon another occasion an *Actor* saith, *Where am I? In Hell? I'll pray myself out again.*

The *Scriptures* describing the most Glorious *Majesty* of GOD, express it thus: (*r*) *There went up a Smoke out of his Nostrils, and Fire out of his Mouth devoured; Coals were kindled at it. He bowed the Heavens also, and came down; and Darkness was under his Feet. And he rode upon a Cherub, and did fly; yea, he did fly upon the Wings of the Wind. He made Darkness his secret place; his Pavilion round about him were dark Waters, and thick Clouds of the Skies. At the Brightness which was before him, his thick Clouds passed, Hail-Stones and Coals of Fire. The LORD also thunder'd in the Heavens, and the Highest gave his Voice: Hail-Stones and Coals of Fire.* The *Play-house* endeavours to ridicule all this Divine Grandeur and Majesty, by representing the *Devils* like GOD, and making their Prison to out-vie his Throne, in this manner (*s*):

Oh! what a gaudy Kingdom is this Hell?
Courts made of burning Brass and dropping Gold;
Gallants a riding in hot Em'rald Coaches,
Shining like Meteors in the fiery Region,
With Horses that have Flames instead of Wings.
Ladies that scorching Planets have for Eyes,
Freckled all o'er with Carbuncles and Rubies,
That glow like Stars, and crackle with the Heat.

(*m*) *Matth.* 25. 46.
(*n*) 2 *Thess.* 1. 9.
(*o*) *Matth.* 16. 26. *Mark* 8. 36, 37.
(*p*) Hercules, *p.* 40. *Scene* 6. *p.* 46. *l.* 9.
(*q*) The Apparition, *p.* 57. *l.* 38.
(*r*) *Psal.* 18. 8, 9, 10, 11, 12, 13.
(*s*) Jane Gray, *p.* 68. *l.* 24.

There's sumptuous Bagnios carv'd of rocky Ice,
Here Ponds of liquid Chrystal made to bathe in,
That's colder in degree than Hell is hot.
Who would not be a Knave to be so tortur'd?

The *Apostle* saith, (t) *Knowing therefore the Terrour of the LORD, we persuade Men:* but when these Terrours are ridicul'd, it is a *sad sign that they cannot be persuaded*; but that they are ripe for, and hast'ning unto that Destruction which they make so light of.

CHAP. XVII.

Other Ways whereby the Devil is also honoured, and his Interest directly promoted by the Stage.

BEside those Methods already mentioned, there are several other Ways whereby the *Devil* is also honoured, and his *Interest* is directly promoted on the *Stage*.

The first Method is, the using such *Phrases* and Expressions, which seem to intimate, that there is no such Being. If we can once believe this, then all the Accounts which the *Scriptures* give of him must appear to be false, and consequently those sacred Oracles can be look'd on as no other than *romantick Stories*. If we can believe that there is no *Devil*, because we do not see him, we may for the same reason be prevailed upon to believe that there is no GOD, since he also is invisible. And if we can believe that there is no *Devil*, then he may carry on his own Designs for our Destruction, without any resistance or endeavours on our parts to prevent them.

But tho such a Notion is of a most dangerous Consequence in reference to all *Religion*; yet it is often insinuated into the Minds of those Persons who frequent the *Play-houses*, by using this word like a Negative.

(t) 2 *Cor.* 5. 11.

Thus when they ſay, (*a*) *The Devil of any Subſtance*, they mean *no Subſtance*. When they ſay, (*b*) *The Devil a bit*, they mean *not a Bit*. Or when they ſay, (*c*) *The Devil he is*, they mean *he is not*. And this alſo is the Meaning of (*d*) ſeveral other Expreſſions of the ſame nature, too many to be here inſerted.

The next Method is by *confounding* of *Epithets*, and uſing the words *Godlike*, *Divine*, and *Deviliſh* in a promiſcuous manner, when they ſpeak of the ſame Perſons or Things, as if there was no manner of diſtinction. Thus they ſpeak (*e*) of *Men*, (*f*) of *Women*, and (*g*) of *other Creatures*, where (*h*) each of theſe words do ſignify ſomething very great and conſiderable.

Another

(*a*) The Wonders in the Sun, *Act* 1. *p*. 9. *l*. 26.

(*b*) *Sawny* the *Scot*, *p*.6. *l*.20. *p*.15. *l*.32. *p*.28. *l*.34. *p*.50. *l*.9. *p*.59. *l*. 18. *p*.64. *l*.21. The City-Ramble, or, The Playhouſe Wedding, *p*. 56. *l*.23. Earl of *Mar* marr'd, *p*.18. *l*. *antepenult*.

(*c*) *Sawny* the *Scot*, *p*. 53. *l*.22. Perplex'd Couple, *p*. 40. *l*. 4. Wife of *Bath*, *p*.60. *l*. 4. Woman is a Riddle, *p*.84. *l*.8.

(*d*) A City-Ramble, or, The Humours of the Compter, *p*. 4. *l*. 19. A Woman's Revenge, *p*.7. *l*. *antepenult*. Injur'd Love, *a Comedy*, *p*. 27. *l*. *ult*. Marplot, *p*.41. *l*. 29. *p*. 59. *l*. 16. The Comical Lovers, *p*.68. *l*.21. The Contrivances, *p*. 21. *l*. 25. Earl of *Mar* marr'd, *p*. 27. *l*. 9. The *Gotham* Election, *p*.61. *l*.5. The Humours of the Army, *p*.38. *l*.15. The Humours of Purgatory, *p*.44. *l*. *penult*. The Man's bewitch'd, *p*. 59. *l*. 15. Perplex'd Lovers, *p*. 1. *l*. 19. Platonick Lady, *p*. 64. *l*. 1. The Wonder, *p*. 76. *l*. 5. Woman is a Riddle, *p*. 84. *l*. 8.

(*e*) *Godlike*, *ſpoken of Men*; Alarbas, *p*. 30. *l*.17, 20. Ajax, *Act* 2. *Verſe* 6. The Force of Friendſhip, *p*. 18. *l*.20. *Perſian* Princeſs, *p*. 19. *l*. 12. Thomyris, *p*.52. *l*.27. *Divine*, *ſpoken of Men*; Theſeus, *p*.49. *Scene* 4. *l*.17. *Deviliſh*, *ſpoken of Men*; The Rival Fools, *p*. 4. *l*. 26.

(*f*) *Godlike*, *ſpoken of Women*; The Succeſsful Pirate, *p*. 24. *l*.5. *Divine*, *ſpoken of Women*; Thomyris, *p*. 8. *l*. 26. *Deviliſh*, *ſpoken of Women*; Gibraltar, *p*.37. *l*.24. The Man's bewitch'd, *p*.45. *l*.5. Perplex'd Couple, *p*. 8. *l*. 3.

(*g*) *Godlike*, *ſpoken of other Creatures*; The Royal Convert, *p*.22. *Act* 3. *l*.2. *p*. 30. *l*. 33. *Divine*, *ſpoken of other Creatures*; The Humours of the Army, *p*.57. *l*.22. Perplex'd Couple, *p*. 8. *l*.2. *p*.9. *l*.27. *p*. 30. *l*.21. *Deviliſh*, *ſpoken of other Creatures*; Recruiting Officer, *p*.47. *l*.16. Rival Fools, *p*. 69. *l*. 23.

(*h*) *See the Meaning alſo of the word Devil, in* Wit at a pinch,

Another Method is, the *calling* other things *Devils*, as if there was no difference between the one and the other. Thus ſuch Women as are courted and admired upon the *Stage*, are ſometimes call'd (*i*) *Angels*, and ſometimes (*k*) *Devils*. Thus the (*l*) *Cherubims* are call'd (*m*) *cloven-footed Angels*. Thus the *Actors* are frequently call'd (*n*) *Devils*, or (*o*) by ſome other Expreſſion, which ſhews that they are worſe than *Devils*. Two Inſtances may ſatisfy the Reader of their great Civility to the *Clergy*.

(*p*) *This Devil of a Prieſt.*
(*q*) *Devil! worſe, if worſe can be, than Devil; thou very Prieſt.*

Thus they call (*r*) themſelves, and at one time an

---

pinch, *p*.7. *l*. 20. *p*. 34. *l*. 27. *And of the word Deviliſh, in* She wou'd if ſhe cou'd, *p*. 95. *l*. 33. Adventures of Half an Hour, *p*. 18. *l*. 15. Cobler of *Preſton*, *p*.16. *l*.28. The Drummer, *p*.15. *l*. 2. Squire of *Alſatia*, *p*. 33. *l*.12. *p*.66. l.5.

(*i*) The Maid's the Miſtreſs, *p*. 52. *l*. 24. Perplex'd Lovers, *p*.10. *l*.1. *p*.17. *l*.13. Provok'd Wife, *p*.54. *l*. 3. The Relapſe, *p*.31. *l*.28. *p*. 46. *l*.3. A Wife well manag'd, *p*.18. *l*.4. Love's laſt Shift, *p*.16. *l*.21.

(*k*) Injur'd Love, *a Comedy*, *p*.44. *l*.10. Love at firſt ſight, *p*. 50. *l*.*penult*. Love's Contrivance, *p*. 20. *l*. 23. Love Triumphant, *p*.29. *l*.12. Marry or do worſe, *p*.32. *l*.12. Rinaldo, *p*. 51. *l*.13. Careleſs Husband, *p*.27. *l*.33. The different Widows, *p*. 25. *l*.28. The General caſhier'd, *p*.4. *l*.10. The Rival Fools, *p*.34. *l*.24. The Roving Husband reclaim'd, *p*. 42. *l*.26. Vice reclaim'd, *p*.7. *l*.16.

(*l*) *Gen*. 3. 24.

(*m*) The City-Ramble; or, The Playhouſe Wedding, *p*. 60. *l*. 33.

(*n*) *Sawny* the *Scot*, *p*. 26. *l*. 33, 35. *p*. 57. *l*.17. Injur'd Love, *p*. 44. *l*.7. The Apparition, *p*.54. *l*.32. *p*.56. *l*.13, 38. Beaux Stratagem, *p*. 10. *l*. 33. *p*.21. *l*. 20. *p*. 46. *l*.27. The Country Laſſes, *p*. 46. *l*. 9, 11. *p*.51. *l*.9. The Double Gallant, *p*. 45. *l*.12. The Fine Lady's Airs, *p*. 46. *l*.15. The General caſhier'd, *p*. 4. *l*.10. The Modern Prophets, *p*.57. *l*.25. *p*.58. *l*. 8, 11. *p*. 61. *l*. 31.

(*o*) Elfrid, *p*.38. *l*.34. Mackbeth, *p*.47. *l*.1. Rinaldo, *p*.31. *l*. 31. Tartuffe, *p*. 53. *l*. 32. Female Advocates, *p*.37. *l*.13.

(*p*) The Modern Prophets, *p*. 12. *l*. 18.

(*q*) A Wife well manag'd, *p*. 18. *l*.13.

(*r*) Female Advocates, *p*. 36. *l*. 13.

Actor calls (*s*) his own Head by this accursed Name. An *Actress* makes herself (*t*) to be worse than the *Devil*, and saith on this occasion, That ***no Fiend in Hell can match the Fury of a disappointed Woman.*** A (*u*) *Justice* of the Peace, instead of saying he will send a Criminal to Prison, saith that he *will send* him *to the Devil*. And another (*x*) *contemplating upon the Divinity* of his Mistress, (as it is blasphemously express'd) calls her his *Goddess, and the Devil and all.*

To this may be added the various Treatment of *Men* and *Women* upon the *Stage*. Sometimes a Man is call'd (*y*) *a GOD*, (*z*) *like to GOD*, (*a*) *more than half divine*, (*b*) a *Demigod*, and *a Man immortal*. To expose the *Incarnation* of our *blessed Saviour* the more, one *Actor* is represented (*c*) to have been an *Infant GOD*, and another is call'd (*d*) a *Devil incarnate*. And because GOD in Scripture is (*e*) call'd *the King of Kings, and LORD of Lords*, we have also a Man call'd (*f*) *the King of Kings, and General of* Greece; who is saluted with this Scripture-Expression, (*g*) *Hail to the King of Kings!* Accordingly, it is common upon the Stage to speak of (*h*) *adoring* the *Man*, and even (*i*) *his sacred Signet*. They tell us (*k*),

The Gods themselves must be like such a Man.

(*s*) A City-Ramble, or, The Humours of the Compter, *p.* 25. *l.* 9.

(*t*) Love's last Shift, *p.* 49. *l.* 33.

(*u*) A City-Ramble, or, The Humours of the Compter, *p.* 9. *l. penult.*

(*x*) The General cashier'd, *p.* 3. *l.* 20.

(*y*) The Pretender's Flight, *p.* 6. *l.* 23.

(*z*) The Victim, *p.* 19. *l.* 17. *p.* 31. *l.* 6. *p.* 41. *l.* 22. *p.* 55. *l.* 9.

(*a*) Ibid. p. 20. l. 17.

(*b*) Ibid. p. 23. l. 5. p. 38. l. 21. p. 55. l. 8.

(*c*) Ibid. p. 38. l. 15.

(*d*) Squire of *Alsatia*, p. 17. l. 18, 26. p. 19. l. *ult.*

(*e*) 1 *Tim.* 6. 15. *Rev.* 17. 14. & 19. 16.

(*f*) The Victim, p. 5. l. 14. p. 63. l. 9.

(*g*) Ibid. p. 4. l. *ult.*

(*h*) *French* Cato, p. 31. l. 4. Pretender's Flight, p. 22. l. 30. The Sultaness, p. 36. l. 30. Titus Manlius, p. 5. l. 3. p. 39. l. 30.

(*i*) The Sultaness, p. 53. l. 15.

(*k*) *French* Cato, p. 3. l. 7.

And (*l*),

In War a Hero, but a God in Peace.

And the Expressions to them are as remarkable. One kneeling, saith, (*m*) *Most ador'd of Princes.* Another, (*n*) *All my Joy is in thee alone.* Another, (*o*) *My Life! my Soul! my Husband!* Another (*p*),

You are the secret Worship of my Soul,
To me so perfect, that you cannot err.

Another, (*q*) *My Life! my Joy! my darling Sin!* And another saith to a Villain, (*r*) *My Life, my Happiness are owing to thee.* Now all these Encomiums cannot but add a greater Emphasis to the Compliment, when (*s*) they are call'd *Devils.* Thus in particular an *Actress* saith, (*t*) *I know he is a Devil; but he has something of the Angel yet undefaced in him, which makes him so charming and agreeable, that I cannot but love him, be he never so wicked.*

But the Treatment of Women upon the *Stage*, is more remarkable. They speak of themselves as (*u*) *Goddesses*, and that (*x*) their *Names* shall be *enroll'd among the Gods.* And therefore it is no wonder if Men are extravagant in their Expressions, and profess (*y*) to *adore*:

(*l*) *French* Cato, p. 32. l. 4.
(*m*) The Cruel Gift, p. 39. l. 32.
(*n*) Myrtillus, p. 21. l. 7.
(*o*) The Drummer, p. 56. l. 31.
(*p*) The Royal Convert, p. 16. l. 14.
(*q*) Man of Mode, p. 179. l. 32.
(*r*) Perfidious Brother, p. 27. l. 5.
(*s*) Love's last Shift, p. 47. l. 30. Man of Mode, p. 195. l. 27.
(*t*) Man of Mode, p. 197. l. 21.
(*u*) Pretender's Flight, p. 6. l. 23.
(*x*) The Victim, p. 39. l. 20.
(*y*) A Woman's Revenge, p. 38. l. *ult.* *French* Cato, p. 17. l. 17. p. 21. l. 11. Love's last Shift, p. 17. l. 18, 28. Lucius, p. 2. l. 14. p. 3. l. 2. p. 6. l. 30. p. 16. l. *ult.* p. 23. l. 30. p. 50. l. 13. Myrtillus, p. 21. l. 11. The Artful Husband, p. 8. l. 6. p. 31. l. *ult.* p. 32. l. 20. p. 42. l. 34.

adore them, and (z) *pay* their *Devotions* there, even in a (a) *kneeling* Posture. In some *Plays* Women are call'd (b) *a Divinity*, (c) something *Divine*, (d) their *Goddess*, (e) *the Sum-Total of* a Man's *Happiness*, (f) *Everlasting Goodness*, (g) *infinitely handsome*, and (h) a *Shrine*, where Men kneel. One saith of a Woman, (i) *She gave Attention to my Prayer*; and, (k) *I have given up both my Soul and Body to her*; and, (l) *In her alone all my Devotion centers.*

The *blasphemous* Expressions of Men to Women upon the *Stage*, are too many to be (m) transcribed; and therefore I shall only produce a few.

(n) *All my Joy is in thee alone.*

(o) *A Hand, a Heart, my Life, my Soul, my Fortune shall all perish to convince you.*

---

l. 34. p. 43. l. 11. The Drummer, p. 40. l. 27. The Fatal Marriage, p. 107. l. *ult.* The Masquerade, p. 24. l. 38 Perfidious Brother, p. 17. l. 10. p. 35. l. 12. Pretender's Flight, p. 14. l. 18. Squire of *Alsatia*, p. 16. l. 12. p. 51. l. 7. The Sultaness, p. 35. l. 2. Wit at a pinch, p. 16. l. 9. Woman is a Riddle, p. 17. l. 5.

(z) She wou'd if she cou'd, p. 97. l. 33. p. 107. l. 11. p. 138. l. 16. The Drummer, p. 40. l. 27.

(a) Lucius, p. 10. l. 1. The Royal Convert, p. 58. l. 30.

(b) The Comical Revenge, p. 15. l. 23.

(c) The Pretender's Flight, p. 14. l. 23. p. 20. l. 21. The Royal Convert, *Epilogue*, p. 2. l. 10. Woman is a Riddle, p. 22. l. 36.

(d) The Artful Husband, p. 28. l. 10.

(e) The Drummer, p. 32. l. 31.

(f) The Fatal Marriage, p. 153. l. 2.

(g) Love's last Shift, p. 17. l. 29.

(h) The Royal Convert, p. 47. l. 18.

(i) The Fatal Marriage, p. 144. l. 3.

(k) Ignoramus, p. 65. l. 16.

(l) Lucius, p. 2. l. 12.

(m) Almyna, p. 42. l. 32. The Rival Brothers, p. 6. l. 29. The Royal Convert, *Epilogue*, l. 32. The Wife of *Bath*, p. 44. l. 30. The Wife's Relief, p. 30. l. 39. The Wonder, p. 50. l. *antepenult.* p. 71. l. 5. The Wonders of the Sun, p. 21. l. 29. *Epilogue*, l. *penult.* Vice reclaim'd, p. 8. l. 1. p. 23. l. 17. Ulysses, p. 28. l. 11. Woman is a Riddle, p. 37. l. 13, 37. p. 47. l. 22. Zelmane, p. 21. l. 8.

(n) Myrtillus, p. 21. l. 7.

(o) The Artful Husband, p. 9. l. 24.

Thy

(p) *Thy Wit's to be ador'd, thy Beauty to be admir'd, but above all, thy Spirit and Generosity charm me. I know not what to say, Words are too light an Offering. Here's my Hand. My Soul! my every Blessing Life affords!*

(q) *My Life, my Happiness, my All is bound up in you.*

(r) *Lowly we bow* to thee, *as to offended Heaven.*

(s) *Thus let me fall, thus lowly to the Earth,*
In humble Adoration of your Goodness.

(t) *You are all that is good and gracious.*

And now, if we would know the *Play-House* Reason of all such *Blasphemies*, it seems to be told us in a late *Comedy:* (u) *The Devil chuses the Shape of a Woman*; and *it is a Form, that best agrees with his infernal Qualities.* Besides, *some affirm, that a Woman hath so much of the Devil in her Nature, that sometimes it would puzzle a Conjurer to distinguish between the one and the other.* In one *Play* it is said of a Woman, That (x) *she is divinely fair, and divinely good*; in another (y) it is thus express'd, *She is devilish young, and devilish handsome.* In one *Play* she is (z) a *dear Angel, and eternal Happiness*; and in others, (a) a *dear Devil.*

Neither do Men express themselves in this manner only (b) when they are affrighted, or (c) in a Passion; but also when they shew the utmost Signs of Respect and Esteem, as may appear from these following Quotations.

(p) The Artful Husband, p.67. l. 17.

(q) The Drummer, p. 37. l. *penult.*

(r) The Royal Convert, p.20. l. *ult.*

(s) Ibid. p.58. l.30.

(t) Ibid. p.59. l.22.

(u) Woman is a Riddle, p.5. l. 5.

(x) The Royal Convert, p.35. l. 2.

(y) The Perplex'd Couple, p. 8. l. 3.

(z) Love's last Shift, p. 16. l. 21.

(a) Injur'd Love, p.44. l.10. Love's Contrivance, p.20. l.33. Love Triumphant, p. 29. l. 13. *Portsmouth* Heiress, p.10. l.26. The Roving Husband reclaim'd, p. 42. l. 26.

(b) Woman is a Riddle, p.32. l. 16.

(c) Love's last Shift, p. 27. l. 4. p. 47. l.26. Squire of *Alsatia*, p. 20. l.27. p. 22. l. 13. p. 62. l. 8.

(*d*) *You dear charming Devil, I can offer up my Devotions at no Altar but yours.*

(*e*) *This Devil still is Mistress of my Heart.*

(*f*) *My dear little She-Infernal, take me into thy Service, and my Soul is thine, without any more ado.*

(*g*) *Say'st thou so, old Satan!* (Spoken to a Woman, who was a Matchmaker.) *Shew me but that, and my Soul is thine.*

(*h*) *Her Eyes are the Devil, that's certain.* This is explain'd by (*i*) another Saying, where the same Person is call'd *Beautiful as the Goddess.*

Thus we may observe, how GOD and the *Devil* are treated and represented alike, especially in such Cases which immediately concern the Soul of Man; and either there is no distinction made between the one and the other, or if there is, the *Devil* hath the Pre-eminence.

Another Method is the *pitying* or *excusing* of the *Devil.* The *Scriptures* do always express the Rebellion of the *Devil* against GOD in Terms of the greatest Destation and Abhorrence, and take occasion from his Punishment to adore the *Divine Justice:* But here he is represented (*k*) as a *poor Devil*, and one who is much to be pity'd, because he is so (*l*) *miserably persecuted.* As *Persecution* is a Suffering for Righteousness sake; so, according to this Language, the *Devil* undertook nothing in his Rebellion against GOD, but what was lawful and commendable: His Cause was like that of the *Martyrs*, his Sufferings were like those who died in defence of the true Religion, and GOD must be a Tyrant for inflicting such a Sentence upon him.

Another Method is by *Epithets*, which they give to the *Devil.* Sometimes they speak of him in a negative

(*d*) Love's Contrivance, p.20. l. 33.

(*e*) The Careless Husband, p. 27. l. 33.

(*f*) The *Portsmouth* Heiress, p.10. l.26.

(*g*) The Relapse, p.10. l.35.

(*h*) Vice reclaim'd, p.7. l.16.

(*i*) Ibid. p. 7. l. 15.

(*k*) The Modern Prophets, p. 20. l. 9. The Wonders in the Sun, p. 44. l. 32.

(*l*) The Wonders in the Sun, p. 44. l. 32.

manner,

manner, and then he is (m) not ſo bad as ſome Men are; he is (n) not ill-natur'd, eſpecially when he is compared with ſome Men; he is (o) *not to be blamed*, (p) not ſubject to *Diſtraction*, and (q) not to be fear'd nor ſhunn'd. *I declare it* (ſaith an Actor) *that he who runs away from the Devil, ſhould be brought to a Court-Martial, and condemn'd for a Coward.*

Sometimes they give him *poſitive Epithets*, and then he is (r) a *dear*, or (s) a *dear dear Devil*, a (t) *dear damnable*, a (u) *dear charming Devil*, or (x) a *dear Infernal*; or the Expreſſion is, (y) *Dear Devil, have pity upon me.* Sometimes he is (z) a *very harmleſs*, (a) a *loving*, (b) a *coaxing*, and (c) an *handſome* Devil. Sometimes he is (d) a *fine*, (e) a *fair*, (f) an *honeſt*, and (g) a *very honeſt Devil*; and ſometimes he is a (h) *little, virtuous*, a (i) *lovely witty*, and (k) a *ſweet Devil*.

Sometimes the *Devils* are deſcrib'd as (l) *ruling* in the Air. Sometimes he is repreſented as (*) governing all

---

(m) The Humours of Purgatory, *p.* 7. *l. ult.*

(n) She wou'd if ſhe cou'd, *p.* 143. *l.* 34.

(o) The Apparition, *p.* 34. *l.* 12.

(p) Mackbeth, *p.* 35. *l.* 13.

(q) The Humours of the Army, *p.* 12. *l.* 14.

(r) Injur'd Love, *a Comedy*, *p.* 44. *l.* 10. Ignoramus, *p.* 21. *l.* 11.

(s) The Country Laſſes, *p.* 51. *l.* 9.

(t) The Roving Husband reclaim'd, *p.* 42. *l.* 26.

(u) Love's Contrivance, *p.* 20. *l.* 33.

(x) Love Triumphant, *p.* 29. *l.* 13.

(y) Injur'd Love, *a Comedy*, *p.* 44. *l.* 10.

(z) Rinaldo, *p.* 51. *l. ult.*

(a) The General caſhier'd, *p.* 4. *l.* 10.

(b) The Rival Fools, *p.* 39. *l.* 20.

(c) Ibid. *p.* 34. *l.* 24.

(d) She wou'd if ſhe cou'd, *p.* 150. *l.* 30.

(e) A Woman's Revenge, *p.* 22. *l.* 4.

(f) Love at firſt ſight, *p.* 50. *l. penult.*

(g) Marry or do worſe, *p.* 31. *l.* 28.

(h) Ibid. *p.* 32. *l.* 12.

(i) The different Widows, *p.* 35. *l.* 28.

(k) Love Triumphant, *p.* 29. *l.* 12.

(l) The Unfortunate Dutcheſs of *Malfi*, *p.* 15. *l.* 27.

(*) The *Gotham* Election, *p.* 28. *l.* 18. Perplex'd Couple, *p.* 18. *l.* 21.

things, according to his Will and Pleasure; and (n) this makes an *Actor* displeased, because the *Devil* did not assist him. In one *Play* these (o) *black Fiends* are call'd,

> (p) *The Spirits that see into the latent Seeds*
> *Of Time, and know th' unripe Event of things.*

Sometimes they call these *Spirits*, the (q) *assisting*, the (r) *awful*, the (s) *eternal*, and (t) the *swift executing Furies*, or (u) the *Furies of the amorous Hell*: And it is observable, that this word is never join'd to an Epithet of Disesteem.

Sometimes they give the *Devil* a Title of Intimacy, and then he is call'd by an (x) *Actor*, his *old Friend*. Sometimes they give him a Title of Respect, and then he is call'd (y) *Master Beelzebub*. In one *Play* a Son ridicules our *Baptismal Vow*, (z) saying, *I defy the Devil and all his Works*: But he is reprimanded by his Father in a different Language, (a) *Hold your peace! the Devil cannot put in a word for you, I think.*

In one *Play*, a Master seeing the *Devil*, saith to his Man, (b) *Silence, you Rogue, and down upon your knees! see who comes yonder!* Because our Superiours are to be respected, he is call'd (c) *Alderman Beelzebub*: And because we are commanded in *Scripture* (d) to *rise up before the hoary Head, and honour the Face of the old Man*; therefore the *Devil* is call'd (e) *old Beelzebub*, and (f) *old Satan*. One saith, (g) the *Devil* and *your humble Ser-*

(n) A Woman's Revenge, p. 46. l. 7.
(o) The *Persian* Princess, p. 27. l. 8.
(p) Ibid. p. 27. l. 19.
(q) Ajax, p. 37. l. 5.
(r) Electra, p. 6. l. 13.
(s) The Gamester, p. 6. l. 1.
(t) Ajax, p. 37. l. 13.
(u) Antiochus, p. 46. l. 18.
(x) The Artful Husband, p. 11. l. *antepenult.*
(y) The Man's bewitch'd, p. 59. l. 20.
(z) Hob, p. 9. l. 7.
(a) Ibid. p. 17. l. 6.
(b) The Wonders in the Sun, p. 10. l. 34.
(c) *Tunbridge*-Walks, p. 54. l. 28.
(d) *Levit.* 19. 32.
(e) The Man's bewitch'd, p. 53. l. 17.
(f) The Succesful Pirate, p. 43. l. 11.
(g) The *Gotham* Election, p. 43. l. 29.

vant,

vant, in the ſame Breath. And laſtly, an *Actor* ſpeaks thus to the *Devil* both for himſelf and another; (*h*) *Old Gentleman, we are both your humble Servants:* without conſidering, that theſe words are too true to be made a Jeſt of upon the Stage.

CHAP. XVIII.

The Bleſſed GOD treated with Contempt upon the Stage.

THE *Players* treating the *Devil* with ſo much Reſpect and Eſteem, it is the leſs to be wonder'd at, if they treat the *Everbleſſed* GOD with Contempt and Reproach. Theſe (*a*) are *two Maſters*, whom *no Man can ſerve:* for if we *love the one*, we muſt *hate the other*; and if we *hold to the one*, we muſt *deſpiſe the other.* And indeed here we may obſerve the vileſt *Blaſphemies* of this kind, that ever were heard or ſuffer'd ſince the World began.

The firſt Method is, The uſing the Name of GOD at all in the *Plays.* The *Names* whereby the *Supreme Being* is known, are ſo ſacred, that they ought not to be mention'd, but with a ſuitable Reverence and Devotion. (*b*) *Jupiter* the Heathen Deity was repreſented as one, who could not attend on Trifles; and we debaſe *the Great Creator of Heaven and Earth*, when he is mention'd by the Name of (*c*) GOD, or (*d*) LORD, in the paltry

(*h*) The Female Advocates, p. 15. l. 4.

(*a*) *Mat.* 6. 24.

(*b*) *Non vacat exiguis rebus adeſſe Jovi.* Ovid.

(*c*) Careleſs Husband, p. 4. l. 18, 25. p. 37. l. 19, 20. p. 55. l. 2, 3. The Confederacy, p. 32. l. *ult.* p. 61. l. 5. Northern Laſs, p. 17. l. 15. p. 19. l. 14. p. 23. l. 28. Roving Husband reclaim'd, p. 10. l. 25. p. 11. l. 9. The Stage-Beaux toſs'd in a Blanket, p. 2. l. 41, &c.

(*d*) A Woman's Revenge, p. 43. l. 12, p. 51. l. 7, 21. p. 55. l. 4.

paltry Concerns of the *Stage*, especially in *Comedies*, where they make it their business to render every thing ridiculous, and whence they banish whatsoever hath a tendency to a grave or serious Thought. It was certainly the opinion of our Legislative Power, that all such words ought to be omitted, as appears from (*l*) the following *Statute* made for that purpose.

" *For the preventing and avoiding the great Abuse of*
" *the holy Name of GOD in Stage-Plays, and Interludes,*
" *be it enacted, That if at any time or times after the*
" *end of this present Session of Parliament, any Person or*
" *Persons do, or shall in any Stage-Play, Interlude, or*
" *Shew, jestingly or profanely speak or use the holy Name*
" *of GOD, or of* Christ Jesus, *or of the Trinity, which*
" *are not to be spoken but with Fear and Reverence; he or*
" *they shall forfeit for every such Offence, by him or them*
" *committed, Ten Pounds; the one Moiety thereof to the*
" *King's Majesty, his Heirs and Successors; the other*
" *Moiety thereof to him or them that will sue for the same*
" *in any Court of Record at* Westminster, *wherein no*
" *Essoign, Protection or Wager of Law shall be allowed.*"

Besides, the *Poets* also alter these sacred Names, that so they may droll upon them in a foppish, fantastical, and ridiculous manner, and (*m*) in a *Tone* or Dialect which they use when they would have any Person or Saying appear contemptible. The best Construction

---

l.4. Cobler of *Preston*, p. 19. *l. penult.* p.11. l.29. p.21. l.5. p.35. l. 2. Fatal Marriage, p. 101. l.12. p.125. l.8. p.127. l. 33. Humours of Purgatory, p. 10. l.1. p.18. l.5. p.33. l.18. p.45. l. 14. Man of Mode, p. 178. l. *ult.* p.179. l.34. p.218. l. 26. p.219. l.18. p.223. l.11, 19. p.236. l.36,37. p.237. l. 6, 11,28. p.241. l.28. p.245. l.17. p.247. l.7. p. 248. l.18. Pretender's Flight, p.21. l.25. p.23. l.3. Squire of *Alsatia*, p.2. l.12. p.3. l.18. p. 15. l.7. p.16. l.1. p.27. l.13. p.32. l.29. p.33. l. 39, *antepenult.* p. 36. l.27. p. 40. l. 13, 30. p.44. l.32. Wit at a Pinch, p.30. l.1. p.32. l.10, p.46. l.1. p.50. l.13. Woman is a Riddle, p. 25. l.19. p.36. l. 30,32. p. 35. l. 27. p. 50. l.9. p.51. l.11. p.83. *l.*22. p. 90. l. 24. p.92. l.16. p.95. l.5.

(*l*) *Statute of* 3 Jac. 1, chap. 21.

(*m*) *See* The Lord *Foppington's* Discourse in The Relapse, *and also in* The Careless Husband, *p.*20. *l.*1. *p.*28. *l.*35, *&c.*

which can be made of this, is a (*n*) *jesting* or trifling with *holy Things*, which was always reckon'd an unsafe, if not a vicious Practice. When they speak the Name of GOD, they speak it so affectedly, as to make it the Jest of the *Stage*; but when they speak of the *Devil*, they speak with such an *Emphasis* as may command Respect and Attention. And thus they run into such Sins which have a plain tendency to *Atheism*, and strike more directly at the supreme Authority. As *Fops* or *Fools* speak on other occasions, so the *Players* generally speak when they mention *The Great Creator of Heaven and Earth*; tho they cannot but know, that such a Familiarity with his Transcendent Majesty, and at such a Time, or even in such a Place, is too apt to breed a Contempt. Sometimes the word (*o*) *Gad*, or (*p*) *Ged*, is apishly used in-

---

(*n*) *Non tutum est ludere cum sacris.*

(*o*) The Adventures of half an Hour, *p*.17. *l*.26, 29. The artful Husband, *p*. 28. *l*.15. *p*.30. *l*.36. *p*.37. *l*.25. *p*.42. *l*.9,23. *p*. 43. *l*.2. *p*.45. *l*.9, 13, 18. *p*.46. *l*.34. *p*.47. *l*. 22, 33. *p*. 66. *l*.1. *p*.67. *l*.27. The careless Husband, *p*.14. *l*.3. The cruel Gift, *Epilogue*, *l*. 6. The fatal Marriage, *p*.98. *l*.25. *p*. 142. *l*. 17. The Female Wits, *p*.31. *l*.11,14. *p*.39. *l*. 24,25. The Humours of Purgatory, *p*.40. *l*.4. Man of Mode, *p*. 178. *l*.31. *p*.179. *l*. 9, 20. *p*.181. *l*.30. *p*.182. *l*.13. The Masquerade. *p*.5. *l*.24. The *Portsmouth* Heiress, *p*.11. *l*.32. *p*.55. *l*.5. *p*.66. *l*.13. Squire of *Alsatia*, *p*.57. *l*.27. The Stage Beaux toss'd in a Blanket, *p*.59. *l*.8. The Wonder, *p*.49. *l*.28. Woman is a Riddle, *p*.12. *l*.12. *p*.47. *l*.34. *p*.85. *l*.3. *Ah Gad!* The Lawyer's Fortune, *p*. 64. *l*. 13. *By Gad!* The Female Wits, *p*.33. *l*.18. *Before Gad!* The Confederacy, *p*. 17. *l*. 13. *Gad forgive me*, The Confederacy, *p*.7. *l*.9. *p*.45. *l*.28. The Female Wits, *p*. 34. *l*.8. Stage Beaux toss'd in a Blanket, *p*. 51. *l*. 20. *O Gad!* The Female Wits, *p*.22. *l*.8. *p*.32. *l*.9. *p*.50. *l*. 24.

(*p*) *Eh! Ged!* (*Spoken affectedly and ridiculously by an affected Hypocrite, Coquet and Jilt, and one whose Reputation hath not been without notorious Blemishes in the very Eye of the World*) The Stage Beaux toss'd in a Blanket, *p*.4. *l*.33,41. *p*.12. *l*.16, 32. *p*.14. *l*.1. *p*.43. *l*. *penult*. *p*.44. *l*.26. *p*.51. *l*. 1,16. *p*.52. *l*.12. *p*.54. *l*.14. *p*. 56. *l*. 9. *p*. 58. *l*. 19. *p*. 59. *l*.5. *Oh Ged!* (*Spoken by a Coxcomb that loves to be the first in all Foppery*) Love's Last Shift, *p*.17. *l*. *antepennlt*. *p*. 20. *l*. 7, 29, 37. *p*.21. *l*. 7. *p*.27. *l*.17. *See the* Drama *in both*.

ſtead of GOD, and (*q*) *Lard*, or (*r*) *Laird*, or (*s*) *Laud*, or (*t*) *Lerd*, or (*u*) *Lud*, inſtead of LORD. And to make it the more ridiculous, (*x*) *The LORD knows what*, is ſpoken in ſuch a *Scotch Tone*, which (*y*) in the Page before is called in Deriſion *an Heathen Dialect*. I need not to multiply Quotations for this purpoſe, ſince (*z*) the ſacred Name of GOD is thus expoſed near fifty times in one *Comedy*, by a paltry Footman of the *Scotch* Nation.

The next Inſtance which I ſhall mention, is the joining of the Name of GOD with the Name of the *Devil*. The Deſign hereof can be no other, but either to make the *Bleſſed GOD* deſpiſed and abhorred as the *Devil* ought to be, or elſe to cauſe the *Devil* to be honoured and adored like GOD himſelf. I ſhall not blot this Paper, by tranſcribing of ſuch Sentences; but the Reader may ſee it is the common Practice, by the (*a*) References in the Margin.

It

(*q*) The artful Husband, p.31. l.27. p.32. l.30. p.38. l.21. p. 68. l. 15. Careleſs Husband, p.26. l.25. p.50. l. *ult*. p.51. l.8. p.56. l. 31. The Confederacy. p.7. l.25. p.24. l.36. p.65.l.18. The Maſquerade, p. 5. l. *ult*. Roving Husband reclaim'd, p.18. l.14. *Eh! Lard! (ridiculouſly)* Stage-Beaux toſs'd in a Blanket, p.13. l.22. *Good Lard!* The Confederacy, p. 13. l. 4. *O Lard!* The Confederacy, p. 13. l.7. Roving Husband reclaim'd, p.26. l.22. Stage-Beaux toſs'd in a Blanket, p.45.l.19.

(*r*) The Pretender's Flight, p. 21. l.*penult*.

(*s*) The Drummer, p. 25. l. *penult*. The Maſquerade, p.27. l. 24.

(*t*) *Oh! Lerd!* Stage-Beaux toſs'd in a Blanket, p.45. l.19.

(*u*) Cobler of *Preſton*, p. 28. l. 6, 19. p.30. l.11. p.36. *l.penult*.

(*x*) The Wonder, p.44. l.11.

(*y*) Ibid. p.43. l.29.

(*z*) *Sawny* the *Scot*, p.6. l.5, 16. p.7. l.3,9,30. p.8. l. 9, 12, 24. p.9. l.7. p.11. l.30. p.14. l.18. p.15. l.1,32. p.16. l. 5, 8. p.17. l.15,29. p.18. l.3. p.19. l.15. p.20. l.3. p.28. l.34. p. 32. l.25,28,35. p.33. l.6. p.35. *l*.13, *ult*. p.36. l.13. p.38. l.2. p.40. l.18. p.49. l.24. p.50. l. 29,30. p.53. l.27,30. p. 54. l. 26. p.59. l.18. p.61. l.26. p. 62. l.11,17. p.63. l. 19, 33, 34. p.65. l.21. p.66. l.11. p.67.l.3. p.69. l. *antepenult*. p. 72. l. 3. p.74. l.6.

(*a*) A Woman's Revenge, p. 28. l. *antepenult*. Elfrid, p.21. l.28. Love in a Wood, p.33. l.17. Marplot, p.16. l. 24. Hob, p.16. l.*ult*. Cruel Gift, p. 57. l.7.

It may be observ'd, that in some of these Quotations the *Devil* seems to be preferred before GOD himself. Thus an *Actor* calls him (c) his *old Friend*, when the Name of GOD is mentioned by the by without any such Title; but the Name of the *Devil* is repeated again and again, as if he was *Alpha and Omega, the Beginning and the Ending, the First and the Last.*

In (d) another *Play*, the *Poet*, to shew his Rhetorick, proceeds by a *Climax* from the least in esteem to the highest. The first Expression is, O LORD! This Object being not worth another Thought, he invokes a Woman for Help, as if she was *Christ* himself; *Pray, Madam, save me!* The calling upon GOD is only to be a witness of the following Blasphemy; and then he proceeds to his *Ne plus ultra, O the Devil!* as being the Object of his last Devotions.

Besides, their Compliments to each other are as remarkable as their Prayers. Thus one saith, (e) *GOD be with you*; and the other answers, *Go* to the *Devil.* And in another *Play* there is this Expression, (f) *GOD be with you in the Devil's Name.*

Another Method whereby the Great GOD is contemn'd, is the treating of *Men* and *Women* as if they were really *Gods*. Here we have the Mistresses advanced *above the Stars*, made *like the most High*, or preferr'd before him, adored with Zeal and Faith, and worshipped up to Martyrdom, whilst they return the Compliments in the same Language. Here (g) *Men* are said to have this Honour paid to them (h) *by all the Earth.* Accordingly, they frequently swear by *Men*, by (i) *the Souls of those who begat them*, by (k) *the Souls of their*

---

l. 7. *Sawny the Scot*, p. 32. l. *antepenult.* p. 59. l. 18. The Female Advocates, p. 62. l. 6, 10. Modern Prophets, p. 71. l. 41. Perplex'd Couple, p. 8. l. 2. Perplex'd Lovers, p. 30. l. 10. Platonick Lady, p. 30. l. 27. Rival Fools, p. 35. l. 32. The Wonder, p. 74. l. 7. Woman is a Riddle, p. 31. l. 31.

(c) Love in a Wood, p. 33. *l.* 17.

(d) The double Gallant, p. 56. l. 15.

(e) The Wonder, p. 74. l. 7.

(f) Contrivances, p. 19. l. 15.

(g) Alexander, p. 44. l. *penult.*

(h) Ibid. p. 103. l. 29.

(i) Gibraltar, p. 12. l. 20.

(k) Solon, p. 38. l. 2.

great

great Anceſtors, by (*l*) their Father's Tomb, and (*m*) *injur'd Shade*; by (*n*) *the Majeſty of* Pekin *in* China; by (*o*) *the Great Lama*, in *China*; by (*p*) *the moſt Potent and Serene Cham*, in *China*; by (*q*) their *Hopes of Catiline*; by (*r*) *Saint George*; by (*s*) *Saint Patrick*, and by (*t*) *the great Ulyſſes*. I really believe, that they had not invented ſo many, and ſuch ſtrange ſorts of *Oaths*, but only becauſe our *Saviour* and St. *James* have forbidden them (*u*) to *ſwear at all*.

It is generally owned by (*x*) *Commentators*, that *Joſeph* ſinned, when he ſwore *by the Life of* Pharaoh, and that neither the Cuſtom of the Place, nor the Vehemency of the Occaſion, could excuſe the Fact. But it is moſt certain, that (*y*) *Polycarp*, when he ſuffer'd Martyrdom, might have been releas'd, if he would have ſworn, *by the Fortune of* Cæſar; and gave this reaſon for his refuſal, *If thou requireſt this, hear freely, I am a Chriſtian.* However, the Reader needs not to wonder at theſe *Oaths*, if he peruſeth ſome Expreſſions (*z*) which mention their reaſon for them.

It was *Lucifer*'s Pride to affect (*a*) a Likeneſs to GOD, for which he was caſt out of Heaven. But now the Epithet *Godlike* is frequently beſtowed by one *Actor* on another. Some Expreſſions at large of this nature I ſhall venture to tranſcribe.

(*b*) *Like* Mars *he look'd as terrible and ſtrong*;
Like Jove *majeſtick, like* Apollo *young*:

(*l*) Love the Leveller, p. 13. l. 24.
(*m*) The Faithful General, p. 68. l. 38.
(*n*) The Biter, p. 19. l. 27. p. 25. l. 4. p. 52. l. 20.
(*o*) The Biter, p. 20. l. 10.
(*p*) Ibid. p. 53. l. 23.
(*q*) The Female Wits, p. 39. l. 21.
(*r*) The Roving Husband reclaim'd, p. 15. l. 5.
(*s*) Stage-Coach, p. 4. l. 17.
(*t*) Ulyſſes, p. 2. l. 24.
(*u*) *Matt.* 5. 34. *James* 5. 12.
(*x*) *See* Pool's *Synopſis* upon *Gen.* 42. 16.
(*y*) *Euſebius*'s Eccleſiaſtical Hiſtory, *Book* 4. *Chap.* 15.
(*z*) *Perolla* and *Izadora*, p. 4. l. 27. p. 27. l. 7. p. 62. l. 27. Solon, p. 19. l. 14. The cruel Gift, p. 41. l. 28. Ulyſſes, p. 2. l. 5. p. 39. l. 3. p. 52. l. 7.
(*a*) *Iſa.* 14. 12, 13, 14.
(*b*) *Britiſh* Enchanters, p. 11. l. 23.

With

With all their Attributes divinely grac'd,
And sure their Thunder in his Arm was plac'd.
c) *Were* Amadis *restor'd to my esteem,*
I cou'd reject a Deity for him.

This is spoken of other Men; let us therefore see what an *Actor* saith of himself. (*d*)

Our Priests have better learn'd what now is ill;
Can when I please be good; and none shall dare
Preach or expound, but what their King would hear.
E'er they interpret, let them mark my Nod;
My Voice their Thunder, this Right Arm their God.

And as they *swear* by Men, so they also frequently *swear* by Women; (*e*) *By our Lady*, or the *Virgin Mary*; (*f*) *By the Life of* their *dear Princess*; and by (*g*) others present upon the *Stage*. Nay, the Expressions which they use to Women, savour of such *Blasphemy*, as is dreadful to relate, and would meet with a just Resentment in any place but a *Play-house*, where it passeth for fine Language. Of which I shall give some Instances.

(*i*) *You have fix'd me yours to the last Existence of my Soul's eternal Entity.*

(*k*) *Tell her, I am all hers; tell her, my Body is hers; tell her, my Soul is hers; and tell her, my Estate is hers.*

In other places, their *Mistresses* are (*l*) *ador'd*, as (*m*) the *Idols* of their Heart. Accordingly, every Per-

---

(*c*) *British* Enchanters, p. 35. l. 3.

(*d*) Ibid. p.6. l.23.

(*e*) The Loyal Subject, p.43. l. 15. The Mistake, p.6. l. 23. Northern Lass, p.54. l. *ult*.

(*f*) Love the Leveller, p.42. l. 2.

(*g*) Solon, p.64. l.15.

(*i*) Careless Husband, p. 35. *l*. 36.

(*k*) The Confederacy, p. 28. l. 28.

(*l*) Almahide, p.14. l.19. p. 54. l. 20. Arsinoe, p. 16. l.2. Camilla, p.5. l.32. p.21. l.33. p.25. l.31. p.26. l.24. Clotilda, p.24. l. *penult*. Hydaspes, p.44. l.31. Love's Triumph, p. 6. l. 10,18. p.18. l.15. *Pyrrhus* and *Demetrius*, p.8. l.1,13. p.23. l. 22. p.31. l. 4, 12. p.55. l.31. *British* Enchanters, p. 7. l. 29. Thomyris, p. 12. l.14. p. 16. l. 15.

(*m*) Camilla, *p*.28. *l*.14. Hydaspes, *p*.6. *l*.16.

ſon who is diſcourſed of, or addreſs'd to in this manner, is repreſented as (*n*) one who *walks and ſpeaks a Deity*; that is, who is known to be a *divine Perſon*, by her Gait and Speech; as (*o*) a *Goddeſs*, or (*p*) as *a bright Goddeſs*, (*q*) of a *Race divine*, (*r*) divine in each Feature, (*s*) of no mortal Race, but (*t*) wearing an heavenly Form, (*u*) with an heavenly Beauty, and for this reaſon (*x*) every Feature is to be adored. They are repreſented with (*y*) Eyes ſhooting forth Lightning, (a ſatirical Expreſſion, did not the profane Alluſion make it paſs for a Compliment.) Their *Charms* are ador'd by (*z*) *Crowds* of Lovers; and (*a*) they are endued with ſuch Graces, which will turn the very Tables of the *Law* into the reverſe, and inſtead of their worſhipping of GOD, the *Gods* ſhould worſhip them; and therefore (*b*) Kings themſelves do kneel on this occaſion. I ſhall add ſome more of the Expreſſions uſed by the *Actors* on the *Stage*, and let the *pious Reader* obſerve if his Blood doth not turn cold at the peruſal of them.

(*c*) *The charming Idol of my Heart.*
(*d*) *My Life! my Soul! my Joy!*
(*e*) *The Soul of my Deſire.*
(*f*) *To thee, as unto GOD, I bow.*
(*g*) *I ſwear by all that's Good. My Life! my Love!*

I could fill (*h*) ſeveral Pages with more of this Language; but he who deſires it, may turn to the Quo-

(*n*) Arſinoe, *p*.3. *l. penult.*
(*o*) Arſinoe, *p*.16. *l*.2. Camilla, *p*.3. *l*. 9, 15. Thomyris, *p*. 15. l. *penult*. p. 28. *l*.16. *p*. 32. *l*.11.
(*p*) Camilla, *p*.3. *l*.15. The Wonders of the Sun, *Epilogue*, *p*.2. *l. penult.*
(*q*) Camilla, *p*.2. *l*.30.
(*r*) Thomyris, *p*.7. *l*.24.
(*s*) Camilla, *p*.25. *l*.31.
(*t*) Ibid. *p*.25. *l*.31.
(*u*) Ibid. *p*.26. *l*.2.
(*x*) Arſinoe, *p*.16. *l*.2.
(*y*) *Exod*. 20. 18. *Rev*.1.14. *Rev*.4.5. *Rev*.18.19,19.
(*z*) Camilla, *p*.5. *l*.32.
(*a*) Camilla, *p*.21. *l*.33. Love's Triumph, *p*.6. *l*.10.
(*b*) *Britiſh* Enchanters, *p*.39. *l*. 35.
(*c*) Clotilda, *p*.8. *l*.8.
(*d*) Love's Triumph, *p*. 37. *l*. 27.
(*e*) *Pyrrhus* and *Demetrius*, *p*.10. *l*.13.
(*f*) Ibid. *p*.38. *l*.5.
(*g*) Arſinoe, *p*.29. *l*.5.
(*h*) Abra-Mule, *Epilogue*, *l*.3. Arſinoe, *p*.1. *l*.6. *p*.3. *l. penult. p*.4.

Quotations in the Margin, where his Curiosity will be abundantly gratified. And certainly the reason why a Man is represented as *GOD*, and a Woman as a *Goddess*, can only be this, that the *Poets* by openly commending the one, may secretly undervalue the other.

And now, instead of resenting such unusual and extravagant Expressions, as they do justly deserve, the *Female Sex* on the *Stage* are taught by the same *Poets* to lay aside all *Modesty*; to take all as if spoken in reality, and to act and speak their Parts accordingly; and which is more to be admir'd, the *Ladies*, who make a great part of the Audience, are pleas'd when their Sex is rais'd to that Height which *Lucifer* once attempted. Besides, the *Actresses* on the *Stage* are almost as guilty as the other Sex. The *Fear* of GOD, the *Shame* of the *World*, and the *Sense* of *Religion*, lays no Restraint upon them, from being guilty in their turns of the same *Blasphemy*. They also (*r*) frequently adore the Men; and without any regard to *Life*, *Nature*, or *Decency*, (which certainly ought to be observed in these Performances) call their *Suitors*, whilst in a single State, (*s*) the Delight of their Souls. They call them (*t*) the *Sun* which gives them Light, and cherishes them with its Heat; the (*u*) *Jewel of* their *Hearts*, which *alone is*

---

*p.*4. *l.*9. *p.*16. *l.*1. Gibraltar, *p.* 58. *l.*12. *p.*13. *l.* 30. *spoken of an intriguing Pimp.* Liberty asserted, *p.*40. *l.*9. Love the Leveller, *p.*62. *l.* 31. *p.*63. *l.*7. *p.* 65. *l.*11,22. Solon, *p.*20. *l.*23. *p.*64. *l.*15. The Amorous Miser, *p.*5. *l.*27. *p.* 57. *l.* 18. *British* Enchanters, *p.*15. *l.*13. Careless Husband, *p.*27. *l.*33. *p.* 65. *l.*1. Conquest of *Spain*, *p.* 12. *l.* 5. Fair Example, *p.*18. *l.*15. The faithful General, *p.*21. *l.*16. Female Wits, *p.* 54. *l.* 23. The Gamester, *p.*5. *l.* 11. *p.*41. *l.*19. *p.*61. *l.*1. Lawyer's Fortune, *p.* 16. *l.*28. *p.*46. *l. penult. Portsmouth* Heiress, *p.*26. *l.*12. *spoken by one in a Parson's Habit.* *p.*10. *l.* 28. *p.* 52. *l.* 22. Rival Brothers, *p.*6. *l.*27, *to* 37. *p.*15. *l.*19. *p.*82. *l.*11. The Roving Husband reclaim'd, *p.* 47. *l.*14. Zelmane, *p.*6. *l.*6. *p.*70. *l.*10.

(*r*) Arsinoe, p. 20. l.9. Hydaspes, p. 44. l. 31. *Pyrrhus* and *Demetrius*, p.16. l.20.

(*s*) Hydaspes, p. 44. l. *antepenult.*

(*t*) Arsinoe, p.33. l.9. *Pyrrhus* and *Demetrius*, p.60. l.25.

(*u*) Arsinoe, p.25. l.12.

worth their *Care*, the *Loss* whereof is intolerable, when all other *Losses* may be endured; (x) the *Idol* of their Souls, and (y) the *Soul* of Pleasure; and one prays another (z) to teach her absent Lord to adore her.

The Prophet *Isaiah* asks no less than three times, (a) *To whom shall we liken GOD? or make him equal? or compare him, that he may be like?* But he who is acquainted with our modern *Plays*, may observe him compared with Creatures, and even with those of an ordinary Character.

And as it is natural to fall from one Wickedness to another; so the *Poets* go farther yet, and represent our holy and just GOD, as one who delights in Uncleanness. This will be evident in another part of this Chapter. In the mean time, it may be observed, that in *Scripture*, (b) *the Grace of GOD teacheth all Men to deny worldly Lusts, and to live soberly.* In the *Play-house*, (c) one concludes with this Exhortation, *Now consider what hath been said, and Heaven give you Grace to put it in practice*; that is, to play the Whore. At another time, a Woman that refuseth to be a Whore, is (d) charg'd with want of *Grace* for that very reason, and (e) is thus threatned, *Well, well, the Sin of Ingratitude is great. Where do you think to go when you die?* As if GOD would punish her for this. Another saith of *Whoredom*, (f) *It is no Sin, but a vile Imposition upon the Law of Nature*, (that is, the Law of GOD) *contriv'd by cunning avaritious Fathers to stop the rapid Tide of generous Love, and tie it down to sordid Interest. What did* (GOD in the) *Creation mean a Woman for, but Pleasure? And Pleasure is the end of all we either do or wish. Desire is a Law, set down by Nature's* (that is, by GOD's) *Counsel, and not to be disputed.* And (g) again, *Dull Custom I de-*

(x) *Pyrrhus* and *Demetrius*, p. 60. l. 25.
(y) Temple of Love, p. 6. l. 18.
(z) *Pyrrhus* and *Demetrius*, p. 8. l. 13.
(a) *Isa.* 40. 18, 25. *Isa.* 46. 5.
(b) *Tit.* 2. 11, 12.
(c) The Relapse, p. 43. l. 17.
(d) A Woman's Revenge, p. 31. l. 23, *ult.*
(e) Ibid. p. 31. l. 30.
(f) Ibid. p. 14. l. 20.
(g) Ibid. p. 15. l. 4.

spise.

spise. I'll follow Nature's (that is, GOD's) *Laws. Beauty was made for use. It gives Desire, Desire is natural, and what is natural cannot be a Sin.* One (*h*) *Actor* desires *for Heaven's* (*viz.* for GOD's) *sake,* that care may be taken for the committing *Adultery* in private. Another (*i*), when upon the Attempt to debauch an *Actress,* puts up this Ejaculation:

Bless'd Heav'n, assist me but in this dear Hour.

In one *Play* an *Actor* invokes the Assistance of GOD's sacred *Majesty* (*k*) to carry on a drunken, and another (*l*) a whoring Intrigue, and others (*m*) upon ridiculous occasions. And to omit all other Instances, in another an *Adulterer* (*n*) prays to GOD for the Accomplishment of his villanous Intention; and to make a Jest of Devotion, desires GOD (*o*) to forgive his Frailties, whilst he goes on to the uttermost without Repentance, as if *Adultery* in GOD's sight was no Frailty at all. Now, what is all this, but a representing of our *Creator* as assisting and delighting in Iniquity, and Men as wallowing in Uncleanness under the pretence of obeying his Laws, and acting thro his Assistance? The *Psalmist* (*p*) speaking of some who were *Partakers with the Adulterers,* adds, *These things hast thou done,* (saith GOD) *and I kept silence. Thou thoughtest that I was altogether such a one as thy self; but I will reprove thee, and set before thee the things which thou hast done.*

[And GOD grant that this Reproof may not be by some Publick Calamity.]

Another way whereby *the Blessed GOD* is treated with Contempt, is by undervaluing his Power, and intimating as if he was not the Supreme Being. Thus one who obtains his Mistress, saith, (*q*) he *hath all that*

(*h*) The Confederacy, p. 28. l. 33.
(*i*) The Orphan, p. 31. l. 14.
(*k*) Gibraltar, p. 5. l. 1.
(*l*) Ibid. p. 22. l. 19.
(*m*) Squire Trelooby, p. 20. l. 1, *antepenul.* p. 21. l. 10. The Lawyer's Fortune, p. 8. l. 29.
(*n*) Love in a Sack, p. 54. l. 14.
(*o*) Ibid. p. 34. l. 6.
(*p*) *Psal.* 50. 18, 21.
(*q*) Hydaspes, p. 72. l. 23.

Heaven can grant. Another ſpeaking of a Sword preſerv'd, uſeth the ſame Language (*r*):

> *In this diſtracted State of our Affairs,*
> *'Tis all that Heaven could grant.*

Another being told by his Miſtreſs, that *Heaven* or GOD permits her to love him no more, anſwers, (*s*) *Why then doth it permit us Life and Thought? Are we deceived in its Omnipotence? Or is it reduc'd to find its Pleaſures in its Creatures Pains?*

Theſe are ſly Inſinuations on ſuch an occaſion; and he who would have an Anſwer to ſuch Queſtions, muſt ſeek for it in another place.

At another time we are told, (*t*) That *the envious Gods have done their worſt*; when no more is meant, but the diſappointing a King on the *Stage* of his Miſtreſs.

One asks, (*u*) *How angelically inſpiring would that divine Form appear?* As if *Angelical* was ſomething more than divine. Another prays (*x*),

> ——————*May Heav'n, and above all,*
> *Your own prevailing Genius guard your Age.*

What is meant by this *prevailing Genius*, is not ſo evident; but any one may obſerve, that it is a better *Guard* to Man than *Heaven* or GOD himſelf.

Another ſwears, (*y*) *By* Allah, *and by a greater Power.*

The word *Allah* in the *Arabick Language* is derived from a *Verb* which ſignifies to *worſhip religiouſly*, and is always uſed for the true GOD, who is thus to be *worſhip'd.* It is therefore very plain, what the *Poet* means by *Allah*, when he lays the *Scene* in *Turkey.* And indeed he himſelf unfolds it, when (*z*) more than once he

---

(*r*) Lucius, *p.*21. *l.*5.

(*s*) The Falſe Friend, *p.* 28. *l.* 30.

(*t*) The Royal Convert, *p.*81. *l.* 21.

(*u*) The Wiſe's Relief, *p.* 63. *l.* 19.

(*x*) Love Triumphant, p. 3. l. 5.

(*y*) Faithful Bride of *Granada*, p. 8. l. 18.

(*z*) Ibid. p. 6. l. 5. p. 51. l. 4.

makes

makes an *Actor* offer to *swear* by *Allah* upon the *Alcoran*, (a) pray to him for Help, and call him (b) *the Great, the Righteous Allah.* But then this greater Power is the Mystery. It must be something greater than GOD; and if the *Poets* can deprive him of his Omnipotency and Supremacy, they may also deprive him of his *Godhead.*

Another Method whereby the *blessed GOD* is vilified, is by giving the Titles of our LORD JESUS CHRIST to Men. The word (c) *Redeemer* is always in *Scripture*, and the word (d) *Saviour* is always in the New Testament apply'd to GOD or *Christ.* (e) *I, even I* (saith he) *am the LORD, and besides me there is no Saviour.* For this reason these adorable Names among *Christians* are appropriated to *our Blessed Saviour* and *Redeemer Jesus Christ* alone, and like the *Jewish Tetragrammaton* peculiarly reserved to the *Deity.* How grating then must it be to any Man, who hath not worn out all Sense of *Religion*, to hear a pretended *High-Priest* compliment an *Actor* on the *Stage* with such Language as this?

(f) *You gave the Proof of a concurring God,*
And are esteem'd and stil'd our Great Redeemer.

Or this (g);

———*Thy former Acts,*
That have aloud proclaim'd thee Thebes's *Saviour.*

In *Scripture* our *blessed Saviour Jesus Christ* is represented as (h) our *Advocate with the Father*, and (i) our

(a) Faithful Bride of *Granada*, p. 47. l. 8.

(b) Ibid. p. 53. l. 20.

(c) *Job* 19. 25. *Psal.* 19. 14. & 78. 35. *Prov.* 23. 11. *Isa.* 41. 14. & 43. 14. & 44. 6, 24. & 47. 4. & 49. 7, 26. & 54. 5, 8. & 59. 20. & 60. 16. & 63. 16. *Jer.* 50. 34.

(d) *Luke* 1. 47. & 2. 11. *John* 4. 42. *Acts* 5. 31. & 13. 23. *Ephes.* 5. 23. *Phil.* 3. 20. 1 *Tim.* 1. 1. & 2. 3. & 4. 10. 2 *Tim.* 1. 10. *Tit.* 1. 3, 4. & 2. 10, 13. & 3. 4, 6. 2 *Pet.* 1. 1, 11. & 2. 20. & 3. 2, 18. 1 *John* 4. 14. *Jude, verse* 25.

(e) *Isa.* 43. 11. & 45. 21. *Hos.* 13. 4.

(f) Oedipus, *Act* 1. *Ver.* 46.

(g) Ibid. *Act* 1. *Ver.* 56.

(h) 1 *John* 2. 1.

(i) *Gal.* 3. 19, 20. 1 *Tim.* 2. 5. *Heb.* 8. 6. & 9. 15. & 12. 24.

only Mediator; and it is an Office peculiar to him and to the *Holy Ghost*, to (*k*) *make Intercession* for his People. And for this reason, these words have by other Writers been peculiarly appropriated to these Persons. Upon the *Stage* the word (*l*) *Advocate* is apply'd to one, who assists in an amorous Suit: And (†) a *Jilt*, who persuades her Mistress to *Adultery*, is call'd *a proper Advocate*. A Man offers himself upon the same occasion (*m*) to be a *Mediator*, and (*n*) *Cupid* is represented as a *Mediator* between Man and Wife, like *Christ* between GOD and Man, and is pray'd to as such. And we have not only Men and Women said (*o*) to intercede for one another in the Intrigues of the *Stage*, but there is also (*p*) this Petition; (to whom it is made, let the Reader judge.)

Fair Empress of the Elysian *Shades, intercede for me.*

But the *Play-House Epithets* and *Expressions* compared together, will let the Reader see the different Respect which is there paid. In the *Play-House* it is (*a*) a *dear dear Devil*, and (*b*) an *envious*, or (*c*) a *lurking* GOD; or (*d*) a *loving Devil*, and (*e*) an *unjust*, or (*f*) an *injurious* GOD.

(*k*) *Isa.* 53. 12. & 59. 16. *Rom.* 8. 26, 27, 34. *Heb.* 7. 25.

(*l*) Abra-Mule, *p.* 25. *l.* 24. Perplex'd Couple, *p.* 60. *l.* 3. Provok'd Wife, *p.* 65. *l.* 23. Woman is a Riddle, *p.* 29. *l.* 6.

(†) The Fair Example, *p.* 44. *l.* 23.

(*m*) The Perplex'd Lovers, *p.* 6. *l.* 22.

(*n*) The *Portsmouth* Heiress, *p. ult. l. antepenult.*

(*o*) The Biter, *p.* 62. *l.* 10. The Country Lasses, *p.* 24. *l.* 30. Force of Friendship, *p.* 20. *l.* 21. The Gamester, *p.* 23. *l.* 19. Humours of the Age, *p.* 17. *l.* 7. The Maid the Mistress, *p.* 54. *l.* 30, 31. *Tunbridge*-Walks, *p.* 14. *l.* 28. Ulysses, *p.* 48. *l.* 38.

(*p*) The Fickle Shepherdess, *p.* 18. *l.* 10.

(*a*) The Country Lasses, *p.* 51. *l.* 9.

(*b*) The Royal Convert, *p.* 38. *l.* 5.

(*c*) *Venus* and *Adonis*, *p.* 19. *l.* 17.

(*d*) The General cashier'd, *p.* 4. *l.* 10.

(*e*) The Fatal Marriage, *p.* 173. *l.* 9.

(*f*) The Successful Pirate, *p.* 12. *l.* 6.

In the *Play-House* it is (g) an *honest*, or (h) a *very honest Devil*; but (i) a *vain* GOD: A (k) *virtuous Devil*, but (l) *a GOD averse to Innocence and Love.* In the *Play-House* it is (m) a *coaxing*, and (n) a *sweet Devil*; but (o) an *harsh*, and (p) an *injurious* GOD. The one is (q) an *old Friend*, and the other is (r) a *changing Deity*. The one (s) governs all things according to his Will and Pleasure, and (t) the other is a *sleeping* GOD.

Thus one saith, (u) *The Devil is a very modest Person, he seeks no body unless they seek him first.* And another (x) hath this Expression, *My Father always taught me to fear GOD and a Serjeant*; as if they were both alike, and the Business of both consisted in contriving to do us a mischief.

But perhaps the most daring, and certainly the most constant Method is yet behind, by which GOD himself is contemn'd; namely, The using of other Words to signify GOD himself, ascribing to such Words his *incommunicable Attributes* and *Acts*, and at another time treating these Words in the most sordid, vile and disingenuous manner, and bringing them for Examples of the most detestable Crimes. This is the way to burlesque him, who is eternal, and even to apply *Omnipotence* to Acts of Infamy. The *Attributes* or *Titles* of GOD are the same with his Being, and only different Words to express one Thing; and when we add them to any Word, we make that Word to signify the true GOD: so that all Contempt thereof is a Contempt of

---

(g) Love at first sight, *p.* 50. *l. penult.*

(h) Marry or do worse, *p.* 31. *l.* 28.

(i) Ulysses, *p.* 20. *l.* 32.

(k) Marry or do worse, *p.* 32. *l.* 12.

(l) Ulysses, *p.* 18. *l.* 16.

(m) The General cashier'd, *p.* 4. *l.* 10.

(n) Love Triumphant, *p.* 29. *l.* 12.

(o) Electra, *p.* 40. *l.* 4.

(p) *Appius* and *Virginia*, *p.* 35. *l.* 33.

(q) The Artful Husband, *p.* 11. *l. antepenult.*

(r) Lucius, *p.* 22. *l.* 4.

(s) The *Gotham* Election, *p.* 28. *l.* 18. Perplex'd Couple, *p.* 18. *l.* 21.

(t) The Fatal Marriage, *p.* 173. *l.* 10.

(u) The Recruiting Officer, *p.* 50. *l.* 32.

(x) The Litigants, *p.* 21. *l.* 33.

GOD himself. It is no Excuse to say, that such a Word of itself doth not signify GOD; for it must be taken as it is represented. A Piece of *Pageantry* is not a *King*; but if it wears a *Crown*, is dress'd up in *Royal Robes*, and is own'd as such, then all Disrespects shewn afterward to it, is a Disrespect to that King whose *Picture* it is, and will be resented as an Affront. And can we think, that GOD is not as jealous of his Honour? When we give his Name, his Titles, and his Worship to *Pagan Images*, or Words of our own devising, this alone is a Crime of an high nature; but the vilifying them afterward, is a most terrible Aggravation: And yet this is the general Practice.

To begin with *Jupiter* or *Jove*: He is (*n*) pray'd to, and praised with *Hymns* on the *Stage*, and worshipped in a magnificent Temple with Incense and Sacrifices. The Descriptions of him at large are such as these:

(*o*) He in *his sublime Abode*
Shook Earth and Seas with his Imperial Nod;
Abroad his unresisted Lightning hurl'd,
And with vindictive Thunder scar'd the trembling World.
(*p*) *Who in his Hand doth roll the three-fork'd Bolt*,
Preparing to discharge the fatal Thunder.
(*q*) *So* Jove *look'd down upon the War of Atoms*,
And rude tumultuous Chaos; *when as yet*
Fair Nature, Form, and Order had not Being,
But Discord and Confusion troubled all:
Calm and serene upon his Throne he sate,
Fix'd there by the eternal Law of Fate;
Safe in himself, because he knew his Power,
And knowing what he was, he knew himself secure.
(*r*) *Fix'd as the Law by which Imperial* Jove,
According to his Prescience and his Power,
Ordains the Sons of Men to Good or Evil.

It is he (saith an *Actor*) who (*s*) *knows the Crimes*

(*n*) The Faithful General, *p*. 25.
(*o*) Abra-Mule, *p*. 35. *l*. 16.
(*p*) *Appius* and *Virginia*, *p*. 9. *l*. 13.
(*q*) Ulysses, *p*. 42. *l*. 1.
(*r*) Ibid. *p*. 59. *l*. 10.
(*s*) Ibid. *p*. 3. *l*. 9.

and

and Injuries of others. It is he (*t*) who *scourgeth the flagitious World, and then forgives.* His (*u*) *Majesty is awful.* His (*x*) *Hand formed* all things. His (*y*) *Will* is *eternal,* and (*z*) his *Thunder sacred.* He is call'd (*a*) *impartial* Jove, *that lords it o'er the World*; or (*b*) *Supreme, First Cause, Eternal Source of Being.* And the Epithets bestow'd on him are (*c*) *Almighty,* (*d*) *Avenger,* (*e*) *Creator of the World,* (*f*) *Dread,* (*g*) *Eternal,* (*h*) *Father,* (*i*) *Father of Gods and Men,* (*k*) *Great,* (*l*) *Immortal,* (*m*) *Imperial,* (*n*) *In Grandeur above,* (*o*) *Just,* (*p*) *King of Gods,* (*q*) *King of Gods and Men,* (*r*) *Mighty,* (*s*) *Olympian,* (*t*) *Supreme,* (*u*) *the Thunderer,* (*x*) *Thundering,* and (*y*) *Vindictive Jove, who prepares his Thunder.*

(*t*) Fortune in her Wits, *p.* 19. *l.* 15.

(*u*) *Phadra* and *Hippolytus, p.* 7. *l.* 15.

(*x*) *Appius* and *Virginia, p.* 12. *l.* 30.

(*y*) Ibid. *p.* 46. *l.* 14.

(*z*) Injur'd Virtue, *p.* 13. *l.* 22.

(*a*) The *Persian* Princess, *p.* 48. *l.* 5.

(*b*) The Faithful General, *p.* 26. *l.* 12.

(*c*) Ajax, *p.* 18. *l. penult.* Solon, *p.* 12. *l.* 16. The Faithful General, *p.* 26. *l.* 13.

(*d*) Ulysses, *p.* 30. *l.* 3.

(*e*) The Faithful General, *p.* 26. *l.* 12.

(*f*) Solon, *p.* 40. *l.* 28.

(*g*) Oedipus, *p.* 44. *l.* 5. The Faithful General, *p.* 26. *l.* 12.

(*h*) The Victim, *p.* 45. *l.* 26.

(*i*) Ibid. *p.* 45. *l.* 26.

(*k*) Ajax, *p.* 42. *l.* 22. *Appius* and *Virginia, p.* 10. *l. ult. p.* 51. *l.* 25. *p.* 56. *l.* 16. Ulysses, *p.* 28. *l.* 22. Electra, *p.* 10. *l.* 10.

(*l*) Oedipus, *p.* 25. *l.* 17. *Perolla* and *Izadora, p.* 46. *l.* 29, 33. The Faithful General, *p.* 25. *Act* 3. *l.* 1. The Victim, *p.* 2. *l.* 24. *p.* 50. *l.* 19.

(*m*) *Phadra* and *Hippolytus, p.* 32. *l.* 30. *p.* 33. *l.* 9. *British* Enchanters, *p.* 30. *l.* 33. The Faithful General, *p.* 25. *Act* 3. *l.* 1.

(*n*) Arsinoe, *p.* 48. *l.* 1.

(*o*) Ulysses, *p.* 3. *l.* 9.

(*p*) *British* Enchanters, *p.* 30. *l.* 33. The Faithful General, *p.* 25. *Act* 3. *l.* 1.

(*q*) The Faithful General, *p.* 65. *l.* 40.

(*r*) Alarbas, *p.* 15. *l.* 15. *p.* 20. *l.* 28. *Appius* and *Virginia, p.* 52. *l.* 11. Love and Liberty, *p.* 57. *l.* 32. *Pyrrhus* and *Demetrius, p.* 31. *l.* 8. Solon, *p.* 12. *l.* 16. Ulysses, *p.* 35. *l.* 10.

(*s*) Electra, *p.* 10. *l.* 10.

(*t*) *Appius* and *Virginia, p.* 5. *l.* 4. *p.* 9. *l.* 13. The Faithful General, *p.* 26. *l.* 12.

(*u*) The Faithful General, *p.* 26. *l.* 13. Ulysses, *p.* 34. *l.* 35.

(*x*) *Phadra* and *Hippolytus, p.* 12. *l.* 26.

(*y*) Ulysses, *p.* 34. *l.* 35.

And to what purpose doth *Jupiter* thus appear in the Majesty of *Jehovah?* Why is he represented with the *Attributes* of the Supreme Being? Why is he furnish'd with *Omnipotence*, and made both the *Creator* and *Judge* of the World? Why are all the Functions of *Providence* put into his hands? Or why is he described with the Majesty of the true GOD? All this is only that he may set off *Vice* with a greater Lustre, and recommend it more effectually to our Practice by his own Example.

One *Vice* which I shall mention, is *Disobedience* to Parents. Thus an *Actor* saith, (z) *Did not* Jupiter *turn his Father* Saturn *out of Heaven, and leave it to us Mortals for a laudable Example to walk by?*

But that which I shall chiefly insist on, is the abominable Sin of *Whoredom* and *Adultery*. Thus an *Actor* in (a) two different *Plays* pleads, to carry on his base Designs, *I am* Jupiter *in love, and you shall be my* Alcmena. And the Strains in Verse are more remarkable.

> (b) *That celebrated King, the mighty* Jove,
> *Fatigu'd with Empire, left his Throne above,*
> *And for a while, enjoy'd the Sweets of Love.*
> (c) *A Face like thine has made* Jove *oft unjust,*
> *And oft intrench upon the Marriage-Vow.*
> (d) *To thee, like* Jove *to* Semele, *I'll come,*
> *And will with Lightning and with Thunder clasp thee.*
> (e) *Remember* Jove, *and think on unregarded* Juno;
> *His Wife was ne'er so happy as his Mistress.*
> (f) *Three Nights (the Poets say) Almighty* Jove
> *Indulg'd the Pleasures of licentious Love,*
> *For Beauty left the Heav'ns imperial Throne,*
> *And laid the sacred Weight of Empire down.*

When an *Actor* is forc'd to use a Disguise for such a leud Purpose, he is not wanting for an Example to make

---

(z) Solon, *p*. 4. *l*. 4.
(a) Love in a Chest, *p*. 52. *l*. 10. The Beaux Stratagem, *p*. 58. *l*. *antepenult*.
(b) Abra-Mule, *p*. 35. *l*. 12.
(c) *Appius* and *Virginia*, *p*. 16. *l*. 1.
(d) Ibid. *p*. 16. *l*. 28.
(e) Clotilda, *p*. 10. *l*. 3.
(f) Irene, *p*. 9. *l*. 25.

the

the matter more commendable: For (g) Jove *himself hath submitted to Disguises, to carry on his Amours*; and, (h) *Thus* Jove *within the milk-white Swan enjoy'd his* Leda.

And to divert their Hearers, they have also the same Strains in *Heroick Verse*.

(i) *Thus* Jove *within the Serpent's scaly* **Fold**
Twin'd round the Macedonian *Queen.*
(k) *Great* Jove, *they say, descending from above,*
T' enjoy the Pleasures of almighty Love,
Did condescend to lay aside his Rod,
Forget his Glory, and eclipse the God,
Thought no Disguise too safe, no Toil too great,
To please the Fair, and favour his Retreat;
Sometimes appear'd to her like Bull or Swan,
But oftner in the lordly Shape of Man.
And thus the mighty Thunderer was seen
To appear below in Shapes so base and mean.
(l) *So, fir'd by* Venus' *Son, the Thund'rer* Jove,
Of Right regardless, rushes on his Love;
By Fraud or Force he gains the beauteous Prize,
Tasting in various Forms as various Joys:
Now as Alcmena's *Lord, their Bed he stains;*
Then Spartan Leda, *like a Swan, he gains:*
Europa *by a lovely Bull's betray'd,*
And in a golden Show'r th' imprison'd Maid:
A Dragon curls in bright Olympia's *Arms,*
Nor can chaste Vows protect Calisto's *Charms.*
Hence Men by Fraud and Artifice succeed,
And Jove's *Example justifies the Deed.*

But lest the Example of *Jove* should not be sufficient to *justify* such Crimes, the *Poets* take care to add more of the same nature: witness the following Quotations.

(g) Woman is a Riddle, *p.* 54. *l.* 25.
(h) Three Hours after Marriage, *p.* 58. *l.* 21.
(i) Ibid. *p.* 58. *l.* 26.
(k) Love in a Sack, *Epilogue, l.* 1.
(l) Lucius, *p.* 8. *l.* 15.

Behold,

(*m*) *Behold, what Shapes Love makes us put on! But Gods (or Poets feign) taught us poor Mortals first to intrigue in counterfeit Shapes.*

(*n*) *What then? Gods and Demigods have assumed viler Shapes, to make a Cuckold.*

(*o*) *Nor can the Gods my fervent Passion blame,*
Since every God himself has been the same.
Phœbus *would oft the charming* Daphne *woo,*
And through the Grove the flying Nymph pursue.
Jove *through the* Hellespont Europa *bore,*
And fell in Danae's *Lap a golden Show'r.*

(*p*) *A Face less beautiful than that which now*
Compels me Empire to forsake for Love,
Has oft from Heav'n allur'd the gazing Gods,
And made them stoop, to be more happy here.

I do not blame the *Poets* for representing the *Pagan* Idols as they were represented by *Pagans*; but they ought not to be proposed as Examples. (*q*) We *have not so learn'd Christ*. Much less should they be treated on other occasions like the true GOD, whom we worship; for this is making a Confusion, and representing both as if they were alike.

But to proceed to other *Idols* among the Heathens. Sometimes *Cupid* is represented as (*r*) a GOD, or (*s*) the GOD of *Love*. Accordingly he is call'd (*t*) a *gentle* GOD, (*u*) a *liberal* GOD, and (*x*) a GOD *who commands*, and also (*y*) *an Infant, but a powerful* GOD. He is call'd (*z*) *Almighty*, (*a*) *Great*, (*b*) *Mighty*, and

---

(*m*) Love in a Chest, *p.* 54. *l.* 5.

(*n*) Three Hours after Marriage, *p.* 28. *l.* 10.

(*o*) Alarbas, *p.* 15. *l. penult.*

(*p*) *Appius* and *Virginia*, *p.* 15. *l.* 12.

(*q*) *Ephes.* 4. 20.

(*r*) Arsinoe, *p.* 16. *l.* 12, 20.

(*s*) Hydaspes, *p.* 16. *l.* 28. *p.* 26. *l.* 19. *p.* 48. *l.* 15, 17. Love's last Shift, *p.* 82. *l.* 16.

(*t*) Hydaspes, *p.* 78. *l.* 8.

(*u*) Injur'd Love, *a Comedy*, *p.* 16. *l.* 7.

(*x*) The Perplex'd Lovers, *p.* 38. *l. ult.*

(*y*) The Cares of Love, *p.* 19. *l.* 20.

(*z*) Liberty asserted, *p.* 52. *l.* 1. Manlius Capitolinus, *p.* 19. *l.* 8. The Perplex'd Couple, *p.* 36. *l.* 26. The Roving Husband reclaim'd, *p.* 29. *l.* 10.

(*a*) Liberty asserted, *p.* 46. *l.* 27. *Pyrrhus* and *Demetrius*, *p.* 22. *l.* 23.

(*b*) Solon, *p.* 9. *l.* 12. *p.* 29. *l.* 29.

Power-

(c) *Powerful:* (d) *The Greatest Power that Nature knows;* (e) *The Creator,* and *Parent of Heaven and Earth; the Delight of GODS above, to whom all Nature owes her Birth:* One (f) *whom no Power can withstand,* but he *rules from the Skies to the Center.* (g) One, who alone *hath conquer'd the Learned and the Brave, and frustrated their Resolutions;* and (h) *the GOD of resistless Fires, who oft in Female Hearts with Triumph sees the unlook'd-for Changes of his wanton Power.*

They tell us (i) of *the mighty,* and (k) *the almighty Power of Love;* and extol him in this manner (l):

To Love, that governs all, our Praises must we give.

And now if we would know who is thus ador'd, and advanc'd above all, we are told in the same and in other *Plays,* that he is (m) a *Boy,* (n) a *trifling Boy,* (o) a *blind Archer,* (p) a *cruel GOD,* (q) a *blind GOD,* (r) a *blind Deity,* (s) a *raging Deity,* (t) a *little Deity,* (u) a *subtle and a fantastick GOD,* (x) a *cruel GOD,* (y) a *froward*

(c) Liberty asserted, p. 46. l. 23. Love's last Shift, p. 83. l. 4. The Cares of Love, p. 19. l. 18.

(d) Love Triumphant, p. 21. l. 2.

(e) *British* Enchanters, p. 16. l. 31.

(f) Ibid. p. 19. l. 29.

(g) The Cares of Love, p. 19. l. 18. *Compare this with Job* 5. 12, 13.

(h) *Perolla* and *Izadora*, p. 27. l. 31.

(i) The Female Advocates, p. 44. l. *antepenult.*

(k) *Pyrrhus* and *Demetrius*, p. 38. l. 28. Conquest of *Spain*, p. 54. l. 24.

(l) Titus Manlius, p. 55. l. 31.

(m) Love and Liberty, p. 21. l. 19.

(n) Arsinoe, p. 23. l. *penult.*

(o) Etearchus, p. 8. l. 9.

(p) Hydaspes, p. 58. l. 14.

(q) Almahide, p. 14. l. 12. p. 16. l. 4. Arsinoe, p. 17. l. 5. Gibraltar, p. 13. l. 30. Hydaspes, p. 36. l. 2. Rinaldo, p. 5. l. *ult.* The Cares of Love, p. 17. l. 14.

(r) The Rival Brothers, p. 16. l. 10.

(s) Love and Liberty, p. 21. l. 21.

(t) Woman is a Riddle, p. 36. l. 6.

(u) Love and Liberty, p. 27. l. 28.

(x) Love's last Shift, p. 82. l. 16. *Phædra* and *Hippolytus*, p. 6. l. 16.

(y) Ulysses, p. 17. l. *ult.*

GOD,

GOD, (z) a *little GOD*, and (a) a *little impertinent GOD*. He is (b) a *little Tyrant*, (c) a *relentless Tyrant*, (d) a *little blind Bastard*, and (e) a *little sneaking Bastard*. They call him (f) *little Cupid*, or (g) *cruel Love*. Sometimes they call him more at large, (h) *Blind Love, that blinds his captive Slaves, and is the Parent of all human Evils*; (i) *ungrateful, cruel, unkind*, and *Plague of our Minds*; (k) that *interloping, blind, mischief-making Bastard, that Disturber of our Peace, that Curse of our Sex, the eyeless Brat*; or (l) a *little, blind, straggling Urching, as unsteady as his Votaries*. And certainly if the *Poets* treat him at this rate, they should never dress him up in the former Equipage.

If at one time *Venus* is represented as a (m) *beauteous Goddess*, at another (n) she shall be *cruel*. And thus there is hardly a Name to which a Divine Title is annex'd, but it also meets with a Character of Reproach.

The word GOD in the *singular Number* being forbidden by the *Statute*, a due care is taken to mention it in the *plural*; and accordingly we have (o) *auspicious*, (p) *awful*, (q) *blessed*, and (r) *bounteous GODS*. We have (s) the *dreadful GODS, who reign beneath*; who

---

(z) The Humours of the Army, p. 47. l. 8.
(a) The Relapse, p. 69. l. 8.
(b) Love and Liberty, p. 25. l. 25.
(c) Faithful Bride of *Granada*, p. 11. l. 11.
(d) The False Friend, p. 24. l. 3.
(e) Perplex'd Lovers, p. 12. l. *ult.*
(f) City-Ramble, p. 54. l. 11.
(g) Comical Revenge, p. 63. l. 13.
(h) Etearchus, p. 60. l. 15.
(i) *Pyrrhus* and *Demetrius*, p. 57. l. 6.
(k) The Generous Husband, p. 12. l. 18.
(l) The Maid the Mistress, p. 8. l. antepenult.
(m) *Venus* and *Adonis*, p. 10. l. 25.
(n) *Phaedra* and *Hippolytus*, p. 6. l. 11.
(o) The Faithful General, p. 69. l. 35.
(p) Injur'd Virtue, p. 9. l. 25. *Phaedra* and *Hippolytus*, p. 11. l. 11. Ulysses, p. 12. l. 6. p. 20. l. 23.
(q) The Conquest of *Spain*, p. 14. l. 26.
(r) *Appius* and *Virginia*, p. 5. l. 12. Etearchus, p. 54. l. 17. *Perolla* and *Izadora*, p. 47. l. 6. *Phaedra* and *Hippolytus*, p. 38. l. 23. The Distress'd Mother, p. 67. l. 18. The Victim, p. 17. l. 28. Thomyris, p. 52. l. 31.
(s) The Royal Convert, p. 51. l. 7.

are

are (*t*) *equal*, and (*u*) *eternal GODS*, *who govern this great World*, *and rule the Heart of Man*. We have the (*x*) *good*, (*y*) *gracious*, (*z*) *great*, (*a*) *immortal*, (*b*) *just*, (*c*) *kind*, and (*d*) *knowing GODS*. We have the (*e*) *merciful* and (*f*) *mighty GODS*, who (*g*) *ordain* whatever ſhall happen. We have (*h*) the *pitying*, and (*i*) the *powerful GODS*, even (*k*) the *powerful* ſacred *GODS* of *Heaven*; and alſo (*l*) the *righteous* and the (*m*) *unerring GODS*. We are told, that (*n*) their *Voice* is *ſacred*, (*o*) they *always guard the Just*, and (*p*) *favour Right*;

(*t*) The Force of Friendſhip, p.27. l.23.

(*u*) *Appius* and *Virginia*, p. 17. l.30.

(*x*) Etearchus, p.66. l. 26. Diſtreſs'd Mother, p. 31. l. 16. Falſe Friend, p. 42. l. 25. Succeſsful Pirate, p.50. l. 17. *Perſian* Princeſs, p. 40. l. 2.

(*y*) *Appius* and *Virginia*, p. 20. l. 7. Ulyſſes, p. 36. l. 36. p.47. l.22. p. ult. l. penult.

(*z*) Oedipus, p.48. l.2. p.71. l. 10. Manlius Capitolinus, p. 58. l. 4.

(*a*) *Appius* and *Virginia*, p. 5. l. penult. p.26. l. 8, penult. p. 27. l.21. p.55. l.34. Arminius, p.5. l.31. Arſinoe, p.39. l.22. *French* Cato, p.13. l.8. p.21. l.7. p.29. l. 5. Crœſus, p. 7. l. ult. Oedipus, p. 37. l. 13. *Phædra* and *Hippolytus*, p. 12. l.15. p.49. l.16. Manlius Capitolinus, p. 36. l. antepenult. *Britiſh* Enchanters, p.15. l.21. Faithful General, p.34. l.19. p. 52. l.27. p.64. l.36. p.68. l.4. The Victim, p.4. l.10. p.29. l.2. Ulyſſes, p.28. l. 7.

(*b*) *French* Cato, p.10. l.12. p.43. l.14. Injur'd Virtue, p.32. l.20. p.54. l. penult. Love and Liberty, p. 22. l.18. Oedipus, p.68. l.1. Manlius Capitolinus, p.1. l. ult. p. 37. l. 9. *Britiſh* Enchanters, p. 30. l. 33. Falſe Friend, p.37. l.23. The Victim, p.41. l.23. p.56. l.26.

(*c*) Manlius Capitolinus, p.14. l. 10. *Perſian* Princeſs, p. 33. l. 14.

(*d*) Titus Manlius, p.17. l.9.

(*e*) The Victim, p.59. l.10.

(*f*) *French* Cato, p.28. l.27. Lucius, p. 17. l. 21. Force of Friendſhip, p.20. l.18. Succeſsful Pirate, p.36. l.21. The Victim, p.41. l.33. p.53. l.4.

(*g*) Ajax, p.21. l.27.

(*h*) *Phædra* and *Hippolytus*, p.32. l.16. p.63. l.34. Faithful General, p.28. l. 3.

(*i*) Titus Manlius, p. 27. l.3. p. 51. l. 8.

(*k*) Ibid. p.27. l. 3.

(*l*) Cato, p.58. l.10. *French* Cato, p.15. l. ult. Oedipus, p. 28. l. 9. *Phædra* and *Hippolytus*, p.38. l. penult. p.48. l.16. p.64. l. 28. Force of Friendſhip, p.23. l. 12. The Victim, p.32. l.33. Ulyſſes, p.1. l.19. p.11. l.1. p.57. l.30.

(*m*) *Phædra* and *Hippolytus*, p. 38. l. 18.

(*n*) *French* Cato, p. 36. l.22.

(*o*) Hydaſpes, p.22. l. 4.

(*p*) Ulyſſes, p.30. l.31.

and their (q) *Prescience* is also mentioned upon the *Stage*. On the other hand, these very GODS are (r) *churlish*, (s) *cruel*, and (t) *envious*; nay (u) they *envy Mankind*. They are (x) *flattering*, (y) *injurious*, (z) *merciless*, and (a) *partial*. They are (b) *perverse*, (c) *pityless*, (d) *rigid*, and (e) *sleeping*. They are (f) *unassisting*, (g) *unequal*, or unjust, (h) unperforming, and (i) *unpitying*. *The GODS* is a word which will include the true GOD, as well as the false; and the *Poets* give no Caution to their Auditors, but that they may take it in its utmost Latitude if they think fit, or at least if they can but be pleased with so gross a *Blasphemy*.

Thus also they speak of the *Deities*, and call them (k) the *Supreme*, or (l) the *Sacred Deities of Heaven*; but at another time it is (m) the *Blind Deity*, or more grossly thus:

> (n) *He's mad, whoe'er believes you,*
> *O ye fallacious Deities.*

(q) Ulysses, p.34. l.30.

(r) *Persian* Princess, p. 12. l. 1.

(s) Camilla, p.30. l.23. *French* Cato, p.12. l.20. p.41. l.22. p. 48. l.17. p.59. l.13. *Phædra* and *Hippolytus*, p.35. l.5. p.51. l. 29. Rinaldo, p. 61. l. 18. Manlius Capitolinus, p.53. l.20. Distressed Mother, p. 31. l. 10. The faithful General, p.20. l.27. Ulysses, p.60. l.21.

(t) *French* Cato, p. 57. l. 9. Royal Convert, p.81, l.21.

(u) *French* Cato, p.57. l.9.

(x) *Venus* and *Adonis*, p. 12. l. 13.

(y) Successful Pirate, p. 12. l. 6.

(z) *French* Cato, p. 56. l.11. The Victim, p.46. l.12.

(a) *French* Cato, p.57. l.20. The Victim, p.14. l.19. Ulysses, p.16. l.25. p.46. l.34.

(b) Oedipus, p.20. l.13.

(c) Ulysses, p.34. l.11.

(d) The Victim, p.33. l.14. p.43. l. *penult*.

(e) Fatal Marriage, p. 173. l. 12.

(f) Electra, p.14. l.4. Oedipus, p. 34. l.8.

(g) *French* Cato, p.62. l.21. Oedipus, p.41. l.2. Fatal Marriage, *p*.173. *l*.9.

(h) *Persian* Princess, p. 58. l. 9.

(i) *French* Cato, p.43. l.22.

(k) Arminius, p.63. *l*.18.

(l) Ibid. p.23. l.13.

(m) Rival Brothers, p. 16. l. 10.

(n) Titus Manlius, p.39. l.10.

The

The word (o) *Heaven*, or (p) *Heavens*, is uſed in *Scripture* to ſignify the true GOD. Accordingly, the *Poets* ſeem to catch at this occaſion, that ſo they may more directly treat the true GOD, ſometimes with Reſpect, and ſometimes with Reproach, even as they treat the *Pagan Idols*. Sometimes it is (q) the *good*, (r) *gracious*, (s) high, and (t) *indulgent Heaven*. Sometimes, the (u) *juſt*, (x) *kind*, (y) *righteous*, (z) *ſweet*, and (a) *unerring Heaven*, and (b) *that which ſearcheth all our Thoughts*. But then at other times they change their Language. One (c) *thanks Heaven* for the Follies on the *Earth*. Another (d) ſaith, *Heaven was unkind to ſet ſo ſtrict a Bound*; that is, to forbid Brother and Siſter from marrying.

(e) *I did not hope to find*
Juſtice in Earth, 'tis not in Heaven neither.
(f) *Caſt not your Eyes up to yon azure Firmament,*
Nor hope Relief from thence. The GODS are pityleſs.
(g) *'Twas the rancorous Malignity*
Of all ill Stars combin'd, of Heaven and Fate.
(h) *The rigid Will of Heaven.*
(i) *Shall I truſt Heaven? No, I ſcorn a Proxy.*

(o) *Luke* 15. 21.
(p) *Dan.* 4. 26.
(q) Cobler of *Preſton*, p.12. l.30. Cruel Gift, p.35. l.21. Fatal Marriage, p.154. l.17. The Sultaneſs, p.9. l. *penult.* p.29. l. 34. The Victim, p.7. l.27.
(r) Cruel Gift, p.10. l.5. p. 17. l.29. p. 24. l. 22. Royal Convert, p.33. l.3.
(s) The Victim, p.43. l.3.
(t) Perfidious Brother, p.12. l. 17.
(u) Manlius Capitolinus, p.41. l. *antepenult.* Royal Convert, p.30. l.15. p.61. l.6. The Victim, p.32. l.24.
(x) Royal Convert, p.[illegible]1. l. *ult.*
(y) The Sultaneſs, p.22. l.16. p.28. l.11. p.52. l.28.
(z) Fatal Marriage, p. 172. l. 17.
(a) *French* Cato, p.10. l.10.
(b) The Sultaneſs, p.47. l.1.
(c) Man of Mode, *Prologue*, *l.* 24.
(d) *Compare* Love Triumphant, p.20. l.25. *with Levit.* 18. 9.
(e) Fatal Marriage, p. 173. l. 10.
(f) Ulyſſes, p.34. l.11.
(g) Fatal Marriage, p. 159. l. 20.
(h) The Victim, p.51. l.21.
(i) Don Sebaſtian, p.9.

(*k*) *Heaven has all Eyes, and no Tongue.* That is, GOD sees Wickedness, but conceals it.

(*l*) *Answer me, Heaven; but hold, what will Heaven answer?*

Answer me, Hell, for Heaven will damn Desire,
And be a Hell within me.

In (*m*) one *Play* the word is droll'd upon in a ridiculous Tone by a Country Clown; and in another (*n*) two different *Actors* say, *Heaven forbid!* But lest this should be too respectful, a *Romish Saint* is put upon the same Level in these words, (*o*) *Saint Anthony forbid!*

Besides, there are several other words which the *Poets* use in the same manner. Some of which they have borrowed from the Writings of the Heathens, and some they have invented of themselves. Thus at one time we meet with (*p*) the *Fate* or *Fates*, as *decreeing*, (*q*) *determining* or (*r*) *dooming* whatsoever shall happen, particularly (*s*) *decreeing* a Man *for high Command.* They are (*t*) *dread*, (*u*) *eternal*, (*x*) *impartial*, and (*y*) *propitious*, and Thanks are returned to them accordingly. They (*z*) *appoint* our *Death*, and (*a*) the *Law* which they make is *unalterable.* But then at other times these *Fates* are (*b*) *blind*, (*c*) *cross*, (*d*) *cruel*, and (*e*) *too cruel.*

(*k*) The Mock Astrologer, p. 37.

(*l*) Elfrid, p. 21. l. 27.

(*m*) Squire of *Alsatia*, p. 5. l. 33.

(*n*) The Wonder, p. 10. l. 6. p. 53. l. 10.

(*o*) Ibid. p. 54. l. 13.

(*p*) *French* Cato, p. 56. l. 9. Titus Manlius, p. 1. l. 8.

(*q*) Force of Friendship, p. 43. l. 10.

(*r*) Force of Friendship, p. 40. l. 6. Perfidious Brother, p. 49. l. 5. Royal Convert, p. 59. l. 8.

(*s*) *French* Cato, p. 3. l. 12.

(*t*) Hydaspes, p. 30. l. 2.

(*u*) Force of Friendship, p. 40. l. 6. Royal Convert, p. 59. l. 8.

(*x*) Conquest of *Spain*, p. 27. l. 14.

(*y*) Irene, p. 32. l. 31.

(*z*) Arsinoe, p. 38. l. *antepenult.*

(*a*) *French* Cato, p. 26. l. 1.

(*b*) Successful Pirate, p. 16. l. *penult.*

(*c*) Arminius, p. 55. l. 12. Titus Manlius, p. 9. l. 13.

(*d*) *French* Cato, p. 57. l. 6. Crœsus, p. 17. l. 6. p. 25. l. 23. p. 27. l. 18. p. 35. l. 8. Liberty asserted, p. 49. l. 26. *British* Enchanters, p. 23. l. 8. Perfidious Brother, p. 55. l. 17. Titus Manlius, p. 9. l. 13.

(*e*) Hydaspes, p. 46. l. 31. Love and Liberty, p. 35. l. 2.

They

They are (*f*) *envying*, (*g*) *envious*, (*h*) *inexorable*, and (*i*) *malevolent*. They are (*k*) *malignant*, (*l*) *outrageous*, (*m*) *partial*, and (*n*) *perfidious*. They are (*o*) *relentless*, (*p*) *remorsless*, (*q*) *rigid*, (*r*) *too rigid*, (*s*) *too too rigid*, and (*t*) *rigorous*. They are (*u*) *Tyrants*, (*x*) *vile*, (*y*) *uncertain*, (*z*) *unequal*, and (*a*) *unlucky*. And we are also told of (*b*) *the ingenious Malice*, (*c*) *the rancorous Malignity*, and (*d*) *the random Lots* of the *Fates*. And this is the Respect that is paid to such Names as are honoured with the *Divine Attributes*.

The next word which I shall mention is *Fortune*. In the *Poets* Language *Fortune* is extoll'd as (*e*) *the bright Queen of the Skies*, (*f*) who *predestinates* all that happens; (*g*) is *kind*, and prayed to for this reason, and is extolled in this manner:

(*h*) *To* Fortune *give immortal Praise,*
Fortune *deposes, and can raise.*
All is as Fortune *shall bestow.*
'Tis Fortune *governs all below.*

And if we would know what this Person is that is thus extoll'd, we are also told from the same *Poets*, that

(*f*) Oedipus, p.43. l.6.
(*g*) Theseus, p.13. l.8.
(*h*) Alarbas, p.40. l.18.
(*i*) Woman is a Riddle, p.49. l.22.
(*k*) Ulysses, p.51. l.16.
(*l*) Manlius Capitolinus, p.15. l.16.
(*m*) Successful Pirate, p.35. l. *antepenult*. The Sultaness, p. 35. l. *antepenult*.
(*n*) Croesus, p.17. l.9.
(*o*) Abra-Mule, p.24. l.23.
(*p*) Force of Friendship, p. 24. l. 6.
(*q*) Successful Pirate, p. 21. l. 34.
(*r*) Love and Liberty, p.34. l. 11.
(*s*) Faithful Bride of *Granada*, p.5. l.15.
(*t*) Manlius Capitolinus, p.12. l. 17.
(*u*) Etearchus, p.64. l.23.
(*x*) Craesus, p.17. l.9.
(*y*) Alarbas, p.6. l.7.
(*z*) Force of Friendship, p.38. l. 6.
(*a*) Arminius, p.55. l.12.
(*b*) Abra-Male, p.66. l.12.
(*c*) Fatal Marriage, p. 159. l. 20.
(*d*) Zelmane, p. 50. l. *antepenult*.
(*e*) Clotilda, p.5. l.26.
(*f*) The Biter, p.7. l 30.
(*g*) The Perplex'd Lovers, p. 31. l.13. p.40. l. 13. Clotilda, p.6. l.26.
(*h*) *British* Enchanters, p.28. l. *penult*. p.29. l.9.

(*i*) she *acts maliciously*, is (*k*) *blind*, (*l*) a *blind Deity*, and (*m*) *always blind*. She is (*n*) *cruel*, (*o*) a *damn'd Jade*, (*p*) a *damn'd Jilt*, (*q*) *false*, (*r*) a *fickle Goddess*, and (*s*) a *fickle Jade*. She is (*t*) a *Jade*, and (*u*) a *Jilt*, (*x*) *impious*, and (*y*) *invidious*. She is (*z*) *like a wanton Gipsy*, (*a*) *maliciously*. (*b*) *niggard*, (*c*) *partial*, and (*d*) *scanty*. She is also (*e*) a *squinting Hag*, (*f*) a *Strumpet*, (*g*) a *Tyrant*, and (*h*) *unsteddy*; and (if we allow the word *Destiny* to be taken in the same sense) she is (*i*) *inexorable*, and (*k*) *insulting*. We are told of (*l*) *the Bitch-Tricks of Madam* Fortune, and (*m*) *the blind Events of giddy Chance*; and an *Actor* saith, (*n*) *Ten thousand Plagues upon that Jilt Fortune*. The *Poets* pretend to fine *Language*, and they may use it upon other occasions; but all which they can pick up at *Billingsgate*, is spent upon those Beings which they worship as a GOD.

(*i*) The Wonder, p. 2. l. 11.

(*k*) Ernelinda, p. 17. l. 3. *Pyrrhus* and *Demetrius*, p. 54. l. 10. Successful Pirate, p. 30. l. *penult*.

(*l*) City Ramble, p. 8. l. 10.

(*m*) The Lying Lover, p. 1. l. 9.

(*n*) Thomyris, p. 24. l. *penult*.

(*o*) The Man's bewitch'd, p. 54. l. 28. Modish Husband, p. 35. l. 13.

(*p*) Modern Prophets, p. 10. l. 2.

(*q*) Arminius, p. 65. l. *penult*.

(*r*) City Ramble, p. 7. l. *penult*.

(*s*) The Man's bewitch'd, p. 42. *l. ult*.

(*t*) Modern Prophets, p. 48. *l*. 4.

(*u*) Fortune in her Wits, p. 49. *l*. 11.

(*x*) Hamlet, p. 4. l. 8. p. 44. l. *ult*.

(*y*) Successful Pirate, p. 41. *l. ult*.

(*z*) Camilla, p. 32. l. 12.

(*a*) Rival Brothers, p. 14. l. 8.

(*b*) Conquest of *Spain*, p. 55. *l*. 17.

(*c*) *Persian* Princess, p. 11. *l*. 25.

(*d*) Conquest of *Spain*, p. 55. *l*. 17.

(*e*) Amorous Miser, p. 14. *l*. 13.

(*f*) Rinaldo, p. 9. l. 1.

(*g*) Etearchus, p. 64. l. 23.

(*h*) *Persian* Princess, p. 26. *l*. 2.

(*i*) Love and Liberty, p. 19. *l*. 22.

(*k*) Almahide, p. 14. l. 8.

(*l*) The Confederacy, p. 5. *l*. 13.

(*m*) Abra-Mule, p. 41. l. 10.

(*n*) The different Widows, p. 60. *l*. 11.

The

The next word which I ſhall mention, is *Nature.* The *Law* of *Nature* among the *Poets* ſignifies (*o*) the Rule which GOD placed at the *Creation* of the World, for all his Creatures to walk by, which is (*p*) ſometimes call'd *the ſacred Laws of Nature.* Accordingly, ſome of the *Epithets* beſtowed on her, are (*q*) *almighty*, (*r*) *bounteous*, and (*s*) *great*, and (*t*) the *Beſtower* of all that is *good.* She is often own'd as (*u*) the *Creator* of Man, and (*x*) the *Faſhioner* of our *Form.* Thus they ſay particularly, (*y*) that

Nature form'd us of her ſofter Mould.

And (*z*),

Nature's unerring Laws are ſtill the ſame,
As when ſhe form'd the Order of the World.

Now the Return of Thanks which the *Poets* make for all this, is peculiar to themſelves. They call her in ſhort, (*a*) a *Bawd*, (*b*) *partial*, (*c*) a *partial Goddeſs*, (*d*) *ſportive*, and (*e*) unequal; or more largely thus:

(*f*) *Nature hath been provident only to Bears and Spiders.*

(*g*) *Nature the Gipſy is but unkind.*

(*h*) *Nature doats with Age*; that is, *the Creator* of the World is become a Fool, or grown twichild.

(*i*) *Nature hath given me my portion of Senſe, with a Pox to her.*

(*o*) The cruel Gift, p.43. l.1.
(*p*) Fatal Marriage, p. 172. l. 12.
(*q*) Solon, p.35. l.24.
(*r*) Mackbeth, p.29. l.4.
(*s*) Liberty aſſerted, p.27. l.14. p.44. l.25. p.65. l.17.
(*t*) Perplex'd Lovers, p. 18. l. 25.
(*u*) Love the Leveller, p. 43. l. 22.
(*x*) Royal Convert, p.27. l.27.
(*y*) Cato, p.14. l.23.
(*z*) The Platonick Lady, p. 54. *S.ene* l.2.
(*a*) The Wife's Relief, p.11. l. 13.
(*b*) Royal Convert, p. 49. l. *ult.* The Wife's Relief, *Prologue*, l.3.
(*c*) Royal Convert, p.83. l.5.
(*d*) Irene, p.3. l.9.
(*e*) The unfortunate Dutcheſs of *Malfi*, p.25. l.22.
(*f*) Love for Love, p. 23. l. 14.
(*g*) The Lady's Laſt Stake, *Epilogue*, l.35.
(*h*) Love Triumphant, p.33. l. 22.
(*i*) Ibid. p.17. l.13.

The next word which I shall mention, is *Powers*. This word upon the *Stage* is taken in a double sense. Sometimes it signifies GOD, and at other times it signifies the *Devil*, but generally it may be taken for either; and this seems to be the reason that it is so crouded with *Epithets* of Respect and Esteem. Sometimes they (k) are the *Powers above*, and sometimes (l) the *Powers beneath*. Sometimes (m) *celestial*, and sometimes (n) *infernal*; for the *Poets* make no difference. However, they are (o) *all-kind*, (p) *almighty*, (q) *all seeing*, (r) *attesting*, and (s) *awful*. They are (t) *blessed*, (u) *blissful*, (x) *divine*, and (y) *eternal*. They are (z) *gracious*, (a) *ever-gracious*, (b) *heavenly*, and (c) *holy*. They are (d) *immortal*, (e) *indulgent*, —— ——

(k) Arsinoe, p.26. l.15. Liberty asserted, p.39. l. *ult*. p.47. l.35. Comical Revenge, p.44. l.13. p.46.l.30. p.47. l.6. Cruel Gift, p.9.l.28. p.12.l.33. p.53. l.8. Faithful Bride of *Granada*, p.30. l.26. The Victim, p.44. l. 10. Thomyris, p. 8. l. 24. Zelmane, p.13. l.2. p.47. l.23. p.62. l.28.

(l) Metamorphosis, p.14. l.9.

(m) Oedipus, p.49. l.6. Ulysses, p.63. l.10.

(n) Electra, p.13, l 12. *Phædra* and *Hippolytus*, p.21. l.21. *Theseus*, p.53. l.21. p.67. l.15.

(o) *Persian* Princess, p.28.l.12.

(p) *Appius* and *Virginia*, p.13. l.31. The faithful General, p.59. l.42.

(q) *Phædra* and *Hippolytus*, p.8. l.35. Solon, p.40. l.4.

(r) *Perolla* and *Izadora*, p.44. l. 22.

(s) *Perolla* and *Izadora*, p.27. l.3. The Cruel Gift, p 23. l.37.

(t) Oedipus, p.49. l.6. The *Persian* Princess, p.33. l.6.

(u) Successful Pirate, p.8.l.15.

(x) *Cinna*'s Conspiracy, p.36. l.12. *British* Enchanters, p. 30. l. 32.

(y) Hydaspes, p. 14. l. 12. Liberty asserted, p.16. l.7. p.61. l. 6. Love and Liberty, p. 2?. l. 17.

(z) *Appius* and *Virginia*, p. 18. l. 33. Perfidious Brother, p. 16. l. 3. p. 40. l. 17. p. 56. l. *ult*.

(a) Fickle Shepherdess, p. 34. l. 11.

(b) Clotilda, p.36. l.23. Etearchus, p.32. l.9. Lucius, p.29. l. 26. Oedipus, p. 33. l. 17. Faithful Bride of *Granada*, p.26. l. 18. Fatal Marriage, p. 172. l. 33.

(c) Royal Convert, p.38. l.8. Ulysses. p.47. l.25.

(d) Cato, p. 58. l. 30. Injur'd Virtue, p.78. l.8. Liberty asserted, p.29. l.12. p.39. l.17, 35. p.40. l.8,20. Lucius, p.23. l.28. The faithful General, p. 28. l.36. p.29. l.1. The Fickle Shepherdess, p.38. l.5. Perfidious Brother, p.56. l.2. Temple of Love, p.9. l.18. The Victim, p.49. l.32. p.54. l.30. The Wife of *Bath*, p.45. l.22.

(e) *Perolla* and *Izadora*, p.26. l.29.

juster,

(*f*) *juster*, or (*g*) *just* and *merciful*. They are (*i*) *mighty*, (*k*) *over-ruling*, (*l*) *pitying*, and (*m*) *propitious*. They are (*n*) *Protectors of the Chaste*, (*o*) *Righteous*, (*p*) *Sacred*, even (*q*) the *sacred Powers above*, and (*r*) the *sacred Powers of Heaven*. They are (*s*) *solemn*, (*t*) *spotless*, (*u*) *supreme*, and (*x*) *unerring*. They are (*y*) the *Guardian Powers*, who (*a*) are *impartial*, who (*b*) *formed human Nature*; they (*c*) *guard the Good*, and (*d*) are *the Guardians of the Just*. They (*e*) *reign on High*. They (*f*) *take Regard of*, and (*g*) *favour Innocence*. They (*h*) guide our Lives, and pre-ordain our *Fates*. They (*i*) *see, and rule this World*. They (*k*) *grant* Success. They (*l*) *view the inmost Thoughts of Mortals*. They (*m*) *calm the Conduct of our Passions*, and they

---

(*f*) The faithful Bride of *Granada*, p.57. l.7. Conquest of *Spain*, p.54. l.28.

(*g*) Conquest of *Spain*, p.13. l.36. Zelmane, p.35. l.21. p.38. l. 23.

(*h*) Mackbeth, p.16. l.6.

(*i*) Elfrid, *Prologue*, l. 18. Lucius, p.11. l.34. p.37. l.33. p.48. l.22. The faithful Bride of *Granada*, p.15. l.8.

(*k*) Ulysses, p.64. l.6.

(*l*) *Phædra* and *Hippolytus*, p. 64. l.13.

(*m*) The City Ramble, p.65. l. 32.

(*n*) *Appius* and *Virginia*, p.26. l. 21.

(*o*) Perfidious Brother, p. 24. l. 2.

(*p*) Solon, p. 56. l.5. Conquest of *Spain*, p.13. l.26. p.39. l.21. p.53. l.13. The Cruel Gift, p.62. l.3. The faithful Bride of *Granada*, p. 37. l. 20. Rival Brothers, p.84. l.30.

(*q*) Oedipus, p.56. l. *antepenult*. The Rival Fools, p. 57. l. 17.

(*r*) Oedipus, p.41. l.4.

(*s*) The Biter, p.14. l.5. p.16. l.22. p.22. l.19.

(*t*) The Force of Friendship, p.31. l.*penult*.

(*u*) The Fickle Shepherdess, p.24. l.6. Force of Friendship, p.30. l.24.

(*x*) The faithful Bride of *Granada*, p.31. l.27. p.35. l.7.

(*y*) Lucius, p.2. l.8.

(*a*) Conquest of *Spain*, p.25. l. 2.

(*b*) *Appius* and *Virginia*, p. 13. l.31.

(*c*) Cato, p.58. l.30.

(*d*) Ulysses, p.47. l.25. p.63. l. 10.

(*e*) Elfrid, *Prologue*, *l.*18.

(*f*) The faithful Bride of *Granada*, p.57. l.7.

(*g*) Ibid. p.15. l.8.

(*h*) The Cruel Gift, p.62. l.3.

(*i*) Ibid. p.33. l.17.

(*k*) Thomyris, p.6. l.14.

(*l*) *Appius* and *Virginia*, p.39. l. 19.

(*m*) The Force of Friendship, p.31. l.*penult*.

(*n*) are prayed to accordingly. Here we are told of (*o*) *the eternal Juſtice of the Powers*, and particularly (*p*) *that immortal Power, whoſe deathleſs Spirit informs this Earth.* But all this muſt not paſs off ſo. We are alſo told, that they are (*q*) *cruel*, (*r*) *malicious*, (*s*) *niggard*, and (*t*) *partial.* They are (*u*) *remorſleſs*, (*x*) *rigid*, (*y*) *too rigid*, and (*z*) *ſullen.* They are (*a*) *unpitying*, and (*b*) *wrathful.* And leſt we ſhould interpret theſe *Epithets* of thoſe *Powers* which are the *Poets* Favourites, we are (*c*) particularly told, for diſtinction ſake, That theſe *wrathful Powers* are the *Powers* above.

The laſt word which I ſhall mention, is *Stars.* Theſe are called (*d*) the *auſpicious*, and (*e*) our *Guardian Stars*, which (*f*) *ordain* whatſoever ſhall happen. Theſe are alſo (*g*) *cruel*, (*h*) *diſaſtrous*, (*i*) *envious*, and (*k*) *guilty.* They are (*l*) *too long inveterate*, (*m*) *malicious*, (*n*) *ma-*

(*n*) Lucius, p. 14. l. 3. p. 27. l. 33. p. 28. l. 16. p. 35. l. 28. The Cruel Gift, p. 33. l. 34. p. 39. l. *ult.* Perfidious Brother, p. 31. l. 11. p. 40. l. 22. *Venus* and *Adonis*, p. 17. l. 1.

(*o*) *Perſian* Princeſs, p. 40. l. *penult.*

(*p*) The Victim, p. 49. l. 32.

(*q*) Oedipus, p. 63. l. 17. *Phædra* and *Hippolytus*, p. 6. l. 10. Thomyris, p. 14. l. 21. p. 20. l. 15.

(*r*) *Phædra* and *Hippolytus*, p. 6. l. 10.

(*s*) Oedipus, p. 14. l. 2.

(*t*) Conqueſt of *Spain*, p. 29. l. 5. The Victim, p. 18. l. 18.

(*u*) *Perolla* and *Izadora*, p. 30. l. 22.

(*x*) The Force of Friendſhip, p. 24. l. 6. Perfidious Brother, p. 53. l. 10.

(*y*) Love and Liberty, p. 28. l. 6.

(*z*) Ulyſſes, p. 36. l. 16.

(*a*) *Pyrrhus* and *Demetrius*, p. 31. l. 4.

(*b*) Liberty aſſerted, p. 39. l. *ult.*

(*c*) Ibid.

(*d*) The *Perſian* Princeſs, p. 32. l. 4.

(*e*) Zelmane, p. 4. l. 18. p. 11. l. 18. p. 20. l. 25. p. 33. l. 25.

(*f*) Zelmane, p. 63. l. 3.

(*g*) The Sultaneſs, p. 54. l. 5. Thomyris, p. 30. l. 4.

(*h*) The Force of Friendſhip, p. 26. l. 22.

(*i*) Ulyſſes, p. 59. l. 2.

(*k*) The Force of Friendſhip, p. 28. l. 13.

(*l*) The faithful Bride of *Granada*, p. 57. l. *penult.*

(*m*) Conqueſt of *Spain*, p. 37. l. 7. The faithful Bride of *Granada*, p. 14. l. *ult.* Zelmane, p. 35. l. 19. p. 68. l. 4.

(*n*) The Succeſsful Pirate, p. 15. l. 34. Zelmane, p. 28. l. 26. p. 44. l. 4.

lignant,

lignant, (*o*) *partial*, *too* (*) *partial*, and (*p*) *unkind*. We are told of the (*q*) *rancorous Malignity of ill Stars*, especiall in ſuch Language as this (*r*) in Proſe:

Malignant Stars, which conſpire to *ſhed down their poiſonous Venom.*

Or thus (*s*) in Verſe:

Conſpiring Stars! who ſeem to dart
Their utmoſt Malice on my Heart.

All theſe are common and daring Strokes; the vileſt *Pagans* would not preſume to treat the GODS which they made, in ſuch a manner. But our *Poets* being far worſe than they, ſet up what they pleaſe in the place of the true GOD, that by aiming at the one they may reflect upon the other: and ſince they cannot perſecute the true GOD by Name or in Perſon, they ſeem reſolved to effect it by their Reſemblances.

[Correct us, O LORD, but in Judgment, not in thine Anger, leſt thou bring us to nothing.]

(*o*) Etearchus, p.42. l.17.
(*) Zelmane, p.15. l.12.
(*p*) Antiochus, p. 66. l. 14. Fortune in her Wits, p.5. l. *antepenult.*
(*q*) The fatal Marriage, p. 59. l.20.
(*r*) Zelmane, p.44. l.4.
(*s*) Hydaſpes, p. 50. l. *penult.*

CHAP.

CHAP. XIX.

The Works of Creation and Providence exposed by the Stage.

IN the last Chapter I gave a most dismal Account how the blessed GOD is treated with Contempt upon the *Stage*, particularly in reference to his own Essence. In this Chapter I shall give another Instance of the Contempt which is daily cast upon him, by misrepresenting of his Works. Now the Works of GOD are of two sorts, either the Work of *Creation*, or the Work of *Providence*. The Work of *Creation* is the Execution of GOD's Decree, wherein he did (*a*) make of nothing the World and all things therein, for himself and his Glory, in the Beginning, by the Word of his Power, within the space of six Days, when the *Creatures* thus made by him were all very good. In *Scripture* Language GOD made the *Creatures*, the *Play-house* Language is the Reverse. For sometimes the *Actors* ascribe the Work of *Creation* to themselves. Thus one *Actor* saith of another

(*b*) *I first created him this GOD on Earth.*

And another saith, (*c*) *The Cravat-String, the Garter, the Sword-Knot,* &c. *were all created by me.*

And sometimes they ascribe the Work of *Creation* to other *Actors*; as, (*d*) *That Blood*, which your Birth created. Or, (*e*) *Thou hast new-created me*; that is, given him hopes of his Mistress's Favour.

At the first opening of the *Play-House* in the *Hay-*

(*a*) *Heb.* 11. 3. *Prov.* 16. 4. *Gen. ch.* 1, 2.

(*b*) The Victim, p. 34. l. 14.

(*c*) Love's last Shift, p. 25. l. 13.

(*d*) Jane Gray, p. 10. l. 6.

(*e*) Fortune in her Wits, p. 45. l. 18.

market,

market, the *Prologue* then spoken was most notoriously *blasphemous*, and enough to make all Lovers of *Religion* abhor the Place. In the very first words the (f) *Builder* was compared to GOD; and the *Building* to the *Creation* of the World:

Such was our Builder's Art, that soon as (g) nam'd,
This Fabrick, like the Infant World, was fram'd.

No *Jest* serves the turn like a Droll upon the *Holy Scriptures* and the *Works* of GOD, since thereby they are the less regarded at another time. Besides, it was the Ambition of the fallen *Angels* to affect a Likeness with GOD, for which they were turn'd out of *Heaven*; and yet (I think) the *Poet* exceeds that in the following Lines:

The Architect must on dull Order wait;
But 'tis the Poet only can create.

Had he said, *GOD and the Poet only can create*, it had been more modest; for then the *Supreme Being* had been join'd as a Partner with the *Poet's* Abilities, whereas now he is totally excluded as *dull* and insignificant.

Tho such a scandalous and profane Expression is enough to raise the Blood at the reading thereof; yet a *Stage-Poet* was so fond of it, that he inserted it in the Title-Page of (h) a *Comedy*, as a choice Quotation, and so apply'd it to his own Performance.

But besides this, the *Poets* in other *Plays* deny the Honour of the *Creation* to GOD, or contradict the Account which the Scriptures give of it. One *Actor* saith, (i) *Why truly, I don't well understand what you meant by your Doctrine to me just now, that every thing we saw was made by Chance.* To this it is answer'd, *Oh! I shall have Time enough to read you such Lectures of Motions, Atoms, and Nature, that you shall learn to think as freely as the best of us, and be convinc'd that all about us*

(f) *Prologue*, l. 1.
(g) *Gen.* 1, 3, 6, 9, 11, 14, 15, 20, 24, 26, 29.
(h) The Fair Example.
(i) The Drummer, p. 10. l. 11.

is

is Chance-Work. This is *Free-Speaking*, and not *Thinking* only.

The first Verse of the whole *Bible* is this, (*k*) *In the Beginning GOD created the Heaven and the Earth.* The *Actors* (*l*) ridicule the word *Creature*, as if they believed no such thing, but that either the World was eternal, or made by an accidental Concourse of Atoms. *Creature! What! Your own Cousin a Creature! What! —a Creature! Nay, now I am sure you are ignorant.*

But to proceed to the *Creation* of Man: (*) *The LORD GOD formed* Adam *out of the Dust of the Ground, and breathed into his Nostrils the Breath of Life; and so Man became a living Soul.* I need not multiply fresh Quotations out of the *Plays*, since an old one may dispatch all at once.

> (†) *What Stuff are Men compos'd of?*
> *Sure the Account of their Creation's false.*

I cannot omit another flagrant Impiety in one of our *English Poets*, tho I do not blame the *Stage* for that, which is the ascribing the Work of *Creation* to the *Devil.* Accordingly in one of our late *Poems*, printed with many others in several *Volumes* to poison the good Notions and Morals of the Nation, and so concurring in the *Play-House* Design, we are told (*m*) of a *Scholar*, who was guilty of *Adultery*, with several other vile Tricks, disguised under the pretence of *Religion.* By his Actions he was a Child of *Satan*, and his Studies were devoted to this purpose. For (*n*),

> *To doubtful Questions he could answer right,*
> *Made plain to him by a* Demoniack *Light.*
> (*o*) *And could, assisted by the Power of* Hell,
> *Th' Events of every rolling Month foretell.*

And as if this Power which instructed him was his GOD, and the *Creator* of the World,

---

(*k*) Gen. 1. 1.

(*l*) The Tender Husband, p. 20. l. 26.

(*) Gen. 2. 7.

(†) The Relapse, p. 63. l. 32.

(*m*) Wit and Mirth, or Pills to purge Melancholy, *Vol.* 5. *printed Anno* 1714. p. 325.

(*n*) P. 325. l. 7.

(*o*) P. 325. l. 13.

(p) *Then to the trembling Strings his Voice he rais'd,*
And in Angelick Hymns his Maker prais'd.

Another thing remarkable, not only among the *Poets* in general, but also the *Stage-Poets* in particular, is, that when they ascribe the Works of *Creation* to GOD, they take care to blame him for whatever they think amiss in them. And we need not to read far in the Books of *Moses*, before we shall find a Text thus grosly abused.

After the *Creation* of Man, the *Scriptures* give us in the next (s) *Chapter* a particular Account how the Woman also was formed by GOD: now on this occasion the *Poets* complain most heavily (t),

That *Providence, which form'd the Fair*
In such a charming Skin,
Their Outside made his only Care,
And never look'd within.

Here the *Poet* tells us, that *Providence* makes Mankind by halves, huddles up the Soul, and takes the least care of his own Image. This is a direct *Blasphemeing* of the *Creation*, and a *Satire* upon GOD Almighty as the *Creator*. However, as we owe our Being to GOD alone, so in *Scripture* it is represented as such a Miracle of Mercy, that we cannot be too much affected with it. And therefore the *Psalmist* saith to GOD, (u) *I will praise thee, for I am fearfully and wonderfully made; marvellous are thy Works, and that my Soul knoweth right well.* The *Players* express our *Creation* thus:

(x) *The blind Work of Chance, which produced a Monster.*
(y) *I am, as Haste ordain'd me, a thing slubber'd.*
(z) ——*Nature form'd us here alike,*

(p) P. 326. l. 1.
(s) *Gen.* 2. 21, 22, 23.
(t) Don *Quixot*, Part the first, p. 20.
(u) *Psal.* 139. 14.
(x) Female Wits, p. 62. l. 16.
(y) Wit without Money, p. 9. l. 14.
(z) The Royal Convert, p. 28. l. 29.

Save

Save that her partial Hand gave all the Majesty
And Greatneſs to my King, and left me rich
Only in Friendſhip, Plainneſs, Truth and Tenderneſs.

Thus *Friendſhip, Truth,* and ſuch-like Virtues are not worth giving thanks to GOD for; but his Partiality is complain'd of, becauſe he gave nothing elſe. So that if this is right, the Rich Man in the *Goſpel* had a better Portion than *Lazarus.*

Beſides, the Gratitude of the *Poets* and *Actors* is ſhewn in Language of the ſame nature. One reads us this Leſſon upon the *Creation:* (*a*) *And if this Rogue was anatomiz'd and diſſected, he hath his Veſſels of Digeſtion and Concoction, and ſo forth. Theſe things are unaccountable and unreaſonable. Why was I not a Bear, that my Cubs might have liv'd upon ſucking their Paws? Nature* (that is, GOD) *hath been provident only to Bears and Spiders; the one hath his Nutriment only in his own hands, and the other ſpins his Habitation out of his Entrails.* Another in the ſame *Play* gives GOD thanks for the Advantage of his Being, by calling the Effects of his immortal Soul, even *Reaſon, Thought, Paſſions, Inclinations, Affections, Appetites* and *Senſes,* an *invincible and a craving Retinue, and ſo many Devils, that will have Employment.* And it is obſervable, that this *Actor* was the *Poet's* chief Favourite, and crown'd with the utmoſt Succeſs. A third, (*c*) who was bred at the *Univerſity,* calls the natural Inclinations to Eating and Drinking (*d*) *Whoreſon Appetites.* All this is ſtrange Language. The *Manicheans,* who affirm'd ſome part of the *Creation* to have been the Work of the *Devil,* could ſcarcely have been ſo coarſe in their *Compliments.* And if a Mother cannot but be affronted when ſuch an Epithet is given to her Child, can we imagine that GOD will not be angry, when it is given to ſuch things which he created?

From the Works of *Creation* I ſhall proceed to the Works of *Providence.* Theſe are the ſubſequent Actions

---

(*a*) Love for Love, p.23. l.9.
(*b*) Ibid. p.22. l.12.
(*c*) Ibid. p.1. l.14. p.68. l. 37, 39.
(*d*) Ibid. p. 22. l. 32.

of

of GOD, or the second Part of the Execution of his eternal Decree, by which he preserves and governs all his Creatures in a most holy, wise, and powerful manner, directing them, and effectually disposing of them, with all that belongs to them, for his own Glory, and for all good Ends. He takes such care of the World, that even (e) *a Sparrow doth not fall to the ground without* his Providence, (f) *the very Hairs of* our *Heads are all numbred*, and (g) *the Disposal* of *Lots is* from him. *Jacob* own'd (h) that it was GOD who *fed* him *all* his *life-long*; and *Joseph* said, that (i) *GOD sent* him into *Egypt, to save* their *Lives by a great Deliverance.* Thus (k) *his Kingdom ruleth over all.* (l) His *Works* are *manifold*, and *made in Wisdom*; and *the Earth is full of* his *Riches.* (m) *All things continue according to* his *Ordinances*; and *all are* his *Servants.* (n) His *Eyes are in every place, beholding the Evil and the Good.* (o) He *is righteous in all his Ways, and holy in all his Works.* (p) He *is wonderful in Counsel, and excellent in working.* (q) He *upholdeth all things by the Word of his Power.* (r) He *led his People through the Wilderness, to make himself a glorious Name.* (s) His *Eyes run to and fro throughout the whole Earth.* (t) He *worketh all things after the Counsel of his own Will.* And (u) as *all things are of him, and to him, and through him*; so *to* him must the *Glory* of all *be* ascribed *for ever and ever.* But the *Players* say of a remarkable Story, (x) It is *as the Devil would have it*; or (y) *just as Luck hits, or the Devil would have it.* If any thing happens more than ordinary, (z) the *Devil is in it*;

(e) *Mat.* 10. 29.
(f) *Mat.* 10. 30.
(g) *Prov.* 16. 33.
(h) *Gen.* 48. 15.
(i) *Gen.* 45. 7.
(k) *Psal.* 103. 19.
(l) *Psal.* 104. 24.
(m) *Psal.* 119. 21.
(n) *Prov.* 15. 3.
(o) *Psal.* 145. 17.
(p) *Isa.* 28. 29.
(q) *Heb.* 1. 3.
(r) *Isa.* 63. 14.
(s) *Zech.* 4. 10.
(t) *Ephes.* 1. 11.
(u) *Rom.* 11. 36.
(x) The *Gotham* Election, p. 28. l. 18.
(y) The Perplex'd Couple, p. 18. l. 21.
(z) Love in a Sack, p. 36. l. 12. Marplot, p. 55. l. 15. *Sawny* the *Scot*, p. 19. l. 1. The Amorous Widow, p. 7. l. 5.

it; and thus he is represented as one, who orders all things. According to the *Play-House* Language he is (*a*) our *Director* in Difficulties, our (*b*) *Protector* in Dangers, and (*c*) one who *cures the Wounds of* our *disorder'd Souls*. He (*d*) *provides a Wife* for one who is single, and (*e*) orders the Affairs of Life and Death. When a Man escapes Dangers, (*f*) *the Devil is in him* to assist him in his Flight, or (*g*) he is said to *deal with* this infernal *Fiend*. And hence the *Devils* are call'd (*h*) *assisting Furies*. When an *Actor* hath good Success, this Observation is made; (*i*) *I see the Devil doth stand his Friend*; or, (*k*) *Sure he can conjure, and hath the Devil for his* Assistant; or else (*l*) it is said to be like the *Devil*.

When any thing is prevented, either (*m*) *the Devil is in it*, or (*n*) *the Devil would not suffer it*. When Success is hoped for, they say, (*o*) *It may be so*, or (*p*) *Matters go rarely, if no Devil cross it*. And when a Man acts amiss, there is this Excuse, (*q*) *What could I do? The Devil* was concerned to bring it about, *and who could help it?*

And now, (*r*) if GOD will not suffer his *Glory* to be

The Beaux Stratagem, p. 27. l. 14. p. 54. l. 7. The City Ramble, or the Play-House Wedding, p. 56. *l. antepenult*. The Double Gallant, p. 45. l. 12. The Man's bewitch'd, p. 61. l. 24. The Perplex'd Couple, p. 39. l. 4. Wit without Money, p. 58. l. *ult*.

(*a*) *Pyrrhus* and *Demetrius*, p. 42. l. 14.

(*b*) Ibid. p. 42. l. 17.

(*c*) *Pyrrhus* and *Demetrius*, p. 42. l. 16. Rinaldo, p. 11. l. 25.

(*d*) The Artful Husband, p. 3. l. 22.

(*e*) The *Persian* Princess, p. 19. l. 25.

(*f*) Love in a Wood, p. 24. l. 24. The Amorous Widow, p. 54. *l. penult*. The Litigants, p. 24. l. 9.

(*g*) Marplot, p. 13. l. 13.

(*h*) Ajax, *Act* 4. *Verse* 23.

(*i*) The Perplex'd Couple, p. 53. l. 10.

(*k*) Wit without Money, p. 44. l. 23.

(*l*) The Platonick Lady, p. 21. l. 4.

(*m*) The Beaux Stratagem, p. 27. l. 14. The Platonick Lady, p. 63. l. 11.

(*n*) The Platonick Lady, p. 26. l. 16.

(*o*) The Man's bewitch'd, p. 3. l. 26.

(*p*) The Platonick Lady, p. 58. l. 7.

(*q*) The Successful Pirate, p. 43. l. 27.

(*r*) *Isa*. 42. 8.

given

given to another, and (*s*) is a *jealous GOD*; how can we expect he will endure that we should ascribe his *Attributes* and *Works* to the *Devil*, and not make us feel the severest Marks of his Displeasure, unless we prevent it by a speedy Reformation?

But the Inferences made from hence in the *Play-House* are most dreadful and amazing. The first is, the ascribing of our Success to the *Devil*. From the Consideration of GOD's *Providence*, the *Psalmist* speaks in this holy Rapture; (*t*) *The LORD also will be a Refuge for the Oppressed, a Refuge in time of Trouble. And they that know thy Name will put their Trust in thee: for thou, LORD, hast never failed them that seek thee.* But the Inference which the Players make, is, (*u*) That *the Devil never fail'd a Woman at a pinch.*

The other Impiety, which flows from this Topick, is the owning the *Devil* as a GOD, and treating him with the same Reverence and Esteem, which is mention'd in the Scriptures as proper to the true GOD, and *vowing* something to him in Adversity, and paying the same in Prosperity. The Consideration of GOD's *Providence* to us in Dangers, and his delivering us from them, hath occasion'd these Duties to be paid to him alone in *Scripture*. To this purpose there are several Directions in (*x*) the *Mosaical Law*. Besides, this was the Practice of (*y*) several before the Time of *Moses*. A *Vow* was made by (*z*) *Jacob*, which (*a*) GOD accepted, and (*b*) required the performance of it. This was a Duty under the Law, practised by (*c*) the whole Nation of the *Israelites* in general, and particularly by (*d*) *Jephthah*, (*e*) *Hannah*, (*f*) *David*, (*g*) *Jonah*, and

(*s*) *Exod.* 20. 5.
(*t*) *Psal.* 9. 9, 10.
(*u*) The Wonder, p. 72. l. 34.
(*x*) *Levit.* 7. 16. & 22. 18, 21, 22, 23. & 23. 38. & 27. 2——28. *Numb.* 6. 1——22. & 15. 3, 8. & *chap.* 30. *Deut.* 12. 6, 11, 17, 26. & 23. 18, 19, 20, 21, 22, 23.
(*y*) *Job* 22. 27.
(*z*) *Gen.* 28. 20.
(*a*) *Gen.* 31. 13.
(*b*) *Gen.* 35. 1.
(*c*) *Numb.* 21. 2.
(*d*) *Judges* 11. 30, 39.
(*e*) 1 *Sam.* 1. 11, 21.
(*f*) *Psal.* 22. 25. & 56. 12. & 61. 5, 8. & 66. 13. & 116. 14. 18. & 132. 2.
(*g*) *Jonah* 2. 9.

(*h*) others; and not only by the *Jews*, but by (*i*) the very *Heathens*; and laſtly, by (*k*) the *Chriſtians* in the *Apoſtles* Days. The *Prophets* (*l*) ſpoke frequently of it, and (*m*) conſtantly inſiſted on the Performance thereof to GOD alone.

When GOD delivered the ten Commandments to the *Iſraelites*, the *Preface* ran thus; (*n*) *I am the LORD thy GOD, who brought thee out of the Land of* Egypt, *out of the Houſe of Bondage:* and the firſt *Commandment* follows thereupon; (*o*) Therefore ſaith GOD, *Thou ſhalt have no other Gods before me.* And *Hezekiah* praying, hath this Expreſſion; (*p*) *O LORD of Hoſts, GOD of* Iſrael, *that dwelleſt between the Cherubims, art not thou GOD, even thou alone? Now therefore, O LORD our GOD, ſave us, that all the Kingdoms of the Earth may know that thou art the LORD, even thou only.* And even before the Time of the Law, (*q*) *Jacob* in his Neceſſity *vowed a Vow, ſaying, If GOD will be with me, and will keep me in the way that I ſhall go, and will give me Bread to eat, and Rayment to put on, ſo that I come unto my Father's Houſe in peace; then ſhall the LORD be my GOD.*

But the *Players* ſpeak of the *Devil* as *all-knowing:*

> (*r*) *Theſe Infernals*
> *By a dire Contract with the* Stygian *Gods,*
> *From ſtalking Ghoſts extort th' uncertain Knowledge*
> *Of hid Futurity.*
> (*s*) *Theſe Spirits ſee into the latent Seeds*
> *Of Time, and know th' unripe Event of things.*

They are acknowledged by the *Actors* as (*t*) *all-kind*, as *powerful* Beings, who help us, and (*u*) as Gods.

(*h*) 2 *Sam.* 15. 7, 8.
(*i*) *Jonah* 1. 16.
(*k*) *Acts* 18. 18. & 21. 23.
(*l*) *Prov.* 7. 14. & 20. 25. & 31. 2. *Mal.* 1. 14.
(*m*) *Pſal.* 50. 14. & 65. 1. *Eccleſ.* 5. 4. *Iſa.* 19. 21. *Jer.* 44. 25.
(*n*) *Exod.* 20. 2.
(*o*) *Exod.* 20. 3.
(*p*) *Iſa.* 37. 16, 20.
(*q*) *Gen.* 28. 20, 21.
(*r*) The *Perſian* Princeſs, *p.* 27. *l.* 8.
(*s*) Ibid. *p.* 27. *l. antepenult.*
(*t*) Ibid. *p.* 28. *l.* 12.
(*u*) The *Perſian* Princeſs, *p.* 8. *l.* 3. The *Britiſh* Enchanters, *p.* 12. *l.* 22.

For these reasons they are pray'd to in such Language as this (*x*):

> *Help now, ye Powers, whether from Heaven or Hell,*
> *Descend, ascend, I care not.*
> (*y*) *Tell me, ye Infernals.*

For these Reasons the *Actors* vow to them in Difficulties, they own the *Devil* as a *God*, and make a Compact with him for the gratifying of their *Revenge*; and lest Men should be ignorant how to ruin their Souls to all Eternity, this (*z*) *blasphemous Sentence* is spoken for their Imitation:

> *See it perform'd,——and thou shalt be,*
> *Dire Instrument of Hell, a God to me.*

[From Hardness of Heart, and *from such a* Contempt of thy Word, and *especially of thy first* Commandment, Good LORD deliver us.]

And when such *Compacts* or *Vows* are made, then the *Devil* frequently expects the Performance, as an *Actor* assures his Votaries (*a*) in these words:

> ——*Sir, the infernal Powers exact*
> *The Tribute, you by solemn Oath declar'd*
> *To pay their Deities.*

And this Tribute is no less than an *Hecatomb of Slaves*, which perhaps may be as many as there are *Actors* in the *Play-House*.

It cannot be deny'd, but sometimes the word *Providence* is taken in a good Sense upon the *Stage*, and can signify only GOD himself. Thus one saith, (*b*) that *Providence disapproves* of his *Choice*, and therefore he

---

(*x*) Jane Gray, *p*. 16. *l*. 4.

(*y*) The Faithful Bride of *Granada*, *p*. 55. *l*. 20.

(*z*) The *British* Enchanters, *p*. 12. *l*. 22.

(*a*) The *Persian* Princess, *p*. 8. *l*. 1.

(*b*) The Perplex'd Couple, *p*. 18. *l*. 3.

must not proceed. Another saith, (c) *For our Good, kind Providence provides.* Thus the things that are here below, are call'd (d) *the Work,* and (e) *the Care of Providence,* even (f) of *eternal Providence.* But then such Expressions make others wound the deeper, and aggravate the Crime, when *Providence* is burlesqu'd and ridicul'd. Thus *Sots* also (g) speak of a *Providential Bottle,* and add, (h) *The Man is providentially drunk, and that's enough.* In one *Play* an (i) *Actor* speaking of an Intrigue for *Adultery,* and persuading the Husband with a Bribe to consent, urges this as an Argument; *See, there's a Providence in it, which nothing can resist.* Another exposing a Fop, throws dirt at our *Creator,* and saith, (k) *How careful is Nature in furnishing the World with necessary Coxcombs?*

But the Inference which is made from hence, is most amazing; namely, the blaming of GOD for all the *Miscarriages* and *Faults* which happen in the World, and excusing all our Sins, because he might have prevented them if he would. When things succeed well, the *Devil* goes off with the Honour; and when things succeed ill, the Cause of all the Mischief is ascribed to GOD. This was a Crime peculiar (l) to one, who (m) lived not to see the Happiness foretold. And it is observable, that holy *Job* (n) who was *perfect and upright, one that feared GOD, and eschewed Evil,* (o) resisted all Temptations of this nature, and *in* the midst of *all* his Miseries (p) he *sinned not,* by *charging GOD foolishly* for what he suffer'd. This is a Crime which chills the Blood when we think of it, and makes the Hand tremble whilst we describe it. When our first Parents sinn'd, *Adam* laid the

---

(c) The Platonick Lady, p. 72. l. 29.

(d) The Fatal Marriage, p. 118. l. 10.

(e) The Faithful Bride of *Granada,* p. 33. l. 11.

(f) Love and Liberty, p. 46. l. 12.

(g) Love at first sight, p. 52. l. 27.

(h) Ibid. p. 52. l. 32.

(i) Love the Leveller, p. 8. l. 12.

(k) The Man of Mode, p. 187. l. 18.

(l) 2 *Kings* 6. 33.

(m) 2 *Kings* 7. 2, 19, 20.

(n) *Job* 1. 1.

(o) *Job* 2. 9, 10.

(p) *Job* 1. 22.

blame

blame upon *Eve*, and *Eve* upon the *Devil*, and neither of these durst lay the blame upon GOD. But here it is remarkable, that tho each of them did wickedly in excusing themselves; yet in this respect our present *Stage* exceeds them all. One (*q*) speaking of *Lust* in a marry'd Woman to commit *Adultery*, softens it with the name of *Love*, and saith, *He that creates Love, if it was so bad a thing, no doubt he would prevent it.* Thus GOD is blam'd for our Miscarriages, and the Fault laid on him, but not on ourselves.

Another saith, (*r*) *If Heaven would have had Men more virtuous and chaste, it should have made Women less charming.*

Another saith, (*s*) *If we confine ourselves to one Woman, our Honour is not safe; if we run at all, our Health's in danger: yet busy Nature will not permit us a Neutrality.*

Another saith, (*t*) *Nature is very pitiful to Whores, in giving them few Children, and these Plurality of Fathers.*

I have spoken too much concerning these detestable Sins, and the most detestable Method which the *Poets* take to excuse them. The Reader may observe by the following Quotations how they vilify the *Attributes* of GOD, and even fly at his face upon other occasions.

(*u*) *For shame, ye Pow'rs, give o'er your Providence,*
And let this little Globe of Earth become
A Play-thing to be toss'd about by Fortune.
Chance may connive at Villains, murder'd Kings,
And Usurpation, yet be well excus'd;
Because it wants the Thunder to revenge:
But Heav'n, that has the Power to redress,
In an Extreme of Mercy blasts its Justice.

(*x*) *Why was that Coxcomb* (an elder Brother) *thrust into the World before me? O Fortune! Fortune! thou art a Bitch, by GOD.*

(*q*) The Roving Husband reclaim'd, *p.* 19. *l. penult.*

(*r*) The Humours of the Age, *p.* 27. *l.* 20.

(*s*) Injur'd Love, *a Comedy*, *p.* 30. *l.* 21.

(*t*) Injur'd Love, *a Tragedy*, *p.* 9. *l.* 31.

(*u*) The *Persian* Princess, *p.* 43. *l.* 1.

(*x*) The Relapse, *p.* 6. *l.* 25.

(y) *Nature hath made ſome difference between you and I.* Anſw. *Yes, ſhe hath made you older: Pox take her.*

(z) *You want a noble Birth.* Anſw. *That's Nature's fault.*

Here we may obſerve the Language of *Hell* with its utmoſt Virulence, even *blaming*, *blaſpheming*, and *curſing* GOD himſelf. The words are enough to infect the Air, and breed the *Plague* in a City where they are uttered. I ſhall add but one Inſtance more of the Treatment which our holy GOD meets with upon the *Stage*, and that is, the repreſenting him as the *Author* of *Sin*. One ſaith, (a) that this was the very Deſign of our Creation, and Men muſt be contented when the Marriage-Bed is diſhonour'd, it being a thing inevitable. For

Woman was form'd to cheat her Tyrant Man.

And in another *Comedy* we have this Expreſſion concerning *Adultery*;

(b) *Never think 'tis a Sin; of a truth I do know*
'Tis the Will of the Fates, and they will have it ſo.

I ſhall add but one Quotation more, where the *Poet* treats our *Maker* in ſuch *Billinſgate* Language, that I leave the Reader to judge if the *Devils* themſelves could have invented any thing more blaſphemous:

(c) *When the World firſt knew Creation,*
A Rogue was a top Profeſſion.

In the Beginning of the *Creation*, even upon the *firſt* Day, there was no rational Being except GOD, whoſe Employment was then to make the World out of nothing. Upon the ſixth Day (d) *GOD ſaw every thing*

(y) The Relapſe, *p.* 28. *l.* 10.
(z) The Wonder, *p.* 2. *l.* 16.
(a) Gibraltar, *Epilogue*, *l.* 9.
(b) The Roving Husband reclaim'd, *p.* 59. *l.* 7.
(c) Don Quixot, *p.* 37. *This Song (to make it more publick) is alſo repeated in* The Pills to purge Melancholy, *Vol.* 3. *p.* 182.
(d) *Gen.* 1. 31.

that

that he had made, and behold it was very good. And therefore what a Compliment this is to the Maker of Heaven and Earth, concerning what he did *in the first Beginning* of the World, I tremble to think. And now that the Words must be restrain'd to that very Time, appears from the following Verses:

> *When there was no more in all Nature but four,*
> *There were two of them in Transgression.*

All Expositors upon the Articles of our *Creed* agree, that by *Christ's Descent* into *Hell* is not meant his being buried, because a Tautology in so short an Epitome would be most absurd. And for the same reason, we cannot think, that in this little Song, which contains the History of the World from the beginning to the end, the two first Strains should be cotemporary: and therefore, as the latter speaks of *Adam*'s Fall, which (e) is allow'd to be on the *sixth* Day of the *Creation*; so the other speaks of something which happen'd before, even at the first Beginning, and that not as accidentally, but a settled *Profession*, Purpose, or Design.

In these last words the *Poet* makes a Jest of the *Fall*, and rails upon *Adam* and *Eve*, according to the usual Language of the *Stage*. He might easily have seen that the Fall of our first Parents was before the Birth of *Cain* and *Abel*; but I suppose, that he desired no more Knowledge of the *Scriptures*, but what might serve to expose them.

Thus we see, how the *Poet* speaks of the Works of *Creation*; let us next inquire how he speaks of the Works of *Providence*. Accordingly, he burlesques what GOD did, and is willing to teach the *all-wise Being* what he ought to have done.

> *He who first, to mend the matter,*
> *Made Laws to bind our Nature,*
> *Should have found the way*
> *To make Wills obey,*
> *And have modelled the new Creature.*

(e) *See* Lightfoot, *Vol.* 2. *p.* 1323, 1324.

Accordin g

According to this, all the *Scripture*-Rules are a Jeſt. The way for Men to be better, was for GOD to have made them better at firſt. And if you ask, why GOD did not take the *Poet's* Direction in this Caſe? he hath already very audaciouſly told the Reaſon; becauſe

When the World firſt knew Creation,
A Rogue was a top Profeſſion.

This is a *daring Blaſphemy*, which every one who hears or reads muſt be amaz'd at; and no one could imagine that any *Creature* could preſume to charge his *Creator* at ſuch a rate. But it is too evident, that the literal Senſe of the *Poem*, and the Coherence of the whole, will naturally bear the vileſt Conſtruction.

It muſt be own'd, that no one, who hath any Senſe of Religion, could without plain Proof imagine, that any *Creature* on this ſide *Hell* can be guilty of ſuch aggravating and complicated *Blaſphemies*. They are ſo daring, that I believe the like was never heard or ſuffer'd before, eſpecially in a Chriſtian Nation. Our *Engliſh* Stage at firſt was much more modeſt and cautious; and then went on to leſſer Crimes. But Length of Time brought in this Corruption by degrees; and it being unpuniſh'd at firſt, the *Poets* ſeem to ſtrive ever ſince, who ſhall carry this *Profaneneſs* to the higheſt pitch. And he is but a dull *Poet* in this Age, who cannot carry on the War againſt Heaven, and ſet GOD at defiance. Theſe Expreſſions are a Scandal to our Nation, and many may think, that they ought to be concealed for ſhame. But whilſt they are as publick as the *Stage* or *Preſs* can make them, and are the Diverſion of others; I hope I may be pardon'd for ſuch Quotations, the only Deſign being to excite a juſt Indignation againſt them.

How far the *Poet* ridicules the *Scripture*-Notion of Converſion, and the *(f)* Saying of St. *Paul*, That *if any Man be in Chriſt, he is a new Creature*, let others judge. It will be too tedious to examine every Particular.

(*f*) 2 *Cor.* 5. 17.

Imme-

Immediately upon this, the *Poet* either falls foul upon the Doctrine of *Original Sin*, and from thence excuseth all actual Transgressions; or else he lays the whole Blame upon GOD, who might have made us better. The words will bear both Constructions.

For the Savage in Man
From th' Original ran,
And in spite of Confinement now reigns as't began.

To prevent this, GOD was pleased to endue us with *Reason*, and give us his *Word* and *Ordinances*. He affords us the *Means* of *Grace*, and promiseth *Grace* in the use of the *Means* to recover us out of this Condition. But this (saith the *Poet*) he might have let alone. 'Tis all but *Trick*, *Cheat* and *Juggle*. It signifies nothing, and was designed only to excuse our Maker.

Here's Preaching and Praying, and Reason displaying;
Yet Brother with Brother is killing and slaying.

The Conclusion follows:

Then blame not the Rogue, who free Sense doth enjoy;
That falls like a Log, and believes he shall lie.

He that dies like a Beast, and believes that he shall rise again no more, is very much in the *Poet*'s Favour. And when Men are guilty of the vilest Enormities, the *Poets* would not have us blame them, but blame the GOD that made them, because he did not make them better.

And now, if we should ask the Apostle's Question, (g) *Shall the thing formed say to him that formed it, Why hast thou made me thus?* It may soon be answer'd, That the *English Poets* are arriv'd to this daring height of Impudence, as to quarrel with GOD upon this account, and give him the vilest Character of Reproach for all his pains.

(g) *Rom.* 9. 20.

Thus

Thus we see that these Performances are such, which no Pen is able to describe, and no Christian can sufficiently detest. These Insolencies have for a long time cried for Vengeance. They defy the GOD of Heaven. They dare him to do his worst; and they so provoke him to send the fiercest of his Wrath upon a distracted Nation, that without a speedy Repentance, we can expect nothing but Destruction.

CHAP. XX.

The Holy Scriptures burlesqu'd by the Stage.

IN our *Church-Catechism* we are told, that our *Duty to GOD is, to honour his holy Name, and his Word*; and therefore, as I have shewn the Honour which the *Actors* pay to the one, so I shall give some Instances of that which they pay to the other.

As in all Arts and Sciences, so in *Divinity*, there are several Words which by custom are appropriated thereunto. And these are generally such Words as are frequently found in *Scripture*, (however I shall take notice of no other) and therefore before I speak of particular Texts, I shall first speak of such Words as are generally used in *Scripture*, and appropriated to a sacred Meaning: and then omitting such *Texts* which have been already mentioned, I shall add some more, in which either the *Name* of GOD is most solemnly mentioned, some weighty Duty pressed, some necessary Doctrine proposed, or where the Honour of GOD is more directly opposed in the *Play-house*.

The first Word which I shall mention, is *Adoration*. This is allowed by all to be a *Religious* Worship due to GOD alone. In the *Play-house*, it is frequently referred (a) to *Women*, and sometimes to Men, and even upon trifling Occasions.

(a) Man of Mode, *Epilogue*, 39. *Persian* Princess, *p.*4. *l.*4. *l.*27. The Masquerade, *p.*24. *l.*

But

But to proceed: By (*b*) *Agony* is usually meant the great Sufferings of our *Blessed* LORD and *Saviour* in the Garden before his Crucifixion. This is frequently (*c*) mentioned in the paltry Concerns of the *Stage*, and not only (*d*) the *Agonies of Death*, but also (*e*) of a *Lover*, (*f*) upon a Report of another kill'd, or (*g*) for a Charge upon another; and also (*h*) *the very Agony of good Breeding*, signifies no more than for a Woman to make herself ridiculous with affected Words.

An *Altar* in *Scripture* was a place built by the Appointment of GOD to offer *Sacrifices* upon; and as it was a Type, so (*i*) *we*, who are *Christians*, *have an Altar*, even *Christ Jesus*, by whom we are to *offer the Sacrifice of Praise to GOD continually*. Upon the *Stage* it is (*k*) the *Altar* of a Man's *fierce Revenge*.

An *Atonement* in *Scripture* is something to appease the Wrath of GOD conceived against Sin, which (*l*) was *made* by the *Priests* in the *Jewish* Law. And therefore among us *Christians*, (*m*) *we receive the Atonement*, *by our LORD Jesus Christ*. The word upon the *Stage* is (*n*) commonly used in *Love-Intrigues*, and in other ridiculous and trifling matters.

Blas-

(*b*) *Luke* 22. 44.

(*c*) The faithful General, *p*.59. *l*. 34. The Maid's the Mistress, *p*. 23. *l*. 3. Modish Husband, *Prologue*, *l*. 7. Royal Convert, *p*.67. *l*.24. The Victim, *p*.61. *l*.24. Ulysses, *p*.27. *l*.1. *p*.49. *l*. 20.

(*d*) Rinaldo, *p*.20. *l*.1. The faithful Bride of *Granada*, *p*.51. *l*.30. Rival Brothers, *p*.93.*l*.15. Ulysses, *p*. 50. *l*.27.

(*e*) Fair Quaker of *Deal*, *p*. 41. *l*.5.

(*f*) Ibid. *p*.3. *l*.3.

(*g*) Ibid. *p*.45. *l*.1.

(*h*) Comical Lovers, *p*.69. *l*.7.

(*i*) *Heb*. 13. 10, 15.

(*k*) Rinaldo, *p*.31. *l*.8.

(*l*) *Levit*.4.20,26,31,35. *Levit*.5.6,10,13,16,18. *Levit*. 6.7. *Levit*.12.8. *Levit*.14.18,19,20, 21,29,31. *Levit*.15.15,30. *Lev*. 16.6,30,32. *Levit*. 19. 30, 32. *Num*.15.15,28.

(*m*) *Rom*. 5.11.

(*n*) *Phædra* and *Hippolytus*, *p*.28. *l*.25. *p*.59. *l*.5. Jane Gray, *p*.39. *l*.34. *p*.49. *l*.13. The Apparition, *p*.64. *l*.23. Beaux Stratagem, *p*.36. *l*.9. Ernelinda, *p*. 5. *l*. 10. Hamlet, *p*. 18. *l*. 24. Hydaspes, *p*.74. *l*. *penult*. Jane Shore, *p*.17. *l*.14. Injur'd Love, *a Comedy*, *p*.60. *l*.12. Love and Liberty, *p*.17. *l*.10. *p*.44. *l*. *antepenult*. The fair Example, *p*. 60. *l*.32. Faithful General, *Epilogue*,

Blasphemy in *Scripture* (*o*) usually signifies some words spoken against the Majesty and Dignity of GOD. Upon the *Stage*, (*p*) this Question is asked, *How darest thou blaspheme the Honour of a Soldier?*

In the old Law, GOD appointed *Circumcision* as (*q*) a *Token of the Covenant* between him and his People, and therefore the *Apostle* applies the word itself (*r*) to *Christians* also. This word is (*s*) exposed upon the *Stage*, as a Mark of a foul Distemper; and another (*t*) saith in Derision, *I'll circumcise the Dog.*

The Notion of *Conversion* among Divines, is a turning from *Sin* unto GOD, or from *Paganism* to *Christianity*; and (*u*) the *Scriptures* favour the same. Sometimes the word is spoken (*x*) in Derision, sometimes it signifies being in Love, when the Woman is represented as GOD; and sometimes it signifies turning from *Religion* to a Course of *Sin*, as appears from the following Expressions.

(*y*) *Her Beauty will make thy Joys immortal.* Answ. *I can't believe either in the Immortality of her Beauty, or your Passion.* Reply, *Look on her then, and be converted.*

---

logue, *l*.23. *p*.9. *l*.36. *p*.18. *l*.36. *p*.63. *l*.17. *p*.67. *l*.13. *p*.70. *l*.8. Female Wits, *p*.66. *l. antepenult.* The Maid's the Mistress, *p*.23. *l*.3. Man of Mode, *p*.229. *l*. 13. Modern Prophets, *p*. 66. *l*. 4. Platonick Lady, *p*.64. *l*.2. Thomyris, *p*. 10. *l*.21. Vice reclaim'd, *p*.34. *l*.14. Ulysses, *p*.27. *l*.17. *p*.63. *l*.9. Zelmane, *p*.40. *l*.28. *p*.54. *l*.14. *Persian* Princess, *p*. 5. *l*. 22.

(*o*) *Levit.* 24.11,16. 2 *Kings* 19.6,22. *Psal.*74.10,18. *Isa.*37. 6,23. *Isa.*52.5. *Isa.*65.7. *Ezek.* 20.27. *Matth.* 12.31. *Mark* 3. 28,29. *Luke* 12. 10. *Rom.*2.24. 1 *Tim.*6.1. *Tit.*2.5. *James* 2.7. *Revel.*13.6. *Rev.* 16 9,11,21.

(*p*) Female Advocates, *p*. 17. *l. penult.*

(*q*) *Gen.* 17. 10, 11, 12, 13, 14.

(*r*) *Philip*.3. 3. *Coloss.* 2.11.

(*s*) Sir Courtly Nice, *Epilogue*, *l*.34. The Country House, *p*. 17. *l*.28. The Wife's Relief, *p*.35. *l*. 29.

(*t*) Hampstead-Heath, *p*. 33. *l* 4.

(*u*) *Psal.* 51. 13. *Isa.* 6. 10. *Isa.*60.5. *Matth.*13.15. *Matth.* 18.3. *Mark* 4.12. *Luke* 22. 32. *John* 12. 40. *Acts* 15. 3. *Acts* 3. 19. *Acts* 28.27. *Jam.* 3. 10. *Jam.* 5. 19.

(*x*) The different Widows, *p*. 35. *l*. 18. Man of Mode, *p*.187. *l*. 3. Woman is a Riddle, *p*.41. *l*. 29.

(*y*) The Country Lasses, *p*.41. *l*. 4.

I

(z) *I was an Infidel, till you converted me.*
(a) *I'm converted, I'm convinced, I'll go to a Wench immediately.*

Despair (b) usually signifies to have no hope of GOD's Favour. In the *Play-house* it signifies (c) to have no hope of a Mistress's Favour.

A (d) *devout Man* is one who dischargeth his Duty to GOD. In the *Play-house* (e) *Devotion* either relates to a *Mistress*, or signifies a Resolution to commit Adultery.

Divine (f) signifies something belonging to GOD. In the *Play-house* (g) *Divinity* is applied to *whoring*, or (h) else to Men, and (i) to one of an ordinary Character.

In (k) several places of *Scripture* there is mention made of *Edification*, as the Design and End of all, but especially of our religious Actions. Upon the *Stage* we are told of (l) *rich edifying Smoak*, or (*) Cherry-Brandy; (m) *whistling to Horses*, that they may *edify*. It is (n) spoken on a ridiculous occasion, and (o) sometimes it only signifies Success in a whoring Intrigue.

In *Scripture*, *Faith in Christ* is frequently pressed upon us as (p) the chief thing necessary to Salvation; and

---

(z) Vice Reclaim'd, *p.* 55. *l.* 32.
(a) Modern Prophets, *p.* 63. *l. penult.*
(b) 2 *Cor.* 4. 8.
(c) Double Gallant, *p.* 60. *l.* 9. Faithful General, *p.* 28. *l.* 51.
(d) *Luke* 2. 25. *Act.* 2. 5. *Act.* 8. 2. *Act.* 10. 2, 7. *Act.* 13. 50. *Act.* 17. 4, 17. *Act.* 22. 12.
(e) Love the Leveller, *p.* 19. *l. antepenult.* She wou'd if she cou'd, *p.* 97. *l.* 34. *p.* 107. *l.* 12. *p.* 138. *l.* 17.
(f) *Heb.* 9. 1. 2 *Pet.* 1. 3, 4.
(g) Humours of the Age, *p.* 27. *l. penult.*
(h) Cato, *p.* 37. *l.* 33. Modern Prophets, *p.* 65. *l. ult.*
(i) Sir Courtly Nice, *p.* 48. *l.* 4.
(k) *Rom.* 14. 19. *Rom.* 15. 2. 1 *Cor.* 8. 1. 1 *Cor.* 10. 23. 1 *Cor.* 14. 3, 4, 5, 12, 26. 2 *Cor.* 10. 8. 2 *Cor.* 12. 19. 2 *Cor.* 13. 10. *Eph.* 4. 12, 16, 29. 1 *Thess.* 5. 11. 1 *Tim.* 1. 4.
(l) The Wonders of the Sun, *p.* 13. *l.* 18.
(*) Squire of *Alsatia*, *p.* 60. *l.* 37.
(m) Wit without Money, *p.* 5. *l.* 14.
(n) The Quacks, *p.* 17. *l. penult.*
(o) The Wonder, *p.* 50. *l.* 2.
(p) *Mark* 16. 16. *Act.* 16. 31. *Act.* 20. 21. *Act.* 24. 24. *Rom.* 3. 22, 25. *Gal.* 2. 16, 20. *Phil.* 3. 9. 2 *Tim.* 3. 15. *Heb.* 12. 2. *Rev.* 14. 12.

an

(*q*) an *Infidel* is one who doth not believe the Doctrines of *Christianity*. Upon the *Stage*, the words (*r*) *Faith*, (*s*) to believe, and (*t*) an *Unbeliever*, are applied either to trifling Matters, or amorous Intrigues, where a Woman is the Object of all. Thus they alſo uſe the word (*u*) *Infidel*. Perhaps ſome Quotations may bear the Light on this occaſion.

(*x*) *An Infidel to all Finery.*

(*y*) *He's grown ſuch an Atheiſt of late, he'll believe nothing*, in trifling matters.

(*z*) *Gold! I'll not believe it.* Anſw. *Periſh then in thy Infidelity.*

(*a*) *I was an Infidel* (to a Woman) *till you converted me.*

The word *Hail* in *Scripture* is an Expreſſion uſed to ſignify a great Eſteem. It was (*b*) uſed by *Chriſt* himſelf to his Diſciples after his *Reſurrection*, and (*c*) by the *Angel* to the Virgin *Mary*, when he brought the News of *Chriſt's Conception*. Upon the *Stage* it is given to (*d*) *Men*, in ſuch Language as this:

(*e*) *Hail to the King of Kings, great* Agamemnon:
Or, *All Hail*, Triumpher, Saviour of the State.

Sometimes it is given (*f*) to other Creatures, ſometimes to (*g*) *Pagan Deities*, and (*h*) ſometimes to the *Devil*.

(*q*) 2 *Cor*.6.15. 1 *Tim*.5.8.

(*r*) Marplot, *p*.56. *l*.26. The Apparition, *p*. 35. l. 4. Artful Husband, *p*.10.l.30. *p*.28. *l*.21. The Cid, *p*.3. l. 10. Provok'd Wife, *p*.67. l.1. Roving Husband reclaim'd, *p*.43. *l*.19. The Wonder, *p*.40. *l*.27.

(*s*) Artful Husband, *p*.10. *l*. 32, 33. The Wife's Relief, *p*. 14. *l*.30.

(*t*) Injur'd Love, *a Tragedy*, *p*.17. *l*.17.

(*u*) The Apparition, *p*.48. *l*. 17. Artful Husband, *p*.28. *l*.18. The Wonder, *p*.18. *l*. 5. Vice reclaim'd, *p*.11. *l*.13.

(*x*) Double Gallant, *p*. 29. *l*. 1.

(*y*) Provok'd Wife, *p*.66. *l*. *penult*.

(*z*) The Wife's Relief, *p*.14. *l*. 30.

(*a*) Vice reclaim'd, *p*. 55. *l*. 32.

(*b*) *Matth*. 28. 9.

(*c*) *Luke* 1. 28.

(*d*) The Victim, *p*.7. *l*.6. *p*.11. *l*. 25.

(*e*) The Victim, *p*.4. *l*. *ult*.

(*f*) Lucius, *p*.33. *l*.4.

(*g*) *Venus* and *Adonis*, *p*. 1. *l*. 1.

(*h*) Metamorphoſis, *p*.14.

To

To be *Incomprehensible*, is one of the *Attributes* of GOD. Upon the *Stage* they ſay (*i*) *an incomprehenſible Coxcomb.*

To be (*k*) *Infinite* is alſo another of his *Attributes*. This word is often (*l*) uſed in very inconſiderable matters. The hopes of being married is called (*m*) an *infinite Joy*. A Woman is not only ſaid to be (*n*) *infinitely handſome*, but even (*o*) *every Glance affords an infinite variety of Charms.*

(*p*) *Juſtification* is an Act of GOD's free Grace unto Sinners, through Chriſt, in which he pardons all their Sins, and accepts of their Perſons as righteous in his ſight. Our Language is not barren of words; but yet (*q*) the *Stage* ſeem to affect this more than any other in their Concerns, when an opportunity preſents.

(*i*) Relapſe, *p.*8. *l.*22.

(*k*) *Pſal.* 147. 5.

(*l*) The Lady's Laſt Stake, p. 14. l.28. p.18. l.30. Lawyer's Fortune, p. 15. l. *antepenult.* Maſquerade, p.20. l. 14. Northern Laſs, p.6. l.3. p.21. l.13. Perplex'd Couple, p. 33. l. 28. *Portſmouth* Heireſs, p.47. l. 30. Squire of *Alſatia*, p.35. l.22. p. 59. l.23. Succeſsful Pirate, p.7. l.23. p.55. l.20. Wife of *Bath*, p.50. l.11. p.54. l.22. Wife's Relief, p.9. l.7. p.51. l.1. Three Hours after Marriage, p.14. l.22. *Tunbridge*-Walks, p. 54. l. 8. Vice reclaim'd, p.23. l.20. Woman is a Riddle, p.49. l.8. p.56. l. 4.

(*m*) Sir Courtly Nice, p. 57. l. 15.

(*n*) The Cares of Love, p.31. l. 27.

(*o*) Humours of the Age, p. 13. l.2.

(*p*) *Luke* 18.14. *Acts* 18. 39. *Rom.* 2. 13. *Rom.* 3. 4,20,24,26, 28, 30. *Rom.* 4.5,25. *Rom.* 5.1, 16, 18. *Rom.*8.30,33. 1 *Cor.* 6.11. *Gal.*2.16,17. *Gal.*3.8,11, 24. *Gal.*5.4. *Tit.*3.7.

(*q*) Injur'd Love, *a Comedy*, p. 58. l. 19. Faithful Bride of *Granada*, p. 17. l. 4. Female Wits, p. 41. l. 27. p. 50. l.14. Humours of the Army, p.65.l.2. Man of Mode, p.211. l.37. p. 252. l.33. Platonick Lady, p. 28. l.20. Provok'd Wife, p.2. l.2. Roving Husband reclaim'd, p.60. l.7. School-Boy, p.10. l. 27. Squire of *Alſatia*, p.23.l.2. Wife's Relief, p.13. l.3. The Wonder, p.52. l.9,10. p.75. l. 26, 30. p.76. l. 17. Vice reclaim'd, p.11. l.13. Wit at a Pinch, p.12. l. *penult.* p.13. l.6. Wit without Money, p.20. l.1. Woman is a Riddle, p.50. l.26. p.55. l.21. Zelmane, p. 39. l. 31. p.41. l.14.

When the *Israelites* were in the Wilderness, (r) GOD fed them with *Manna*. But to make the Miracle mean, we are told, (s) that *a Touch of* Leonora'*s Hand is like* Manna *from Heaven.*

A *Martyr* (t) signifies one who suffers a violent Death for the Cause of *Christianity.* In the *Play-house* Language, (u) *Virginity* is a *Load of Martyrdom*; and Men are said to be *Martyrs*, not only (x) *for their Country*, but also (y) to *Folly*, (z) to *Honour*, (a) for *Intriguing*, (b) *for Love*, (c) to *Good-Manners*, (d) to *Pride*, (e) for a *Secret*, and (f) for *Whoring.*

It was the peculiar Character of *Canaan*, (k) that it was *a Land flowing with Milk and Honey.* In a *Comedy*, (l) it is thus burlesqu'd; *The Land of* Canaan, *that flowed with strong Beer, and Chines of Beef.*

In the old *Law*, there is frequent mention of (m) *offering Peace-Offerings unto the LORD.* An *Actor* saith, (n) to a *Woman of Intrigue*, *To shew how I repent, take this Watch as a Peace-Offering.* And she adds on the

---

(r) *Exod.* 16. 15, 31, 33, 35. *Numb.* 11.6,7,9. *Deut.* 8. 3, 16. *Neh.* 9.20. *Psal.* 78.24. *John* 6. 31.49,58.

(s) Sir Courtly Nice, p. 48. l. 8.

(t) *Acts* 22. 20. *Revel.* 2.13. *Rev.* 17.6.

(u) City Ramble, p.40. l.21.

(x) Love and Liberty, p. 6. l. 6.

(y) The Wife's Relief, p. 15. l. 26.

(z) Faithful General, p. 49. l. 28.

(a) Marplot, p.6. l.21.

(b) Arsinoe, p.13. l.17. Gibraltar, p.45. l.29. Cruel Gift, p.56. l.3. p.60. l.18. The Force of Friendship, p.32. l.2. p.36. l.30. p.39. l.7. The Gamester, p.19. l.11. Successful Pirate, p. 24. l.13. p.26. l.7. The Wife's Relief, p.43. l.16.

(c) Sir Courtly Nice, p. 43. l. 5.

(d) *Pyrrhus* and *Demetrius*, p.31. l.20. Country Lasses, p. 69. l.8.

(e) Injur'd Love, *a Comedy*, p.56. l.1.

(f) Love for Love, p. 42. l. 3.

(k) *Exod.* 3. 8,17. *Exod.* 13. 5. *Exod.* 33. 3. *Levit.* 20. 24. *Numb.* 14.8. *Numb.* 16. 13, 14. *Deut.* 6.3. *Deut.* 11.9. *Deut.* 26. 9,15. *Deut.* 27.3. *Deut.* 31. 20. *Numb.* 13.17. *Jos.* 5.6. *Jer.* 11. 5. *Jer.* 32.22. *Ezek.* 20.6,15.

(l) Country Lasses, p. 20. l. 11.

(m) *Exod.* 20.24. *Exod.* 24.5. *Levit.* 3.1,3,6,9. *Numb.* 6.14,17, 18. *Deut.* 27.7.

(n) Roving Husband reclaim'd, p.43. l.4.

same

same occasion, (o) *No one, that hath Money, is ever despised. The best wy of shewing Faith, is by plentiful Offerings.*

Persecution (p) in *Scripture* is a suffering for Righteousness sake. In the *Play-house* (q) the Punishment is inconsiderable, and the Cause very different.

Prayer is a Duty which we owe to GOD. In the *Play-house* (r) it signifies addressing to the Ladies: and one saith (s) of an *Actress*, *If she would give ear to my Prayer*, (that is, commit Adultery) *I would make her my Saint.*

The *preaching* of the Word of GOD is (o) one of the ordinary Means of Salvation. The *Players* speak in Derision upon impertinent occasions; (u) *Sirrah! leave your Preaching.*

(x) *I don't question but you were preaching a Sermon to her.* Or,

(y) *Preach no more upon this Text; I am determin'd, and there is no hopes of my Conversion.*

Predestination is (z) the eternal Decree and Purpose of GOD concerning the Salvation of Mankind. The word is (a) applied upon the *Stage* to their Concerns. A (b) Woman *ordains* what shall happen. A (c) Whore to one is *predestin'd* to doat upon another; and (d) an accidental meeting is said to be *the very Predestination of good Fortune.*

(o) The Roving Husband reclaim'd, p.43. l.19.

(p) *Matth.*5.10,11,12. *John* 15.20. *Rom.*12.14.

(q) She wou'd if she cou'd, p.103. l.3. Man of Mode, p. 213. l.3.

(r) Abra-Mule, *Epilogue*, *l.*3. Fatal Marriage, p. 144. l.3.

(s) The Roving Husband reclaim'd, p.47. l.14.

(t) *Rom.*10.14,15,17. 1 *Cor.* 1.17,18,23,24.

(u) Love's Last Shift, p. 1. l. 1.

(x) Ibid. p.8. l. *antepenult.*

(y) Man of Mode, p. 187. l. 3.

(z) *Rom.* 8. 26, 30. *Eph.* 1. 5, 11.

(a) The Earl of *Mar* marr'd, p.20. l.1.

(b) Alexander, p.67. l. 17.

(c) A Woman's Revenge, p. 36. l.25.

(d) The Biter, p.7. l.30.

In *Scripture*, (e) *Purity* is much recommended. Our *Saviour* saith, (f) *Blessed are the pure in Heart, for they shall see GOD*; and St. *John* adds, (g) *Every one that hath this hope in him, purifieth himself, even as he is pure.* Upon the *Stage* it is said, (h) *You cannot be too pure a Temple for Love*, that is, Adultery: And not only (i) *pure*, but also (k) *purest pure*, signifies a Whore.

As *Christ Jesus* is our only *Redeemer* from Sin, Death and Hell; so the words (l) *to redeem*, and (m) *Redemption*, do usually refer to him alone, except upon the *Stage*, where they (n) affect to use the word, when they might have others, and always refer to a created Being. Besides, they have frequently this Phrase, (o) *utterly ruin'd beyond Redemption*; which I shall not strain into its worst Sense, but leave the Reader to judge of it.

(e) 2 *Sam*.22.27. *Ps*. 18.26. *Prov*.21.8. *Acts* 15.9. 2 *Cor*.6. 6. 1 *Tim*. 3. 19. 1 *Tim*. 5. 22. *Tit*.2.14. *Heb*.9.13,14,23. *Jam*. 3.17. *Jam*.4.8. 1 *Pet*.1.22.

(f) *Matth*.5.8.

(g) 1 *John*.3.3.

(h) The Roving Husband reclaim'd, p.45. l.12.

(i) Squire of *Alsatia*, p. 27. l.4,15,38. p.36. l.30.

(k) Ibid. p.56. l.15.

(l) *Luke* 1. 68. *Luke* 24. 21. *Gal*. 3. 13. *Gal*.4.5. *Tit*. 2.14. 1 *Pet*. 1. 18. *Rev*.5.9. *Rev*.14. 3, 4.

(m) *Luke* 2. 38. *Rom*. 3. 24. *Ephes*.1.7. *Coloss*.1.14. *Heb*.9. 12, 15.

(n) Love and Liberty, p. 48. l.26. Love the Leveller, p.41. l.16. p.42. l. 19. *Perolla* and *Izadora*, p. 33. l.34. p.37. l.8. p. 49. l. 29. p. 58. l. 21. She wou'd if she cou'd, p.107. l.21. *British* Enchanters, p. 29. l. 23. Conquest of *Spain*, p.38. l. 28. Fair Quaker of *Deal*, p.60. l. *penult*. The Faithful General, p. 18. l.22. p.19. l.23. The False Friend, p.59. l.23. Fatal Marriage, p.122. l.11. Humours of the Army, p.67. l.3. The Lawyer's Fortune, p.30. l. *antepenult*. The Maid's the Mistress, p.26. l.16. The Man's bewitch'd, p.42. l.3. Northern Lass, p.11. l. 19. p. 45. l. 24. Perfidious Brother, p.57. l.18. p.57. l.10. Relapse, p.50. l. *penult*. Rival Fools, p.34. l.19. p.40. l. *antepenult*. The Sultaness, p. 21. l. 7. The Victim, p. 49. l.24. Ulysses, p.62. l.36.

(o) The Apparition, p.25. l. *ult*. Busy-Body, p.45. l.22. p. 59. l.14. Double Gallant, p.1. l.10. p.36. l.34. p.76. l.4. The Gamester, p.64. l.7. Lawyer's Fortune, p. 60. l. 19. Modern Prophets, p.69. l.18. Perplex'd Lovers, p. 49. l. 9. Provok'd Wife, p.34. l.12. *Spanish* Fryar, p.7. l.27. Squire of *Alsatia*, p. 40. l. 3. The Wonder, p. 71. l. 12.

One

One *Actor* saith, (p) *Must I go into that nasty Hole, which I call'd by way of Joke the Gate of Hell?* And the Answer is, *Even thither, till you are redeem'd.* Another saith, (q) *She may redeem all yet*; meaning, by being a Whore. We are told (r) that *Play-Money is a Sacred Thing, and not to be profaned. It is consecrated to Pleasure,* and *it will be Sacrilege* to apply it otherwise. And it is a shame, that they have not the same regard for those Words, which by Use are appropriated to GOD or *Christ*.

By *Religion* (s) is meant the Way whereby GOD is worshipped. Upon the *Stage*, it signifies (t) a cunning Intrigue.

There is (u) a *Reverence* peculiarly due to the *Name* and Sanctuary of GOD. An *Actor* (x) accepting of a Present, saith, *I receive it on my Knees with Reverence and Devotion.*

The words (c) *Reprobate* and (d) *Cast-away*, do properly signify such as are rejected by GOD, and out of favour with him. In the *Play-House* (e) it is wish'd for, (f) a Master is call'd so by his Maid, and (g) it signifies one who is out of favour with the Women.

The word *Sacred* signifies something devoted to GOD; in (h) our *Plays* it is used upon trifling Occasions.

A *Sacrifice* in the *Jewish Law* (i) was a Beast slain and offered

(p) Fortune in her Wits, p. 20. l. 25.

(q) Love the Leveller, p. 21. l. 21.

(r) The Confederacy, p. 15. l. 32.

(s) *Acts* 13. 43. *Acts* 26. 5. *Gal.* 1. 13, 14. *James* 1. 26, 27.

(t) Marplot, p. 56. l. 26.

(u) *Levit.* 19. 30. & 26. 2. *Psal.* 2. 11. & 89. 7. *Heb.* 12. 28.

(x) Love the Leveller, p. 19. l. *antepenult.*

(c) *Jer.* 6. 30. *Rom.* 1. 28. 2 *Cor.* 13. 5, 6, 7. 2 *Tim.* 3. 8. *Tit.* 1. 16.

(d) 1 *Cor.* 9. 27.

(e) The Artful Husband, p. 67. l. 33.

(f) She wou'd if she cou'd, p. 133. l. 5.

(g) The Comical Lovers, p. 63. l. 36.

(h) The Faithful General, p. 30. l. 5. The Man of Mode, *Epilogue*, l. 25. The *Portsmouth* Heiress, p. 46. l. 22. The Wife's Relief, p. 32. l. 39.

(i) *Exod.* 3. 18. & 5. 3, 8, 17. & 8. 8, 25, 27, 28. & 10. 25. & 12. 27. & 13. 15. & 18. 12. *Levit.* 9. 4. *Numb.* 6, 8, 13, 19. & 29. 6.

offered unto GOD. They were all Types of *Christ*, who (*k*) is call'd *our Sacrifice*; and therefore GOD was angry when they were (*l*) offered to any other. In the *Play-House* we are pester'd with (*m*) *Victims*, and (*n*) *Sacrifices*

---

2. 5. 1 *Sam.* 16. 2. 1 *Kings* 8. 6. 2 *Kings* 17. 36. 1 *Chron.* 29. 21. 2 *Chron.* 7. 12.

(*k*) *Ephes.* 5. 2. 1 *Cor.* 5. 7.

(*l*) *Exod.* 22. 20. & 32. 8. & 34. 15. *Deut.* 32. 17. 1 *Kings* 3. 2, 3. & 11. 8. 2 *Kings* 5. 17. & 12. 3. & 14. 5. & 15. 4, 35. & 17. 35. *Levit.* 17. 7. 2 *Kings* 16. 4. 2 *Chron.* 28. 4, 23. & 33. 17, 32. *Psal.* 106. 37, 38. *Isa.* 57. 7, 8. *Ezek.* 20. 28. *Hos.* 4. 13, 14. *Hos.* 11. 2. 1 *Cor.* 8. 4. & 10. 19, 20, 28.

(*m*) Hydaspes, *p.* 14. *l.* 8. *p.* 48. *l.* 17. *p.* 52. *l.* 14. Irene, *p.* 14. *l.* 18. Love and Liberty, *p.* 9. *l.* 23. *p.* 45. *l.* 4. Love for Love, *p.* 67. *l.* 3. Marplot, *p.* 4. *l.* 34. *Cinna*'s Conspiracy, *p.* 44. *l.* 10. *p.* 49. *l.* 2. *p.* 52. *l.* 26. Ajax, *p.* 12. *l.* 3. *Phædra* and *Hippolytus*, *p.* 6. *l.* 4. *p.* 59. *l.* 6. *p.* 60. *l.* 12. *p.* 63. *l.* 4. Rinaldo, *p.* 31. *l.* 8. *p.* 33. *l.* 5. *p.* 20. *l.* 1. *p.* 59. *l.* 12. Manlius Capitolinus, *p.* 39. *l.* 2. *p.* 43. *l. penult.* *p.* 45. *l.* 23. Solon, *p.* 33. *l.* 2. *p.* 56. *l.* 31. *British* Enchanters, *p.* 13. *l.* 8. *p.* 24. *l. ult.* *p.* 33. *l.* 2. The Cid, *p.* 29. *l.* 13. Comical Revenge, *p.* 63. *l.* 16. Conquest of *Spain*, *p.* 72. *l.* 19. Cruel Gift, *p.* 2. *l.* 25. Distress'd Mother, *p.* 9. *l.* 27. *p.* 25. *l.* 5. *p.* 50. *l.* 9. Faithful Bride of *Granada*, *p.* 20. *l.* 17. *p.* 41. *l. ult.* Faithful General, *p.* 28. *l.* 48. False Friend, *p.* 52. *l.* 6. Fine Lady's Airs, *p.* 50. *l.* 23. Force of Friendship, *p.* 6. *l. penult.* *p.* 27. *l.* 22. *p.* 31. *l.* 30. Humours of the Age, *Epilogue*, *l.* 15. Modish Husband, *p.* 60. *l.* 18. Perfidious Brother, *p.* 33. *l.* 32. *p.* 46. *l.* 14. Perplex'd Couple, *p.* 37. *l.* 21. The Sultaness, *p.* 16. *l.* 24. *p.* 21. *l.* 7. *p.* 44. *l.* 6. Wife of *Bath*, *p.* 45. *l.* 9. Theseus, *p.* 17. *l.* 17. *p.* 27. *l.* 5. Thomyris, *p.* 48. *l.* 4. *p.* 50. *l. penult.* Titus Manlius, *p.* 35. *l.* 19. Ulysses, *p.* 56. *l.* 10.

(*n*) *Appius* and *Virginia*, *p.* 23. *l.* 1. Arminius, *p.* 65. *l.* 34. *p.* 81. *l.* 20. Arsinoe, *p.* 2. *l.* 19. *p.* 33. *l.* 27. Camilla, *p.* 24. *l. antepenult.* Alexander, *p.* 69. *l.* 17. Cato, *p.* 29. *l.* 10. *Cinna*'s Conspiracy, *p.* 4. *l.* 35. *p.* 21. *l.* 29. *p.* 24. *l.* 2, 20. *p.* 31. *l.* 20. *p.* 36. *l.* 17. Clotilda, *p.* 50. *l.* 23. Hamlet, *p.* 34. *l. penult.* Hydaspes, *p.* 68. *l.* 12. Jane Gray, *p.* 40. *l.* 23. *p.* 82. *l.* 12. Injur'd Love, *a Comedy*, *p.* 12. *l.* 28. *p.* 25. *l.* 7. Injur'd Love, *a Tragedy*, *p.* 66. *l.* 1. Injur'd Virtue, *p.* 30. *l.* 11. Irene, *p.* 32. *l.* 30. *p.* 45. *l. penult.* Liberty asserted, *p.* 22. *l. antepenult.* *p.* 23. *l.* 12. Love and Liberty, *p.* 7. *l. penult.* *p.* 9. *l.* 3. Manlius Capitolinus, *p.* 8. *l.* 5, 6. *p.* 18. *l.* 26. *p.* 38. *l.* 22. *p.* 45. *l.* 23. Marplot, *p.* 6. *l.* 26. *Perolla* and *Izadora*, *p.* 41. *l.* 6. *p.* 60. *l. ult.* *p.* 62. *l.* 16. *Phædra* and *Hippolytus*, *p.* 9. *l.* 21. *p.* 26. *l.* 29. Rinaldo, *p.* 47. *l.* 12.

Solon

crifices to any thing that comes uppermost; as to (o) *Ambition*, (p) to their *Appetites*, (q) to *Beauty*, (r) to a *Game at Cards*, (s) to *Diversion*, or (t) to the *Fates*; (u) to a *Fop*, (x) a *Fool*, (y) *Friendship*, or (z) *Glory*; (a) to a *Goddess*, (b) to *Honour*, (c) to *Humour*, or (d) to the Idol *Mammon*; (e) to *Jealousy*, (f) to *Ignorance*,

---

Solon, *p.* 13. *l.* 21. *p.* 37. *l.* 23. *p.* 62. *l.* 21. She wou'd if she cou'd, *p.* 133. *l.* 10. The Amorous Miser, *p.* 10. *l. ult.* The Artful Husband, *p.* 56. *l.* 20. *p.* 62. *l. penult.* *British* Enchanters, *p.* 25. *l.* 4. *p.* 39. *l.* 33. Busy Body, *p.* 31. *l.* 2. The Cid, *p.* 25. *l.* 18. *p.* 26. *l.* 20. *p.* 34. *l.* 9. *p.* 50. *l.* 25. Comical Lovers, *p.* 51. *l.* 18. Comical Revenge, *p.* 47. *l.* 6. Conquest of *Spain*, *p.* 33. *l.* 28. *p.* 58. *l.* 25. *p.* 65. *l.* 15. The Contrivances, *p.* 22. *l. ult.* Cruel Gift, *p.* 21. *l.* 22. Distress'd Mother, *p.* 18. *l.* 8. *p.* 41. *l.* 8. *p.* 47. *l.* 16. *p.* 59. *l.* 24. The different Widows, *p.* 23. *l.* 38. Faithful Bride of *Granada*, *p.* 16. *l.* 4. *p.* 18. *l.* 16. *p.* 25. *l.* 1. Faithful General, *p.* 8. *l.* 39. *p.* 17. *l.* 16. Female Advocates, *p.* 19. *l.* 10. Force of Friendship, *p.* 24. *l.* 21. *p.* 31. *l. antepenult.* Humours of the Army, *p.* 37. *l.* 8. The Maid's the Mistress, *p.* 40. *l.* 21. *p.* 48. *l.* 14. *p.* 54. *l.* 18. Modish Husband, *p.* 64. *l.* 25. Perplex'd Couple, *p.* 37. *l.* 6. *Portsmouth* Heiress, *p.* 37. *l.* 31. *p.* 38. *l.* 23. *p.* 50. *l.* 7. Pretender's Flight, *p.* 2. *l.* 20. Provok'd Wife, *p.* 41. *l.* 19. The Relapse, *p.* 53. *l.* 14. Rival Brothers, *p.* 3. *l.* 4. Roving Husband reclaim'd, *p.* 63. *l. antepenult.* Successful Pirate, *p.* 58. *l.* 11. The Sultaness, *p.* 24. *l.* 17. *p.* 27. *l.* 1. *p.* 28. *l.* 17. *p.* 41. *l.* 30. *p.* 50. *l.* 21. *p.* 53. *l.* 12. Tender Husband, *p.* 51. *l.* 8. Wife of *Bath*, *p.* 33. *l.* 20. The Wife's Relief, *p.* 65. *l.* 13. The Wonder, *p.* 7. *l.* 3. The Wonders of the Sun, *p.* 60. *l.* 13. Theseus, *p.* 43. *l.* 14. Thomyris, *p.* 47. *l.* 10.

(o) *French* Cato, p. 16. l. 5. *Cinna*'s Conspiracy, p. 3. l. 31. p. 50. l. 11. Faithful Bride of *Granada*, p. 15. l. 14.

(p) The Beaux Stratagem, p. 6. l. 16.

(q) Ernelinda, p. 17. l. 6.

(r) The Tender Husband, p. 3. l. 10.

(s) The Man of Mode, p. 226. l. 23.

(t) Solon, p. 59. l. 11.

(u) The Artful Husband, p. 10. l. 9.

(x) The Wonder, p. 3. l. 8.

(y) The Faithful General, p. 65. l. 6.

(z) *Appius* and *Virginia*, p. 42. l. 28. Hydaspes, p. 30. l. 6. The Faithful General, p. 71. l. 49.

(a) *Appius* and *Virginia*, p. 40. l. 21.

(b) Love and Liberty, p. 18. l. 26.

(c) The Fair Quaker of *Deal*, p. 22. l. 1.

(d) The Amorous Miser, p. 19. l. 19.

(e) Arsinoe, p. 23. l. 20.

(f) The Wife of *Bath*, p. 8. l. 18.

(*g*) to their own *Interest*, or (*h*) to their *Parents Interest* and *Pleasure*; (*i*) to *Laughter*, (*k*) to *Love*, (*l*) to a *Man*, or (*m*) to a *Man's Tongue*; (*n*) to a *Monastery*, (*o*) to a *Monkey*, (*p*) to the *Muses*, or (*q*) to *Persons murder'd*; (*r*) to *Pleasure*, (*s*) to *Pride*, (*t*) to *publick Feuds*, or (*u*) to the *publick Good*; (*x*) to a *Rabble*, (*y*) to *Rage*, (*z*) to *Revenge*, or (*a*) *Resentment*; to a (*b*) *Rival*, (*c*) to *Rome*, (*d*) to *Vanity*, or (*e*) *Violence*; (*f*) to a Man's own *Will*, (*g*) to *Wit*, (*h*) to a *Whore*, or

---

(*g*) The Perplex'd Couple, p. 3. *l.* 9.

(*h*) The Amorous Miser, p. 21. l. 31.

(*i*) Love's last Shift, p. 23. l. 26.

(*k*) *Appius* and *Virginia*, p. 41. l. ult. Arsinoe, p. 23. l. 20. *Cinna*'s Conspiracy, p. 29. l. 30. Love and Liberty, p. 59. l. 17. Love at first sight, p. 65. l. 16. The General cashier'd, p. 14. l. 25. The Masquerade, p. 9. l. 14.

(*l*) Britannicus, p. 48. l. 13. Injur'd Love, *a Tragedy*, p. 65. l. *antepenult*. The City-Ramble, p. 26. l. 12. p. 40. l. 20. Cruel Gift, p. 23. l. 4. The Fair Example, p. 48. l. 2. The Faithful General, p. 46. l. 35. The Wife's Relief, p. 13. l. 10. p. 19. l. 36. The Wonder, p. 19. l. 2. *Tunbridge*-Walks, p. 4. l. 30. p. 11. l. *antepenult*. Ulysses, p. 25. l. 2. Force of Friendship, p. 22. l. 22. Humours of the Army, p. 34. l. 23, 29.

(*m*) The General cashier'd, p. 29. l. 16.

(*n*) The Wife of *Bath*, p. 59. l. 20.

(*o*) The Fine Lady's Airs, p. 10. l. 15.

(*p*) The Wife of *Bath*, p. 54. l. 10.

(*q*) Irene, p. 14. l. 1. Love and Liberty, p. 45. l. *ult*. Conquest of *Spain*, p. 55. l. 12.

(*r*) Woman is a Riddle, p. 13. l. 25.

(*s*) Marry or do worse, p. 40. l. 31. The Fair Example, p. 14. l. 16.

(*t*) *French* Cato, p. 46. l. *antepenult*.

(*u*) Successful Pirate, p. 45. l. 35.

(*x*) Squire of *Alsatia*, p. 31. l. 26.

(*y*) Love and Liberty, p. 59. l. 17.

(*z*) Hydaspes, p. 14. l. 8. Comical Revenge, p. 55. l. 4. Faithful Bride of *Granada*, p. 13. l. 9. p. 16. l. 27. Squire of *Alsatia*, p. 62. l. 12.

(*a*) The *Gotham* Election, p. 61. l. 23.

(*b*) The Wonder, p. 79. l. 19.

(*c*) *Appius* and *Virginia*, p. 42. l. 28.

(*d*) The Wife's Relief, p. 30. l. 19.

(*e*) Conquest of *Spain*, p. 17. l. 8.

(*f*) Hamlet, p. 66. l. 31.

(*g*) Fortune in her Wits, p. 39. l. *antepenult*.

(*h*) A Woman's Revenge, p. 32. *l. penult*.

(*i*) to any other *Woman*; and alſo (*k*) to *Happineſs*, or (*l*) to *Quiet*. The Reader muſt be tired with ſuch a multitude of Quotations; but he may obſerve, that as *Sacrificing* was always appropriated both by *Jews* and *Gentiles* to ſuch, whom they thought to be *Gods*; ſo if the word is taken in a literal ſenſe, our *Stage* can outdo either *Pagan Rome* or *Athens* in the Number of their Gods, and may in time make them vie with the *Romiſh Saints*. But if it is taken in a *Metaphorical Senſe*, yet here is a confounding of GOD and his Creatures, and treating them all alike. Every thing which is common, is treated as ſacred upon the *Stage*; and every thing which is ſacred, is uſed as common. The *Poets* rack their Wits to bring all *Scripture-Words* and *Phraſes* upon the *Stage*, that whilſt they are there uſed for Diverſion, it may wholly take off the Seriouſneſs which ought to be, when we hear them in another place, or upon another occaſion.

But to proceed: In *Scripture*, to *ſacrifice* ſignifies to offer up ſomething to GOD; in the *Play-Houſe* it ſignifies (*m*) to be guilty of Murder, (*n*) to ſpoil a Cauſe, (*o*) to betray a Man, or (*p*) to ſcandalize a Woman. To be *ſacrificed* ſignifies (*q*) to be unhappily married, or (*r*) to die by Revenge. To be made a *Sacrifice*, is (*s*) to be rejected by another. A Woman is ſaid to ſacrifice herſelf, when (*t*) ſhe marries unfortunately; and a Man (*u*) ſacrificeth himſelf, when he is his own Executioner. One ſaith, (*x*) *I'll offer up an early Sacrifice,*

(*i*) *Appius* and *Virginia*, p.40. l. 21, 34. Marplot, p.56. l.28. The Biter, p.62. l.5. Comical Revenge, p.46. l.24. The Man of Mode, p.259. l.11. Modern Prophets, p.14. l.3. *Portſmouth* Heireſs, p. 27. l. 24. Roving Husband reclaim'd, p.45. l.27.

(*k*) Faithful General, p. 55. l. 9.

(*l*) The Wonder, p.47. l.32.

(*m*) Abra-Mule, p. 24. l.37.

(*n*) *Cinna*'s Conſpiracy, p. 2. l. 5.

(*o*) Abra-Mule, p.5. l.37.

(*p*) Love for Love, p. 11. l. 36.

(*q*) Comical Lovers, p. 37. l. 22.

(*r*) Antiochus, p.54. l. 5.

(*s*) The Female Advocates, p. 12. l. 24.

(*t*) The Wife of *Bath*, p.48. l. 4.

(*u*) Antiochus, p. 56. l. *antepenult.*

(*x*) Irene, p.36. l. *antepen.*

when he only means *Murder*. In (*y*) one *Play* we are told, that the *Swains are come to pay their Morning-Sacrifices before* Clorinda: And in another, (*z*) a Woman weeping is complimented in this Language;

> *Waste not those precious Tears: Oh! weep no more.*
> *Should Heaven frown, the World would be too poor*
> *(Robb'd of the sacred Treasure of your Eyes)*
> *To pay for Mercy one fit Sacrifice.*

I suppose that the *Poet* never thinks on the *Sacrifice* of *Christ Jesus* to appease the Wrath of GOD against sinful Man, or otherwise he would not be so profane; but it is strange, that not one of the Auditors shall express a Resentment on such an occasion.

The *Prophet Isaiah*, (*a*) speaking of the Crucifixion of our *Saviour*, saith, *He was led as a Lamb to the Slaughter*; and St. *Peter* adds, (*b*) that we *were redeemed by the precious Blood of Jesus Christ, as a Lamb without blemish and without spot*. An *Actress* (*c*) talking very immodestly, compares herself at the same time to a *tame Lamb for Sacrifice*.

St. *Paul* saith, (*d*) That *Christ offered up himself a Sacrifice without spot to GOD, to bear the Sins of many*; and St. *Peter* tells (*e*) us the same: and (*f*) we who are *Christians* are intreated by *the Mercies of GOD, that* we *present* our *Bodies a living Sacrifice, holy and acceptable unto him*. Upon the *Stage* an *Actor* having been guilty of (*g*) the *Vanity and Lewdness of Youth*, particularly *Drunkenness* and *Whoredom*, comes to his Father with these words; *I offer myself at your feet as a Sacrifice, without a blemish*.

I shall dispatch the following Words more briefly. The next in order is *Salvation*. This in several places

(*y*) The Fickle Shepherdess, p. 8. l. 14.

(*z*) The Comical Revenge, p. 24. l. 29.

(*a*) *Isa.* 53. 7.

(*b*) 1 *Pet.* 1. 18, 19.

(*c*) Love's last Shift, p. 16. l. 14.

(*d*) *Heb.* 9. 9, 14, 28.

(*e*) 1 *Pet.* 1. 18, 19.

(*f*) *Rom.* 12. 1.

(*g*) Squire of *Alsatia*, p. 73. l. 23.

of

of *Scripture* (too many to be refer'd to) ſignifies the Delivery of Man from Sin, Death and Hell, and making us for ever happy in the Kingdom of Heaven; and is therefore call'd (*h*) *eternal Salvation*, or (*i*) *the End of our Faith, even the Salvation of our Souls.* An *Actor* ſaith, (*k*) *I would not be abſent* (from the Houſe of Lords) *for the Salvation of Mankind.* Upon the *Stage* the (*l*) Word ſignifies the being made eaſy in Love-Affairs; (*m*) *to ſave* is to commit *Adultery*, and *to deſtroy* is to be honeſt. St. *James* ſaith, (*n*) That *he who converteth a Sinner from the Error of his Way*, ſhall *ſave a Soul from Death*: But (*o*) this Phraſe is uſed in the *Play-Houſe* in a different Meaning.

St. *Paul* (*p*) *beſeecheth* us, *that* we *walk worthy of the Vocation wherewith* we *are called.* In the *Play-Houſe* Language, (*q*) to *labour honeſtly in their Vocation* is to pimp for their Miſtreſſes; and (*r*) to be *diligent* in their *Vocation*, is to be taken up in reading of *Plays* and *Romances.*

In *Scripture*, *Worſhip* is an Act, (*s*) which is due to GOD alone. In the *Play-Houſe* it is ſaid, (*t*) *The Mobile ſhall worſhip thee*, an *Actor*; and another ſaith of his Miſtreſs, (*u*) She is *the Idol of my Soul, and I am her conſtant zealous Worſhipper.*

Laſtly, *Zeal* is (*x*) an Earneſtneſs of the Soul to perform the Service of GOD, and promote his Glory. In our *Plays* it is (*y*) an *Earneſtneſs* for *Villany*, (thus

(*h*) *Heb.* 5. 9.
(*i*) 1 *Pet.* 1. 9.
(*k*) The Relapſe, p. 9. l. 31.
(*l*) The Man of Mode, p. 186. l. 30.
(*m*) Love in a Cheſt, p. 57. l. 27.
(*n*) *James* 5. 20.
(*o*) The Sultaneſs, p. 39. l. *penult.*
(*p*) *Epheſ.* 4. 1.
(*q*) The Fair Example, p. 62. l. 9.
(*r*) The Comical Lovers, p. 30. l. *penult.*
(*s*) *Mat.* 4. 10. *Rev.* 22. 8, 9.
(*t*) The Squire of *Alſatia*, p. 3. l. 6.
(*u*) The Generous Husband, p. 39. l. 15.
(*x*) *Numb.* 25. 11, 13. *Pſal.* 69. 9. & 119. 139. *John* 2. 17. *Acts* 22. 3. *Rom.* 10. 2. 1 *Cor.* 14. 12. 2 *Cor.* 7. 11. 2 *Cor.* 9. 2. *Coloſſ.* 4. 13. *Tit.* 2. 14. *Revel.* 3. 19.
(*y*) *Phædra* and *Hippolytus*, p. 52. l. 28.

(z) one ſaith, he *plunder'd* another *out of pure Zeal)* or elſe it is (*a*) an Endeavour to help another to an Opportunity of Whoring: However (*b*) the Word is always uſed upon trifling Occaſions, when (*c*) ſometimes it is call'd *unweary'd Zeal.*

I ſhall only add two other *Play-Houſe* Sentences. The firſt is ſpoken of two *Actors.* (*d*) The *daily Contemplation* of the one, *nay his Salvation, is his Looking-Glaſs; for there he finds eternal Happineſs. The other's Heaven, at leaſt his Prieſt, is his Claret-Glaſs; for to that he confeſſeth all his Sins, and from it receives Abſolution and Comfort. But his Damnation is a Looking-Glaſs; for there he finds an eternal Fire in his Noſe.* Here is *daily Contemplation, Salvation, eternal Happineſs, Heaven,* a *Prieſt, Confeſſion of Sins, Abſolution* and *Comfort, Damnation* and *Eternal Fire* jumbled together, that the Audience may laugh at them all at once.

But as the *Poets* ſtrive to outdo one another in Wickedneſs, ſo another puts (*e*) the following words into the mouth of a fine Lady, when ſhe ſpeaks of herſelf: *Men are generally Hypocrites and Infidels. They pretend to worſhip, but have neither Zeal nor Faith: How few, like* Valentine, *would perſevere unto Martyrdom!* Here we have *Hypocrite, Infidel, Worſhip, Zeal, Faith,* and *Martyrdom*; and the *Poet* crams the Lady with them like a Capon, that ſo he may make himſelf and her, and alſo the *Scripture-Expreſſions,* ridiculous at the ſame time.

But the *Poets* take care not only to expoſe *Scripture*-Words, but even the *Scriptures* themſelves, that they may render them and the *Authors* of them contemptible, or of no force with us. One *Actor* ſaith to another,

---

(z) The Humours of the Army, p. 63. l. 21.

(*a*) She wou'd if ſhe cou'd, p. 91. l. 4.

(*b*) The Apparition, p. 35. l. 36. p. 36. l. 27. The Country Laſſes, p. 16. l. 25. Faithful Bride of *Granada,* p. 20. l. *ult.* Provok'd Wife, p. 9. l. 3. The Sultaneſs, p. 25. l. 4.

(*c*) The different Widows, p. 58. l. 1. The Faithful General, p. 28. l. *antepenult.*

(*d*) Sir *Courtly Nice,* p. 12. l. 37.

(*e*) Love for Love, p. *ult.* l. 26.

ther, (*f*) *You are as mad as a Prophet, you have always before your eyes a Vision of Horns and Whores.* This is intolerable. Another saying, (*g*) *We must return Good for Evil*, is thus answer'd, *That may be a Mistake in the Translation.* And by this Method an *Atheist* may object against all the rest. And a third, more daring than any, saith, (*h*) *It is a Question would puzzle an Arithmetician, if you should ask him, Whether the BIBLE saves more Souls in* Westminster-Abby, *or damns more in* Westminster-Hall? *For my part I am Truth, and cannot tell.* And now, who can forbear to shew Resentment under such Provocations? Who can be silent when the Oracles of Truth, and the Laws of Omnipotence, are thus laugh'd at and despised? When the *Poets* are suffer'd to play upon the Bible; when *Christianity* shall be hooted off the *Stage*; and an *Actor* shall apply to himself, what is spoken of *Christ* only, to rail more effectually at the whole *Gospel*. But this is not all: (*i*) The whole *Scripture is* said to be *given by Divine Inspiration*, and these *Holy Men of GOD spake as they were guided by the Holy Ghost*. But to put other Beings upon the same level with this blessed *Person* of the *Trinity*, the *Poets* tell us, that (*k*) *Arguments*, (*l*) a *Cause*, (*m*) *Courage*, (*n*) *Drinking a Health*, or (*o*) an *Example*, will inspire. That (*p*) *Friends*, (*q*) a *Genius*, (*r*) *Glory*, or (*s*) *ill Usage* will inspire. That (*t*) *Malice* will inspire, which is pray'd to accordingly for such a Purpose. That (*u*) an *Occasion*,

---

(*f*) Sir *Courtly Nice*, p. 28. l. 1.

(*g*) The Provok'd Wife, p. 3. l. *penult.*

(*h*) Love for Love, p. 51. l. 5.

(*i*) 2 *Tim.* 3. 16. 2 *Pet.* 1. 21.

(*k*) Love's last Shift, p. 56. l. 25.

(*l*) The Pretender's Flight, p. 36. l. 16.

(*m*) The Lawyer's Fortune, p. 55. l. 15.

(*n*) Love's last Shift, p. 52. l. 30.

(*o*) The Faithful General, p. 22. l. 34.

(*p*) The Pretender's Flight, p. 17. l. 32.

(*q*) The Faithful General, p. 46. l. 8.

(*r*) Ibid. p. 45. *l. penult.*

(*s*) The Perplex'd Lovers, p. 17. l. 10.

(*t*) The Perplex'd Couple, p. 20. l. 16.

(*u*) The Tender Husband, p. 38. l. 18.

(x) a *Project*, (y) the *soft Dreams of Love*, and (z) the *Voices of Birds*, and (*) *warlike Notes*, or (†) *Words*, or (‖) *Wrongs*, will inspire. So that all this being put together, whatever is meant by Inspiration, must be a very insignificant matter. Besides, as the *Poets* make Women to be worship'd and adored, and give them the Honour due to GOD alone; so on this occasion they tell us, that (a) *Love* inspires (b) with an unusual Warmth, and that (c) the Person, or (d) the Beauty of *Women* doth inspire others. One saith to a Woman, (e) *My Soul with Rapture feels more powerful Inspirations from thine Eyes*: and to carry it off more boldly, we are told, (f) that *Poets may well be said to be inspired, when a* fine *Lady employs their Thoughts*. And that we may look upon these Sacred Writers to be either *mad* or *drunk*, we are inform'd that either (g) *Wine*, or (h) *Ale and Toast*, or (i) *Rage*, or (k) *Folly* will inspire a Man. One tells his *Lady*, (l) he *finds Passion coming upon* him *by Inspiration*. And another saith, (m) *Don't be inspired, but give a Man a rational Answer*; as if *Inspiration* bereft Men of their *Sense* and *Reason*; and if so, then their Writings ought to be little regarded.

(x) The Lying Lover, p. 39. l. *penult*.

(y) *Venus* and *Adonis*, p. 17. l. 9.

(z) Ibid. p. 17. l. 11.

(*) Love's last Shift, p. 82. l. 6.

(†) The Provok'd Wife, p. 20. l. 13.

(‖) The Faithful General, p. 33. l. 45.

(a) The Force of Friendship, p. 5. l. 4, 16. The Lady's last Stake, p. 51. l. 29. Ulysses, p. 4. l. 3.

(b) The Force of Friendship, p. 2. l. 6.

(c) The Distress'd Mother, p. 14. l. 18. The Fatal Marriage, p. 113. l. 5. The Lying Lover, p. 41. l. 6. The Perplex'd Couple, *Prologue*, l. 10, 12.

(d) The Modern Prophets, p. 32. l. *ult*. Woman is a Riddle, p. 46. l. 19. p. 47. l. *ult*.

(e) The Faithful General, p. 31. l. 2.

(f) The Fickle Shepherdess, *Dedication*, p. 1. l. 4.

(g) The Lying Lover, p. 41. l. 6.

(h) The Lady's last Stake, *Epilogue*, l. 20.

(i) Zelmane, p. 33. l. 12.

(k) Love's last Shift, *Prologue*, l. *antepenult*.

(l) The Double Dealer, p. 19.

(m) The Wife of *Bath*, p. 60. l. 31.

Besides, in the *Poets* Language, *to inspire* signifies (*n*) to bring People to a Resolution, (*o*) to teach Revenge, to (*p*) make People in love, (*q*) to make a Woman think well of a Man, or (*r*) bring a Man to a Resolution of committing Adultery. This can serve only to make the Word contemptible, and represent our GOD as an Assister in Iniquity.

I suppose that the Reader will not think it a Digression, if I add one Quotation out of those many scandalous Volumes of *Songs*, which are printed and dispersed abroad to poison the whole Nation. The *Tune* (like the rest) is very easy, and fit for a Country Capacity. The *Song* declares for *Atheism*, and gives this Reason, because the *Scriptures* are a Cheat.

The Assertion is (*s*),

Gods there are none.

The Reason immediately follows:

For all the Books of Moses
Were nothing but Supposes;
And he deserv'd Rebuke, Sir,
Who wrote the Pentateuch, *Sir:*
'Twas nothing but a Sham.

And as for Father Adam,
With Mistress Eve, *his Madam;*
And what the Serpent *spoke, Sir,*
Was nothing but a Joke, Sir,
And a well-invented Flam.

I shall trouble the Reader but with one Instance more, which was observ'd by (*t*) a late eminent Writer. *One of these Champions of Vice is the reputed Author of a detestable Paper, that hath lately been handed about in*

(*n*) The Sultaness, *p.* 43. *l.* 18.

(*o*) The Perplex'd Lovers, *p.* 14. *l.* 5.

(*p*) The Sultaness, *Prologue, l.* 5. *Venus* and *Adonis, p.* 17. *l.* 11.

(*q*) The Modish Husband, *p.* 12. *l. ult.*

(*r*) Ibid. *p.* 7. *l.* 1.

(*s*) Pills to purge Melancholy, *Vol.* 5. *printed* Anno 1714. *p.* 82. *l.* 15.

(*t*) Sir *Richard Blackmore's* Essays, *Vol.* 2. *p.* 270.

Manu-

Manuscript, and now appears in Print, in which the godless Author has burlesq'd the First Psalm *of* David *in so obscene and profane a manner, that perhaps no Age ever saw such an insolent Affront offer'd to the establish'd Religion of their Country; and this, Good Heaven! with Impunity. A sad Demonstration this, of the low Ebb to which the* British *Virtue is reduced in these degenerate Times.*

From the Usage which the *Scriptures* meet with in general, I shall now proceed to treat of particular Texts. And omitting those *Texts* which have been already mention'd, I shall add some more, in which either the *Name* of GOD is most solemnly mention'd, some weighty Duty press'd, or some necessary Doctrine proposed; or where the Honour of GOD is more directly opposed in the *Play-House.*

To begin then with the Books of *Moses:* The first *Chapter* of *Genesis* begins with the *Creation* of the World; but of this I have given a melancholy Account already.

The (*u*) next Chapter treats of the *Creation* of our *First Parents Adam* and *Eve*, and the placing of them in *Paradise.* But tho they are the common Parents of all Mankind; yet (*x*) it doth not give them an Exemption from being frequently lampoon'd by the *Stage.*

When *Adam* was created, GOD (*y*) placed him in *Paradise:* This is join'd (*z*) with the *Poetical Dreams* of *Elysium.*

When *Adam* was in *Paradise*, GOD said, (*a*) *It is not good that Man should be alone: I will make him an Helpmeet for him.* Accordingly (*b*) he created *Eve*, and (*c*) instituted Marriage. When an *Actor* (*d*) useth this Expression in a good Sense, he is thus reprimanded:

(*u*) *Gen.* chap. 2.

(*x*) Marry or do worse, p.12. l. 18. Adventures of half an Hour, p.8. l. *penult.* p.19. l.14. Amorous Widow, p. 62. l. 22. The Apparition, p. 30. l. 24. The Country Lasses, p.27. l.*antepenult.* The Lady's last Stake, p.4. l.3. The Provok'd Wife, p.70. l.36. Woman is a Riddle, p.4. l.33.

(*y*) *Gen.* 2. 8, 9, 15.

(*z*) The Royal Convert, p.1. l. 7.

(*a*) *Gen.* 2. 18.

(*b*) *Gen.* 2. 21, 22.

(*c*) *Gen.* 2. 24.

(*d*) Squire of *Alsatia*, p. 49. l. 41, *antepenult.*

Come,

Come, leave off your Canaanitish *Dialect, and talk like the Inhabiters of this World.* Because *Eve* was made of the Rib of *Adam*, therefore a Woman is (*e*) deridingly called *the Hoop of an Hogshead.* GOD appointed *Matrimony.* An *Actor* saith to a Whore, (*f*) *Woman is but half a Creature till she be join'd to Man; now thou art whole and perfect.* GOD saith, *They two shall be one Flesh.* The (*g*) Comment is remarkable, *As Man and Wife are one Flesh, so Repentance and Wedlock are inseparable.* Or more daring thus:

> (*h*) *Well had it been, yes, wondrous well for Man,*
> *If Nature ne'er had form'd his Female Mate:*
> *Love poisons oftner than it gives us Joy.*

The third *Chapter* of *Genesis* gives us an Account of the Fall of our first Parents by the Instigation of the *Devil*, and their being cast out of *Paradise*. How far these Texts are perverted in favour of our *Grand Enemy*, hath been already mentioned. I shall only add, that after their *Fall*, the *Players* represent them still as innocent. (The greatest Crime against GOD is accounted among them as nothing.) GOD saith, (*i*) that when they had forfeited their Innocency, *they sewed Fig-leaves together, and made themselves Aprons.* An *Actor* saith, (*k*) *Freemen ought to appear like innocent old* Adam; *a Fig-leaf's sufficient.*

But to proceed no farther Chapter by Chapter. When (*l*) *there were Giants in the Earth*, occasioned by an unnatural Copulation, the Wickedness of Man was so great, that it brought the Flood to destroy them. The *Actors* (*m*) threaten the same, in terms of the highest *Blasphemy*, without any regard to the Vengeance which may follow.

(*e*) Cobler of *Preston*, p. 26. l. 14.

(*f*) Squire of *Alsatia*, p. 15. l. 24.

(*g*) Artful Husband, p. 58. l. 20.

(*h*) Cruel Gift, p. 43. l. 38.

(*i*) *Gen.* 3. 7.

(*k*) Wit without Money, p. 40. l. 18.

(*l*) *Gen.* 6. 4.

(*m*) The Amorous Widow, p. 26. l. 34.

We'll beget a Race of People that ſhall be immortal. A Race, that ſhall create a ſecond War with Jove, *and raiſe* Olympus' *Top equal with the Seat of him that hurls the Thunder.*

And another courts his Miſtreſs with this Expreſſion, (*n*) *I thought you the propereſt Perſon to apply to, that we may produce a Race of* Alexanders, *that ſhall rattle thro the World like a Peal of Thunder, wage Wars, deſtroy Cities, and ſend old Women head-long to the Devil.*

In the ſame Chapter, (*o*) GOD threatens to *deſtroy the Earth* with a *Flood.* This, and (*p*) the building of the Tower of *Babel*, is (*q*) burleſqued at the ſame time. Neither can (*r*) *Abraham*'s interceding for *Sodom* (*s*) eſcape the ſame Treatment.

Abraham (*t*) adjured his Servant with this Expreſſion, *Put, I pray thee, thy Hand under my Thigh; and I will make thee ſwear by the LORD, the GOD of Heaven, and the GOD of the Earth.* This (*u*) Form is uſed by a *Damſel* to her *Suitor*, with a great deal of immodeſt Diſcourſe, to make it more ridiculous, and to wreſt the *Scriptures*, if poſſible, to deliver an obſcene Thought.

Jacob's Expreſſion (*x*) of *bringing down* his *grey Hairs with ſorrow to the Grave*, is (*y*) alſo uſed in the *Play-houſe.*

Moſes propheſied of *Iſſachar*, (*z*) that he ſhould be *a ſtrong Aſs.* An *Actor*, (*a*) to repreſent a *Cuckold*, ſhews *a Cap with Ears*, and adds this Expreſſion :

Gallants, look here, this Fool's Cap has an Air,
Goodly and ſmart, with Ears of Iſſachar.

(*n*) Fine Lady's Airs, p. 40. l. 14.

(*o*) *Gen.* 6. 17.

(*p*) *Gen.* 11. 9.

(*q*) Three Hours after Marriage, p. 61. l. 16.

(*r*) *Gen.* 18. 20, 28, 32.

(*s*) Three Hours after Marriage, p. 18. l. 13.

(*t*) *Gen.* 24. 2, 3.

(*u*) Beau Merchant, p. 54. *in fine*, &c.

(*x*) *Gen.* 42. 38.

(*y*) Fatal Marriage, p. 111. l. 33.

(*z*) *Gen.* 49. 14.

(*a*) Three Hours after Marriage, *Prologue*, p. 2. l. 5.

It was the Tyranny of *Pharaoh*, to force the *Israelites* to (*b*) *make Brick* without *Straw*. This *Text* (*) is perverted in the *Play-house* to an immodest purpose.

To omit (*c*) the *Mosaical* Ceremonies; The History informs us, (*d*) that *GOD opened the Mouth of* Balaam's *Ass*: The *Player* burlesque the Miracle, (*e*) *Lawyers and Chambermaids, like* Balaam's *Ass, never speak, unless they see an Angel*; or (*f*) *an Ass hath spoken at a less Injury than this.*

In the *Scripture*, GOD (*g*) positively forbids *the Woman to wear that which appertaineth to a Man*, and also *the Man* to *put on a Woman's Apparel*; and gives this reason, *For all that do so are an Abomination to the LORD.* The *Players* often transgress this Command for the sake of the Jest, where sometimes (*h*) *Women*, and (*i*) sometimes Men are scandalously guilty in this particular. *David*

(*b*) *Exod.* 5. 6, 7, 8.

(*) She wou'd if she cou'd, p. 111. l. 30.

(*c*) *Compare* Numb. 5. 11. *to the end, with* Three Hours after Marriage, p. 32. l. 4.

(*d*) *Numb.* 22. 22, *to* 36.

(*e*) Woman is a Riddle, p. 44. l. 10.

(*f*) *Portsmouth* Heiress, p. 47. l. 28.

(*g*) *Deut.* 22. 5.

(*h*) Gibraltar, p. 44. *Sheet* F. l. 32. p. 55. *Sheet* G. l. 3. Injur'd Love, *a Comedy, Dramatis Personæ*, Ogle *and* Frolick. Love and Liberty, p. 58. l. 7. Love for Love, *Prologue*. Marplot, *Dramatis Personæ*, Isabinda, & p. 26. l. 18. Marry or do worse, p. 28. l. 11. The Apparition, p. 59. l. 25. The artful Husband, p. 33. l. 22, &c. *who courts, marries, and beds, Epilogue*, l. 1, &c. Comical Lovers, p. 43. l. 33. p. 47. l. 27. p. 49. l. 18. p. 62. l. 1. The different Widows, p. 39. l. 1. Double Gallant, p. 69. l. 4. Fair Quaker of *Deal*, p. 49. l. 2. Fatal Marriage, p. 128. l. 15. p. 134. l. 34. Fickle Shepherdess, *compare the* Title-Page *with Dramatis Personæ*, Damon, Alexis, Menalchas, Adrastus, Claius *a Shepherd, and* Dorilas. The Gamester, p. 53. l. 15. The General cashier'd, *Dramatis Personæ*, Orind, p. 38. l. 31. Generous Husband, *Dramatis Personæ*, Fictitia *and* Viola, *and* Epilogue. Humours of the Army, *Dramatis Personæ*, Belvidera *and* Clara, p. 26. l. 4. Lady's Last Stake, p. 40. l. 5. The Mistake, *Dramatis Personæ*, Camillo. Modish Husband, p. 53. l. 22. Recruiting Officer, p. 34. l. 19. Rival Fools, p. 27. l. 9. p. 41. l. 1. Squire of *Alsatia*, p. 70. l. 12. Tender Husband, *Dramatis Personæ, and* Fainlove, *fere per totum.* Vice Reclaim'd, p. 39. l. 16.

(*i*) Gibraltar, p. 47. *Sheet* F. l. 8. Injur'd Love, *a Comedy, Epilogue*,

David ſpeaking of his Death as near, ſaith, (*k*) *I go the way of all the Earth.* This Text in the *Play-houſe* is (*l*) ridiculouſly applied to *carnal Copulation.*

In *Scripture* we are commanded to (*m*) *ſerve the LORD with fear, and rejoice with reverence*; (*n*) to *worſhip the LORD our GOD only*, and (*o*) to *work out our own Salvation with fear and trembling.* Upon the *Stage* we are told of (*p*) whoring *with fear and reverence.* An *Actor* ſaith, (*q*) *The Ladies worſhip me with awe and trembling:* and another adds, (*r*) *I worſhip Junia.*

David ſaith, (*s*) *Into thy hands I commend my Spirit; for thou haſt redeemed me, O LORD, thou GOD of Truth.* An *Actor* ſaith, (*t*) *Ladies both, into your hands I commit myſelf.*

David ſaith, (*u*) *And now, LORD, what is my Hope? truly, my Hope is even in thee.* An *Actor* ſaith thus:

> (*x*) *We hope not Safety from our ſelves, but thee:*
> *In thee our King we truſt, in thee our Hero.*

Or thus:

> (*y*) Florella, *in thee lies all my Hopes.*

David ſaith to GOD, (*z*) *I have ſworn, and I will perform it, that I will keep thy righteous Judgments.* An *Actor*

Epilogue, l. 11. p. 62. l. 18. Love in a Cheſt, p. 55. l. 1. p. 58. l. 22. Marry or do worſe, p. 54. l. 7. Squire Trelooby, p. 47. l. 2. The Apparition, p. 55. l. 39. City Ramble, p. 17. l. 14. p. 23. l. 2. The Contrivances, p. 11. l. 6. Country Laſſes, p. 56. l. 13. Different Widows, p. 8. l. 3. Walking-Statue, p. 49. l. 1. Woman is a Riddle, p. 50. l. 17.

(*k*) 1 *Kings* 2. 2. See alſo *Joſhua* 23. 14.

(*l*) The Stage-Coach, *p.* 12. *l.* 21.

(*m*) *Pſal.* 2. 11.

(*n*) *Matth.* 4. 10. *Revel.* 22. 8, 9.

(*o*) *Philip.* 2. 12.

(*p*) Sir Courtly Nice, *p.* 11. *l. penult.*

(*q*) An Act at *Oxford*, *p.* 7. *l.* 7.

(*r*) Britannicus, *p.* 21. *l.* 15.

(*s*) *Pſal.* 31. 5.

(*t*) Comical Lovers, *p.* 4. *l.* 6.

(*u*) *Pſal.* 39. 7.

(*x*) Ulyſſes, *p.* 61. *l.* 9.

(*y*) Perplex'd Lovers, *p.* 14. *l.* 8.

(*z*) *Pſal.* 119. 106.

Actor swears (*a*) by *Heavens*, upon a ridiculous occasion; and adds, *I have sworn, and I will keep my Oath.*

Solomon tells us, (*b*) that *to every thing there is a season; and a time for every purpose under the Sun.* This Expression the *Players* repeat, and make a blasphemous Inference, (*c*) that *a Bottle is good in the Evening, and a Whore doth well in the Morning.*

Solomon saith of Friendship, (*d*) *A three-fold Cord is not easily broken.* This an *Actor* (*) repeats with much Ridicule, and applies it to an untimely End.

Solomon, speaking of Death, saith, (*e*) *The Spirit shall return unto GOD, who gave it.* An *Actor* describes it (*f*) three times, by *going to the Devil.*

These are the *Play-house* Comments upon *Moses* and the *Prophets*; and upon Inquiry we shall find, that it fares no better with *Christ* and his *Apostles*.

The *New Testament*, being originally written in *Greek*, makes the knowledge of that Language much more necessary for the understanding of the sacred Text; and therefore all Translations are only valid as they agree with this. But to dispatch the *Original* all at once, (*g*) a pretended *Priest* saith upon the *Stage*, *Greek is turned Turk; we are only to be saved by the* Helvetick *Translation.*

But to instance in some Particulars. Our *Blessed Saviour* is very positive in forbidding us to *commit Adultery*, saying, that for this reason we should avoid every Provocation thereto; and that (*h*) *he who looketh on a Woman to lust after her, hath committed Adultery with her already in his Heart.* But if we should have such Inclinations, tho they are as dear to us as an *Eye* or a *Foot*, yet he commands us to part with them under the Penalty of *Hell-Fire*. The *Players* tell us, that if we have a lustful Thought, we may go on to the utmost:

(*a*) *Sawny* the *Scot*, *p.* 30. *l.* 33.

(*b*) *Eccles.* 3. 1.

(*c*) Gibraltar, *p.*39. *Sh.*E. *l.*37.

(*d*) *Eccles.* 4. 12.

(*) A Woman's Revenge, *p.* 57. *l.*11.

(*e*) *Eccles.* 12. 7.

(*f*) Humours of Purgatory, *p.*31. *l.*7, 10, 13.

(*g*) Unfortunate Dutchess of *Malfi*, *p.*49. l.4.

(*h*) *Matth.*5.27, 28, 29.

For, say they, (*i*) *What signifies a Woman's being chaste in the Flesh, if she is a Whore in her Spirit? And to what purpose is it to keep herself from the World, if she hath suffered her self before-hand to be debauch'd by the Devil?*

Our *Blessed Saviour* exhorts us, (*k*) that *whatsoever we would that Men should do to us*, we should *do so to them; For this is the Law and the Prophets.* This *Text* is used by the *Players* (*l*) in vindication of *Adultery.*

Our *Blessed Saviour* (*m*) saith, that in matters of *Religion*, there must be no Neutrality. The *Players* jest with this Expression; and one in a Captain's Habit saith, (*n*) *He that is not for us, is against us; therefore plunder.*

Our *Saviour* saith (*o*) of St. *Peter*'s Confession, *Upon this Rock will I build my Church.* To this an *Actor* (*p*) alludes, when he saith, It is *founded upon the Rock of a Woman's Inconstancy.*

Our *Blessed Saviour* commands us (*q*) to *render unto* Cesar *the things which are* Cesar's, *and unto GOD the things which are GOD's.* These *Texts* are applied by the *Stage* to encourage *Whoring.* It is but laying the Child to the right Father. *But*, (*r*) saith an Actress, *if I receive their Flames, what if I should grow soft upon it, and receive a dangerous Impression?* To this it is answer'd, *Why then you must be rendered to the Man, whose Image you bear.* Concluding with an Exhortation, to *fear nothing.*

When *our Saviour* was born, the *Angels* said unto the Shepherds, (*u*) *I bring you Glad-tidings of great Joy, which shall be to all People.* Upon the *Stage*, (*x*) a part of this Expression is most impudently applied by a Pimp to his success in discovering a supposed Mistress.

(*i*) Gibraltar, *p*.3. *l*.34.
(*k*) *Matth*.7.12. *Luke* 6.31.
(*l*) Gibraltar, *p*.16. *l*.14.
(*m*) *Matth*. 12.30.
(*n*) Amorous Miser, *p*. 53. *l*. 25.
(*o*) *Matth*. 16.18.
(*p*) Woman is a Riddle, *p*.22. *l*. 16.
(*q*) *Matth*. 22.21. *Mark* 12.17. *Luke* 20.25.
(*r*) *Portsmouth* Heiress, *p*.19. *l*. 14.
(*u*) *Luke* 2.10.
(*x*) The Wonder, *p*.63. *l*.24.

Our

Our *Saviour*, (y) ſpeaking of the *Joy* which *there is in Heaven for one Sinner that repenteth*, compares him to *a loſt Sheep*, which is *found*. The *Stage* Comment is this, (z) *whoſe loſt Sheep is a Lover.*

When the *Prodigal Son* returned, he ſaid, (a) *Father, I have ſinned againſt Heaven, and before thee.* An *Actreſs* ſaith thus to her Lover, (b)

> *Here on my Knees I've ſinn'd, I muſt confeſs,*
> *Againſt your Love, and my own Happineſs.*

In (c) the *Goſpel*, *Christ* compares himſelf to a *Carcaſe* to which the Eagles fly; and thus is he our ſpiritual Food and Delight. An *Actor* (d) ſaith of himſelf, *I'll ſtick to the old Proverb, Where the Carrion is, the Crows will be. So long as I have Youth and Beauty, they'll all follow.*

When our *Saviour* was riſen from the Dead, he asked St. *Peter* three times this Queſtion, (e) Simon, *Son of* Jonas, *loveſt thou me?* Who anſwered as often, *Yea, LORD, thou knoweſt that I love thee.* But theſe Expreſſions are out-done in the *Play-houſe*: (f) *Doſt thou not love me,* Damaris? *Thou knoweſt I love thee with all my Heart.*

To proceed to the *Apoſtles*, St. *Paul* argues very ſeriouſly, (g) *What ſhall we ſay then? Shall we continue in Sin, that Grace may abound? GOD forbid! How ſhall we that are dead unto Sin, live any longer therein?* The Language of the *Stage* is thus: (h) *Such a Kindneſs would encourage us to ſin again.* Anſwer, *And if it ſhould!* Reply, *'Twould give occaſion for the pleaſing Exerciſe of Mercy.* Anſwer, *Right! And ſo we act the Part of Heaven and Earth together, and taſte of both their Pleaſures.* Here *Sin* is commended, and the *Mercy* of GOD is

---

(y) *Matt.* 18.12. *Luke* 15.4.
(z) Comical Lovers, *p.* 40. *l.* 28.
(a) *Luke* 15.18,21.
(b) Comical Revenge, p. 64. l. *penult.*
(c) *Matth.* 24. 28. *Luke* 17. 37.
(d) Roving Husband Reclaim'd, p.10. l.2.
(e) *John* 21.15,16,17.
(f) Amorous Widow, p.50. l. 14.
(g) *Rom.* 6.1,2.
(h) The Miſtake, p.44. l.15.

droll'd upon, being made the occasion of our Security. It is the *Pleasure* of Men in the *Play-house*-Language, not to be Religious, but to run on in *Sin*, after Oaths and Vows to the contrary; and the *Pleasure* of GOD to pardon such presumptuous *Sinners*.

St. *Paul* cries out with Admiration, (*i*) *O the depth of the Riches both of the Wisdom and Knowledge of GOD! How unsearchable are his Judgments, and his Ways past finding out!* An *Actor* exclaims thus, (*k*) *O Cupid, how unsearchable are thy Mysteries?*

The same *Apostle* tells us, (*l*) that *Marriage* was appointed by GOD as a Means *to avoid Fornication*; and therefore (*m*) it is *honourable among all Men, and the Bed undefiled; but Whoremongers and Adulterers GOD will judge.* The *Actors* (*n*) professedly render it as dishonourable as they can, and as the unhappiest State in the World; they expose it by all the ridiculous Similitudes imaginable, and complain of GOD's Providence in this particular. I have not said half which may be observed from the (*o*) Quotations in the Margin, nor cited the fourth part of those which I might have done. In short, *Marriage* is a Means to prevent *Whoring*, for

---

(*i*) *Rom.* 11. 33.

(*k*) A Woman's Revenge, p. 9. l.30.

(*l*) 1 *Cor.* 7. 2, 9.

(*m*) *Heb.* 13. 4.

(*n*) The Drummer, *Epilogue*, p.2. l.5.

(*o*) A City Ramble, or, The Humours of the Compter, p.21. *per totum.* An Act at *Oxford*, p.14. l.12. p.20. l.11. p.54. l.4. A Woman's Revenge, p.20.l.16. *French* Cato, *Epilogue*, l. 4. Fortune in her Wits, p.50. l. *penult.* Gibraltar, p.3. l.3. p.38. *Sheet* E. l.6. p.58. l.33. Hampstead-Heath, p.16. l.29. p.22. l.22. Love at first sight, p. 1. l. 1. p.6. l.33. p.45. l.4. Love the Leveller, p.17. l.19. Love's Last Shift, p. 28. l. 32. Marry or do worse, p.12. l. 18. She wou'd if she cou'd, p.92. l.26. p.93. l.13. p.130. l. 13. p.148. l.10. Artful Husband, p.1. p.2. p.3. *British* Enchanters, p. 28. l.7. Careless Husband, p. 2. l. 37. p.4. l.3. p.18. l.7,33. p.20. l.30. p.52. l.23. The Cares of Love, p.3. l.24. p.48. l. 5, 13. The Confederacy, p.25. l.33. *to the end.* p.26. *from* l.1. *to* 33. The Gamester, *Epilogue*, l. 5. Lawyer's Fortune, p. 63. l. 17. Man of Mode, p.185. l.37. The *Portsmouth* Heiress, p.19. l.30. p.31. *l. ult.* p.*ult.* l. 22. Three Hours after Marriage, p.33. l.28. Woman is a Riddle, p.5. l.14. p.11. l.23.

which reaſon they ſo exclaim againſt it. Since GOD calls it an honourable State, therefore they render it contemptible. And as (*p*) *Whores* in *Scripture* are accounted abominable, ſo in the *Play-houſe* they are repreſented as deſirable.

The ſame *Apoſtle* ſaith, (*q*) that *GOD ſhall be all in all.* An *Actor* ſaith, (*r*) *A rich Gentleman, and that's all in all.*

He ſaith, (*s*) *If any Man be in Chriſt, he is a new Creature.* An *Actreſs* ſaith of a fantaſtical ridiculous Fellow, (*t*) *He is the new-made Creature.*

The ſame *Apoſtle* is alſo very warm (*u*) againſt ſuch as ſlander'd them, that they *walked according to the Fleſh*; and he ſaith, *For tho we walk in the Fleſh, we do not walk after the Fleſh.* An *Actor* ſaith upon the *Stage,* (*x*) *I am Fleſh as well as Spirit; and my Body muſt have ſome Converſation* (ſpoken of Whoring) *as well as my Soul.*

The ſame *Apoſtle* gives us this Charge, (*y*) *See then that ye walk circumſpectly, not as Fools, but as Wiſe; redeeming the Time, becauſe the Days are Evil.* An *Actor* ſaith of a Lady, (*z*) *Out of Religion and good Conduct,* ſhe will *provide a wiſe Man to beget a witty Son to recover the Eſtate his Father had ſpent: For the tender Sex love to walk circumſpectly.* And another ſaith of himſelf, (*a*) *I intend to redeem the Time. As how? Is the Wine good? Are the Women kind?*

The Apoſtle exhorts (*b*) *Husbands* to *love* their *Wives.* An *Actor* ſaith (*c*) of a bad Husband, *If you did but know what an odious thing it is to be thought to love a Wife in good Company, you would forgive him.*

(*p*) *Deut.*23.17,18.

(*q*) 1 *Cor.* 15.28.

(*r*) The artful Husband, p.37. l.6.

(*s*) 2 *Cor.* 5.17.

(*t*) The artful Husband, p.30. l.28.

(*u*) 2 *Cor.*10.2,3,4,5.

(*x*) Gibraltar, *Sheet* E. p.36. l.28.

(*y*) *Epheſ.* 5.15, 16. *Coloſſ.* 4.5.

(*z*) The Roving Husband reclaim'd, p.8. l.9.

(*a*) She wou'd if ſhe cou'd, p. 91. l.31.

(*b*) *Epheſ.* 5.25, 28. *Coloſſ.* 3.19.

(*c*) She wou'd if ſhe cou'd, p. 134. l.29.

The *Apostle* saith also of our *Blessed Saviour*, (*d*) that he is *touched with the feeling of our Infirmities*, and proposeth it for our Comfort. An *Actor* (*e*) saith to a *Widow* upon the *Stage* in a different Sense; *Ay, ay, we should have a fellow-feeling of one another, indeed.*

He also saith, (*f*) that *Jesus Christ* is *the same yesterday, and to-day, and for ever.* An *Actor* saith, (*g*) *the Pleasures of* London *yesterday, and to-day, and to-morrow, are eternally the same.*

To instance but in one *Apostle* more. St. *John* (*h*) informs us, that *if we say that we have no Sin, we deceive our selves, and the Truth is not in us.* In a Comedy (*i*) an *Actor* being examin'd, *what Sins he had been guilty of, which had drawn a Judgment upon him*, makes this Answer, *None, Sir, none; I never committed any Sin in my Life.* And having afterward own'd himself guilty of *Cheating*, *Lying*, *Betraying a Trust*, and *Aspersing his Neighbour*, he was again asked, (*k*) *Are these no Sin?* To which he readily answers, *Why, No! I have been told, that nothing is a Sin, but Swearing and Sabbath-breaking.* And certainly, since *Swearing* is a Sin by their own Confession, their Guilt in this one particular is enough to condemn them to Hell to all Eternity.

Thus we see how the Oracles of the most High GOD are burlesqu'd and ridicul'd, and sometimes contradicted. Without the profane Allusion, all the Wit, and frequently the very Sense, is lost. This is a Method to regale the *Atheist*, and harden the Libertine. One *Actor* saith, (*l*) *I would not have you rally things which are serious:* But he is answer'd with an *Oath*, *Well enough! where's the Jest of rallying any thing else?* It is a melancholy Thought, and a worse Prospect, that we have (*m*) such Companies of *ungodly and unstable Men*, who continually *wrest the Scriptures*; and [GOD grant, that it neither may be to their own, nor the Nation's Destruction.]

(*d*) *Heb.* 4. 15.

(*e*) The Comical Revenge, p. 36. l. 15.

(*f*) *Heb.* 13. 8.

(*g*) Country Lasses, p. 2. l. 22.

(*h*) 1 *John* 1. 8.

(*i*) Fair Example, p. 64. l. 33.

(*k*) Ibid. p. 65. l. 11.

(*l*) The Drummer, p. 11. l. 28.

(*m*) 2 *Pet.* 3. 16.

CHAP.

CHAP. XXI.

The Opinion of ſome late Writers concerning the Stage.

TO what hath been ſaid in this Treatiſe concerning the *Stage*, I ſhall crave leave to add ſome Quotations from a few of our modern and eminent Writers upon the ſame Subject.

The firſt whom I ſhall mention is (*a*) Archbiſhop *Tillotſon*, who hath theſe words:

'I ſhall only ſpeak a few words concerning *Plays*; 'which as they are now ordered among us, are a migh-'ty Reproach to the Age and Nation.

'To ſpeak againſt them in general, may be thought 'too ſevere, and that which the preſent Age cannot ſo 'well brook, and would not perhaps be ſo juſt and rea-'ſonable, becauſe it is very poſſible that they might be 'ſo framed, and governed by ſuch Rules, as not only to 'be innocently diverting, but inſtructing and uſeful to 'put ſome Vices and Follies out of countenance, which 'cannot perhaps be ſo decently reproved, nor ſo effec-'tually expoſed and corrected any other way. But as 'now the *Stage* is, they are intolerable, and not fit to be 'permitted in a civiliz'd, much leſs a Chriſtian Nation. 'They do moſt notoriouſly miniſter to Infidelity and 'Vice. By the Profaneneſs of them, they are apt to 'inſtil bad Principles into the Minds of Men, and to 'leſſen that Awe and Reverence which all Men ought 'to have for GOD and Religion; and by their Lewd-'neſs they teach Vice, and are apt to infect the Minds 'of Men, and diſpoſe them to lewd and diſſolute 'Practices. And therefore I do not ſee how any Per-'ſons pretending to Sobriety and Virtue, and eſpecially 'to the pure and holy Religion of our Bleſſed Saviour,

(*a*) In his Sermon upon *Corrupt Communication.*

'can without great Guilt and open Contradiction to 'his holy Profession, be present at such lewd and im-'modest *Plays*, much less frequent them, as too many 'do, who yet would take it very ill to be shut out of 'the Community of Christians, as they would most 'certainly have been in the first and purest Ages of 'Christianity.'

Another Writer (*b*) argues thus:

'Here is a large Collection of Debauchery; such 'Pieces as are rarely to be met with. 'Tis sometimes 'painted at length too, and appears in great variety 'of Progress and Practice. It wears almost all sorts of 'Dresses to engage the Fancy, to fasten upon the Me-'mory, and keep up the Charm from languishing. 'Sometimes you have it in Image and Description; 'sometimes by way of Allusion; sometimes in Disguise, 'and sometimes without it. And what can be the 'meaning of such a Representation, unless it be to tinc-'ture the Audience, to extinguish Shame, and make 'Lewdness a Diversion? This is the natural Conse-'quence, and therefore one would think it was the In-'tention too. Such licentious Discourse tends to no 'Point, but to stain the Imagination, to awaken Folly, 'and to weaken the Defences of Virtue.

'But the danger of such an Entertainment is but part 'of the Objection; 'tis all Scandal and Meanness into 'the bargain. It doth in effect degrade human Nature, 'sinks Reason into Appetite, and breaks down the dis-'tinction between Man and Beast. Goats and Monkeys, 'if they could speak, would express their Brutality in 'such Language as this.

'To argue the matter more at large.

'Smuttiness is a fault in Behaviour, as well as in Re-'ligion. 'Tis a very coarse Diversion, the Entertain-'ment of those who are generally least both in Sense 'and Station. The looser part of the *Mob* have no 'true relish of Decency and Honour, and want Educa-'tion and Thought to furnish out a genteel Conversation.

(*b*) *Collier*'s Short View of the Immorality and Profaneness of the *English* Stage, *Chap.* 1. *viz.* The Immodesty of the Stage, *Pag.* 4.

'Bar-

'Barrenneſs of Fancy makes them often take up with 'theſe ſcandalous Liberties. A *vicious* Imagination may 'blot a great deal of Paper at this rate with eaſe enough. 'And 'tis poſſible, Convenience may ſometimes invite 'to the Expedient. The modern *Poets* ſeem to uſe 'Smut as the old ones did *Machines*, to relieve a fainting 'ing Invention. When *Pegaſus* is jaded, and would 'ſtand ſtill, he is apt, like other *Tits*, to run into every 'Puddle.'

'Obſcenity in any Company is a ruſtick uncreditable 'Talent, but among Women 'tis particularly rude. 'Such Talk would be very affronting in Converſation, 'and not indur'd by any Lady of Reputation. Whence 'then comes it to paſs, that thoſe Liberties, which diſ'oblige ſo much in Converſation, ſhould entertain upon 'the *Stage?* Do the Women leave all the regard to 'Decency and Conſcience behind them, when they 'come to the *Play-houſe?* Or doth the Place transform 'their Inclinations, and turn their former Averſions 'into Pleaſures? Or were their pretences to Sobriety 'elſewhere, nothing but Hypocriſy and Grimace? Such 'Suppoſitions as theſe are all Satire and Invective. They 'are rude Imputations upon the whole Sex. To treat 'the Ladies with ſuch Stuff, is no better than taking 'their Money to abuſe them. It ſuppoſes their Imagi'nations vicious, and their Memories ill furniſhed; 'that they are practiſed in the Language of the Stews, 'and pleaſed with the Scenes of Brutiſhneſs: When at 'the ſame time the Cuſtoms of Education and the Laws 'of Decency are ſo very cautious in regard to Women; 'I ſay, ſo very reſerved, that 'tis almoſt a fault for them 'to underſtand that they are ill uſed. They cannot 'diſcover their Diſguſt without diſadvantage, nor bluſh 'without diſſervice to their Modeſty. To appear with 'any Skill in ſuch Cant, looks as if they had fallen upon 'ill Converſation; or managed their Curioſity amiſs. In 'a word, he that treats the Ladies with ſuch Diſcourſe, 'muſt conclude, either that they like it, or they do 'not. To ſuppoſe the firſt, is a groſs Reflection upon 'their *Virtue:* and as for the latter caſe, it entertains 'them with their own Averſion; which is Ill-Nature 'and Ill Manners enough in all Conſcience. And in 'this particular, *Cuſtom* and *Conſcience*, the Forms of

'*Breeding*,

'*Breeding*, and the Maxims of *Religion*, are on the same
'side. In other Instances, *Vice* is often fashionable;
'but here a Man can't be a Sinner, without being a
'Clown.'

And again (*c*),

'By what hath been offer'd it appears, that the *pre-*
'*sent English Stage* is superlatively scandalous. It exceeds
'the Liberties of all Times and Countries. It hath
'not so much as the poor Plea of a *Precedent*, to which
'most other ill things may claim a pretence. 'Tis
'mostly mere Discovery and Invention: A new World
'of Vice found out and planted with all the Industry
'imaginable. *Aristophanes* himself, how bad soever in
'other respects, doth not amplify and flourish, and run
'through all the Topicks of Lewdness like these Men.
'The *Miscellany Poems* are likewise horribly licentious.
'They are sometimes Collections from Antiquity, and
'often the worst Parts of the worst *Poets*: And to
'mend the matter, the *Christian Translation* is more
'nauseous than the *Pagan Original*. Such Stuff, I be-
'lieve, was never seen, and never suffer'd before. In
'a word, if Poverty and Diseases, the Dishonour of
'Families, and the debauching of Kingdoms are such
'valuable Advantages; then I confess these Books de-
'serve Encouragement: But if the Case is otherwise, I
'humbly conceive the Proceeding should be so too.'

And again (*d*),

'I could give the Reader some more of these fine
'Sentences; but they are too much out of Order to
'appear. The truth is, our *Stage-Poets* seem to fence
'against Censure by the Excess of Lewdness; and to
'make the overgrown Size of a Crime, a Ground for
'Impunity. As if a Malefactor should project his
'Escape, by appearing too scandalous for publick Tryal.
'However, this is their Armour of Proof; this is the
'Strength, which they retreat to. They are fortified
'in Smut, and almost impregnable in Stench; so that
'where they deserve most, there is no coming at them.'

(*c*) *Collier*'s short View of the Immorality and Profaneness of the *English* Stage, *p*. 54.

(*d*) P. 178.

Sir

Sir *Richard Blackmore* complains thus (*e*):

'I have revived my old Controversy with the *Stage*, 'the Entertainments of which, as they are still ma-'naged, are highly prejudicial to the Interests of Reli-'gion and Virtue, as having an apparent Tendency to 'produce profane Principles and Corruption of Man-'ners. I have in the following *Essay upon Wit* shew'd 'how that Talent is abused and prostituted to unworthy 'Purposes in Dramatick Performances, and what a 'pernicious Influence it must needs have, whilst so em-'ploy'd on the Minds and Actions of Men. I know, 'it is alledg'd in defence of our *Comedies*, that they 'are proper to expose the Fool, and reform the Liber-'tine; to recommend Decency and Virtue, and put 'Foppery and Immorality out of countenance. But as 'to the Correction of Vice, and propagating of Sobriety 'of Manners, it is evident by long Experience, that it 'hath not that Effect in any degree, and indeed is not 'an adequate and competent Means for that End.'

And again (*f*):

'As the amorous Fictions owe their birth to the '*Milesians*, the most profligate and vicious Nation that 'ever appear'd upon the face of the Earth; so they 'have a great Influence upon all People, where they are 'generally received and applauded, by corrupting their 'Manners, dissolving their Minds, and destroying their 'Taste of useful and solid Learning.'

And again (*g*):

'The most extensive Abuse of Parts and Ingenuity 'appears in the loose Productions of our Writers to the '*Stage*. It was the Complaint of the celebrated Wit 'of *Spain*, *Michael de Cervantes*, that the *Comedies* in 'his time were not only extravagant and monstrous 'in their Contrivance, but likewise the Exemplars of 'Vice and Representations of Lewdness. But had the '*Plays* of *Spain* at that time been as immoral and un-'chaste as the daily Entertainments of the *British*

(*e*) *In his* Essays, *Vol.* I. Preface, *p.* 44. *printed Anno* 1716.

(*f*) Essay upon Epick Poetry, *Vol.* I. *p.* 29.

(*g*) Essay upon Wit, *Vol.* I. *p.* 218.

'*Theatre*,

'*Theatre*, which have a manifeſt Tendency to vitiate 'the Taſte of the People, fill their Imaginations with 'obſcene Ideas, and their Lives with Levity, Idleneſs 'and Luxury; I ſay, if that great Man, whoſe Judg-'ment was equal to his admirable Genius, had ſeen Re-'ligion and Virtue ſo derided, and Modeſty, Reſerved-'neſs and Decency ſo inſulted and expoſed, his Zeal 'for the Honour of his Country, and his Love of Man-'kind, would have animated him to have attack'd the 'Comick Poets with the ſame Spirit, with which he 'aſſaulted the prevailing Folly of his Age, the roman-'tick Atchievements of Knights Errant: his Wit and 'good Senſe would have made thoſe merry Authors as 'odious for poiſoning the People with their looſe and 'immoral Writings, as he made the others ridiculous 'for their extravagant and idle Tales.

'No doubt a Comedy may be ſo contriv'd, that it 'may at once become delightful, and promote Pru-'dence and Sobriety of Manners; that is, when the 'principal Action contains an inſtructive Moral, and all 'the Parts, in a regular Connection, Dependence and 'Proportion, illuſtrate and ſupport each other, and have 'a manifeſt Influence on the main Event, and when 'the Diction is chaſte and inoffenſive to the modeſt and 'virtuous Hearers. So regular and beautiful a Piece as 'this, cannot but greatly pleaſe and divert, as well as 'inſtruct the Audience. Nor is it, I imagine, for want 'of Knowledge in the Rules of Writing, nor of ſuffi-'cient Genius, in which the Nation abounds, that ſo 'few Comedies diſtinguiſh'd by theſe Perfections have 'been produced: But this Defect ariſeth partly from 'this, that the Comick Poets are often Men of looſe 'Manners, and therefore unlikely Perſons to undertake 'the Encouragement and Promotion of Virtue, of 'which they have no Taſte; and to diſcountenance 'Imprudence and Immorality, when by doing ſo, they 'muſt expoſe their own Character to deriſion: tho 'ſometimes it may happen, that a looſe Poet, merely 'from his juſt Manner of Thinking, and his Senſe of 'Decency in forming Diſcourſes becoming each Cha-'racter, may entertain the Audience with laudable Per-'formances.

'Ano-

'Another, and the chief Cauſe of the Immorality of 'the Theatre, is the ill Taſte of the People, who, not-'withſtanding they have applauded ſeveral clean and 'regular *Tragedies*, ſuch as thoſe which have of late 'appear'd, that are worthy of the greateſt Commen-'dation, eſpecially *Cato*, and the *Plays* for the moſt 'part of Mr. *Rowe*, as great a Genius for Tragedy as 'any Nation in any Age has produced; yet ſtill fre-'quent and encourage the looſeſt *Comedies*. It happens, 'that the greateſt part of Men of Wit and Humour, 'who not being eaſy in their Fortunes, work for the '*Stage*, and are Day-Labourers for the Muſes, lie under 'a neceſſity of bringing thoſe Productions to a Mar-'ket, which are in faſhion, and therefore vendible; 'whilſt others, tho of ever ſo much greater Value, 'would be turned back upon their hands; nor would 'the *Actors*, who live by their Employments, as the 'Comick Writers do by theirs, undertake to repreſent 'an innocent, and much leſs a *Comedy* of yet higher 'Merit.

'Tho ſeveral Aſſaults have been made upon the *Co-'mick Poets* in faſhion, and many Batteries have been 'raiſed againſt the *Theatre*, yet hitherto they have 'proved unſucceſsful: the *Stage* is become impregna-'ble, where looſe *Poets*, ſupported by Numbers, Power 'and Intereſt, in defiance of all Rules of Decency and 'Virtue, ſtill provide new Snares and Temptations to 'ſeduce the People, and corrupt their Manners. Not-'withſtanding the earneſt Cries of this great City, that 'importune theſe Writers to reform the *Theatre*, and 'no longer to infect her Youth, and draw their Inclina-'tions from their Profeſſions and Employments; not-'withſtanding the Sighs and Tears of many once flou-'riſhing, but now diſconſolate Families, ruin'd by the 'diſſolute Lives of their chief Branches, who loſt their 'Virtue by frequenting the fatal Entertainments of the 'Theatre; notwithſtanding the wiſe and ſober part of 'the Kingdom earneſtly ſollicite them to ſpare the Peo-'ple, to ſtop the ſpreading Plague, and ſtay the de-'ſtroying Pen, they perſevere with intrepid Reſolution 'and inexorable Cruelty to poiſon the Minds, and ruin 'the Morals of the Nation.

'The *Actors*, we may ſafely conclude, are not re-
'ſtrained by ſuch rigorous Precepts of Virtue, but that
'they will always be inclin'd to preſent thoſe Perfor-
'mances, which will beſt fill the Houſe, and promote
'their Intereſt; and therefore they will readily humour
'the vitiated Taſte of the Audience, by acting the moſt
'immoral *Plays*, whilſt they find their account in doing
'ſo: And that which confirms this Obſervation, is, that
'they never, as far as I have heard, rejected any *Come-*
'*dy* merely for its Looſeneſs; tho, I believe, they
'have refuſed many for want of that entertaining Qua-
'lity.

'It would therefore prove an effectual Remedy for
'this Evil, if the Ladies would diſcountenance theſe
'Comedies, by expreſſing their Diſlike, and refuſing to
'be preſent when they are acted. And this, no doubt,
'they would do, were they inform'd that the *Come-*
'*dies*, which they encourage by their Appearance at
'the *Theatre*, are full of wanton Sentiments, obſcene
'Alluſions, and immodeſt Ideas, contain'd in Expreſ-
'ſions of a double Meaning: For it cannot be ima-
'gined, they would bear with Unconcernedneſs, much
'leſs with Pleaſure, Diſcourſes in publick, which they
'deteſt as unſufferable in private Converſation, if they
'knew them to be unchaſte. And ſhould the Ladies
'aſſert their Eſteem of Virtue, and declare openly on
'the ſide of Modeſty, the moſt attractive Beauty of
'the Fair Sex, as certainly they would do, if they un-
'derſtood how much theſe amiable Qualities have been
'expoſed and affronted by our moſt eminent Comick
'Poets, this would lay the Ax to the Root, and at one
'blow deſtroy this pernicious Practice. For after this,
'what Writer would tranſgreſs the Rules of Decency
'and Purity of Expreſſion, when he knows, that by
'his immodeſt Mixtures he ſhall fright the Ladies from
'the Houſe?

'The Poets and Players would ſoon find themſelves
'obliged to reſtrain their licentious Conduct, reform
'the Theatre, and preſent to the Town, if not in-
'ſtructive, at leaſt inoffenſive and unſhocking Diver-
'ſions. And it is very deſirable, that this Expedient
'were ſet on foot, that the Honour of the *Engliſh The-*
'*atre* may be retriev'd; that while we juſtly boaſt of
'our

'our Priority of Wit and Humour to our Neighbours, 'we may not be obliged to acknowledge the great Inferiority of our *Comedies* in reſpect of Cleanneſs and 'moral Beauty; that we may not be reproach'd, that 'while we profeſs a reformed and pure Religion, we 'encourage an immodeſt and unreform'd *Theatre*; and 'that we are very defective in the Practice of Virtue 'and Regularity of Manners, while theſe Abominations 'are indulg'd, and theſe unhallow'd Groves and High 'Places of Immorality are frequented without diſtur-'bance.'

And again (*h*):

'In one Inſtance, and that of great moment, our 'Taſte continues unreform'd, and that deſpicable ſort 'of Wit is ſtill received with Pleaſure and Applauſe; 'and that is, when Words of a double Signification, 'which is the Foundation of the old exploded way of 'facetious Writing, are apply'd to looſe and immodeſt 'Purpoſes: for then they are ſtill very agreeable, and 'made the moſt entertaining Parts of the *Comedy*, 'which is ſenſleſs and inſipid, if not animated and 'heighten'd by thoſe impure Mixtures. And thus far 'the Taſte of the preſent Age, however otherwiſe po-'lite, is altogether coarſe and uncultivated. And I 'cannot imagine, but the ingenious Writers of ſuch 'looſe Pieces are themſelves conſcious, that this eaſy 'and almoſt unavoidable kind of Wit (which reſults 'only from a Congruity of Words in Sound, but not 'in Meaning, and which they deſpiſe and deride when 'they are uſed upon other Subjects, and for other Pur-'poſes than to raiſe obſcene Ideas, and gratify the vitia-'ted Taſte of a degenerate Age) is low and contemp-'tible.'

And again (*i*):

'It is from a falſe Taſte, that Men of Literature 'employ their ingenious Talents in looſe and profane 'Productions; for this contradicts the End, and de-'ſtroys the Uſefulneſs of Writing, which is to delight

(*h*) Sir *Richard Blackmore's* Eſſays, *Vol.* 2. An Eſſay upon Writing, *p.* 264. *printed* Anno 1717.

(*i*) P. 267.

'and improve the Mind; or, in fuller Expression, to 'convey to it moral Instruction, by the insinuating 'Force of Pleasure. Nor is it a less Corruption of 'Taste in the People, who encourage and applaud 'those shameless Pens, which are prostituted to the Ser-'vice of Irreligion and Vice, and engaged to oppose, 'with the utmost Malice and Rancour, the Interest of 'Heaven and Virtue; and by propagating Impiety and 'degenerate Manners, are labouring to pull down their 'own Altars, and bring Destruction upon themselves, 'their native Land, and late Posterity.'

And again (*k*):

'Men of true Taste and critical Judgment could not 'without Pain and Indignation observe, that a petulant 'Set of Writers, who have no way to Popularity and 'Fame, but by making their court to the Vices and 'Follies of the Age, from a rooted and inflexible En-'mity to Piety and Virtue, and immortal Hatred to 'good Men, had undertaken by their immodest and 'flagitious Papers to defeat the good and great Design 'of such Writers, who wish'd well to their Country 'and Religion; to efface the laudable Impressions, 'which they had made on the Minds of Men; and re-'store the vitiated Taste, from which they seem'd in a 'good degree to have been delivered. Pity it is, if we 'regard the Honour and Welfare of Religion, or the 'Safety and flourishing State of the Kingdom, that 'such malignant Pens should be suffered to pour down 'their Poison on the wholesom Seeds of Morality, 'blast in the Bud the generous Plants, and destroy our 'Expectations from that promising Nursery of virtuous 'and wise Instruction, which the others had cultivated 'and improv'd with so much Application, Zeal and In-'genuity. Pity it is, that these intrepid Conspirators 'against Heaven and Religion, animated with deliberate 'Malice, should go on by their impious Turns of Wit 'and Raillery, to expose all modest and prudent Be-'haviour, and give the last Blow, if they are able, to 'Sobriety of Manners: and thus by recovering and 'confirming the vitiated Relish of the Nation, undo

(*k*) Sir *Richard Blackmore*'s Essay upon Writing, *p.* 269.

'all

'all that the other Writers, by their excellent Labours, 'have to their great honour done, in the Service of 'Virtue and their Country.'

And again (*l*):

'Since the *Essay* upon *Writing* was printed, tho not 'publish'd, a new *Comedy* hath been acted, so empty 'of Wit and Sense, and so redundant in shameless Im-'morality, that perhaps no *Dramatick* Representation 'did ever so much disgrace the *Stage*, nor affront a '*British* Audience. The Author———hath not only 'discovered his own vitiated Judgment, but with an 'arrogant Assurance hath taken it for granted, that 'the Nation hath the same degenerate and corrupt 'Taste. I cannot therefore but take notice with Satis-'faction, that the People have asserted their Honour, 'and vindicated their Capacity and Discernment, by 'expressing universally their Contempt and Detestation 'of that Performance. And it is to be hoped, that 'after the publick Mortification, which such a Con-'spirator against Virtue and Decency hath received, our '*Comick Poets* will desist from such audacious Attempts 'on the good Sense of the Audience; and the rather, 'because it cannot be presumed, but that those who are 'intrusted with the Care of *Theatrical* Entertainments, 'will interpose their Authority, and suffer no more 'such *Comedies* to sink the Reputation of *Poetry*, and 'insult the Judgment of the Town.'

I have quoted Archbishop *Tillotson* on this occasion, to shew the Opinion of so eminent a Divine, and one who was justly raised to so high a Station. I have quoted Mr. *Collier* concerning the *Immodesty* of the *Stage*; be-cause the *Vice* is still the same in our modern *Comedies*, or rather worse than ever. And indeed the Expressions are intolerable, and not fit to be produced. The whole Plot and Contrivance of the *Plays* turn upon Lewdness. The Methods of forming such Intrigues are drawn up into a *Science*, and set off with the utmost advantage to be put in practice: And then the greatest *Debauchees* are rewarded with Success in the *End*. And as these Re-

---

(*l*) *Volume* II. *Preface*, p. 46. *Anno* 1717.

presentations seem to please the Humour of the Nation where they are acted; so they are a sad Indication how loose we are in our Morals, and how ripe for Destruction. We may therefore too sadly apply to ourselves the Words of the Prophet; (*m*) *Except the Lord of Hosts had left unto us a very small Remnant, we should have been as* Sodom, *and we should have been like unto* Gomorrah. It is a wonder that they, who run daily into these *Temptations*, do not fall into all manner of *Evil*. And it must be wholly owing to the *restraining Grace* of GOD (whom such do daily tempt) and to his Providence, which prevents the Opportunities, that they who see with pleasure such *vile Representations*, do not also proceed to the *vilest Actions*. The exposing the Wickedness of this nature in our late *Plays*, would fill a Volume as large as what I have written; but it would be a most nauseous Employment. And as the Monsters are too deformed to be produced; so I shall forbear, and leave the *Reader* only to consider, whether they who are guilty of the former Impieties, can be supposed to scruple the greatest Immoralities.

I have also added the preceding Sentences from Sir *Richard Blackmore*'s *Essays*, because they were printed so very lately; and do therefore serve as a corroborating Evidence, That our present *Stage* is as bad as ever; and all the Methods which have been hitherto used for their Reformation, have proved ineffectual. And this naturally produceth another melancholy Consideration, That the Great GOD, who hath been so long, so often, and so grievously provoked, will not always be mocked; and we may greatly fear, that his Mercy thus abused, will be turned into Justice.

(*m*) *Isa.* 1. 9.

CHAP.

CHAP. XXII.

The Opinion of the Stage-Poets concerning their own Plays.

TO what hath been ſaid by other Authors, I ſhall add the Opinion of the *Stage-Poets* themſelves. And certainly, if ever any People, being (a) *ſubverted*, were afterward *condemned* by their own Confeſſion, theſe are the Men. They own themſelves guilty, and yet go on with the greateſt Obſtinacy. Thus they aggravate their Crimes, (b) they *glory in their Shame*, and deſerve not the leaſt Favour from GOD or Man.

The *Epithets* that they beſtow, are the firſt Particular which I ſhall take notice of. Accordingly the *Play-Houſes* are call'd by them, (c) *The common Refuge of all the young idle People*, (d) the *Devil's Forge*, (e) thoſe *Nurſeries of Debauchery, the two lewd Play-Houſes*; (f) the *ſad Play-Houſes*, or (g) *thoſe Marts for Lewdneſs*. The *Actors* are call'd (h) a *pack of wicked Players*, (i) thoſe little inſignificant Creatures the Players, or (k) a *Company of wild Players*; and their Performances, (l) *Plays*, and *ſuch idle Stuff*, or (m) *Plays which are worſe than nothing*. The being preſent at them, is (n) the *Vanity of ſeeing Plays*; and the *Poets* are deſcribed to be

(a) *Tit.* 3. 10.
(b) *Phil.* 3. 19.
(c) The Man of Mode, *p.*213. *l.* 32.
(d) The City-Ramble, or the Play-Houſe Wedding, *p.*70. *l.*13.
(e) The City-Ramble, *p.* 2. *l.* 16.
(f) The Fair Quaker of *Deal*, *p.* 51. *l.* 32.
(g) Ibid. *Epilogue*, *l.* 14.
(h) The City-Ramble, or the Play-Houſe Wedding, *p.*2. *l.*26.
(i) The Man of Mode, *p.*197. *l.* 18.
(k) The Female Wits, *p.* 15. *l.* 23.
(l) The Amorous Miſer, *p.* 5. *l.* 26.
(m) The Maſquerade, *p.* 4. *l.* 14.
(n) The Fair Quaker of *Deal*, *Epilogue*, *l.* 12.

(*o*) *as insolent as the rest of the Scriblers of the Town,* (*p*) who *will allow no Man Wit, who doth not play the fool like themselves.* One of the *Poets,* speaking of his Translation out of the *French,* (*q*) adds, that *the better to fit it to the* English *Taste,* he hath *made some few Deviations*; that is, he hath made it more bold, daring and profane: and this I suppose an *Author* well versed in these Writings calls (*r*) the *British Fire*; Fire indeed! and enough, without a Miracle of Mercy, to lay the Kingdom in ashes. A *Poet* speaking of the Design to reform the *Vices* of the *Stage,* by putting the Laws in execution, calls it (*s*) *the Censure and Strictness of the Times,* when *Plays, as tho they were not dull enough before, must (to oblige the affected Zeal and Humour of some kind of People) be robb'd of all the Life and Pertness* (that is, the Blasphemy and Profaneness) *in them.* Indeed one saith, (*t*) *It is a pleasure to the Muses to think, that there are some Men of too delicate Understandings, to give into the Taste of a depraved Age.* But (to use his own Phrase) it is a *mortifying Thought* to consider how few the Number is. Another (*u*) saith, *The* English, *I must confess, ought a little to restrain their fiery Imagination beneath the Yoke of Rules: They should not give such a Loose to Metaphors: They should beware of falling into certain Meannesses, which the* Greek *Poets did not sufficiently avoid; and they should bid adieu to their Romantick Ideas.* These things are not right; but yet there are Crimes of a higher nature to charge them with, from their own Confessions, which I shall only produce to the Reader with very little Comment upon them.

'(*x*) Should I trust you to your self, you might find 'the way to some little blind Bawdy-House, or which 'is worse, to the great one, the Play-House.'

(*o*) The Fair Quaker of *Deal, Epilogue, in fine.*

(*p*) The Man of Mode, *p.*215. *l.* 25.

(*q*) Manlius Capitolinus, *Preface,* p. 2.

(*r*) The Distress'd Mother, *Prologue, l.* 24.

(*s*) The *Portsmouth* Heiress, *Preface,* p. 1. l. 2.

(*t*) The Royal Convert, *Dedication,* p. 2. l. 19.

(*u*) *A Parallel between the two Tragedies of* Cato, *at the end of the* French Cato, *p.* 3. *l.* 25.

(*x*) As you find it, p. 15. l. 13.

' Whores

'(y) Whores in *London* are ſo dog-cheap, a Man
' may but ſtep into the *Play-houſe* Paſſage, and fetch up
' half a dozen for half a Crown.'

'(z) Poetry in its firſt Inſtitution was principally de-
' ſigned to correct and rectify Manners. But tho the
' Writers of later Ages have in a great meaſure, not to
' ſay in a ſcandalous manner, deviated from the Foot-
' ſteps and Examples of their Predeceſſors; yet they
' have found Protection and Favour from thoſe, who
' have been ſo generous as to aſcribe the Faults of the
' *Poets* to the Degeneracy of the Age wherein they
' lived.'

'(a) The beſt Criticks have long and juſtly com-
' plained, that the Coarſeneſs in moſt Characters in our
' late *Comedies* have been unfit Entertainments for Peo-
' ple of Quality, eſpecially the Ladies: and nothing
' hath lately appear'd which might reform the Town to
' a better Taſte.'

'(b) The licentious Pens of *Poets* have brought thoſe
' monſtrous Births into Light which now ſhame the
' World.'

'(c) 'Tis your Jilts and your Gipſies, your Wan-
' tons and your Libertines, that the looſe Scriblers of
' this Age dreſs up ſo lovely, which is the crying Shame
' of the *Stage*.'

'(d) The reprobate Scriblers of this Age are ſuch a
' ſenſeleſs pack of Rogues, that they bewray their own
' Neſts, and ſtuff ſo many villanous lewd Characters
' into their *Plays*, till they have almoſt undone the very
' *Stage* they live by.'

'(e) Theſe *Players* have marr'd more Lawyers than
' ever *Weſtminſter-Hall* made. [*Anſwer*] With Submiſ-
' ſion, Sir, I think a *Play-houſe* rightly underſtood, is a
' very good School of Morality. [*Reply*] Morality!
' Ay! picking up Whores is a very moral Buſineſs in-
' deed. I tell you, Sir, an honeſt Neighbour of mine,

(y) Gibraltar, p.6. l.8.

(z) The Baſſet-Table, *Dedication.*

(a) The Careleſs Husband, *Dedication.*

(b) The City Ramble, or The Play-houſe Wedding, *Dedication.*

(c) Ibid. p.30. l.34.

(d) Ibid. p.58. l.27.

(e) The fair Example, p. 20. l. 29.

' that

'that had never ſeen *London* before, runs to the *Play-*
'*houſe*, and picks up an Orange-Wench. To the Ta-
'vern they go. He gives her a Couple of Guineas; ſhe
'gives him a Favour; down into the Country he brings
'it. He gives it his Wife, ſhe gives it the Doctor, and
'now the whole Pariſh is in a Diet-Drink. And there's
'the *Play-houſe* for ye! [*Anſwer*] The beſt things may
'be perverted to an ill uſe. [*Reply*] What! you are
'for the *Play-houſes* too, are you? A fine ſight 'tis in-
'deed, to ſee a Company of Ladies cracking their Sides
'at a dull *Play*, and ſleeping all Church-time at an ex-
'cellent moral Sermon.'

'(*f*) In *Rome* and *Athens* the name of *Poet* was held
'ſacred, whilſt he taught nothing which contradicted
'the Conſtitution he liv'd under, or the Religion of his
'Country. In the Declenſion of theſe two Empires,
'*Poetry* too got into licence, and help'd to debauch and
'vitiate thoſe Morals it had before improv'd. But now
'the *Poets* find the Palates of their Gueſts ſo vitiated,
'that they neglect the more ſubſtantial Food which
'was deſign'd for their Nouriſhment. Methinks thoſe
'Gentlemen who have the management of the *Thea-*
'*tres*, ſhould agree to baniſh every thing that could be
'thought the leaſt below the Dignity of the *Stage*. But
'this I fear we can hardly hope to ſee, whilſt the two
'Houſes are open.'

'(*g*) A vitious Strain doth uſually attend the *Comick-*
'*Muſe*.'

'(*h*) The *Play-houſe*! Ay, that's the place where
'ſuch bold Sluts are nurs'd up in their Impudence. A
'ſcandal to all Morality, and a ſhame to your Sex.'

'(*i*) Reformation is a mere Pretence to deceive the
'wiſer ſort, who would fain ſuppreſs the *Stage*. But
'were it ſo, *Poets* are too lewd themſelves to pretend
'to correct others. No, to reform is the leaſt Aim of
'the *Poet*: 'Tis to pleaſe, to indulge the Fancy, and to
'ſooth the Appetite. The *Stage* gives the Faſhions,

(*f*) The Force of Friendſhip, *Preface*.

(*g*) The Gameſter, *Dedication*, l. 14.

(*h*) Humours of the Age, p. 38. l. 20.

(*i*) Ibid. p. 46. l. 14.

'and

'and Vice is represented more for Example than Ridi-
'cule.'

'(k) *Plays* are endeavoured to humour the Times
'and the Company that attend them; and therein they
'have an eye to comply with the greater number of Peo-
'ple, who for the most part are ill-bred Citizens, *Jews*,
'and Merchants Apprentices. For that cause, they have
'spices of Profaneness, and rather encourage Vice, by
'setting it off with a Lustre, than blacken it; and ren-
'der Virtue rather Folly, than shew the Beauty of
'it.'

'(l) Tho it ought to be the care of all Governments,
'that publick Representations should have nothing in
'them but what is agreeable to the Manners, Laws,
'Religion and Policy of the Place and Nation in which
'they are exhibited; yet it is the general Complaint
'of the more learned and virtuous among us, that the
'*English Stage* has extremely offended.'

'(m) It is high time that we should no longer draw
'Occasions of Mirth from those Images, which, the Reli-
'gion of our Country tells us, we ought to tremble at
'with Horror.'

'(n) The *Poets* corrupt our Manners with their bad
'Characters; and always reward a profligate Whore-
'master with a good Fortune.'

'(o) Your *Wits* now-a-days are the most ridiculous
'part of Mankind; censorious, scurrilous, and ill-man-
'ner'd to the last degree; bright in nothing but their
'scoffing at *Religion* and *Government*, or defending *A-*
theism, and abusing the *Clergy*.'

'(p) You that are an Advocate for *Comedy*, one would
'think, had liv'd in an Age when Intriguing was most
'in fashion, since nothing is so commodious for that as
'our present Diversion.'

'(q) In our modern *Comedies* Wit is quite lost, and
'moral Instruction expung'd. The Gentlemen which

(k) The Lawyer's Fortune, p. 37. l.16.

(l) The Lying Lover, *Preface*, p.1. l.1. *By Sir* Richard Steel.

(m) Ibid. p.2. l.20.

(n) The Maid's the Mistress, p. 53. l.1.

(o) The Masquerade, p.4. l.2.

(p) Ibid. p.23. l.15.

(q) Ibid. p.24. l.5.

'they

'they draw for the Patterns of the Age, are always
'great Rogues, and yet the only Perſons rewarded.
'Buffoonry ſupplies the place of Wit, and Scandal and
'Detraction that of Satire. [*Anſwer*] We owe theſe
'Conſequences to the corrupted Taſte of the Town,
'to which our Writers ſuit their Works: For ſo long
'as it is eaſy to raiſe Applauſe from Party-Strokes, and
'laſcivious double Entenders, Men will never rack
'their Brains to produce more laſting Diverſions.'

'(r) Looſe Intriguing and Cuckold-making, *&c.* generally ſtuff the *Plays*.'

'(s) The reading of *Plays* and *Romances* has quite
'turn'd her Head. The *Poets* do this Miſchief. The
'Goddeſs of Beauty muſt be a Whore. And in all
'their wicked Fictions, the very fineſt Lady, the Heroine
'of all the Story, muſt be the greateſt Strumpet.'

'(t) In the *Theatres* now and then, and but now and
'then, a good *Play* appears; whilſt bad ones, like Thiſtles,
'ſpring up ſo faſt, that they choak both the
'Houſes.'

'(u) The Age declines from her primitive Virtue,
'and the ſilken Wits of the Time diſgracing Nature
'and harmonious Poeſy, are tranſported with many
'illiterate and prodigious Births.'

'(x) Theſe *Stage-Plays* are plaguy dangerous things.'

'(y) Bad *Plays* do oft ſucceed.'

'(z) The *Poets* drop the Deſign of *Comedy* with the
'publick Good, for their private Intereſt; and Fear or
'Gain, or both, make them rather countenance than
'laſh the Vices of the Age: they ſtudy nothing now,
'but to advance the Profits of the third Day, and ſo
'get their abominable Stuff ſupported.'

(r) Modern Prophets, *Preface*, p. 1. l. 30.

(s) Perplex'd Couple, p. 9. l. 18.

(t) The School-Boy, *Preface*, l. 7.

(u) Stage-Coach, *Dedication*, p. 1. l. 1.

(x) What-d'ye-call-it, p. 40. l. 17.

(y) The Wife's Relief, *Prologue*, l. 21.

(z) Woman is a Riddle, p. 3. l. 36.

Here

Here are Quotations enough in Prose to find them all guilty; but to these I shall add some others in Verse.

'(a) But this Poetick Licence of the Age
'Has with stiff Nonsense so debauch'd the *Stage*,
'And writ you into such a vicious Taste,
'That what is Sterling Wit, to you's Bombast.
'And since elsewhere your Favour we observe,
'Sure Wit and Virtue too our House would starve.'
'(b) If we to Virtue lean, the Bullies huff;
'And then they cry, 'tis damn'd dull fustian Stuff.'
'(c) Too long has Marriage, in this tasteless Age,
'With ill-bred Raillery supply'd the Stage:
'No little Scribler is of Wit so bare,
'But has his Fling at the poor wedded Pair.'
'(d) The *Stage* its primitive Use should know, design'd
'At once to please, and to instruct Mankind:
'But such base Offsprings have of late been shewn,
'That Sense or Modesty would blush to own.'
'(e) *Play* should reform, and *Satire* should correct;
'But modern Wits the antient Rules neglect:
'A loose Extravagant obtains your Praise,
'And the bold huffing Hero shares the Bays.'
'(f) What a dull Business is my virtuous Part?'
'(g) ———— Mere Virtue here
'Makes up my hideous frightful Character.'
'(h) From late Experience taught, we slight the Rule
'Of Profit with Delight.'
'(i) *Poets* in former days, without Disputes,
'Turn'd Men to Gods, transform'd the Gods to Brutes:
'Our *Poets* change the *Scene*, but with this odds,
'Make Men the Brutes, make nothing of the Gods.'

(a) As you find it, *Prologue*, l. 5, 13.

(b) Love the Leveller, *Epilogue*, l. 15.

(c) The Drummer, *Epilogue*, l. 31.

(d) The fair Example, *Prologue*, l. 19.

(e) Faithful Bride of *Granada*, *Epilogue*, l. 3.

(f) The Maid's the Mistress, *Epilogue*, l. 2.

(g) Ibid. l. 9.

(h) Rival Fools, *Prologue*, l. 36.

(i) Stage-Coach, *Prologue* l. 1.

And

And now, if we ſhould ask what good can be expected from the *Stage* as an Equivalent for ſo many Affronts offer'd to GOD, ſo many Injuries to Religion, and ſo much Miſchief done to their Country? They tell us, that their higheſt Aim is to pleaſe and divert the Company. One calls the writing of *Plays*, (*k*) an *Attempt to pleaſe*; and confeſſes in his own caſe, (*l*) that *his ſole Aim is to divert* the *Spleens* of the Auditory. Another ſaith, (*m*) *Diverſion is the Buſineſs of the* Stage, and (*n*) *Our true Intent is all for your Delight*. A third ſaith, (*o*) *To divert the Patrons of the* Stage *is my ſole Aim, in all which I attempt.*

A fourth adds in an *Epilogue*, (*p*)

Poor Wheedle *hopes h' as giv'n you all Content;*
Here he proteſts, 'tis that he only meant.

And a fifth in a *Prologue*, (*q*)

Our Author for himſelf all Fears diſclaims,
Since he alone at your Diverſion aims;
And counts it Merit, if he can but move
His Pit by Laughter, his poor Scenes t' approve.

And therefore, ſince this is the general caſe, we may make that Inference which one of their own *Poets* hath (*r*) already made;

When *Poets aim at nought but to delight,*
Fidlers have to the Bays an equal Right.

If then Religion muſt be thus expoſed, and our GOD affronted only for Diverſion; this highly provokes him to take ſuch Methods which his Juſtice ſhall think fit, to ſpoil our *Paſtime*, and vindicate his own Honour.

(*k*) A Woman's Revenge, *Prologue*, l.11.
(*l*) Ibid. l.28.
(*m*) The Comick Maſque, *Preface*, l.1.
(*n*) Ibid. p.5. l.24.
(*o*) Humours of Purgatory, *Dedication*, p.2. l.15.
(*p*) Man of Mode, *Epilogue*, l. 8.
(*q*) Woman is a Riddle, *Prologue*, l.13.
(*r*) Squire of *Alſatia*, *Prologue*, l.33.

CHAP.

CHAP. XXIII.

Objections answered.

THE *Stage* being found guilty from so many Testimonies of its Friends the *Poets*, it will be easy to answer the Objections which are frequently raised in its Vindication. And First, It may be objected, that several of these Expressions, which I have quoted, are spoken by *Madmen* or *Drunkards*, and therefore their Freedoms ought to go for nothing. This is in some cases Matter of Fact. But it may be answer'd, That such Expressions of *Blasphemy* ought not to be spoken upon any pretence whatsoever. Such hideous Sentences, which are enough to violate the Ear of a *Pagan*, and turn the Blood of a *Christian* into Water, should not be put into the Mouth of the *Devil*; and that which is not fit to be heard, is not fit to be utter'd. If they are mad or drunk who act, they ought to be kept in dark Rooms, and without Company; but to shew them, or to let them loose, is somewhat unreasonable. We are not willing to trust such with Swords or Poison, for fear of the Injury which may be done to Man; and why should we arm their Tongues with *Blasphemy*, and set them up in Defiance of GOD, and in Rebellion against him? The *Poets* are in their Wits when they write, and the *Actors* when they speak; so that if they take this liberty on the *Stage*, they ought to be accountable for it in another place. However, this Excuse will amount to a Confession, that such Persons who are represented as sober, and in their right Minds, ought to converse otherwise; so that if this Objection excuses one Sentence in twenty, it effectually condemns all the rest. Besides, the Madness is not always supposed to be real, but it oftentimes appears to be only feigned, and the Persons guilty are never reproved for it. They are the principal *Actors*; and tho they are either mad or drunk, yet they are sure to be rewarded with the utmost Success at the

the end of the *Play*. And therefore whilst this must serve for an Apology, the whole *Plot* is, That this *Hellish Language* may be more deeply imprinted in the Minds of the Audience, and set off with the greatest advantage. And then this politick Contrivance shall only serve to skreen the *Blasphemy* from any farther Censure. However (*a*) *Profaneness*, tho ever so well corrected, is not to be endured. It ought to be banish'd without Proviso or Limitation. No Pretence of *Character* or Punishment can excuse it; or any *Stage*-Discipline make it tolerable. 'Tis grating to *Christian* Ears, dishonourable to the Majesty of GOD, and dangerous in the Example. In a word, it tends to no Point, unless it be to wear off the Horrour of the Practice, to weaken the Force of Conscience, and to teach the Language of the Damn'd.

Another Objection is, That the *Play-House* exposeth *Vice*, for Men to abhor it, and not to imitate it. But this is false in Fact, and their own *Poets* do tell us the contrary. Here *Vice* is exposed, as a Tradesman exposeth his Goods, to make it more common and desirable, to make a gain by it, and disperse it through the Nation. It hath been constantly proved, and it is still as evident as ever, that the *Stage-Poets* make their principal Persons vicious, and reward them at the end of the *Play*. They put Lewdness and Profaneness into a thriving Condition, give it an Equipage of Quality, and treat it with such Ceremony and Respect, as shews that their Design is to confound the Understanding, to fortify the Charm, and to make the Mischief invincible. Besides, take it at best, the *Antidote* is not strong enough for the Poison. When Profaneness and Debauchery have run through all the *Scenes*, and met with several Successes and Applause, a slight Example at the end, or a moral Sentence of six Lines, is not sufficient. It stands there only for an Excuse, and is just as if a Man should set an House in a flame, and think to make amends by crying *Fire!* in the streets; and as if a Man should pay a *Shilling* for robbing on the Highway, or be set in the Stocks for Murder. However, there is no necessity to be made sick for the sake of the *Physick*,

(*a*) *Collier*'s Short View, *p*. 96.

to

to have our Heads broken for the ſake of a *Plaſter*, or that the *Sacred Name* of GOD ſhould be diſhonoured, becauſe the Offenders are puniſhed. This is at beſt but (*b*) *doing Evil that Good may come of it*; and the *Condemnation* of ſuch Men *is juſt*. But if we grant this Objection to be true; yet it will not affect any part of the preceding Chapters: For none of theſe Expreſſions do meet with any Reproof or Diſcouragement at all. And they are therefore ſo many Arguments, that either the *Players* look upon them to be no Crimes, or elſe that they are reſolved to go on to the uttermoſt.

Another Objection is, That all theſe Expreſſions muſt be taken only in jeſt. But theſe things are not to be jeſted with. It was always reckoned an unſafe, if not a vitious Practice, to ſport and trifle with ſerious things. We know, that (*c*) our *GOD will not be mocked*; and why then ſhould we treat him in ſuch a manner? Beſides, the *Scriptures* directly condemn ſuch Practices. *Solomon* ſaith, (*d*) that they are *Fools*, who thus *make a mock at Sin*, and (*e*) that *a Companion of* ſuch *Fools ſhall be deſtroyed*. And (*f*) that *as a Madman, who caſteth Firebrands, Arrows, and Death; ſo is he that deceiveth his Neighbour, aud ſaith, Am not I in ſport?* And St. *Paul* (*g*) ſpeaking of ſome things which were not to be *named among* Chriſtians, mentions the three *Stage-Vices*, namely, *Filthineſs*, *Fooliſh Talking*, and *Jeſting*, *which* he again tells us *are not convenient*. The Vindicators of the *Play-Houſe* excuſe all that is ſaid, becauſe it is only a *jeſting matter*; and St. *Paul* condemns it for the ſame reaſon: ſo that if their Argument is good, the *Apoſtle* is miſtaken. Beſides, the *Stage* jeſts with ſuch things, as are not to be jeſted with. Can we *ſwear*, *curſe*, *blaſpheme*, *mock GOD*, *ridicule Religion*, and *burleſque the Scriptures* in jeſt? Can we honour the *Devil*, and aſcribe the *divine Attributes* to him in jeſt? Can we expoſe *Religion*, and plead for *Vice*, and ſay, it is all in jeſt? Can we make a jeſt of *Heaven*, and not forfeit our Right to it? Or can we make a Jeſt of *Hell*, and not expoſe ourſelves to the Miſeries of that Place? Theſe *Sports* and *Jeſts* call for *Judgments* in earneſt. A

(*b*) *Rom.* 3. 8.
(*c*) *Galat.* 6. 7.
(*d*) *Prov.* 14. 9.
(*e*) *Prov.* 13. 20.
(*f*) *Prov.* 26. 18, 19.
(*g*) *Epheſ.* 5. 3, 4.

Tempest on the *Stage* may afterward be ſent upon the Nation. *Magical Repreſentations* may *provoke* GOD, until the *Devil* is let looſe to act more diſmal *Tragedies*. When *Devils* carry Men to *Hell* in jeſt, and the *Stage* opens for this purpoſe, we may dread the Fate of *Korah*, *Dathan*, and *Abiram*; and whilſt *Fire* and *Brimſtone* is raining in the *Play-Houſe*, we may tremble to think on *Sodom* and *Gomorrah*.

Beſides, GOD himſelf hath given us (*h*) a Rule, whereby we may know, whether it is right or not: *Is it not evil? Offer it now unto thy Governour. Will he be pleaſed therewith, or accept thy Perſon? ſaith the Lord of Hoſts.* Suppoſe then, that the *Stage* did ſet up a *Pretender* to theſe Realms, give him the Honour which is due to the *King* himſelf, reward his Votaries with Succeſs, and never reprove them, and pervert the *Statute-Book* for this purpoſe; and afterward ſay, That all this was but a Jeſt: Can we think that others would take it ſo? Can any one look on it as a ſufficient Excuſe? Would not the Government reſent it, and puniſh ſuch Inſolence to the utmoſt? How then can we think the Affront to GOD leſs than that, which in the like caſe would be offered to Man? Is not the *Devil* a Rebel againſt GOD? And why then ſhould he be thus reſpected? Is not GOD as jealous of his Honour, and as able to puniſh, as any human Authority? And why ſhould he be thus affronted? And is not the profane wreſting of the *Scriptures* as bad as expoſing the *Statute-Book*? *Atheiſts* may fancy what they pleaſe; but GOD will ariſe, maintain his own Cauſe, and vindicate his own Honour in due time. He (*i*) *remembers how the fooliſh Man blaſphemes* him *daily*. Nay, he cannot *forget the Voice of* his *Enemies*, whilſt *the Preſumption of them that hate him increaſeth more and more*. And (*k*) *when* his *Judgments are* again *upon the Earth, the Inhabitants thereof will learn Righteouſneſs.*

The laſt Objection which I ſhall take notice of, is, That the *Play-Houſes* are much reform'd of late, by the great Care that is taken of them. But ſuppoſing

---

(*h*) *Mal.* 1. 8.
(*i*) *Pſal.* 74. 22, 23.
(*k*) *Iſa.* 26. 9.

the

the best, there is such a Stream daily let in, which is enough to spoil all. He who will be at the pains to read over the *Advertisements* in the *Daily Courant*, may easily observe, that they continually act the most *profane* and debauched of all the old *Plays*, especially such as have been already exposed, and for which the *Actors* have been found guilty in *Westminster-Hall*. How then can they be (*l*) *a new Lump*, whilst the old *Leven* is still retain'd? Or what signifies it to cleanse a Puddle, whilst a filthy Stream is daily let into it?

However, the Matter of Fact is false; for the new *Plays* are not reform'd. Those which were printed off the two Years last past, have added a considerable Number to the Quotations of this Book. They declare themselves utter Enemies to all Reformation either in themselves or others, and expose it to the uttermost; and how then can we imagine, that they are reform'd? A late *Comedy*, call'd *Sawny* the *Scot*, is said in the *Title-Page* to be altered and improv'd by a Servant to *his Majesty*. But notwithstanding these Improvements and Alterations, it is full of most dreadful *Oaths*, and horrid *Curses*. The Name of GOD is ridiculed by a paltry Footman, almost as often as he speaks. The Alterations seem to be made (*m*) *In the Devil's Name*, according as it is expressed in the *Play* itself. The pretended *Reformation* shews us to be ripe for utter Destruction; and he who will compare this Performance with the Original, will find it ten times more the Child of Hell than the first. But the *Moral* in either is good for nothing.

The *Original* in *Shakespear* is free from *Cursing*; but it is frequently added in (*n*) the other by way of Improvement. The *Original* doth make (*o*) an *Oath* by a Creature the most solemn of all *Oaths*. It doth not jest upon (*p*) *Adam*, *Eve* or (*q*) *Noah*, or (*r*) the *Sacred*

(*l*) 1 *Cor.* 5. 7.

(*m*) *Sawny* the *Scot*, p. 7. l. 1. p. 36. l. 18. p. 49. l. 15.

(*n*) P. 6. l. 9. p. 7. l. 13. p. 8. l. 35. p. 16. l. 9. p. 17. l. 20, *penult*. p. 23. l. *antepenult*. p. 39. l. 30. p. 42. l. 3. p. 50. l. 8, 11. p. 55. l. 18. p. 62. l. 29. p. 64. l. 22.

(*o*) *Sawny* the *Scot*, p. 30. l. 2.

(*p*) Ibid. p. 60. l. 3.

(*q*) Ibid. p. 60. l. 7.

(*r*) Ibid. p. 30. l. 33.

Scriptures; neither doth it ridicule (s) *ſaying Grace* before Meat, with the *Devil's* Name to it, like the late Alterations. The *Original* hath no praying to the *Devil*, no *Ejaculation* in his Name, and no drolling upon an *Article* of our *Faith*, like the other. *Grumio* in *Shakeſpear* is but (t) once uncivil to his *Miſtreſs*, which ſeems to be by his Maſter *Petruchio*'s Order. He (u) makes uſe of the Name of GOD but twice, and (theſe things excepted) is ſeldom out of *Character*. He argues, (x) *Was it fit for a Servant to uſe his Maſter thus?* But *Sawny* is rude and impertinent to both *Maſter* and *Miſtreſs*, and indeed upon all occaſions. He (y) *ſwears*, he (z) *curſes*, he (a) *adjures* in the *Devil's* Name, and (b) ridicules the Name of GOD; he (c) prays to the *Devil*, and (d) is continually talking of him. He burleſques

(s) *Sawny* the *Scot*, p. 36. l. 13.

(t) *Shakeſpear*, p. 223. col. 2.

(u) Ibid. p. 212. col. 2.

(x) Ibid. p. 212. col. 2.

(y) *Sawny* the *Scot*, p. 6. l. 5, 13, 15, 25, *antepen.* p. 7. l. 3, 4, 9, 30. p. 8. l. 9, 12, 24, 31. p. 9. l. 7, 8. p. 10. l. 8. p. 11. l. 30. p. 13. l. *penult.* p. 14. l. 18. p. 15. l. 1, 32, 33. p. 16. l. 5, 8. p. 17. l. 15, 20, 29. p. 18. l. 2, 3. p. 19. l. 15. p. 20. l. 3. p. 25. l. 17. p. 27. l. 32. p. 28. l. 34. p. 32. l. 25, 29, *antepenult.* p. 33. l. 1, & 6, *twice.* l. 18, 24, 32. p. 34. l. 1, 11, 16. p. 35. l. 1, 13, *ult.* p. 36. l. 13, 37. p. 38. l. 2, 23, 28. p. 39. l. 10, *antepenult.* p. 40. l. 3, 18. p. 48. l. 23. p. 49. l. 16, 24. p. 50. l. 29, 30, 31. p. 52. l. *antepenult.* p. 53. l. 27, 30. p. 54. l. 26. p. 56. l. 7, *twice.* p. 58. l. 7, 27. p. 59. l. 18. p. 61. l. 25. p. 62. l. 11, 16. p. 63. l. 19, 33, 34. p. 64. l. *penult.* p. 65. l. 21. p. 66. l. 11. p. 67. l. 3. p. 69. l. *antepenult.* p. 70. l. 19. p. 72. l. 3. p. 73. l. 11, 30. p. 74. l. 6.

(z) Ibid. p. 6. l. 9. p. 7. l. 13. p. 8. l. 35. p. 16. l. 9. p. 17. l. 20, *penult.* p. 39. l. 30. p. 42. l. 3. p. 50. l. 8. p. 55. l. 18. p. 62. l. 29. p. 64. l. 22.

(a) Ibid. p. 7. l. 1. p. 36. l. 18. p. 49. l. 15.

(b) Ibid. p. 6. l. 5, 17. p. 7. l. 3, 9, 30. p. 8. l. 9, 12, 24. p. 9. l. 7. p. 11. l. 30. p. 14. l. 18. p. 15. l. 1, 32. p. 16. l. 5, 8. p. 17. l. 15, 29. p. 18. l. 3. p. 19. l. 15. p. 20. l. 3. p. 28. l. 34. p. 32. l. 25, 28, *antepenult.* p. 33. l. 6. p. 34. l. 16. p. 35. l. 13, *ult.* p. 36. l. 13. p. 38. l. 2. p. 40. l. 18. p. 49. l. 24. p. 50. l. 29, 30. p. 53. l. 27, 30. p. 54. l. 26. p. 59. l. 18. p. 61. l. 26. p. 62. l. 11, 17. p. 63. l. 19, 32, 33. p. 65. l. 21. p. 66. l. 11. p. 67. l. 3. p. 69. l. *antepen.* p. 72. l. 3. p. 74. l. 6.

(c) Ibid. p. 58. l. 28.

(d) Ibid. p. 6. l. 9, 20. p. 7. l. 1, 13. p. 8. l. 35. p. 14. l. 19. p. 15. l. 32. p. 16. l. 9. p. 17. l. 20, *penult.* p. 28. l. 34. p. 32. l. 34, 36. p. 33. l. 6. p. 39. l. 30. p. 42. l. 3, 15. p. 49. l. 15, 23. p. 50. l. 8, 9. p. 55. l. 18. p. 58. l. 28. p. 59. l. 18. p. 62. l. 29. p. 64. l. 16, 21, 22.

(*e*) the *Articles* of our Faith, and (*f*) exposes *Religion*. And perhaps for these Reasons he is honoured to have his Name in the *Title-Page*, which was omitted in the *Original*.

The *Play* call'd *The What-d'ye-call-it* had in a little time two Editions, and a *Key* was printed, to make it more intelligible. This *Key* observes it to be notoriously (*g*) guilty of *Smut*, that the Actions add an Efficacy to the Words, and make a deeper Impression: and that (*h*) it places *Popery* and *Knitting* together, as things of equal importance.

In the *Play* itself there is *swearing* (*i*) by GOD, (*k*) by their *Faith*, and (*l*) by all that's *Good*. Here we have (*m*) the *Clergy* frequently vilified and ridiculed; and (*n*) a *Bottle-Skrew* is sent to the *Vicar*, instead of the *Supervisor* of the *Stage*.

The three *Justices* of the *Peace*, who make up the *Quorum*, are represented as (*o*) most simple and ridiculous in their Discourse, and as (*p*) minding little more than the *large Tankard*, which is set before them. And for the Service of *his Majesty*, here is a Caution given, that if Men are impress'd for the Army, the *Magistrates* shall be haunted by (*q*) their *Ghosts*, (*r*) their *Wives Ghosts*, and (*s*) the *Ghosts* of their *Children* yet unborn; intending thereby (*t*) to banter those *Gentlemen* out of their power in raising of Men for the Publick, when the Exigency of the Nation shall require it.

(*e*) *Sawny* the *Scot*, *p.* 67. *l.* 30.

(*f*) Ibid. *p.* 36. *l.* 13. *p.* 56. *l.* 8.

(*g*) The What-d'ye-call-it, *p.* 36. *l.* 10. The Key to the What-d'ye-call-it, *p.* 30. *l.* 16.

(*h*) The What-d'ye-call-it, *p.* 26. *l.* 11. The Key to the What-d'ye-call-it, *p.* 22. *l.* 3.

(*i*) The What-d'ye-call-it, *p.* 3. *l. penult.*

(*k*) Ibid. *p.* 4. *l.* 18.

(*l*) P. 10. l. 19.

(*m*) P. 38. l. 11, 20, *antepenult.* p. 39. l. 15, 22.

(*n*) P. 28. l. 4.

(*o*) P. 4, 5, 17, 18, 38, *&c.*

(*p*) P. 6, 9, 10, 12, 15.

(*q*) P. 16.

(*r*) P. 16.

(*s*) P. 17.

(*t*) The Key to the What-d'ye-call-it, *p.* 32.

There is but one Line of the *Play* commended in the Preface, as proper, and according to Character; namely, this bitter Curse (*u*):

> *Ye Dog, die like a Soldier, and be damn'd.*

The *Epilogue* is contained in this *Distich*:

> *Our Stage-Play has a Moral, and no doubt*
> *You all have Sense enough to find it out.*

But to help their *Sense*, the *Preface* (*x*) adds, That *this Moral seems intirely calculated to flatter the Audience in their Vanity and Self-conceitedness.*

In short, the Pretence to a *Reformation* is only to amuse the World, whilst they carry on the same Designs as formerly against GOD and *Religion*, and strive to pull the one out of his Throne, and root the other out of the Kingdom.

(*u*) *Compare* The What-d'ye-call-it, *p.*21. *Scene* 2. *l.*2. *with the* Preface *p.* 6.

(*x*) The What-d'ye-call-it, Preface, *p.* 2.

CHAP.

CHAP. XXIV.

The Conclusion.

AND now, who can expreſs himſelf with a Warmth ſuitable to this Occaſion? When the *Bleſſed GOD* is affronted, who can be ſilent? And when the *Devil* himſelf is adored, who can be neuter? Are not theſe Expreſſions ſcandalous in themſelves to the laſt degree? And is not the Guilt increaſed, when they are ſpoken by Characters of Diſtinction, and without Reproof? It is lamentable to conſider, how the *Authority* of GOD is provoked on the *Stage*; how the Intereſt of the *Devil* is publickly advanced, and in a *Chriſtian* Nation; how the *Attributes* of GOD, and the Works of *Creation* and *Providence* are abuſed; how *Religion* is undermined, and the *Scriptures* moſt notoriouſly perverted. And if we are ſilent, can we think that our GOD will hold his peace? Is this the Return which we make to him for ſo many Deliverances, when we were at the brink of Ruin? If we ſay, like thoſe of old, (a) *Tuſh, the LORD ſhall not ſee, neither ſhall the GOD of* Jacob *regard it*; we may find ourſelves miſtaken at laſt. We are not ſo ſecure, but he can ſend his Judgments; and never did any Nation provoke him as we have done. How juſtly may GOD expoſtulate with us, as he did with the *Iſraelites*? and ſay, (b) *Did I not ſave you from them that oppreſſed you? And ye cried unto me, and I delivered you out of their hand. Yet ye have forſaken me, and ſerved other Gods; wherefore I will deliver you no more. Go, and cry unto the Gods, which ye have choſen: let them deliver you in the time of your Tribulation.* GOD hath ſaved us from thoſe who worſhip graven Images; and we requite him for his Kindneſs, by paying

(a) *Pſal.* 94. 7. (b) *Judges* 11. 11,12, 13, 14.

divine Adoration to the *Devil.* And is not this enough to make him once more let looſe the ſame Enemies upon us, until we are again carry'd away captives by the *ſpiritual Babylon?* We juſtly abhor the *Popiſh Maſs*, becauſe of the *Prayers* to *Saints departed*; and can we think it a leſs Crime to be preſent in thoſe Aſſemblies where *Satan* himſelf is invok'd, and his Name is ſo frequently mentioned in their *Ejaculations?* If it was the Honour of our *Forefathers* to oppoſe the *worſhipping of Saints*, and the *Ave-Marias* even to death, their Memory will be a Diſgrace to us, if we oppoſe not thoſe who worſhip the *Devil* with an *Hail Powers beneath!* as if we thought that ſuch Abominations did not deſerve our Reſentments. I know not what can excuſe our Remiſſneſs, unleſs we imagine that the *Devils* in *Hell* ought to have that Reſpect which we juſtly deny to the *Virgin Mary* and to the *Bleſſed Saints* in *Heaven.* But let us *not be deceived*, for *GOD will not* always thus *be mocked.* Let us not be ſecure, for theſe Crimes do cry aloud for Judgments. Nay, I muſt add, that they are *National Sins*, and do therefore call for *National Calamities.* When there are good *Laws* made againſt *Vice*, and ſuch a care taken in the execution of them that they cannot be broken in publick; then the Sins of particular Perſons light only upon their own Heads, and they alone muſt anſwer for their own Deeds: But when there are no *Laws* made, or the *Laws* are defective, or for want of a due Information of the Crime, or Execution of the Penalty, ſuch Sins are open and publick; then the Guilt goes farther, it becomes a *publick Fault*, and it calls for a *publick Vengeance.* Where the Defect lies, I ſhall not pretend to determine; but it is certain that theſe Crimes are acted in a very publick manner. Houſes are erected for this purpoſe in the *Metropolis* of this Nation, and ſet apart with *Prologues* and *Muſick*, and ſuch a Joy and Solemnity at their firſt Opening, as if they were *Churches*, and dedicated to the Service of that GOD, whom the *Auditors* adore. Their Numbers increaſe. Their Abuſes grow worſe and worſe. Theſe things are acted before great Companies of People: and to make it more publick, Tickets are diſperſed to private Perſons, and others are fixed up in publick Places. Advertiſements are mentioned in the Prints, and eſpeci-

ally

ally in the *Daily-Courant*, of the *Plays* which ſhall be acted: The frequenting of theſe places is made the Mode and Faſhion of the Age, and all poſſible Methods are taken to bring more Company to them. And to ſet up theſe Performances in oppoſition to the Worſhip of GOD, People are frequently told by the Encouragers of the *Stage*, That they can be edified as well, and learn as much Good, by the *hearing* of a *Play*, as by the *hearing* of a *Sermon*. The *Plays* thus acted, are afterward printed; that even thoſe who do not hear them, may be poiſon'd by them. Beſides, other *Actors* fix at ſome of the chief Cities of this Nation, as particularly at *Bath* and *Briſtol*, and in times when there is the greateſt Concourſe of People there. Others ſtrole about in other places; neither have the *Univerſities* themſelves been always free from the Infection, eſpecially in their greateſt Solemnities. And to make it more abominable, when they thus provoke GOD to Wrath, and gratify the *Devil*, theſe Men ſhall tell the World upon all occaſions, and even in print, that they are *His Majeſty's Servants*, and ſometimes *His Majeſty's ſworn Servants*. And can we then think, that all this is nothing but a private Guilt? Or if this is only ſo, what can be National? Or can we ſerve our GOD, our *King*, or our *Country* better, than by ſhewing our Abhorrence and Deteſtation of ſuch flagrant Impieties? Or can we expect that our *Cities* and *Univerſities* will ever proſper (unleſs their *Proſperity* is a Judgment) if theſe Abominations are continued, or ſuffered to come among them? If he is the beſt Subject, who is the beſt *Chriſtian*; then ſuch Places and Entertainments as theſe, muſt be a diſſervice to our *King*, our *Church*, and our *Conſtitution*. Such ſcandalous Diverſions muſt of neceſſity unſettle our Minds, diſpirit our Zeal, and make us neither fit for the Service of GOD or Man. In ſhort, what hath been aſſerted by (*c*) another Pen, is plainly evident from the former Chapters, That to frequent the *Play-houſe*, is inconſiſtent with the Duties and Character of a *Chriſtian*. The Guilt of the place muſt in a great meaſure fall upon the Audience, ſince without their Company it could not be ſupported. To be preſent at the *Abuſe*

(*c*) *Collier's* Diſſuaſive from the Play-houſe, *p.* 13.

of *Religion*, after Warning given, amounts to Conſent and Approbation. And not only (*d*) the *Scorners* and *Deriders* of GOD and *Religion* are condemned, but even ſuch as *ſit in the Seat* with them, or have patience to hear them. To delight in ill *Company*, is to become a part of it. To aſſiſt and encourage a Murderer, is a capital Crime. The bare concealing of Treaſon againſt a temporal Prince, brings a Man in Guilty. And ſhall we think that where the Majeſty and Honour of the Great GOD is concerned, People are not accountable for the Profaneneſs which they hear with Pleaſure, and for their Diverſion? Every one knows, that it is the Company which ſupports the *Play-houſes*. Without a numerous Audience they would be forced to diſband, to ſurrender their Buſineſs, and perhaps be diſcouraged into a Reformation. And are we then to aſſiſt ſuch places of *Profaneneſs* by our Purſes and Perſons? Muſt we keep up the Credit of Debauchery? Muſt we make a Contribution for *Blaſphemy*, and raiſe a Tax for the Government of Hell? To countenance ſuch Practices, muſt inevitably communicate the Guilt, and heighten the Provocation. And when Wickedneſs is thus flaming and outrageous, we cannot expect but Vengeance will quickly follow.

When you are tempted to go to the *Play-houſe*, conſider your *Baptiſmal Vow*. The very firſt *Promiſe* which was made in your *Name*, was, that you ſhould *renounce the Devil and all his Works, the Pomps and Vanities of this wicked World, and all the ſinful Luſts of the Fleſh, ſo that you would not follow, nor be led by them.* Our *Church-Catechiſm* tells us, that we our *ſelves, when* we *come of Age, are bound to perform* this *Promiſe*. Nay, *Baptiſm* is a *Covenant*, and we are only intitled to the *Bleſſing* upon the performance of our Part: ſo that if we break our Conditions, GOD is not bound to obſerve his. If we expect to be *Members of Chriſt, the Children of GOD*, or *Inheritors of the Kingdom of Heaven*, we muſt renounce theſe things. If the Words and Actions had been inoffenſive, I could not have urged this matter ſo far; but as the *Stage* is now managed, there is not any

(*d*) לֵצִים *Deriſores, Pſal.* 1. 1.

Argument used by the *Primitive Christians* against the *Theatres* in their Times, but it is as conclusive on this occasion.

A Postscript of Questions proposed.

Quest. 1. CAN we imagine that the *Players*, who are guilty of such Crimes as these, will ever scruple to be guilty of any others, even the worst which can be expressed in Words, or shewn by Representations?

Quest. 2. Whether the acting such things in *publick*, and in the chief Cities of the Nation, doth not make them National Crimes? And consequently, whether it may not justly bring upon us National Judgments, unless it is speedily regulated?

Quest. 3. As our *Plays* have been so vile and abominable for these many Years past, whether the Judgments which they justly call for, may not be likely to be most severe?

Quest. 4. When (a) *GOD delivered the Children of* Israel *out of* Egypt, *he afterward destroyed them that repented not:* And therefore it may be justly asked, whether our late Deliverances will not aggravate these Crimes, and heighten our Condemnation?

Quest. 5. When *Achan*, tho but a private Person, stole the *Golden Wedge*, GOD said, (b) *I will not be with you any more, except you destroy the accursed thing from among you.* How then can we expect a Blessing from GOD, whilst he is daily and publickly provoked to Anger, in Houses built and set apart for this very purpose?

It is an Observation of (c) a late eminent *Author*, That *the Priests of the Church of* Rome, *from a just Observation of human Nature, do (not without Reason) attempt to draw Men off from the Belief of Religion in gene-*

(a) *Jude, Ver.* 5.
(b) *Josh.* 7. 12.
(c) Sir *Richard Blackmore's* Essays, *Vol.* 2. *Pag.* 139.

ral,

ral, in order to the bringing them over to their own Persuasion. For they are satisfied, that very few are so stupid in great Straits, or when their Consciences shall be rouzed, as not to lay hold on any Religion that offers them Safety: and being so far gone in Impiety that they can hardly come up to the Conditions of the Gospel-Covenant, as mentioned in all the *Protestant Reformed Churches*, they are willing to be of a Religion which offers them Salvation upon easier Terms.

Hence (saith the same Author) *it is very probable that to procure their End, they maintain in this as well as other Countries, artful Emissaries, loose Wits, and petulent Poets, to poison the People with irreligious Principles, to mock and expose the Scriptures, and all things sacred, serious and divine; and by their vile Writings and loose Conversation to spread Vice and Immorality, till by degrees many become impious in Principle, and then they are prepared to receive such Impressions, and embrace such Doctrines.* And therefore,

Quest. 6. Whether the Endeavours to reconcile *Popery* with the *Protestant Churches* by some, the extenuating and excusing it by others, and the want of Zeal against it in most, is not in a great measure owing to the Corruption of our Morals? And whether if this Deluge of *Atheism*, *Profaneness* and *Impiety* had not been let in among us, our Enemies would have presumed to have taken the other Method?

Quest. 7. How can we answer it to GOD, to our own *Consciences*, and to our Posterity, if we do not endeavour to prevent the Designs of our Enemies, by a more effectual care to stop this Deluge which breaks in upon us, and by which they intend our Ruin?

The first Attempt of bringing the *Israelites* to *Idolatry*, began with poisoning their Morals. Before this, there was no such (*d*) *Iniquity* or *Perverseness* in them. But when they (*e*) *began to commit Whoredom with the Daughters of* Moab, *then they called the People to the Sacrifices of their Gods; and the People did eat, and bowed down to their Gods. And* Israel *joined themselves unto*

(*d*) *Numb.* 23. 21.
(*e*) *Numb.* 25. 1,2,3,9. *Psal.* 106.28,29.

Baal-

Baal-Peor. *And the Anger of the LORD was kindled against them*, insomuch that four and twenty thousand Men died of the Plague; which could not be appeased, but by the Prayer of *(f) Phinehas*, joined with his *Zeal* to execute Justice on such Immoralities. And therefore,

Quest. 8. If *these (g) things were written for our Admonition and Example*, how can we expect an Abhorrence of the vilest *Religion* in the World, or that GOD should give us his Blessing, whilst such *Scenes* of *Immorality* are continued with Impunity?

Quest. 9. When the *Children of* Israel committed *Idolatry*, they were often oppressed by those People whose *Idols* they worshipped. And (h) when they affected the *Babylonish Finery*, they were afterward punished with the *Babylonish Fetters*. As therefore we have now many of our *Plays*, our *Musick* and *Scenes* from *Italy*, even from *(i) Babylon the Great, the Mother of Harlots, and Abominations of the Earth*; and as we copy after her *Originals* in these *Abominations*, may we not fear a Scourge from those Kingdoms without a speedy Reformation, especially since there is a Person in that Communion who still pretends a Right to the *British Throne?* Or can we think our selves secure from GOD's Judgments, whilst we also consider, that (k) such *Things* as *these are written for our Admonition and Example?*

Quest. 10. When the *Plays* were corrupted in *Athens*, an Heathen People, they severely felt the Consequence of it: For (l) it so exhausted their Treasure, that they had no Money to set forth their Ships, or defend their Country. And by this means their Enemies prevailed against them. To prevent this, the *Athenians (m)* appointed several Inspectors for its better Regulation. When this did not succeed, (n) they passed a farther Censure, and made a Law, that no *Magistrate*, or *Judge*

(f) *Numb.* 25.4,5,6,7,8,10, 11,12,13. *Psal.* 106.30,31.

(g) 1 *Cor.* 10. 6, 8,11.

(h) *Zeph.* 1. 8.

(i) *Revel.* 17. 5.

(k) 1 *Cor.* 10.6,8,11.

(l) Plutarch. *De Gloria Atheniensium.*

(m) Ibid.

(n) Ibid.

of

of the *Areopagus*, should make a *Comedy*, because it was a disreputable Employment. After this, they (o) enacted, that *common Actors* should be reputed Infamous; and at last, (p) they totally suppressed the *Theatre*. How then will they (q) *rise up in Judgment against* us, *and condemn* us, if we are remiss in this Matter?

Quest. 11. When the *Plays* were corrupted in *Heathen Rome*, (r) a very early Law was made against them, in which they were declared Infamous; and it was enacted, That no *Actor* should be admitted to the *Court*, the *Bar*, or the *Senate*, and should also be uncapable of any Military or other Honour or Esteem: and therefore when GOD enters into Judgment for these things, will it (s) not *be more tolerable for* them, *than* it will be *for* us?

Quest. 12. In a former *Evening-Post*, from Tuesday *January* 10, to Thursday *January* 12, we had this printed Account.

Vienna, December 21. *A Youth of sixteen Years of Age, condemn'd for blaspheming GOD and his Providence, was executed this Day Sevennight. His Tongue was first cut out, and then he was beheaded.* How then must such an Example in a Popish Country rise up in Judgment against us, who pretend to be reformed, if such *Blasphemies* against GOD and his Providence are heard among us, before great Companies of People, where they pass for nothing, or at most to make Diversion, and to be laugh'd at?

Quest. 13. Can we ever expect any Reformation of *Swearing*, *Cursing*, *Blasphemy*, or any *lewd* and *filthy Talk*, whilst it is spoken publickly in those *Places*, which are proposed as Patterns of fine Language?

Quest. 14. Can we ever expect, but that the Cities where our *Plays* are acted, will be always full of the worst *Vices*, whilst they are represented with the ut-

(o) *Chrysostom. Hom.* 13. in 1 *Cor.* 4. *Tom.* 10.

(p) *Horat. de Arte Poeticâ.*

(q) *Matth.* 12. 41, 42. *Luke* 11. 30, 31, 32.

(r) *Tertulliani libro de Spectaculis*, pag. 699. *Edit. Basil.* 1562.

(s) *Matth.* 11. 20, 21, 22, 23, 24.

most

most Advantage to the *Audience*, and the Persons thus guilty are caress'd, and crown'd with Success?

Quest. 15. Can we reconcile the going to such places with our *Baptismal Vow*, whilst they continue thus to reproach our GOD, and honour the *Devil?* And if not, can we be real *Christians?* Can we walk worthy of our *Baptism?* Or can we be fit to receive the *LORD's-Supper*, until we resolve to be wholly absent from them?

Quest. 16. Can any Person, who values his GOD, his *King*, or his Nation, or who hath any *Modesty* left, be present in those places, where so much Debauchery is represented to the Life, and so much *Blasphemy*, *Profaneness*, and *filthy Communication* is continually heard?

SOLI DEO GLORIA.

FINIS.

BOOKS printed for Henry Hammond *in* Bath.

THREE Sermons preach'd on three particular Subjects, *viz.* I. King *GEORGE* the Security of the Church of *England.* On *Iſa.* 63. 10. II. The Church of *England* the Standard to regulate all other Churches by, at the Fall of Popery. On *Iſa.* 2. 2. III. An Exhortation to Love and Peace, as the means to fit us for ſuch Bleſſings. On *Luke* 19. part of Ver. 42. By *Arthur Bedford,* M. A.

The Doctrine of Obedience and Non-Reſiſtance due to the Higher Powers, explain'd, ſtated, and vindicated; with proper Inferences from the ſame: In a Sermon preach'd at the Aſſizes held at *Taunton* in the Town of *Somerſet,* on Tueſday *March* 19. 171$\frac{6}{7}$. By the ſame Author.

The Obligations which lie both upon Magiſtrates and others, to put the Laws in execution againſt Immorality and Profaneneſs: In a Sermon preach'd at the Aſſizes held at *Wells* in the County of *Somerſet,* on Wedneſday the 28th Day of *Auguſt,* in the Year of our Lord 1717. before Sir *Robert Eyre* and Sir *James Montague,* being his Majeſty's Judges for the ſaid Circuit. By the ſame Author.

Scholæ Bathonienſis Primitiæ: ſeu Excerpta quædam è Walleri & Miltoni Poematibus, latino Carmine, à Scholaribus quibuſdam Scholæ Grammaticalis Bathonienſis, donata.

Practical Diſcourſes on the ſeveral Parts and Offices of the Liturgy of the Church of *England.* Wherein are laid open the Harmony, Excellency, and Uſefulneſs of its Compoſure. In four Parts, bound in 5 Vol. Uſeful for all Families.

A Practical Expoſition of the Church Catechiſm: in ſeveral Diſcourſes on all the Parts of it. In two Volumes. Uſeful for all Families. The ſecond Edition.

Six Diſcourſes on ſeveral Occaſions.

Theſe three by the Revd *Matthew Hole,* D. D. Rector of *Exeter-College* in *Oxford.*

A Practical Diſſertation on *Bath-Waters.* Treating of the Antiquity of Bathing. Of the Original of Springs. Of the Cauſe of the Heat of *Bath-Waters*; and of their Ingredients. Of Drinking *Bath-Waters.* Of Bathing. Of the City of *Bath,* its Situation, Bath, *&c.* By *William Oliver,* M. D. and F. R S.